MATH TEACHING SERIES
STUDENTS • TEACHERS • PARENTS

A step-by-step
MATH TEACHING SERIES
for
Students, Teachers, **AND** Parents

GRADE LEVEL

6

ABOUT THE AUTHOR:

Nicholas Aggor is a parent and an ex-senior engineer with a master's degree
in engineering, fully trained in the prestigious Six Sigma Blackbelt
of Problem Solving, and a National Dean's List Scholar

www.MathTeachingSeries.com
Published by Nicholas Aggor Publisher, LLC.

Welcome to the Math Teaching Series

IF YOU ARE AN EDUCATOR...

This text and every text in the Math Teaching Series provide new "tools" designed to assist you in teaching mathematics. After listening and working with educators to assist all students, even those who struggle with math, we were able to build a step-by-step method to improve the delivery of effective instruction.

IF YOU ARE A PARENT...

We will guide your student to build skills and they will become competent. Study will progress with less stress and more peace as the student and you are able to work together toward success. Pride in accomplishment can come early and stay during the study effort with the system.

IF YOU ARE A STUDENT...

These texts were built to assist all students and allow them to earn respect for their efforts. Those who struggle can get the help they need in a process built to avoid becoming lost and stuck. You are guided and the course is designed to allow you to build competence in skills, which will allow you to feel confident!

Nicholas Aggor, an Author, an Engineer, a Parent

This series of texts is dedicated to making the playing field a more fair and equal process to all students with a well-constructed platform to deliver the lessons.

I believe there are always at least three parties to the success of education. With the student supported with a text built to this level of support, we are confident that the educators of the world will now receive "hands on" help as well for the student with parents, relatives, and others who are dedicated to the journey that can use this text.

I wish to thank all the teachers who help in the real life struggle to teach.

We have designed a new set of tools for students, teachers, and parents.

Nicholas Aggor

Texas Instruments images used with permission of the copyright owner.

Material extracted from TI-Nspire™ Math and Science Learning Technology and TI-Nspire™ Learning Handheld Quick Reference with permission of the publisher Copyright (2007), Texas Instruments Incorporated

ISBN: 978-0-9840609-1-7

School to Home Connection

You promise to work and I promise you will not get lost.

Math Teaching Series Lesson One

LEARN WHY TO WORK AND YOU WILL SUCCEED

- You are as rich and as intelligent as anyone while studying this book.
- Stay with me and work daily and you will see improved results.
- This is all about effort, so follow the pathways and you will improve.

LEARN HOW TO WORK AND YOU WILL SUCCEED

- Peace and quiet will allow focus. NO radio, television, games, and phones.
- Expect to win, to progress and keep score daily and results will improve.
- Your teachers are there to help and teach, so show them your work daily.

Daily Score Card

1. Students grade parents for providing scheduled studies time, homework time, bed time, quiet place to study, quiet place to do homework, and food.
2. Parents grade students for the effort the students make during the scheduled studies time, homework time, and bed time.
3. Teachers grade students during quizzes, homework, and tests.

Days	Studies Time	Quality Control at Home		Quality Control at School	Steps to Improve
		Students' Grading	Parents' Grading	Teachers' Grading	Improvement
Mon					
Tue					
Wed					
Thu					
Fri					
Sat					
Sun					

- Students earn good results with good work habits. Take pride in your efforts.
- Share your daily effort with your parents, guardians, your family, and friends.
- Seek advice and help from your math teachers on your journey to success.
- Parents should make copies of the score card for monitoring progress.

How to Use This Book Most Effectively

There is a consistent teaching method in the text to follow.

Your book contains Examples, with step-by-step demonstration of "how to" do the math problems. As you study, focus on learning the "how to" properly and the solutions offered throughout your text will teach you the methods to use.

Practice the Examples and come to know how to do the work. The Examples section will "teach you" the process in a step-by-step manner. This way, learning the correct methods will prevent you from getting lost or stuck. You will find each step to be connected and the pace will allow you to progress with confidence.

After following the Examples offered with understanding, work the chapter Exercise Problems. As you do the Exercise Problems, use the "hints" provided, as you need them, sending you back to the Examples. This will allow you to advance, and as you learn the steps properly, your confidence will strengthen.

Challenge questions are designed for you to excel in the area of study. Allow yourself time to work the Challenge Questions as they will strengthen your skills.

Word Problems provide Real World applications of the methods you are learning. You are provided with the "how to" method again, showing the step-by-step solutions to solve these questions properly. This will help to improve your math reasoning skills.

Learn to use the Table of Contents (front) and the Index of Terms (back) in this book. These are reference aids to quickly direct you to solutions.

TABLE OF CONTENTS - GRADE 6

Chapter 14: Fractions 193

Chapter 32: Circles 775

Chapter 33: Circumference 783

Chapter 34: Similar And Congruent Figures 787

Chapter 35: Symmetric Figures 801

ORDER OF OPERATIONS

Quick Cumulative Review

1. Mary said that to divide by a fraction is the same as to multiply by the reciprocal of the fraction. Is her statement correct? Explain your answer. Hint: Review the section of the Math Teaching Series on Dividing by a Fraction.

2. Explain what is meant by the reciprocal of a number. Hint: Review the section of the Math Teaching Series on the Reciprocal of Numbers.

3. John said that $\dfrac{2}{3} \div \dfrac{1}{6} = 8$. Is his statement correct? Give reasons for your answer.

4. Evaluate:

   a. $\dfrac{3}{4} \div \dfrac{1}{4} =$ 　　　　**b.** $10 \div \dfrac{1}{5} =$ 　　　　**c.** $\dfrac{3}{5} \times \dfrac{2}{3} =$ 　　　　**d.** $\dfrac{3}{5} + \dfrac{2}{3} =$

   Hint: Review the sections on Fractions in the Math Teaching Series.

5. The measure of a side of a square is 3 m.
   a. What is the perimeter of the square?
   b. What is the area of the square?
   Hint: Review the sections on Perimeter and Area in the Math Teaching Series.

6. If the product of two numbers is zero, then the value of at least one of the numbers is _____. Give reasons for your answer. Hint: Review the chapter on the Multiplication of Whole Numbers in the Math Teaching Series for grade 5.

New Terms
order of operations, "PERMDAS", exponents, square root

Order of Operations
The order of operations is the sequence to follow in solving expressions involving parentheses, exponents, roots, multiplication, division, addition, and subtraction.

What have I learned so far?

Explaining the Order of Operations

Example 1
Explain the order of operations by:
a. Finding the total number of balls by addition only
b. Finding the total number of balls by using additions and multiplication. Show that

the answer in **a** is the same as the answer in **b**.
c. Showing that if the addition operation is done before the multiplication operation in equation [A] of solution **b**, a wrong answer is obtained.

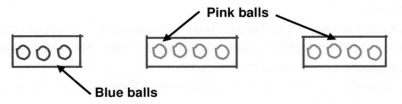

Pink balls

Blue balls

Solution
a The total number of balls by addition only = 3 blue balls + 4 pink balls + 4 pink balls.

= 11 balls.

b. Alternate method:

Since there are 2 sets of 4 pink balls the total number of pink balls = 2 × 4 pink balls. There are 3 blue balls also, therefore, the total number of balls

$$= 3 + 2 \times 4 \underline{\hspace{5cm}}[A]$$
$$= 3 + 8$$
$$= 11 \text{ balls.}$$

Therefore, the answer in the Solution **a** is the same as the answer in Solution **b**.

c. Note that in the Solution **b**, the answer 11 is obtained because the multiplication operation was done before the addition operation in equation [A]. If the addition operation is done first before the multiplication operation in equation [A], a different and a wrong answer is obtained as shown:

3 + 2 x 4

5 x 4 = 20 **(This is a different and a wrong answer).**

Conclusion
We can conclude from Example 1 that the expression 3 + 2 × 4 could result in more than one value as the solution but only one value is the correct answer. Therefore, mathematicians have agreed on an order to follow when performing operations and this order is known as the **order of operations**.

The order of operations may be simplified as **PERMDAS** where:

Rule 1: **P** = Parentheses: Do the operations within the ( ) first if there are any.

Rule 2: **E** = Exponents: Do exponents second if there are any.

Rule 3: **R** = Roots: Do roots third if there are any. The roots refers to all types of roots.
(Examples of types of roots are: $\sqrt{}$, $\sqrt[3]{}$, $\sqrt[4]{}$, ...)

Rule 4: **M** = Multiplication and **D** = Divide from left to right: Do multiplication and division from left to right if there are any.

Rule 5: **A** = Add and **S** = Subtract from left to right: Do addition and subtraction from left to right if there are any.

I can solve the problems too if only
I understand the concepts.

Addition and Subtraction
Example 2
Find the value of each expression.

a. 3 + 2 - 1   **b.** 22 - 2 + 4   **c.** 10 - 2 - 3

Solution
PERMDAS, specifically Rule 5 which states "**A** = Add and **S** = Subtraction from left to right" should be used to find the values of **a**, **b**, and **c**.

a. Using Rule 5 from left to right, we have to do the addition first before the subtraction step-by-step as shown:

$$3 + 2 - 1 = 5 - 1 \qquad (3 + 2 = 5)$$
$$= 4$$

b. Using Rule 5 from left to right, we have to subtract first before the addition step-by-step as shown:

$$22 - 2 + 4 = 20 + 4 \qquad (22 - 2 = 20)$$
$$= 24 \qquad (20 + 4 = 24)$$

c. Using Rule 5 from left to right, we have to do the subtraction on the left first, and then do the second subtraction step-by-step as shown:

$$10 - 2 - 3 = 8 - 3 \qquad (10 - 2 = 8)$$
$$= 5 \qquad (8 - 3 = 5)$$

Multiplication and Division
Example 3
Find the value of each expression

a. 9 · 2 ÷ 3   **b.** 24 ÷ 3 · 2   **c.** 60 ÷ 10 ÷ 2

Solution
PERMDAS, specifically Rule 4, which states "**M** = Multiplication and **D** = Division from left to right" should be used to find the values of questions **a**, **b**, and **c**.

a. Using Rule 4 from left to right, we should do the multiplication before the division step-by-step as shown:

$$9 \cdot 2 \div 3 = 18 \div 3 \qquad (9 \cdot 2 = 18)$$
$$= 6 \qquad (18 \div 3 = 6)$$

b. Using Rule 4 from left to right, we should do the division before multiplication step-by-step as shown:

$$24 \div 3 \cdot 2 = 8 \cdot 2 \qquad (24 \div 3 = 8)$$
$$= 16 \qquad (8 \cdot 2 = 16)$$

c. Using Rule 4 from left to right, we should do the division at the left side first before doing the second division step-by-step as shown:

$$60 \div 10 \div 2 = 6 \div 2 \qquad (60 \div 10 = 6)$$

$$= 3 \qquad (6 \div 2 = 3$$

Addition, Subtraction, Multiplication, and Division
Example 4
Find the value of each expression.

a. $5 \cdot 3 - 4$ **b.** $24 - 4 \cdot 2$ **c.** $60 \div 10 + 5$
d. $7 - 60 \div 10$ **e.** $10 - 2 \cdot 3 + 4$ **f.** $10 + 2 \cdot 3 - 4$
g. $20 - 3 \cdot 4 + 6 \div 3$ **h.** $20 \div 5 \cdot 2 + 6 - 2$ **i.** $2 \cdot 8 \div 4$
j. $16 \div 4 \cdot 2$ **k.** $21 \div 3 + 3 \cdot 10$ **l.** $9 + 6 - 4 \cdot 2$ **m.** $2 + 4 \cdot 6$

Solution
PERMDAS, specifically Rule 4 which states, **M** = Multiplication and **D** = Division from left to right" and Rule 5 which states, "**A** = Add and **S** = Subtract from left to right" should be used to find the values of questions **a, b, c, d, e, f, g, h, i, j, k, l, and m** as shown:

a. Using **PERMDAS**, the multiplication should be done before subtraction step-by-step as shown:
$$5 \cdot 3 - 4 = 15 - 4 \qquad (5 \cdot 3 = 15)$$
$$= 11 \qquad (15 - 4 = 11)$$

b. Using **PERMDAS**, multiplication should be done before subtraction step-by-step as shown:
$$24 - 4 \cdot 2 = 24 - 8 \qquad (4 \cdot 2 = 8)$$
$$= 16 \qquad (24 - 8 = 16)$$

c. Using **PERMDAS**, division should be done before the addition step-by-step as shown:
$$60 \div 10 + 5 = 6 + 5 \qquad (60 \div 10 = 6)$$
$$= 11 \qquad (6 + 5 = 11)$$

d. Using **PERMDAS**, division should be done before subtraction step-by-step as shown:
$$7 - 60 \div 10 = 7 - 6 \qquad (60 \div 10 = 6)$$
$$= 1 \qquad (7 - 6 = 1)$$

e. Using **PERMDAS**, do multiplication, subtraction, and then addition step-by-step as shown:
$$10 - 2 \cdot 3 + 4 = 10 - 6 + 4 \qquad (2 \cdot 3 = 6)$$
$$= 4 + 4 \qquad (10 - 6 = 4)$$
$$= 8 \qquad (4 + 4 = 8)$$

f. Using **PERMDAS**, do multiplication, addition, and then subtraction step-by-step as shown:
$$10 + 2 \cdot 3 - 4 = 10 + 6 - 4 \qquad (2 \cdot 3 = 6)$$
$$= 16 - 4 \qquad (10 + 6 = 16)$$
$$= 12 \qquad (16 - 4 = 12)$$

g. Using **PERMDAS**, do the multiplication, division, subtraction, and then addition step-by-step as shown:
$$20 - 3 \cdot 4 + 6 \div 3 = 20 - 12 + 6 \div 3 \qquad (3 \cdot 4 = 12)$$

$$= 20 - 12 + 2 \qquad (6 \div 3 = 2)$$
$$= 8 + 2 \qquad (20 - 12 = 8)$$
$$= 10 \qquad (8 + 2 = 10)$$

h. Using **PERMDAS**, do the division, multiplication, addition, and then subtraction step-by-step as shown:

$$20 \div 5 \cdot 2 + 6 - 2 = 4 \cdot 2 + 6 - 2 \qquad (20 \div 5 = 4)$$
$$= 8 + 6 - 2 \qquad (4 \cdot 2 = 8)$$
$$= 14 - 2 \qquad (8 + 6 = 14)$$
$$= 12 \qquad (14 - 2 = 12)$$

i. Using **PERMDAS**, do the multiplication, and then the division step-by-step as shown:

$$2 \cdot 8 \div 4 = 16 \div 4 \qquad (2 \cdot 8 = 16)$$
$$= 4 \qquad (16 \div 4 = 4)$$

j. Using **PERMDAS**, do the division, and then the multiplication step-by-step as shown:

$$16 \div 4 \cdot 2 = 4 \cdot 2 \qquad (16 \div 4 = 4)$$
$$= 8 \qquad (4 \cdot 2 = 8)$$

k. Using **PERMDAS**, do the division, multiplication, and then the addition step-by-step as shown:

$$21 \div 3 + 3 \cdot 10 = 7 + 3 \cdot 10 \qquad (21 \div 3 = 7)$$
$$= 7 + 30 \qquad (3 \cdot 10 = 30)$$
$$= 37 \qquad (7 + 30 = 37)$$

l. Using **PERMDAS**, do multiplication, addition, and then subtraction step-by-step as shown:

$$9 + 6 - 4 \cdot 2 = 9 + 6 - 8 \qquad (4 \cdot 2 = 8)$$
$$= 15 - 8 \qquad (9 + 6 = 15)$$
$$= 7 \qquad (15 - 8 = 7)$$

m. Using **PERMDAS**, do multiplication before addition step-by-step as shown:

$$2 + 4 \cdot 6 = 2 + 24 \qquad (4 \cdot 6 = 24)$$
$$= 26 \qquad (2 + 24 = 26)$$

It is not difficult, if I make the time to practise, I can become a "MathMaster".

Addition, Subtraction, Multiplication, Division, and Parentheses
Example 5
Find the value of each expression.

a. $2 \cdot (4 + 2)$ **b**. $(5 - 3) \cdot 3$ **c**. $24 \div (10 + 2)$ **d**. $(25 - 5) \div 4$

e. $(11 + 4) \cdot 2 + 3$ **f**. $6 + (10 - 3)$ **g**. $12 \div 3 \cdot (6 - 2)$ **h**. $3 \cdot (7 + 3) \div 5$

i. $6 \cdot 2 \div (8 - 6)$ **j**. $(16 + 4) \times (7 - 2)$ **k**. $13 + 8 \div (18 - 16)$ **l**. $(4 + 2 \cdot 5) \div 2$

m. $3 \cdot (11 - 2 \cdot 3 \div 6) \div (20 \div 4 - 3)$ **n**. $15 - (7 + 2)$ **o**. $(36 + 4) \times (5 - 2)$

p. $(19 - 9) - (7 - 5)$ **q**. $(23 - 19) + (7 + 3)$

Solution

Note: The symbol for a **parenthesis** is ( ). The plural of **parenthesis** is **parentheses**.

PERMDAS is used to find the values of questions **a** to **q** as shown:

a. Do the addition inside of the **parenthesis**, and then multiply step-by-step as shown:

$$2 \cdot (4 + 2) = 2 \cdot 6 \qquad\qquad (4 + 2) = 6$$
$$= 12 \qquad\qquad\qquad (2 \cdot 6 = 12)$$

b. Do the subtraction inside of the **parenthesis**, and then multiply step-by-step as shown:

$$(5 - 3) \cdot 3 = 2 \cdot 3 \qquad\qquad (5 - 3) = 2$$
$$= 6 \qquad\qquad\qquad (2 \cdot 3 = 6)$$

c. Do the addition inside of the **parenthesis**, and then divide step-by-step as shown:

$$24 \div (10 + 2) = 24 \div 12 \qquad\qquad (10 + 2) = 12)$$
$$= 2 \qquad\qquad\qquad (24 \div 12 = 2)$$

d. Do the subtraction inside of the **parenthesis**, and then divide step-by-step as shown:

$$(25 - 5) \div 4 = 20 \div 4 \qquad\qquad (25 - 5) = 20$$
$$= 5 \qquad\qquad\qquad (20 \div 4 = 5)$$

e. Do the addition inside of the **parenthesis**, multiply, and then add step-by-step as shown:

$$(11 + 4) \cdot 2 + 3 = 15 \cdot 2 + 3 \qquad\qquad (11 + 4) = 15$$
$$= 30 + 3 \qquad\qquad\qquad (15 \cdot 2 = 30)$$
$$= 33 \qquad\qquad\qquad (30 + 3 = 33)$$

f. Do the subtraction inside of the **parenthesis**, and then add step-by-step as shown:

$$6 + (10 - 3) = 6 + 7 \qquad\qquad (10 - 3) = 7$$
$$= 13 \qquad\qquad\qquad (6 + 7 = 13)$$

g. Do the subtraction inside of the **parenthesis**, do the division, and then multiply step-by-step as shown:

$$12 \div 3 \cdot (6 - 2) = 12 \div 3 \cdot 4 \qquad\qquad (6 - 2 = 4)$$
$$= 4 \cdot 4 \qquad\qquad\qquad (12 \div 3 = 4)$$
$$= 16 \qquad\qquad\qquad (4 \cdot 4 = 16)$$

h. Do the addition inside of the **parenthesis**, do the multiplication and then do the division step-by-step as shown:

$$3 \cdot (7 + 3) \div 5 = 3 \cdot 10 \div 5 \qquad\qquad (7 + 3) = 10$$
$$= 30 \div 5 \qquad\qquad\qquad (3 \cdot 10 = 30)$$
$$= 6 \qquad\qquad\qquad (30 \div 5 = 6)$$

i. Do the subtraction inside the **parenthesis**, do the multiplication, and then do the division step-by-step as shown:

$$6 \cdot 2 \div (8 - 6) = 6 \cdot 2 \div 2 \qquad\qquad (8 - 6) = 2$$
$$= 12 \div 2 \qquad\qquad\qquad (6 \cdot 2 = 12)$$
$$= 6 \qquad\qquad\qquad (12 \div 2 = 6)$$

j. Do the addition inside of the **parenthesis** on the left side, do the subtraction in the

parenthesis on the right side, and then multiply step-by-step as shown:

$$(16 + 4) \times (7 - 2) = 20 \times (7 - 2) \qquad (16 + 4 = 20)$$
$$= 20 \times 5 \qquad (7 - 2 = 5)$$
$$= 100 \qquad (20 \times 5 = 100)$$

k. Do the subtraction inside of the **parenthesis**, do the division, and then do the addition step-by-step as shown:

$$13 + 8 \div (18 - 16) = 13 + 8 \div 2 \qquad (18 - 16) = 2$$
$$= 13 + 4 \qquad (8 \div 2 = 4)$$
$$= 17 \qquad (13 + 4 = 17)$$

l. Do the multiplication inside the **parenthesis**, do the addition inside of the **parenthesis**, and then do the division step-by-step as shown:

$$(4 + 2 \cdot 5) \div 2 = (4 + 10) \div 2 \qquad (2 \cdot 5 = 10)$$
$$= 14 \div 2 \qquad (4 + 10 = 14)$$
$$= 7 \qquad (14 \div 2 = 7)$$

m. Do the operations inside of the **parenthesis** on the left side according to PERMDAS by multiplying, dividing, and subtracting, then do the operations inside of the **parenthesis** on the right side according to PERMDAS by dividing and then subtracting. Finally, multiply and divide as shown step-by-step:

$$3 \cdot (11 - 2 \cdot 3 \div 6) \div (20 \div 4 - 3) =$$

$$3 \cdot (11 - 2 \cdot 3 \div 6) \div (20 \div 4 - 3)$$

$$= 3 \cdot (11 - 6 \div 6) \div (20 \div 4 - 3) \qquad (2 \cdot 3 = 6)$$

$$= 3 \cdot (11 - 1) \div (20 \div 4 - 3) \qquad (6 \div 6 = 1)$$

$$= 3 \cdot 10 \div (20 \div 4 - 3) \qquad (11 - 1 = 10)$$

$$= 3 \cdot 10 \div (5 - 3) \qquad (20 \div 4 = 5)$$

$$= 3 \cdot 10 \div 2 \qquad (5 - 3 = 2)$$

$$= 30 \div 2 \qquad (3 \cdot 10 = 30)$$

$$= 15 \qquad (30 \div 2 = 15)$$

n. Do the addition inside of the **parenthesis** and then do the subtraction step-by-step as shown:

$$15 - (7 + 2) = 15 - 9 \qquad (7 + 2 = 9)$$
$$= 6 \qquad (15 - 9 = 6)$$

o. Do the addition inside of the **parenthesis** at the left side, do the subtraction inside of the **parenthesis** at the right side, and then multiply step-by-step as shown:

$$(36 + 4) \times (5 - 2) = 40 \times (5 - 2) \qquad (36 + 4 = 40)$$
$$= 40 \times 3 \qquad (5 - 2 = 3)$$
$$= 120 \qquad (40 \times 3 = 120)$$

p. Do the subtraction inside of the **parenthesis** at the left side, do the subtraction inside of the **parenthesis** at the right side, and then do the subtraction step-by-step as shown:

$$(19 - 9) - (7 - 5) = 10 - (7 - 5)$$
$$= 10 - 2$$
$$= 8$$

$$(19 - 9 = 10)$$
$$(7 - 5 = 2)$$
$$(10 - 2 = 8)$$

q. Do the subtraction inside of the **parenthesis** at the left side, do the addition inside of the **parenthesis** at the right side and then do the addition step-by-step as shown:

$$(23 - 19) + (7 + 3) = 4 + (7 + 3)$$
$$= 4 + 10$$
$$= 14$$

$$(23 - 19 = 4)$$
$$(7 + 3 = 10)$$
$$(4 + 10 = 14)$$

Addition, Subtraction, Multiplication, Division, Parentheses, Exponents, and Roots

Quick Review

Exponents show repeated multiplication. Therefore, an exponent tells how many times a base is used as a factor as shown:

(a).

Exponent form.   Factor form.

Standard form.   Exponent

$$4^3 = 4 \cdot 4 \cdot 4 = 64$$ $$4^3$$

Base   4 is used as a factor 3 times.

(b). $2^3 = 2 \cdot 2 \cdot 2 = 8$

An example of a "**Root**" is a **square root**.

If $A = x^2$, then x is the square root of A. The square root of x^2 is written as $\sqrt{x^2} = x$ where $\sqrt{\ }$ is the symbol for square root. (**Note**: Finding the square root is similar to finding the length of a side of a square when the area of the square is known.) Review the section on the area of a square. Review the section on square root also.

For examples:

a. $\sqrt{4} = \sqrt{2^2} = 2$ **b.** $\sqrt{9} = \sqrt{3^3} = 3$ **c.** $\sqrt{16} = \sqrt{4^2} = 4$

d. $\sqrt{25} = \sqrt{5^2} = 5$ **e.** $\sqrt{36} = \sqrt{6^2} = 6$ **f.** $\sqrt{49} = \sqrt{7^2} = 7$

g. $\sqrt{64} = \sqrt{8^2} = 8$ **h.** $\sqrt{81} = \sqrt{9^2} = 9$ **i.** $\sqrt{100} = \sqrt{10^2} = 10$

Example 6

Find the value of each expression.

a. $(3^2 - \sqrt{9}) - \sqrt{16} + 2^2$ **b.** $2^2 \times \sqrt{25} + \sqrt{16}$ **c.** $\sqrt{36} + 4^2 - \sqrt{9}$

d. $(2^3 + \sqrt{25}) - (3^2 - \sqrt{36})^2$　　**e.** $(\sqrt{81} - 2^2 + \sqrt{16}) \times (6^2 - 4^2 - 3^2) \div 2$

Solution

PERMDAS is used to find the values of questions **a** to **e** as shown:

a. Do the **exponent** and the **root** inside of the **parenthesis**, and then subtract inside of the **parenthesis**, do the **exponent outside the parenthesis**, do the **root outside the parenthesis**, subtract, and then add step-by-step as shown:

$$(3^2 - \sqrt{9}) - \sqrt{16} + 2^2 = (9 - \sqrt{9}) - \sqrt{16} + 2^2 \qquad\qquad 3^2 = 9$$
$$= (9 - 3) - \sqrt{16} + 2^2 \qquad\qquad \sqrt{9} = 3$$
$$= 6 - \sqrt{16} + 2^2 \qquad\qquad 9 - 3 = 6$$
$$= 6 - \sqrt{16} + 4 \qquad\qquad 2^2 = 4$$
$$= 6 - 4 + 4 \qquad\qquad \sqrt{16} = 4$$
$$= 2 + 4 \qquad\qquad 6 - 4 = 2$$
$$= 6 \qquad\qquad 2 + 4 = 6$$

b. Do the **exponent**, do the **roots**, multiply, and then add step-by-step as shown:

$$2^2 \times \sqrt{25} + \sqrt{16} = 4 \times \sqrt{25} + \sqrt{16} \qquad\qquad 2^2 = 4$$
$$= 4 \times 5 + 4 \qquad\qquad \sqrt{25} = 5, \sqrt{16} = 4$$
$$= 20 + 4 \qquad\qquad 4 \times 5 = 20$$
$$= 24 \qquad\qquad 20 + 4 = 24$$

c. Do the **exponent**, do the **roots**, add, and then subtract step-by-step as shown:

$$\sqrt{36} + 4^2 - \sqrt{9} = \sqrt{36} + 16 - \sqrt{9} \qquad\qquad 4^2 = 16$$
$$= 6 + 16 - 3 \qquad\qquad \sqrt{36} = 6, \sqrt{9} = 3$$
$$= 22 - 3 \qquad\qquad 6 + 16 = 22$$
$$= 19 \qquad\qquad 22 - 3 = 19$$

d. Do the **exponent** and the **root** inside of the **parenthesis** on the left side and then add, do the **exponent** and the **root** inside of the **parenthesis** on the right side and then subtract, do the **exponent** inside of the **parentheses** on the right side. Finally, subtract as shown step-by-step:

$$(2^3 + \sqrt{25}) - (3^2 - \sqrt{36})^2 = (8 + \sqrt{25}) - (3^2 - \sqrt{36})^2 \qquad 2^3 = 2 \cdot 2 \cdot 2 = 8$$
$$= (8 + 5) - (3^2 - \sqrt{36})^2 \qquad\qquad \sqrt{25} = 5$$
$$= 13 - (3^2 - \sqrt{36})^2 \qquad\qquad (8 + 5) = 13$$
$$= 13 - (9 - \sqrt{36})^2 \qquad\qquad 3^2 = 9$$
$$= 13 - (9 - 6)^2 \qquad\qquad \sqrt{36} = 6$$
$$= 13 - 3^2 \qquad\qquad (9 - 6)^2 = 3^2$$
$$= 13 - 9 \qquad\qquad 3^2 = 9$$
$$= 4 \qquad\qquad 13 - 9 = 4$$

e. Do the **operations** inside of the **parenthesis** at the left side according to **PERMDAS**, do the **operations** inside of the **parenthesis** at the right side according to **PERMDAS**, multiply the results, and then divide as shown step-by-step:

$$(\sqrt{81} - 2^2 + \sqrt{16}) \times (6^2 - 4^2 - 3^2) \div 2$$

$$= (\sqrt{81} - 4 + \sqrt{16}) \times (6^2 - 4^2 - 3^2) \div 2 \qquad\qquad 2^2 = 4$$

$$= (9 - 4 + 4) \times (6^2 - 4^2 - 3^2) \div 2 \qquad\qquad \sqrt{81} = 9,\ \sqrt{16} = 4$$

$$= (5 + 4) \times (6^2 - 4^2 - 3^2) \div 2 \qquad\qquad 9 - 4 = 5$$

$$= 9 \times (6^2 - 4^2 - 3^2) \div 2 \qquad\qquad 5 + 4 = 9$$

$$= 9 \times (36 - 16 - 9) \div 2 \qquad\qquad 6^2 = 36,\ 4^2 = 16,\ 3^2 = 9$$

$$= 9 \times (20 - 9) \div 2 \qquad\qquad 36 - 16 = 20$$

$$= 9 \times 11 \div 2 \qquad\qquad 20 - 9 = 11$$

$$= 99 \div 2 \qquad\qquad 9 \times 11 = 99$$

$$= 49\frac{1}{2} \qquad\qquad 99 \div 2 = 49\frac{1}{2}$$

The notes and the generous worked examples have provided me with the conceptual understanding and the computational fluency to do my homework.

Exercises

1. What is meant by the order of operations?

2. What does PERMDAS stand for?

3. Find the value of each expression. Hint: See Example 2.
   Match similar exercises with similar examples.

   a. 8 + 4 - 3   **b.** 16 - 7 + 3   **c.** 16 - 5 - 8

   d. 32 - 10 + 5   **e.** 13 + 2 - 7   **f.** 24 - 6 - 10

4 Find the value of each expression. Hint: See Example 3.
   Match similar exercises with similar Examples.

   a. 10 · 2 ÷ 4   **b.** 15 ÷ 5 · 3   **c.** 36 ÷ 6 ÷ 6

   d. 28 ÷ 7 · 3   **e.** 24 ÷ 4 ÷ 3   **f.** 8 · 2 ÷ 4

5. Find the value of each expression. Hint: See Example 4.
   Match similar exercises with similar examples.

   a. 6 · 4 - 3   **b.** 36 - 5 · 2   **c.** 30 ÷ 3 + 4

   d. 8 - 30 ÷ 5   **e.** 12 - 4 · 2 + 6   **f.** 5 + 3 · 4 - 2

   g. 16 - 2 · 5 + 4 ÷ 2   **h.** 14 ÷ 7 · 3 + 8 - 3   **i.** 4 · 6 ÷ 3

   j. 12 ÷ 3 · 4   **k.** 18 ÷ 6 + 2 · 6   **l.** 6 + 12 - 3 · 4   **m.** 7 + 2 · 4

6. Find the value of each expression. Hint: See Example 5.
   Match similar exercises with similar examples.

   a. 4 · (7 + 3)   **b.** (7 - 5) · 2   **c.** 36 ÷ (4 + 2)

   d. (18 - 3) ÷ 5   **e.** (13 + 2) · 2   **f.** 8 + (24 - 9)

   g. 16 ÷ 4 · (8 - 6)   **h.** 2 · (5 + 4) ÷ 6   **i.** 8 · 3 ÷ (12 - 8)

j. $(12 + 6) \times (9 - 7)$ **k**. $11 + 3 \div (4 - 2)$ **l**. $(5 + 3 \cdot 5) \div 2$

m. $4 \cdot (12 - 3 \cdot 4 \div 3)$ **n**. $8 - (3 + 5)$ **o**. $(14 + 2) \times (6 - 4)$

p. $(9 - 3) - (13 - 7)$ **q**. $(15 - 8) + (4 + 8)$

7. Find the value of each expression. Hint: See Example 6.
  Match similar exercises with similar examples.

  a. $(2^2 - \sqrt{4}) - \sqrt{4} + 3^2$ **b**. $3^2 \times \sqrt{16} + \sqrt{9}$ **c**. $\sqrt{64} + 3^2 - \sqrt{9}$

  d. $(3^3 + \sqrt{9}) - (2^3 - \sqrt{25})^2$ **e**. $(\sqrt{100} - 3^2 + \sqrt{25}) \times (5^2 - 3^2 - 2^2)$

Challenge Questions

8 Find the value of each expression.

  a. $10 - 3 - 4$ **b**. $17 - 8 + 2$ **c**. $18 + 3 - 9$ **d**. $36 \div 6 \div 3$

  e. $9 \cdot 2 \div 3$ **f**. $15 \div 3 \cdot 3$ **g**. $10 - 4 \div 2$ **h**. $8 - 2 \cdot 4 + 5$

  i. $18 - 11 \cdot 2$ **j**. $12 \div 4 + 3$ **k**. $8 \cdot 4 - 5$ **l**. $5 \cdot 4 \div 2$

  m. $12 - 3 \cdot 2 + 4 \div 2$ **n**. $24 \div 6 \cdot 2 + 9 - 7$ **o**. $16 \div 4 \cdot 3$

  p. $24 \div 4 + 3 \cdot 4$ **q**. $8 + 3 \cdot 5$ **r**. $10 + 4 - 2 \cdot 4$ **s**. $3 \cdot 4 \div 2$

9. Find the value of each expression.

  a. $6 \cdot 3 \div (9 - 6)$ **b**. $(8 + 3) \cdot 4$ **c**. $24 \div (5 + 3)$ **d**. $3 \cdot (5 + 6)$

  e. $15 \div 3 \cdot (7 - 3)$ **f**. $3 \cdot (4 + 3) \div 3$ **g**. $(12 - 3) - (10 - 4)$

  h. $(10 - 4) \times (7 + 3)$ **i**. $(8 + 4 \div 2) \div 5$ **j**. $6 \cdot (14 - 3 \times 4 \div 3)$

  k. $(14 - 8) + (3 + 7)$ **l**. $3 \cdot (16 - 4 \cdot 2 \div 8)$ **m**. $(7 + 5 \cdot 5) \div 4$

10. Find the value of each expression.

  a. $\sqrt{81} - 2^3 + \sqrt{4}$ **b**. $3^2 \cdot \sqrt{4} - \sqrt{9}$ **c**. $4^2 - \sqrt{100} \div 2$

  d. $(4^2 + \sqrt{81}) - (2^3 - \sqrt{9})^2$ **e**. $(3^3 - \sqrt{16}) - \sqrt{16} + 3^2$

  f. $\sqrt{81} + 3^2 - \sqrt{16}$ **g**. $(4^2 - \sqrt{16}) - \sqrt{9} + 3^2$ **h**. $3^3 \cdot \sqrt{25} + \sqrt{36}$

Answers to Selected Questions

3a. 9   **4a**. 5   **5a**. 21   **6a**. 40   **7a**. 9

Extension of the Order of Operations Using PERMDAS

(A). Fraction Bar

The order of operations using PERMDAS can be extended to include a fraction bar.
A fraction bar indicates that the operations in the numerator are done separately using
PERMDAS and the operations in the denominator are also done separately using
PERMDAS. Finally, the numerator is divided by the denominator.

Example 7

Find the value of each expression.

a. $\dfrac{24 \div (7 - 3)}{9 - 3}$ **b.** $\dfrac{(16 - 4) - 2}{5 - 12 \div 4}$ **c.** $\dfrac{(15 - 7) \cdot 4}{16 - 4 \cdot 3}$ **d.** $\dfrac{3 \cdot 4 + 10}{12 \div 3 - 1}$

Solution

a. Considering the **numerator** using PERMDAS, do the subtraction inside of the **parenthesis**, and then do the division. Considering the **denominator** using PERMDAS, do the subtraction, and then dividing the **numerator** by the **denominator** as shown step-by-step:

$$\frac{24 \div (7 - 3)}{9 - 3} = \frac{24 \div 4}{9 - 3} \qquad\qquad (7 - 3) = 4$$

$$= \frac{6}{9 - 3} \qquad\qquad 24 \div 4 = 6$$

$$= \frac{6}{6} \qquad\qquad 9 - 3 = 6$$

$$= 1 \qquad\qquad 6 \div 6 = 1$$

b. Considering the **numerator**, using PERMDAS, do the subtraction inside of the **parenthesis**, and then do the subtraction outside the parentheses. Considering the **denominator**, using PERMDAS, do the division, and then the subtraction. Finally, divide the **numerator** by the **denominator** as shown step-by-step:

$$\frac{(16 - 4) - 2}{5 - 12 \div 4} = \frac{12 - 2}{5 - 12 \div 4} \qquad\qquad (16 - 4) = 12$$

$$= \frac{10}{5 - 12 \div 4} \qquad\qquad 12 - 2 = 10$$

$$= \frac{10}{5 - 3} \qquad\qquad 12 \div 4 = 3$$

$$= \frac{10}{2} \qquad\qquad 5 - 3 = 2$$

$$= 5 \qquad\qquad 10 \div 2 = 5$$

c. Considering the **numerator**, and using **PERMDAS**, do the subtraction inside the **parenthesis**, and then multiply. Considering the **denominator**, and using PERMDAS, do the multiplication, and subtraction. Finally, divide the **numerator** by the **denominator** step-by-step as shown:

$$\frac{(15 - 7) \cdot 4}{16 - 4 \cdot 3} = \frac{8 \cdot 4}{16 - 4 \cdot 3} \qquad\qquad (15 - 7) = 8$$

$$= \frac{32}{16 - 4 \cdot 3} \qquad\qquad 8 \cdot 4 = 32$$

$$= \frac{32}{16 - 12} \qquad\qquad 4 \cdot 3 = 12$$

$$= \frac{32}{4} \qquad\qquad 16 - 12 = 4$$

$$= 8 \qquad\qquad 32 \div 4 = 8$$

d. Considering the **numerator**, using PERMDAS, multiply, and then add.
Considering the **denominator**, using PERMDAS, divide, and subtract.
Finally, divide the numerator by the denominator step-by-step as shown:

$$\frac{3 \cdot 4 + 10}{12 \div 3 - 1} = \frac{12 + 10}{12 \div 3 - 1} \qquad\qquad 3 \cdot 4 = 12$$

$$= \frac{22}{12 \div 3 - 1} \qquad\qquad 2 + 10 = 22$$

$$= \frac{22}{4 - 1} \qquad\qquad 12 \div 3 = 4$$

$$= \frac{22}{3} \qquad\qquad 4 - 1 = 3$$

$$= 7\frac{1}{3} \qquad\qquad 22 \div 3 = 7\frac{1}{3}$$

(B). Parentheses and Brackets

The symbol for parentheses is ( ) and the symbol for a bracket is [ ]. The brackets
may be considered as another type of parentheses, and that the operations
inside of the **parentheses** are done first according to PERMDAS **before** the
operations inside of the **brackets** are done according to PERMDAS,
and then we should do the remaining operations according to PERMDAS. The
parentheses and brackets are used in expressions when further groupings of
the numbers in the expression are necessary. **Note that the operations should
always be done within the innermost grouping symbols first**.

Example 8
Find the value of each expression.
a. [(9 - 5) + 3] $\cdot$ 2   **b.** [(19 - 4) $\div$ (12 - 9)] $\cdot$ 3
Solution
a. Do the subtraction inside of the **parentheses**, do the addition inside of the **bracket**

next, and then multiply step-by-step as shown:

$$[(9 - 5) + 3] \cdot 2 = [4 + 3] \cdot 2$$
$$= 7 \cdot 2$$
$$= 14$$

$$(9 - 5) = 4$$
$$[4 + 3] = 7$$
$$7 \cdot 2 = 14$$

b. Do the subtractions inside of **both parentheses**, do the division inside of the **bracket** next, and then multiply step-by-step as shown:

$$[(19 - 4) \div (12 - 9)] \cdot 3 = [15 \div 3] \cdot 3$$
$$= 5 \cdot 3$$
$$= 15$$

$$(19 - 4) = 15, (12 - 9) = 3$$
$$[15 \div 3] = 5$$
$$5 \cdot 3 = 15$$

Example 9

Find the value of each expression.

a. $[(7 - 5)^2 + 3] \cdot 3$ **b**. $[(10 - 8)^3 \div (9 - 7)^2] \cdot 3$ **c**. $[(11 - 9)^2 \times (24 - 23)^2]^2 \cdot 2$

Solution

a. Do the operation inside of the **parenthesis**, do the operation in the **bracket**, and then multiply step-by-step as shown:

$$[(7 - 5)^2 + 3] \cdot 3 = [2^2 + 3] \cdot 3$$
$$= [4 + 3] \cdot 3$$
$$= 7 \cdot 3$$
$$= 21$$

$$(7 - 5)^2 = 2^2$$
$$2^2 = 4$$
$$[4 + 3] = 7$$
$$7 \cdot 3 = 21$$

b. Do the operations inside of both **parentheses**, do the operations in the **bracket**, and then multiply step-by-step as shown:

$$[(10 - 8)^3 \div (9 - 7)^2] \cdot 3 = [2^3 \div 2^2] \cdot 3$$
$$= [8 \div 4] \cdot 3$$
$$= 2 \cdot 3$$
$$= 6$$

$$(10 - 8)^3 = 2^3, (9 - 7)^2 = 2^2$$
$$2^3 = 2 \cdot 2 \cdot 2 = 8, 2^2 = 2 \cdot 2 = 4$$
$$[8 \div 4] = 2$$
$$2 \cdot 3 = 6$$

c. Do the operations inside of both **parentheses**, do the operations in the bracket, square the simplification inside the bracket, and then multiply step-by-step as shown:

$$[(11 - 9)^2 \times (24 - 23)^2]^2 \cdot 2 = [2^2 \times 1^2]^2 \cdot 2$$
$$= [4 \times 1]^2 \cdot 2$$
$$= 4^2 \cdot 2$$
$$= 16 \cdot 2$$
$$= 32$$

$$(11 - 9)^2 = 2^2, (24 - 23)^2 = 1^2$$
$$2^2 = 4, 1^2 = 1$$
$$[4 \times 1]^2 = 4^2$$
$$4^2 = 4 \times 4 = 16$$
$$16 \cdot 2 = 32$$

━━━━━━━━━━━━━━ The notes and the generous worked examples have provided me with the conceptual understanding and the computational fluency to do my homework.

Exercises

1. Find the value of each expression. Hint: See Example 7. Match similar exercises with similar examples.

a. $\dfrac{18 \div (11 - 9)}{17 - 14}$ **b.** $\dfrac{(19 - 3) - 4}{6 - 9 \div 3}$ **c.** $\dfrac{(27 - 23) \cdot 4}{18 - 7 \cdot 2}$ **d.** $\dfrac{5 \cdot 3 + 5}{9 - 20 \div 5}$

2. Find the value of each expression. Hint: See Example 8. Match similar exercises with similar examples.

    a. $[(12 - 7) + 4] \cdot 3$ **b.** $[(14 - 6) \div (16 - 12)] \cdot 2$

3. Find the value of each expression. Hint: See Example 9.
Match similar exercises with similar examples.

    a. $[(9 - 7)^2 + 6] \cdot 2$ **b.** $[(5 - 1)^2 \div (11 - 9)^2] \cdot 2$ **c.** $[(18 - 16)^2 \times (7 - 5)^2]^2 \cdot 2$

Challenge Questions

4. Find the value of each expression.

    a. $\dfrac{4 \cdot 3 + 8}{11 - 36 \div 6}$ **b.** $\dfrac{(7 - 4) \cdot 5}{9 - 4}$ **c.** $[(7 - 3) + 2] \cdot 4$

    d. $[(6 - 4)^3 \div (5 - 3)^2] \cdot 2$ **e.** $[(14 + 10) \div (8 - 2)] \cdot 2$ **f.** $[(3 + 1)^2 \times (13 - 11)^2] \cdot 2$

Answers to Selected Questions

1a. 3   **2b.** 4   **3a.** 20

Cumulative Review

1. $8.48 \times 6 =$ **2.** $90 \div 3 =$ **3.** $43 - 7.9 =$

2. Multiply, add, or subtract.

    a. $\begin{array}{r} 77.3 \\ -\ 59.4 \\ \hline \end{array}$ **b.** $\begin{array}{r} 603 \\ +\ 697 \\ \hline \end{array}$ **c.** $\begin{array}{r} 326 \\ \times\ \ \ 4 \\ \hline \end{array}$

    d. $\begin{array}{r} 148 \\ \times\ \ \ .6 \\ \hline \end{array}$ **e.** $\begin{array}{r} 2.34 \\ \times\ 1.32 \\ \hline \end{array}$ **f.** $125 \div 5 =$

3. Find the value of each expression.

    a. $7 \cdot 5 - 30 =$ b. $28 - 10 \cdot 2 =$ c. $36 \div 4 + 9 =$

    d. $25 - 36 \div 4 =$ e. $9 - 1 \cdot 5 + 6 =$ f. $8 \cdot 3 \div (4 + 2) =$

4. A triangle has a base of 4 ft. Find the area of the triangle if the height is 12 ft.

5. The length of a rectangle is 6 cm. Find the area of the rectangle if the width is 5 cm.

6. The diameter of a circle is 10 m. Find the radius of the circle. Hint: Review the chapter on Circles in the Math Teaching Series for grade 5.

7. Complete each equation.

    a. 36 in. = ? ft   b. 2 ft = ? in.   c. 3 ft = ? yd

Hint: Review the chapter on Customary Unit of Length in the Math Teaching Series for grade 5.

FACTORS

New Term: Factor

A **factor** is a number that can divide another number evenly. For example, 2 can divide 4 evenly, and therefore, 2 is a factor of 4. A **factor** can also be said to be a number that can be multiplied by another number to obtain a product. For example, the factors of 12 are 1, 2, 3, 4, 6, and 12 because:

$$1 \times 12 = 12$$
$$2 \times 6 = 12$$
$$3 \times 4 = 12$$

Rule 1: A number will always have 1 and itself as a factor, and therefore, always begin the factors with 1, and then check in order for pairs of factors.

Rue 2: To find all the factors of a number, list all the numbers that can divide into it evenly including 1 and the number itself. List the factors from the least to the greatest.

Example 1

What are the factors of 9?

Solution

Using Rules 1 and 2, the factors of 9 are:

$$1 \times 9 = 9$$
$$3 \times 3 = 9$$

Note that the factor 3 pairs with itself, such that $3 \times 3 = 9$ and that 9 is also one of the factors, and therefore, 3 is used once as a factor instead of twice.

Therefore, the factors of 9 are 1, 3, and 9.

Example 2

What are the factors of 24?

Solution

Using Rules 1 and 2, the factors of 24 are:

$$1 \times 24 = 24$$
$$2 \times 12 = 24$$
$$3 \times 8 = 24$$
$$4 \times 6 = 24$$

The factors of 24 are 1, 2, 3, 4, 6, 8, 12, and 24.

Exercises

1. List all the factors of each number. Hint: See Examples 1 and 2 and Rules 1 and 2.

(a) 10	(b) 4	(c) 16	(d) 21	(e) 14
(f) 25	(g) 13	(h) 11	(i) 27	(j) 45
(k) 32	(l) 7	(m) 17	(n) 20	(o) 28

2. Explain what is meant by a factor?

Common Factors and Greatest Common Factor (GCF)

Two or more numbers can have factors that are the same and these factors are called **common factors**.

The **greatest common factor** (**GCF**) of two or more numbers is the greatest factor shared by the numbers.

Example 1

Find the (a) factors of 12 and 16.

(b) common factors of 12 and 16. Show your solution on a Venn diagram.

(c) greatest common factor of 12 and 16

Solution

(a) Using rules 1 and 2, the factors of 12 and 16 are as follows:

$$1 \times 12 = 12 \qquad 1 \times 16 = 16$$
$$2 \times 6 = 12 \qquad 2 \times 8 = 16$$
$$3 \times 4 = 12 \qquad 4 \times 4 = 16$$

Note that the factor 4 pairs with itself, such that $4 \times 4 = 16$ and that 16 is also one of the factors, and therefore, 4 is used once as a factor instead of twice.

From the factors above, the factors of 12 are 1, 2, 3, 4, 6, 12.

From the factors above, the factors of 16 are 1, 2, 4, 8, 16.

(b) Comparing the factors of 12 and 16, the factors that are common to both 12 and 16 are 1, 2, and 4, and therefore, the common factors of 12 and 16 are 1, 2, and 4 and this can be put in a Venn diagram as shown:

The overlapping region has the factors 1, 2, and 4 which are common to both 12 and 16.

This circle contains the factors of 16 which are 1, 2, 4, 8, and 16.

This circle contains the factors of 12 which are 1, 2, 3, 4, 6, and 12.

The diagram above is called venn diagram

(c) From solution (b), the common factors of 12 and 16 are 1, 2, and 4. The greatest common factor from the common factors 1, 2, and 4 is 4. Therefore, the greatest common factor (GCF) of 12 and 16 is 4.

Example 2
Find the (a) factors of 8, 10, and 15.
        (b) common factors of 8, 10, and 15.
        (c) greatest common factors of 8, 10, and 15.

Solution
(a) Using Rules 1 and 2, the factors of 8, 10, and 15 are as shown:

Factors of 8	Factors of 10	Factors of 15
$1 \times 8 = 8$	$1 \times 10 = 10$	$1 \times 15 = 15$
$2 \times 4 = 8$	$2 \times 5 = 10$	$3 \times 5 = 15$

From the factors above, the factors of 8 are 1, 2, 4, and 8.
From the factors above, the factors of 10 are 1, 2, 5, and 10.
From the factors above, the factors of 15 are 1, 3, 5, and 15.

(b). Comparing the factors of 8, 10, and 15, the factors that are common to 8, 10, and 15 is just 1.

(c). From the solution of (b), the common factor of 8, 10, and 15 is 1, and therefore, the greatest common factor (GCF) of 8, 10, and 15 is 1.

Rule 3: To find the greatest common factor (GCF) of two or more numbers, follow the three steps as shown:
    1. Find the factors of the numbers.
    2. Find the common factors of the numbers.
    3. Select the greatest common factor (GCF) from the common factors.

Check for Understanding
(a) A number will always have itself and 1 as factors. True or False?
(b) To find all the factors of a number list all the numbers that can divide into it evenly

including 1 and itself. True or False?

Exercises

1. Explain how you can find the factors of two numbers .
2. Explain how you can find the common factors of two numbers.
3. Explain how you can find the greatest common factor(GCF) of two numbers.
4. Find the factors, common factors and the greatest common factor (GCF) of each set of numbers. Hint: See Example 1.

   (a) 4 and 12   (b) 9 and 18   (c) 12 and 18
   (d) 18 and 24   (e) 12 and 18   (f) 8 and 15
   (g) 12 and 16   (h) 7 and 12   (i) 11 and 19
   (j) 25 and 15   (k) 3 and 10   (l) 13 and 5
   (m) 16 and 20   (n) 21 and 7   (0) 8 and 20

5. Find the greatest common factor (GCF) of 24 and 42 and show your solution on a Venn diagram. Hint: See Example 1.
6. Find the factors, common factors and the greatest common factors (GCF) of each set of numbers. Hint: See Example 2.

   (a) 6, 8, and 10   (b) 4, 12, and 16   (c) 8, 12, and 15
   (d) 12, 18, and 24   (e) 8, 12, and 24   (f) 12, 16, and 24
   (g) 7, 9, and 11   (h) 5, 10, and 15   (i) 11, 16, and 21

Challenge Questions

7. Show the solutions to question 4(a) to 4(c) on a Venn diagram.
8. Find the factors, common factors and the greatest common factor (GCF) of each set of numbers:

   (a) 5, 12, and 13   (b) 9 and 15   (c) 10, 16, and 21
   (d) 8, 16, and 24   (e) 12 and 15   (f) 3 and 14

Answers to Selected Questions

4(a) GCF is 4   5. GCF is 6

PRIME FACTORIZATION

Every composite number can be expressed as the product of prime factors and this product is the **prime factorization** of the number. Recall from the chapter on the "prime numbers and composite numbers" that a composite number is a number (other than 0) that has more than two factors, that is, a composite number has more than 1 and itself as factors.

Rule 1: To write a composite number as a product of prime numbers is to write the prime factorization of the number.

What is a factor tree? A **factor tree** is a step-by-step method for factoring a number by using a diagram as shown in Example 1.

Example 1

Use a factor tree to find the prime factorization of 24. Express your answer in the exponential form.

Solution

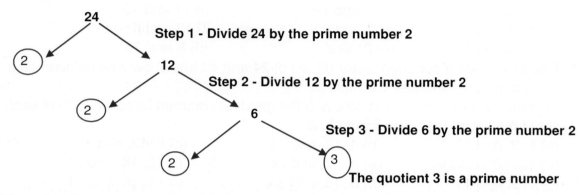

Step 1 - Divide 24 by the prime number 2

Step 2 - Divide 12 by the prime number 2

Step 3 - Divide 6 by the prime number 2

The quotient 3 is a prime number

The prime factorization of 24 is 2 · 2 · 2 · 3 which can be written in the exponential form as $2^3 \cdot 3^1$ or simply $2^3 \cdot 3$. The exponent 3 tells how many times the base 2 is used as a factor. Review the chapter on "the power of numbers".

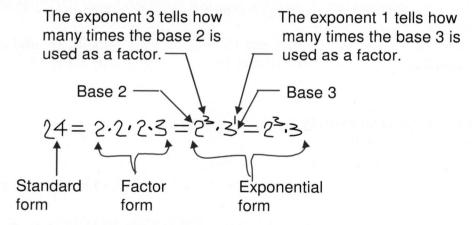

The exponent 3 tells how many times the base 2 is used as a factor.

The exponent 1 tells how many times the base 3 is used as a factor.

Base 2   Base 3

$$24 = 2 \cdot 2 \cdot 2 \cdot 3 = 2^3 \cdot 3^1 = 2^3 \cdot 3$$

Standard form   Factor form   Exponential form

From the solution of Example 1 note that:

(a) 24, 12, and 6 are all divided by the least possible prime number of 2 until we obtain the final quotient of 3 which is a prime number.

(b) When 6 is divided by 2, the quotient is 3 and 3 is a prime number, and therefore, the division cannot go on any further.

(c) All the factors are prime.

Rule 2: **To find the prime factorization of any number, divide the number by prime numbers only in order starting from the least possible prime number until**

the final quotient is a prime number.

Example 2
Use a factor tree to find the prime factorization of 60. Express your answer in the exponential form.
Solution
Using rule 2, we can write the prime factorization of 60 as shown:

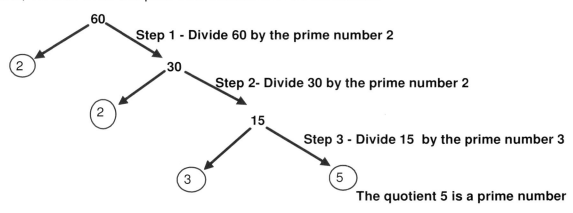

The prime factorization of 60 is 2 · 2 · 3 · 5 which is written in the exponential form as 2^2 · 3 · 5. See the explanation for the exponential form in Example 1.

Example 3
(a) From the solution of Example 2, complete the prime factorization:
$$60 = 2 \cdot 2 \cdot 15$$
$$= 2 \cdot 2 \cdot ? \cdot 5$$
(b) Complete the prime factorization:
$$54 = 2 \cdot 27$$
$$= 2 \cdot 3 \cdot 9$$
$$= 2 \cdot 3 \cdot ? \cdot 3$$
Solution
(a) From the solution of Example 2, the prime factorization can be completed as shown:
$$60 = 2 \cdot 2 \cdot 3 \cdot 5 \text{ because one of the prime factors of 15 is missing which is 3}$$
(b) The prime factorization of 54 is:
$$54 = 2 \cdot 3 \cdot 3 \cdot 3 \text{ because one of the prime factors of 9 is missing, which is 3.}$$

Exercises
1. Give the prime factorization of each number by using the factor tree. Express your answer in the exponential form. Hint: See Examples 1 and 2.
   (a) 12   (b) 18   (c) 20   (d) 28
   (e) 44   (f) 32   (g) 58   (h) 48

(i) 64	(j) 36	(k) 45	(l) 50
(m) 25	(n) 54	(o) 49	(p) 30
(q) 34	(r) 65	(s) 42	(t) 27

2. Find the prime factorization without using a factor tree. Express your answer in the exponential form. Hint: See Example 3.

(a) 15	(b) 16	(c) 21	(d) 35
(e) 9	(f) 35	(g) 40	(h) 26

Challenge Questions

3. Find the prime factorization of each number by using a factor tree. Express your answer in the exponential form.

(a) 45	(b) 72	(c) 27	(d) 180

4. Find the prime factorization without using a factor tree. Express your answer in the exponential form.

(a) 64	(b) 54	(c) 85	(d) 90

Answers to Selected Questions

1(a) $12 = 2 \cdot 2 \cdot 3 = 2^2 \cdot 3$ 2(a) $15 = 3 \cdot 5 = 3^1 \cdot 5^1 = 3 \cdot 5$

Cumulative Review

1. What is a factor tree?
2. What does PERMDAS stands for?
3. Explain the following terms:

a. median	b. scientific notation
c. mode	d. mean
e. average	f. sum
g. dividend	h. quotient

Hint: Review the Math Teaching Series for grade 5.

4. What is the sum of the measures of the angles in a triangle?
5. What is the sum of the measures of the angles in a rectangle?
6. Mary said that the opposite sides of a rectangle are parallel. Is her statement correct? Explain. Review the Math Teaching Series for grade 5.

(The answers to the above Cumulative Review problems can also be found in the Math Teaching Series for grade 6. Refer to the Table of Contents and the Index.)

POWER OF NUMBERS

In the grid diagram, there are 5 rows and 5 columns of blocks. The total number of blocks in the grid can be written as 5 · 5 where the dot (·) means multiplication.

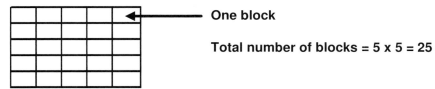

One block

Total number of blocks = 5 x 5 = 25

The total number of the blocks is 5×5 which may be written as $5 \cdot 5$ which may further be written as 5^2 where the 5 is the base and 2 is the exponent as shown below:

$$5 \cdot 5 = 5^2 \quad \nearrow \text{exponent}$$
$$\nwarrow \text{base}$$

The **exponent** 2 shows how many times the base 5 is used as a factor
5^2 is known as "5 squared" or 5 to the second power. Similarly, instead of writing the same factor several times, the factor can be written once and the exponent can be used as shown:

$$5 \cdot 5 \cdot 5 = 5^3 \qquad \text{which is 5 to the third power}$$
$$5 \cdot 5 \cdot 5 \cdot 5 = 5^4 \qquad \text{which is 5 to the fourth power}$$
$$5 \cdot 5 \cdot 5 \cdot 5 \cdot 5 = 5^5 \qquad \text{which is 5 to the fifth power}$$

In general, $n \cdot n \cdot n \cdot n \cdot n \cdot n \cdot \ldots = n^x$ which is n to the xth power

Rule 1: The value of any number or any representation of a number such as a, b, n, x, or y to the power 0 is 1. For example, $1^0 = 1$, $2^0 = 1$, $100^0 = 1$, $n^0 = 1$, $x^0 = 1$, and $y^0 = 1$.

Example 1
How do you read 10^4 ?
Solution
10^4 is read as "10 to the power 4."

Example 2
(a) Write 8 in the exponential form.
(b) Write 24 in the exponential form.
(c) Write 60 in the exponential form.
Solution
(a) Use the prime factorization method under the section of prime factorization to find

the prime factors of 8 as shown:

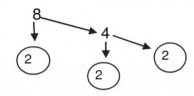

The prime factorization of 8 is 2 · 2 · 2.

Factor form

Therefore, $8 = 2 \cdot 2 \cdot 2 = 2^3$

Standard form.   Exponential form

(b) From the chapter on prime factorization Example 1, the prime factors of 24 are:

2 · 2 · 2 · 3

Therefore, the exponential form of 24 is:

$24 = 2 \cdot 2 \cdot 2 \cdot 3 = 2^3 \cdot 3$

Standard form   Exponential form

(c) From the chapter on prime factorization, Example 2, the prime factors of 60 are:

2 · 2 · 3 · 5.

Therefore, the exponential form of 60 is:

$60 = 2 \cdot 2 \cdot 3 \cdot 5 = 2^2 \cdot 3 \cdot 5$

Standard form.   Exponential form

Example 3
(a) Find the value of 4^3
(b) Find the value of 3^4
(c) Find the value of $2 \cdot 3^2$
(d) $2 \cdot 3^2 \cdot 4^2 =$
(e) Find the value of $2^2 \cdot 3 \cdot 5^2$

Solution
(a) $4^3 = 4 \times 4 \times 4 = 64$
(b) $3^4 = 3 \times 3 \times 3 \times 3 = 81$
(c) $2 \cdot 3^2 = 2 \times 3 \times 3 = 18$
(d) $2 \cdot 3^2 \cdot 4^2 = 2 \times 3 \times 3 \times 4 \times 4 = 288$
(e) $2^2 \cdot 3 \cdot 5^2 = 2 \times 2 \times 3 \times 5 \times 5 = 300$

Example 4

(a) Find the value of 6^1

(b) Find the value of 4^0

(c) Find the value of $6^1 \cdot 4^0 \cdot 2^2$

(e) Find the value of $3^0 \cdot 20^0 \cdot x^0$

Solution

(a) $6^1 = 6$

(b) $4^0 = 1$　　**Notice that any number to the power of 0 is equal to 1, therefore, $4^0 = 1$.**

(c) $6^1 \cdot 4^0 \cdot 2^2 = 6 \times 1 \times 2 \times 2 = 24$　　Note $4^0 = 1$

(d) $2^0 \cdot 5^1 \cdot 6^2 = 1 \times 5 \times 6 \times 6 = 180$　Note $2^0 = 1$

(e) $3^0 \cdot 20^0 \cdot x^0 = 1 \times 1 \times 1 = 1$　　　Note $3^0 = 1$, $20^0 = 1$, $x^0 = 1$

Example 5

Complete each equation

(a) $a \cdot a \cdot b \cdot b \cdot b = a^2?$ 　　　　　(b) $2 \cdot 2 \cdot 3 \cdot 5 \cdot 5 = 2^2 \cdot 3?$

(c) $2 \cdot x \cdot 4 \cdot y \cdot x = 8x^2?$ 　　　　(d) $3 \cdot x \cdot y \cdot 2 \cdot y = ?x?$

(e) $a^0 \cdot 4 = ? \cdot 4$ 　　　　　　　　(f) $a^0 \cdot b^0 \cdot 3 \cdot 3 \cdot 4 = ? \, ? \, 3^2 \cdot 4$

Solution

(a) $a \cdot a \cdot b \cdot b \cdot b = a^2 b^3$　　(b^3 because there are 3 bases of b).

　　　　　　　　　　　　　　　(a^2 because there are 2 bases of a).

(b) $2 \cdot 2 \cdot 3 \cdot 5 \cdot 5 = 2^2 \cdot 3 \cdot 5^2$　　(5^2 because there are 2 bases of 5).

　　　　　　　　　　　　　　　(2^2 because there are 2 bases of 2).

　　　　　　　　　　　　　　　(3 because there is 1 base of 3).

(c) $2 \cdot x \cdot 4 \cdot y \cdot x = 8x^2 y$　　　(y because there is 1 base of y).

　　　　　　　　　　　　　　　(x^2 because there are 2 bases of x).

　　　　　　　　　　　　　　　(8 because $2 \cdot 4 = 8$).

(d) $3 \cdot x \cdot y \cdot 2 \cdot y = 6xy^2$　　　(6 and y^2 because $3 \times 2 = 6$ and there are 2 bases of y).

　　　　　　　　　　　　　　　(x because there is 1 base of x).

(e) $a^0 \cdot 4 = 1 \cdot 4$　　　　　(Note: $a^0 = 1$)

(f) $a^0 \cdot b^0 \cdot 3 \cdot 3 \cdot 4 = 1 \cdot 1 \cdot 3^2 \cdot 4$　(Note: $a^0 = 1$, and $b^0 = 1$)

　　　　　　　　　　　　　　　(3^2 because there are 2 bases of 3).

Exercises

1. Explain what is meant by the base and the exponent of a number in the exponential form.

2. How do you read the following: Hint: See Example 1.

　　(a) 2^5 　　　　　(b) 3^4 　　　　　(c) 10^3 　　　　　(d) 100^2

(e) 9^1 (f) 12^3 (g) 5^3 (h) 2^6

3. Write the following in the exponential form. Hint: See Example 2.

    (a) 9   (b) 12   (c) 16   (d) 18   (e) 20

    (f) 32   (g) 45   (h) 25   (i) 36   (j) 27

    (k) 21   (l) 27   (m) 35   (n) 99   (o) 64

4. Find the following values. Hint: See Example 3.

    (a) 2^4 (b) 8^2 (c) $2^3 \cdot 3^2$ (d) $3^2 \cdot 4^2$

    (e) $2 \cdot 3^2 \cdot 5^2$ (f) $2^2 \cdot 4 \cdot 5^2$ (g) $2 \cdot 3^2 \cdot 4$ (h) $2^3 \cdot 3 \cdot 4^2$

    (i) $3 \cdot 4 \cdot 5^2$ (j) $2 \cdot 3^2 \cdot 6$ (k) $2 \cdot 2 \cdot 4^2$ (l) $2^2 \cdot 3^2 \cdot 4$

    (m) 10^2 (n) 9^2 (o) $2 \cdot 10^3$ (p) $3^2 \cdot 8^2$

5. Find the following values. See Example 4.

    (a) 100^0 (b) 9^1 (c) $2^0 \cdot 3^2$ (d) $2^2 \cdot 4^0 \cdot 5^1$

    (e) $2^2 \cdot 3 \cdot 4^2$ (f) $2^3 \cdot 3^0 \cdot 4^2$ (g) $3^2 \cdot 5^0 \cdot 6^2$ (h) $4^0 \cdot 2^2 \cdot 3^2$

    (i) $2^0 \cdot 3^1 \cdot 5^0$ (j) $6^0 \cdot 10^0 \cdot 15^0$ (k) $2^0 \cdot 3^0 \cdot 5^0$ (l) $2^2 \cdot 6^2 \cdot 9^0$

    (m) $3^2 \cdot 5^0 \cdot 8^0$ (n) $2^3 \cdot 3^2 \cdot 4^0$ (o) $100^0 \cdot 200^0 \cdot 300^0$ (p) $10^2 \cdot 4^2$

6. Complete each equation. See Example 5.

    (a) $a \cdot a \cdot b \cdot b = a^2\,?$ (b) $2 \cdot 3 \cdot 3 \cdot 5 = 2 \cdot ? \cdot 5$ (c) $2 \cdot 2 \cdot 2 \cdot x \cdot x = ?\,x^2$

    (d) $3 \cdot x \cdot 2 \cdot y \cdot x = ? \cdot x^2 \cdot y$ (e) $2 \cdot a \cdot b \cdot 3 \cdot a \cdot = 6\,?\,b$ (f) $4 \cdot x \cdot y \cdot 2 \cdot y = 8\,x\,?$

    (g) $a \cdot a \cdot a \cdot b = ?\,b$ (h) $3 \cdot a \cdot x \cdot 4 \cdot a \cdot x = ?\,a^2\,?$ (i) $a^0 \cdot b^0 \cdot 2 \cdot 2 = 1\,?\,2^2$

    (j) $2 \cdot 2 \cdot 4^0 \cdot a^0 = 2^2 \cdot ? \cdot 1$ (k) $x^0 \cdot y^0 \cdot z^0 = ?\,?\,?$ (l) $4 \cdot y \cdot x \cdot b \cdot 2 \cdot y \cdot b = ?\,?\,x\,y^2$

Challenge Questions

7. Find each value.

    (a) $7^2 \cdot 9^0 =$ (b) $150^0 =$ (c) $2^0 \cdot 5^2 \cdot 7^0 =$ (d) $5^2 \cdot a^0 \cdot b^2 =$

8. Complete the equation.

    (a) $3 \cdot a \cdot b \cdot a \cdot b = 3a^2\,?$ (b) $4 \cdot a \cdot b \cdot 3 \cdot a \cdot b = ?\,a^2 b^2$

Answers to Selected Questions

    3(a). 3^2 4(a). 16   5(a). 1

EXPONENTS

An exponent shows how many times a base is used as a factor. For example,

$$1000 = 10 \cdot 10 \cdot 10 = 10^3$$

10 is the base
3 is the exponent

The exponent of 3 shows that the base which is 10 is used as a factor of 1000 three times. "10^3" is read as 10 to the third power or "10 cubed."

Multiplying Powers With the Same Base

The factors of any power such as 5^4 may be grouped in different ways as follows:

$5 \cdot 5 \cdot 5 \cdot 5 = 5^4$ ————————————————[A]

$(5 \cdot 5 \cdot 5) \cdot 5 = 5^3 \cdot 5^1 = 5^4$ ————————————[B]

$(5 \cdot 5) \cdot (5 \cdot 5) = 5^2 \cdot 5^2 = 5^4$ ———————————[C]

$5 \cdot (5 \cdot 5 \cdot 5) = 5^1 \cdot 5^3 = 5^4$ ————————————[D]

By observing equation [A], we can write:

$5 \cdot 5 \cdot 5 \cdot 5 = 5^1 \cdot 5^1 \cdot 5^1 \cdot 5^1 = 5^{1+1+1+1} = 5^4$

By observing equation [B], we can write:

$(5 \cdot 5 \cdot 5) \cdot 5 = 5^3 \cdot 5^1 = 5^{3+1} = 5^4$

By observing equation [C], we can write:

$(5 \cdot 5) \cdot (5 \cdot 5) = 5^2 \cdot 5^2 = 5^{2+2} = 5^4$

By observing equation [D], we can write:

$5 \cdot (5 \cdot 5 \cdot 5) = 5^1 \cdot 5^3 = 5^{1+3} = 5^4$

Therefore, observing equations [A], [B], [C], and [D], to multiply powers with the same base, use the same base, and then add the exponents such that in general,

$\mathbf{b}^m \cdot \mathbf{b}^n = \mathbf{b}^{m+n}$

Example 1

Multiply and write each product as one power.

a. $6^2 \cdot 6^7$ **b.** $7^3 \cdot 3^2$ **c.** $8^3 \cdot 8$ **d.** $4^2 \cdot a^2 \cdot 4^3 \cdot a^5$ **e.** $7^2 \cdot 7^6 \cdot 7^4$

Solution

a. $6^2 \cdot 6^7 = 6^{2+7}$ Add the exponents since the bases 6 and 6 are the same.

Generally, $\mathbf{b}^m \cdot \mathbf{b}^n = \mathbf{b}^{m+n}$

$\quad\quad = 6^9$ $2 + 7 = 9$

b. $7^3 \cdot 3^2 = 7^3 \cdot 3^2$ The bases 7 and 3 are not the same so their exponents cannot be combined.

c. $8^3 \cdot 8 = 8^3 \cdot 8^1$ 8 is the same as 8^1

      $= 8^{3+1}$ Add the exponents since the bases 8 and 8 are the same.
Generally, $\mathbf{b}^m \cdot \mathbf{b}^n = \mathbf{b}^{m+n}$

     $= 8^4$ $3 + 1 = 4$

d. $4^2 \cdot a^2 \cdot 4^3 \cdot a^5 = (4^2 \cdot 4^3) \cdot (a^2 \cdot a^5)$ Grouping the like bases together.

          $= 4^{2+3} \cdot a^{2+5}$ Add the exponents of the like bases.

          $= 4^5 \cdot a^7$ $2 + 3 = 5$ and $2 + 5 = 7$. The bases **4** and **a** are not the same so we cannot combine them.

e. $7^2 \cdot 7^6 \cdot 7^4 = 7^{2+6+4}$ Add the exponents because the bases 7, 7, and 7 are the same.

       $= 7^{12}$ $2 + 6 + 4 = 12$.

Example 2
Multiply using exponents.
a. $9^3 \cdot x^4 \cdot 2^4 \cdot 9 \cdot x^3 \cdot 2^n$
b. $n^2 \cdot k^3 \cdot n^4 \cdot k^2 \cdot n$

Solution

a. $9^3 \cdot x^4 \cdot 2^4 \cdot 9 \cdot x^3 \cdot 2^n = (9^3 \cdot 9) \cdot (x^4 \cdot x^3) \cdot (2^4 \cdot 2^n)$ Grouping the like bases.

           $= (9^3 \cdot 9^1) \cdot (x^4 \cdot x^3) \cdot (2^4 \cdot 2^n)$ Note: 9 is the same as 9^1.

           $= 9^{3+1} \cdot x^{4+3} \cdot 2^{4+n}$ Add the exponents of the like bases.

           $= 9^4 \cdot x^7 \cdot 2^{4+n}$ We can no longer combine the exponents because the bases 9, x, and 2 are not the same.

b. $n^2 \cdot k^3 \cdot n^4 \cdot k^2 \cdot n = (n^2 \cdot n^4 \cdot n) \cdot (k^3 \cdot k^2)$ Grouping the like bases of n and k.

         $= (n^2 \cdot n^4 \cdot n^1) \cdot (k^3 \cdot k^2)$ Note: n is the same as n^1.

         $= n^{2+4+1} \cdot k^{3+2}$ Add the exponents of the like bases.

         $= n^7 \cdot k^5$ We can no longer combine the exponents because the bases n and k are not the same.

Dividing Powers With the Same Base
Let us observe what happens when we divide powers with the same base as shown:

$$\frac{4^6}{4^4} = \frac{4 \cdot 4 \cdot 4 \cdot 4 \cdot 4 \cdot 4}{4 \cdot 4 \cdot 4 \cdot 4} = \frac{\cancel{4} \cdot \cancel{4} \cdot \cancel{4} \cdot \cancel{4} \cdot 4 \cdot 4}{\cancel{4} \cdot \cancel{4} \cdot \cancel{4} \cdot \cancel{4}} = 4 \cdot 4 = 4^2 \underline{\hspace{2cm}} [\text{A}]$$

It should then be observed from equation $[\text{A}]$ that $\dfrac{4^6}{4^4} = 4^{6-4} = 4^2$

Therefore, to divide powers with the same base, use the same base and then subtract the exponents, such that in general $\dfrac{b^m}{b^n} = \mathbf{b}^{m-n}$, and $b \neq 0$. The symbol $\neq$ means "is

not equal to." Note that $b \neq 0$ because if $b = 0$, then $\dfrac{b^m}{b^n} = \dfrac{0^m}{0^n}$, but it is impossible to

divide by 0.

Example 3
Divide and write each quotient as one power.

a. $\dfrac{6^5}{6^3}$ **b.** $\dfrac{n^5}{n^2}$ **c.** $\dfrac{m^6}{n^4}$

Solution

a. $\dfrac{6^5}{6^3} = 6^{5-3} = 6^2$ Subtract the exponents since the bases 6 and 6 are

the same. Generally, $\dfrac{b^m}{b^n} = \mathbf{b}^{m-n}$, $b \neq 0$.

b. $\dfrac{n^5}{n^2} = n^{5-2} = n^3$ Subtract the exponents since the bases n and n

are the same. Generally, $\dfrac{b^m}{b^n} = \mathbf{b}^{m-n}$, $b \neq 0$.

c. $\dfrac{m^6}{n^4}$ Cannot combine the exponents because the bases

m and n are not the same.

Example 4
Simplify each expression. Your answer should be in exponents.

a. $\dfrac{3^4 \cdot n^6}{n^2 \cdot 3^2}$ **b.** $\dfrac{x^7 \cdot y^8 \cdot 2^8}{y^6 \cdot 2^5 \cdot x^3}$ **c.** $\dfrac{12^7 \cdot n^6 \cdot y^5 \cdot x^4}{12^4 \cdot y^2 \cdot x \cdot k^2}$

Solution

a. $\dfrac{3^4 \cdot n^6}{n^2 \cdot 3^2} = 3^{4-2} \cdot n^{6-2}$ Subtract the exponents of the like bases.

$\dfrac{3^4}{3^2} = 3^{4-2}$, $\dfrac{n^6}{n^2} = n^{6-2}$. Generally, $\dfrac{b^m}{b^n} = \mathbf{b}^{m-n}$, $b \neq 0$.

$\qquad\qquad = 3^2 \cdot n^4$ $4 - 2 = 2$ and $6 - 2 = 4$.

b. $\dfrac{x^7 \cdot y^8 \cdot 2^8}{y^6 \cdot 2^5 \cdot x^3} = x^{7-3} \cdot y^{8-6} \cdot 2^{8-5}$ Subtract the exponents of the like bases.

$$\frac{x^7}{x^3} = x^{7-3}, \quad \frac{y^8}{y^6} = y^{8-6}, \quad \frac{2^8}{2^5} = 2^{8-5}$$

$$= x^4 \cdot y^2 \cdot 2^3 \qquad 7-3 = 4, \; 8-6 = 2, \text{ and } 8-5 = 3.$$

c. $\dfrac{12^7 \cdot n^6 \cdot y^5 \cdot x^4}{12^4 \cdot y^2 \cdot x \cdot k^2} = \dfrac{12^{7-4} \cdot n^6 \cdot y^{5-2} \cdot x^{4-1}}{k^2}$ Subtract the exponents of

the like bases.

$$= \frac{12^3 \cdot n^6 \cdot y^3 \cdot x^3}{k^2}$$ For example: $\dfrac{12^7}{12^4} = 12^{7-4} = 12^3$

$$\frac{y^5}{y^2} = y^{5-2} = y^3$$

$$\frac{x^4}{x} = \frac{x^4}{x^1} = x^{4-1} = x^3$$

Note that $x = x^1$.

Zero Power
It can be shown that 1 can be expressed as a fraction with the numerator and the denominator of the fraction having the same base and the same exponents and subtracting the exponents will result in a zero exponent as shown:

$$1 = \frac{3^2}{3^2} = 3^{2-2} = 3^0$$

Therefore, $1 = 3^0$

Therefore, the zero power of any number except 0 equals 1 such that in general
$b^0 = 1$ and $b \neq 0$.

Example 5
Evaluate

a. 7^0 **b.** $5^6 \cdot 5^{-6}$ **c.** $\dfrac{10^4}{10^4}$ **d.** $\dfrac{n^5}{n^5}$

e. $\dfrac{12^7 \cdot y^5 \cdot 4^3}{12^7 \cdot y^5 \cdot 4^2}$ **f.** $\dfrac{4^5 \cdot 3^4 \cdot n^9 \cdot 3^{-4}}{4^5 \cdot n^9}$

Solution

a. $7^0 = 1$ The zero power of any number except 0 equals 1.

b. $5^6 \cdot 5^{-6} = 5^{6 + (-6)}$ To multiply powers with the same base, use the same base, and then add the exponents such that in general,

$$b^m \cdot b^n = b^{m+n}.$$

$$5^6 \cdot 5^{-6} = 5^{6-6}$$

Note: + (- = -, therefore, 6 + (-6) = 6 - 6.

$$= 5^0$$

6 - 6 = 0.

$$= 1$$

The zero power of any number except 0 is 1.

c. $\dfrac{10^4}{10^4} = 10^{4-4}$

To divide powers with the same base, use the same base,

and then subtract the exponents such that in general

$$\dfrac{b^m}{b^n} = b^{m-n} \text{ and } b \neq 0.$$

$$= 10^0$$

4 - 4 = 0

$$= 1$$

The zero power of any number except 0 is 1

d. $\dfrac{n^5}{n^5} = n^{5-5}$

To divide powers with the same base, use the same base,

and then subtract the exponents such that in general

$$\dfrac{b^m}{b^n} = b^{m-n}, \text{ and } b \neq 0.$$

$$= n^0$$

5 - 5 = 0

$$= 1$$

The zero power of any number except 0 is 1.

e. $\dfrac{12^7 \cdot y^5 \cdot 4^3}{12^7 \cdot y^5 \cdot 4^2} = 12^{7-7} \cdot y^{5-5} \cdot 4^{3-2}$

To divide powers with the same base, use the same base, and then subtract the exponents such that in general

$$\dfrac{b^m}{b^n} = b^{m-n} \text{ and } x \neq 0.$$

$$= 12^0 \cdot y^0 \cdot 4^1$$

7 - 7 = 0, 5 - 5 = 0, and 3 - 2 = 1.

$$= 1 \cdot 1 \cdot 4$$

$12^0 = 1$, $y^0 = 1$, and $4^1 = 4$.

$$= 4$$

f. $\dfrac{4^5 \cdot 3^4 \cdot n^9 \cdot 3^{-4}}{4^5 \cdot n^9} = 4^{5-5} \cdot 3^{4+(-4)} \cdot n^{9-9}$

To divide powers with the same base, use the same base, and then subtract the

31

exponents such that in general $\dfrac{b^m}{b^n} = \mathbf{b}^{m\,-\,n}$

and $b \neq 0$. For examples: $\dfrac{4^5}{4^5} = 4^{5\,-\,5}$

$$\dfrac{n^9}{n^9} = n^{9\,-\,9}$$

To multiply powers with the same base, use the same base, and then add the exponents such that in general $b^m \cdot b^n = b^{m\,+\,n}$.
For example: $3^4 \cdot 3^{-4} = 3^{4\,+\,(-4)}$.

$= 4^0 \cdot 3^{4\,-\,4} \cdot n^0$

$= 4^0 \cdot 3^0 \cdot n^0$

$= 1 \cdot 1 \cdot 1$

$= 1$

Note: $+ (- = -$,for an example $3^{4\,+\,(-4)} = 3^{4\,-\,4}$.
$5 - 5 = 0$, $4 - 4 = 0$, and $9 - 9 = 0$.
The zero power of any number except 0 is 1.

Negative Exponents and Dividing With Exponent

We can show that $10^{-1} = \dfrac{1}{10}$ as shown:

$$\dfrac{10^2}{10^3} = \dfrac{10 \cdot 10}{10 \cdot 10 \cdot 10}$$

$$\dfrac{10^2}{10^3} = \dfrac{\overset{1}{\cancel{10}} \cdot \overset{1}{\cancel{10}}}{\underset{1}{\cancel{10}} \cdot \underset{1}{\cancel{10}} \cdot 10} \qquad\qquad \text{Divide by 10}$$

$$\dfrac{10^2}{10^3} = \dfrac{1}{10} \underline{\hspace{5cm}}[\text{A}]$$

But $\dfrac{10^2}{10^3} = 10^{2\,-\,3}$

To divide powers with the same base, use the same base, and then subtract the exponents such that in general $\dfrac{b^m}{b^n} = b^{m\,-\,n}$ and $b \neq 0$. For an example,

$$\dfrac{10^2}{10^3} = 10^{2\,-\,3}.$$

32

$$\frac{10^2}{10^3} = 10^{-1} \underline{\hspace{6cm}}[B]$$

Note: 2 - 3 = -1.

Comparing equation [A] and equation [B], it can be written that:

$$10^{-1} = \frac{1}{10^1} = \frac{1}{10}$$ Note that equation [A] is the same as equation [B].

Therefore, in general, $b^{-n} = \frac{1}{b^n}$ for all real numbers and $b \neq 0$. It can therefore, be stated in general that: **A base with a negative exponent is equal to I divided by that base with a positive exponent.**

Example 6

Evaluate.

a. 4^{-3} **b.** $(-4)^{-3}$ **c.** $\dfrac{(-4)^2}{(-4)^3}$ **d.** $\dfrac{(6-4)^3}{(9-7)^6}$ **e.** $(4 \cdot 3)^4 \cdot (2 \cdot 6)^{-6}$ **f.** $2^3 \cdot 2^{-2} \cdot 2^{-3}$

Solution

a. $4^{-3} = \dfrac{1}{4^3}$ In general, $b^{-n} = \dfrac{1}{b^n}$, $b \neq 0$.

$= \dfrac{1}{4 \cdot 4 \cdot 4}$ $4^3 = 4 \cdot 4 \cdot 4$

$= \dfrac{1}{64}$ $4 \cdot 4 \cdot 4 = 64$

b. $(-4)^{-3} = \dfrac{1}{(-4)^3}$ In general, $b^{-n} = \dfrac{1}{b^n}$, and $b \neq 0$.

$= \dfrac{1}{(-4) \cdot (-4) \cdot (-4)}$ $(-4)^3 = (-4) \cdot (-4) \cdot (-4)$

$= \dfrac{1}{-64} = -\dfrac{1}{64}$ Note: $(-4) \cdot (-4) = +16 = 16$, but $(-4) \cdot (-4) \cdot (-4) = -64$

because the product of odd number negative signs is negative. Therefore, $(-) \cdot (-) \cdot (-) = -$. Hint: Review multiplication involving negative numbers.

c. $\dfrac{(-4)^2}{(-4)^3} = (-4)^{2-3}$ To divide powers with the same base, use the same base

and then subtract the exponents, such that in general

$$\frac{b^m}{b^n} = b^{m-n} \text{ and } b \neq 0.$$

$$\frac{(-4)^2}{(-4)^3} = (-4)^{-1} \qquad \text{Note: } 2 - 3 = -1$$

$$= \frac{1}{(-4)^1} \qquad \text{In general, } b^{-n} = \frac{1}{b^n}, \text{ and } b \neq 0.$$

$$= \frac{1}{-4} \qquad \text{Note: } \frac{1}{(-4)^1} = \frac{1}{(-4)} = \frac{1}{-4}. \qquad \text{Any number with exponent 1 is}$$

the same number.

d. $\dfrac{(6-4)^3}{(9-7)^6} = \dfrac{2^3}{2^6}$ Do the operations inside the parentheses first.

Hint: See the section on the Order of Operations.
6 - 4 = 2 and 9 - 7 = 2.

$$= 2^{3-6} \qquad \text{To divide powers with the same base, use the same}$$

base, and then subtract the exponents, such that in general

$$\frac{b^m}{b^n} = b^{m-n}, \text{ and } b \neq 0.$$

$$= 2^{-3} \qquad 3 - 6 = -3$$

$$= \frac{1}{2^3} \qquad \text{In general, } b^{-n} = \frac{1}{b^n}, b \neq 0$$

$$= \frac{1}{2 \cdot 2 \cdot 2} \qquad 2^3 = 2 \cdot 2 \cdot 2$$

$$= \frac{1}{8} \qquad 2 \cdot 2 \cdot 2 = 8.$$

e. $(4 \cdot 3)^4 \cdot (2 \cdot 6)^{-6}$ $= 12^4 \cdot 12^{-6}$ Do the operations inside the parentheses first.
Hint: See the section on order of operations.

$$= 12^{4 + (-6)} \qquad \text{To multiply powers with the same base, use}$$

the same base and then add the exponents,
such that in general, $b^m \cdot b^n = b^{m+n}$

$$= 12^{4-6} \qquad \text{Note: } + (- = -, \text{ for example, } 12^{4 + (-6)} = 12^{4-6}.$$

$$= 12^{-2} \qquad 4 - 6 = -2$$

$$= \frac{1}{12^2} \qquad \text{In general, } b^{-n} = \frac{1}{b^n}, \text{ and } b \neq 0.$$

34

$$= \frac{1}{12 \cdot 12} \qquad 12^2 = 12 \cdot 12 = 144.$$

$$= \frac{1}{144}$$

f. $2^3 \cdot 2^{-2} \cdot 2^{-3} = 2^{3 + (-2) + (-3)}$

To multiply powers with the same base, use the same base and then add the exponents, such that in general, $b^m \cdot b^n = b^{m+n}$.

$$= 2^{3-2-3}$$
Note: $+(- = -$, such that $+ (-2) = -2$ and $+ (-3) = -3$.
$$= 2^{3-5}$$
$-2 - 3 = -5$.
$$= 2^{-2}$$
$3 - 5 = -2$.
$$= \frac{1}{2^2}$$
In general, $b^{-n} = \frac{1}{b^n}$, and $b \neq 0$.
$$= \frac{1}{2 \cdot 2}$$
$2^2 = 2 \cdot 2$
$$= \frac{1}{4}$$
$2 \cdot 2 = 4$

Example 7
Simplify

$$\frac{5}{3^{-2}}$$

Solution
$$\frac{5}{3^{-2}} = \frac{5}{\frac{1}{3^2}}$$

In general, $b^{-n} = \frac{1}{b^n}$, and $b \neq 0$. Therefore, $3^{-2} = \frac{1}{3^2}$.

$$= 5 \div \frac{1}{3^2}$$

$$= 5 \times \frac{3^2}{1}$$

To divide by a fraction, multiply by the reciprocal of the fraction. Hint: Review division by fractions.
$3^2 = 3 \times 3$

$$= 5 \times 3 \times 3$$
$$= 45$$

Example 8
Simplify. $\dfrac{15x^5y^3}{5x^2y}$

Solution

$$\frac{15x^5y^3}{5x^2y} = \frac{\overset{3}{\cancel{15}}x^5y^3}{\underset{1}{\cancel{5}}x^2y} = \frac{3x^5y^3}{x^2y}$$

Divide the numerical coefficients by 5.

$$= \frac{3x^5y^3}{x^2y} = 3x^{5\,-\,2}y^{3\,-\,1}$$

Subtract the exponents of the powers

of the denominator from the exponents of the powers with the same base in the numerator. Note that $y = y^1$.

$$= 3x^3y^2$$

Example 9

Simplify.   **a.** $\dfrac{-36a^5bc^4}{6a^2bc^3}$ **b.** $\dfrac{18p^5k^9}{-6p^2k^6}$

Solution

a. $\dfrac{-36a^5bc^4}{6a^2bc^3} = \dfrac{\overset{-6}{\cancel{-36}}a^5bc^4}{\underset{1}{\cancel{6}}a^2bc^3} = \dfrac{-6a^5bc^4}{a^2bc^3}$

Divide the numerical coefficients by 6.

$$= \frac{-6a^5bc^4}{a^2bc^3} = -6a^{5\,-\,2}b^{1\,-\,1}c^{4\,-\,3}$$

Subtract the exponents of the powers of the denominator from the exponents of the powers with the same base in the numerator. Note that $b = b^1$.

$$= -6a^3b^0c^1$$
$$= -6a^3 \cdot 1 \cdot c^1 \qquad\qquad b^0 = 1.$$
$$= -6a^3c \qquad\qquad\qquad c^1 = c.$$

b. $\dfrac{18p^5k^9}{-6p^2k^6} = \dfrac{\overset{3}{\cancel{18}}p^5k^9}{\underset{-1}{\cancel{-6}}p^2k^6} = \dfrac{3p^5k^9}{-p^2k^6}$

Divide the numerical coefficients by 6.

$$= -3p^{5\,-\,2}k^{9\,-\,6}$$

36

Subtract the exponents of the powers of the denominator from the exponents of the powers with the same base in the numerator. Note that in general, $\dfrac{a}{-b}$ = a certain negative number and $b \neq 0$.

$$= -3p^3k^3$$

Example 10

Simplify $\dfrac{-24p^7k^5}{-8p^3k^2}$

Solution

$$\dfrac{-24p^7k^5}{-8p^3k^2} = \dfrac{\overset{3}{-24}p^7k^5}{\underset{1}{-8}p^3k^2} = \dfrac{3p^7k^5}{p^3k^2}$$

Divide the numerical coefficients by -8.

$$= \dfrac{3p^7k^5}{p^3k^2} = 3p^{7-3}k^{5-2}$$

Subtract the exponents of the powers of the denominator from the exponents of the powers with the same base in the numerator. Note -8 ÷ (-8) = 1, -24 ÷ (-8) = 3.

$$= 3p^4k^3 \qquad 7 - 3 = 4 \text{ and } 5 - 2 = 3.$$

Exercises

1. What is an exponent?

2. What is a base?

3. Multiply and write each product as one power. Hint: See Examples 1a, 1c, and 1e.

a. $3^4 \cdot 3^7$ **b**. $9^5 \cdot 9$ **c**. $5^4 \cdot 5^6 \cdot 5^3$

d. $4^4 \cdot 4^2$ **e**. $5^4 \cdot 5^6 \cdot 5^3$ **f**. $6^2 \cdot 6 \cdot 6^4$

4. Multiply and write each product as one power. Hint: See Example 1b and 1d.

a. $3^4 \cdot n^5$ **b**. $5^3 \cdot 4^6$ **c**. $a^4 \cdot b^3$

5. Multiply using exponents. Hint: See Example 2a.

a. $4^3 \cdot n^5 \cdot 3^4 \cdot n^2 \cdot 4^2$ b. $k^4 \cdot 7^2 \cdot k^3 \cdot 7^4 \cdot k^5$

6. Multiply using exponents. Hint: See Example 2a.

a. $b^4 \cdot w^4 \cdot n \cdot b^2 \cdot n^3 \cdot w^2$ **b**. $x^4 \cdot v \cdot k^2 \cdot v^2 \cdot x^2$

c. $p^4 \cdot n^7 \cdot d^2 \cdot p^2 \cdot n^2$ **d**. $a^2 \cdot b^4 \cdot c^3 \cdot a^3 \cdot c^2$

7. Divide and write each quotient as one power. Hint: See Example 3a.

a. $\dfrac{4^7}{4^2}$ **b.** $\dfrac{9^{14}}{9^6}$ **c.** $\dfrac{7^4}{7^3}$ **d.** $\dfrac{6^6}{6^4}$

8. Divide and write each quotient as one power. Hint: See Example 3b.

a. $\dfrac{n^9}{n^4}$ **b.** $\dfrac{w^5}{w^2}$ **c.** $\dfrac{k^8}{k^5}$ **d.** $\dfrac{b^5}{b^3}$

9. Divide and write each quotient as one power. Hint: See Example 3c.

a. $\dfrac{k^4}{m^3}$ **b.** $\dfrac{12^5}{11^4}$ **c.** $\dfrac{x^7}{b^5}$ **d.** $\dfrac{7^5}{6^4}$

10. Simplify each expression. Hint: See Example 4a and 4b.

a. $\dfrac{5^8 \cdot k^5}{k^3 \cdot 5^4}$ **b.** $\dfrac{4^4 \cdot x^5 \cdot y^6}{y^2 \cdot x^3 \cdot 4^2}$ **c.** $\dfrac{w^7 \cdot u^5 \cdot x^4 \cdot 3^3}{x^2 \cdot u^3 \cdot 3^2 \cdot w^7}$

11. Simplify each expression. Hint: See Example 4c.

a. $\dfrac{11^6 \cdot w^9 \cdot y^5 \cdot 6^5}{y^3 \cdot w^6 \cdot 11^4 \cdot 6^3 \cdot v^2}$ **b.** $\dfrac{k^6 \cdot 2^2 \cdot 10^3}{10^9 \cdot 2^4 \cdot k^3 \cdot x}$

12. Evaluate. Hint: See Example 5a.

a. 10^0 **b.** 1^0 **c.** 29^0 **d.** 100^0

13. Evaluate. Hint: See Example 5b.

a. $2^7 \cdot 2^{-7}$ **b.** $6^{10} \cdot 6^{-10}$ **c.** $8^5 \cdot 8^{-5}$ **d.** $9^8 \cdot 9^{-8}$

14. Evaluate. Hint: See Example 5c.

a. $\dfrac{3^4}{34}$ **b.** $\dfrac{8^7}{8^7}$ **c.** $\dfrac{5^9}{5^9}$ **d.** $\dfrac{2^{10}}{2^{10}}$

15. Evaluate. Hint: See Example 5d.

a. $\dfrac{k^8}{k^8}$ **b.** $\dfrac{n^{10}}{n^{10}}$ **c.** $\dfrac{p^5}{p^5}$ **d.** $\dfrac{j^8}{j^8}$

16. Evaluate. Hint: See Example 6a.

a. 5^{-2} **b.** 4^{-2} **c.** 6^{-3} **d.** 3^{-3}

17. Evaluate. Hint: See Example 6b.

a. $(-3)^{-2}$ **b.** $(-2)^{-3}$ **c.** $(-5)^{-3}$ **d.** $(-4)^{-4}$

18. Evaluate. Hint: See Example 6c.

a. $\dfrac{(-3)^2}{(-3)^3}$ **b.** $\dfrac{(-3)^2}{(-3)^4}$ **c.** $\dfrac{(-5)^2}{(-5)^4}$ **d.** $\dfrac{(-4)^2}{(-4)^4}$

19. Evaluate. Hint: See Example 6d.

a. $\dfrac{(5-3)^2}{(6-4)^3}$ **b.** $\dfrac{(7-5)^3}{(8-6)^5}$ **c.** $\dfrac{(9-6)^2}{(7-4)^4}$ **d.** $\dfrac{(5-1)^2}{(9-5)^4}$

20. Evaluate. Hint: See Example 6e.

a. $(3 \cdot 2)^3 \cdot (6 \cdot 1)^{-5}$ **b.** $(4 \cdot 4)^4 \cdot (8 \cdot 2)^{-6}$

c. $(2 \cdot 2)^4 \cdot (4 \cdot 1)^{-6}$ **d.** $(2 \cdot 6)^{-6} \cdot (4 \cdot 3)^4$

21. Evaluate. Hint: See Example 6f.

  a. $2^4 \cdot 2^{-6} \cdot 2^{-2}$ **b.** $3^{-2} \cdot 3^4 \cdot 3^{-3}$ **c.** $4^2 \cdot 4^{-3} \cdot 4^2 \cdot 4^{-2}$

22. Simplify. Hint: See Example 7.

  a. $\dfrac{4}{3^{-2}}$ **b.** $\dfrac{3}{2^{-4}}$ **c.** $\dfrac{12}{3^{-3}}$ **d.** $\dfrac{5}{4^{-2}}$

23. Simplify. Hint: See Example 8

  a $\dfrac{16x^4y^5}{4x^2y}$ **b** $\dfrac{25x^6y^3}{5x^2y^2}$ **c** $\dfrac{9p^7k^3}{3p^2k}$ **d** $\dfrac{12x^{15}y^3}{4x^{12}y}$

24. Simplify. Hint: See Example 9

  a. $\dfrac{-12a^9bc^{14}}{6a^3bc^6}$ **b.** $\dfrac{30w^{15}x^{11}}{-10w^2x^6}$ **c.** $\dfrac{-18a^5b^3c^{10}}{2a^2bc^6}$ **d.** $\dfrac{36wp^{12}x^{13}}{-9wp^2x^6}$

25. Simplify. Hint: See Example 10

  a. $\dfrac{-24p^7k^5}{-8p^3k^2}$ **b.** $\dfrac{-21x^9k^7}{-7x^5k^2}$ **c.** $\dfrac{-36s^{17}k^8}{-9s^3k^2}$ **d.** $\dfrac{-22x^7k^5}{-11x^3k^5}$

Challenge Questions

26. Multiply using exponents.

  a. $n^4 \cdot 3^3 \cdot 4^2 \cdot 3^2 \cdot 4^2$ **b.** $x^6 \cdot y^4 \cdot x^2 \cdot y$

27. Evaluate

  a. 17^0 **b.** 10^{-2} **c.** $11^{-12} \cdot 11^{-12}$ **d.** $\dfrac{2}{3^{-2}}$

  e. $\dfrac{4}{3^{-2}}$ **f.** $k^4 \cdot k^{-4}$ **g.** $\dfrac{(-2)^2}{(-2)^4}$ **h.** $(4 \cdot 3)^2 \cdot (2 \cdot 6)^{-4}$

  i. $2^{-3} \cdot 2^{-2} \cdot 2^3$ **j.** $3^{-3} \cdot 3^2 \cdot 3^{-3}$ **k.** $4^4 \cdot 4^{-6}$ **l.** $(3 \cdot 2)^2 \cdot (2 \cdot 3)^{-4}$

  m. $\dfrac{v^5}{v^2}$ **n.** $\dfrac{9^7}{9^5}$ **o.** $(-3)^{-3}$ **p.** 3^{-3}

  q. $\dfrac{2^3}{2^3}$ **r.** $\dfrac{2}{4^{-2}}$ **s.** $\dfrac{m^n}{m^x}$ **t.** $\dfrac{9^0 \cdot n^{-7} \cdot w^5 \cdot k^{-4}}{n^{-2} \cdot w^{-2} \cdot k^2 \cdot 7^0}$

28. Simplify

  a. $4^6 \cdot y^4 \cdot x^5$ **b.** $\dfrac{(7-6)^3}{(8-6)^2}$ **c.** $\dfrac{(9-7)^2}{(7-5)^4}$ **d.** $\dfrac{(5-2)^2}{(9-6)^3}$

e. $\dfrac{5^0 \cdot n^3 \cdot p^5}{n^{-4} \cdot w^2}$ **f.** $\dfrac{t^{-3}}{t^3}$ **g.** $\dfrac{t^3}{t^{-3}}$ **h.** $(2 \cdot 6)^{-6} \cdot (4 \cdot 3)^6$

i. $x^3 \cdot x^5 \cdot x^0 \cdot x$ **j.** $x^4 \cdot c^9 \cdot y^3 \cdot c^9 \cdot y^0$ **k.** $y \cdot y^0$

29. Simplify.

a $\dfrac{24x^8y^9}{4x^3y}$ **b.** $\dfrac{42w^{12}x^7}{-6w^5x^3}$ **c.** $\dfrac{18x^{10}y^4}{3x^4y^2}$ **d.** $\dfrac{-28x^7k^9}{-7x^4k^2}$

e. $\dfrac{-15x^5k^8}{-3x^5k^2}$ **f.** $\dfrac{-18a^6b^7c^{10}}{3a^2bc^8}$ **g.** $\dfrac{-32s^{11}k^7}{-8s^3k^5}$ **h.** $\dfrac{28x^{18}y^9}{4x^{10}y^6}$

Answers to Selected Questions

3a. 3^{11} **4a.** Cannot combine as one power because the bases are different.

6a. $b^6 \cdot w^6 \cdot n^4$

9a. Quotient cannot be written as one power because the bases are different.

13a. 1   **18a.** $-\dfrac{1}{3}$ **22a.** 36

Cumulative Review

1. John said that the range of 8, 6,1, 20, and 18 is 19. Is his statement correct?
   Explain your answer. Hint: Find the range and compare your answer to 19.
2. Find the range of the following sets of numbers:
   a. 4, 12, 4, 6, 3   b. 26, 6, 9, 5, 26, 11   c. 15, 9, 17, 20, 22, 9
3. Find the mode of each of the following numbers.
   a. 4, 12, 4, 6, 3   b. 26, 6, 9, 5, 26, 11   c. 15, 9, 17, 20, 22, 9

.

(Do you find the generous examples of the Math Teaching Series helpful?)

CHAPTER 5

SCIENTIFIC NOTATION

Scientific notation can be used to write large numbers in the standard form **more easily**. A large number written in scientific notation is a mathematical statement expressed as **a product of two factors** as shown:
   The first factor is a number that is at least 1 but less than 10 and the second factor is a power of 10.
So, to change the standard form of a number to scientific notation, multiply the first factor (that is at least 1 but less than 10) by the second factor (that is a power of 10) as shown:
   Standard form = Scientific notation
   = **(first factor that is at least 1 but less than 10)** × **(second factor that is a power of 10.)**

Example 1
Write 640,000,000 in scientific notation.
Solution
Step 1: Find the first factor of 640,000,000 by counting the number of places the decimal point in the standard form must be moved to the left to form a number that is at least 1 but less than 10 as shown:

First factor

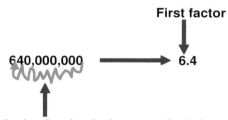

640,000,000 ⟶ 6.4

Move the decimal point 8 places to the left.

   Note that there is an imaginary decimal point after every whole number, review the chapter on decimals.
Step 2: Find the second factor of 640,000,000 by using the fact that since the decimal point in step 1 is moved 8 places to the left, the exponent of 10 is 8. The exponent of 10 is 8 and can be written as shown:

Second factor

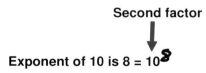

Exponent of 10 is 8 = 10^8

Step 3: Write the number (640,000,000) in the scientific notation as the product of the two factors of 6.4 and 10^8 as shown:

$$640,000,000 = 6.4 \times 10^8$$

Example 2
Write 72,000,000,000 in the scientific notation.
Solution
Step 1: Find the first factor of 72,000,000,000 by counting the number of places the decimal point in the standard form must be moved to the left to form a number that is at least 1 but less than 10 as shown:

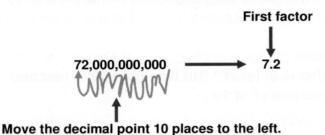

First factor

72,000,000,000 ⟶ 7.2

Move the decimal point 10 places to the left.

Note that there is an imaginary decimal point after every whole number, review the chapter on decimals.

Step 2: Find the second factor of 72,000,000,000 by using the fact that since the decimal point in step 1 is moved 10 places to the left, the exponent of 10 is 10. The exponent of 10 is 10 and can be written as shown:

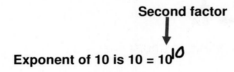

Second factor

Exponent of 10 is 10 = 10^{10}

Step 3: Write the number (72,000,000,000) in the scientific notation as the product of the two factors of 7.2 and 10^{10} as shown:

$$72,000,000,000 = 7.2 \times 10^{10}$$

Example 3
Write 3,960,000 in the scientific notation.
Solution
Step 1: Find the first factor of 3,960,000 by counting the number of places the decimal point in the standard form must be moved to the left to form a number that is at least 1 but less than 10 as shown:

CHAPTER 4

First factor

3,960,000 ⟶ 3.96

Move the decimal point 6 places to the left.

Note that there is an imaginary decimal point after every whole number, review the chapter on decimals.

Step 2: Find the second factor of 3,960,000 by using the fact that since the decimal point in step 1 is moved 6 places to the left, the exponent of 10 is 6. The exponent of 10 is 6 and can be written as shown:

Second factor

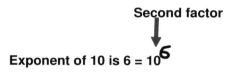

Exponent of 10 is 6 = 10^6

Step 3: Write the number (3,960,000) in the scientific notation as the product of the two factors of 3.96 and 10^6 as shown:

$$3,960,000 = 3.96 \times 10^6$$

Example 4
Write 59,738,100,000,000 in the scientific notation.
Solution
Step 1: Find the first factor of 59,738,100,000,000 by counting the number of places the decimal point in the standard form must be moved to the left to form a number that is at least 1 but less than 10 as shown:

First factor

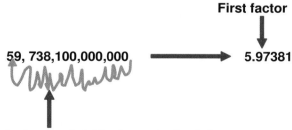

59, 738,100,000,000 ⟶ 5.97381

Move the decimal point 13 places to the left.

Note that there is an imaginary decimal point after every whole number, review the chapter on Decimals.

Step 2: Find the second factor of 59,738,100,000,000 by using the fact that since the decimal point in step 1 is moved 13 places to the left, the exponent of 10 is 13. The exponent of 10 is 13 and can be written as shown:

Second factor

↓

Exponent of 10 is 13 = 10^{13}

Step 3: Write the number 59,738,100,000,000 in the scientific notation as the product of the two factors of 5.97381 and 10^{13} as shown:

$$59,738,100,000,000 = 5.97381 \times 10^{13}$$

Example 5
Explain why each of the numbers is not written in the scientific notation.

a. $7.5 + 10^6$ **b.** 15×10^7 **c.** 6.2×8^5 **d.** 0.876×10^9

Solution

a. The scientific notation is written as the product of two factors but $7.5 + 10^6$ is not a product, but rather an addition.

b. The scientific notation is written as the product of two factors such that the first factor must be at least 1 but less than 10, but in 15×10^7, the first factor which is 15 is rather more than 10.

c. The scientific notation is written as the product of two factors such that the second factor is an exponent or power of 10, but in 6.2×8^5, the second factor is 8^5 but 8^5 is not an exponent or power of 10.

d. The scientific notation is written as the product of two factors such that the first factor must be at least 1 but less than 10, but in 0.876×10^9, the first factor which is 0.876 is less than 1.

How to Write Scientific Notations of Numbers Less Than 1
In order to write the scientific notation of numbers that are less than 1, the decimal point in the number **must be moved to the right and must be placed behind the first non-zero digit so as to obtain a number that is at least 1.**

Since the decimal point is moved to the right, **the exponent must be negative**. Recall that a scientific notation is still a mathematical statement expressed as the product of two factors such that the first factor is at least 1 but less than 10 and the second factor is a power of 10.

Example 6
Write 0.0000004 in the scientific notation.
Solution

Step 1: Find the first factor of 0.0000004 by counting the number of places the decimal point in the decimal notation **must be moved to the right** to form a number that is at least 1 but less than 10 as shown:

First factor

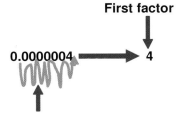

0.0000004 ⟶ 4

Move the decimal point 7 places to the right.

Step 2: Find the second factor of 0.0000004 by using the fact that since the decimal point in step 1 is moved 7 places to the **right**, the exponent of 10 is **-7**. The exponent of 10 is -7 and can be written as shown:

Second factor

Exponent of 10 is -7 = 10^{-7}

Step 3: Write the number 0.0000004 in the scientific notation as the product of the two factors 4 and 10^{-7} as shown:

$$0.0000004 = 4 \times 10^{-7}$$

Example 7

Write 0.000001426 in the scientific notation.

Solution

Step 1: Find the first factor of 0.000001426 by counting the number of places the decimal point must be **moved to the right** to form a number that is at least 1 but less than 10 as shown:

First factor

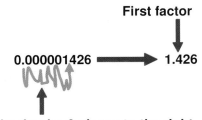

0.000001426 ⟶ 1.426

Move the decimal point 6 places to the right.

Step 2: Find the second factor of 0.000001426 by using the fact that since the decimal point in step 1 is moved 6 places to the right, the exponent or the power of 10 is -6. The exponent of 10 is -6 can be written as shown:

Second factor

Exponent of 10 is -6 = 10^{-6}

Step 3: Write the number 0.000001426 in the scientific notation as the product of the two factors 1.426 and 10^{-6} as shown:

$$0.000001426 = 1.426 \times 10^{-6}$$

How to Write Scientific Notation in the Standard Notation
In order to write the scientific notation as the standard notation, two rules should be followed:
Rule 1: If the exponent of the base of the scientific notation is positive, it means that the decimal point in the scientific notation should be moved to the **right** according to the magnitude of the exponent. Hint: See Example 8a.

Example of the scientific notation with positive exponent is:

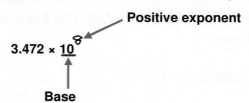

Positive exponent

$3.472 \times \underline{10}^{8}$

Base

Rule 2: If the exponent of the base of the scientific notation is negative, it means that the decimal point in the scientific notation should be moved to the **left** according to the magnitude of the exponents. Hint: See Example 8b.

Example of the scientific notation with negative exponent is:

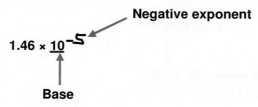

Negative exponent

$1.46 \times \underline{10}^{-5}$

Base

Example 8
Write each scientific notation in the standard notation.
a. 3.472×10^{8} **b.** 1.46×10^{-5} **c.** -6.3×10^{6}
Solution
a. $3.472 \times 10^{8} = 3.472 \times 100,000,000$ $10^{8} = 100,000,000$

= 3.472

**Move the decimal point 8 places to the right.
See rule 1.**

Write the zeros here as place holders.
　　　　　　Review the chapter on decimals.

= 3.4720 0 0 0 0 0

**Move the decimal point 8 places to the right.
See rule 1.**

347,200,000

Note that a detailed explanation is provided for the understanding of the concept, however, the detailed explanation may not be necessary in solving your homework exercises. The student should understand and apply how the decimal point may be moved to the right or left as needed in order to solve their exercises.

b. $1.46 \times 10^{-5} = 1.46 \times \dfrac{1}{10^5}$

In general, $b^{-n} = \dfrac{1}{b^n}$ and $b \neq 0$.

Review the chapter on Exponents.

$$= 1.46 \times \frac{1}{100,000}$$

$$= \frac{1.46}{100,000}$$

1.46

**Move the decimal point 5 places to the left.
See rule 2.**

Write the zeros here as place holders.
Review the chapter on decimals.

$$= 0\,0\,0\,0\,1.46$$

Move the decimal point 5 places to the left.
See rule 2.

$$= 0.0000146$$

Note that the detailed explanation is provided for the understanding of the concept, however, the detailed explanation may not be necessary in solving your homework exercises. The student should understand and apply how the decimal point may be moved to the right or left as needed in order to solve their exercises.

c. $\qquad -6.3 \times 10^6 = -6.3 \times 1{,}000{,}000$ $\qquad\qquad\qquad 10^6 = 1{,}000{,}000$

$$= -6.3$$

Move the decimal point 6 places to the right.
See rule 1.

Write zeros here as place holders.
Review the chapter on decimals.

$$= -6.3\,0\,0\,0\,0\,0$$

Move the decimal point 6 places to the right.
See rule 1.

$$= -6{,}300{,}000$$

Note that the detailed explanation is provided for the understanding of the concept, however, the detailed explanation may not be necessary in solving your homework exercises. The student should understand and apply how the decimal point may be moved to the right or left as needed in order to solve their exercises.

Exercises

1. Describe how you would write 4.8969×10^7 in the standard notation. Hint: See the preceding notes.

2. Describe how you would write 0.00038 in the scientific notation. Hint: See Example 6.

3. The scientific notation can be used to write large numbers in standard form more easily. True or False? Hint: See the preceding notes.

4. The scientific notation is made up of two factors. True or False?
Hint: See the preceding notes.

5. Write the following numbers in the scientific notation. Hint: See Example 1.

    a. 530,000,000   **b.** 720,00   **c.** 480,000,000
    d. 940,000,000,000   **e.** 670,00   **f.** 110,000,000

6. Write the following numbers in the scientific notation. Hint: See Example 2.

    a. 64,000,000   **b.** 55,000,000   **c.** 78,000
    d. 12,000,000   **e.** 99,000   **f.** 84,000,000,000

7. Write the following numbers in the scientific notation. Hint: See Example 3.

    a. 5,870,000   **b.** 7,250,000   **c.** 6,740,000
    d. 2,940,000,000   **e.** 4,390,000,000   **f.** 8,390,000

8. Write the following numbers in the scientific notation. Hint: See Example 4.

    a. 47,891,200,000   **b.** 98,147,300,000   **c.** 57,284,000
    d. 64,734,300,000,000   **e.** 38,234,400,000   **f.** 49,195,000

9. Explain why each number is not written in the scientific notation. Hint: See Example 5.

    a. $2.9 + 10^7$ **b.** 12×10^4 **c.** 4.5×9^{10}
    d. 0.491×10^8 **e.** $5.7 + 10^8$ **f.** 0.34×10^7

10. Write the following numbers in the scientific notation. Hint: See Example 6.

    a. 0.000006   **b.** 0.00009   **c.** 0.000002
    d. 0.0008   **e.** 0.0003   **f.** 0.0000007

11. Write the following numbers in the scientific notation. Hint: See Example 7.

    a. 0.00004135   **b.** 0.000741   **c.** 0.000000148
    d. 0.00000278   **e.** 0.00389   **f.** 0.0091

12. Write each scientific notation in the standard form. Hint: See Example 8.

a. 4.731×10^5	**b.** 1.246×10^{-7}	**c.** -5.71×10^4
d. 9.81×10^7	**e.** 3.46×10^{-5}	**f.** 8.1×10^8
g. 1.2×10^{-6}	**h.** -5.7×10^4	**i.** 3.481×10^9
j. 4.793×10^6	**k.** -7.4×10^7	**l.** 7.34×10^{-4}
m. -9.31×10^7	**n.** 5.712×10^5	**o.** 6.341×10^{-7}

Answers to Selected Questions

5a. 5.3×10^8 **6a.** 6.4×10^7 **7a.** 5.87×10^6 **8a.** 4.78912×10^{10}

10a. 6×10^{-6} **11a.** 4.135×10^{-5} **12a.** 473100

Challenge Questions

13. Write each number in the scientific notation.

a. 72,000,000	**b.** 0.000002	**c.** 0.0000192
d. 94,000,000	**e.** 1,000,000,000	**f.** 4000,000,000
g. 77,000,000	**h.** 142,000,000	**i.** 298,000
j. 8,000,000,000	**k.** 272,000	**l.** 0.00078
m. 0.00000418	**n.** 0.0009	**o.** 22,000,000,000

14. Explain why each of the following is not in scientific notation.

a. 0.491×10^4	**b.** $3.7 + 10^{16}$	**c.** 38×10^4
d. 4.81×6^5	**e.** 4.9×7^8	**f.** 50×10^6

15. Write each number in the standard notation.

a. 3.12×10^6	**b.** 1.7×10^9	**c.** 1.48×10^{-4}
d. -2.4×10^5	**e.** 3.6×10^4	**f.** -4.8×10^4
g. 7.1×10^{-5}	**h.** 4.2×10^{-4}	**i.** -2.2×10^6

Cumulative Review

1. Add or subtract:

a. 12.78	**b.** 6.87	**c.** 9.55
+ 2.55	- 1.91	+ 6.77

2. $5^2 \times 3 =$ **3.** $3^2 \times 2^2 =$ **4.** $7.5 - 2.6 =$

AVERAGE, MEAN, RANGE, MODE, AND MEDIAN

Average

Explanation 1

In its simplest form, an average is to share or divide anything equally. For example, how can we share or divide 6 oranges equally between 2 girls? We can share the 6 oranges equally so that each girl will receive 3 oranges as shown:

Six oranges to be shared equally.

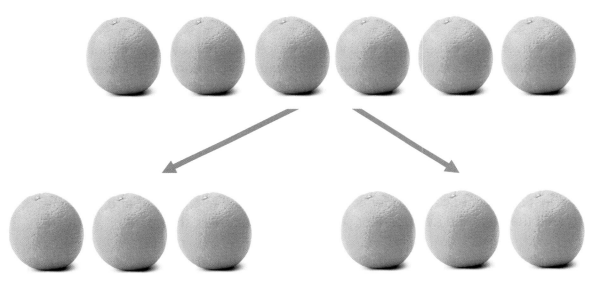

Equal share of 3 oranges   **Equal share of 3 oranges**

From the above picture, we are able to divide 6 oranges equally between 2 girls by dividing the total number of the oranges by the number of people who are to receive the share. Similarly, **an average is the total number divided by the number of the numbers**, and in this case the number of the numbers involves 2 girls which can be written as shown:

$$\text{Average} = \frac{\text{Total number of oranges}}{\text{Number of people}} = \frac{6}{2} = 3 \text{ oranges}$$

Explanation 2

Assume that a girl has 2 oranges and another girl has 4 oranges and they are requested to share the oranges equally, then they have to add the oranges together and then divide the total number of the oranges or the sum of the oranges by 2 or the number of the girls. Similarly, sharing the oranges equally is the same as finding the average which can be stated as follows: **an average is the sum of numbers divided by the number of the numbers**. This average can be written as shown:

$$\text{Average} = \frac{\text{Sum of oranges}}{\text{Number of people}} = \frac{2+4}{2} = \frac{6}{2} = 3$$

Conclusion from Explanations 1 and 2

In Explanation 1, we find the average by dividing "Total number of oranges" by "Number of people," but in Explanation 2, the average is found by dividing the "Sum of oranges" by "Number of people." We can then combine Explanations 1 and 2 together to write that **an average is the total or the sum of the numbers divided by the number of the numbers**. Therefore, there are two methods of finding averages as explained by Examples 1 and 2, and stated in the rule below:

Rule: An average can be found by dividing the total number by the number of the numbers if the total number is given in the question, otherwise the average can be found by dividing the sum of the numbers by the number of the numbers if the individual numbers are given in the question.

Understanding Average

When students from schools take part in the external examinations, the schools are rated by the average performance of the students in each school by dividing the sum of the test scores of all the students in a specific school by the number of students who took the test. The average test score can be written as shown:

$$\text{Average test score} = \frac{\text{Sum of the test scores}}{\text{Number of the students who took the test}} \quad\text{———}\ [A]$$

Group Exercise

The class should be divided into four groups and without using any students' names, each group should be given the test scores of the last weekly test. Each group should find the average test score of the last weekly test by completing the tables as shown and using the average equation, which is equation $[A]$.

Test scores:

Student #	1	2	3	4	5	6	7	8	. . .	N
Test score	?	?	?	?	?	?	?	?	. . .	?

Each group should report out the average test score to the whole class.
Each group should discuss the following 4 questions and to list and report out their answer with reasons to the whole class.
1. Are the average test scores from the 4 groups the same?

2. How could the average test score be improved? When each student's test score is increased by 2, what happens to the average test score? Is the average test score higher when the individual test score is increased by 2?
3. Could you name some external tests that your school participates in?
4. What factors will lower the average test score? When the individual test score is lowered by 2, does the average test score become lower?

Example 1
(**a**). The test scores of five students out of a maximum score of 10 are
8, 7, 9, 10, and 6. Find the average test score of the students.
(**b**). The total age of 5 boys is 20 years. What is their average age?
Solution
(**a**). Using the formula, the average test score is:

$$\text{Average test score} = \frac{\text{Sum of the test scores}}{\text{Number of the students that took the test}} \quad\text{———— [A]}$$

Sum of the test scores = 8 + 7 + 9 + 10 + 6 = 40
Number of the students that took the test = 5

$$\text{Average test score} = \frac{40}{5} \qquad \text{See equation } [A]$$

$$= \frac{\overset{8}{\cancel{40}}}{\underset{1}{\cancel{5}}} \qquad \text{Divide by 5.}$$

Therefore, the average test score is 8.
(**b**). The total age of the 5 boys = 20 years
The number of the boys = 5
Using the formula:

$$\text{Average} = \frac{\text{Total number (ages)}}{\text{Number of people}} = \frac{20}{5}$$

$$= \frac{\overset{4}{\cancel{20}}}{\underset{1}{\cancel{5}}} \qquad \text{(Divide by 5).}$$

Therefore, the average age of the 5 boys is 4 years.

Example 2

Find the average of the following numbers:

$$1\frac{1}{2}, 2\frac{3}{4}, 3\frac{2}{3}, 2\frac{1}{2}$$

Solution

Using the formula, the average of the numbers is:

$$\text{Average number} = \frac{\text{Sum of the numbers}}{\text{Number of the numbers}} \qquad \text{————————— [A]}$$

Sum of the numbers $= 1\frac{1}{2} + 2\frac{3}{4} + 3\frac{2}{3} + 2\frac{1}{2}$

Number of the numbers $= 4$ (There are 4 numbers involved.)

Add the numbers as shown: (Review the Addition of Mixed Numbers.)

$$1\frac{1}{2} = 1\frac{1}{2} \times \frac{6}{6} = 1\frac{6}{12}$$

$$2\frac{3}{4} = 2\frac{3}{4} \times \frac{3}{3} = 2\frac{9}{12}$$

$$3\frac{2}{3} = 3\frac{2}{3} \times \frac{4}{4} = 3\frac{8}{12}$$

$$2\frac{1}{2} = 2\frac{1}{2} \times \frac{6}{6} = 2\frac{6}{12}$$

$$8\frac{29}{12} = 8 + 2\frac{5}{12} = 10\frac{5}{12} \quad \text{(Review Division of Fractions)}$$

Sum of the numbers $= 10\frac{5}{12}$

Using equation [A]:

$$\text{Average number} = \frac{10\frac{5}{12}}{4} \qquad \text{(There are 4 numbers.)}$$

$$= 10\frac{5}{12} \div 4$$

$$= 10\frac{5}{12} \times \frac{1}{4} \qquad \text{(Review the Division of Fractions - multiply by reciprocal of 4.)}$$

Note: The reciprocal of any number $= 1 \div$ the number

54

$$= \frac{125}{12} \times \frac{1}{4} \qquad \text{(Review the Multiplication of Mixed Fractions.)}$$

$$= \frac{125}{48} = 2\frac{29}{48}$$

Therefore, the average number is $2\frac{29}{48}$

Example 3

The average age of 8 children is 9 years. If the ages of seven of the children are 6, $8\frac{1}{2}$, 4, 10, 11, 12, and 9, how old is the 8th child?

Solution

Sum of the ages of the 7 children $= 6 + 8\frac{1}{2} + 4 + 10 + 11 + 12 + 9 = 60\frac{1}{2}$ years.

Total ages of the 8 children $= 8 \times$ average age of the 8 children.

$$= 8 \times 9 \text{ years}$$
$$= 72 \text{ years.}$$

Age of 8th child = Total age of the 8 children − Sum of the ages of the 7 children

$$= 72 \text{ years} - 60\frac{1}{2} \text{ years}$$

$$= 11\frac{1}{2} \text{ years.}$$

Therefore, the age of the 8th child is $11\frac{1}{2}$ years.

Mean, Range, Mode, and Median

The **mean** is the same as the average.

The **range** is the difference between the biggest number and the smallest number in a data.

Example 4

The table shows the ages of 9 students.

Students #	1	2	3	4	5	6	7	8	9
Ages	16	14	13	14	17	15	14	12	11

a. Find the range of the ages of the students.

b. Find the mean age of the students.

c. By conducting a group exercise, find the range of the data by using a line plot.

d. Find the mode of the data.

e. By using the line plot in Example 4c, how would you find the mode of the data?

f. Find the median age of the students.

g. By using the line plot of Example 4c, how would you find the median age of the students?

Solution

a. From the table, the student # 5 has the highest age of 17 years and the student # 9 has the lowest age of 11 years.

Therefore, the range = Highest age - Lowest age

= 17 years - 11 years = 6 years.

b. Let us find the mean age of the students as follows:

Sum of the ages of the students = 16 + 14 + 13 + 14 + 17 + 15 + 14 + 12 + 11

= 126 years

The number of students = 9   From the table, 9 students are listed.

The mean of the ages of the students = $\dfrac{\text{Sum of the ages of the students}}{\text{Number of the students}}$

= $\dfrac{126 \text{ years}}{9}$

= 14 years   Review the Division of Integers.

Therefore, the mean age of the students is 14 years.

c. Group Exercise

The class should be divided into four groups. Each group should complete the line plot of the ages of all the 9 students, using x for each mark as started below.

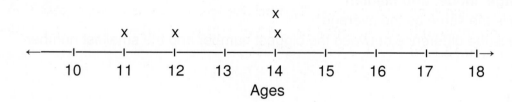

Ages

How could the range be determined from the line plot?

Answer: The x at the extreme left side of the line plot indicates the lowest age and the x at the extreme right side of the line plot indicates the highest age.

Subtract the lowest age from the highest age to obtain the range.

d. The **mode** is the number that occurs most often. From the table, the age 14 years occurs 3 times which is the age that occurs most often, and therefore 14 is the mode.

e. Group Exercise

From the completed line plot, how could you find the mode?

Answer: **The age column which has the most "x" indicates the mode**. Which age column has the most "x"? What is the mode from the line plot? The mode is the data that appears most.

f. The **median** is the middle number when data is listed in numerical order. Numerical order means to list the data from the least number to the greatest number, in order without omission. We can write the ages of the 9 students in numerical order as shown:

11, 12, 13, 14, 14, 14, 15, 16, 17

↑

This 14 is the middle number when the data is listed in numerical order and therefore, this 14 is the median.

g. Group Exercise

From the completed line plot, how could you find the median?

Answer: The xs on the line plot are already in numerical order, and therefore, by counting the xs from left to right on the line plot, **we should be able to locate the x which is at the middle of the data and this middle x is the median.** What is the median from the line plot?

Special Method for Finding Median

The median is the middle number when data is listed in numerical order. However, if the data is an even number of numbers, there will be no middle number as the median as shown:

6, 8, 12, 14

The numbers 6, 8, 12, and 14 have no middle number because the number of the numbers is 4 which is an even number. **To find the median of an even number of numbers, the median is the average of the two middle numbers.** The two middle numbers of 6, 8, 12, and 14 are 8 and 12 and so,

the average of 8 and 12 $= \dfrac{8 + 12}{2} = \dfrac{20}{2} = 10.$

Therefore, the median of 6, 8, 12, and 14 is 10.

How to Solve Multi-Step Problems Involving Mean

Example 5

The mean of the ages of 3 boys is 5 years. How old should the fourth boy be such that the mean of the 4 boys will be 8 years?

Solution

The method of solving this problem involves finding the total ages of the 3 boys and then let x represents the age of the fourth boy. We can then find the sum of the ages of all the 4 boys, we can also find the mean of the ages of all the four boys. Finally, we can equate the mean of the ages of the 4 boys to 8 years, and then solve for x which is the age of the fourth boy as shown:

Total ages of the 3 boys = 3 × Mean age of the 3 boys.

$$= 3 \times 5 \text{ years} \qquad \text{Mean age of the 3 boys} = 5 \text{ years.}$$

$$= 15 \text{ years}$$

Let the age of the fourth boy = x years

Total age of all the 4 boys = 15 years + x years

Mean of the ages of the 4 boys $= \dfrac{\text{Sum of the ages of the 4 boys}}{\text{Total number of boys}}$

$$= \dfrac{15 + x}{4}$$

Since the question gives us the mean of the 4 boys is 8 years, we can equate $\dfrac{15 + x}{4}$ to 8, and then solve for x which is the age of the fourth boy as shown:

$$\frac{15 + x}{4} = 8$$

$$\frac{15 + x}{4} = \frac{8}{1} \qquad \text{8 is the same as } \frac{8}{1}.$$

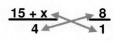

Cross products of a proprotion are equal. A proportion is a statement that two ratios are equal. Review the chapter on Proportion.

$(15 + x) \times 1 = 4 \times 8$ Review the chapter on proportion.

$15 \times 1 + x \times 1 = 4 \times 8$ Multiply to eliminate the bracket.

$15 + x = 32$ $4 \times 8 = 32$.

$15 - 15 + x = 32 - 15$ Subtract 15 from both sides of the equation $15 + x = 32$ in order to obtain x.

$0 + x = 17$ $15 - 15 = 0$ and $32 - 15 = 17$.

$x = 17$

Therefore, the fourth boy should be 17 years.

The notes and the generous worked examples have provided me with conceptual understanding and computational fluency to do my homework.

Exercises

1. (**a**) Explain what is meant by average, mean, range, mode, and median.
   (**b**) Six boys are given $24. What is the average amount each boy will receive? Hint: See Example **1**(**a**).
   (**c**). If 8 students are to share 16 apples, what is the average number of the apples each student will receive? Hint: See Example **1**(**b**).

2. What is the average of 4, 5, 2, and 1? Hint: See Example **1**(**a**).

3. Find the average of the following numbers: Hint: See Examples **1**(**a**) and 2.

   (**a**) 2.1, 6.4, 2.8, 1.2, 2.5   (**b**) $1\frac{1}{2}$, $6\frac{2}{3}$, $1\frac{5}{6}$

   (**c**) 22, 5, 14, 6, 8   (**d**) 4, 7, 8, 11, 2, 6, 3, 9, 13
   (**e**) 14, 16, 8, 10, 7, 5   (**f**) 77, 43

   (**g**) $2\frac{2}{3}$, $1\frac{3}{4}$, $3\frac{1}{4}$, $\frac{1}{3}$ (**h**) 1, 3, 9, 11, 4, 3, 12

   (**i**) 14, 24, 31, 16   (**j**) 5, 10, 12, 14, 6
   (**k**) 8, 5, 2   (**l**) 10, 6, 8, 4   (**m**) 2, 7, 5, 1, 10

4. From the given data, find the range. Hint: See the section under Range. See Example **4a**.

   (**a**) 3, 4, 7, 28   (**b**) 101, 7, 2, 94
   (**c**) 38, 49, 86, 99, 31, 2   (**d**) 2, 8, 4, 35, 44
   (**e**) 39, 98, 401, 30, 11   (**f**) 15, 25, 7, 5

5. Find the median. Hint: See the section on Median, see Example **4f**.

   (**a**) 4, 8, 1, 6, 4   (**b**) 9, 5, 8,   (**f**) 7, 12, 3

   (**g**) 4.2, 3.1, 6.4, 1.8, 6.2   (**h**) $7\frac{1}{2}$, $6\frac{1}{3}$, $8\frac{3}{4}$, $6\frac{2}{3}$, $7\frac{1}{4}$ (**i**) 6.3, 4.7, 8.4

6. Find the median. Hint: See the section on the Special Method of Finding the Median.

   (**a**) 2, 8, 5, 3   (**b**) 3, 7, 8, 1   (**c**) 12, 2, 4, 6, 1, 3
   (**d**) 12, 4   (**e**) 4, 6   (**f**) 3, 4, 8, 2, 7, 9

   (**g**) 110, 112, 100, 98   (**h**) 2.4, 2.8, 4.2, 6.4   (**i**) $7\frac{1}{2}$, $6\frac{2}{3}$, $2\frac{2}{3}$, $1\frac{3}{4}$

7. Find the mode. Hint: See the section on Mode. See Example 4d.

   (**a**) 2, 3, 7, 8, 2, 9, 3, 2   (**b**) 4, 1, 6, 9, 4, 2, 4, 1
   (**c**) 9, 11, 6, 7, 9, 4, 9   (**d**) 1, 4, 6, 1, 7, 1, 2, 6, 4

(e) 4, 1, 5, 1, 6, 5, 8, 5   (f) 2, 6, 9, 4, 6, 2, 6

8. Find the mode and the range. Hint: See the section on Mode and Range.
   See Examples **4a** and **4d**.

   (a) 12, 14, 4, 12, 3, 1, 12, 14   (b) 19, 24, 6, 19, 4, 2
   (c) 3, 6, 9, 10, 6, 24, 4   (d) 1, 4, 5, 6, 5, 13, 5

   (e) 2.5, 6.8, 4.1, 3, 6.8, 7.2   (f) $4\frac{1}{2}$, $1\frac{7}{8}$, $6\frac{4}{5}$, $1\frac{7}{8}$, 2

   (g) $2\frac{3}{4}$, $1\frac{1}{2}$, $8\frac{3}{7}$, $2\frac{3}{4}$, 6, $2\frac{3}{4}$ (h) 1.5, 7.5, 2.5, 2.5, 1.5, 2.5, 1.5

9. The mean of 3 numbers is 2. What is the fourth number such that the mean of
   all the four numbers should be 5. Hint: See Example **5**.

10. The mean age of 2 girls is 4 years. What should be the age of the third girl
    such that the mean of all three girls should be 6 years? Hint: See Example **5**.

11. The mean of 5 numbers is 7, what should be the sixth number for the mean
    of all the 6 numbers to be 4? Hint: See Example **5**.

12. The mean of the ages of 3 girls is 14 years, what should be the age of the fourth
    girl such that the mean age of all the 4 girls should be 12 years? Hint: See
    Example **5**.

Challenge Questions

13. Find the average. Round off your answer to the nearest whole number.

    (a) 2, 6, 14   (b) 14, 28, 31, 43   (c) 2.4, 6.9, 1.3
    (d) 1.6, 10.4   (e) 36, 54, 104, 64   (f) 3, 7, 8, 4, 9

    (g) $2\frac{3}{4}$, 3, $4\frac{1}{2}$, $2\frac{1}{4}$ (h) $10\frac{3}{4}$, $11\frac{1}{4}$ (i) 4.4, 6.9, 3.3

14. Find the range and the mode.

    (a) 1, 7, 6, 1, 4, 1, 9   (b) 14, 2, 8, 1.4   (c) 2.2, 4.8, 2.2, 4
    (d) 8, 10, 17, 10, 34, 10   (e) 2, 2, 4, 8, 4, 9, 4   (f) 6, 7, 11, 14, 7

15. Find the mean.

    (a) 2, 3, 4   (b) 10, 22   (c) 1.2, 4.3, 3.5
    (d) $14\frac{2}{6}$, $82\frac{2}{3}$, 2   (e). 31, 3   (f). 12, 6, 12

16. Find the mean.

(a) 2, 9, 7, 1, 4   (b) 1, 6, 8, 2, 10, 3   (c) 2, 4, 1, 8

(d) 2.2, 4.2, 6.8, 1.8   (e) $1\frac{1}{4}$, $6\frac{1}{2}$, $2\frac{1}{4}$ (f) 7, 9

17. The mean of 3 numbers is 6. What should be the fourth number such that the mean of all the four numbers should be 10?

Answers to Selected Questions

1(b) $4.00   **3(a)** 3   **4(a)** 25   **9.** 14

REAL WORLD APPLICATIONS - WORD PROBLEMS

1. The average test score of 5 students is 12. If the test scores of 4 students are 10, 13, 10, and 14, what is the test score of the 5th student?
Hint: See Example **3** under the chapter Average.

2. The ages of three students are 9, 10, and 11 years. Find their average age.
Hint: See Example **1** under the chapter for Average.

Challenge Questions

3. The average age of 6 employees is 25 years. If the ages of 4 of the employees are 20, 21, 30, and 23 years, what is the total ages of the 2 remaining employees?

4. The weekly test scores of 6 students are 90%, 78%, 89%, 98%, 86%, and 65%. What is the average test score of the students?

5. Make a line plot of the following data and using the line plot explain how you would obtain the mode, range, mean, and the median. Hint: Number the number line from 0 to 30.

8, 12, 16, 28, 2, 18, 12, 4, 8, 12, 10, 12, 2, 2, 28.

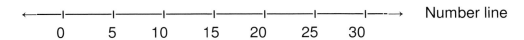

Number line

ALGEBRAIC EXPRESSIONS

An algebraic expression is formed by numbers, variables and the operations of addition, subtraction, division, multiplication, powers and roots as shown in Table 1:

Table 1

Word Phrases	Operations needed	Examples of expressions
1. A number **plus** 2. 2. A number **increased** by 2. 3. 2 **more** than a number. 4. **Add** 2 to a number.	+	Let x be the number, and therefore, the expression is **x + 2.**
1. **Subtract** 3 from a number. 2. A number **decreased** by 3. 3. 3 **less** than a number. 4. A number **minus** 3. 5. **Difference** of a number and 3.	—	Let n be the number, and therefore, the expression is **n - 3.**
1. 4 **divided** into a number. 2. A number **divided** by 4. 3. **Quotient** of a number and 4.	÷	Let k be the number, and therefore, the expression is **k ÷ 4.**
1. **Product** of 5 and a number. 2. 5 **multiplied** by a number. 3. 5 **times** a number.	×	Let y be the number, and therefore, the expression is **5 × y = 5y.**
1. A number to the **power** a.	Power	Let 2 be the number, and therefore, the expression is 2^a.
1. **Root** of a number x.	√	Let x represent the number, and therefore, the expression is $\sqrt{x}$.

Key point: Understand and know the relationship between the words in **bold** under the "word phrase" column and the corresponding "operations needed" column in Table 1. For example, **more** means addition and **less** means subtraction.

Exercises or Group Exercises

1. Write an algebraic expression for each word phrase. Hint: See examples of the expressions in table 1.

a. 10 more than k.	**b.** 8 less than x.	**c.** P minus 6.
d. w decreased by 15.	**e.** the quotient of 6 and p.	**f.** Product of 2 and k.
g. 7 multiplied by v.	**h.** Difference of 9 and b.	**i.** Subtract 1 from n.
j. 5 times k.	**k.** Add 11 to y.	**l.** Increase 12 by x.
m. z to the power 6.	**n.** Root of k.	**o.** 8 to the power w.

Complex Word Phrases

It is possible to combine some of the word phrases in Table 1 to form complex word phrases as shown in Table 2:

Table 2

Key Words	Word Phrases	Examples of expressions
more, products	2 **more** than the **product** of 4 and k.	4k is the **product** of 4 and k, and therefore, the expression is 4k + 2.
less, product	4 **less** than the **product** of 6 and k.	6k is the **product** of 6 and k, and therefore, the expression is 6k - 4.
less, divide	10 **less** than m **divided** by 7.	m **divided** by 7 is m ÷ 7, and therefore, the expression is m ÷ 7 - 10.
more, divide	10 **more** than m **divided** by 7.	m **divided** by 7 is m ÷ 7, and therefore, the expression is m ÷ 7 + 10.
times, sum	3 **times** the **sum** of n and 5.	The **sum** of n and 5 is n + 5, and therefore, the expression is 3(n + 5).
times, difference	8 **times** the **difference** of x and 6.	The **difference** of x and 6 is x - 6, and therefore, the expression is 8(x - 6).
times, product	2 **times** the **product** of k and 5.	The **product** of k and 5 is 5k, and therefore, the expression is 2 × 5k = 10k.
times, quotient	**Twice** the **quotient** of p and 58.	The **quotient** of p and 58 is p ÷ 58, and therefore, the expression is 2(p ÷ 58).
plus, product	2 **plus** the **product** of 3 and y.	The **product** of 3 and y is 3y, and therefore, the expression is 3y + 2.
minus, product	2 **minus** the **product** of 3 and y.	The **product** of 3 and y is 3y, and therefore, the expression is 2 - 3y.
fraction, sum	**Five-sixth** the **sum** of k and 3.	The **sum** of k and 5 is k + 5, and therefore, the expression is $\frac{5}{6}$(k + 3).

Key Points: 1. Understand and know the relationship among the "key words" column the "word phrase column," and the "examples of expressions column."

2. Note that each complex word phrase has at least two operations and it is important that the student should know which operation should be done first. In Table 2, the operations to be done first are in bold under the column "examples of expressions."

Exercises

1. Write an algebraic expression for each word phrase. Hint: See the examples in

Table 2 and also watch for the key words in Table 2.

a. 10 more than the product of 7 and w.　　　　**b**. 1 less than the product of 8 and k.

c. 3 less than k divided by 6.　　　　　　　　**d**. 6 times the sum of w and 10.

e. 4 times the difference of y and 2.　　　　　**f**. 7 plus the product of 6 and k.

g. 20 minus the product of 5 and w.　　　　　**h**. 2 more than k divided by 6.

i. 8 times the product of m and 10.　　　　　**j**. Twice the quotient of 60 and w.

k. Four times the quotient of 100 and p.　　　　**l**. One-third the sum of w and 12.

m. One-third the difference between 32 and p.

Challenge Questions

2. Write the expression for the following word phrases.

a. w more than 5 times k.　　　　　　　　**b**. 11 more than p times n.

c. n less than 4 times b.　　　　　　　　**d**. 100 decreased by 3 times w.

e. w less than twice n.　　　　　　　　　**f**. Half the quotient of w and k.

g. 6 times the product of p and k.　　　　**h**. Half the difference between k and 3.

(Once you understand how to write expressions, you can then write and solve equations in the chapter on equations using an "equal to" symbol to show that two expressions are equal.)

Evaluation of Expressions
Example 1

Evaluate each expression for $a = 2$, $b = 3$, $c = 2.1$, and $d = 4$.

a. $a + d$　　　**b**. $\dfrac{b}{a}$　　　**c**. $(ac) + 10$　　　**d**. $\dfrac{14}{a} - 3$

e. $\dfrac{d}{a} + c$　　　**f**. $3bc$　　　**g**. $(d - c) - a$　　　**h**. $b + \dfrac{d}{a}$

Solution

a. Substitute 2 for a and 4 for d into the expression $a + d$ as shown:

$$a + d = 2 + 4$$
$$= 6$$

b. Substitute 3 for b and 2 for a into the expression $\dfrac{b}{a}$ as shown:

$$\frac{b}{a} = \frac{3}{2}$$
$$= 1\frac{1}{2}$$

c. Substitute 2 for a and 2.1 for c into the expression $(ac) + 10$ as shown:

$$(ac) + 10 = (2 \times 2.1) + 10$$
$$= 4.2 + 10$$
$$= 14 \cdot 2$$

64

d. Substitute 2 for a into the expression $\dfrac{14}{a}$ - 3 as shown:

$$\dfrac{14}{a} - 3 = \dfrac{14}{2} - 3$$
$$= 7 - 3 \qquad\qquad 14 \div 2 = 7$$
$$= 4$$

e. Substitute 4 for d, 2 for a, and 2.1 for c into the expression $\dfrac{d}{a}$ + c as shown:

$$\dfrac{d}{a} + c = \dfrac{4}{2} + 2.1$$
$$= 2 + 2.1$$
$$= 4.1$$

f. Substitute 3 for b and 2.1 for c into the expression 3bc as shown:
$$3bc = 3 \times 3 \times 2.1$$
$$= 9 \times 2.1 \qquad\qquad 3 \times 3 = 9$$
$$= 18.9$$

g. Substitute 4 for d, 2,1 for c and 2 for a into the expression (d - c) - a as shown:
$$(d - c) - a = (4 - 2.1) - 2$$
$$= 1.9 - 2 \qquad\qquad 4 - 2.1 = 1.9$$
$$= -.1 \qquad\qquad\quad 1.9 - 2 = -.1$$

h. Substitute 3 for b, 4 for d and 2 for a into the expression b + $\dfrac{d}{a}$ as shown:

$$b + \dfrac{d}{a} = 3 + \dfrac{4}{2}$$
$$= 3 + 2 \qquad\qquad 4 \div 2 = 2$$
$$= 5$$

Exercises

1. Evaluate each expression for a = 8, b = 2, c = 1, and d = 4. Hint: Match similar exercises with the similar examples in Example 1.

a. db   **b.** $\dfrac{a}{d}$ + b   **c.** d + c   **d.** (ab) + 4

e. $\dfrac{12}{b}$ + 4   **f.** $\dfrac{d}{c}$ + b   **g.** (a - d) - b   **h.** c + $\dfrac{d}{b}$

Challenge Questions

2. Evaluate each expression for m = 9, n = 2, w = 3, and p = 4.

a. mn   **b.** $\dfrac{18}{w}$ - p   **c.** (m - p) - w   **d.** n + $\dfrac{m}{w}$

e. $\dfrac{p}{n}$ + m   **f.** $\dfrac{24}{p}$ + m   **g.** p + nw   **h.** mp + n

EQUATIONS

New words: equations, variable, solution, and solve

An **equation** uses an "equal to" symbol to show that two expressions are equal.
The examples of equations are:

$2x + 1 = 4 - x$, $w + 4 = 10$, $5n = 15$, and $\dfrac{25}{5} = 5$.

An equation is therefore, similar to a seesaw such that the weight of the people on one side of the seesaw **is equal to** the weight of the people at the other side of the seesaw when the beam of the seesaw is horizontal or balanced.

Beam of the seesaw

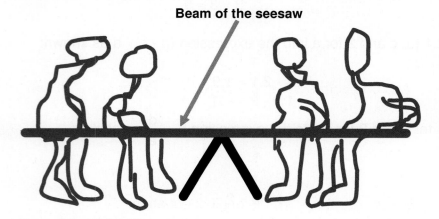

Group Exercise
The class may be divided into four groups and under the supervision of the teacher, and other adults, the students should balance the beam of a seesaw to demonstrate that an equation is similar to a balanced beam of a seesaw.

The **variable** in an equation is the unknown value in an equation. For example, x is the variable in the equation $2x + 1 = 4 - x$.
The **solution** to an equation is the value of the variable in the equation. To **solve** an equation means that we should **find the value of the variable**.

Solving Equations Using Addition
We can simply state the "**addition property of equality**" as shown:
When the same number is added to both sides of an equation, the resulting equation still has equal values at both sides of the equation.

Addition Property of Equality

Adding the same number to both sides of an equation.	Algebra
Add 4 to both sides of the equation 3 + 6 = 9 as shown: $$3 + 6\ = 9$$ $$\underline{\ \ +4\ \ \ \ +4\ \ }$$ $$3 + 10 = 13$$ Note that the resulting value of both sides of the equation after adding 4 to both sides of the equation is the same, which is 13	$X = W$ $X + Z = W + Z$

Example 1

Solve for n in the equation n - 6 = 12. Check your answers.

Solution

The basic method of solving for n is to isolate the variable n.

$n - 6 = 12$

$n - 6 + 6 = 12 + 6$ Add 6 to both sides of the equation in order to isolate the variable n.

$\quad\quad\quad n = 18$ -6 + 6 = 0

Check Your Answer

$n - 6 = 12$

$18 - 6 = 12$ Substitute 18 for n in the original equation.

$\quad\quad 12 = 12$ Since the right side of the equation is equal to the left side, the answer is correct.

Example 2

Solve for t in the equation 8 = t - 4. Check your answer.

Solution

The basic method for solving for t is to isolate t.

$8 = t - 4$

$8 + 4 = t - 4 + 4$ Add 4 to both sides of the equation in order to isolate t.

$12 = t + 0$ 8 + 4 = 12 and -4 + 4 = 0

$12 = t$

Check Your Answer

$8 = t - 4$

$8 = 12 - 4$ Substitute 12 for t in the original equation.

$8 = 8$ Since the left side of the equation is equal to the right side of the equation, the answer is correct.

Example 3

Solve for w in the equation 10 = -2 - w. Check your answer.

Solution

The basic method for solving for w is to isolate w.

10 = -2 - w	
10 + 2 = -2 + 2 - w	Add 2 to both sides of the equation in order to isolate w.
12 = 0 - w	-2 + 2 = 0
12 = -w	
12(-1) = -w(-1)	Multiply both sides of the equation by -1 in order to change -w to w because we are asked to solve for w but not -w.
-12 = w	Note: 12(-1) = -12 and -w(-1) = +w = w.

Check Your Answer

10 = -2 - w	
10 = -2 - (-12)	Substitute w = -12, into the original equation.
10 = -2 + 12	-(-12) = +12
10 = 10	-2 + 12 = 10
	Since the left side of the equation is equal to the right side of the equation, the answer is correct.

Solving Equations Using Subtraction

We can simply state the "**subtraction property of equality**" as shown:

When the same number is subtracted from both sides of an equation, the resulting equation still has equal values at both sides of the equation.

Subtraction Property of Equality

Subtract the same number from both sides of an equation.	Algebra
Subtracting 4 from both sides of the equation 10 + 8 = 18 as shown: 10 + 8 = 18 - 4 - 4 10 + 4 = 14 Note that the resulting value of both sides of the equation after subtracting 4 from both sides of the equation is the same which is 14.	x = w x - z = w - z

Example 4

Solve for x in the equation x + 3 = 16. Check your answer.

Solution

The basic method for solving for x is to isolate x.

x + 3 = 16

x + 3 - 3 = 16 - 3   Add 3 to both sides of the equation in order to isolate x.

x + 0 = 13   +3 - 3 = 0

x = 13

Check Your Answer

x + 3 = 16

13 + 3 = 16   Substitute x = 13 into the original equation.

16 = 16   Since the left side of the equation is equal to the right side of the equation, the answer is correct.

Example 5

Solve for y in the equation 12 = 3 + y. Check your answer.

Solution

The basic method for solving for y is to isolate y.

12 = 3 + y

12 - 3 = 3 - 3 + y   Subtract 3 from both sides of the equation in order to isolate y.

9 = 0 + y   12 - 3 = 9 and 3 - 3 = 0.

9 = y

Check Your Answer

12 = 3 + y

12 = 3 + 9   Substitute y = 9 into the original equation.

12 = 12   Since the left side of the equation is equal to the right side of the equation, the answer is correct.

Applications

Example 6

The sum of two numbers is 19. One of the numbers is 11. What is the other number?

Solution

Let the other number be n.

The sum of the two numbers is 19 therefore:

n + 11 = 19

n + 11 - 11 = 19 - 11   Subtract 11 from both sides of the equation in order to isolate n.

n + 0 = 8   +11 - 11 = 0 and 19 - 11 = 8.

n = 8

Example 7

When 2 is subtracted from a number the difference is 13. What is the number?

Solution

Let the number be n.

When 2 is subtracted from the number the difference is 13 therefore:

$n - 2 = 13$

$n - 2 + 2 = 13 + 2$ Add 2 to both sides of the equation to isolate n.

$n + 0 = 15$ $-2 + 2 = 0$ and $13 + 2 = 15$.

$n = 15$

Exercises

1. What is a variable in an equation?

2. What is meant by the solution of an equation?

3. Solve for the variable in each equation. Check your answer.
   Hint: See Example 1 and Example 2.

   a. $x - 4 = 10$ **b.** $w - 3 = 11$ **c.** $15 = y - 5$

   d. $p - 7 = -3$ **e.** $8 = 6 + y$ **f.** $w - 6 = 14$

4. Solve for the variable in each equation. Check your answer.
   Hint: See Example 3.

   a. $14 = 2 - k$ **b.** $8 = 6 - w$ **c.** $4 - w = 12$

   d. $3 - p = 9$ **e.** $12 = w + 4$ **f.** $7 + w = 14$

5. Solve for the variable in each equation. Check your answer.
   Hint: See Example 4 and Example 5.

   a. $x + 2 = 6$ **b.** $x + 14 = 14$ **c.** $11 = p + 10$

   d. $13 = 14 + t$ **e.** $12 = w + 4$ **f.** $7 + w = 14$

6. The sum of two numbers is 25. One of the numbers is 15. What is the other number? Hint: See Example 6.

7. When 4 is subtracted from a number, the difference is 29. What is the number? Hint: See Example 7

Challenge Questions

8. Solve for the variable in each equation.

   a. $n + 14 = 16$ **b.** $12 - p = 14$ **c.** $x - 5 = 9$ **d.** $12 - t = 4$

   e. $2 - e = 7$ **f.** $w + 2 = 6$ **g.** $6 + w = 10$ **h.** $9 + t = 11$

9. When 13 is subtracted from a number, the difference is 24. What is the number?

10. The sum of two numbers is 55. One of the numbers is 27. What is the other number?

11. Mary's age in years minus 8 is 29. How old is Mary. Hint: Let x = Mary's age in years.

Solving Equations by Dividing

To solve for the variable in an equation where the variable forms a multiplication equation, use the "**division property of equality**" to obtain the solution.

We can simply state **the division property of equality** as:

When the same non-zero number is used to divide both sides of an equation, the resulting equation still has equal values on both sides of the equation.

Division Property of Equality

Divide both sides of the equation by the same non-zero number.	Algebra
Dividing both sides of the equation $5 \times 4 = 20$ by the same non-zero number of 2 as shown: $$\frac{5 \times 4}{2} = \frac{20}{2}$$ $$10 = 10$$ Note that the resulting value of both sides of the equation after dividing both sides of the equation by 2 is the same which is 10	$$w = p$$ $$\frac{w}{x} = \frac{p}{x}$$ x is a non-zero number.

Example 8

Solve and check your answer.

a. $5n = 25$ **b.** $21 = 3x$

Solution

a. The basic method to solve for n is to isolate n.

$$5n = 25$$

$$\frac{5n}{5} = \frac{25}{5}$$ Divide both sides of the equation by 5 in order to isolate n.

$$\frac{\overset{n}{\cancel{5}n}}{\underset{1}{\cancel{5}}} = \frac{\overset{5}{\cancel{25}}}{\underset{1}{\cancel{5}}}$$

$$n = 5.$$

Check Your Answer

$5n = 25$

$5 \cdot 5 = 25$ Substitute 5 for n in the original equation.

$25 = 25$ Since the left side of the equation is equal to the right side
of the equation, the answer is correct

b. The basic method to solve for x is to isolate x.

$21 = 3x$

$$\frac{21}{3} = \frac{3x}{3}$$ Divide both sides of the equation by 3 in order to isolate x.

$$\frac{\overset{7}{21}}{\underset{1}{3}} = \frac{\overset{x}{3x}}{\underset{1}{3}}$$

$7 = x$

Check Your Answer

$21 = 3x$

$21 = 3 \cdot 7$ Substitute 7 for x in the original equation.

$21 = 21$ Since the left side of the equation is equal to the right side
of the equation, the answer is correct.

Solving Equations by Multiplication

To solve for the variable in an equation where the variable forms a division equation,
use the "**multiplication property of equation**," to obtain the solution.

We can simply state the **multiplication property of equality** as:

when the same number is used to multiply both sides of an equation, the resulting
equation still has equal values on both sides of the equation.

Multiplication Property of Equality

Multiplying both sides of the equation by the same number.	Algebra
Multipying both sides of the equation $4 \times 3 = 12$ by the same number 2 as shown: $4 \times 3 = 12$ $4 \times 3 \times \mathbf{2} = 12 \times \mathbf{2}$ $12 \times \mathbf{2} = 12 \times \mathbf{2}$ $24 = 24$ Note that the resulting value of both sides of the equation after multiplying both sides of the equation by 2 is the same, which is 24	$w = p$ $w\mathbf{x} = p\mathbf{x}$

Example 9

Solve for x and check your answer.

a. $\dfrac{x}{4} = 7$ **b.** $\dfrac{5}{x} = \dfrac{1}{2}$

Solution

a. The basic method for solving for x is to isolate x.

$$\frac{x}{4} = 7$$

$$\frac{x}{4} \times 4 = 7 \times 4$$ Multiply both sides of the equation by 4 in order to isolate x. The 4 on the left side cancels out as shown below.

$$\frac{x}{\underset{1}{\cancel{4}}} \times \overset{1}{\cancel{4}} = 28$$

$$x = 28$$

Check Your Answer

$$\frac{x}{4} = 7$$

$$\frac{28}{4} = 7$$ Substitute 28 for x in the original equation

$$\frac{\overset{7}{\cancel{28}}}{\underset{1}{4}} = 7 \qquad \text{Divide by 4.}$$

$$7 = 7 \qquad \text{Since the left side of the equation is equal to the right side of the equation, the answer is correct}$$

b. The basic method for solving for x is to isolate the x.

$$\frac{5}{x} = \frac{1}{2}$$

$$\frac{5}{x} \cdot x = \frac{1}{2} \cdot x \qquad \text{Multiply both sides of the equation by x in order to eliminate the x on the left side of the equation as a denominator when the x cancels out on the left side of the equation as shown:}$$

$$\frac{5}{\underset{1}{\cancel{x}}} \cdot \overset{1}{\cancel{x}} = \frac{1}{2} \cdot x$$

$$5 = \frac{x}{2}$$

$$5 \cdot 2 = \frac{x}{2} \cdot 2 \qquad \text{Multiply both sides of the equation by 2 in order to isolate x when the 2 cancels out on the right side of the equation as shown:}$$

$$5 \cdot 2 = \frac{x}{\underset{1}{\cancel{2}}} \cdot \overset{1}{\cancel{2}}$$

$$10 = x$$

Check Your Answer

$$\frac{5}{x} = \frac{1}{2}$$

$$\frac{5}{10} = \frac{1}{2}$$ Substitute 10 for x in the original equation.

$$\frac{\overset{1}{5}}{\underset{2}{10}} = \frac{1}{2}$$

$$\frac{1}{2} = \frac{1}{2}$$ Since the left side of the equation is equal to the right side of the equation, the answer is correct.

Applications

Hint: Review the chapter on "Algebraic Expressions."

Example 10

A number divided by 4 equals 8. What is the number? Hint: See Example **9a**.
Solution

Let the number be x. The number divided by 4 equals 8, therefore, $\frac{x}{4} = 8$.

The basic method for obtaining x **is to isolate the x**.

$$\frac{x}{4} \cdot 4 = 8 \cdot 4$$ Multiply both sides of the equation by 4 in order to isolate the x. when the 4 cancels out on the left side of the equation as shown:

$$\frac{x}{\underset{1}{4}} \cdot \overset{1}{4} = 8 \cdot 4$$

$$x = 32$$

Example 11

a. John scored 3 times as many points as Nick. If John scored 24 points, how many points did Nick score? Hint: See Example 8.
b. A CD cost 3 times as much as an LP. If the CD cost $18.00 how much did the LP cost? Hint: See Example 8.
Solution
a. **Step 1**: Set up the equation.
Let the number of the points scored by Nick = x.
John scored 3 times as many points as Nick and John scored 24 points.
Therefore:

$$3x = 24$$

Step 2: Solve the equation. The basic method for solving for x is to isolate the x.

$$\frac{3x}{3} = \frac{24}{3}$$ Divide both sides of the equation by 3 in order to isolate the x.

$$\frac{\overset{x}{\cancel{3x}}}{\underset{1}{3}} = \frac{\overset{8}{\cancel{24}}}{\underset{1}{3}}$$

$$x = 8 \text{ points.}$$

b. Step 1: Set up the equation. Hint: Review the chapter on the "Algebraic expressions."
Let the cost of the LP = x.
A CD cost 3 times as much as an LP and the CD cost $18.00, therefore:
$$18 = 3x$$

Step 2: Solve the equation.
The basic method for solving for x is to isolate the x by dividing both sides of the equation by 3 as shown:
$$18 = 3x$$

$$\frac{18}{3} = \frac{3x}{3}$$ Divide both sides of the equation by 3 in order to isolate the x.

$$\frac{\overset{6}{\cancel{18}}}{\underset{1}{3}} = \frac{\overset{x}{\cancel{3x}}}{\underset{1}{3}}$$

$$6 = x$$
$$x = \$6.00$$

Exercises
1. Solve and check your answer. Hint : See Example 8.

   a. $3x = 15$ **b.** $12 = 4x$ **c.** $36 = 9y$

   d. $4p = 28$ **e.** $3y = 27$ **f.** $5w = 45$

2. Solve and check your answer. Hint : See Example 9.

   a. $\frac{x}{3} = 10$ **b.** $\frac{y}{5} = 2$ **c.** $\frac{p}{4} = 3$ **d.** $\frac{w}{5} = 6$

e. $\dfrac{3}{x} = \dfrac{1}{3}$ **f.** $\dfrac{2}{y} = \dfrac{1}{5}$ **g.** $\dfrac{1}{4} = \dfrac{3}{w}$ **h.** $\dfrac{p}{3} = 6$

3. A number divided by 3 equals 21.
   What is the number? Hint: See Example 10.
4. Elizabeth has 3 times as many CD's as Nancy.
   If Elizabeth has 9 CD's how many CD's does Nancy have? Hint: See Example 11.
5. A number divided by 5 equals 9. What is the number? Hint: See Example 10.

Challenge Questions
6. Solve for the variable and check your answer.

   a. $6x = 42$ **b.** $\dfrac{p}{5} = 3$ **c.** $64 = 4x$ **d.** $\dfrac{4}{p} = \dfrac{1}{3}$

7. A number divided by 4 equals 6. What is the number?
8. Samuel made 4 times as much money this week for baby-sitting as George.
   If Samuel made $36.00, how much did George make?

Solving Two-Step Equations
Example 12
Solve $2x + 1 = 9$.
Solution
Step 1: Isolate 2x by subtracting 1 from both sides of the equation.

    $2x + 1 = 9.$

    $2x + 1 - 1 = 9 - 1$ Subtract 1 from both sides of the equation in order to
                         isolate the term with x in it which is 2x.

         $2x = 8$

Step 2: Isolate x by dividing both sides of the equation by 2.

    $\dfrac{2x}{2} = \dfrac{8}{2}$ Divide both sides of the equation by 2 in order to isolate the x.

    $\overset{x}{\underset{1}{\dfrac{2x}{2}}} = \overset{4}{\underset{1}{\dfrac{8}{2}}}$

    $x = 4$

Example 13

Solve: **a.** $3y - 5 = -20$ **b.** $\dfrac{w}{8} + 6 = 2$ **c.** $12 = \dfrac{n}{3} - 4 \cdot 2$ **d.** $28 = 10n - 12$

Solution
a. $3y - 5 = -20$
Step 1: Isolate 3y.

$$3y - 5 + 5 = -20 + 5$$ Add 5 to both sides of the equation in order to isolate the term with y which is 3y.

$$3y + 0 = -15$$ $-5 + 5 = 0$ and $-20 + 5 = -15$.

$$= -15$$

Step 2: Isolate y

$$3y = -15$$

$$\frac{3y}{3} = -\frac{15}{3}$$ Divide both sides of the equation by 3 in order to isolate the y.

$$\frac{\overset{y}{\cancel{3y}}}{\underset{1}{\cancel{3}}} = -\frac{\overset{5}{\cancel{15}}}{\underset{1}{\cancel{3}}}$$

$$y = -5$$

b. $\dfrac{w}{8} + 6 = 2$

Step 1: Isolate $\dfrac{w}{8}$.

$$\frac{w}{8} + 6 - 6 = 2 - 6$$ Subtract 6 from both sides of the equation in order to isolate the term with w which is $\dfrac{w}{8}$.

$$\frac{w}{8} + 0 = -4$$ $6 - 6 = 0$ and $2 - 6 = -4$

$$\frac{w}{8} = -4$$

Step 2: Isolate w.

$$\frac{w}{8} \times 8 = -4 \times 8$$ Multiply both sides of the equation by 8 in order to eliminate the 8 as a denominator and then isolate w.

$$\frac{w}{\underset{1}{\cancel{8}}} \times \overset{1}{\cancel{8}} = -4 \times 8$$ Divide by 8.

$$w = -32$$

c. $12 = \dfrac{n}{3} - 4 \cdot 2$

Step 1: Isolate $\dfrac{n}{3}$.

$12 + 4 \cdot 2 = \dfrac{n}{3} - 4 \cdot 2 + 4 \cdot 2$ Add $4 \cdot 2$ to both sides of the equation in order to isolate the term with n which is $\dfrac{n}{3}$.

$12 + 8 = \dfrac{n}{3} + 0$ $4 \cdot 2 = 8$ and $-4 \cdot 2 + 4 \cdot 2 = 0$ or $-8 + 8 = 0$.

$20 = \dfrac{n}{3}$

Step 2: Isolate n.

$20 \times 3 = \dfrac{n}{3} \times 3$ Multiply both sides of the equation by 3 in order to eliminate the 3 as a denominator, and then isolate n.

$$20 \times 3 = \dfrac{n}{\overset{1}{\cancel{3}}} \times \overset{1}{\cancel{3}}$$

$60 = n$

d. $28 = 10n - 12$

Step 1: Isolate 10n.

$28 + 12 = 10n - 12 + 12$ Add 12 to both sides of the equation in order to isolate the term with n which is 10n.

$40 = 10n$ $28 + 12 = 40$ and $-12 + 12 = 0$.

Step 2: Isolate n.

$\dfrac{40}{10} = \dfrac{10n}{10}$ Divide both sides of the equation by 10 in order to isolate n.

$$\dfrac{\overset{4}{\cancel{40}}}{\underset{1}{\cancel{10}}} = \dfrac{\overset{n}{\cancel{10n}}}{\underset{1}{\cancel{10}}}$$

$4 = n$

REAL WORLD APPLICATIONS - WORD PROBLEMS
Applications and Solving Two-Step Equations

Hint: Review the chapter on Algebraic Expression.

Example 14
Gertrude wants to buy a DVD for $45.00. She already has $5.00. If she earns $4.00 an hour for baby-sitting, how many hours must she work to earn the money she needs?
Solution
Step 1: Let n be the number of hours that Gertrude must work.

Step 2: Write an equation based on the information.

She earns $4.00 an hour for baby-sitting and from Step 1, she must work for n hours, and therefore, the total money that she makes baby-sitting is:
$$4n \text{ dollars.}$$
But she already has $5.00 therefore, the total money that she needs is 4n + 5 dollars. The total money that she needs which is 4n + 5 dollars must be equal to the cost of the DVD which is $45.00. Therefore;
$$4n + 5 = 45$$

Step 3: Solve the equation by isolating the n.

(Note that once the equation is set up, we can then use the two-step equation solving method such as in Example 12 and Example 13 to find n.)

$$4n + 5 = 45$$

$4n + 5 - 5 = 45 - 5$	Subtract 5 from both sides of the equation in order to isolate the term with n, which is 4n.
$4n = 40$	$+5 - 5 = 0$ and $45 - 5 = 40$.

$$\frac{4n}{4} = \frac{40}{4} \qquad \text{Divide both sides of the equation by 4 in order to isolate n.}$$

$$\frac{\overset{n}{\cancel{4n}}}{\underset{1}{\cancel{4}}} = \frac{\overset{10}{\cancel{40}}}{\underset{1}{\cancel{4}}}$$

$$n = 10 \text{ hours.}$$

Example 15
If a number is divided by 5 and then 3 is subtracted, the result is 2. What is the number?
Solution
Step 1: Let x be the number

Step 2: Write an equation based on the information in the question.

The number is divided by 5 and from step 1, the number is x, and therefore,

the number divided by 5 = $\dfrac{x}{5}$.

If 3 is subtracted from the number divided by 5, the result is 2, and therefore,

$$\dfrac{x}{5} - 3 = 2$$

Step 3: Solve the equation by isolating the x.

(Note that once the equation is set up, we can then use the two-step equation solving method such as in Example 12 and Example 13 to find x.)

$$\dfrac{x}{5} - 3 = 2$$

$$\dfrac{x}{5} - 3 + 3 = 2 + 3$$ Add 3 to both sides of the equation in order to isolate the term in x which is $\dfrac{x}{5}$.

$$\dfrac{x}{5} = 5$$ $-3 + 3 = 0$ and $2 + 3 = 5$.

$$\dfrac{x}{5} \times 5 = 5 \times 5$$ Multiply both sides of the equation by 5 in order to isolate x.

$$x = 25$$

Example 16

If you divide a number by 4 and 5 is added to the result, you get 11. What is the number?

Solution

Step 1: Let p be the number.

Step 2: Write an equation based on the information in the question. The number is divided by 4 and from Step 1, the number is p, and therefore, the number

divided by 4 = $\dfrac{p}{4}$.

If 5 is added to the number divided by 4, the result is 11, and therefore,

$$\dfrac{p}{4} + 5 = 11$$

Step 3: Solve the equation by isolating the p.

(Note that once the equation is set up, we can then use the two-step equation solving method such as in Example 12 and Example 13 to find p.)

$$\dfrac{p}{4} + 5 = 11$$

$$\frac{p}{4} + 5 - 5 = 11 - 5$$ Subtract 5 from both sides of the equation in order to isolate the term in p which is $\frac{p}{4}$.

$$\frac{p}{4} = 6$$ $+5 - 5 = 0$ and $11 - 5 = 6$.

$$\frac{p}{4} \times 4 = 6 \times 4$$ Multiply both sides of the equation by 4 in order to isolate p.

$$\frac{p}{\overset{}{\underset{1}{4}}} \times \overset{1}{4} = 6 \times 4$$

$$p = 24$$

Example 17

Four more than the product of 8 and a number is 36. What is the number?

Solution

Step 1: Let the number be m.

Step 2: Write an equation based on the information in the question.

The product of 8 and the number is 8m because, from Step 1, the number is m. Therefore, 4 more than the product of 8 and the number is $8m + 4$. Then if 4 more than the product of 8 and the number is 36, this statement can be written as:

$8m + 4 = 36$

Step 3: Solve the equation by isolating the m.

(Note that once the equation is set up, we can then use the two-step equation solving method such as in Example 12 and Example 13 to find m.)

$8m + 4 = 36$

$8m + 4 - 4 = 36 - 4$ Subtract 4 from both sides of the equation in order to isolate the term with m, which is 8m.

$8m = 32$ $+4 - 4 = 0$ and $36 - 4 = 32$

$$\frac{8m}{8} = \frac{32}{8}$$ Divide both sides of the equation by 8 in order to isolate m.

$$\frac{\overset{m}{8m}}{\underset{1}{8}} = \frac{\overset{4}{32}}{\underset{1}{8}}$$

$$m = 4$$

Example 18

Five less than the product of 6 and a number is 31. What is the number?

Solution

Step 1: Let the number be x.

Step 2: Write an equation based on the information in the question.

The product of 6 and the number will be 6 · x or 6x because, from Step 1, the number is x. Therefore, 5 less than the product of 6 and the number will be 6x - 5. Then, if five less than the product of 6 and the number is 31, the statement will be:

$$6x - 5 = 31$$

Step 3: Solve the equation by isolating the x.

(Note that once the equation is set up, we can then use the two-step equation solving method such as in Example 12 and Example 13 to find x.)

$$6x - 5 = 31$$

$$6x - 5 + 5 = 31 + 5$$ Add 5 to both sides of the equation in order to isolate the term in x which is 6x.

$$6x = 36$$ -5 + 5 = 0 and 31 + 5 = 36

$$\frac{6x}{6} = \frac{36}{6}$$ Divide both sides of the equation by 6 in order to isolate x.

$$\frac{\overset{x}{\cancel{6x}}}{\underset{1}{\cancel{6}}} = \frac{\overset{6}{\cancel{36}}}{\underset{1}{\cancel{6}}}$$

$$x = 6$$

Example 19

John earned $30.00 washing cars. He earned $6.00 less than 3 times what Mary earned. How much did Mary earn?

Solution

Step 1: Let k be the money that Mary earned.

Step 2: Write an equation based on the information in the question.

3 times what Mary earned = 3k because from Step 1, k is the money that Mary earned. The expression $6.00 less than 3 times what Mary earned can be stated as: 3k - 6.

$30.00 is $4.00 less than 3 times what Mary earned and this statement can be written as: 3k - 6 = 30

Step 3: Solve the equation by isolating the k.

$$3k - 6 = 30$$

$$3k - 6 + 6 = 30 + 6$$
     Add 6 to both sides of the equation in order to isolate the term in k which is 3k.

$$3k = 36$$
     -6 + 6 = 0 and 30 + 6 = 36.

$$\frac{3k}{3} = \frac{36}{3}$$
     Divide both sides of the equation by 3 in order to isolate the k.

$$\frac{\overset{k}{\cancel{3k}}}{\underset{1}{\cancel{3}}} = \frac{\overset{12}{\cancel{36}}}{\underset{1}{\cancel{3}}}$$

$$k = \$12$$

Exercises

1. Solve for x, y, w, or p in each equation.
Hint: See Example 12.

 a. $4x + 3 = 15$ **b.** $2y + 4 = 12$ **c.** $5 + 3p = 20$

 d. $2p + 6 = 18$ **e.** $4w + 4 = 24$ **f.** $5w + 6 = 26$

2. Solve for x, y, w, or p in each equation.
Hint: See Examples **13a** and **13d**.

 a. $4x - 3 = 9$ **b.** $3p - 6 = 24$ **c.** $5y - 3 = 12$

 d. $6p - 5 = 19$ **e.** $4w - 4 = 16$ **f.** $-4 + 3y = 11$

 g. $-3 + 3w = 12$ **h.** $-5 + 4x = 15$ **j.** $3p - 3 = 18$

3. Solve for x or w. Hint: See Examples **13b** and **13c**.

 a. $24 = \frac{x}{3} + 4.1$ **b.** $\frac{w}{5} - 2 = 7$ **c.** $13 = \frac{w}{2} - 7$ **d.** $8 = \frac{x}{3} + 6.3$

4. Solve for w or p. Hint: See Example **13d**.

 a. $12 = 3w - 3$ **b.** $9 = 4p - 1$ **c.** $7 = 5p - 8$ **d.** $6 = 3w - 3$

5. Mary wants to buy a camera for $64. She already has $14. If she earns $5 an hour for baby-sitting how many hours must she work to earn the money she needs? Hint: See Example 14.

6. If a number is divided by 4 and then 5 is subtracted the result is 4. What is the number? Hint: See Example 15.

7. If you divide a number by 3 and add 6 to the result, you get 16. What is the number? Hint: See Example 16.

8. Seven more than the product of 6 and a number is 31. What is the number? Hint: See Example 17.

9. Three less than the product of 5 and a number is 22. What is the number? Hint: See Example 18

10. Judith earned $24 baby-sitting. She earned $4 less than twice what Mary earned. How much did Mary earned? Hint: See Example 19.

Challenge Questions

11. Solve for x, y, w, or p in each equation.

a. $3w - 7 = 23$	**b.** $4x + 5 = 41$	**c.** $6x - 2 = 22$
d. $-4 + 4p = 28$	**e.** $6 + 7p = 27$	**f.** $4y + 3 = 27$

g. $9 = \dfrac{w}{4} + 8$	**h.** $\dfrac{y}{4} - 2.4 = 3$	**j.** $8 = 4p - 8$

12. Five less than the product of 8 and a number is 27. What is the number?

13. Nine more than the product of 4 and a number is 19. What is the number?

14. If you divide a number by 4 and add 11 to the result, you get 15. What is the number?

15. Nick earned $36 baby-sitting. He earned $18 less than three times what John earned. How much did John earned?

16. George wants to buy a copy of the "Mathmasters series" book for $37. He already has $17. If he earns $6 an hour baby-sitting, how many hours does he have to work to earn the money he needs?

Answers to Selected Questions

2f. $\qquad -4 + 3y = 11$

$-4 + 4 + 3y = 11 + 4 \qquad$ Add 4 to both sides of the equation to isolate 3y.

$\qquad\qquad 3y = 15$

$$\frac{3y}{3} = \frac{15}{3} \qquad \text{Divide both sides of the equation by 3 in order to isolate y.}$$

$\qquad\qquad y = 5$

MULTI-STEP EQUATION SOLVING

Equations With Like Terms or Variables

Equations with like terms are equations with the same types of variables. For example in the equation $6x + 2x = 24$, the terms 6x and 2x have the same type of variable in x, and therefore, we say that the equation $6x + 2x = 24$ has like terms in x. The general method for solving equations with like terms is to isolate all the like terms to one side of the equation add or subtract the like terms, then divide to isolate the variable.

Example 1

Solve for x, k, or w.

a. $6x + 2x = 24$ **b.** $5k - 2k = 9$ c. $3w + 12 = 5w$

Solution

a. $6x + 2x = 24$

Step 1: Add the like terms.

$$8x = 24 \qquad\qquad 6x + 2x = 8x$$

Step 2: Divide both sides of the equation by 8 to isolate x.

$$\frac{8x}{8} = \frac{24}{8}$$

$$\frac{\overset{x}{\cancel{8}x}}{\underset{1}{\cancel{8}}} = \frac{\overset{3}{\cancel{24}}}{\underset{1}{\cancel{8}}}$$

$$x = 3$$

b. $5k - 2k = 9$

Step 1: Subtract the like terms.

$$3k = 9 \qquad\qquad 5k - 2k = 3k.$$

Step 2: Divide both sides of the equation by 3 to isolate k.

$$\frac{3k}{3} = \frac{9}{3}$$

$$\frac{\overset{k}{\cancel{3}k}}{\underset{1}{\cancel{3}}} = \frac{\overset{3}{\cancel{9}}}{\underset{1}{\cancel{3}}}$$

$$k = 3$$

c. $3w + 12 = 5w$

Step 1: Isolate all the like terms to one side by subtracting 3w from both sides of the equation.

$$3w - 3w + 12 = 5w - 3w$$

$$12 = 2w \qquad\qquad\qquad 3w - 3w = 0 \text{ and } 5w - 3w = 2w.$$

Step 2: Divide both sides of the equation by 2 in order to isolate w.

$$\frac{12}{2} = \frac{2w}{2}$$

$$\begin{array}{cc} 6 & w \\ \dfrac{12}{2} & = \dfrac{2w}{2} \\ 1 & 1 \end{array}$$

$$6 = w$$

Example 2

Solve for x, k, or w.

a. 8x - 1 -3x = 24   **b**. 9w + 3 = 6w + 15   **c**. -8k - 5 = 4k - 29

Solution

a. 8x - 1 - 3x = 24

Step 1: Isolate the like terms to one side of the equation by adding 1 to both sides of the equation.

8x - 1 + 1 - 3x = 24 + 1

8x - 3x = 25   -1 + 1 = 0

Step 2: Combine the like terms by subtracting 3x from 8x.

5x = 25   8x - 3x = 5x

Step 3: Isolate x by dividing both sides of the equation by 5.

$$\frac{5x}{5} = \frac{25}{5}$$

$$\begin{array}{cc} x & 5 \\ \dfrac{5x}{5} & = \dfrac{25}{5} \\ 1 & 1 \end{array}$$

$$x = 5$$

b. 9w + 3 = 6w + 15

Step 1: Isolate the like terms to one side of the equation by subtracting 6w from both sides of the equation and also subtracting 3 from both sides of the equation.

9w + 3 - 3 - 6w = 6w - 6w + 15 - 3

9w - 6w = 12   3 - 3 = 0, 6w - 6w = 0, and 15 - 3 = 12.

Step 2: Combine the like terms by subtracting 6w from 9w.

3w = 12   9w - 6w = 3w

Step 3: Isolate w by dividing both sides of the equation by 3.

$$\frac{3w}{3} = \frac{12}{3}$$

$$\frac{\overset{w}{\cancel{3w}}}{\underset{1}{\cancel{3}}} = \frac{\overset{4}{\cancel{12}}}{\underset{1}{\cancel{3}}}$$

$$w = 4$$

c. -8k -5 = 4k - 29

Step 1: Isolate the like terms to one side of the equation by adding 8k to both sides of the equation and also by adding 29 to both sides of the equation.

-8k + 8k -5 + 29 = 4k + 8k -29 + 29

24 = 4k + 8k   -8k + 8k = 0, -5 + 29 = 24

and -29 + 29 = 0.

Step 2: Combine the like terms by adding 4k to 8k.

24 = 12k

Step 3: Isolate k by dividing both sides of the equation by 12.

$$\frac{24}{12} = \frac{12k}{12}$$

$$\frac{\overset{2}{\cancel{24}}}{\underset{1}{\cancel{12}}} = \frac{\overset{k}{\cancel{12}}}{\underset{1}{\cancel{12}}}$$

2 = k or k = 2

Example 3

Solve for x, y, or w.

a. $\dfrac{4}{5} = x + \dfrac{3}{4}$ **b.** $y - 1\dfrac{1}{2} = 2\dfrac{1}{3}$ **c.** $\dfrac{6}{7} = w - \dfrac{2}{3}$

Solution

a. $\dfrac{4}{5} = x + \dfrac{3}{4}$ **Type of equation: Addition type**

Step 1: Isolate x by subtracting $\dfrac{3}{4}$ from both sides of the equation.

$$\frac{4}{5} - \frac{3}{4} = x + \frac{3}{4} - \frac{3}{4}$$

$$\frac{4}{5} - \frac{3}{4} = x \qquad\qquad \frac{3}{4} - \frac{3}{4} = 0$$

Step 2: Subtract $\dfrac{3}{4}$ from $\dfrac{4}{5}$ to obtain the value of x.

$$\dfrac{4}{5} - \dfrac{3}{4} = x$$

$$\dfrac{16 - 15}{20} = x \qquad\qquad \text{LCD (least common denominator)} = 20.$$

$$\dfrac{1}{20} = x \qquad\qquad 16 - 15 = 1$$

b. $y - 1\dfrac{1}{2} = 2\dfrac{1}{3}$ \qquad\qquad **Type of equation: Subtraction type**

Step 1: Isolate y to one side of the equation by adding $1\dfrac{1}{2}$ to both sides of the equation.

$$y - 1\dfrac{1}{2} + 1\dfrac{1}{2} = 2\dfrac{1}{3} + 1\dfrac{1}{2}$$

$$y = 2\dfrac{1}{3} + 1\dfrac{1}{2} \qquad\qquad -1\dfrac{1}{2} + 1\dfrac{1}{2} = 0$$

Step 2: Add $2\dfrac{1}{3}$ to $1\dfrac{1}{2}$ to obtain the value of y.

$$y = 2\dfrac{1}{3} + 1\dfrac{1}{2}$$

$$2\dfrac{1}{3} \cdot \dfrac{2}{2} = \dfrac{2}{6} \swarrow \text{LCD} \qquad\qquad \text{Review Addition of Fractions.}$$

$$+ 1\dfrac{1}{2} \cdot \dfrac{3}{3} = \dfrac{3}{6} \swarrow \text{LCD} \qquad\qquad \text{Review Addition of Fractions.}$$

$$3\dfrac{5}{6} \qquad\qquad\qquad 2 + 1 = 3 \text{ and } \dfrac{2}{6} + \dfrac{3}{6} = \dfrac{5}{6}$$

$$y = 3\dfrac{5}{6}$$

c. $\dfrac{6}{7} = w - \dfrac{2}{3}$ \qquad\qquad **Type of equation: Subtraction type**

Step 1: Isolate w to one side of the equation by adding $\dfrac{2}{3}$ to both sides of the equation.

$$\frac{6}{7} + \frac{2}{3} = w - \frac{2}{3} + \frac{2}{3}$$

$$\frac{6}{7} + \frac{2}{3} = w \qquad\qquad -\frac{2}{3} + \frac{2}{3} = 0$$

Step 2: Add $\frac{6}{7}$ to $\frac{2}{3}$ in order to obtain the value of w.

$$\frac{6}{7} + \frac{2}{3} = w$$

$$\frac{18 + 14}{21} = w \qquad\qquad LCD = 21$$

$$\frac{32}{21} = w \qquad\qquad \text{Review Addition of Fractions.}$$

$$1\frac{11}{21} = w$$

Example 4

Solve for m and w.

a. $2.4 = m - 0.17$ **b**. $w + 1.5 = 3.16$

Solution

a. $2.4 = m - 0.17$ **Type of equation: Subtraction type**

Step 1: Isolate m to one side of the equation by adding 0.17 to both sides of the equation.

$$2.4 + 0.17 = m - 0.17 + 0.17$$
$$2.4 + 0.17 = m \qquad\qquad -0.17 + 0.17 = 0$$

Step 2: Add 2.4 to + 0.17 in order to obtain the value of m.

$$\begin{array}{r} 2.4 \\ + \underline{0.17} \\ 2.57 \end{array}$$

Therefore, $2.57 = m$ or $m = 2.57$

b. $w + 1.5 = 3.16$ **Type of equation: Addition type**

Step 1: Isolate w to one side of the equation by subtracting 1.5 from both sides of the equation.

$$w + 1.5 - 1.5 = 3.16 - 1.5$$

$$w = 3.16 - 1.5 \qquad\qquad 1.5 - 1.5 = 0$$

Step 2: Subtracting 1.5 from 3.16 to obtain the value of w.

```
  3.16
- 1.5
------
  1.66
```

$$w = 1.66$$

Exercises

1. What is meant by like terms?

2. Solve for x, y, or k in each equation. Hint: See Example 1.

    a. $4x + 3x = 21$ **b**. $7y - 2y = 25$ **c**. $2k + 18 = 5k$

    d. $3y + 27 = 12y$ **e**. $6k + 2k = 32$ **f**. $5x - 2x = 30$

3. Solve for x, k, or w. Hint: See Example 2.

    a. $7x - 2 - 4x = 31$ **b**. $4w + 4 = 2w$ **c**. $-5k - 3 = 3k - 27$

    d. $6w + 12 = 3w$ **e**. $-6k - 4 = 2k - 20$ **f**. $3w + 4 - 2x = 23$

4. Solve for w, x, or y. Hint: See Example 3.

    a. $\dfrac{4}{5} = x + \dfrac{1}{2}$ **b**. $y - 1\dfrac{1}{3} = 2\dfrac{1}{4}$ **c**. $\dfrac{4}{5} = w - \dfrac{1}{2}$

    d. $w - 1\dfrac{1}{4} = 3\dfrac{1}{2}$ **e**. $\dfrac{3}{4} = y + \dfrac{1}{3}$ **f**. $\dfrac{2}{3} = x - \dfrac{2}{3}$

5. Solve for m or w. Hint: See Example 4.

    a. $3.8 = m - 0.24$ **b**. $w + 1.7 = 4.19$ **c**. $w + 1.5 = 3.21$

    d. $4.2 = w - 0.33$ **e**. $m + 2.8 = 3.18$ **f**. $5.3 = w - 0.12$

Challenge Questions

6. Solve for x, y, or w in each equation.

    a. $5y - 7 - 3y = 10$ **b**. $6.7 = x - 2.4$ **c**. $4w - 2w = 6$

    d. $-4y - 2 = 3y - 16$ **e**. $8.4 = x - 2.33$ **f**. $\dfrac{3}{4} = w + \dfrac{1}{2}$

    g. $x - 2\dfrac{1}{2} = 1\dfrac{3}{4}$ **h**. $3y + 16 = 7y$ **i**. $\dfrac{4}{5} = w - \dfrac{1}{3}$

Distributive Property with Equations

The distributive property states that for any number a, b, and c:

$$a(b + c) = ab + ac$$
$$a(b - c) = ab - ac.$$

This distributive property is used in simplifying expressions.

Distributive Law with a Positive on the Outside

Example 1
Simplify each expression.

a. $2(x + 4)$ **b.** $2(x - 4)$ **c.** $3(2n + 6)$ **d.** $6(4 - 2g)$

Solution

a. $2(x + 4)$

$2(x + 4) = 2 \cdot x + 2 \cdot 4$ Distributive property; $a(b + c) = ab + ac$.
$ = 2x + 8$

b. $2(x - 4)$

$2(x - 4) = 2 \cdot x - 2 \cdot 4$ Distributive property; $a(b - c) = ab - ac$.
$ = 2x - 8$

c. $3(2n + 6)$

$3(2n + 6) = 3 \cdot 2n + 3 \cdot 6$ Distributive property; $a(b + c) = ab + ac$
$ = 6n + 18$

d. $6(4 - 2g)$

$6(4 - 2g) = 6 \cdot 4 - 6 \cdot 2g$ Distributive property; $a(b - c) = ab - ac$.
$ = 24 - 12g.$

Exercises
Simplify each expression. Hint: See Example 1.

1. $4(a + 2)$ **2.** $3(2x - 6)$ **3.** $6(y + 2)$ **4.** $8(2w - 5)$
5. $4(10 - 3a)$ **6.** $3(w - 1)$ **7.** $5(3g - 4)$ **8.** $3(a + 5)$
9. $7(2x + 4)$ **10.** $4(3y - 5)$ **11.** $6(2 - 46)$ **12.** $4(3 + 2x)$
13. $5(2a + 1)$ **14.** $6(a + b)$ **15.** $2(3c - 2)$ **16.** $3(2y - 8)$

Distributive Law with a Negative on the Outside
During multiplication or division (see Example 2):

       1. If all the symbols are positive the answer is positive.
       2. If the number of negative symbols is an even number, then the answer is positive.
       3. If the number of negative symbols is an odd number, then the answer is negative.

Example 2

Simplify each expression.

   a. -2(3 + 4x)   **b**. -3(-4 + 2a)   **c**. -4(-2x - 6)

   d. -(-2a - 4)   **e**. -(2a + 6)   **f**. -(-3x + 5)

Solution

a. -2(3 + 4x)

-2(3 + 4x) = -2 · 3 + (-2)(4x)	Distribution property; **-a**(**b** + **c**) = **-ab** + (**-a**)**c**.
= -6 - 8x	Note, odd number of negative symbols = -

(-)(+) = -, therefore, -2 · 3 = -6

        ↓ ↓

       (-) (+) = -

Note, odd number of negative symbols = -

    +(-)(+) = -, therefore, + (-2)(4x) = -8x

       ↓ ↓ ↓

     + (-) (+) = -

b. -3(-4 + 2a)

-3(-4 + 2a) = (-3)(-4) + (-3)(2a)	Distributive property; **-a**(**-b** + **c**) = (**-a**)(**-b**) + (**-a**)(**c**).
= 12 - 6a	Note, even number of negative symbols = +

(-)(-) = +, therefore, (-3)(-4) = +12 = 12.

Note, odd number of negative symbols = -

    +(-)(+) = -, therefore, + (-3)(2a) = -6a.

       ↓ ↓ ↓

     + (-) (+) = -

c. -4(-2x - 6)

-4(-2x - 6) = (-4)(-2x) - (-4)(6)	Distributive property; **-a**(**-b** - **c**) = (**-a**)(**-b**) - (**-a**)(**c**).
= 8x + 24	Note, even number of negative symbols = +

(-)(-) = +, therefore, (-4)(-2x) = +8x = 8x.

        ↓ ↓

       (-) (-) = +

Note, even number of negative symbols = +

    (-)(-)(+) = +, therefore, -(-4)(6) = +24 = 24

       ↓ ↓ ↓

     - (-) (+) = +

d. -(-2a - 4)

-(-2a - 4) = -2(-a) - (-4)	Distributive property; -(**-b** - **c**) = -(**-b**) - (**-c**)
= 2a + 4	Note, even number of negative symbols = +

(-)(-) = +, therefore, -2(-a) = +2a = 2a.

        ↓ ↓

       (-) (-) = +

Note, even number of negative symbols = +

    (-)(-) = +, therefore, - (-4) = +4 = 4.

        ↓ ↓

       (-) (-) = +

e. -(2a + 6)

-(2a + 6) = -(2a) + (-)(6)   Distributive property; -(**b** + **c**) = -**b** + (-)(**c**).
       = -2a - 6   Note, odd number of negative symbols = -
                                       Hint: See Example 2a.

f. -(-3x + 5)

-(-3x + 5) = -(-3x) + (-)(5)   Distributive property
        = 3x - 5   See the preceding examples.

Exercises

1. Simplify each expression. Hint: See Example **2a**.
   a. -2(4 + 5a)   **b**. -4(3 + 4x)   **c**. -3(4x + 2)
   d. -5(3y + 6)   **e**. -6(2 + 3w)   **f**. -3(2w + 4)

2. Simplify each expression. Hint: See Example **2b**.
   a. -2(-2 + 2w)   **b**. -3(-4 + 6a)   **c**. -4(-5 + 3w)
   d -5(-6 + 3a)   **e** -2(-3 + 2x)   **f**. -3(-3 + 4a)

3. Simplify each expression. Hint: See Example **2c**.
   a. -3(-3x - 2)   **b**. -2(-6x - 4)   **c**. -5(-7a - 6)
   d. -4(-4y - 3)   **e**. -6(-2w - 5)   **f**. -3(-5w - 5)

4. Simplify each expression. Hint: See Example **2d**.
   a. -3(3a - 3)   **b**. -(-4w - 5)   **c**. -(-6y - 7)
   d. -(-5x - 4)   **e**. -(-7a - 6)   **f**. -(4x - 5)

5. Simplify each expression. Hint: See Example **2e**.
   a. -(3x + 4)   **b**. -4(w + 7)   **c**. -(3a + 6)
   d -(-4y + 5)   **e**. -4(a + 6)   **f**. -(5w + 3)

6. Simplify each expression. Hint: See Example **2f**.
   a. -(-4a + 2)   **b**. -(-3y + 4)   **c**. -(-5w + 3)
   d. -(-3x + 4)   **e**. -(-6y + 2)   **f**. -(-2x + 8)

Challenge Questions

7. Simplify each expression.
   a. -(-3a - 4)   **b**. -2(-4 - 3y)   **c**. -4(6 + 7w)
   d. -(-3w + 6)   **e**. -3(-2w - 3)   **f**. -2(-5 + 3a)

Answers to Selected Questions

1a. -8 - 10a   **2a**. 4 - 4w   **3a**. 9x + 6
4a. -9 + 9a   **5a**. -3x - 4   **6a**. 4a - 2

Distributive Law with Equations
Example 1
Solve for y.   2(4 + y) = 12

Solution

$2(4 + y) = 12$

Step 1: Simplify the equation.

$2 \cdot 4 + 2 \cdot y = 12$	Distributive property
$8 + 2y = 12$	$2 \cdot 4 = 8$

Step 2: Isolate 2y by subtracting 8 from both sides of the equation.

$8 - 8 + 2y = 12 - 8$	
$2y = 4$	$8 - 8 = 0$ and $12 - 8 = 4.$

Step 3: Isolate y by dividing both sides of the equation by 2.

$$\frac{2y}{2} = \frac{4}{2}$$

$$\frac{\overset{y}{\cancel{2y}}}{\underset{1}{\cancel{2}}} = \frac{\overset{2}{\cancel{4}}}{\underset{1}{\cancel{2}}}$$

$$y = 2$$

Rules

Two rules are needed when dividing as shown:

Rule 1: If the symbols (+, -) of the numerator and the denominator are the same, the symbol of the answer is **positive**.

For example, $\dfrac{-a}{-a} = +1 = 1$ and $\dfrac{+a}{+a} = \dfrac{a}{a} = 1.$

Rule 2: If the symbols (+, -) of the numerator and the denominator are different, the symbol of the answer is **negative**.

For example, $\dfrac{-a}{a} = -1$ and $\dfrac{a}{-a} = -1$

Example 2

Solve for x. $-3(2x + 3) = -15$

Solution

$-3(2x + 3) = -15$

Step 1: Simplify the equation.

$-3 \cdot (2x) -3 \cdot (+3) = -15$	Distributive property.
$-6x - 9 = -15$	Note, odd number of negative symbols = -

Step 2: Isolate -6x to one side of the equation by adding 9 to both sides of the equation.

$-6x - 9 + 9 = -15 + 9$	
$-6x = -6$	$-9 + 9 = 0$ and $-15 + 9 = -6.$

Step 3: Isolate x to one side of the equation by dividing both sides of the equation

by -6.

$$\frac{-6x}{-6} = \frac{-6}{-6}$$

$$\frac{\overset{x}{\cancel{-6}x}}{\underset{1}{\cancel{-6}}} = \frac{\overset{1}{\cancel{-6}}}{\underset{1}{\cancel{-6}}}$$ Hint: Rule 1 is used here.

$$x = 1$$

Example 3

Solve for w. $-2(2w - 3) = 12$

Solution

$-2(2w - 3) = 12$

Step 1: Simplify the equation.

$-2 \cdot 2w - 2 \cdot (-3) = 12$ Distributive property.

$-4w + 6 = 12$ Note, odd number of negatives = -

$-(+) = -$, therefore, $-2 \cdot (2w) = -4w$.

↓   ↓

-   (+) = -

Note, even number of negatives = +.

$-(-) = +$, therefore, $-2 \cdot (-3) = +6 = 6$.

↓   ↓

-   (-) = +.

Step 2: Isolate -4w to one side of the equation by subtracting 6 from both sides of the equation.

$-4w + 6 - 6 = 12 - 6$

$-4w = 6$ $+6 - 6 = 0$ and $12 - 6 = 6$.

Step 3: Isolate w to one side of the equation by dividing both sides by -4.

$$\frac{-4w}{-4} = \frac{6}{-4}$$

$$\frac{\overset{w}{\cancel{-4}w}}{\underset{1}{\cancel{-4}}} = \frac{\overset{3}{\cancel{6}}}{\underset{-2}{\cancel{-4}}}$$ Hint: Rule 1 is used for $\frac{-4w}{-4}$ and Rule 2 is used for $\frac{6}{-4}$.

$$w = \frac{3}{-2}$$

96

$$w = -1\frac{1}{2}$$

Example 4

Solve for w.   -(2w - 4) = -14

Solution

-(2w - 4) = -14

Step 1: Simplify the equation.

   -(2w - 4) = -14
   (-)2w - (-)4 = -14   Distributive property.
   -2w + 4 = -14   Note, odd number of negative numbers = -.
                               -(+) = -, therefore, -(2w) = -2w.
                               ↓ ↓
                               - (+) = -
                   Note, even number of negatives = +
                   -(-) = +, therefore, -(-4) = +4 = 4
                               ↓ ↓
                               - (-) = +

Step 2: Isolate -2w to one side of the equation by subtracting 4 from both sides of the equation.

   -2w + 4 - 4 = -14 - 4
   -2w = -18   +4 - 4 = 0 and -14 - 4 = -18.

Step 3: Isolate w to one side of the equation by dividing both sides of the equation by -2.

$$\frac{-2w}{-2} = \frac{18}{-2}$$

$$\frac{\overset{w}{\cancel{-2w}}}{\underset{1}{\cancel{-2}}} = \frac{\overset{-9}{\cancel{18}}}{\underset{1}{\cancel{-2}}}$$

Hint: Rule 1 is used for $\frac{-2w}{-2}$ to obtain +w = w and Rule 2 is used for $\frac{18}{-2}$ to obtain -9.

$$w = -9$$

Example 5

Solve for b.   2b + 3(b - 4) = 4

Solution

2b + 3(b - 4) = 4

Step 1: Simplify the equation.

$2b + 3 \cdot 2b - 3 \cdot 4 = 4$ \hspace{2cm} Distributive property

$2b + 6b - 12 = 4$

Step 2: Combine the like terms.

$8b - 12 = 4$ \hspace{3cm} $2b + 6b = 8b$.

Step 3: Isolate 8b to one side of the equation by adding 12 to both sides of the equation.

$8b - 12 + 12 = 4 + 12$

$8b = 16$ \hspace{3cm} $-12 + 12 = 0$ and $4 + 12 = 16$

Step 4: Isolate b to one side of the equation by dividing both sides of the equation by 8.

$$\frac{8b}{8} = \frac{16}{8}$$

$$\frac{\cancel{8}b}{\cancel{8}} = \frac{\cancel{16}^{2}}{\cancel{8}_{1}}$$

$$b = 2$$

Example 6

Solve for x. \hspace{2cm} $9x + 5 - 2(3x + 6) = 14$

Solution

$9x + 5 - 2(3x + 6) = 14$

Step 1: Simplify the equation.

$9x + 5 - 2(3x) + (-2)(6) = 14$ \hspace{1cm} Distributive property

$9x + 5 - 6x - 12 = 14$

Step 2: Combine the like terms.

$3x - 7 = 14$ \hspace{3cm} $9x - 6x = 3x$ and $5 - 12 = -7$

Step 3: Isolate 3x to one side of the equation by adding 7 to both sides of the equation.

$3x - 7 + 7 = 14 + 7$

$3x = 21$ \hspace{3cm} $-7 + 7 = 0$ and $14 + 7 = 21$

Step 4: Isolate x by dividing both sides of the equation by 3.

$$\frac{3x}{3} = \frac{21}{3}$$

$$\frac{\cancel{3}x}{\cancel{3}_{1}} = \frac{\cancel{21}^{7}}{\cancel{3}_{1}}$$

$x = 7$

Example 7

Solve for n. $2(3 - n) = 16 - 2(3 + 2n)$

Solution

$2(3 - n) = 16 - 2(3 + 2n)$

Step 1: Simplify the equation.

$2 \cdot 3 - 2 \cdot n = 16 - 2 \cdot 3 + (-2)(2n)$ Distributive property.

$6 - 2n = 16 - 6 - 4n$ $+ (-2)(2n) = -2(2n) = -2 \cdot 2n = -4n$

Step 2: Isolate the like terms to the left side of the equation by adding 4n to both sides of the equation and also subtracting 6 from both sides of the equation.

$6 - 6 - 2n + 4n = 16 - 6 - 6 - 4n + 4n$

$-2n + 4n = 4$ $6 - 6 = 0, 16 - 6 - 6 = 4,$ and $-4n + 4n = 0$

$2n = 4$

Step 3: Isolate n to one side of the equation by dividing both sides of the equation by 2.

$$\frac{2n}{2} = \frac{4}{2}$$

$$\frac{\overset{n}{\cancel{2n}}}{2} = \frac{\overset{2}{\cancel{4}}}{2}$$
$$\quad n \qquad 1$$

$$n = 2$$

Example 8

Solve for n. $8n - 3(4 - 2n) = 6(n + 1)$

Solution

$8n - 3(4 - 2n) = 6(n + 1)$

Step 1: Simplify the equation.

$8n - 3 \cdot 4 - (-3)(2n) = 6 \cdot n + 6 \cdot 1$ Distributive property.

$8n - 12 + 6n = 6n + 6$ Hint: See previous examples.

Step 2: Isolate the like terms to the left side of the equation by subtraction 6n from both sides of the equation and also by adding 12 to both sides of the equation.

$8n - 12 + 12 + 6n - 6n = 6n - 6n + 6 + 12$

$8n = 6 + 12$ $-12 + 12 = 0$ and $6n - 6n = 0$.

$8n = 18$

Step 3: Isolate n by dividing both sides of the equation by 8.

$$\frac{8n}{8} = \frac{18}{8}$$

$$\frac{\overset{n}{\cancel{8n}}}{\underset{1}{\cancel{8}}} = \frac{18}{8} \qquad \text{Divide right side of the equation by 8.}$$

$$n = 2\frac{2}{8} = 2\frac{1}{4} \qquad \text{Review the reduction of fractions to the lowest term.}$$

Group Exercises

1. Using Rule 1, give the correct answer.

    a. $\dfrac{-6}{-2} =$ **b.** $\dfrac{-10}{-5} =$ **c.** $\dfrac{8}{4} =$ **d.** $\dfrac{-64}{-8} =$

2. Using Rule 2, give the correct answer:

    a. $\dfrac{-8}{-2} =$ **b.** $\dfrac{10}{-5} =$ **c.** $\dfrac{-8}{4} =$ **d.** $\dfrac{64}{-8} =$

Exercises

1. Solve for x, y, or w. Hint: See Example 1.

    a. $3(2 + x) = 12$ **b.** $4(5 + w) = 28$ **c.** $2(3 + y) = 15$

2. Solve for x, y, or w. Hint: See Example 2.

    a. $-2(3x + 3) = -12$ **b.** $-4(3y + 2) = -32$ **c.** $-5(2w + 1) = -15$

3. Solve for x, y, or w. Hint: See Example 3.

    a. $-3(2w - 4) = 24$ **b.** $-4(3y - 2) = 32$ **c.** $-5(2x - 2) = 30$

4. Solve for x, y, or w. Hint: See Example 4.

    a. $-(3w - 3) = -15$ **b.** $-(4y - 5) = -29$ **c.** $-(5x - 6) = -31$

5. Solve for y. Hint: See Example 5.

    a. $3y + 3(3y - 4) = 12$ **b.** $2y + 4(2y - 5) = 10$ **c.** $5y + 3(4y - 2) = 11$

6. Solve for w, x, or y. Hint: See Example 6.

    a. $10w + 7 - 3(2w + 3) = 14$ **b.** $14x + 10 - 4(3x + 2) = 6$ **c.** $15y - 3(4y + 4) + 8 = 8$

7. Solve for w, x, or y. Hint: See Example 7.

    a. $3(4 - w) = 30 - 4(2 + w)$ **b.** $2(5 - 3x) = 28 - 3(3 + 3x)$ **c.** $4(2 - 2y) = -2(4 + 5y) + 28$

8. Solve for w, x, or y. Hint: See Example 8.

    a. $5w - 2(3 - 2w) = 4(w + 1)$ **b.** $2y - 2(8 - 3y) = 3(4 - 2y)$ **c.** $4x - 3(4 - 2x) = 2(2x + 2)$

Challenge Questions

9. Solve for w, x, or y.

    a. $-(3x + 16) = 1$ **b.** $-2(2w - 3) = -10$ **c.** $6y + 2(2y - 3) = 14$

    d. $2(3 - 2w) = 20 - 3(2 + 4w)$ **e.** $6w - 3(1 - w) = 3(w + 3$

Answers to Selected Questions
1a. 2   **2a.** 1   **3a.** -2

REAL WORLD APPLICATIONS - WORD PROBLEMS

Review the section on "**Algebraic Expressions**" first so that you may be able to write the equations correctly.

Group Review

Write the following phrases in mathematical terms.

1. 8 less than three times **a** is: 3**a** - 8

2. x decreased by 4 times a number is: x - 4n where n is the number.

3. y more than 3 times k is: 3k + y

4. 4 less than 10 times a number is: 10n - 4 where n is the number.

Example 1

If 4 is increased by twice a number, the result is 20.
What is the number?

Solution

Setup: Let the number be x, and therefore, twice the number = 2x. We can write 4 increased by 2x as 4 + 2x.

The result of 4 increased by 2x is 20 therefore,

$$4 + 2x = 20$$

Step 1: Isolate 2x to one side of the equation by subtracting 4 from both sides of the equation.

$$4 - 4 + 2x = 20 - 4 \qquad 4 - 4 = 0 \text{ and } 20 - 4 = 16$$
$$2x = 16$$

Step 2: Isolate x to one side of the equation by dividing both sides of the equation by 2.

$$\frac{2x}{2} = \frac{16}{2}$$

$$\frac{\overset{x}{\cancel{2x}}}{\underset{1}{\cancel{2}}} = \frac{\overset{8}{\cancel{16}}}{\underset{1}{\cancel{2}}}$$

$$x = 8$$

Example 2

3 times a number is subtracted from 8 more than 5 times the number the result

101

is 48.

a. What is the number?

b. Check your answer.

Solution

a. **Setup**: Let the number be n. Therefore, 3 times the number is 3n. We can write 8 more than 5 times the number as 5n + 8. We can write 3n subtracted from 5n + 8 as 5n + 8 - 3n, and therefore, we can write that the result of 5n + 8 - 3 is 48 as:

$$5n + 8 - 3n = 48$$

Step 1: Isolate the like terms to one side of the equation by subtracting 8 from both sides of the equation.

$$5n + 8 - 8 - 3n = 48 - 8$$
$$5n - 3n = 40$$

Step 2: Combine like terms by subtracting 3n from 5n.

$$2n = 40$$

Step 3: Isolate n to one side of the equation by dividing both sides of the equation by 2.

$$\frac{2n}{2} = \frac{40}{2}$$

$$\frac{\overset{n}{\cancel{2n}}}{\underset{1}{\cancel{2}}} = \frac{\overset{20}{\cancel{40}}}{\underset{1}{\cancel{2}}}$$

$$n = 20$$

b. To check the answer n = 20 substitute 20 for n in the original equation 5n + 8 - 3n = 48 to see if the result will be 48 or not. If the result is 48 then the answer n = 20 is correct but if the result is not 48 then the answer n = 20 is not correct.

$$5n + 8 - 3n = 48 \text{ then becomes } 5 \times 20 + 8 - 3 \times 20 = 48$$
$$100 + 8 - 60 = 48$$
$$108 - 60 = 48 \quad \text{Review Order of Operations.}$$
$$48 = 48$$

The answer n = 20 is correct.

Example 3

If 4 times Mary's age is increased by 10 more than 3 times her age the result is 59.

a. How old is Mary?

b. Check your answer.

Solution

a. Setup: Let Mary's age be x, and therefore, 4 times Mary's age = 4x. We can write 10 more than 3 times her age as 3x + 10. The result of 4x increased by 3x + 10 is 59 can be written as:

4x + 3x + 10 = 59

Step 1: Isolate the like terms to one side of the equation by subtracting 10 from both sides of the equation.

4x + 3x + 10 - 10 = 59 - 10

4x + 3x = 49   10 - 10 = 0 and 59 - 10 = 49.

Step 2: Combine the like terms by adding 4x and 3x together.

7x = 49

Step 3: Isolate x to one side of the equation by dividing both sides of the equation by 70.

$$\frac{7x}{7} = \frac{49}{7}$$

$$\frac{\overset{x}{\cancel{7x}}}{\underset{1}{\cancel{7}}} = \frac{\overset{7}{\cancel{49}}}{\underset{1}{\cancel{7}}}$$

x = 7 years.

b. To check the answer x = 7 years, substitute 7 for x in the original equation 4x + 3x + 10 = 59 to see if the result will be 59 or not. If the result is 59 then the answer x = 7 years is correct, but if the result is not 59, then the answer x = 7 years is not correct.

4x + 3x + 10 = 59 then becomes 4 × 7 + 3 × 7 + 10 = 59

28 + 21 + 10 = 59

59 = 59

The answer x = 7 years is correct.

Exercises

1. If 6 is increased by twice a number, the result is 40. Find the number.
   Hint: See Example 1.

2. If 8 is increased by 4 times a number, the result is 24. Find the number.
   Hint: See Example 1.

3. If 4 times a number is subtracted from 12 more than 6 times the number, the result is 36.
   a. Find the number.   **b.** Check your answer.
   Hint: See Example 2.

4. If 3 times John's age is increased by 10 more than 5 times his age, the result is 74.
   a. How old is John?   **b.** Check your answer.
   Hint: See Example 3.

Challenge Questions

5. If 2 is increased by twice a number, the result is 20. Find the number.

6. If 4 times Chase's age is increased by 8 more than twice his age, the result is 44.

a. How old is Chase?　　　**b**. Check your answer.

7. If twice Samuel's age is increased by 4 more than 4 times his age, the result is 48.

　　a. How old is Samuel?　　　**b**. Check your answer.

Cumulative Review

1. Write 13,000,000 in the scientific notation.

2. Write 935,000,000 in the scientific notation.

3. The formula for the area of a rectangle is $A = L \times W$, where A = area, L = length, and W = width. Find L in terms of A and W. Hint: Divide both sides of the equation by W.

4. What is the formula for finding the area of:

　　a. A parallelogram?　　　　　**b**. A triangle?

5. Find the measure of the angle for x in each triangle.

a.
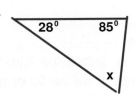

b.
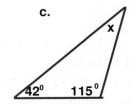

c.

d.
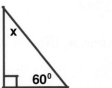

e.
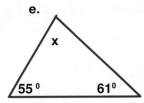

f.
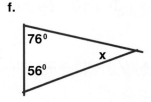

6. Find the value of x in each diagram.

a.

b.

c.
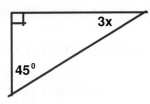

104

INEQUALITY

The statement that uses > and < to show that two quantities are not equal is an **inequality**. The symbols for inequalities, their meanings, examples, and their solutions are shown in the table below:

Table 1

Symbols	Meaning	Examples	Solutions
<	is less than.	x < 10 means x is less than 10.	Every number less than 10 is a solution.
>	is greater than	x > -3 means x is greater than -3.	Every number greater than -3 is a solution.
≤	is less than or equal to.	x ≤ 6 means x is less than or equal to 6.	Every number less than 6 or equal to 6 is a solution.
≥	is greater than or equal to.	y ≥ -2 means y is greater than or equal to -2.	Every number greater than -2 or equal to -2 is a solution.

Conclusions From Table 1

1. Notice that the information under the column "Solutions" shows that:
   a. An inequality may have **more than one solution**.
   b. Values that make **the inequality true** are solutions of the inequality.
2. Notice that the information under the column "Examples" shows that:
   a. An inequality may contain a variable, as in the inequality x < 10. In this inequality, x is the variable.
   b. An inequality may not contain a variable, as in the inequality 3 > -3.

Example 1
a. Is the number 2 one of the solutions of x < 8?

b. Are -9, 0, and $9\frac{1}{2}$ also solutions of x < 10?

Solution
a. Yes, the number 2 is one of the solutions of x < 8, because 2 < 8 is true. Hint: The meaning of the symbol < in Table 1 is used in deciding the solution.

b. Yes, -9, 0, and $9\frac{1}{2}$ are also solutions of x < 10 because -9, 0 and $9\frac{1}{2}$ are less than 10. Hint: The meaning of the symbol < in Table 1 is used in deciding the solution.

Example 2
Are $-2\frac{1}{2}$, 0, and 100 also solutions of x > -3?

Solution

Yes, $-2\frac{1}{2}$, 0, and 100 are also solutions of x > -3 because $-2\frac{1}{2}$, 0, and 100 are greater than -3. Hint: The meaning of the symbol > in Table 1 is used in deciding the solution.

Example 3
Are -99, 0, and $\frac{1}{4}$ also solutions of $x \leq \frac{1}{3}$?

Solution
Yes, -99, 0, and $\frac{1}{4}$ are also solutions of $x \leq \frac{1}{3}$ because -99, 0, and $\frac{1}{4}$ are less than $\frac{1}{3}$. Hint: The meaning of the symbol $\leq$ in Table 1 is used in deciding the solution.

Example 4
a. Are $\frac{1}{8}$, 0, and 50 also solutions of $y \geq -\frac{1}{4}$?

b. Are -10, −1, and $-\frac{3}{4}$ also solutions of $y \geq -\frac{1}{4}$?

Solutions
a. Yes, $\frac{1}{8}$, 0, and 50 are also solutions of $y \geq -\frac{1}{4}$ because $\frac{1}{8}$, 0, and 50 are greater than $-\frac{1}{4}$. Hint: The meaning of the symbol $\geq$ in Table 1 is used in deciding the solution.

b. No, -10, −1, and $-\frac{3}{4}$ are not also solutions of $y \geq -\frac{1}{4}$ because -10, −1, and $-\frac{3}{4}$ are less than $-\frac{1}{4}$. Hint: The meaning of the symbol $\geq$ in Table 1 is used in deciding the solution, additionally, the graphical solution of inequalities on a number line (which is the next section) may help more in the understanding of the solution of example 4b.

How to Graph the Solutions of Inequalities on the Number Line
There are three main steps in graphing all the solutions of inequalities as follows:
Step 1: Draw a number line as shown:

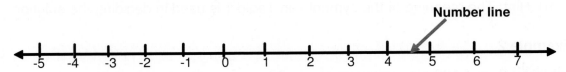

Step 2: Find the solutions of the inequality and use:
       a. a hollow dot to show that a specific number is not a solution as shown:

The hollow dot shows that 4 is not a solution.

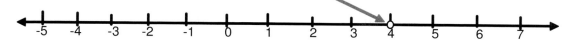

b. a solid dot to show that a specific number is also a solution as shown:

The solid dot shows that 4 is a solution.

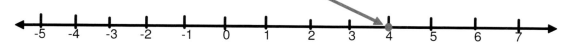

Step 3: Start at the:

    a. hollow dot and color over the solutions you have found as shown:

The hollow dot shows that 4 is not a solution.

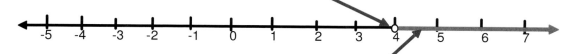

Color over the solutions that you have found.
For example, the red color is the solution for x > 4.

    b. solid dot and color over the solutions you have found as shown:

The solid dot shows that 4 is also a solution.

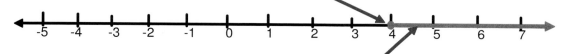

Color over the solutions that you have found.
For example, the red color is the solution for x ≥ 4.

Note: **1.** You may combine Step 1, Step 2, and Step 3 in solving problems.
    2. The red color arrow on the number line shows that the solutions go on forever.

Example 5

Graph the solution of x < 6 on a number line.
Solution
Every number less than 6 is a solution of x < 6. Let us graph the solution as shown:

The hollow dot shows that 6 is not a solution

Example 6

Graph the solution of x > 3 on a number line.
Solution

Every number greater than 3 is a solution to x > 3. Let us graph the solution as shown:

The hollow dot shows that 3 is not a solution

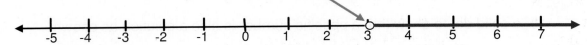

Example 7

Graph the solution of $x \leq \dfrac{1}{3}$ on a number line.

Solution

Every number less than $\dfrac{1}{3}$ or equal to $\dfrac{1}{3}$ is a solution to $x \leq \dfrac{1}{3}$. Let us graph the solution as shown:

The solid dot shows that $\dfrac{1}{3}$ is also a solution.

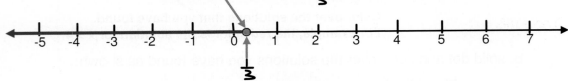

Example 8

Graph the solution of $y \geq -\dfrac{1}{4}$ on a number line.

Solution

Every number that is greater than or equal to $-\dfrac{1}{4}$ are solutions to $y \geq -\dfrac{1}{4}$. Let us graph the solution as shown:

The solid dot shows that $-\dfrac{1}{4}$ is also a solution.

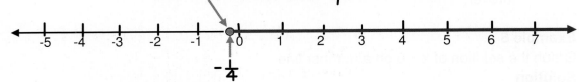

Exercises or Group Exercises

1. List the four symbols of inequality and state what each symbol means.
   Hint: See the Table 1.

2. If x < 6, is 5 a solution? Explain. Hint: See Example 1.

3. If x < 3, are -11 and 0 also solutions? Hint: See Example 1.

4. If x < 8, is 10 a solution? Explain. Hint: See Example 1.

5. If x > 2, is 10 a solution? Explain. Hint: See Example 2.

6. If x > 2, is 0 a solution? Explain. Hint: See Example 2.

7. If y > 14, is 13 a solution? Explain. Hint: See Example 4b.

8. Are -50, 0, and $\frac{1}{4}$ also solutions to $x \le \frac{1}{2}$? Explain. Hint: See Example 3.

9. Are -1, 0, and $\frac{1}{8}$ also solutions to $x \le \frac{2}{3}$? Explain. Hint: See Example 3.

10. Are 0, 1, and 20 also solutions to y ≥ -1? Explain. Hint: See Example **4a**.

11. Are -2, 0, 1 and 100 also solutions to y ≥ -3? Explain. Hint: See Example **4a**.

12. Graph the solutions of the following inequalities on a number line.
   Hint: See Example 5.
   a. x < 4   **b**. x < 7   **c**. y < 2   **d**. x < -3

13. Graph the solutions of the following inequalities on a number line.
   Hint: See Example 6.
   a. x > 2   **b**. x > 5   **c**. x > -2   **d**. y > 0

14. Graph the solutions of the following inequalities on a number line.
   Hint: See Example 7.
   a. $x \le \frac{1}{2}$ **b**. x ≤ 4   **c**. y ≤ -2   **d**. x ≤ 5

15. Graph the solutions of the following inequalities on a number line.
   Hint: See Example 8.
   a. $y \ge -\frac{1}{2}$ **b**. y ≥ 3   **c**. x ≥ -2   **d**. y ≥ 1

Challenge Questions

16. Graph the solutions of the following inequalities on a number line.
   a. x ≥ 0   **b**. x ≤ 0   **c**. x ≥ -1   **d**. x < -2
   e. y ≤ -5   **f**. y < -6   **g**. y > 6   **h**. x > -4

17. Explain why -2 is one of the solutions of x ≥ -3

18. Explain why -4 is not a solution of x ≥ -3

How to Solve Inequalities

How to solve inequalities is much the same as how to solve equations, but the **only difference is that when both sides of an inequality are multiplied or divided by a negative number, the inequality symbol must be reversed. Regard this as Rule 1**.

Example 1

Solve for x.

x + 7 ≤ 3

Solution

x + 7 ≤ 3

x + 7 - 7 ≤ 3 - 7   Subtract 7 from both sides of the equation in order to eliminate the 7 at the left side of the equation so

$x + 0 \leq -4$

$\quad x \leq -4$

that x alone will remain at the left side of the equation.
$7 - 7 = 0$ and $3 - 7 = -4$.

Example 2
Solve for x.

$x - 5 \leq -6$

Solution

$x - 5 \leq -6$

$x - 5 + 5 \leq -6 + 5$

Add 5 to both sides of the equation in order to eliminate the -5 from the left side of the equation so that only x remains at the left side of the equation.
$-5 + 5 = 0$ and $-6 + 5 = -1$.

$x + 0 \leq -1$

$x \leq -1$

Example 3
Solve for n

$n + 6 \geq -4$

Solution

$n + 6 \geq -4$

$n + 6 - 6 \geq -4 - 6$

Subtract 6 from both sides of the inequality so that only n remains at the left side of the inequality.
$6 - 6 = 0$ and $-4 - 6 = -10$

$n + 0 \geq -10$

$n \quad \geq -10$

Example 4
Solve for t.

$\dfrac{t}{4} \geq -8$

Solution

$\dfrac{t}{4} \geq -8$

$\dfrac{t}{4} \times 4 \geq -8 \times 4$

Multiply both sides of the inequality by 4 in order to eliminate the denominator of 4 from the left side of the inequality so that only t should remain at the left side of the inequality.

$\dfrac{t}{\underset{1}{4}} \times \overset{1}{4} \geq -32$

Divide by 4 and also $-8 \times 4 = -32$

$t \geq -32$

Example 5
Solve for y. -2y ≤ - 5
Solution
-2y ≤ -5

$$\frac{-2y}{-2} \geq \frac{-5}{-2}$$

↑
(Reverse the symbol).

Divide both sides of the inequality by -2 and **reverse** the inequality symbol so that only y should remain at the left side of the equation. **See Rule 1**.

$$\frac{\cancel{-2}y}{\cancel{-2}} \geq \frac{\cancel{-5}}{\cancel{-2}}$$

Note: The negative symbols attached to the numerators and the denominators cancel out each other.

$$y \geq \frac{5}{2}$$

$$\geq 2\frac{1}{2}$$

Example 6
Solve for k.

$$\frac{k}{-3} > 6$$

Solution

$$\frac{k}{-3} > 6$$

$$\frac{k}{-3} \times (-3) < 6 \times (-3)$$

↑
(Reverse the symbol).

Multiply both sides of the inequality by -3 in order to eliminate the denominator on the left side of the inequality so that only k remains at the left side of the inequality. **See Rule 1**.

$$\frac{k}{\cancel{-3}} \times (\cancel{-3}) < -18$$

Note: The negative symbols at the left side of the inequality cancel out and also 6 × (-3) = -18.

k < -18

Example 7
Solve for p.

$- 4p \geq 12$

Solution

$-4p \geq 12$

$$\frac{-4p}{-4} \leq \frac{12}{-4}$$

    ↑
(Reverse the symbol).

Divide both sides of the inequality by -4 in order to

eliminate the -4 from the left side of the inequality so that only p should remain at the left side of the inequality and then **reverse** the inequality symbol. **See Rule 1.**

$$\frac{\cancel{-4}\,p}{\cancel{-4}} \leq -3$$
(with p over the $-4p$ and 1 under the -4)

Note: The negative symbols that are attached to the

inequality cancel out to give positive p which is simply written as p, also $4p \div 4 = p$ and $12 \div (-4) = -3$.

$p \leq -3$

Exercises

1. Judith said that when both sides of an inequality are multiplied or divided by a negative number, the symbol of the inequality is reversed.
Is her statement true or false?

2. Solve for x, n, and k. Hint: See Example 1, 2, and 3.

    a. $x + 10 \leq 12$ **b**. $n + 2 \geq 3$ **c**. $k - 4 \leq -3$

    d. $n + 11 \geq -3$ **e**. $x - 3 \leq 4$ **f**. $k + 3 < -5$

3. Solve for x, n, and k. Hint: See Example 4.

    a. $\dfrac{k}{6} \geq -2$ **b**. $\dfrac{n}{4} \leq 3$ **c**. $\dfrac{x}{2} > 4$

    d. $\dfrac{n}{3} < -6$ **e**. $\dfrac{k}{3} > -4$ **f**. $\dfrac{x}{5} \leq 4$

4. Solve for x, n, and k. Hint: See Examples 5 and 7.

    a. $-2y < -8$ **b**. $-3n < 12$ **c**. $-4k \geq 16$

    d. $-3x \geq -2$ **e**. $-5y > 25$ **f**. $-6k \leq 36$

    g. $-4k \geq 8$ **h**. $-2n \leq -24$ **i**. $-7x > -21$

5. Solve for x, n, and k. Hint: See Example 6.

    a. $\dfrac{k}{-4} < 2$ **b**. $\dfrac{n}{-3} \geq 3$ **c**. $\dfrac{n}{-5} \leq -2$

    d. $\dfrac{n}{-5} > -3$ **e**. $\dfrac{x}{-4} < -12$ **f**. $\dfrac{n}{-2} > 0$

Challenge Questions

6. Solve for x, n, and k.

a. $\dfrac{x}{3} > 5$ **b.** $\dfrac{k}{-2} \leq -1$ **c.** $\dfrac{n}{-5} \geq -2$

d. $k + 4 \geq -7$ **e.** $n - 6 < 3$ **f.** $x - 8 \leq -4$

Answers to Selected Questions

2a. $x \leq 2$ **3a.** $k \geq -12$ **4a.** $y > 4$ **5a.** $k > -8$

Cumulative Review

1. Solve for w in each equation.

     a. $2w = 12$ **b.** $\dfrac{w}{5} = 4$ **c.** $\dfrac{2}{3} \times w = 6$

2. The average age of two boys is 8 years. What is their total ages? Hint: You may use the formula for finding averages.

3. $25 \times 5 =$ **4.** $2.5 \times 5 =$ **5.** $2.5 \times .5 =$

4. Find the measure of the angles for b and x in each parallelogram.

a.

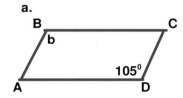

b.

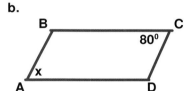

c.

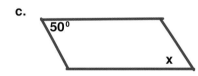

d.

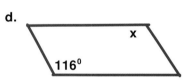

5. By considering each right angle, find the measure of x.

a..

b.

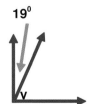

c.

d.

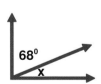

e.

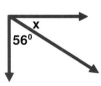

f.

SQUARE ROOTS

The square root of a number x is a number y such that when y is multiplied by itself, equals the original number x. The symbol for square root is $\sqrt{}$.

$$\text{If } x = y \cdot y,$$
$$\text{then } \sqrt{x} = \sqrt{y \cdot y}$$
$$= y$$

Example 1
Find the square root of 4.
Solution
Step 1: To find the square root of 4, find the factors of 4 such that when the factor is multiplied by itself, equals 4. This factor is the square root of 4.
The factors of 4 are: 4×1
$$2 \times 2$$
Step 2: Select the factor that, when multiplied by itself equals 4.
The factors $2 \times 2 = 4$, therefore, the square root of 4 is 2.
We can write the square root of 4 is 2 mathematically as $\sqrt{4} = 2$.

Example 2
Find the $\sqrt{25}$.
Solution
Step 1: To find the $\sqrt{25}$, find the factors of 25 such that the factor multiplied by itself equals 25 is the square root.
The factors of 25 are: 25×1 and 5×5
Step 2: Select the factor that, when multiplied by itself equals 25.
The factor $5 \times 5 = 25$, therefore,
$$\sqrt{25} = \sqrt{5 \times 5}$$
$$= 5$$

Important Rules.
For any number represented by x and y:
Rule 1: If $x = y \cdot y = y^2$, then
$$\sqrt{x} = \sqrt{y \cdot y} = \sqrt{y^2}$$
$$= y$$
Rule 2: If $x = y \cdot y = y^2$, then

$$-\sqrt{x} = -\sqrt{y \cdot y} = -\sqrt{y^2}$$
$$= -y$$

Rule 3: If $x = y \cdot y = y^2$ then
$$\pm\sqrt{x} = \pm\sqrt{y \cdot y} = \pm\sqrt{y^2}$$

Rule 4: $\sqrt{0} = 0$ and $\sqrt{1} = 1$

Example 3

Find the $\sqrt{11^2}$.

Solution

Using Rule 1, $\sqrt{11^2} = 11$

Example 4

Find the $-\sqrt{25}$.

Solution

Using Rule 2, $-\sqrt{25} = -\sqrt{5 \times 5} = -\sqrt{5^2}$
$$= -5$$

Example 5

Find the $\pm\sqrt{100}$.

Solution

Using Rule 3, $\pm\sqrt{100} = \pm\sqrt{10 \times 10} = \pm\sqrt{10^2}$
$$= \pm10$$

Exercises

1. Describe how you can find the square root of a number.

2. Find the value. Hint: See Examples 1, 2, and Rule 1.

   a. $\sqrt{9}$ **b.** $\sqrt{16}$ **c.** $\sqrt{36}$ **d.** $\sqrt{49}$ **e.** $\sqrt{64}$

3. Find the value. Hint: See Example 3 and Rule 1.

   a. $\sqrt{3^2}$ **b.** $\sqrt{6^2}$ **c.** $\sqrt{p^2}$ **d.** $\sqrt{9^2}$ **e.** $\sqrt{12^2}$

4. Find the value. Hint: See Examples 4.

   a. $-\sqrt{9}$ **b.** $-\sqrt{36}$ **c.** $-\sqrt{4^2}$ **d.** $-\sqrt{81^2}$ **e.** $-\sqrt{100}$

5. Find the value. Hint: See Example 5 and Rule 3.

a. $\pm\sqrt{25}$ **b.** $\pm\sqrt{25}$ **c.** $\pm\sqrt{25}$ **d.** $\pm\sqrt{25}$ **e.** $\pm\sqrt{25}$

Challenge Questions
6. Find the value.

a. $\sqrt{81}$ **b.** $-\sqrt{132}$ **c.** $\pm\sqrt{64}$ **d.** $\sqrt{100}$ **e.** $\pm\sqrt{16}$

Notes
1. The symbol $\sqrt{}$ is the square root and it is also called the radial symbol.

2. $\sqrt{2}$ for an example is known as the radical number.

3. $\sqrt{4}$ for an example is read as the positive square root of 4.

4. $-\sqrt{4}$ for an example is read as the negative square root of 4.

5. $\pm\sqrt{4}$ for an example is read as positive or negative square root of 4.

6. The square roots of numbers that can be found easily without decimals such as $\sqrt{4} = 2$, $\sqrt{9} = 3$, and $\sqrt{25} = 5$ are called **perfect squares**. Therefore, any number that is the square of an integer is called a **perfect square**.

How to Solve Expressions Involving the Square Root Symbol

To solve for the expression involving the square root symbol such as $\sqrt{x^2 + y^2}$,

Step 1: Find the square root of each number, and then add the squares of the numbers together. Let's assume that $x^2 + y^2 = z$, then,
$$\sqrt{x^2 + y^2} = \sqrt{z}$$

Step 2: Find the value of $\sqrt{z}$.

Example 6
Find the value of $\sqrt{8^2 + 6^2}$

Solution

Step 1: Find the square of each number, and then add the squares of each of the numbers together.
$$\sqrt{8^2 + 6^2} = \sqrt{8 \cdot 8 + 6 \cdot 6}$$
$$= \sqrt{64 + 36}$$
$$= \sqrt{100}$$

Step 2: Find the value of $\sqrt{100}$.
$$\sqrt{100} = \sqrt{10 \cdot 10} = \sqrt{10^2}$$
$$= 10 \qquad \text{Rule 1 is used.}$$

116

Example 7

Find the value of $\sqrt{3^2 + 1^2 + 1^2 + 2^2 + 1^2}$.

Solution

Step 1: Find the square of each number, and then add the squares of the numbers together.

$$\sqrt{3^2 + 1^2 + 1^2 + 2^2 + 1^2} = \sqrt{3 \cdot 3 + 1 \cdot 1 + 1 \cdot 1 + 2 \cdot 2 + 1 \cdot 1}$$
$$= \sqrt{9 + 1 + 1 + 4 + 1}$$
$$= \sqrt{16}$$

Step 2: Find the value of $\sqrt{16}$.

$$\sqrt{16} = \sqrt{4 \cdot 4} = \sqrt{4^2}$$
$$= 4 \qquad\qquad \text{Rule 1 is used.}$$

Exercises

1. Find the values. Hint: See Example 6.

    a. $\sqrt{4^2 + 3^2}$ **b.** $\sqrt{12^2 + 5^2}$ **c.** $\sqrt{6^2 + 8^2}$

2. Find the values. Hint: See Example 7.

    a. $\sqrt{6^2 + 3^2 + 2^2}$ **b.** $\sqrt{2^2 + 1^2 + 4^2 + 2^2}$

REAL WORLD APPLICATIONS - WORD PROBLEMS

Example 1

Find the perimeter of a square which has an area of 25 ft²

Solution

Setup: Area of a square = side × side.

    Therefore, 25 ft² = side × side.

    25 ft² = s × s   Let a side of the square = s ft.

    25 ft² = s² _____ [A].

Step 1: Find the value of the side or s.

    To find s, find the square root of both sides of equation [A].

$$\sqrt{25 \text{ ft}^2} = \sqrt{s^2}$$
$$\sqrt{5^2 \text{ ft}^2} = \sqrt{s^2}$$
$$5 \text{ ft} = s \qquad\qquad \text{Hint: See Rule 1.}$$
$$\sqrt{5^2 \text{ ft}^2} = 5 \text{ ft. and } \sqrt{s^2} = s.$$

Therefore, the side of the square is 5 ft. long.

Step 2: Find the perimeter of the square.

The perimeter is the distance around the square.

The square has 4 equal sides therefore:

Perimeter of the square = 4 × s   where s = length of a side of the square.
$$= 4 \times 5 \text{ ft} \quad s = 5 \text{ ft}$$
$$= 20 \text{ ft}$$

Exercises - Applications

1. The area of a square is 16 cm^2. Find the perimeter of the square. Hint: See Example 1.
2. Find the perimeter of a square which has an area of 49 m^2 Hint: See Example 1.
3. A square swimming pool has an area of 100 m^2. Find the perimeter of the swimming pool. Hint: See Example 1.
4. Find the perimeter of each of the **square** diagrams.

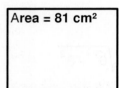

Area = 81 cm²   Area = 100 ft²   Area = 144 m²

Note: All the diagrams in this book are not drawn to scale.

Hint: See Example 1.

5. Find the perimeter of a square which has an area of 36 m^2. Hint: See Example 1.

Answer to a Selected Question

1. 16 cm.

Cumulative Review

1. Simplify:
   a. $4^2 - 3^2 =$ **b**. $5^2 + 2^2 =$ **c**. $4^2 \div 2^2 =$
   d. $6^2 \div 2^2 =$ **e**. $3^2 \cdot 3^2 =$ **f**. $50 \div 5^2 =$

2. Find each square root.
   a. $\sqrt{16} =$ **b**. $\sqrt{25} + 6 =$ **c**. $\sqrt{36} + \sqrt{9} =$

3. What is the sum of the measures of the angles on a line?

4. Simplify: $\sqrt{49} + 4^2 - 20 =$

RATIOS

Ratio Concepts

Kofi and Ama have 12 pencils. They have agreed to divide the pencils such that Kofi will have 8 pencils and Ama will have the remaining 4 pencils. To find out how many times more pencils Kofi has than Ama, divide 8 by 4.

$$8 \div 4 = 2$$

Therefore, Kofi has twice as many pencils as Ama. In the above statement we are comparing two quantities which are the number of Kofi's pencils and the number of Ama's pencils by division. Similarly, **a ratio is the comparison of two quantities by division**. The ratio of the number of Kofi's pencils to Ama's pencils can be expressed in three ways as shown:

      1). Using "to" method (8 to 4).

      2). Using fraction method ($\frac{8}{4}$).

      3). Using a colon(:) method (8 : 4).

The ratio $\frac{8}{4}$ can be reduced to the simplest form as $\frac{2}{1}$ by dividing both the numerator and the denominator by 4. Note carefully that a ratio should always have a denominator, and therefore, if the denominator is 1, we must always write the denominator as 1.

Rule 1: To find the ratio of one number to another number, write the first number as the numerator and the second number as a denominator, and then reduce to the lowest term if possible. For example, the ratio of x to y is $\frac{x}{y}$ or x : y and y is a non-zero number.

More Ratio Concepts

Recall from the section on fractions that reducing a fraction to the lowest terms, the value of the fraction is not changed, and similarly, reducing a ratio to the lowest term does not change the value of the ratio.

REAL WORLD APPLICATIONS - WORD PROBLEMS
Example 1

A class consists of 13 girls and 12 boys.
(a) What is the ratio of the girls to the boys?
(b) What is the ratio of the boys to the girls?
(c) What is the ratio of the boys to the whole class?
(d) What is the ratio of the girls to the whole class?
(e) What is the ratio of the total class to the number of girls?

(f). What is the ratio of the total class to the number of boys?

Solution

(a) The number of girls = 13

The number of boys = 12

Using Rule 1, which states, " To find the ratio of one number to another number, write the first number as the numerator and the second number as the denominator and then reduce to the lowest terms if possible," the ratio of the girls to the boys is:

$$\frac{\text{Number of girls}}{\text{Number of boys}} = \frac{13}{12} \text{ or } 13 : 12$$

(b) Using Rule 1, the ratio of the boys to the girls is:

$$\frac{\text{Number of boys}}{\text{Number of girls}} = \frac{12}{13} \text{ or } 12 : 13$$

(c) The total number of students in the whole class = 12 + 13 = 25

Using Rule 1, the ratio of the number of boys to the whole class is:

$$\frac{\text{Number of boys}}{\text{Total number of students}} = \frac{12}{25} \text{ or } 12 : 25$$

(d) The total number of students in the whole class = 12 + 13 = 25.

Using Rule 1, the ratio of the number of the girls to the whole class is:

$$\frac{\text{Number of girls}}{\text{Total number of students}} = \frac{13}{25} \text{ or } 13 : 25$$

(e) The total number of students in the whole class is 12 + 13 = 25.

Using Rule 1, the ratio of the whole class to the number of girls is:

$$\frac{\text{Total number of students}}{\text{Number of girls}} = \frac{25}{13} \text{ or } 25 : 13$$

(f). The total number of students in the whole class is 12 + 13 = 25.

Using Rule 1, the ratio of the whole class to the number of boys is:

$$\frac{\text{Total number of students}}{\text{Number of boys}} = \frac{25}{12} \text{ or } 25 : 12$$

Example 2

The ratio of rabbits to birds in a small zoo is 7 : 3.

If the total population of the rabbits and the birds at the zoo is 30,

(a) how many rabbits are in the zoo?

(b) how many birds are in the zoo?

Solution

Step 1: Find the total ratio.

Total ratio $= 7 + 3 = 10$

Step 2: Find the fractions of the rabbits and the birds.

$$\text{The fraction of the rabbits} = \frac{\text{The ratio of the rabbits}}{\text{Total ratio}} = \frac{7}{10}$$

$$\text{The fraction of the birds} = \frac{\text{The ratio of the birds}}{\text{Total ratio}} = \frac{3}{10}$$

(a)

Step 3: To find the number of rabbits in the zoo, multiply the fraction for the rabbits by the total population of the zoo.

$$\text{Therefore, the number of rabbits at the zoo} = \frac{7}{10} \times 30$$

$$= \frac{7}{\overset{}{\underset{1}{10}}} \times \overset{3}{30} \quad \text{Divide the numerator and the denominator by 10.}$$

$$= 7 \times 3 = 21 \text{ rabbits}$$

(b)

Step 4: To find the number of birds at the zoo, multiply the fraction for birds by the total population of the zoo.

$$\text{Therefore, the number of birds at the zoo} = \frac{3}{10} \times 30$$

$$= \frac{3}{\overset{}{\underset{1}{10}}} \times \overset{3}{30} \quad = 9 \text{ birds.} \quad \text{Divide the numerator and the denominator by 10.}$$

$$= 3 \times 3 = 9 \text{ birds}$$

Example 3

Mr. Jones is 45 years old. His son is 10 years old.

What is the ratio of Mr. Jones age to his son's age?

Solution

Using Rule 1, the ratio of Mr. Jones' age to his son's age is:

$$\frac{45}{10} \text{ or } 45:10$$

$$= \frac{\overset{9}{\cancel{45}}}{\underset{2}{\cancel{10}}} \qquad \text{Reduce } \frac{45}{10} \text{ to the lowest term by dividing by 5.}$$

$$= \frac{9}{2}$$

Therefore, the ratio of Mr. Jones' age to his son's age is $\frac{9}{2}$ or $9:2$

Example 4
What is the ratio of 7 days to 3 weeks?
Solution
Before a ratio can be written, make sure that both the numerator and the denominator of the ratio have the same unit. In this example, the units are days and weeks. We cannot express days as a ratio of weeks. Convert 7 days to 1 week by dividing 7 days by 7 because 7 days = 1 week .
Solution
Using Rule 1, the ratio of 7days to 3 weeks is:

$$\frac{7 \text{ days}}{3 \text{ weeks}} = \frac{1 \text{ week}}{3 \text{ weeks}}$$

$$= \frac{1 \cancel{week}}{3 \cancel{weeks}}$$

$$= \frac{1}{3} \text{ or } 1:3$$

Therefore, the ratio of 7 days to 3 weeks $= \frac{1}{3}$ or $1:3$

Note: A ratio also compares more than two numbers by division as shown in Example 5.

Rule 2: To find a number which is equivalent to a ratio when the total number is given, multiply the fraction of the ratio by the total number.

Example 5
John, Eric and Janet had a joint business, and they shared the profit of the business which was $150.00 in the ratio 2 : 3 : 5 respectively.

(a) What are the fractions of the shares of John, Eric, and Janet in the profit?

(b) What is John's share of the profit?

(c) What is Eric's share of the profit?

(d) What is Janet's share of the profit?

Solution

(a) The word "respectively" in the problem means that the ratios are matched with the names John, Eric, and Janet in order.

Since the total ratio $= 2 + 3 + 5 = 10$, and the ratio parts are 2, 3, and 5, the ratio $2 : 3 : 5$ can also be written as a fraction as $\dfrac{2}{10}$, $\dfrac{3}{10}$, and $\dfrac{5}{10}$.

(b) The total ratio $= 2 + 3 + 5 = 10$

Using Rule 2, John's share of the profit $= \dfrac{2}{10} \times \$150$

$$= \dfrac{2}{\cancel{10}} \times \$\cancel{150}^{15} \qquad \text{Divide by 10}$$

$$= 2 \times \$15 = \$30$$

Using Rule 2, Eric's share of the profit $= \dfrac{3}{10} \times \$150$

$$= \dfrac{3}{\cancel{10}} \times \$\cancel{150}^{15} \qquad \text{Divide by 10}$$

$$= 3 \times \$15 = \$45$$

Using Rule 2, Janet's share of the profit $= \dfrac{5}{10} \times \$150$

$$= \dfrac{5}{\cancel{10}} \times \$\cancel{150}^{15} \qquad \text{Divide by 10}$$

$$= 5 \times \$15 = \$75$$

Exercises

1. Explain what is meant by the ratio of two numbers.

2. Change each expression to a ratio in a fraction form, and reduce to the lowest term if possible. Hint: See Examples 1(a) and 1(b).

    (a) 4 to 7   (b) 5 to 8   (c) 3 to 9   (d) 5 to 20
    (e) 15 : 25   (f) 12 : 4   (g) 16 : 4   (h) 27 : 3
    (i) 49 : 7   (j) 3 to 36   (k) 18 to 3   (l) 24 : 4
    (m). 25 : 75   (n) 75 :35   (0). 11 : 99   (p) 64 : 8

3. A class consists of 10 boys and 13 girls.
    (a) What is the ratio of the number of boys to the number of girls? Hint: See Examples 1(a) and 1(b).
    (b) What is the ratio of the number of girls to the number of boys? Hint: See Examples 1(a) and 1(b).

4. A company has 50 employees. The ratio of the number of the men to the number of women is 2 : 3, find:
    (a) the number of men working for the company. Hint: See Example 2.
    (b) the number of women working for the company. Hint: See Example 2 .

5. A clinic has 3 male nurses and 7 female nurses. What is the ratio of the
    (a) male nurses to the female nurses?
    (b) female nurses to the male nurses?
    (c) female nurses to the total number of nurses at the clinic?
    (d) male nurses to the total number of nurses at the clinic?
    (e) total number of nurses to the male nurses?
    (f) total number of nurses to the female nurses?
     Hint: See Example 1.

6. Judith scored 100% on a test, John scored 95% on the same test. What is the ratio of the test score of Judith to that of John? Reduce your answer to the lowest term. Hint: See Example 3.

7. What is the ratio of 10 minutes to 1 hour? Hint: The units of a ratio must be the same, 60 minutes =1 hour, see Example 4.

8. What is the ratio of 2 feet to 6 inches? Hint: The unit of a ratio must be the same, 12 inches = 1 foot, see Example 4.

9. What is the ratio of 3 weeks to 3 months? Hint: The unit of a ratio must be the same, 4 weeks = 1 month, see Example 4 .

10 Nick, Jones, and George shared $250 in the ratio 5 : 12 : 8, respectively.
    (a) What is the total ratio?
    (b) What is the fraction of the money that Nick received?
    (c) What is the fraction of the money that Jones received?
    (d) What is the fraction of the money that George received?
    (e) What is the money that Nick received?
    (f) What is the money that Jones received?
    (g) What is the money that George received?

Hint: See Example 5.

Challenge Questions

1. What is the ratio of 2 hours to 30 minutes?

2. What is the ratio of 6 feet to 10 inches?

3. A woman is 35 years old and her son is 5 years old. What is the ratio of the woman's age to the son's age?

4. There are 600 students in a certain school. The ratio of the girls to the boys at the school is 6 : 4.

(a) Find the fraction of the student population that are girls?

(b) Find the fraction of the student population that are boys?

(c) How many students are girls in the school?

(d) How many students are boys in the school?

5. What is the ratio of 2 weeks to 2 months?

6. Three students shared $100.00 in the ratio 6 : 3 : 1. How much did each student receive?

7. What is the ratio of 6 inches to 2 feet?

EQUIVALENT RATIOS

Equivalent ratios are ratios that represent the same thing or the same value. For example the ratios $\frac{1}{2}$, $\frac{2}{4}$, and $\frac{4}{8}$ are equivalent ratios because all of them represent the same value of $\frac{1}{2}$ when all the ratios are reduced to the lowest terms.

Understanding the Concept of Equivalent Ratios.

The concept of the equivalent ratios can further be explained by observing the equal areas of the squares of figure 1, figure, 2 and figure 3. In figure 1, the square is divided into two parts and the area of the triangle BCD represents $\frac{1}{2}$ of the area of the square ABCD. The square ABCD in figure 2 is divided into 4 parts and the same area triangle BCD is now represented by 2 parts(areas of triangles BCE and CDE) which can be written as $\frac{2}{4}$ parts of the same square ABCD which can be reduced to the lowest terms to obtain $\frac{1}{2}$. The square ABCD in figure 3 is divided into 8 parts and the same triangle BCD is now represented by 4 parts which can be written as $\frac{4}{8}$ parts of the same square ABCD which can be reduced to the lowest term to obtain $\frac{1}{2}$.

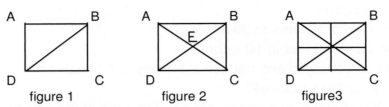

figure 1   figure 2   figure3

The logic is the fact that the same area of triangle BCE is represented as $\frac{1}{2}$ in figure 1 and it is represented as $\frac{2}{4}$ in Figure 2 and it is represented as $\frac{4}{8}$ in Figure 3, and therefore, all the ratios of $\frac{1}{2}$, $\frac{2}{4}$, and $\frac{4}{8}$ represent the same area of the triangle BCD, similarly equivalent ratios are ratios that represent the same thing or value. Equivalent ratios can be expressed or written as equivalent fractions. Cross products of equivalent fractions are equal and this will help us to solve many problems as illustrated in the following examples.

Rule 1: **Equivalent ratios can be expressed or written as equivalent fractions and the cross products of equivalent fractions are equal**.

Example 1
a). There are 205 animals and 37 birds at a certain zoo. Write the ratio of the number of the birds to the number of the animals in 3 different ways.

b). Complete to get equivalent or equal ratios: $\frac{3}{2} = \frac{12}{?}$

c). Complete to get equivalent or equal ratios: 4 : 1 and ? : 4

Solution
The number of birds = 37, the number of animals = 205.
Ratios can be written in three different ways by using "to," a fraction bar, or a colon.

The ratio of the birds to the animals is: 37 to 205, $\frac{37}{205}$, or 37 : 205.

b). There are two methods to solve this problem. They are by "cross products," or by inspection.

Cross Products Method:
$\frac{3}{2} = \frac{12}{?}$ can be written as $\frac{3}{2} = \frac{12}{y}$ so that we can solve for y.

Cross products of equivalent ratios or fractions are equal, and therefore,

$\frac{3}{2} \diagdown \frac{12}{y}$ is $3 \times y = 2 \times 12$

$$3y = 24 \qquad\qquad\qquad\qquad [A]$$

Divide each side of equation $[A]$ by 3 to obtain y as shown:

$$\frac{3y}{3} = \frac{24}{3}$$

$$\frac{\overset{y}{\cancel{3}y}}{\underset{1}{\cancel{3}}} = \frac{\overset{8}{\cancel{24}}}{\underset{1}{\cancel{3}}}$$

$$y = 8$$

Therefore, the equivalent ratios of $\frac{3}{2} = \frac{12}{?}$ are $\frac{3}{2} = \frac{12}{8}$.

Inspection Method

Let us inspect the ratio $\frac{3}{2}$ and $\frac{12}{?}$ and find out how the numerator 3 can be changed to the numerator 12. We should find that the numerator 3 is multiplied by 4 to obtain the numerator of 12 and similarly we have to multiply the denominator of 2 by the same number 4 to give us a denominator of 8.

multiply by the same number.

$$\frac{3}{2} = \frac{3 \times ?}{2 \times ?} = \frac{3 \times 4}{2 \times 4} = \frac{12}{8}$$

multiply by the same number.

Therefore, the equivalent ratio $\frac{3}{2} = \frac{12}{?}$ should be $\frac{3}{2} = \frac{12}{8}$

c). In order for 4 : 1 and ? : 4 to be equal ratios , then 4 : 1 = ? : 4 and the ratio

can be written in a fraction form as $\frac{4}{1} = \frac{?}{4}$

There are two methods to solve this problem which is by "cross products " or by inspection.

Cross Products Method

The cross product of equivalent ratios or fractions are equal, and therefore:

$$\frac{4}{1} \diagup\!\!\!\!\diagdown \frac{?}{4} \quad \text{is } 4 \times 4 = 1 \times ?$$

$$16 = ?$$

Therefore, the equivalent ratio of $\frac{4}{1} = \frac{?}{4}$ is $\frac{4}{1} = \frac{16}{4}$

Inspection Method

Let us inspect the equivalent ratio $\frac{4}{1} = \frac{?}{4}$ to find out how the denominator 1 in the first ratio changes to the denominator 4 in the second ratio. The denominator 1 is multiplied by 4 to get the denominator 4 in the second ratio and similarly, the numerator 4 of the first ratio should be multiplied by the same number 4 to obtain the numerator of 16 in the second ratio as shown:

$$\frac{4}{1} = \frac{?}{4} \quad , \qquad \frac{4}{1} = \frac{4 \times ?}{1 \times ?} = \frac{4 \times 4}{1 \times 4} = \frac{16}{4}$$

↗ multiply by the same number

↘ multiply by the same number

↑   ↑

1st ratio   2nd ratio

Therefore, the equivalent ratio is $\frac{4}{1} = \frac{16}{4}$.

Example 2

a). State four ways to show that one ratio is equivalent to the other?

b). Show that $\frac{2}{4}$ and $\frac{4}{8}$ are equivalent ratios.

Solution

a). The four ways to show that one ratio is equivalent to another ratio are:
by multiplying each term in the smaller ratio by the same number that will be equal to the bigger ratio, by dividing each term of the bigger ratio by the same number that will be equal to the smaller ratio, by reducing each ratio to the lowest terms or by finding the cross products of the ratios. The cross product of equivalent ratios are equal.

b). Let us use each of the four methods in solution (a) to solve the problem.

Method 1:

What same number can multiply the terms of the smaller ratio (the smaller ratio is $\frac{2}{4}$) in order to obtain the bigger ratio (the bigger ratio is $\frac{4}{8}$)? This can be expressed as shown:

↗ what number that can multiply 2 to obtain 4?

$$\frac{2}{4} = \frac{2 \times ?}{4 \times ?} = \frac{4}{8}$$

smaller ratio ↗   ↘ bigger ratio

what number can multiply 4 to obtain 8?

Since the terms of the smaller ratio can be multiplied by the same number, which is 2 to obtain the bigger ratio, the two ratios are equivalent.

Note: Recall that when the terms of a ratio are multiplied by the same number, the value of the ratio does not change, and that equivalent ratios have equivalent fractions.

Method 2:

What same number can divide the terms of the bigger ratio (the bigger ratio is $\frac{4}{8}$) in order to obtain the smaller ratio. This can be expressed as shown:

what number can divide 4 to obtain 2?

$$\frac{4}{8} = \frac{4 \div ?}{8 \div ?} = \frac{2}{4}$$ smaller ratio

bigger ratio

what number can divide 8 to obtain 4?

$$\frac{4}{8} = \frac{4 \div 2}{8 \div 2} = \frac{2}{4}$$

Since the terms of the bigger ratio can be divided by the same number, which is 2 to obtain the smaller ratio, the two ratios are equivalent.

Note: Recall that when the terms of a ratio are divided by the same number, the value of the ratio does not change, and that equivalent ratios have equivalent fractions.

Method 3:

Reduce each ratio to the lowest term, and if the lowest terms are equal, then the ratios are equivalent.

Reduce $\frac{2}{4}$ to the lowest term by dividing the terms by 2 .

Therefore, $\dfrac{2}{4} = \dfrac{\overset{1}{2}}{\underset{2}{4}} = \dfrac{1}{2}$

Reduce $\frac{4}{8}$ to the lowest term by dividing the terms by 4.

Therefore, $\dfrac{4}{8} = \dfrac{\overset{1}{4}}{\underset{2}{8}} = \dfrac{1}{2}$

Since $\dfrac{2}{4} = \dfrac{1}{2}$ and $\dfrac{4}{8} = \dfrac{1}{2}$, both ratios are equivalent.

Method 4:

The cross products of equivalent fractions are equal, and therefore,

$$\dfrac{2}{4} \diagdown\diagup \dfrac{4}{8}$$

$$2 \times 8 = 16$$
$$4 \times 4 = 16$$

Since the cross products of the fractions are equal, the fractions are equivalent fractions, and therefore, the ratios are equivalent ratios.

Example 3

It is a fact that equivalent ratios can be written as equivalent fractions. Show that the ratio 15 : 6 is equivalent to 5 : 2.

Solution

The ratios 15 : 6 and 5 : 2 can be written as fractions as shown:

$$15 : 6 = \dfrac{15}{6} \text{ and } 5 : 2 = \dfrac{5}{2}$$

The fractions $\dfrac{15}{6}$ and $\dfrac{5}{2}$ are equivalent because the terms in $\dfrac{15}{6}$ can be divided by

3 to obtain $\dfrac{5}{2}$ as shown:

$$\dfrac{\overset{5}{\cancel{15}}}{\underset{2}{\cancel{6}}} = \dfrac{5}{2} \quad \text{or} \quad \dfrac{15}{6} = \dfrac{15 \div ?}{6 \div ?} = \dfrac{5}{2}$$

Therefore, the ratio 15 : 6 is equivalent to 5 : 2. Note that the style of the solution to Example 2(b) Method 2 is used to solve this problem.

Alternative Method

This problem can simply be solved by using Rule 1, which states that the equivalent ratios can be written as equivalent fractions and the cross products of equivalent fractions are equal.

Let us check if the cross products of the equivalent fractions are equal or not, as shown:

$$\dfrac{15}{6} = \dfrac{5}{2}, \text{ and the cross products are:}$$

$$\dfrac{15}{6} \diagdown\diagup \dfrac{5}{2}$$

Therefore, $15 \times 2 = 30$, $6 \times 5 = 30$
Since the cross products are equal the ratios are equivalent.

Example 4

Are the ratios $\dfrac{1}{6}$ and $\dfrac{5}{31}$ equivalent?

Solution

The ratios $\dfrac{1}{6}$ and $\dfrac{5}{31}$ are already written in the fraction form, and therefore, let us find out if the two fractions $\dfrac{1}{6}$ and $\dfrac{5}{31}$ are equivalent or not. We should find what same number that can multiply the terms of $\dfrac{1}{6}$ in order to obtain the ratio $\dfrac{5}{31}$ as shown:

$$1 \times 5 = 5$$

$$\frac{1}{6} = \frac{1 \times \, ?}{6 \times \, ?} = \frac{5}{31}$$

$$6 \times 5 = 30. \text{ Note that 30 is not 31.}$$

Since 5 can not be multiplied by the terms of $\dfrac{1}{6}$ which are 1 and 6 in order to obtain 5 and 31, $\dfrac{1}{6}$ and $\dfrac{5}{31}$ are not equivalent fractions, and therefore, the ratios $\dfrac{1}{6}$ and $\dfrac{5}{31}$ are not equivalent ratios.

Alternative Method

This problem can simply be solved by using Rule 1 which states that " Equivalent ratios can be written as equivalent fractions and the cross products of equivalent fractions are equal." Let us check if the cross products of the equivalent fractions are equal or not, as shown:

$$\frac{1}{6} = \frac{5}{31}$$

$$\frac{1}{6} \bowtie \frac{5}{31} \qquad 1 \times 31 = 31$$
$$6 \times 5 = 30 \qquad \text{Note that 30 is not equal to 31.}$$

Since the cross products are 31 and 30, and $31 \neq 30$, the ratios $\dfrac{1}{6}$ and $\dfrac{5}{31}$ are not equivalent. Note that the symbol $\neq$ means "is not equal to."

Example 5

Find a ratio that is equivalent to $\dfrac{6}{9}$ and explain your reasons.

Solution

There are two ways to solve this problem. One way is to divide the numerator and the denominator of $\dfrac{6}{9}$ by the same number and the quotient will give us the solution to the problem as shown:

$$\frac{6}{9} = \frac{6 \div 3}{9 \div 3} = \frac{2}{3}$$

Therefore, the equivalent of $\dfrac{6}{9}$ is $\dfrac{2}{3}$

Alternative Method

Another way to solve the problem is to multiply the numerator and the denominator of $\dfrac{6}{9}$ by the same number as shown:

$$\frac{6}{9} = \frac{6 \times ?}{9 \times ?} = \frac{6 \times 2}{9 \times 2} = \frac{12}{18}$$
Note: Both the numerator and the denominator are multiplied by the same number 2.

Therefore, the equivalent of $\dfrac{6}{9}$ is $\dfrac{12}{18}$

Exercises

1. Ratios can be written in three ways using "to," "colons," or fractions. Write each of the following ratio statements in three ways. Hint: See Example 1.
   (a) A class consists of 11 boys and 13 girls. What is the ratio of boys to girls?
   (b) There are 2 oranges and 6 apples in a room. What is the ratio of apples to oranges?
   (c) There are 4 vans and 9 cars at the school. What is the ratio of the vans to the cars?
2. State the four ways by which it can be shown that one ratio is equivalent to another ratio. Hint: See Example 2(a).
3. Complete the following statement:
   Equivalent ratios can be written as ———————————— Hint: See Rule 1.
4. Explain what is meant by equivalent ratios.
5. Explain what is meant by equivalent fractions.
6. Show that the following ratios are equivalent, use the cross products method. Hint: See Examples 2 and 3.
   (a) 1 : 2 and 2 : 4   (b) 2 : 4 and 4 : 8   (c) 2 : 4 and 8 : 16

(d) 3 : 6 and 9 : 18   (e) 3 : 9 and 9 : 27   (f) 6 : 12 and 12 : 24

(g) $\dfrac{9}{15}$ and $\dfrac{3}{5}$ (h) $\dfrac{3}{5}$ and $\dfrac{12}{20}$ (i) $\dfrac{1}{6}$ and $\dfrac{2}{12}$

(j) $\dfrac{3}{4}$ and $\dfrac{9}{12}$ (k) $\dfrac{12}{16}$ and $\dfrac{3}{4}$ (l) $\dfrac{5}{15}$ and $\dfrac{10}{30}$

7. Are the ratios $\dfrac{1}{2}$ and $\dfrac{2}{5}$ equivalent? Hint: See Example 4.

8. Determine if the following ratios are equivalent or not. Hint: See Examples 3 and 4.

(a) $\dfrac{1}{2}$ and $\dfrac{8}{16}$ (b) $\dfrac{1}{3}$ and $\dfrac{3}{8}$ (c) $\dfrac{3}{2}$ and $\dfrac{9}{6}$

(d) 6 : 2 and 12 : 4   (e) 1 : 3 and 2 : 6   (f) 2 :3 and 5 : 6

(g) 1 : 5 and 2 : 10   (h) 4 : 1 and 16 : 3   (i) 4 : 2 and 8 : 4

(j) $\dfrac{2}{3}$ and $\dfrac{4}{6}$ (k) $\dfrac{5}{2}$ and $\dfrac{25}{10}$ (l) $\dfrac{7}{2}$ and $\dfrac{21}{3}$

Challenge Questions

9. A class has 6 girls and 5 boys.
  (a) What is the ratio of the boys to the girls?
  (b) What is the ratio of the girls to the boys?
  (c) What is the ratio of the boys to the number of students in the whole class?

10. Show that the following ratios are equivalent:

(a) $\dfrac{5}{1}$ and $\dfrac{25}{5}$ (b) $\dfrac{1}{4}$ and $\dfrac{4}{16}$ (c) $\dfrac{2}{7}$ and $\dfrac{6}{21}$

(d) 8 : 2 and 16 : 4   (e) 3 : 7 and 9 : 21   (f) $\dfrac{4}{3}$ and $\dfrac{12}{9}$

11. Determine which ratios are equivalent or not:

(a) $\dfrac{1}{3}$ and $\dfrac{2}{7}$ (b) $\dfrac{8}{1}$ and $\dfrac{64}{8}$ (c) $\dfrac{2}{3}$ and $\dfrac{1}{2}$

(d) $\dfrac{2}{9}$ and $\dfrac{6}{27}$ (e) 4 : 3 and 12 : 9   (f) 2 : 1 and 6 : 3

12. Complete the equations to obtain equivalent or equal ratios:

(a) $\dfrac{2}{4} = \dfrac{?}{8}$ (b) $\dfrac{4}{3} = \dfrac{8}{?}$ (c) $\dfrac{?}{2} = \dfrac{5}{6}$

(d) $\dfrac{3}{8} = \dfrac{9}{?}$ (e) $\dfrac{4}{?} = \dfrac{12}{15}$ (f) $\dfrac{1}{3} = \dfrac{?}{9}$

PROPORTION

A **proportion** is an equation stating that two ratios are equal.

For example, $\dfrac{30}{10} = \dfrac{15}{5}$ is a proportion because when each ratio $\dfrac{30}{10}$ and $\dfrac{15}{5}$ are reduced to the lowest terms, it can be seen that both ratios are equal as shown:

$\dfrac{30}{10} = \dfrac{\overset{3}{\cancel{30}}}{\underset{1}{\cancel{10}}} = 3,$ the ratio $\dfrac{30}{10}$ is reduced to the lowest term by dividing by 10.

$\dfrac{15}{5} = \dfrac{\overset{3}{\cancel{15}}}{\underset{1}{\cancel{5}}} = 3,$ the ratio $\dfrac{15}{5}$ is reduced to the lowest term by dividing by 5.

By reducing $\dfrac{30}{10}$ and $\dfrac{15}{5}$ to the lowest terms, it can be seen that each ratio is equal to 3, and therefore, both ratios are equal and we can then conclude that $\dfrac{30}{10} = \dfrac{15}{5}$ is a proportion. In fact we have written a proportion by writing that $\dfrac{30}{10} = \dfrac{15}{5}$ or $30 : 15 = 15 : 5$, and in each equation we are showing that the relationship of the numbers 30 to 10 is the same as the relationship of the numbers 15 to 5.

Note that the ratio $30 : 10$ has the same value as the ratio $15 : 5$ because when ratios are reduced to the lowest terms, their values are not changed.

Property of Proportion

Rule 1: The cross products of a proportion are equal, such that if $\dfrac{a}{b} = \dfrac{c}{d}$, then $ad = bc$, and that b and d are non-zero numbers.

If $\dfrac{a}{b} = \dfrac{c}{d}$, then the cross products are:

$$\dfrac{a}{b} \diagdown\!\!\!\!\diagup \dfrac{c}{d}$$

which is ad = bc and b ≠ 0 and d ≠ 0
where ≠ means "not equal to".

Cross product means to multiply diagonally as shown above.

Note: To make sure that ratios are **equal**, or are **a proportion**, we multiply the cross products and compare the value of each cross product, and if the cross products are equal, then the ratios are equal or are a proportion. We can also show that two ratios are equal by reducing each ratio to the lowest term. If the lowest terms are equal, then the two ratios are equal.

Summary
The two methods used to identify proportions are:
1. cross products.
2. lowest terms.

Example 1
Are the ratios $\dfrac{2}{3} = \dfrac{3}{4}$ a proportion?

Solution
Using the rule, the cross products of a proportion are equal.
The cross products are shown:

$$\dfrac{2}{3} \diagdown\!\!\!\!\diagup \dfrac{3}{4}$$

$$2 \times 4 \neq 3 \times 3$$
$$8 \neq 9 \quad \text{The sign} \neq \text{means not equal to.}$$

Since 8 is not equal to 9, the ratio $\dfrac{2}{3} = \dfrac{3}{4}$ is not a proportion.

Example 2
Mr. Johnson drove 60 miles in 2 hours. On the next day, he drove 90 miles in 3 hours. Write a proportion and determine if the proportion is true or false.
Solution
The proportion can be written as:

$$60 : 2 = 90 : 3 \text{ or } \dfrac{60}{2} = \dfrac{90}{3}$$

Using Rule 1, the cross products of a proportion are equal, and therefore, we can use cross products to determine if the proportion is true or false.

$$\dfrac{60}{2} \diagdown\!\!\!\!\diagup \dfrac{90}{3}$$

$$60 \times 3 = 2 \times 90$$
$$180 = 180$$

Since the cross products of the ratios are equal, the proportion is true.

Example 3

Last year, Blengo Middle School was cleaned by 6 people in 10 days. This year, the school was cleaned by 4 people in 12 days working at the same rate as that of last year. Write a proportion and determine if the proportion is true or false.

Solution

The proportion can be written as:

$$6 \text{ people : } 10 \text{ days} = 4 \text{ people : } 12 \text{ days} \quad \text{or} \quad \frac{6}{10} = \frac{4}{12}$$

Using the Rule 1, the cross product of a proportion are equal, determine if the proportion is true or false.

$$\frac{6}{10} \times\!\!=\!\!\times \frac{4}{12}$$

$$6 \times 12 \neq 10 \times 4 \quad (\neq \text{ means not equal}).$$
$$72 \neq 40$$

Since the cross products are not equal, the proportion is false.

Rule 2

To find a missing number (y) in a proportion, find the cross products, and then divide as needed.

Example 4

Find the value of y in the proportion $\dfrac{y}{4} = \dfrac{5}{2}$

Solution

Using Rule 2, which states that, "to find a missing number (y) in a proportion, find the cross products, and then divide as needed," solve the problem as shown:

$$\frac{y}{4} \times\!\!=\!\!\times \frac{5}{2} \qquad \text{or } y \times 2 = 4 \times 5$$

$$2y = 20 \quad \rule{2cm}{0.4pt} \; [A]$$

Divide each side of equation $[A]$ by 2 to obtain y.

$$\frac{2y}{2} = \frac{20}{2}$$

$$\frac{\overset{y}{\cancel{2y}}}{\underset{1}{\cancel{2}}} = \frac{\overset{10}{\cancel{20}}}{\underset{1}{\cancel{2}}}$$

Divide by 2.

$$y = 10$$

Example 5

Solve the proportions:

(a) $\dfrac{2}{5} = \dfrac{y}{100}$ 　　　(b) $\dfrac{2}{1.8} = \dfrac{4}{y}$

Solution

(a) Using Rule 2,

$$\frac{2}{5} \diagdown \frac{y}{100} \qquad \text{or } 2 \times 100 = 5 \times y$$

$$200 = 5y \quad\text{———————— [A]}$$

Divide each side of equation [A] by 5 to obtain y.

$$\frac{200}{5} = \frac{5y}{5}$$

$$\frac{\overset{40}{\cancel{200}}}{\underset{1}{\cancel{5}}} = \frac{\overset{y}{\cancel{5y}}}{\underset{1}{\cancel{5}}}$$

$$40 = y, \text{ or } y = 40.$$

(b) Using Rule 2,

$$\frac{2}{1.8} \diagdown \frac{4}{y} \qquad \text{or } 2 \times y = 1.8 \times 4$$

$$2y = 7.2 \quad\text{———— [B]}$$

Divide each side of equation [B] by 2 in order to obtain the value of y.

$$\frac{2y}{2} = \frac{7.2}{2}$$

$$\frac{\overset{y}{\cancel{2y}}}{\underset{1}{\cancel{2}}} = \frac{\overset{3.6}{\cancel{7.2}}}{\underset{1}{\cancel{2}}}$$

$$y = 3.6$$

Example 6
Solve the proportions:

(a) $\dfrac{y+2}{5} = \dfrac{y}{4}$ 　　　　　　(a) $\dfrac{y+3}{y} = \dfrac{8}{6}$

Solution
(a) Using Rule 2,

$$\dfrac{y+2}{5} \diagup\!\!\!\!\diagdown \dfrac{y}{4}$$ 　　or $(y + 2) \times 4 = 5 \times y$

$$y \times 4 + 2 \times 4 = 5 \times y$$
$$4y + 8 = 5y \;\;\text{————}[A]$$

Subtract 4y from each side of equation $[A]$ in order to obtain the value of y as shown:

$$4y + 8 - 4y = 5y - 4y$$
$$8 = y$$ 　　　　(Note: $4y - 4y = 0,\;\; 5y - 4y = y$)
$$y = 8$$

(b) Using Rule 2,

$$\dfrac{y+3}{y} \diagup\!\!\!\!\diagdown \dfrac{8}{6}$$ 　　or $(y + 3) \times 6 = y \times 8$

$$y \times 6 + 3 \times 6 = y \times 8$$
$$6y + 18 = 8y \;\;\text{————}[B]$$

Subtract 6y from each side of equation $[B]$ in order to eliminate the 6y at the left side of the equation $[B]$ as shown:

$$6y + 18 - 6y = 8y - 6y$$ 　　(Note: $6y - 6y = 0$, and $8y - 6y = 2y$)
$$18 = 2y \;\;\text{———————————}[C]$$

Divide each side of equation $[C]$ by 2 to obtain the value of y as shown:

$$\dfrac{18}{2} = \dfrac{2y}{2}$$

$$\dfrac{\overset{9}{\cancel{18}}}{\cancel{2}_1} = \dfrac{\overset{y}{\cancel{2y}}}{\cancel{2}_1}$$

$$9 = y,\text{ or } y = 9$$

Example 7

Find the value of y in the following proportions.

(a) $\dfrac{4}{y-2} = \dfrac{5}{y+5}$

(b) $\dfrac{y-6}{y+8} = \dfrac{2}{3}$

Solution

(a) Using Rule 2,

$$\dfrac{4}{y-2} \diagdown \dfrac{5}{y+5} \qquad \text{or} \quad 4 \times (y+5) = (y-2) \times 5$$

$$4 \times y + 4 \times 5 = y \times 5 - 2 \times 5$$

$$4y + 20 = 5y - 10 \;\; \underline{\hspace{3cm}} \; [\text{A}]$$

Subtract from each side of the equation $[\text{A}]$ in order to eliminate 4y from the left side of equation $[\text{A}]$ as shown:

$$4y + 20 - 4y = 5y - 10 - 4y \qquad (\text{Note: } 4y - 4y = 0 \,, \; 5y - 4y = y)$$

$$20 = y - 10 \underline{\hspace{3cm}} \; [\text{B}]$$

Add 10 to each side of equation $[\text{B}]$ in order to obtain y at the right side of equation $[\text{B}]$ as shown:

$$20 + 10 = y - 10 + 10 \qquad (\text{Note: } -10 + 10 = 0)$$

$$30 = y, \text{ or } y = 30$$

(b) Using Rule 2,

$$\dfrac{y-6}{y+8} \diagdown \dfrac{2}{3} \qquad \text{or} \quad (y-6) \times 3 = (y+8) \times 2$$

$$y \times 3 - 6 \times 3 = y \times 2 + 8 \times 2 \qquad \text{Multiply}$$

$$3y - 18 = 2y + 16 \;\; \underline{\hspace{3cm}} \; [\text{C}]$$

Add 18 to each side of equation $[\text{C}]$ in order to eliminate 18 from the left side of equation $[\text{C}]$ as shown:

$$3y - 18 + 18 = 2y + 16 + 18 \qquad (\text{Note: } -18 + 18 = 0)$$

$$3y = 2y + 34 \;\; \underline{\hspace{4cm}} \; [\text{D}]$$

Subtract 2y from each side of equation $[\text{D}]$ in order to eliminate 2y at the right side of equation $[\text{D}]$ as shown:

$$3y - 2y = 2y + 34 - 2y \qquad (\text{Note: } 3y - 2y = y, \; 2y - 2y = 0)$$

$$y = 34$$

Exercises

1. What is a ratio?

2. What is a proportion?

3. Comparing a ratio and a proportion, what is the difference between a ratio and a proportion?

4. Write a ratio that forms a proportion, and then write another ratio that does not form a proportion, and explain your reasoning. Hint: See Examples 1 to 3.

5. Determine which proportions are true or false: Hint: See Examples 1 to 3.

(a) $\dfrac{1}{2} = \dfrac{3}{7}$

(b) $\dfrac{1}{3} = \dfrac{1}{4}$

(c) $\dfrac{1}{2} = \dfrac{3}{6}$

(d) $\dfrac{1}{3} = \dfrac{4}{12}$

6. Solve each proportion for the missing number. Hint: See Examples 4 and 5.

(a) $\dfrac{y}{2} = \dfrac{3}{4}$

(b) $\dfrac{2}{y} = \dfrac{1}{8}$

(c) $\dfrac{2}{3} = \dfrac{y}{6}$

(d) $\dfrac{5}{y} = \dfrac{3}{6}$

(e) $\dfrac{6}{y} = \dfrac{2}{7}$

(f) $\dfrac{3}{4} = \dfrac{y}{8}$

(g) $\dfrac{3}{2} = \dfrac{5}{y}$

(h) $\dfrac{2.5}{5} = \dfrac{y}{3}$

(i) $\dfrac{3}{y} = \dfrac{2.1}{1}$

(j) $\dfrac{4}{y} = \dfrac{4}{7}$

(k) $\dfrac{2}{7} = \dfrac{?}{49}$

(l) $\dfrac{2}{c} = \dfrac{20}{48}$

(m) $2 : 5 = n : 4$

(n) $4 : 3 = 5 : a$

(o) $y : 8 = 1 : 32$

(p) $c : 2 = 3.6 : 6$

7. Solve the proportions. Hint: See Example 6a.

(a) $\dfrac{y+1}{2} = \dfrac{y}{4}$

(b) $\dfrac{2+y}{3} = \dfrac{y}{6}$

(c) $\dfrac{y+3}{4} = \dfrac{y}{2}$

(d) $\dfrac{3+y}{4} = \dfrac{y}{8}$

(e) $\dfrac{y+2}{3} = \dfrac{y}{6}$

(f) $\dfrac{4+y}{4} = \dfrac{y}{3}$

8. Find y in the proportion. Hint: See Example 6b.

(a) $\dfrac{y+2}{y} = \dfrac{2}{3}$

(b) $\dfrac{y+1}{y} = \dfrac{2}{3}$

(c) $\dfrac{y+3}{y} = \dfrac{1}{4}$

(d) $\dfrac{y+4}{y} = \dfrac{4}{3}$

(e) $\dfrac{y+4}{y} = \dfrac{3}{4}$

(f) $\dfrac{y+2}{y} = \dfrac{2}{4}$

9. Solve the proportion. Hint: See Example 7a.

(a) $\dfrac{3}{y-2} = \dfrac{5}{y+5}$

(b) $\dfrac{2}{y-2} = \dfrac{3}{y+1}$

(c) $\dfrac{2}{y-1} = \dfrac{4}{y+2}$

(d) $\dfrac{1}{y-1} = \dfrac{2}{y+2}$

(e) $\dfrac{4}{y-3} = \dfrac{2}{y+3}$

(f) $\dfrac{1}{y-1} = \dfrac{3}{y+4}$

10. Find y in the proportions. Hint: See Example 7b.

(a) $\dfrac{y-1}{y+2} = \dfrac{1}{4}$

(b) $\dfrac{y-2}{y+4} = \dfrac{3}{4}$

(c) $\dfrac{y-2}{y+5} = \dfrac{1}{5}$

(d) $\dfrac{y-3}{y+5} = \dfrac{2}{5}$ (e) $\dfrac{y-5}{y+4} = \dfrac{5}{2}$ (f) $\dfrac{4+y}{y+3} = \dfrac{2}{3}$

Challenge Questions

11. Find the value of y in the proportions.

(a) $\dfrac{y-5}{y+2} = \dfrac{1}{4}$ (b) $\dfrac{6}{y-3} = \dfrac{3}{y+6}$ (c) $\dfrac{y+4}{y} = \dfrac{3}{4}$

(d) $\dfrac{6+y}{6} = \dfrac{y}{4}$ (e) $2 : 7 = 4 : y$ (f) $\dfrac{y}{4} = \dfrac{1}{16}$

(g) $\dfrac{3}{y} = \dfrac{3}{4}$ (h) $\dfrac{3}{16} = \dfrac{y}{32}$ (i) $y : 6 = 3 : 18$

12. Find the missing number.

(a) $\dfrac{2}{3} = \dfrac{\$10}{?}$ (b) $\dfrac{\$15}{y} = \dfrac{3}{4}$ (c) $\dfrac{6\ \text{feet}}{y} = \dfrac{4}{6}$ (d) $\dfrac{12}{3} = \dfrac{y}{4\ \text{days}}$

General Order of a Proportion for Solving Word Problems

Recall that a proportion is an equation stating that two ratios are equal, and in solving word problems, it **is critical to set the terms of the two ratios in order**, otherwise the solution of the problem will not be correct. For example, let us write the proportion for the following information. If 3 packages of pencils cost $8, what is the cost of 7 packages of pencils. The required proportion can be written as shown:

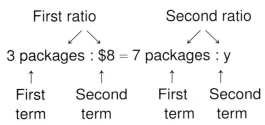

First ratio   Second ratio

3 packages : $8 = 7 packages : y

First   Second   First   Second
term   term   term   term

Let y be the cost of 7 packages of pencils. The general order of the above proportion can be written as shown:

$$\text{packages} : \$ = \text{packages} : \$ \quad \underline{\hspace{3cm}} \ [\text{A}]$$

Note that the left side of the ratio of equation $[\text{A}]$ has "packages" followed by the $ symbol and the **same order** "packages" followed by the $ symbol occurs at the right side of equation $[\text{A}]$. In order to solve word problems in proportion, the **ratios must be written in the same order**.

Note carefully, that if the two ratios are written as a proportion without the correct order of the terms of the ratios as shown:

packages : $ = $: packages,

the proportion will not be correct, and therefore, the answer will not be correct. **It is strongly suggested that in order to solve word problems involving proportions the terms of the ratios must be written in the correct order.**

REAL WORLD APPLICATIONS - WORD PROBLEMS
Proportion

Example 1

Mr. Johnson drove 60 miles in 2 hours. How long will he take to travel 180 miles if he is traveling at the same speed?

Solution

The proportion can be written as:

$$60 \text{ miles} : 2 \text{ hours} = 180 \text{ miles} : y \quad \text{or} \quad \frac{60 \text{ miles}}{2} = \frac{180 \text{ miles}}{y} \quad \text{where } y \text{ is}$$

the time taken to travel 180 miles.

Using Rule 2, which states that, "to find a missing number (y) in a proportion, **find the cross products and divide as needed**," solve the problem as shown:

$$\frac{60}{2} \diagdown \diagup \frac{180}{y} \qquad \text{or } 60 \times y = 2 \times 180$$

$$60y = 360 \quad \text{———————} [A]$$

Divide each side of equation $[A]$ by 60 to obtain the value of y as shown:

$$\frac{60y}{60} = \frac{360}{60}$$

$$\frac{\overset{y}{\cancel{60}y}}{\underset{1}{\cancel{60}}} = \frac{\overset{6}{\cancel{360}}}{\underset{1}{\cancel{60}}}$$

$$\frac{y}{1} = \frac{6}{1} \text{ , or } y = 6 \text{ hours}$$

Therefore, it takes 6 hours to travel 180 miles.

Example 2

If 2 packages of pens cost $6.40, how many packages can be bought for $38.40?

Solution

Let y be the number of the packages of pens that can be bought for $38.40.
The proportion can be written as:

$$2 \text{ packages} : \$6.40 = y : \$38.40 \quad \text{ or } \quad \frac{2 \text{ packages}}{\$6.40} = \frac{y \text{ packages}}{\$38.40}$$

Using Rule 2, **find the cross product**, **and solve the problem** as shown:

$$\frac{2}{6.40} \quad \diagdown \quad \frac{y}{38.40} \quad \text{ or } 2 \times 38.40 = 6.40 \times y$$

$$2 \times 38.40 = 6.40 \times y \quad \text{——————} [A]$$

Divide each side of equation $[A]$ by 6.40 in order to obtain the value of y as shown:

$$\frac{2 \times 38.40}{6.40} = \frac{6.40 \times y}{6.40}$$

$$\frac{2 \times 38.40}{6.40} = \frac{\overset{1}{\cancel{6.40}} \times y}{\underset{1}{\cancel{6.40}}}$$

$$\frac{2 \times \overset{6}{\cancel{38.40}}}{\underset{1}{\cancel{6.40}}} = y \quad \text{You may use a calculator to divide by 6.40.}$$

$$2 \times 6 = y$$
$$12 = y$$

Therefore, 12 packages of the pens can be bought for $38.40.

Example 3

Three shirts cost $10 and 7 shirts cost $25. Is this proportion false or true?

Solution

The proportion can be written as:

$$3 \text{ shirts} : \$10 = 7 \text{ shirts} : \$25 \quad \text{ or } \quad \frac{3}{10} = \frac{7}{25}$$

Using Rule 2, find the cross products, and note that **the cross products of a proportion are equal**, therefore,

$$\frac{3}{10} \quad \diagdown \quad \frac{7}{25} \quad \text{ or } \quad 3 \times 25 \neq 10 \times 7$$

$$75 \neq 70,$$

≠ means not equal to. Since 75 ≠ 70, the cross products are not equal, and therefore, the proportion is false.

Example 4

A store sold 7 oranges for $3, how many similar oranges would be bought for $5.14? Give your answer to the nearest whole number.

Solution

The proportion can be written as:

$$7 \text{ oranges} : \$3 = y : \$5.14 \quad \text{or} \quad \frac{7 \text{ oranges}}{\$3} = \frac{y}{\$5.14}$$

Let y be the number of oranges that can be bought for $5.14.

Using Rule 2, the **cross products of a proportion are equal**, and solve the problem as shown:

$$\frac{7 \text{ oranges}}{\$3} = \frac{y}{\$5.14} \quad \text{or} \quad 7 \text{ oranges} \times \$5.14 = \$3 \times y$$

$$7 \text{ oranges} \times \$5.14 = \$3 \times y \quad \text{————————} \quad [A]$$

Divide each side of equation $[A]$ by $3 in order to obtain the value of y as shown:

$$\frac{7 \text{ oranges} \times \$5.14}{\$3} = \frac{\$3 \times y}{\$3}$$

$$\frac{7 \text{ oranges} \times \$5.14}{\$3} = \frac{\overset{1}{\$3} \times y}{\underset{1}{\$3}}$$

$$\frac{35.98 \text{ oranges}}{3} = y \qquad \text{Divide by 3}$$

$$11.9 \text{ oranges} = y$$

Therefore, 12 oranges (to the nearest whole number) can be bought for $5.14.

Example 5

Red peppers are on sale for $.72 a dozen. What is the price of 32 peppers?

Solution

The proportion can be written as:

$$\text{peppers} : \$ = \text{peppers} : \$ \qquad \text{(general order of the proportion.)}$$
$$12 \text{ peppers} : \$.72 = 32 \text{ peppers} : y \qquad \text{(a dozen = 12)}$$

144

or

$$\frac{12 \text{ peppers}}{\$.72} = \frac{32 \text{ peppers}}{y}$$

Let y be the cost of 32 peppers.

Using Rule 2, **find the cross products, divide as needed**, and solve the problem as shown:

$$\frac{12 \text{ peppers}}{\$0.72} \underset{\longrightarrow}{\overset{\longleftarrow}{}} \frac{32 \text{ peppers}}{y} \qquad \text{or } 12 \text{ peppers} \times y = \$.72 \times 32 \text{ peppers}$$

$$12 \text{ peppers} \times y = \$.72 \times 32 \text{ peppers} \quad \text{———————————} [A]$$

Divide each side of the equation $[A]$ by 12 peppers in order to obtain the value of y as shown:

$$\frac{\overset{1}{\cancel{12 \text{ peppers}}} \times y}{\underset{1}{\cancel{12 \text{ peppers}}}} = \frac{\$.72 \times \overset{\$.06}{\cancel{32 \text{ peppers}}}}{\underset{1}{\cancel{12 \text{ peppers}}}} \qquad \text{You may use a calculator.}$$

$$y = \$.06 \times 32 = \$1.92$$

Therefore, 32 peppers will cost $1.92.

Example 6

If some special peanuts are priced at $1.80 per kg., how many kg. of the same type of the peanut can be bought for $12.60?

Solution

The proportion can be written as:

$$\$: \text{kg.} = \$: \text{kg} \qquad \text{(general order of the proportion).}$$

$$\$1.80 : 1 \text{ kg} = \$12.60 : y \quad \text{or } \frac{\$1.80}{1 \text{ kg}} = \frac{\$12.60}{y}$$

Let y be the number of kg. that will cost $12.60.

Using Rule 2, **find the cross products, divide as needed**, and solve the proportion as shown:

$$\frac{\$1.80}{1 \text{ kg.}} \underset{\longrightarrow}{\overset{\longleftarrow}{}} \frac{\$12.60}{y} \qquad \text{or } \$1.80 \times y = 1 \text{ kg.} \times \$12.60.$$

$$\$1.80 \times y = 1 \text{ kg} \times \$12.60 \quad \text{———————} [A]$$

Divide each side of equation $[A]$ by $1.80 in order to obtain the value of y as shown:

$$\frac{\overset{1}{\cancel{\$1.80}} \times y}{\underset{1}{\cancel{\$1.80}}} = \frac{1 \text{ kg} \times \overset{7}{\cancel{\$12.60}}}{\underset{1}{\cancel{\$1.80}}}$$ You may use a calculator to divide.

$$y = 1 \text{ kg} \times 7 = 7 \text{ kg}.$$
Therefore, 7 kg will cost $12.60.

Example 7
Elizabeth earned $20 for 4 hours of baby-sitting. At this rate, what would she earn for 3 hours of baby-sitting?
Solution
The proportion can be written as:

$: hours = $: hours   (general order of the proportion).

$$\$20 : 4 \text{ hours} = y : 3 \text{ hours} \qquad \text{or} \quad \frac{\$20}{4} = \frac{y}{3}$$

Let y be the amount earned in 3 hours.
Using Rule 2, **find the cross products**, **divide as needed,** and solve the problem as shown:

$$\frac{\$20}{4 \text{ hrs.}} \quad \frac{y}{3 \text{ hrs.}} \qquad \text{or} \quad \$20 \times 3 \text{ hrs.} = 4 \text{ hrs.} \times y$$

$$\$20 \times 3\text{hr.} = 4\text{hr.} \times y \text{ ————————— } [A]$$

Divide each side of equation $[A]$ by 4 hr. in order to obtain the value of y as shown:

$$\frac{\overset{\$5}{\cancel{\$20}} \times 3\cancel{\text{hr.}}}{\underset{1}{\cancel{4 \text{ hr.}}}} = \frac{\overset{1}{\cancel{4 \text{ hr.}}} \times y}{\underset{1}{\cancel{4 \text{ hr.}}}}$$

$$\$5 \times 3 = y \qquad \text{or} \quad y = \$15$$
Therefore, Elizabeth will earn $15 in 3 hours.

Example 8
A certain machine can print 3000 pages in 2 hours. At this rate, how many minutes would it take to print 600 pages?
Solution
The proportion can be written as:

$$\text{pages : hours} = \text{pages : hours} \qquad \text{(general order of the proportion.)}$$

$$3000 \text{ pages : 2 hours} = 600 \text{ pages : y} \qquad \text{or} \qquad \frac{3000 \text{ pages}}{2 \text{ hr.}} = \frac{600 \text{ pages}}{y}$$

Let y be the time taken to print 600 pages.

Using Rule 2, **find the cross products, divide as needed**, and solve the proportion as shown:

$$\frac{3000 \text{ pages}}{2 \text{ hr}} \diagdown \frac{600 \text{ pages}}{y}$$

$$3000 \text{ pages} \times y = 600 \text{ pages} \times 2 \text{ hr.} \rule{3cm}{0.4pt} [A]$$

Divide each side of equation $[A]$ by 3000 pages in order to obtain the value of y as shown:

$$\frac{\overset{1}{\cancel{3000 \text{ pages}}} \times y}{\underset{1}{\cancel{3000 \text{ pages}}}} = \frac{600 \text{ pages} \times 2 \text{ hr.}}{3000 \text{ pages}}$$

$$y = \frac{600 \text{ pages} \times 2 \text{ hr.}}{3000 \text{ pages}}$$

$$y = \frac{600 \text{ pages} \times 120 \text{ minutes}}{3000 \text{ pages}} \qquad (\; 60 \text{ minutes} = 1 \text{ hr}$$

$$2 \text{ hrs} = 60 \times 2 = 120 \text{ minutes})$$

$$y = \frac{\overset{\overset{1}{\cancel{6}}}{\cancel{600 \text{ pages}}} \times 120 \text{ minutes}}{\underset{\underset{5}{30}}{\cancel{3000 \text{ pages}}}} \qquad \text{(Divide by 100, and then by 6)}$$

$$y = \frac{1 \times 120 \text{ minutes}}{5} = 24 \text{ minutes.}$$

Therefore, it will take 24 minutes to print 600 pages.

Example 9

Grace hit 6 home runs in 97 times at bat. At this rate, how many times at bat would she need to hit 9 home runs? Round your answer to the nearest whole number.

Solution

The proportion can be written as :

home runs : # of times at bat = home runs : # of times at bat   (General order)

6 home runs : 97 times at bat = 9 home runs : y,

or

$$\frac{6 \text{ home runs}}{97 \text{ times at bat}} = \frac{9 \text{ home runs}}{y}$$

Let y be the number of times at bat that would be needed to produce 9 home runs. Using Rule 2, **find the cross products**, **divide as needed,** and solve the problem as shown:

$$\frac{6 \text{ home runs}}{97 \text{ times at bat}} \diagdown \diagup \frac{9 \text{ home runs}}{y}$$

or 6 home runs × y = 97 times at bat × 9 home runs   ——————————————— [A]

Divide each side of equation [A] by 6 home runs in order to obtain the value of y as shown:

$$\frac{6 \text{ home runs} \times y}{6 \text{ home runs}} = \frac{97 \text{ times at bat} \times 9 \text{ home runs}}{6 \text{ home runs}}$$

$$\frac{\overset{1}{\cancel{6 \text{ home runs}}} \times y}{\underset{1}{\cancel{6 \text{ home runs}}}} = \frac{97 \text{ times at bat} \times 9 \text{ home runs}}{6 \text{ home runs}}$$

$$y = \frac{97 \text{ times at bat} \times \overset{3}{\cancel{9 \text{ home runs}}}}{\underset{2}{\cancel{6 \text{ home runs}}}} \qquad \text{(Divide by 3)}$$

$$y = \frac{97 \text{ times at bat} \times 3}{2} = \frac{291 \text{ times at bat}}{2} \qquad (97 \times 3 = 291)$$

y = 145.5 times at bat   (Review decimal fractions).

y = 146 times at bat to the nearest whole number. (Review Decimal Fractions).

Therefore, 146 times at bat would be needed to hit 9 home runs.

Exercises

1. Eric drove 45 miles in 3 hours. How long will he take to travel 135 miles if he travels at the same rate? Hint: See Example 1.

2. If 3 packages of candy cost $12.00, how many packages can be bought for

$28.00. Hint: See Example 2.

3. Determine which proportions are false and which are true. Hint: See Example 3.

  (a) $\dfrac{2}{3} = \dfrac{6}{9}$ (b) $\dfrac{2}{3} = \dfrac{4}{7}$ (c) $\dfrac{3}{5} = \dfrac{1}{4}$ (d) $\dfrac{1}{2} = \dfrac{6}{12}$

4. A store sold 5 mangoes for $4.00, how many similar mangoes can be bought for $24.00? Hint: See Example 4.

5. Oranges are on sale for $1.60 per dozen. What is the price of 4 oranges?
Hint: See Example 5.

6. Red peppers are on sale for $.64 a dozen. What is the price of 30 peppers?
Hint: See Example 5.

7. If some special apples are priced at $1.20 per pound, how many pounds of the same type of the of the apples can be bought for $3.00? Hint: See Example 6.

8. Mary earned $63.00 for 7 hours of baby-sitting. At this rate, what would she earn for 2 hours of baby-sitting? Hint: See Example 7.

9. A special machine can print 250 pages in 2 hours. At this rate, how many minutes would it take to print 95 pages? Hint: See Example 8.

10. Judith hit 2 home runs in 13 times at bat. At this rate, how many times at bat will she need to hit 5 home runs? Round off your answer to the nearest whole number. Hint: See Example 9.

Challenge Questions

11. A train covers 80 miles in 2 hours. How long will it take the train to travel 240 miles at the same speed?

12. Five oranges cost $2.00 and three of the same type of oranges cost $4.00. Is the proportion true or false?

13. John earned $30.00 for 5 hours of baby-sitting. At this rate, how much will he earn for 7 hours of baby-sitting?

Answers to Selected Questions

1. 9 hours   6. $1.60

Cumulative Review

1. Find the area of each figure. The figures are triangles and a rectangle.

  a.   **b.**   **c.**

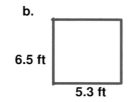

6 cm
7 cm

6.5 ft
5.3 ft

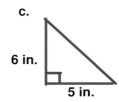

6 in.
5 in.

RATES

Joshua can ride 5 miles in 2 hours on his bicycle. The 5 miles in 2 hours can be written as a ratio as shown:

$$\frac{5 \text{ miles}}{2 \text{ hours}}$$

Note that the ratio above compares two quantities which are 5 and 2 which are measured in two different units which are miles and hours.
Ratios that compare two quantities measured in different units are called rates.

Group Exercise

The class should be divided into four groups. Each group should select 3 students who can represent them in running 100 yards. Each group should have their own stop watch. Each group should time and record how long it takes each of the selected 3 students to run the 100 yards. Each group should complete the chart that follows and also find the speed of each student in 100 yards per __ minutes.

Chart
Group 1, 2, 3, or 4.

Student #	Distance	Time to run 100 yards	Speed $= \dfrac{\text{Distance}}{\text{Time}}$
1	100 yards	_____ minutes	$\dfrac{100 \text{ yards}}{\text{___ minutes}}$
2	100 yards	_____ minutes	$\dfrac{100 \text{ yards}}{\text{___ minutes}}$
3	100 yards	_____ minutes	$\dfrac{100 \text{ yards}}{\text{___ minutes}}$

Each group should report to the whole class about their best speed. Note that the speed which compares distance to time is a rate, and this can be expressed as yards per minute or miles per hour. Similarly, rates can also be expressed as 100 miles in 6 hours, 8 mangoes for $6.00 and printing of 200 pages in 15 minutes.

Complete the Table

Suppose from the group exercise, a student ran 100 yards in 4 minutes, complete the table below that predicts how far the same student can run in 8 and 12 minutes if the student runs at the same rate.

Time in minutes	4	8	12
Distance in yards	100	?	?

Explain how you can predict the distances the student runs in 8 and 12 minutes. The prediction is based on the fact that 8 minutes is twice 4 minutes, 12 minutes is 3 times 4 minutes such that the following rates can be written as shown in (a) and (b).

(a) 4 is multiplied by 2 to obtain 8, therefore, 100 should also be multiplied by 2 to obtain 200.

$$\frac{100}{4} : \frac{?}{8} = \frac{100}{4} : \frac{200}{8}$$

(b) 4 is multiplied by 3 to obtain 12, therefore, 100 should also be multiplied by 3 to obtain 300.

$$\frac{100}{4} : \frac{?}{12} = \frac{100}{4} : \frac{300}{12}$$

The table becomes:

Time in minutes	4	8	12
Distance in yards	100	200	300

The table that we have created is obtained by using the idea of equivalent ratios.
Equivalent ratios are ratios which have equivalent fractions.
Equivalent fractions means fractions that are the same in value or equal and **equivalent ratios** means ratios that are the same in value or equal.
For example,

$$\frac{100 \text{ yards}}{4 \text{ minutes}} \text{ is equivalent to } \frac{200 \text{ yards}}{8 \text{ minutes}} \text{ because each term of}$$

$$\frac{200 \text{ yards}}{8 \text{ minutes}} \text{ can be divided by 2 to obtain } \frac{100 \text{ yards}}{4 \text{ minutes}}.$$

Similarly, $\frac{100 \text{ yards}}{4 \text{ minutes}}$ is equivalent to $\frac{300 \text{ yards}}{12 \text{ minutes}}$ because the terms of

$$\frac{300 \text{ yards}}{12 \text{ minutes}} \text{ can be divided by 3 to obtain } \frac{100 \text{ yards}}{4 \text{ minutes}}.$$

Rule 1 :
Equivalent ratios can be written as equivalent fractions and the cross product of equivalent fractions are equal.

Distance-Time Graph
A distance-time graph is a graph that shows the distance on the y axis and the time on the x-axis. From the distance-time graph, we can tell the time it takes to cover a certain distance and also, we can tell the distance covered in a certain time as shown in Example 1.

Example 1
Using the distance-time graph of a man who is walking slowly,
a. Find the distance walked in 2 hours.
b. How long does it take to walk 3.5 miles?
c. What is the distance walked in $3\frac{1}{2}$ hours?
d. How long did he take to walk 3 miles? Select one of the answers.

   (Answers: **1**. 6 hrs.   **2**. 4 hrs.   **3**. $5\frac{1}{5}$ hrs.).

e. What distance did he walk in 1 hr.?

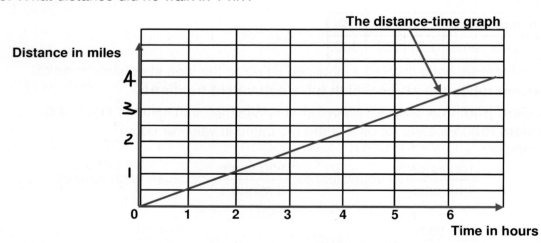

Solution
The important features of the distance-time graph are as shown and this features will help us in understanding how to solve the problem.

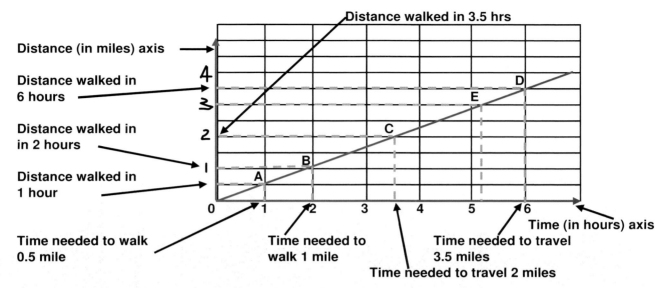

a. To find the distance walked in 2 hr., start from the location of 2 hr. on the "time (in hours) axis" in the diagram, and move vertically up until you meet the graph at point A. Then move horizontally to the "distance (in miles) axis" to meet the "distance (in miles) axis" at the point of value of 1 mile. Therefore, the distance walked in 2 hr. is 1 mile.

b. To find how long it takes to walk 3.5 miles, start from the location of 3.5 miles on the "distance (in miles) axis" in the diagram, and move horizontally until you meet the graph at point D. Then move vertically down until you meet the "time (in hours) axis" at the point of value of 6 hr. Therefore, the time needed to walk 3.5 miles 6 hr.

c. To find the distance walked in $3\frac{1}{2}$ hr., start from the location of $3\frac{1}{2}$ hr. on the "time (in hours) axis" in the diagram, and move vertically up until you meet the graph at C. Then move horizontally until you meet the "distance (in miles) axis" at the point of value of 2 miles. Therefore, the distance walked in $3\frac{1}{2}$ hr. is 2 miles.

d. To find how long it takes to walk 3 miles, start from the location of 3 miles on the "distance (in miles) axis" and move horizontally until you meet the graph at E. Then move vertically down until you meet the "time (in hours) axis" at the point of location of $5\frac{1}{5}$ hours. Therefore, the correct answer is $5\frac{1}{5}$ hours.

Special note: It is difficult to read the exact values of the points on a graph at times. Therefore, we should estimate the values of the points on the graph as the required answers at times as best as we can. For example, the best answer that we obtained in Example 1d is $5\frac{1}{5}$ hr., but $5\frac{1}{5}$ hr. may not be the exact answer, but luckily in this case, $5\frac{1}{5}$ hr. is one of the answers provided.

e. To find the distance walked in 1 hour, start from the location of 1 hr. on the "time (in hours) axis" in the diagram, and move vertically up until you meet the graph at A. Then move horizontally until you meet the "distance (in miles) axis" at the point of value of 0.5 miles. Therefore, the distance walked in 1 hr. is 0.5 mile.

Exercises

1. Using the distance-time graph of a woman who was walking slowly,
   a. Find the distance walked in 2 hours.
   b. How long does it take to walk 6.5 miles?
   c. What is the distance walked in 1 hour?
   d. How long did it take to walk 7 miles? Select one of the answers.

   (Answers: **1**. $4\frac{1}{3}$ hr.   **2**. 4 hr.   **3**. 6 hr.).

   e. What distance did she walk in 3.5 hr.?

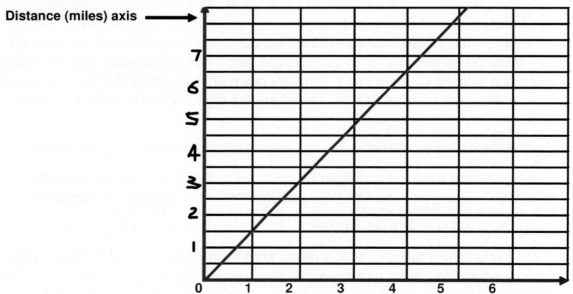

Challenge Question

2. Using the distance-time graph of a girl who was walking slowly,
   a. Find the distance walked in 3 hours.
   b. How long does it take to walk 2 miles?
   c. What is the distance walked in 4 hours?
   d. How long did it take to walk 5 miles? Select one of the answers.

   (Answers: **1**. $4\frac{1}{3}$ hr.   **2**. $2\frac{1}{2}$ hr.   **3**. 4 hr.)

e. What distance did she walk in 1 hr.?

Distance (miles) axis ⟶

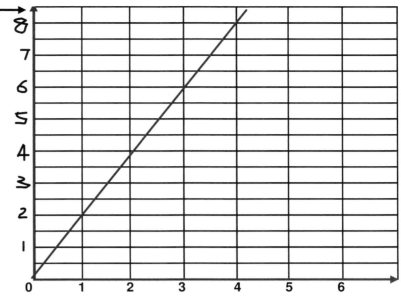

Time (in hours) axis

Answers to Selected Questions

1a. 3 miles.   **1d**. $4\frac{1}{3}$ hr.

REAL WORLD APPLICATIONS - WORD PROBLEMS
Rates

Example 1
What is meant by the statement "John's speed is 10 miles per hour?"
Solution
10 miles per hour (mi/hr) is the rate that describes how fast John can travel in one hour.

Note that **proportion** can be used to set up and solve rate problems as shown in the following examples.

Example 2
Joshua drove his car at a speed of 45 miles per hour.
(a) How far did he travel in 3 hours at that rate?
(b) If he traveled 225 miles at that rate, how many hours did he take to complete the trip.
Solution
(a) We are given in the problem that Joshua traveled 45 miles in every 1 hour, and

we are required to find how long did he take to travel 225 miles. We can use a proportion to set up the solution and solve the problem as shown:

45 miles : 1 hour = n miles : 3 hours,

where n is the distance traveled in 3 hours.
The ratios can be written in the form of a fraction as shown:

$$\frac{45 \text{ miles}}{1 \text{ hour}} = \frac{n}{3 \text{ hours}} \underline{\hspace{3cm}} [A]$$

The cross products of equivalent ratios are equal, and therefore, equation $[A]$ becomes:

$$45 \text{ miles} \times 3 \text{ hours} = 1 \text{ hour} \times n \text{ miles} \underline{\hspace{3cm}} [B]$$

Divide each side of equation $[B]$ by 1 hour in order to obtain the value of n as shown:

$$\frac{45 \text{ miles} \times 3 \text{ hours}}{1 \text{ hour}} = \frac{1 \text{ hour} \times n}{1 \text{ hour}}$$

$$\frac{45 \text{ miles} \times 3 \text{ hours}}{1 \text{ hour}} = \frac{1 \text{ hour} \times n}{1 \text{ hour}}$$

$$45 \text{ miles} \times 3 = n$$
$$135 \text{ miles} = n$$

Therefore, Joshua traveled 135 miles in 3 hours.

(b) We are given in the problem that Joshua traveled 45 miles in every hour and we are required to find how many hours he took to travel 225 miles. We can use proportion to set up the solution and solve the problem as shown:

45 miles : 1 hour = 225 miles : n,

where n is the number of hours taken to travel 225 miles. The ratios can be written in the form of fractions as shown:

$$\frac{45 \text{ miles}}{1 \text{ hour}} = \frac{225 \text{ miles}}{n} \underline{\hspace{3cm}} [C]$$

The cross products of equivalent ratios are equal, and therefore, equation [C] then becomes:

$$\dfrac{45 \text{ miles}}{1 \text{ hour}} \bowtie \dfrac{225 \text{ miles}}{1 \text{ hour}}$$

$$45 \text{ miles} \times n = 1 \text{ hour} \times 225 \text{ miles} \quad\text{————————} [D]$$

Divide each side of equation [D] by 45 miles in order to obtain the value of n as shown:

$$\dfrac{45 \text{ miles} \times n}{45 \text{ miles}} = \dfrac{1 \text{ hour} \times 225 \text{ miles}}{45 \text{ miles}}$$

$$\dfrac{\overset{1}{\cancel{45 \text{ miles}}} \times n}{\underset{1}{\cancel{45 \text{ miles}}}} = \dfrac{1 \text{ hour} \times \overset{5}{\cancel{\underset{}{225 \text{ miles}}}}}{\underset{1}{\overset{45}{\cancel{45 \text{ miles}}}}} \qquad \text{Divide by 5 and then by 9}$$

↑
Divide by 45

$$n = 1 \text{ hour} \times 5$$
$$= 5 \text{ hours}$$

Therefore, Joshua used 5 hours to travel 225 miles.

Example 3

If Eric paid $6.24 for 3 gallons of gasoline, at this price,
(a) how much will he pay for 5 gallons of gasoline?
(b) how many gallons can he buy for $12.48?
(c) how much would 7 gallons cost?

Solution

(a) A proportion can be used to set up the solution as follows:

$6.24 : 3 gallons = ? : 5 gallons

where ? represents the cost for 5 gallons of gasoline.

(Always remember to set the terms of a proportion in order.)

The proportion can be written in a fraction form as shown:

$$\dfrac{\$6.24}{3 \text{ gallons}} = \dfrac{?}{5 \text{ gallons}}$$

Cross products of equivalent ratios are equal, and therefore:

$$\dfrac{\$6.24}{3 \text{ gallons}} \bowtie \dfrac{?}{5 \text{ gallons}}$$

$$\$6.24 \times 5 \text{ gallons} = 3 \text{ gallons} \times ? \quad\rule{2cm}{0.4pt}\quad [A]$$

Divide each side of equation $[A]$ by 3 gallons in order to obtain the value for ?
Equation $[A]$ then becomes:

$$\frac{\$6.24 \times 5 \text{ gallons}}{3 \text{ gallons}} = \frac{3 \text{ gallons} \times ?}{3 \text{ gallons}}$$

$$\frac{\overset{\$2.08}{\cancel{\$6.24}} \times 5 \,\cancel{\text{gallons}}}{\underset{1}{\cancel{3 \text{ gallons}}}} = \frac{\overset{1}{\cancel{3 \text{ gallons}}} \times ?}{\underset{1}{\cancel{3 \text{ gallons}}}}$$

$$\$2.08 \times 5 = ?$$
$$\$10.40 = ?$$

Therefore, 5 gallons of gasoline = $10.40

(b) Proportion can be used to set up the solution as shown:

$$\$6.24 : 3 \text{ gallons} = \$12.48 : n \text{ gallons} \quad\rule{2cm}{0.4pt}\quad [B]$$

where n represents the number of gallons of gasoline that can be bought with $12.48. Equation $[B]$ can be written in a fraction form as shown:

$$\frac{\$6.24}{3 \text{ gallons}} = \frac{\$12.48}{n}$$

Cross products of equivalent ratios are equal, and therefore:

$$\frac{\$6.24}{3 \text{ gallons}} \,\,\bowtie\,\, \frac{\$12.48}{n}$$

Therefore, $\$6.24 \times n = 3 \text{ gallons} \times \$12.48 \quad\rule{2cm}{0.4pt}\quad [C]$

Divide each side of equation $[C]$ by $6.24 in order to obtain the value for n gallons of gasoline as shown:

$$\frac{\$6.24 \times n}{\$6.24} = \frac{3 \text{ gallons} \times \$12.48}{\$6.24}$$

$$\frac{\overset{1}{\cancel{\$6.24}} \times n}{\underset{1}{\cancel{\$6.24}}} = \frac{3 \text{ gallons} \times \overset{2}{\cancel{\$12.48}}}{\underset{1}{\cancel{\$6.24}}}$$

n = 3 gallons × 2
n = 6 gallons
Therefore, 6 gallons can be bought for $12.48.

(c) A proportion can be used to set up the solution as shown:

$6.24 : 3 gallons = n : 7 gallons

where n is the cost for 7 gallons of gasoline.
The ratios can be written in the form of a fraction as shown:

$$\frac{\$6.24}{3 \text{ gallons}} = \frac{n}{7 \text{ gallon}} \quad\quad\quad\quad [D]$$

The cross products of equivalent ratios are equal, and therefore, equation [D] becomes:

$$\frac{\$6.24}{3 \text{ gallons}} \quad\quad \frac{n}{7 \text{ gallons}}$$

$$\$6.24 \times 7 \text{ gallons} = 3 \text{ gallons} \times n \quad\quad\quad\quad [E]$$

Divide each side of equation [E] by 3 gallons in order to obtain the value of n as shown:

$$\frac{\overset{\$2.08}{\$6.24} \times 7 \text{ gallons}}{\underset{1}{3 \text{ gallons}}} = \frac{\overset{1}{3 \text{ gallons}} \times n}{\underset{1}{3 \text{ gallons}}}$$

$2.08 ×7 = n
$14.56 = n
Therefore, 7 gallons of gasoline will cost $14.56.

Example 4
During the first 2 days of her vacation, Elizabeth spent $5.12 on breakfast.
At this rate,
(a) how much did she spend on breakfast for 7 days?
(b) how many days of breakfast could she buy with $23.04?
Solution
(a) We are given in the problem that in 2 days Elizabeth spent $5.12 on breakfast and we are requested to find how much she spent on breakfast in 7 days. We can use a proportion to set up and solve the problem as shown:

2 days : $5: 12 = 7 days : n,

where n is how much money Elizabeth spent on the breakfast for 7 days. The ratios can be written in the form of a fraction as shown:

$$\frac{2 \text{ days}}{\$5.12} = \frac{7 \text{ days}}{n} \quad\rule{4cm}{0.4pt}\quad [A]$$

The cross products of equivalent ratios are equal, and therefore, equation $[A]$ then becomes:

$$\frac{2 \text{ days}}{\$5.12} \quad\underset{\times}{=}\quad \frac{7 \text{ days}}{n}$$

$$2 \text{ days} \times n = \$5.12 \times 7 \text{ days} \quad\rule{4cm}{0.4pt}\quad [B]$$

Divide each side of equation $[B]$ by 2 days in order to obtain the value of n as shown:

$$\frac{2 \text{ days} \times n}{2 \text{ days}} = \frac{\$5.12 \times 7 \text{ days}}{2 \text{ days}}$$

$$\frac{\overset{1}{\cancel{2 \text{ days}}} \times n}{\underset{1}{\cancel{2 \text{ days}}}} = \frac{\$5.12 \times 7 \cancel{\text{ days}}}{2 \cancel{\text{ days}}}$$

$$n = \frac{\$5.12 \times 7}{2} = \frac{\$35.84}{2}$$

$$= \$17.92$$

(b) We are given in the problem that in 2 days Elizabeth spent $5.12 on breakfast and we are requested to find how many days of breakfast she could buy for $23.04. We can use a proportion to set up and solve the problem as shown:

2 days : $5.12 = n : $23.04,

where n represents the number of days of breakfast that could be bought with $23.04. The ratios can be written in the form of fractions as shown:

$$\frac{2 \text{ days}}{\$5.12} = \frac{n}{\$23.04} \quad\rule{4cm}{0.4pt}\quad [C]$$

The cross products of equivalent ratios are equal, and therefore, equation $[C]$ then becomes:

$$\frac{2 \text{ days}}{\$5.12} = \frac{n}{\$23.04}$$

$$2 \text{ days} \times \$23.04 = \$5.12 \times n \quad \text{————————} \, [D]$$

Divide each side of equation $[D]$ by $5.12 in order to obtain the value of n as shown:

$$\frac{2 \text{ days} \times \$23.04}{\$5.12} = \frac{\$5.12 \times n}{\$5.12}$$

$$\frac{2 \text{ days} \times \$23.04}{\$5.12} = \frac{\overset{1}{\$5.12} \times n}{\underset{1}{\$5.12}}$$

$$\frac{2 \text{ days} \times \$23.04}{\$5.12} = n \qquad \text{(You may use a calculator)}.$$

$$9 \text{ days} = n$$

Therefore, Elizabeth can buy breakfast for 9 days with $23.04.

Exercise

1. Explain what is meant by a rate.
2. Explain the statement that Eric's car uses a gallon of gasoline per 18 miles.
   Hint: See Example 1.
3. A bus covers 60 miles in 3 hours, and at this rate:
   (a) How many miles will the bus cover in 10 hours?
   (b) How many hours will the bus take to cover 100 miles?
   (c) How many hours will the bus take to cover 45 miles?
   Hint: See Example 2, you may use a calculator. Round your answer to 2 decimal places.
4. Judith can walk 5 miles in 3 hours, and at this rate:
   (a) How long does she take to walk 15 miles?
   (b) How long does she take to walk 25 miles?
   (c) How many miles can she walk in 10 hours?
   (d) How many miles can she walk in 12 hours?
   Hint : See Example 2. Round your answer to 1 decimal place.

5. Hope bought 3 oranges for $.90.

   (a) How many oranges could she buy for $3.60?

   (b) How much will she pay for 9 oranges?

   (c) How much will she pay for 12 oranges?

  Hint: See Example 4.

Challenge Questions

6. Samuel bought 6 apples for $1.00.

   (a) How many apples could he buy for $3.50?

   (b) How many apples could he buy for $2.25?

   (c) How much will he pay for 10 apples?

   (d) How much will he pay for 24 apples?

   (e) How much will he pay for 36 apples?

   (f) How many apples could he buy for $4.00?

7. Given that Joseph can run 5 miles in 2 hours and at that rate:

   (a) How long does he take to run 20 miles?

   (b) How many miles does he cover in 8 hours?

   (c) How long does he take to run 12 miles?

   (d) How many miles does he cover in 14 hours?

   (e) How long does he take to run 50 miles?

Answers to Selected Questions

3a. 200 miles   **4a.** 9 hr.

Cumulative Review

1. Explain mean, median, and mode.

2. Explain ratio, equivalent ratio, proportion, and rate.

3. Divide:

   a. $\dfrac{3}{5} \div \dfrac{4}{15} =$ **b.** $\dfrac{6}{7} \div \dfrac{3}{14} =$ **c.** $\dfrac{8}{9} \div 4 =$

4. Multiply:

   a. $\dfrac{3}{5} \times 20 =$ **b.** $\dfrac{3}{4} \times \dfrac{4}{15} =$ **c.** $9 \times \dfrac{5}{6} =$

5. The sum of the measures of two angles of a rectangle is 100^0. Find the measure of the third angle of the triangle.

6. Add or subtract:

   a. 9.01 - 2.44 =   **b.** 73.64 + 6. 33 =   **c.** 10.79 - 3.88 =

INTEGERS

Cumulative Review

1. $44 + 17 =$ 2. $33 - 14 =$ 3. $54 + 28 =$ 4. $116 - 97 =$

5. $23 - 17 =$ 6. $12 \div 54 =$ 7. $18 \times 2 =$ 8. $15 \div 3 =$

9. $\begin{array}{r} 12 \\ \times\, 3 \\ \hline \end{array}$ 10. $\begin{array}{r} 9 \\ \times\, 3 \\ \hline \end{array}$ 11. $72 \div 3 =$ 12. $7 + 68 =$

13. $15 + 88 =$ 14. $18 \div 3 =$ 15. $16 - 8 =$ 16. $9 \times 2 =$

17. $35 \div 5 =$ 18. $21 - 15 =$ 19. $30 \div 6 =$ 20. $17 - 8 =$

21. $\begin{array}{r} 25 \\ \times\, 3 \\ \hline \end{array}$ 22. $\begin{array}{r} 18 \\ +\, 19 \\ \hline \end{array}$ 23. $\begin{array}{r} 37 \\ -\, 13 \\ \hline \end{array}$ 24. $\begin{array}{r} 17 \\ \times\, 4 \\ \hline \end{array}$

25. $42 \div 3 =$ 26. $24 \div 8 =$ 27. $12 + 38 =$ 28. $44 - 18 =$

New Terms: **integer, negative integer, positive integer, opposites, and absolute values**.

An **integer** is any negative or positive whole number or zero. We can show integers on the number line as:

The integers on the left side of 0 are less than 0 and are negative integers.   **The integers on the right side of 0 are greater than 0 and are positive integers.**

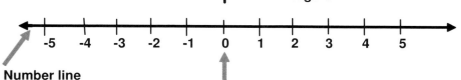

Number line

Zero (The integer 0 is neither negative nor positive).

Negative integers are always written with a – sign, however, positive integers can be written with or without a + sign. Positive and negative integers can be used to represent actual life situations as shown:

a. The temperature 40 degrees below zero can be written as -40^0F.

b. The temperature 52 degrees above zero can be written as $+52^0F$ or 52^0F.

Example 1

a. Express twenty feet below sea level using integers.

b. Express thirty feet above sea level using integers.
Solution
Hint: The sea level is at 0 ft. such that any measurement above the sea level is a positive number and any measurement below the sea level is a negative number.
a. Twenty feet below sea level can be written as –20 ft.
b. Thirty feet above sea level can be written as +30 ft or 30 ft.

Team Project
The class should be divided into four teams and each team should write about two situations that negative or positive integers could be used such as scoring a football game by losing 10 yards or gaining 12 yards. Each team should report to the class about their real life situations with integers.

Graph Integers
Integers can be graphed on a number line by drawing a dot.

Example 2
Graph –4 on the number line.
Solution
Draw a number line and then draw a dot at the position of –4.

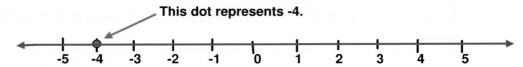

Example 3
Graph +3 on the number line.
Solution
Draw a number line and then draw a dot at the position of +3.

Opposite Integers
The opposite of saving $4.00 in the bank is withdrawing $4.00 from the bank. In both cases, the same amount of $4.00 is involved. Every integer has an opposite and **opposite integers** are at the same distances from 0 on a number line, but in opposite directions.

Example 4

Write the opposite of +3.

Solution

The opposite integers are at the same distance from 0 on a number line, but in the opposite direction as shown:

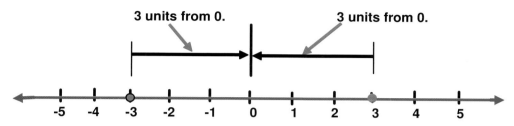

The opposite of +3 is –3.

Example 5

Write the opposite of –4.

Solution

The opposite integers are at the same distance from 0 on a number line, but in the opposite direction.

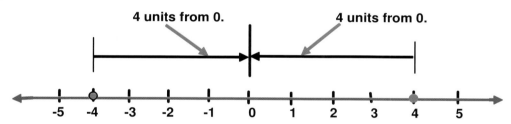

The opposite of –4 is +4 or 4.

Absolute Value

The **absolute value** of an integer is the distance of the integer from 0 on the number line or it is the number of units the integer is from 0 on the number line.

Example 6

Find the absolute value of –4. Find the absolute value of +4.

Solution

The absolute value of an integer is the distance of the integer from 0 on the number line or the number of units the integer is from 0 on the number line. The absolute value of –4 is at a distance of 4 units from 0, and therefore, the absolute value of –4 is +4 or 4.

The absolute value of +4 which is the same as 4 is at a distance of 4 units from 0, and therefore, the absolute value of +4 is 4.

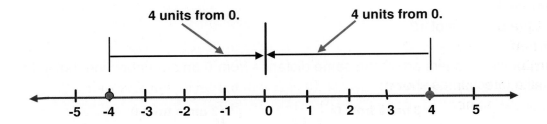

Example 7
Find the absolute value of +3. Find the absolute value of -3.
Solution
The absolute value of an integer is the distance of the integer from 0 on the number line or it is the number of units the integer is from 0. The absolute value of +3 which is the same as 3 is at a distance of 3 units from 0 on the number line, and therefore, the absolute value of +3 is 3.
The absolute value of -3 is at a distance of 3 units from 0 on the number line, and therefore, the absolute value of -3 is 3.

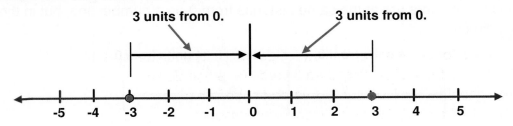

Conclusion
The absolute value of any number **is the same number without any sign in front of the number** as shown:
a. The absolute value of −4 is 4.
b. The absolute value of +4 is 4.
c. The absolute value of −3 is 3.
d. The absolute value of +3 is 3.
| | is the symbol for the absolute value.
|−6| means the absolute value of −6 which is 6.
|−2| means the absolute value of −2 which is 2.
We can conclude that the absolute value of any number is the same number without any sign in front of the number.

Example 8
Find |−5|
Solution
The absolute value of any number is the value of the same number without any sign in front of the number. Therefore, |−5| = 5.

Example 9

Find $|-10| + |-8| + |+2|$

Solution

The absolute value of any number is the value of the same number without any sign in front of the number. Therefore, $|-10| + |-8| + |+2|$

$$= 10 + 8 + 2 \qquad (|-10| = 10, \ |-8| = 8, \ |+2| = 2)$$
$$= 20$$

Example 10

Evaluate: $|+2| - |-9| + 4 + |+2| - |-1|$

Solution

The absolute value of any number is the same number without any sign in front of the number. Therefore,

$$|+2| - |-9| + 4 + |+2| - |-1|$$
$$= 2 - 9 + 4 + 2 - 1 \qquad (|+2| = 2, \ |-9| = 9, \ |+2| = 2, \ |-1| = 1)$$
$$= -2 \qquad\qquad (2 - 9 = -7, \ -7 + 4 = -3, \ -3 + 2 = -1, \ -1 \ -1 = -2)$$

Exercises

1. Express the following statements as integers. Hint: See Example 1.
   a. The school football team gained 5 yards for a first down.
   b. The school football team lost 4 yards on the last play.
   c. John withdrew $10.00 from his checking account.
   d. Mary deposited $20.00 in her checking account.

2. Graph the following on a number line. Hint: See Examples 2 and 3.
   a. −2   **b.** +5   **c.** −6   **d.** +1   **e.** −1

3. Identify the integers graphed. Hint: See Examples 1, 2, and 3.

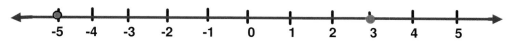

4. Write an integer to represent each situation. Hint: See Example 1.
   a. 90 degrees above 0.   **b.** A lost of 8 yards.
   c. A deposit of $50.00.   **d.** A withdrawal of $100. 00.

5. Graph the opposite of each integer on a number line. Hint: See Examples 4 and 5.
   a. −1   **b.** +2   **c.** −6   **d.** +5   **e.** −5

6. Write the opposite of each integer. Hint: See Examples 4 and 5. Do not indicate your answer on the number line.
   a. −5   **b.** +12   **c.** −20   **d.** +15
   e. −200   **f.** +400   **g.** −1,340   **h.** +5,000

7. Write an integer to represent each situation. Hint: See Example 1.
   a. a gain of 2 pounds.   **b.** 10 feet below sea level.
   c. 10 feet underground.   **d.** 10 feet below ground.

e. a growth of 7 inches.   **f.** 6 points ahead.

8. What is the absolute value of a number?

9. Graph the absolute values of the following numbers on a number line.
   Hint: See Examples 6 and 7.
   a. −1   **b.** −7   **c.** +5   **d.** +6   **e.** −3   **f.** +8

10. Write each absolute value. Hint: See Example 8.
    a. $|-11|$ **b.** $|-24|$ **c.** $|+200|$ **d.** $|-64|$ **e.** $|-1|$
    f. $|0|$ **g.** $|+36|$ **h.** $|-36|$ **i.** $|-89|$ **j.** $|20|$

11. Evaluate the following. Hint: See Example 9.
    a. $|-2| + |-10| =$ **b.** $|+4| + |-1| =$ **c.** $|+12| - |+2| =$
    d. $|-3| + |+4| - |-1| =$ **e.** $|20| - |-4| + |-2| - |5| =$
    f. $|-44| - |+6| - |+18| =$ **g.** $|+2| - |-3| + |-10| - |4| =$

12. Evaluate the following. Hint: See Example 10.
    a. $|-26| + |-1| + |-16| =$ **b.** $|+30| - |-15| - |+15| =$
    c. $|-18| - |-11| + |+6| - |+2| =$ **d.** $|-64| - |+64| =$

Challenge Questions

13. Evaluate the following.
    a. $|-100| - |-100| =$ **b.** $|+58| - |+48| =$ **c.** $16 + |-16| =$

14. Graph the opposite of 10.

15. Graph −7, −8, 0, 2, and 6 on the same number line.

16. Write an integer to describe each situation.
    a. A helicopter rises 100 feet.
    b. A submarine is 20 feet below the surface of the water.

Answers to Selected Questions
10a. 11   **11a.** 12   **12a.** 43   **16a.** +100ft or 100ft

Compare and Order Integers

A time line can be used to show the events of the day. For example, a student's daily time line may include the following:

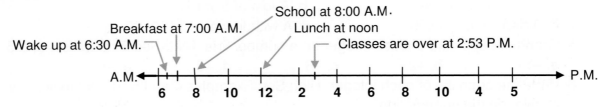

On the above number line, the student wakes up at 6:30 A.M. before having breakfast at 7:00 A.M., Similarly, you can use number lines to compare and order numbers. The numbers to the right on a number line are always greater than the numbers to the left. Alternatively, the numbers to the left on a number line are always less than the numbers to the right. **Notice** that on the number line that follows, −4

168

is to the left of 0, therefore, −4 is less than 0, and also, 0 is greater than −4 since 0 is to the right of −4 on the number line.

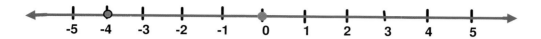

Team Exercise

The class should be divided in to teams and each team should make a typical Monday time line for a student within the team starting from the time the student wakes up to the time that the student goes to bed. The time line should include dinner time, play time, and homework time. Each team should report their time line to the whole class.

1. From your time line, could you say that a time line can help you to order events?
2. Each team should make a time line for a typical Thanksgiving Day and then report the time line to the whole class.

Example 1

Use the number line to order −4, +3, −5, +4, and −2 from the least to the greatest.

Solution

The number line is drawn with the integers −4, +3, −5, +4, and −2 indicated on it as shown:

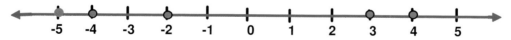

The number to the left on the number line is always less than the number to the right, and therefore, using the number line, the order of the numbers from the least to the greatest is:

$$−5, −4, −2, 3, \text{ and } 4.$$

Example 2

Use the number line to order +5, −1, 0, −4, and +3 from the greatest to the smallest.

Solution

The number line is drawn with the integers +5, −1, 0, −4, and +3 indicated on it as shown:

The number to the right on the number line are always greater than the numbers on the left, and therefore, using the number line, the order of the numbers from the greatest to the least is:

$$+5, +3, 0, -1, \text{ and } -4.$$

Using "greater than" and "less than" symbols

The symbol $>$ means greater than.
The symbol $<$ means less than.

Example 3

Using the number line, replace ? with $<$, $>$ or $=$.

a. $-3 \; ? \; -1$ **b.** $0 \; ? \; -3$ **c.** $+1 \; ? \; -1$

Solution

a. Graph -3 and -1 on a number line.

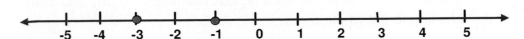

        -3 is to the left of -1 on the number line, so $-3 < -1$

b. Graph 0 and -3 on a number line.

        0 is to the right of -3 on the number line, so $0 > -3$.

c. Graph $+1$ and -1 on a number line.

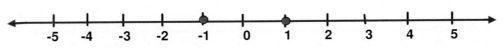

        $+1$ is to the right of -1, so $+1 > -1$.

Example 4

Compare. Write $<$, $>$ or $=$ for each ?.

a. $|-3| \; ? + 3$ **b.** $|-4| \; ? -5$ **c.** $|-2| \; ? + 4$

Solution

$|-3| = 3$ Review absolute numbers.

Therefore, $|-3| \; ? + 3$

      $= 3 \; ? + 3$

        $3 = 3$ The two values are equal.

b. $|-4| = 4$ Review absolute numbers.

Therefore, $|-4| \; ? -5$

      $= 4 \; ? -5$

Graph 4 and -5 on a number line.

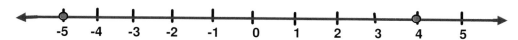

4 is on the right side of –5 on the number line, so 4 > –5

c. |–2| = 2   Review absolute numbers.

   Therefore, |–2| ? +4

         = 2 ? +4

   Graph 2 and +4 on the number line.

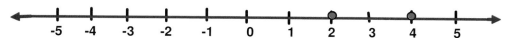

   2 is to the left of +4 on the number line, so 2 < +4.

Exercises

1. Use the number line to order the following numbers from the least to the greatest. Hint: See Example 1.

   a. –3, +5, –4, –1, 0, +2   **b.** +6, 0, –4, –2,

   c. –1, 0, –6, +4, +1,   **d.** +4, –3, 0, +5

2. Use the number line to order the following numbers from the greatest to the least. Hint: See Example 2.

   a. –6, 0, +4, –2   **b.** +5, –1, 0, +2

   c. –1, +1, 0, +5, –4   **d.** 0, +2, –2, +5

3. Using the number line, replace ? by >, <, or =. Hint: See Example 3(a).

   –5 ? –4

4. Using a number line, replace ? by >, < or =. Hint: See Example 3(b).

   0 ? –1

5. Using a number line, replace ? by >, < or =. Hint: See Example 3(c).

   + 4 ? – 3

6. Compare. Write >, < or = for each ?. Hint: See Example 4.

   a. |–5| ? +4   **b.** |–1| ? –6   **c.** |+2| ? –4

Challenge Questions

Compare. Write >, < or = for each?

7. a. |–3| ? |+3| **b.** |–2| ? –2   **c.** 0 ? –1

8. Which number has the least value: 0, –4, +8, –1, or –10?

9. Which number has the greatest value: –14, –2, +9, +100, or –200?

10. What is the absolute value of –1000?

Mixed Review

1. 20% of $100.00 =   **2.** $\frac{2}{3}$ of 18 =   **3.** $\frac{1}{6} \times \frac{18}{25}$ =

4. The inverse of $\frac{3}{4}$ = **5.** The opposite of −6 = **6.** Absolute of -7 =

7. $2 + 4 \div 2 - 1$ = **8.** $6901 - 5999$ = **9.** 25×6 =

10. Write the opposite of each integer.

    a. -99   **b.** +12   **c.** -1   **d.** +32

11. Graph each integer and its opposite on a number line.

    a. -4   **b.** +5   **c.** -6   **d.** +6

12. Name a positive or a negative number to represent each situation.

    a. 13 feet above sea level   **b.** Earning $10

    c. 15^0 below 0   **d.** A decrease of 5 points

13. Compare. Write < or > for ?.

    a. -8 ? 8   **b.** 0 ? -5   **c.** -4 ? -6   **d.** 9 ? 14   **e.** -8 ? 1

14. Order the integers in each set from least to greatest.

    a. 4, -1, 0, -4   **b.** -5, 8, -2, 3   **c.** -4, 7, -11, 0   **d.** 23, -33, 55, -2

ADDITION OF INTEGERS

I can solve the problems too if only I understand the concepts.

New Term

Zero pair

Playing a Board Game - Group Exercises

Example 1

John and Mary decide to play a board game.

    • John starts at 0 and rolls a 4.

    • The fourth square tells him to roll again. His token lands on a square that tells him to move back 4 spaces.

How many spaces from the start is John's token?

Solution

Use red counters to represent negative integers and blue counters to represent positive integers.

    Let (-) represent red counters, which then represent negative integers.

    Let (+) represent blue counters, which then represent positive integers.

Step 1: Use 4 positive (blue) counters to represent John's first roll which can be represented as +4. Place all of the counters on a table.

(+) (+) (+) (+)

Step 2: Use 4 negative (red) counters to represent John's 4 spaces backwards. Place the 4 negative (red) counters on the table with the 4 positives (blue) counters from Step 1.

(+) (+) (+) (+)
(-) (-) (-) (-)   = +4 + (-4)

Step 3: Make as many pairs of one positive and one negative counters. The sum of each pair is zero, and so remove each **zero pair** since it does not change the value on the table.

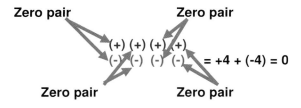

There are no counters left on the table. John's token is 0 spaces from the start which means that John is back to the starting point.

Let us establish an integer addition rule for adding a negative integer to a positive integer. From Example 1, note that +4 + (-4) = 0 is possible if + (- **becomes** - such that +4 + (-4) can be written as +4 - 4 = 0. It is important to note that + (- **becomes** -. We can use absolute values to establish an integer addition rule for adding a negative integer to a positive integer as shown:

> **Adding a negative integer to a positive integer (or adding a positive integer to a negative integer), subtract the smaller absolute value from the larger, and then use the sign of the number with larger absolute value as the sign of the sum. If the two integers are equal, their sum is zero.**

The absolute value of a number is the number itself when the number is positive or zero, and the absolute value of a number is the opposite of the number when the number is negative. (Review the chapter/section on Absolute Values.)

Example 1 can be written as: +4 + (-4) = 0. The absolute of +4 is 4 and the absolute of -4 is 4 (the opposite of -4 is 4), so that 4 - 4 = 0.

Hint: See how Example 1 is solved using a shortcut method in Example 6.

Zero pairs means equal numbers of positive and negative integers such that the addition of each pair is zero.

Example 2
Use counters to find -5 + (-2)

Solution

Use red counters to represent negative integers.

Let (-) represent red counters, which then represent negative integers.

Step 1: Place 5 negative counters on the table to represent -5.
Place 2 more negative counters on the same table to represent adding -2.

(-) (-) (-) (-) (-)
(-) (-)

Step 2: There are no positive counters, and therefore, we cannot remove any zero pairs. Count the total number of counters on the table.

Step 3: There are a total of 7 negative counters on the table and this represents -7. Therefore, -5 + (-2) = -7.

Let us establish an integer addition rule for adding two negative integers. From Example 2, note that -5 + (-2) = -7 is possible if + (- **becomes** - such that -5 + (-2) can be written as -5 - 2 = -7. We can use absolute values to establish an integer addition rule for adding a negative integer to a positive integer as shown:

Adding two negative numbers, **add the absolute values of the numbers**, **and then attach a negative sign to their sum**.

The absolute value of a number is the number itself when the number is positive or zero, and the absolute value of a number is the opposite of the number when the number is negative. (Review the chapter/section on Absolute Values.)

Example 2 can be written as: -5 + (-2) =. The absolute of -5 is 5 (the opposite of -5 is 5), and the absolute of -2 is 2 (the opposite of -2 is 2), so that 5 + 2 = 7. Using the rule, attach a negative sign to this sum, so that the sum becomes -7. Therefore, -5 + (-2) = -7.

Hint: See how Example 2 is solved using a shortcut method in Example 7.

Example 3

Use counters to find -3 + (+4)

Solution

Use red counters to represent negative integers and blue counters to represent positive integers.

Let (+) represent blue counters, which then represent positive integers.
Let (-) represent red counters, which then represent negative integers.

Step 1: Place 3 negative counters on a table
Place 4 positive counters on the same table representing adding +4.

(-) (-) (-)
(+) (+) (+) (+)

Step 2: Make as many pairs of the positive and negative counters. The sum of each pair is zero and so remove each zero pair since it does not change the value on the table.

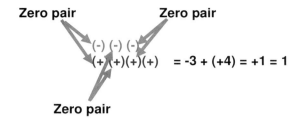

Zero pair   Zero pair

(-) (-) (-)

(+)(+)(+)(+)   = -3 + (+4) = +1 = 1

Zero pair

Count the total number of counters left on the table.

Step 3: There is 1 positive counter left on the table. Therefore, -3 + (+4) = +1 = 1.
Let us establish an integer addition rule for adding a negative integer to a positive integer. From Example 3, note that -3 + (+4) = +1 is possible if + (+ **becomes** + such that -3 + (+4) = +1 can be written as -3 + 4 = +1 = 1. In mathematics, positive signs are not generally attached to a number to indicate that the number is positive, so +1 is written as 1. We can use absolute values to establish an integer addition rule for adding a positive integer to a negative integer as shown:

> **Adding a positive integer to a negative integer (or adding a negative integer to a positive integer), subtract the smaller absolute value from the larger, and then use the sign of the number with larger absolute value as the sign of the sum. If the two integers are equal, their sum is zero.**

The absolute value of a number is the number itself when the number is positive or zero, and the absolute value of a number is the opposite of the number when the number is negative. (Review the chapter/section on Absolute Values.)

Example 3 can be written as: -3 + (+4) =. The absolute of -3 is 3 (the opposite of -3 is 3) and the absolute of +4 is 4 (the absolute value of a number is the number itself when the number is positive), so that 4 - 3 = 1. Using the rule, use the sign of the number with larger absolute value as the sign of the sum, and in this case, the larger absolute number is 4, and the sign of 4 is positive. In general, we do not attach a positive sign to an answer, so that 4 - 3 = +1 = 1.

Hint: See how Example 3 is solved using a shortcut method in Example 8.

Example 4

Use counters to find +1 + (+4)

Solution

Use blue counters to represent positive integers.

Let (+) represent blue counters, which then represent positive integers.

Step 1: Place 1 positive counter on the table to represent +1
        Place 4 positive counters on the table to represent +4

(+)
(+) (+) (+) (+)

Step 2: Since there are no negative counters, we cannot remove any zero pair numbers.

Step 3: Count the total number of counters on the table, which is +5.
Therefore, +1 + (+4) = +5.

Let us establish an integer addition rule for adding two positive integers. From Example 4, note that +1 + (+4) = +5 is possible if + (+ **becomes** + such that +1 + (+4) = +5 can be written as +1 + 4 = 5.

From Example 4, note that +1 + (+4) = +5 means that **to add any two positive integers, add the two integers and attach the positive sign after the addition, which is called the sum**. In this particular case, add 1 to 4 which is 5, and then attach a positive sign to the 5 which is +5. In mathematics, positive signs are not generally attached to a number to indicate that the number is positive, so +5 is written as 5. The rule for adding two positive integers is as shown:

> **To add any two positive integers, add the two integers and attach the positive sign after the addition, which is called the sum.**

Hint: See how Example 4 is solved using a shortcut method in Example 9.

Example 5
Find -6 + (+4)
Solution
Use red counters to represent negative integers and blue counters to represent positive integers.

Let (+) represent blue counters, which then represent positive integers.
Let (-) represent red counters, which then represent negative integers.

Step 1: Place 6 negative counters on the table to represent -6.
Place 4 positive counters on the table to represent +4.

(-) (-) (-) (-) (-) (-)
(+) (+) (+) (+)

Step 2: Make as many pairs of one positive and one negative counters. The sum of each pair is zero, and so remove each zero pair since it does not change the value on the table.

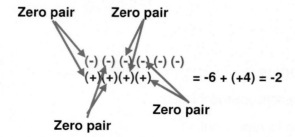

Count the total number of counters left on the table. There are a total of 2 negative counters left on the table, therefore: -6 + (+4) = -2

Let us establish a rule for integer addition of positive and negative integers.
From Example 5, note that -6 + (+4) = -2 is possible if + (+ **becomes** + such that -6 + (+4) = -2 can be written as -6 + 4 = -2.
Notice how the negative sign is attached to the final answer because 6 (not -6) is larger than 4, and 6 has the negative sign. Notice also that, if the question were to be -3 + 4 = , the solution is -3 + 4 = +1 = 1. In this case, there is no negative sign attached to 1 because 3 is less then 4, and although 3 has a negative sign. Notice that the absolute value of -6 is 6 (-6 is the opposite of 6), and the absolute value of +4 is 4, so that 6 - 4 = 2. In example 5, the larger absolute value is 6 and the smaller absolute value is 4, so that 6 - 4 = 2, and the sign of the larger absolute number is -, so that -6 + 4 = -2. We can use absolute values to establish an integer addition rule for adding a positive integer to a negative integer as shown:

> **Adding a positive integer to a negative integer (or adding a negative integer to a positive integer), subtract the smaller absolute value from the larger, and then use the sign of the number with larger absolute value as the sign of the sum. If the two integers are equal, their sum is zero**.

Hint: See how Example 5 is solved using a shortcut method in Example 10.

Summary of the Steps or Rules for Adding Integers
1. **Addition of two integers with like signs**
   a. Find the absolute values of the integers.
   b. Find the sum of the absolute values
   c. Attach the sign common to both integers to the answer.
2. **Addition of two integers with unlike signs**.
   a. Find the absolute values of the integers.
   b. Find the difference of the absolute values.
   c. Attach the sign of the integer with the greater absolute value to the answer.
      If the absolute values of both integers are the same, then their sum is zero.

Let us Use the information Under the Section "Summary of the Steps or Rules for Adding Integers" to Solve Examples 1 to 5.

Example 6
Find the sum.
+4 + (-4)   **This is the same as Example 1**.
Solution
Find the absolute values of +4 and -4. See "Addition of two integers with unlike signs."
$$|+4| = 4$$
$$|-4| = 4$$

Find the **difference** of the absolute values. Hint: Find the **difference** of the absolute values of the integers with **unlike signs**

$$4 - 4 = 0$$ Since the two integers have unlike signs, and their absolute values are the same, their sum is zero. Hint: "See Addition of Two Integers With Unlike Signs."

Example 7
Find the sum.

-5 + (-2)   **This is the same as Example 2**.

Solution

Find the absolute values of -5 and -2. See "Addition of Two Integers With Like Signs."

$$|-5| = 5$$
$$|-2| = 2$$

Find the **sum** of the absolute values. Hint: Find the **sum** of the absolute values of the integers with **like signs**. See "Addition of Two Integers With Like Signs."

$$5 + 2 = 7$$

Attach the sign common to both integers to the answer. So,

-5 + (-2) = -7   Note: The - sign is common to both 5 and 2.
Hint: See the information under the section "Addition of Two Integers With Like Signs."

Example 8
Find the sum.

-3 + (+4)   **This is the same as Example 3**.

Solution

Find the absolute values of -3 and +4. See "Addition of two integers with unlike signs."

$$|-3| = 3$$
$$|+4| = 4$$

Find the **difference** of the absolute values. Hint: Find the **difference** of the absolute values of the integers with **unlike signs**. **Subtract the smaller absolute integer from the larger absolute integer**.

$$4 - 3 = 1$$

Attach the sign of the integer with the greater absolute value to the answer. So,

-3 + (+4) = +1 = 1   Note: +1 is the same as 1.
Hint: See Addition of Two Integers With Unlike Signs.

Example 9
Find the sum.

+1 + (+4)   **This is the same as Example 4**.

Solution

Find the absolute values of +1 and +4. See "Addition of Two Integers With Like Signs."

$$|+1| = 1$$

$|+4| = 4$

Find the **sum** of the absolute values. Hint: Find the **sum** of the absolute values of the integers with **like signs**. See "Addition of Two Integers With Like Signs."

$1 + 4 = 5$

Attach the sign common to both integers to the answer. So,

$+1 + (+4) = +5 = 5$ Note: The + sign is common to both 1 and 4.
Hint: See the information under the section
Addition of Two Integers With Like Signs.

Example 10
Find the sum.

-6 + (+4)   **This is the same as Example 5**.
Solution
Find the absolute values of -6 and +4. See "Addition of two integers with unlike signs."

$|-6| = 6$
$|+4| = 4$

Find the **difference** of the absolute values. Hint: Find the **difference** of the absolute values of the integers with **unlike signs**. **Subtract the smaller absolute integer from the larger absolute integer**.

$6 - 4 = 2$

Attach the sign of the integer with the larger absolute value to the answer. So,

-6 + (+4) = -2   Notice that the integer with the larger absolute value
is 6. The 6 has a - sign, so attach a - sign to the answer.
Hint: "See Addition of Two Integers With Unlike Signs."

The notes and the generous worked examples have provided me with conceptual understanding and computational fluency to do my homework.

Exercises
1. Explain what is meant by zero pairs.
2. Group exercise:
Mary and John decided to play a board game. Mary started at 0 and rolled 5. The fifth square tells her to roll again. Her token lands on a square that tells her to move back 3 spaces. How many spaces back is Mary's token? Hint: See Examples 1 and 6. You may use the integer addition rule for Examples 1 and 6.
3. Group exercise:
Use counters to find the following: Hint: See Examples 2.

    a. -3 + (-2) =   **b**. -7 + (-2) =   **c**. -1 + (-1) =

d. -10 + (-7) =   **e**. -5 + (-4) =   **f**. -6 + (-4) =

g. -3 + (-5) =   **h**. -5 + (-4) =   **i**. -7 + (-7) =

4. Solve Exercise 3 without using counters. Use the rule for adding integers.
   Hint: See the rule for Examples 2 and 7. Note that + (- is -.

5. Use counters to find the following: Hint: See Example 3.

    a.-4 + (+8) =   **b**. -7 + (+2) =   **c**. -1 + (+1) =

    d.-2 + (+6) =   **e**. -9 + (+1) =   **f**. -6 + (+4) =

    g.-4 + (+8) =   **h**. -5 + (+6) =   **j**. -7 + (+7) =

6 Solve Exercise 5 without using counters. Use the rule for adding integers.
   Hint: See Examples 3 and 8. Note that + (+ is +.

7. Use counters to find the following: Hint: See Example 4.

    a. +2 + (+6) =   **b**. +1 + (+9) =   **c**. +7 + (+3) =

    d. +4 + (+7) =   **e**. +8 + (+4) =   **f**. +3 + (+11) =

    g. +6 + (+5) =   **h**. +5 + (+8) =   **j**. +3 + (+7) =

8 Solve Exercise 7 without using counters. Use the rule for adding integers in
   Examples 4 and 9.
   Hint: See Example 4.

9 Use counters to solve the following. Hint: See Example 5.

    a. -5 + (+4) =   **b**. -6 + (+2) =   **c**. -6 + (+1) =   **d**. -8 + (+4) =

    e. -7 + (+5) =   **f**. -5 + (+2) =   **g**. -4 + (+3) =   **h**. -2 + (+1) =

10 Solve Exercise 9 without using counters. Use the rule for adding integers in
    Examples 5 and 10. Hint: See Example 5.

Challenge Questions

11 Solve the following problems.

    a. +6 + (-4) =   **b**. -3 + (-5) =   **c**. -4 + (+) 2 =   **d**. -6 + 0 =

    e. -7 + (-7) =   **f**. +4 + (-6) =   **g**. +7 + (+) 3 =   **h**. +2 - 6 =

12 Compare and write <, > or = for ? Hint: Use Examples 1 to 5 to simplify first
    before comparing. To solve **a**, simplify +2 + (-4) as -2 first, and then compare
    -2 to -3. Since -2 is greater than -3, the correct answer to **a** is +2 + (-4) > -3.

    a. +2 + (-4) ? -3   **b**. -2 + (+8) ? +5   **c**. +4 + (-5) ? +2

    d. +4 + (-3) ? +2   **e**. -4 + (-7) ? +2   **f**. -3 + (-7) ? +3

Answers to Selected Questions

    3a. -5   **3b**. -9   **5a**. 4   **5b**. -5

    7a. 8   **7b**. 10   **9a**. -1   **9b**. -4

Why Do We Need to Know How to Use the Rules For Addition of Integers?
It is useful to know and use the rules for integer addition especially when the
integers are large instead of using counters. For example, it will be difficult to use

counters to add integers involving 300 and -450.

It is possible to use the rules for integer addition or a number line to add integers when the integers are large, as shown in the following examples.

Example 13
Using the rule for adding integers, find +261 + (-200)
Solution
+ (- becomes -, and so that, +261 + (-200) = +261 - 200 = +61 = 61. Notice that +261 - 200 = +61 = 61, when the rule for integer addition for adding a negative integer to a positive integer is used as in Example 3. Recall that absolute values are used in the rule.

Example 14
Using the rule for adding integers, find -261 + (-300).
Solution
From the solution of Example 2, +(- becomes -, therefore, -261 + (-300) = -261 - 300 = -561. Notice that -261 - 300 = -561, when the rule for adding a negative integer to another negative integer is used as in Example 2. Recall that absolute values are used in the rule.

Example 15
Use the number line to find the sum of 300 + (-450).
Solution
Step 1: Draw a number line, and start at 0 and go 300 units in the positive direction (right) as shown.

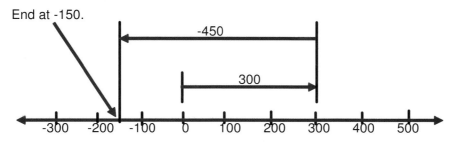

Step 2: From point 300 go 450 in the negative direction (left) as shown. You end at -150, making, 300 + (-450) = -150.

The notes and the generous worked examples have provided me with conceptual understanding and computational fluency to do my homework.

Exercise
1. Use the rule to find the following sums. Hint: See Example 13.

    a. +340 + (-329) =   **b.** -450 + (+200) =   **c.** -701 + (+204) =

    d. +528 + (-224) =   **e.** -178 + (+464) =   **f.** +379 + (-580) =

2. Use the rule to find the following sums. Hint: See Example 14.

    a. -492 + (-321) =   **b.** -209 + (-164) =   **c.** -342 + (-201) =

    d. -239 + (-101) =   **e.** -341 + (-244) =   **f.** -464 + (-100) =

3 Use a number line to find the sum of the following numbers.

    Hint: See Example 15.

    a. 250 + (-200) =   **b.** 100 + (-400) =   **c.** 381 + (-250) =

    d. 98 + (-164) =   **e.** 88 + (-238) =   **f.** 238 + (-108) =

Challenge Questions

4. Find the sum of the following numbers.

    a. 340 + (-264) =   **b.** -277 + (-341)   **c.** +516 + (-201) =

    d. -168 + (-295) =   **e.** 255 + (-179) =   **f.** +209 + (-304) =

Answers to Selected Questions

1a. 11   **2a.** -813   **3a.** 50

SUBTRACTING INTEGERS

The subtraction problems can be solved by using counters as shown in Example 1.

Example 1

Find 5 - 2

Solution

Step 1: Place 5 positive counters on a mat.

    ⊕ ⊕ ⊕ ⊕ ⊕

Step 2: Since subtraction is the opposite of addition, remove 2 of the positive counters from the mat to represent subtracting 2.

        Remove 2 of the positive counters.

          ↗↗

  ⊕ ⊕ ⊕ ⊕ ⊕ = 5 - 2

Step 3: Count the positive counters remaining on the mat.

    ⊕ ⊕ ⊕   = 5 - 2 = 3

    There are 3 positive counters left on the mat and meaning, 5 - 2 = 3.

Rule 1: **To subtract a smaller positive number from a bigger positive number, subtract the smaller number from the bigger number.**

Example 2

Find 2 - 6.

Solution

Step 1: Place 2 positive counters on a mat.

⊕ ⊕ = 2

Step 2: To subtract 6, we must remove 6 positive counters. But we cannot remove 6 positive counters because there are not 6 positive counters on the mat. We must add 6 zero pairs to the mat, and then we can remove 6 positive counters.

⊕ ⊕

⊖ ⊖ ⊖ ⊖ ⊖ ⊖   ↙ (6 negative and 6 positive counters form 6 zero pairs.)

⊕ ⊕ ⊕ ⊕ ⊕ ⊕   ← Remove these 6 positive counters.

Step 3: Pair the positive and negative counters. Remove all zero pairs.

⊕ ⊕

⊖ ⊖ ⊖ ⊖ ⊖ ⊖   = -4

Step 4: The number of the negative counters that remains on the mat is 4, therefore,

2 - 6 = -4

Rule 2: Considering Examples 1 and 2, **to subtract one positive number from another positive number**, **subtract the smaller absolute value of the numbers from the bigger absolute value**, **and then attach the sign of the bigger absolute value number**.

In Example 2, the bigger absolute value number is 6 and the smaller absolute value number is 2. Using the rule, 2 - 6 becomes 6 - 2 = 4, and then a negative sign is attached to the 4 because the sign of the bigger absolute value number is -. So we can write 2 - 6 = -4.

Example 3

Use counters to find -5 - 3

Solution

Step 1: Place 5 negative counters on the mat to represent -5.

⊖ ⊖ ⊖ ⊖ ⊖ = -5

Step 2: To subtract 3 we must remove 3 positive counters, but we cannot remove 3 positive counters because there are none on the mat. Therefore, we must add 3 zero pairs to the mat. We can now remove 3 positive counters. Note that we cannot remove something that we do not have.

⊖ ⊖ ⊖ ⊖ ⊖ = ⊖ ⊖ ⊖ ⊖ ⊖

⊖ ⊖ ⊖   = ⊖ ⊖ ⊖

⊕ ⊕ ⊕   ← Remove these 3 positive counters.

Step 3: There are 8 negative counters remaining on the mat and this represents -8.

Therefore, -5 - 3 = -8.

Rule 3: Considering the answer for Example 3, **to subtract a positive number 3 from a negative number -5, add the absolute values of the numbers together (5 + 3 = 8) and attach negative sign the sum**, for example -8. Note that it is sometimes necessary to add zero pairs in order to subtract. When zero pairs are added, the value of the integers on the mat does not change. Note also that the absolute value of -5 is 5 and the absolute value of 3 is 3.

Example 4 (Subtraction problems involving two negative integers).
Use counters to find -6 - (-2).
Solution
Step 1: Place 6 negative counters on the mat to represent -6.
$\ominus\ominus\ominus\ominus\ominus\ominus$ = -6
Step 2: Remove 2 negative counters from the mat to represent subtracting -2.

Remove these 2 negative counters.
↗↗
$\ominus\ominus\ominus\ominus\ominus\ominus$ = $\ominus\ominus\ominus\ominus$ = -4
Step 3: There are 4 negative counters left on the mat and this represents -4.
Therefore, -6 - (-2) = -4.
Notice that -6 - (-2) = -4 is possible only when - (- becomes +, so that
-6 - (-2) becomes -6 + 2 = -4
Rule 4: Considering Example 4, **to subtract one negative number from another, subtract the smaller absolute value number (2) from the bigger absolute value number (6) and attach the sign of the bigger absolute value number (6) to the subtraction or difference (-4)**.
Considering example 4, the absolute value of -6 is 6 and the absolute value of -2 is 2.

━━━━━━━━━━━━━━━━━━━━ The notes and the generous worked examples have provided me with conceptual understanding and computational fluency to do my homework.

Exercise
1. Find the difference. You may use counters.
   Hint: See Example 1 or Rule 1.
   a. 6 - 2   **b**. 5 - 3   **c**. 7 - 4   **d**. 6 - 2
2. Find the difference. You may use counters.
   Hint: See Example 2 or Rule 2.
   a. 2 - 4   **b**. 3 - 5   **c**. 3 - 7   **d**. 1 - 5
3. Use counters to find the following.

Hint: See Example 3 or Rule 3.

a. -4 - 2 =   **b**. -6 - 4 =   **c**. -5 - 4 =   **d**. -2 - 3 =

e. -1 - 2 =   **f**. -4 - 4 =   **g**. -7 - 3 =   **h**. -2 - 1 =

4. Use counters to find the following:

Hint:See Example 4 or Rule 4.

a. -1 - (-4) =   **b**. -7 - (-3) =   **c**.-2 - (-5) =   **d**. -8 - (-2)=   **e**. -8 - (-5) =

f. -3 - (-4) =   **g**. -3 - (-3) =   **h**. -10 - (-10) =   **i**. -8 - (-9) =

Challenge Questions

5. Find the difference.

a. 3 - 5 =   **b**. 3 - (-5) =   **c**. -4 - (-8) =   **d**. -8 - (-8) =   **e**. 6 - 4 =

f. -6 - 8 =   **g**. 0 - (-6) =   **h**. 7 - (-3) =   **i**. -5 - (-7) =   **j**. -6 - 6 =

k. 4 - (-4) =   **l**. 1 - 7 =   **m**. -3 - (-4) =   **n**. -5 - (-6) =   **o**. -2 - (-2) =

Answers to Selected Questions

1a. 4   **2a**. -2   **3a**. -6   **4a**. 3

REAL WORLD APPLICATIONS - WORD PROBLEMS
Subtraction of Integers

Example 1

The temperature in New York at 7:00 A.M. was -2^0F and at 2:00 P.M., the temperature was 5^0F. Find the change in the temperature.

Solution

To find the change in the temperature, subtract the starting temperature $(-2^0$F$)$ from the ending temperature $(5^0$F$)$ as shown:

$$5 - (-2) = 5 + 2 \qquad\qquad \text{Note: } - (- = +$$
$$= 7^0\text{F}$$

Therefore the change in the temperature $= 7^0$F.

The notes and the generous worked examples have provided me with conceptual understanding and computational fluency to do my homework.

Exercises

1. On December 25 at 6:00 A.M. the temperature was -8^0F and at 12:30 P.M, the temperature was 10^0F. What is the change in temperature?
   Hint: See Example 1.

2. On December 24, 2004 the temperature of a certain city was -1^0F and 8 hours later, the temperature was -7^0F. What was the change in the

temperature? Hint: Set up as follow: Change in temperature = -7 - (-1) and also see Example 1.

Challenge Questions

3. At 12:00 P.M. on January 6, 2005 the temperature was -2⁰F, and at 7:00 P.M. the temperature was -3⁰F. What is the change in the temperature?

4. The temperature of a certain village on December 28,1997 was -6⁰F and about 10 hours later, the temperature was -3⁰F. What is the change in the temperature?

MULTIPLYING INTEGERS

What is multiplication? Multiplication is repeated addition. The symbol for multiplication is ×. For example, 6×3 means $3 + 3 + 3 + 3 + 3 + 3$.

Example 1
Model the multiplication of 6×3 using counters.
Step 1: 6×3 means 6 sets of 3 positive counters. Put these counters on the mat.

⊕ ⊕ ⊕   ⊕ ⊕ ⊕   ⊕ ⊕ ⊕
⊕ ⊕ ⊕   ⊕ ⊕ ⊕   ⊕ ⊕ ⊕

Step 2: Find the number of counters on the mat. There are 18 positive counters on the mat. Therefore, $6 \times 3 = 18$.
Rule 1: **To multiply a positive number by another positive number, just multiply the two numbers together as in Example 1**.

Example 2
Use counters to find $5 \times (-2)$
Solution
Step 1: $5 \times (-2)$ means 5 sets of 2 negative counters as shown on the mat.

⊖ ⊖   ⊖ ⊖   ⊖ ⊖   ⊖ ⊖   ⊖ ⊖

Step 2: There are 10 negative counters on the mat, making $5 \times (-2) = -10$
Rule 2: **To multiply a positive number by a negative number just multiply the two numbers together and attach a negative sign to the product as shown in Example 2, Step 2**. Note also that × (- becomes a multiplication with a negative symbol attach to the product as in Example 2, Step 2.

Example 3
Use counters to find -2×4

Solution

Step 1: Using the fact that -2 is the opposite of 2, -2 × 4 means to remove 2 sets of 4 positive counters. However, we cannot remove 2 sets of 4 positive counters because there are none to remove. We must first add 2 sets of 4 zero pairs, and then we can remove 2 sets of 4 positive counters.

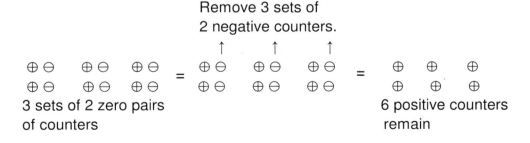

Two sets of 4 zero pairs of counters

Remove 2 sets of 4 positive counters.

Step 2: Find the number of the counters remaining on the mat. There are 8 negative counters remaining on the mat and this represents -8. Therefore, -2 × 4 = -8.

Rule 3: **To multiply a negative number by a positive number, just multiply the two numbers and attach a negative symbol to the product as in Example 3, Step 2.**

Special note: To multiply a negative integer by another integer, remove as many sets of positive counters as possible as in Example 3, Step 1.

Example 4

Use counters to find -3(-2).

Solution

Step 1: Using the fact that -3 is the opposite of 3, -3(-2) means to remove 3 sets of 2 negative counters but there are none to remove. Therefore, we must first add 3 sets of 2 zero pairs and then we can remove 3 sets of 2 negative counters.

Remove 3 sets of 2 negative counters.

3 sets of 2 zero pairs of counters

6 positive counters remain

Step 2: Find the number of the remaining counters on the mat. There are 6 positive counters that remain on the mat, and this represents +6 or 6, and therefore, -3(-2) = 6.

Rule 4: **To multiply one negative number by another negative number, just multiply the two numbers together and their product must be positive**

as shown in example 4, step 2.

Summary of the Signs of the Rules for Multiplying Integers
Considering Examples 1 to 4, when multiplying two numbers that have the same signs, the sign of the product of the numbers is positive. For example, -2(-3) = +6 = 6, and 2(3) = +6 = 6.
Considering Examples 1 to 4, when multiplying two numbers that have different signs, the sign of the product of the numbers is negative. For example, -2(3) = -6, and 2(-3) = -6.

The notes and the generous worked examples have provided me with conceptual understanding and computational fluency to do my homework.

Exercises
1. Explain what is meant by multiplication.
2. Use counters to multiply the following. Hint: See Example 1. You may use Rule 1.
   a. 3×2 **b.** 4×3 **c.** 2×5 **d.** 5×4
3. Use counters to find the following. Hint: See Example 2. You may use Rule 2.
   a. $3 \times (-2)$ **b.** $4 \times (-3)$ **c.** $3 \times (-5)$ **d.** $4 \times (-2)$
4. Use counters to find the following. Hint: See Example 3. You may Use Rule 3.
   a. -3×4 **b.** -2×5 **c.** -4×3 **d.** -5×2
   e. -3×3 **f.** -5×6 **g.** -2×6 **h.** -6×3
5. Use counters to find the followings. Hint: See Example 4. You may use Rule 4.
   a. $-2(-4)$ **b.** $-4(-4)$ **c.** $-3(-3)$ **d.** $-5(-3)$
   e. $-4(-2)$ **f.** $-3(-2)$ **g.** $-4(-5)$ **h.** $-2(-5)$
6. Solve questions 2 to 5 using just the rules.

Challenge Questions
7. Find the following products using the rules of multiplications.
   a. $-6(-6) =$ **b.** $-8 \times 6 =$ **c.** $7 \times (-3) =$ **d.** $9 \times 4 =$
   e. $-5(-5) =$ **f.** $7 \times 3 =$ **g.** $-3 \times 8 =$ **h.** $(-7) =$
   i. $3 \times (-7) =$ **j.** $-3 \times (-7) =$ **k.** $-3(5) =$ **l.** $-4 \times (-9) =$

Answers to Selected Questions
2a. 6   **3a.** -6   **4a.** -12   **5a.** 8   **7k.** -15

Cumulative Review
Find each product, sum or difference.
1. $-6 + 10 =$ **2.** $-8 - (-3) =$ **3.** $-3 + (-4) =$

4. 7 - (-4) =   **5**. -7 × 3 =   **6**. -4 - (-3) =

7. 8 - (-2) =   **8**. -5 × (-2) =   **9**. 6(-3) =

10. Replace each ? with =, < or > to make a true statement. Review the chapter/section on Number Line.

   a. 4 ? -2   **b**. -4 ? -3   **c**. -3 ? 0

   d. -1 ? -1   **e**. -2 ? -1   **f**. 0 ? -1

11. Which problem does not have -4 as its answer?

   A. 8 - 12

   B. -1 + (-3)

   C. 2 - 6

   D. -2(-2)

   E. 2(-2)

Answer to Selected Questions

   10a. 4 > -2   **10c**. -3 < 0   **10d**. -1 = -1

DIVIDING INTEGERS

What is division? Division is separating a quantity into equal-sized groups. For example, 3 girls want to share 9 apples equally, how can this be done?

Step 1: Put 9 counters on a mat, and let 9 counters represent the 9 apples.

   ⊕ ⊕ ⊕ ⊕ ⊕ ⊕ ⊕ ⊕ ⊕

Step 2: Separate the 9 counters into 3 equal-sized groups.

   ⊕ ⊕ ⊕
   ⊕ ⊕ ⊕
   ⊕ ⊕ ⊕

There are 3 equal groups of 3 positive counters each, and therefore, 9 ÷ 3 = 3. Each girl will receive 3 apples.

Example 1

Use counters to find -12 ÷ 4

Solution

Step 1: Put 12 negative counters on the mat to represent -12.

   ⊖ ⊖ ⊖ ⊖ ⊖ ⊖ ⊖ ⊖ ⊖ ⊖ ⊖ ⊖

Step 2: Separate the 12 counters into 4 equal-sized groups.

   ⊖ ⊖ ⊖ ⊖
   ⊖ ⊖ ⊖ ⊖
   ⊖ ⊖ ⊖ ⊖
   4 equal-sized groups.

There are 4 equal-sized groups of 3 negative counters each and meaning

$-12 \div 4 = -3$

Rule 1: From Example 1, **when a negative integer is divided by a positive integer, the quotient is negative**.

Working Backward to Solve Division Problems

Multiplication is the opposite of division. We can therefore, work backward by using multiplication to solve division problems by using the logic of "**what number multiplied by the divisor equals to the dividend**". Examples 2 to 5 will explain how we can divide integers by working backward. Review the section on multiplication of integers and knowing the multiplication tables will be helpful.

Example 2

Find $12 \div 3$.

Solution

To find $12 \div 3$, think of what number times 3 equals to 12?

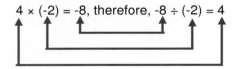

$4 \times 3 = 12$, therefore, $12 \div 3 = 4$

Rule 2: From Example 2, **when a positive integer is divided by a positive integer the quotient is positive**.

Example 3

Find $-8 \div (-2)$.

Solution

To find $-8 \div (-2)$, think of what number times -2 equals to -8?

$4 \times (-2) = -8$, therefore, $-8 \div (-2) = 4$

Rule 3: From Example 3, **when a negative integer is divided by a negative integer the quotient is positive**.

Example 4

Find $-15 \div 3$.

Solution

To find -15 ÷ 3, think of what number multiplied by 3 equals to -15?

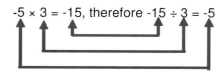

-5 × 3 = -15, therefore -15 ÷ 3 = -5

Rule 4: From Example 4, **when a negative integer is divided by a positive integer, the quotient is negative**.

Example 5
Find 15 ÷ (-3).
Solution
To find 15 ÷ (-3), think of what number multiplied by -3 equals to 15?

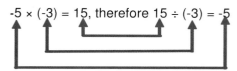

-5 × (-3) = 15, therefore 15 ÷ (-3) = -5

Rule 5: From Example 5, **when a positive integer is divided by a negative integer the quotient is negative**.

Summary of the Signs of the Rules for Dividing Integers
Considering Examples 1 to 5, when dividing an integer by another integer, that have the same signs, the sign of the quotient (answer) is positive. For example, -6 ÷ -2 = 3, and 6 ÷ 2 = 3.
Considering examples 1 to 5, when dividing an integer by another integer, that have different signs, the sign of the quotient (answer) is negative. For example, -6 ÷ 2 = -3, and 6 ÷ (-2) = -3.

The notes and the generous worked examples have provided me with conceptual understanding and computational fluency to do my homework.

Exercises
1. Division is the opposite of multipli_____.
2. Use counters to find the following. Hint: See Example 1. **You may use Rule 1**.

   a. -9 ÷ 3 =   **b**. -10 ÷ 2 =   **c**. -4 ÷ 2 =   **d**. -6 ÷ 3 =
   e. -15 ÷ 5 =   **f**. -18 ÷ 3 =   **g**. -24 ÷ 8 =   **i**. 36 ÷ 6 =
   k. -28 ÷ 4 =   **l**. -50 ÷ 10 =   **m**. -44 ÷ 11 =   **n**. -14 ÷ 7 =

3. Work backward by using multiplication to solve the following division problems. Hint: See Example 2. **You may use Rule 2**.

a. $15 \div 5 =$ **b.** $12 \div 6 =$ **c.** $28 \div 4 =$ **d.** $16 \div 4 =$

e. $18 \div 9 =$ **f.** $21 \div 3 =$ **g.** $24 \div 3 =$ **h.** $48 \div 6 =$

4. Work backward by using multiplication to solve the following division problems. Hint: See Example 3. **You may use Rule 3**.

     a. $-12 \div (-2) =$ **b.** $-8 \div (-4) =$ **c.** $-10 \div (-5) =$ **d.** $-21 \div (-3) =$

     e. $-30 \div (-6) =$ **f.** $-18 \div (-3) =$ **g.** $-28 \div (-4) =$ **h.** $-9 \div (-3) =$

5. Work backward by using multiplication to solve the following division problems. Hint: See Example 4. **You may use Rule 4**.

     a. $-4 \div 2 =$ **b.** $-6 \div 3 =$ **c.** $-9 \div 3 =$ **d.** $-16 \div 4 =$

     e. $-20 \div 5 =$ **f.** $-21 \div 7 =$ **g.** $-36 \div 3 =$ **h.** $-12 \div 6 =$

6. Work backward by using multiplication to solve the following division problems. Hint: See Example 5. **You may use Rule 5**.

     a. $21 \div (-3) =$ **b.** $12 \div (-4.) =$ **c.** $28 \div (-4) =$ **d.** $16 \div (-4) =$

     e. $36 \div (-6) =$ **f.** $18 \div (-3) =$ **g.** $10 \div (-2) =$ **h.** $14 \div (-7) =$

Answers to Selected Questions

2a. -3   **2b.** -5   **3a.** 3   **3b.** 2   **4a.** 6

4b. 2   **5a.** -2   **5b.** –2   **6a.** -7   **6b.** -3

Challenge Questions

7 Find each quotient.

     a. $-32 \div 4 =$ **b.** $21 \div (-3) =$ **c.** $-33 \div (-11) =$ **d.** $24 \div 8 =$

     e. $-15 \div 3 =$ **f.** $-6 \div (-6) =$ **g.** $-36 \div (-4) =$ **h.** $35 \div (-7) =$

8 Find the value of $a \div b$ if $a = -2$ and $b = -1$. Hint: Substitute $a = -2$ and $b = -1$ in the expression $a \div b$, and then divide.

Cumulative Review Exercises

1. Solve the following problems.

     a. $-5 + (-4) =$ **b.** $-3 + (+3) =$ **c.** $+2 + 6 =$ **d.** $-4 \div (-2) =$

     e. $8 \div (-4) =$ **f.** $27 + (-7) =$ **g.** $-3 + 8 =$ **h.** $-6 - (-3) =$

     i. $-3 - 4 =$ **j.** $4 \times (-3) =$ **k.** $-2 \times 7 =$ **l.** $-1 + (-1) =$

     m. $4 - 6 =$ **n.** $-4(-2) =$ **o.** $-5 - 3 =$ **p.** $-2 \times (-3) =$

     q. $-8 - (-2) =$ **r.** $-16 \div 4 =$ **s.** $-16 \div (-4) =$ **t.** $10 - (-4) =$

6. Compare and write $<$, $>$ or $=$ for ?

     a. $+3 + (-2) ? -3$ **b.** $-1 + (+7) ? 6$ **c.** $-1 + (-1) ? 0$ **d.** $+3 + (-3) ? +1$

FRACTIONS

A fraction can be considered a "part of something." A fraction may be defined as a "part of a unit." An apple may be considered one whole or a unit and if some part of the apple is eaten, then the remaining apple is no more a unit, but a part of the whole apple, which is called a **fraction** of the whole apple.

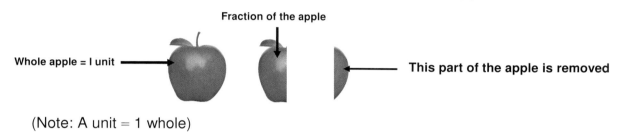

Fraction of the apple

Whole apple = I unit

This part of the apple is removed

(Note: A unit = 1 whole)

A fraction consists of two numbers separated by a fraction bar as shown below. Assume that half of the apple is eaten, then it means that the apple is divided into two parts and one part of it has been eaten. This statement can be written

as half of the apple has been eaten, and the fraction half is written as: $\dfrac{1}{2}$

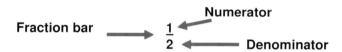

Numerator

Fraction bar $\longrightarrow$ $\dfrac{1}{2}$

Denominator

The numerator indicates how many equal parts are being considered, or how many parts are represented in the fraction. Since the apple is divided into two equal parts and one part is eaten, then we are considering one out of the two equal parts.
The denominator indicates how many equal parts the whole is divided into. The apple is divided into two equal parts.
A fraction therefore, tells us that:
(**a**) The top number (numerator) indicates how many parts are represented or considered by a fraction.
(**b**) The bottom number (denominator) indicates into how many parts the unit has been divided.

Group Exercise
The materials needed for this exercise are oranges and knives.
This exercise is to demonstrate how to divide a whole into two halves. The class

should be divided into pairs of students and with the supervision of the teacher and the parents, each pair of students should put an orange onto a plate. The teacher should give one student per group a knife to cut the orange into approximately two equal parts. These two equal parts of the whole orange are referred to as "one half of a whole orange" as shown in the diagram.

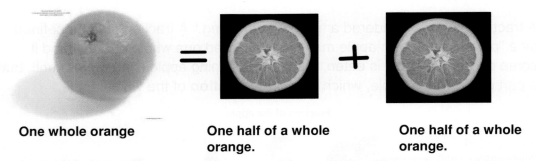

One whole orange   **One half of a whole orange.**   **One half of a whole orange.**

Each member of the group should be given one half of the whole orange to be eaten in order to remember one whole orange can be cut into two equal halves and the two equal halves can be shared by the two students in each group. Also, if we add the two halves of the oranges together, we should get the original whole orange.

UNDERSTANDING FRACTIONS WITH MORE DIAGRAMS
The diagrams below show an egg that is divided into two equal parts.

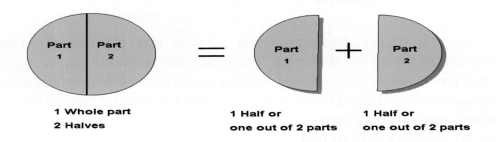

1 Whole part
2 Halves

1 Half or
one out of 2 parts

1 Half or
one out of 2 parts

The diagrams below show a special colored cake that is divided into three equal parts and one part can be written in a fraction form as $\frac{1}{3}$.

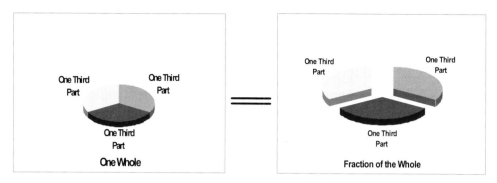

If we are considering two equal parts of the cake out of the total three equal parts, then it can be written in a fraction form as $\dfrac{2}{3}$.

Example 1
How many equal parts are the rectangles divided into?

(a)

(b)

©

Solution
(**a**) The rectangle is divided into 5 equal parts.
(**b**) The rectangle is divided into 4 equal parts.
(**c**) The rectangle is divided into 3 equal parts.

Example 2
Write the shaded or colored part as a fraction of each rectangle.

(a)

(b)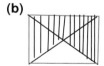

©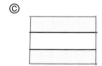

Solution
(**a**) The rectangle is divided into five equal parts. Two parts are shaded, and therefore, two parts are being considered out of a total of five equal parts.
The fraction is therefore,

$\dfrac{2}{5}$ ← Number of equal parts being considered.
← Number of equal parts the whole rectangle is divided into.

(**b**) The rectangle is divided into four equal parts. Three parts are shaded, and therefore, three out of the total of four equal parts are being considered.
The fraction is therefore,

$\dfrac{3}{4}$ ← Number of equal parts being considered.
← Number of equal parts the whole rectangle is divided into.

(**c**) The rectangle is divided into three equal parts. Two parts are shaded, and therefore, two out of the total three equal parts are being considered.
The fraction is therefore,

$$\frac{2}{3}$$ ← **Number of equal parts being considered.**
← **Number of equal parts the whole rectangle is divided into.**

Example 3
A circle is divided into eight equal parts. If three parts are shaded black,
(**a**) What fraction is shaded black?
(**b**) What fraction is not shaded black?

Solution
(**a**) The circle is divided into eight equal parts, and 3 equal parts out of the total of 8 equal parts are shaded black.
Therefore, the fraction shaded black is,

$$\frac{3}{8}$$ ← **Number of equal parts being considered.**
← **Number of equal parts the whole circle is divided into.**

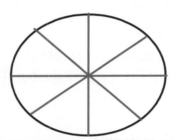 =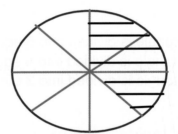

The circle is divided into 8 parts.   **3 out of 8 parts are shaded black.**

(**b**) Since 3 equal parts of the circle is shaded black, the circle is divided into 8 equal parts, the number of equal parts of the circle that are not shaded black is
$$8 - 3 = 5$$
Therefore, the fraction of the circle that is not shaded black is,

$$\frac{5}{8}$$ ← **Number of equal parts being considered.**
← **Number of equal parts the whole circle is divided into.**

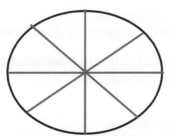 =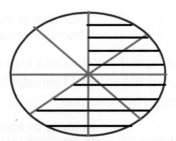

The circle is divided into 8 parts.   **5 out of 8 parts are shaded black.**

Critical Thinking

1. From the solution of Example **3**, note that the circle is divided into eight equal parts and one part is one-eighth of the circle and it is written in a fraction form as $\frac{1}{8}$.

2. In Example **3(a)**, three-eighths of the circle is shaded black and five-eighths is not shaded black. Three-eighths is written in a fraction form as $\frac{3}{8}$, 5-eigths is written in a fraction form as $\frac{5}{8}$ and 8-eigths is written as $\frac{8}{8}$.

Using Example **3(b)** solution, we can then add up fractions with the same denominator as shown:

$$8\text{-eigths} = 5\text{-eigths} + 3\text{-eigths}$$

$$\frac{8}{8} = \frac{5}{8} + \frac{3}{8} \quad\text{———————}\quad [A]$$

The fractions on the right side of equation $[A]$ can be added up by just adding the numerators together putting it over the common denominator of 8. Equation $[A]$ then becomes:

$$\frac{8}{8} = \frac{5}{8} + \frac{3}{8} = \frac{5 + 3}{8} = \frac{8}{8}$$

Common denominator of 8.

In Example **3(b)**, note that 8-eigths of the circle is the same as 1 whole circle and the 8-eigths can be written as $\frac{8}{8}$. Therefore, $\frac{8}{8} = 1$ whole circle. We conclude by stating that whenever the top number of a fraction is the same as the bottom number, then the fraction = 1. Examples are: $\frac{1}{1} = 1$, $\frac{2}{2} = 1$, $\frac{3}{3} = 1$, $\frac{4}{4} = 1$, $\frac{5}{5} = 1$, $\frac{6}{6} = 1$,...

Example 4

There are 24 students in a class in a certain school. If 13 of the students are girls,
(**a**) What fraction of the students are girls?
(**b**) What fraction of the students are boys?
Solution
(**a**) Total number of students = 24

Number of girls = 13

The fraction of girls = $\dfrac{13}{24}$

$= \dfrac{13}{24}$ ╱Number of parts of the whole class being considered.

╱Number of the students in the whole class.

(b) Total number of students = 24

Number of girls = 13

Number of boys = Total number of students − Number of girls.

$= 24 - 13 = 11$

The fraction of boys = $\dfrac{11}{24}$

$= \dfrac{11}{24}$ ╱Number of parts of the whole class being considered.

╱Number of students in the whole class.

Example 5

Mary had 11 out of 12 of her mathematics test questions correct.

(a) What fraction did she have correct?

(b) What fraction did she have wrong?

Solution

(a) Total number of questions = 12

Number of correct questions = 11

Therefore, the fraction correct $= \dfrac{11}{12}$

$= \dfrac{11}{12}$ ╱Number of questions considered to be correct.

╱Total number of questions.

(b) Total number of questions = 12

Number of questions that are correct = 11

The number of wrong questions =

Total number of questions - Number of correct questions.

$= 12 - 11 = 1$

The fraction of the wrong questions $= \dfrac{1}{12}$ ╱Number of wrong questions.

╱Total number of questions.

Group Exercise

The class should be divided into four teams, Team A, Team B, Team C, and Team D. The class may be divided into more teams if needed. With the supervision of a teacher or a parent, each team should order a pizza which should be divided into 8 equal parts.

Team A

Team B

Team C

Team D

1. Team A should remove 5 parts of the pizza to share. What fraction of the pizza is shared and what fraction remains?
2. Team B should remove 7 parts of the pizza to share. What fraction of the pizza is shared and what fraction remains?
3. Team C should remove 6 parts of the pizza to share. What fraction of the pizza is shared and what fraction remains?
4. Team D should remove 4 parts of the pizza to share. What fraction of the pizza is shared and what fraction remains?

Each team should copy and complete Table 1.

Table 1, **Team** _____

Equal parts of pizza	Parts shared	Part remains	Fraction shared	Fraction Remains

Each team should post Table 1 on the blackboard, and then report their answers to the class.

The notes and the generous worked examples have provided me with conceptual understanding and computational fluency to do my homework.

Exercises

Hint: For the solutions to questions 1 - 9, see the preceding notes/information.

1. What is a fraction?
2. A fraction represents a ————————
3. The top number of a fraction is called ————————
4. The bottom number of a fraction is called ————————
5. The top number of a fraction tells us about ————————
6. The bottom number of a fraction tells us about ————————-
7. If the numerator of a fraction is the same as the denominator, the fraction is equal to ————-
8. If a whole apple is divided into seven equal parts, the bottom number of the fraction will be ————————
9. If a circle is divided into five equal parts and 2 parts are removed,
   (**a**) What fraction is removed?
   (**b**) What fraction remains?
10 Write the fraction of the shaded or the colored areas. Hint: See Example **3**.

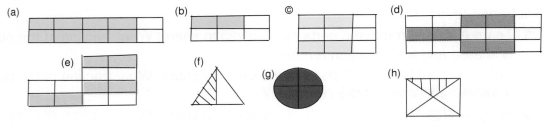

11. If a whole unit, such as a whole circle is divided into ten equal parts, the bottom number of the fraction is _____
12. Write four separate fractions which are equal to 1 or represent a whole unit.
    Hint: Read the section under "Critical thinking."
13. John had 7 out of 10 mathematics problems correct.
    (**a**) What fraction of the questions did John have correct?
    (**b**) What fraction of the questions did John have wrong? Hint: See example 5.
14. There are 20 students in a class. If 3 students were absent one day,
    (**a**) what fraction were absent?
    (**b**) what fraction were present ? Hint: See Example **4**.
15. Mary bought 12 cookies and she gave away 8 of them.
    (**a**) What fraction did she give away?
    (**b**) What fraction remained? Hint: See Example **3**.
16. The school team won 5 out of the last 13 games.

(**a**) What fraction of the games did they win?

(**b**) What fraction of the games did they loose? Hint: See Example **5**.

17. If a fraction is written as $\frac{3}{7}$, into how many parts has the unit been divided?

Hint: See Example **2**.

18. In the picture, what part of the pizza is removed? What part of the picture remains? Hint: See Example 3.

The part of the pizza that remains.

The pizza is divided into 8 parts.

The part of the pizza that is removed.

Challenge Question

19. Mary worked 48 hours last week. If 8 hours were overtime hours, what fraction of the total hours were overtime?

Answers to Selected Questions

14(a) $\frac{3}{20}$ **16(a)** $\frac{5}{13}$

FRACTIONS AS A PART OF A SET

Quick Cumulative Review

Using the graph of blue, pink, green, and yellow rings:

1. How many pink rings are in the graph?

2. How many more blue rings are there in the graph than green rings?

3. Which colors of the rings have the same number of rings?

4. Which color has the greatest number of rings?

5. Which color has the least number of rings?

6. Which color is your favorite and why?

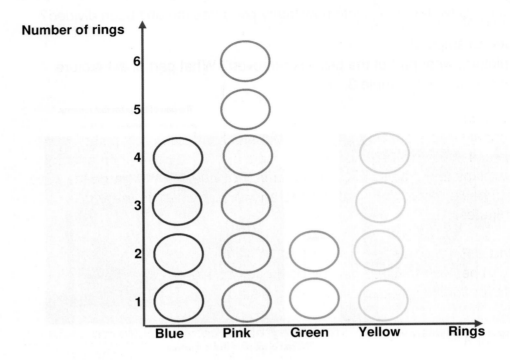

What is a Set?

Recall that we have already discussed fractions as a part of a whole. It is also possible to write fractions as a part of a set. Therefore, a fraction is a number that stands for a part of a whole or a part of a set. A set is things that belong to the same group and all the things that belong to the same group form one whole and can be considered as one. For example, the female students and the male students in grade 5 belong to the same group or belong to the same class or belong to the same set known as students. The female students form a fraction of the class or a fraction of the set or a fraction of the whole. The male students also form a fraction of the class or a fraction of the set or a fraction of the whole. The number of female students and the number of male students form the whole set. **A set is therefore, the sum or the total of things that belong to the same group or a common group**.

Example 1

There are 2 pink rings, 3 green rings, and 1 blue ring. How many rings are in the set?

Solution

The pink rings, green rings and the blue ring belong to the same group or a common

group known as rings. We have already discussed that a set is the sum of the total of things that belong to the same group or a common group.
Therefore:

The number of the rings that belong to the set

$$= \text{sum of the rings}$$
$$= 2 \text{ pink rings} + 3 \text{ green rings} + 1 \text{ blue ring}$$
$$= 6 \text{ rings}$$

Group Exercise

The class should be divided into groups of four students. Each group should put 3 blue counters, 4 yellow counters, 2 blue counters and 1 red counter on a table. Using the explanation of a set, find the number of counters in the set on the table. Each group should record their method and answer to present to the whole class within 10 minutes.

How to Find a Fraction as a Part of a Set

A formula can be used to find a fraction as a part of a set.
The formula for finding a fraction as a part of a set is:

$$\textbf{A fraction as a part of a set} = \frac{\textbf{Number of things being considered in the set}}{\textbf{Total Number of things in the set}}$$

The formula simply means that we are considering and **comparing a certain number of things in the set to the total number of things in the set**.

Example 2

There are 3 blue balls and 1 red ball on the table.
a. What fraction of the set is blue balls?
b. What fraction of the set is red balls?
Solution

We can use the formula for finding the fraction as a part of a set to find the fraction of the blue balls as a part of a set of all the balls as shown:

a. The fraction of the blue balls as a part of a set

$$= \frac{\text{Number of things being considered in the set}}{\text{Total Number of things in the set}}$$

$$= \frac{\text{Number of blue balls in the set}}{\text{Total number of balls in the set}}$$

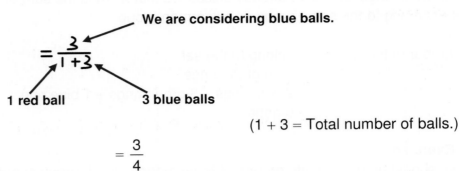

We are considering blue balls.

$= \dfrac{3}{1+3}$

1 red ball   3 blue balls

(1 + 3 = Total number of balls.)

$= \dfrac{3}{4}$

Therefore, $\dfrac{3}{4}$ of the set is blue.

b. We can use the formula for finding the fraction as a part of a set to find the fraction of the red balls as a part of a set of all the balls as shown:

The fraction of red balls as a part of a set

$$= \frac{\text{Number of things being considered in the set}}{\text{Total Number of things in the set}}$$

$$= \frac{\text{Number of red balls in the set}}{\text{Total number of balls in the set}}$$

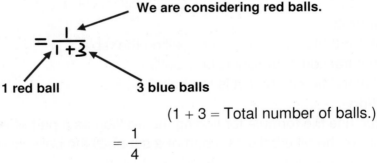

We are considering red balls.

$= \dfrac{1}{1+3}$

1 red ball   3 blue balls

(1 + 3 = Total number of balls.)

$= \dfrac{1}{4}$

Therefore, $\dfrac{1}{4}$ of the set is red.

Example 3
The diagram represents pink, green and blue rings.
a. What fraction of the rings is blue?
b. What fraction of the rings is pink?
c. What fraction of the rings is green?
d. What fraction of the rings is either pink or green?
e. What fraction of the rings is either pink or blue?
f. What fraction of the rings is either green or blue?

Solution

In this solution, we will practise how to use the formula to solve for the fraction as a part of a set.

a.

Number of blue rings in the set = 1.

Total number of rings in the set = 6.

The fraction of the blue rings as a part of a set of all the rings

$$= \frac{\text{Number of blue rings in the set}}{\text{Total number of rings in the set}}$$

$$= \frac{1}{6}$$

Therefore, the fraction of the blue rings as a part of a set of all the rings is $\frac{1}{6}$.

b.

Number of pink rings in the set = 2

Total number of the rings in the set = 6.

The fraction of the pink rings as a part of a set of all the rings

$$= \frac{\text{Number of pink rings in the set}}{\text{Total number of rings in the set}}$$

$$= \frac{2}{6}$$

$$= \frac{\overset{1}{\cancel{2}}}{\underset{3}{\cancel{6}}} \quad \text{Reduce to the lowest term by dividing by 2.}$$

$$= \frac{1}{3}$$

Therefore, the fraction of the pink rings as a part of a set of all the rings is $\frac{1}{3}$.

c.

Number of green rings in the set = 3

205

Total number of rings in the set = 6

The fraction of the green rings as a part of a set of all the rings

$$= \frac{\text{Number of green rings in the set}}{\text{Total number of rings in the set}}$$

$$= \frac{3}{6}$$

$$= \frac{\overset{1}{\cancel{3}}}{\underset{2}{\cancel{6}}} \qquad \text{Reduce to the lowest term by dividing by 3.}$$

$$= \frac{1}{2}$$

Therefore, the fraction of the green rings as a part of a set of all the rings is $\frac{1}{2}$.

d.

Number of pink rings = 2.

Number of green rings = 3.

Number of either pink or green rings in the set

= Number of pink rings + number of green rings.

= 2 + 3

= 5

The fraction of either pink or green rings as a part of the set of all the rings

$$= \frac{\text{Number of either pink or green rings in the set}}{\text{Total number of rings in the set}}$$

$$\overset{\nearrow \text{ Number of either pink or green rings in the set.}}{= \frac{5}{6}}$$

$$\searrow \text{ Total number of rings in the set.}$$

Therefore, the fraction of either pink or green rings as a part of a set of all the rings is $\frac{5}{6}$.

e.

Number of pink rings in the set = 2.

Number of blue rings in the set = 1.

Number of either pink or blue rings in the set

$$= \text{Number of pink rings} + \text{number of blue rings.}$$
$$= 2 + 1$$
$$= 3$$

The fraction of either pink or blue rings as a part of a set of all the rings

$$= \frac{\text{Number of either pink or blue rings in the set}}{\text{Total number of rings in the set}}$$

↙ Number of either pink or blue rings in the set.

$$= \frac{3}{6}$$

↖ Total number of rings in the set.

$$= \frac{\overset{1}{\cancel{3}}}{\underset{2}{\cancel{6}}} \qquad \text{Reduce to the lowest term by dividing by 3.}$$

$$= \frac{1}{2}$$

Therefore, the fraction of either pink or blue rings as a part of a set of all the rings is $\frac{1}{2}$.

f.

Number of green rings in the set = 3.
Number of blue rings in the set = 1.
Number of either green or blue rings in the set

$$= \text{Number of green rings} + \text{number of blue rings.}$$
$$= 3 + 1$$
$$= 4$$

The fraction of either green or blue rings as a part of a set of all the rings

$$= \frac{\text{Number of either green or blue rings in the set}}{\text{Total number of rings in the set}}$$

↙ Number of either green or blue rings in the set.

$$= \frac{4}{6}$$

↖ Total number of rings in the set.

$$= \frac{\overset{2}{\cancel{4}}}{\underset{3}{\cancel{6}}}$$ Reduce to the lowest term by dividing by 2.

$$= \frac{2}{3}$$

Therefore, the fraction of either green or blue rings as a part of a set of all the rings is $\frac{2}{3}$.

Example 4

The Science Club of a middle school consists of 3 boys and 7 girls.

a. What fraction of the club members are boys?

b. What fraction of the club members are girls?

Solution

Both the girls and the boys belong to the Science Club.

The total number of the club members is the set of all the members of the club.

a.

Therefore, we can use the formula for finding the fraction as a part of a set to find the fraction of the boys as a part of a set of the total club members as shown:

The fraction of the boys as a part of a set of club members

$$= \frac{\text{Number of things being considered in the set}}{\text{Total number of things in the set}}$$

$$= \frac{\text{Number of boys in the club}}{\text{Total number of club members}}$$

We are considering boys in the club.

$$= \frac{3}{3 + 7}$$

3 boys ↗   ↖ 7 girls

$$= \frac{3}{10}$$

Therefore, $\frac{3}{10}$ of the club members are boys.

b.

Similar to the solution of 4a, we can use the formula for finding the fraction as a part of a set to find the fraction of the girls as a part of a set of the total club members as shown:

The fraction of the girls as a part of a set of the total club members

$$= \frac{\text{Number of things being considered in the set}}{\text{Total number of things in the set}}$$

$$= \frac{\text{Number of girls in the club}}{\text{Total number of club members}}$$

We are considering girls in the club.

$$= \frac{7}{3 + 7}$$

3 boys ↗   ↖ 7 girls

$$= \frac{7}{10}$$

Therefore, $\frac{7}{10}$ of the set or club members are girls.

The notes and the generous worked examples have provided me with conceptual understanding and computational fluency to do my homework.

Exercises

1. Explain what is meant by a set.

2. Explain what is meant by a fraction as a part of a set.

3. Give two examples of sets.

4. There is 1 red ball, 4 blue balls and 2 green balls. What is the number of balls in the set?
Hint: See Example 1.

5. What is the formula for finding a fraction as part of a set?

6. Use the diagram of rings to answer the questions.
   a. What is the fraction of the green rings?
   b. What is the fraction of the blue ring?
   Hint: See Example 2.

7. Use the diagram of rings to answer the questions.
   a. What is the fraction of the pink rings?
   b. What is the fraction of the blue ring?
   Hint: See Example 2

8. In each set of the diagram, find what fraction of the rings is blue and what fraction of the rings is green? Hint: See Example 2.

   a.

   b.

   c.

   d.

   e.

9. The diagram represents pink, green and blue rings.
   a. What fraction of the rings is blue?
   b. What fraction of the rings is pink?
   c. What fraction of the rings is green?
   d. What fraction of the rings is either pink or green?
   e. What fraction of the rings is either pink or blue?
   f. What fraction of the rings is either green or blue?

   Hint: See Example 3.

10. The diagram represents pink, green, and blue rings.
   a. What fraction of the rings is blue?
   b. What fraction of the rings is pink?

c. What fraction of the rings is green?

d. What fraction of the rings is either pink or green?

e. What fraction of the rings is either pink or blue?

f. What fraction of the rings is either green or blue?

Hint: See Example 3.

11. The Glee Club of a school consists of 11 boys and 15 girls.

a. What fraction of the club members are boys?

b. What fraction of the club members are girls?

Hint: See Example 4.

Challenge Questions

12. The diagram represents pink, green, and blue rings.

a. What fraction of the rings is blue?

b. What fraction of the rings is pink?

c. What fraction of the rings is green?

d. What fraction of the rings is either pink or green?

e. What fraction of the rings is either pink or blue?

f. What fraction of the rings is either green or blue?

13. In each set of the diagram, find what fraction of the rings is pink and what fraction of the rings is green? Hint: See Example 2.

a.

b.

c.

d.

e.

Answers to Selected Questions

6a. $\dfrac{2}{3}$ **7a.** $\dfrac{2}{3}$ **8a.** $\dfrac{1}{5}$ is blue, and $\dfrac{4}{5}$ is green   **9a.** $\dfrac{2}{5}$ **10a.** $\dfrac{2}{7}$

ADDITION OF FRACTIONS
ADDITION OF FRACTIONS THAT HAVE THE SAME DENOMINATORS

Rule: To add fractions that have the same denominators, add the numerators and put the sum or addition of the numerators over the same (common) denominator.

Example 1
Add the following:

(**a**) $\dfrac{1}{6} + \dfrac{2}{6} + \dfrac{1}{6}$ (**b**) $\dfrac{1}{7} + \dfrac{2}{7} + \dfrac{3}{7}$

Solution

(**a**) The numerators are 1, 2, and 1. The denominator of each fraction is 6.

Step 1: Add the numerators: $1 + 2 + 1 = 4$

Step 2: Put the addition (sum) of the numerators over the same denominator as shown: $\dfrac{4}{6}$

Step 3: Therefore, $\dfrac{1}{6} + \dfrac{2}{6} + \dfrac{1}{6} = \dfrac{4}{6}$

(**b**) The numerators are 1, 2, and 3. The denominator of each fraction is 7.

Step 1: Add the numerators: $1 + 2 + 3 = 6$

Step 2: Put the addition (sum) of the numerators over the same common denominator as shown: $\dfrac{6}{7}$

Step 3: Therefore, $\dfrac{1}{7} + \dfrac{2}{7} + \dfrac{3}{7} = \dfrac{6}{7}$

Example 2
Add the following:

(**a**) $\dfrac{2}{9} + \dfrac{1}{9} + \dfrac{4}{9} + \dfrac{3}{9} + \dfrac{5}{9}$ (**b**) $\dfrac{3}{12} + \dfrac{2}{12} + \dfrac{1}{12} + \dfrac{4}{12}$ (**c**) $\dfrac{3}{24} + \dfrac{2}{24} + \dfrac{4}{24} + \dfrac{5}{24}$

Solution
(**a**) The numerators are 2, 1, 4, 3, and 5. The denominator of each fraction is 9.
Step 1: Add the numerators: $2 + 1 + 4 + 3 + 5 = 15$
Step 2: Put the addition (sum) of the numerators over the same common denominator as shown: $\dfrac{15}{9}$.

Step 3: Therefore, $\dfrac{2}{9} + \dfrac{1}{9} + \dfrac{4}{9} + \dfrac{3}{9} + \dfrac{5}{9} = \dfrac{15}{9}$

This book will later discuss how to handle fractions such as how to reduce to the lowest terms and improper fractions.
(**b**) The numerators are 3, 2, 1, and 4. The denominator of each fraction is 12.
Step 1: Add the numerators: $3 + 2 + 1 + 4 = 10$
Step 2: Put the addition (sum) of the numerators over the same common denominator as shown: $\dfrac{10}{12}$

Step 3: Therefore, $\dfrac{3}{12} + \dfrac{2}{12} + \dfrac{1}{12} + \dfrac{4}{12} = \dfrac{10}{12}$

(**c**) The numerators are 3, 2, 4 and 5. The denominator of each fraction is 24.
Step 1: Add the numerators: $3 + 2 + 4 + 5 = 14$
Step 2: Put the addition (sum) of the numerators over the same common denominator as shown: $\dfrac{14}{24}$

Step 3: Therefore, $\dfrac{3}{24} + \dfrac{2}{24} + \dfrac{4}{24} + \dfrac{5}{24} = \dfrac{14}{24}$

REAL WORLD APPLICATIONS - WORD PROBLEMS
Addition of Fractions

Example 3

Eric needs $\dfrac{5}{12}$ foot, $\dfrac{7}{12}$ foot, $\dfrac{11}{12}$ foot, and $\dfrac{8}{12}$ foot of lumber to complete a project. How many feet of the lumber does Eric need?

Solution

The fractions of the lumber are $\dfrac{5}{12}, \dfrac{7}{12}, \dfrac{11}{12},$ and $\dfrac{8}{12}$.

Total feet of lumber needed $= \dfrac{5}{12} + \dfrac{7}{12} + \dfrac{11}{12} + \dfrac{8}{12}$

The numerators are 5, 7, 11, and 8. The denominator of each fraction is 12.

   Step 1: Add the numerators: $5 + 7 + 11 + 8 = 31$

   Step 2: Put the addition (sum) of the numerators over the same common

      denominator as shown: $\dfrac{31}{12}$

   Step 3: Therefore, the total feet of lumber needed

$$= \dfrac{5}{12} + \dfrac{7}{12} + \dfrac{11}{12} + \dfrac{8}{12} = \dfrac{31}{12} \text{ feet.}$$

Example 4

Nicholas bought the following weights of cheese: $\dfrac{6}{16}$ pound, $\dfrac{8}{16}$ pound, $\dfrac{9}{16}$ pound, and $\dfrac{11}{16}$ pound. What was the total weight of cheese that Nicholas bought?

Solution

The fractions of the cheese are:
$$\dfrac{6}{16}, \dfrac{8}{16}, \dfrac{9}{16}, \text{ and } \dfrac{11}{16}$$

The total weight of the cheese $= \dfrac{6}{16} + \dfrac{8}{16} + \dfrac{9}{16} + \dfrac{11}{16}$

The numerators are 6, 8, 9, and 11. The denominator of each fraction is 16.

Step 1: Add the numerators: $6 + 8 + 9 + 11 = 34$

Step 2: Put the addition (sum) of the numerators over the same common

denominator as shown: $\dfrac{34}{16}$

Step 3: Therefore, the total weight of the cheese = $\dfrac{6}{16} + \dfrac{8}{16} + \dfrac{9}{16} + \dfrac{11}{16} = \dfrac{34}{16}$

Critical Thinking

To add fractions is really finding out how many parts are there in all the fractions to be added. For example, in Example **2(c)**, **we are really finding out how many 24ths there are in all the fractions to be added.**

The notes and the generous worked examples have provided me with conceptual understanding and computational fluency to do my homework.

Exercises

Add the following. Hint: See Examples 1 and 2.

(1) $\dfrac{1}{4} + \dfrac{2}{4} + \dfrac{1}{4}$

(2) $\dfrac{1}{5} + \dfrac{3}{5}$

(3) $\dfrac{1}{8} + \dfrac{3}{8} + \dfrac{4}{8}$

(4) $\dfrac{3}{11} + \dfrac{4}{11} + \dfrac{1}{11} + \dfrac{2}{11}$

(5) $\dfrac{1}{10} + \dfrac{3}{10} + \dfrac{6}{10} + \dfrac{4}{10}$

(6) $\dfrac{4}{13} + \dfrac{2}{13} + \dfrac{4}{13} + \dfrac{5}{13}$

(7) $\dfrac{3}{17} + \dfrac{2}{17} + \dfrac{1}{17} + \dfrac{6}{17}$

(8) $\dfrac{5}{15} + \dfrac{1}{15} + \dfrac{4}{15} + \dfrac{3}{15}$

(9) $\dfrac{5}{16} + \dfrac{1}{16} + \dfrac{3}{16} + \dfrac{4}{16}$

(10) $\dfrac{7}{27} + \dfrac{6}{27}$

(11) $\dfrac{2}{31} + \dfrac{5}{31} + \dfrac{7}{31}$

(12) $\dfrac{10}{41} + \dfrac{6}{41} + \dfrac{8}{41}$

(13) $\dfrac{11}{45} + \dfrac{1}{45} + \dfrac{13}{45}$

(14) $\dfrac{7}{35} + \dfrac{2}{35} + \dfrac{10}{35}$

(15) $\dfrac{9}{40} + \dfrac{6}{40} + \dfrac{13}{40}$

(16) $\dfrac{3}{28} + \dfrac{4}{28} + \dfrac{6}{28}$

(17) $\dfrac{2}{9} + \dfrac{4}{9}$

(18) $\dfrac{4}{15} + \dfrac{7}{15}$

(19) Joshua needs $\dfrac{1}{6}$ foot, $\dfrac{2}{6}$ foot, $\dfrac{3}{6}$ foot, and $\dfrac{4}{6}$ foot of wood to complete his project. How many feet of wood does Joshua need? Hint: See Example **3**.

(20) Samuel bought $\dfrac{17}{36}$ yard, $\dfrac{28}{36}$ yard, $\dfrac{25}{36}$ yard, and $\dfrac{33}{36}$ yard of fabric for his school project. How many yards did Samuel buy? Hint: See Example **3**.

(21) Mary bought the following weights of cheese: $\dfrac{9}{16}$ pound, $\dfrac{5}{16}$ pound, $\dfrac{7}{16}$

pound, and $\frac{13}{16}$ pound. What was the total weight of cheese that Mary bought? Hint: See Example **4**.

(**20**) Rose made a cake for her friend. She mixed $\frac{3}{6}$ cup of milk, $\frac{3}{6}$ cup of sugar, $\frac{3}{6}$ cup of shortening, and $\frac{3}{6}$ cup of flour. How many cups did she mix? Hint: See Example 4.

Challenge Question

(**21**) Karen cut off the following pieces of wood: $\frac{4}{9}$ foot, $\frac{7}{9}$ foot, $\frac{5}{9}$ foot, and $\frac{8}{9}$ foot. How many feet of wood did she cut?

Answers to Selected Questions

(**1**) $\frac{4}{4} = 1$, (**19**) $\frac{10}{6} = 1\frac{4}{6} = 1\frac{2}{3}$ feet

TYPES OF FRACTIONS

New Terms
Proper fraction, improper fraction and **mixed fractions**

The three types of fractions are:
      1. **Proper fraction**
      2. **Improper fraction**
      3. **Mixed fraction**

A proper fraction is a fraction where the numerator is less than the denominator. Some examples of proper fractions are: $\frac{1}{2}, \frac{3}{4}, \frac{5}{12}, \frac{99}{100},$ and $\frac{199}{200}$.

An improper fraction is a fraction where the numerator is greater than the denominator. Some examples of improper fractions are: $\frac{7}{4}, \frac{8}{3}, \frac{11}{4}, \frac{12}{7},$ and $\frac{250}{199}$.

A mixed fraction contains both a whole number and a fractional part.

Some examples of mixed fractions are: $1\frac{1}{2}$, $2\frac{3}{4}$, $3\frac{4}{5}$, $4\frac{12}{13}$, and $5\frac{1}{6}$.

RAISING FRACTIONS AND LOWERING FRACTIONS

New term
Equivalent fractions

Equivalent fractions are fractions that have the same values or fractions that represent the same part of a whole.

Group Class Exercise
Divide the class into four groups. Each group should be given three pages of 11 x 8 paper, a ruler and a pencil.
Step 1: Each group should sketch a rectangle with dimensions of 8 inches by 4 inches.

A rectangle is a four sided figure as shown ➡

Label the rectangle ABCD. Let AB and DC be the lengths of the rectangle. Each group should mark point E between A and B such that E should be 4 inches from A. Mark point F between D and C so that F should be 4 inches from D. With a pencil and a ruler, draw a line from E to F.

Note that rectangle EBCF is $\frac{1}{2}$ of rectangle ABCD.

Step 2: Measure and mark the point G between A and E such that G is 2 inches from A. Measure and mark point H between D and F so that H is 2 inches from D. Use a pencil and a ruler to draw a line from G to H. Measure and mark point I between E and B so that I is 2 inches from E. Measure and mark point J between F and C so that J is 2 inches from F. Use a pencil and a ruler to draw a line from I to J. Note that rectangle ABCD is divided into 4 equal parts and rectangle EBCF is:

$$\frac{2}{4} \text{ of rectangle ABCD.}$$

Step 3: Measure and mark point K between A and D so that point K is 2 inches from A. Measure and mark point L between B and C so that L is 2 inches from B.

Use a pencil and a ruler to draw a line from K to L. Note that rectangle ABCD is divided into 8 equal parts and rectangle EBCF is:

$$\frac{4}{8} \text{ of rectangle ABCD.}$$

Summary:

Step 1: Shows that rectangle EBCF = $\frac{1}{2}$ of rectangle ABCD.

Step 2: Shows that rectangle EBCF = $\frac{2}{4}$ of rectangle ABCD.

Step 3: Shows that rectangle EBCF = $\frac{4}{8}$ of rectangle ABCD.

Conclusion: Rectangle EBCF = $\frac{1}{2} = \frac{2}{4} = \frac{4}{8}$ of rectangle ABCD, and these

fractions are known as **equivalent fractions**. Equivalent fractions are fractions that represent the same part of a whole.

How are Equivalent Fractions Obtained?

Rule 1: Equivalent fractions are obtained by multiplying both the denominator and the numerator by the same number.

For example, the fraction $\frac{1}{3}$ can be changed to $\frac{2}{6}$ by multiplying both the

numerator and the denominator by 2 as shown: $\frac{1}{3} = \frac{1}{3} \times \frac{2}{2} = \frac{2}{6}$

Critical Thinking

By multiplying both the numerator and the denominator by 2, we are actually multiplying $\frac{1}{3}$ by 1 because $\frac{2}{2} = 1$, and multiplying $\frac{1}{3}$ by a fraction of $\frac{2}{2}$ which is

equal to 1 does not change the value of $\frac{1}{3}$, but only changes the original

fraction to an equivalent fraction of $\frac{2}{6}$. When $\frac{1}{3}$ is changed to $\frac{2}{6}$ without changing

the value of $\frac{1}{3}$ is called raising $\frac{1}{3}$ to $\frac{2}{6}$, and the fraction with the bigger

denominator or numerator is called the higher equivalent. In this case, the higher

equivalent is $\frac{2}{6}$.

Rule 2: Multiplying both the numerator and the denominator by the same number will not change the value of the fraction.

Example 1

Raise $\frac{1}{5}$ to a higher equivalent that has a denominator of 20.

Solution

The problem can be written as: $\frac{1}{5} = \frac{?}{20}$

Using Rule 1, which states that equivalent fractions are obtained by multiplying both the denominator and the numerator by the same number, let us find what number is multiplied by the denominator 5 to obtain 20.

$$\frac{1}{5} = \frac{?}{20}$$

The denominator of 5 is multiplied by 4 to obtain a higher equivalent denominator of 20, and the numerator of 1 should also be multiplied by the same number 4 to obtain a higher equivalent numerator of 4 as shown:

$$\text{Therefore, } \frac{1}{5} = \frac{4}{20} \leftarrow \text{Higher equivalent fraction}$$

The higher equivalent $= \frac{4}{20}$, and this may also be obtained by simply multiplying the numerator and the denominator by 4 as shown:

$$\frac{1}{5} \times \frac{4}{4} = \frac{4}{20} \leftarrow \text{Higher equivalent fraction}$$

Example 2

Raise $\frac{2}{7}$ to a higher equivalent that has a numerator of 6.

Solution

The problem can be written as: $\frac{2}{7} = \frac{6}{?}$

Using Rule 1, let us find what number is multiplied by the numerator 2 to obtain the higher equivalent numerator of 6. The numerator 2 is multiplied by 3 to obtain the higher equivalent numerator of 6, and therefore, the denominator of 7 should also be multiplied by 3 to obtain the higher equivalent denominator of 21 as shown below:

$$\frac{2}{7} = \frac{6}{21} \leftarrow \text{Higher equivalent fraction}$$

The higher equivalent $= \frac{6}{21}$, and this may also be obtained simply by multiplying the numerator and the denominator of $\frac{2}{7}$ by 3 as shown:

$$\frac{2}{7} \times \frac{3}{3} = \frac{6}{21} \leftarrow \text{Higher equivalent fraction}$$

Example 3

Copy and complete to make a true statement:

(a) $\dfrac{2}{6} = \dfrac{10}{?}$ (b) $\dfrac{3}{?} = \dfrac{6}{8}$ (c) $\dfrac{?}{4} = \dfrac{12}{16}$

Solution

(a) Using Rule 1, let us find what number is multiplied by the numerator 2 to obtain the higher equivalent numerator of 10. The numerator 2 is multiplied by 5 to obtain the higher equivalent numerator of 10, and therefore, the denominator of 6 should also be multiplied by 5 to obtain the higher equivalent denominator of 30 as shown:

$$\frac{2}{6} = \frac{10}{30} \leftarrow \text{Higher equivalent fraction}$$

The higher equivalent fraction is $\dfrac{10}{30}$, and this can also be obtained simply by multiplying the denominator and the numerator by 5 as shown:

$$\frac{2}{6} \times \frac{5}{5} = \frac{10}{30} \leftarrow \text{Higher equivalent fraction}$$

(b) Let us find the number that is used to divide the numerator of 6 in order to obtain the lower equivalent numerator of 3. The numerator of 6 is divided by 2 in order to obtain the lower equivalent numerator of 3, and therefore, the denominator of 8 should also be divided by the same number 2 in order to obtain the lower equivalent denominator of 4 as shown:

$$\text{Lower equivalent fraction} \rightarrow \frac{3}{4} = \frac{6}{8}$$

The lower equivalent is $\dfrac{3}{4}$, and this can also be obtained by dividing the numerator and the denominator of the higher equivalent fraction of $\dfrac{6}{8}$ by 2 as shown:

$$\text{Lower equivalent fraction} \rightarrow \frac{3}{4} = \frac{6 \div 2}{8 \div 2}$$

(c) Let us find the number that is used to divide the higher equivalent denominator of 16 in order to obtain a lower equivalent denominator 4. The higher equivalent denominator of 16 is divided by 4 in order to obtain the lower equivalent denominator of 4, and therefore, the numerator of 12 should also be divided by the same number 4 to obtain the lower equivalent numerator of 3 as shown:

$$\text{Lower equivalent fraction} \rightarrow \frac{3}{4} = \frac{12}{16}$$

The lower equivalent fraction $= \frac{3}{4}$, and this can also be obtained simply by dividing

the numerator and the denominator of the higher equivalent of $\frac{12}{16}$ by 4 as shown:

$$\text{Lower equivalent fraction} \rightarrow \frac{3}{4} = \frac{12 \div 4}{16 \div 4}$$

Critical Thinking

1. Changing from any fraction to a higher equivalent fraction involves the multiplication of the numerator and the denominator by the same number.
2. Changing from any fraction to a lower equivalent fraction involves the division of the numerator and the denominator by the same number which is the same common factor. We will learn more about common factors later.

REAL WORLD APPLICATIONS - WORD PROBLEM
EQUIVALENT FRACTIONS
Example 4

Mary made a pizza and she cut it into 8 slices. If she ate $\frac{1}{4}$ of the pizza, how many

slices did she eat?
Solution
8 slices of pizza is the whole pizza. Therefore, the solution can be set up as shown:

$$\frac{1}{4} = \frac{?}{8}$$

Let us find the number which multiplied the lower equivalent denominator of 4 to obtain the higher equivalent denominator of 8. The lower equivalent denominator of 4 is multiplied by 2 in order to obtain the higher equivalent denominator of 8, therefore, the lower equivalent numerator of 1 should also be multiplied by the same number of 2 in order to obtain a higher equivalent numerator of 2 as shown:

$$\frac{1}{4} = \frac{2}{8} \searrow$$

This is the number of slices eaten by Mary.

Mary eats 2 slices of the pizza, and this can also be solved simply by multiplying the denominator and the numerator of the lower equivalent fraction of $\frac{1}{4}$ by 2 as shown:

$$\frac{1}{4} \times \frac{2}{2} = \frac{2}{8} \searrow$$

Mary ate 2 slices of the pizza.

_____

The notes and the generous worked examples have provided me with conceptual understanding and computational fluency to do my homework.

Exercise
1. What is meant by equivalent fractions?
2. How are equivalent fractions obtained?
3. Write the equivalence of $\frac{1}{4}$ by raising the denominator to 24. Hint: See Example 1.
4. Write the equivalence of $\frac{3}{7}$ by raising the numerator to 12. Hint: See Example 2.
5. Copy and complete to make a true statement. Hint: See Example 3.

(a) $\frac{2}{10} = \frac{?}{40}$ (b) $\frac{1}{8} = \frac{?}{32}$ (c) $\frac{6}{7} = \frac{36}{?}$ (d) $\frac{?}{27} = \frac{1}{3}$ (e) $\frac{5}{6} = \frac{25}{?}$

6. Raise $\frac{2}{3}$ to a higher equivalent fraction that has a denominator of 15. Hint: See Example 1.

7. Copy and complete to make true statements. Hint: See Example 3.

(a) $\frac{1}{6} = \frac{?}{12}$ (b) $\frac{2}{8} = \frac{?}{24}$ (c) $\frac{?}{36} = \frac{2}{6}$ (d) $\frac{4}{?} = \frac{12}{9}$

(e) $\frac{?}{14} = \frac{3}{7}$ (f) $\frac{5}{15} = \frac{1}{?}$ (g) $\frac{12}{?} = \frac{36}{9}$ (h) $\frac{?}{7} = \frac{15}{21}$

8. John made a pizza and cut it into 12 slices. If he ate $\frac{1}{4}$ of the pizza, how many slices did he eat? Hint: See Example 4.

7. In a class of 25 students, $\frac{2}{5}$ are girls. How many students are girls? Hint: The whole class has 25 students . Set up as shown: $\frac{2}{5} = \frac{?}{25}$, and then solve it.

Challenge Questions
8. Complete each pair of equivalent fractions.

(a) $\frac{1}{4} = \frac{?}{12}$ (b) $\frac{2}{?} = \frac{12}{18}$ (c) $\frac{3}{8} = \frac{?}{24}$

222

(d) $\dfrac{?}{21} = \dfrac{9}{7}$ (e) $\dfrac{5}{35} = \dfrac{15}{?}$ (f) $\dfrac{11}{77} = \dfrac{1}{?}$

(g) $\dfrac{24}{36} = \dfrac{6}{?}$ (h) $\dfrac{20}{60} = \dfrac{?}{120}$ (i) $\dfrac{?}{30} = \dfrac{8}{10}$

9. Write an equivalent fraction for each fraction below. You may choose to raise or lower the equivalent fraction.

(a) $\dfrac{1}{2}$ (b) $\dfrac{1}{3}$ (c) $\dfrac{2}{7}$ (d) $\dfrac{2}{5}$ (e) $\dfrac{7}{10}$

(f) $\dfrac{3}{7}$ (g) $\dfrac{6}{12}$ (h) $\dfrac{11}{22}$ (i) $\dfrac{24}{25}$ (j) $\dfrac{21}{34}$

Answers to Selected Questions

3. $\dfrac{6}{24}$ 5(a). 8   9(a). $\dfrac{1}{2} \times \dfrac{2}{2} = \dfrac{2}{4}$

MULTIPLES, LEAST COMMON MULTIPLE, COMMON DENOMINATORS, AND LEAST COMMON DENOMINATOR

1. MULTIPLES
The multiples of a whole number are the product of that number and any other whole number except zero.

Example 1
(a) What are the multiples of 5?
(b) What are the multiples of 3?
Solution:
(a) The multiples of 5 are: $5 \times 1 = 5$, $5 \times 2 = 10$, $5 \times 3 = 15$, $5 \times 4 = 20$, $5 \times 5 = 25$, . . .
    Therefore the multiples of 5 are: 5, 10, 15, 20, 25,...
(b) The multiples of 3 are: $3 \times 1 = 3$, $3 \times 2 = 6$, $3 \times 3 = 9$, $3 \times 4 = 12$, $3 \times 5 = 15$,
    $3 \times 6 = 18$, $3 \times 7 = 21$, ...
    Therefore, the multiples of 3 are: 3, 6, 9, 12, 15, 18, 21, . . .

2. LEAST COMMON MULTIPLES.
Rule 1: The least common multiple (LCM) of two or more numbers is the least or the smallest multiple that is common to all the numbers.

Rule 2: The least common multiple (LCM) of two or more numbers can be found by listing the multiples of each number in order from the smallest to the greatest until a multiple that is common to all the numbers is obtained.

Example 2
What is the least common multiple (LCM) of 3 and 4?
Solution
The multiples of 3 are: $3 \times 1 = 3$
$3 \times 2 = 6$
$3 \times 3 = 9$
$3 \times 4 = 12 \rightarrow (LCM)$
$3 \times 5 = 15$
$3 \times 6 = 18$

Therefore, the multiples of 3 are: 3, 6, 9, 12, 15, 18, . . .

The multiples of 4 are: $4 \times 1 = 4$
$4 \times 2 = 8$
$4 \times 3 = 12 \rightarrow$ Stop here because 12 also appears as a multiple of 3, and 12 is therefore the least common multiple of 3 and 4.

Therefore, the multiples of 4 are: 4, 8, 12, . . .
↑
LCM

The LCM = 12
Note that Rule 2 is used in solving this problem.

Example 3
What is the least common multiple of 4 and 6?
Solution
The multiples of 4 are: $4 \times 1 = 4, 4 \times 2 = 8, 4 \times 3 = 12, 4 \times 4 = 16, 4 \times 5 = 20, . . .$
Therefore, the multiples of 4 are: 4, 8, 12, 16, 20, . . .
The multiples of 6 are: $6 \times 1 = 6, 6 \times 2 = 12, . . .$
↑
Stop here because 12 also appears as a multiple of 4 and therefore, 12 is the least common multiple (LCM) of 4 and 6.

The LCM = 12
Note that Rule 2 is used in solving this problem.

Example 4
Find the least common multiple (LCM) of 6 and 7.

Solution

The multiples of 6 are: 6 × 1 = 6, 6 × 2 = 12, 6 × 3 = 18, 6 × 4 = 24, 6 × 5 = 30,

6 × 6 = 36, 6 × 7 = 42, 6 x 8 = 48, . . .

The multiples of 6 are: 6, 12, 18, 24, 30, 36, 42, 48, . . .

The multiples of 7 are: 7 × 1 = 7, 7 × 2 = 14, 7 × 3 = 21, 7 × 4 = 28, 7 × 5 = 35,

7 × 6 = 42

↑

Stop here because 42 also appears as a multiple
of 6 and so, 42 is the least common multiple
of 6 and 7.

The LCM is 42

Note that Rule 2 is used to solve this problem.

Example 5

Given that the multiples of 4 are: 4, 8, 12, 16, 20, 24, 28, 32, . . . and given that
the multiples of 6 are: 6, 12, 18, 24, 30, 36, . . ., explain why although 24 is
a common multiple of 4 and 6, 24 is not the least common multiple (LCM) of 4
and 6.

Solution

The multiples of 4 are: 4, 8, 12, 16, 20, 24, 28, 32, . . .

The multiples of 6 are: 6, 12, 18, 24, 30, 36, . . .

By observing the multiples of 4 and 6 above, 24 appears as one of the multiples of
4 and 6. It can also be observed that 12 is one of the multiples of 4 and 6 but 12 is
the smallest number that is the multiple of both 4 and 6 and therefore, 12 is the
least common multiple (LCM) of 4 and 6 and 24 is just one of the common
multiples of 4 and 6.

Example 6

Find the least common multiple of 6, 9, and 12.

Solution

The multiples of 6 are: 6 × 1= 6, 6 × 2 = 12, 6 × 3 = 18, 6 × 4 = 24, 6 × 5 = 30,

6 × 6 = 36, 6 × 7 = 42, . . .

The multiples of 9 are: 9 × 1 = 9, 9 × 2 = 18, 9 × 3 = 27, 9 × 4 = 36,

↑

Stop here because 36 is also one of
the multiples of 6.

The multiples of 12 are: 12 × 1 = 12, 12 × 2 = 24, 12 × 3 = 36,

↑

Stop here because 36 is also one of the multiples
of 6 and 9. Since 36 is the smallest multiple which
is common to 6, 9, and 12, 36 is the least common
multiple (LCM) of 6, 9, and 12.

The LCM is 36.

The notes and the generous worked examples have provided me with conceptual understanding and computational fluency to do my homework.

Exercises

1. Explain what is meant by a multiple of a number?
2. List the first eight multiples of each number. Hint: See Examples **1** and **2**.
   (**a**) 5   (**b**) 8   (**c**) 9   (**d**) 4   (**e**) 10   (**f**) 11   (**g**) 12
3. Explain what is meant by the least common multiple of two or more numbers?
4. Find the least common multiple of each set of numbers. Hint: See Examples **2, 3** and **4**.
   (**a**) 2 and 7   (**b**) 3 and 7   (**c**) 4 and 7   (**d**) 5 and 7   (**e**) 6 and 8

   (**f**) 7 and 8   (**g**) 5 and 9   (**h**) 7 and 9   (**i**) 12 and 8   (**j**) 12 and 48

   (**k**) 10 and 7   (**l**) 11 and 4   (**m**) 13 and 4   (**n**) 7 and 4   (**o**) 5 and 7
5. Given that the multiples of 5 are: 5, 10, 15, 20, 25, 30, 35, 40, 45, 50, 55, 60, . . ., and the multiples of 6 are: 6, 12, 18, 24, 30, 36, 42, 48, 54, 60, . . . , explain why 60 cannot be the least common multiple (LCM) of 5 and 6. Hint: See Example **5**.
6. Find the least common multiple (LCM) of each set of numbers. Hint: See Example **6**.
   (**a**) 3, 4, and 6   (**b**) 4, 8, and 24   (**c**) 3, 5, and 6   (**d**) 3, 11, and 33

   (**e**) 4, 7, and 14   (**f**) 9, 4, and 6   (**g**) 6, 9, and 4   (**h**) 6, 5, and 4.
7. Explain the difference between the common multiples of two or more numbers and the least common multiple of two or more numbers. Hint: See Example **5**.

3. COMMON DENOMINATORS

A common denominator is when two or more fractions have the same denominator.

Considering the fractions $\frac{1}{12}$, $\frac{5}{12}$, $\frac{7}{12}$, and $\frac{11}{12}$, the denominator 12 is common to all

the fractions of $\frac{1}{12}$, $\frac{5}{12}$, $\frac{7}{12}$, and $\frac{11}{12}$, and therefore, the common denominator is 12.

The **usefulness of the common denominator** will be discussed fully under comparing fractions.

4. LEAST COMMON DENOMINATOR

The least common denominator of two or more fractions is the least common

multiple (LCM) of their denominators. Hint: Review the topic under the Least Common Multiple (LCM) to fully understand the least common multiple (LCM) of numbers.

Example 1

Find the least common denominator of $\dfrac{1}{3}$ and $\dfrac{2}{7}$.

Solution

The denominators of $\dfrac{1}{3}$ and $\dfrac{2}{7}$ are 3 and 7.

The multiples of 3 are: $3 \times 1 = 3$, $3 \times 2 = 6$, $3 \times 3 = 9$, $3 \times 4 = 12$, $3 \times 5 = 15$, $3 \times 6 = 18$, $3 \times 7 = 21$, $3 \times 8 = 24$, . . .

Therefore, the multiples of 3 are: 3, 6, 9, 12, 15, 18, 21, 24, . . .

The multiples of 7 are: $7 \times 1 = 7$, $7 \times 2 = 14$, $7 \times 3 = 21$, . . .

Stop here because 21 is the smallest number which also appears as a multiple of 3. Therefore, 21 is the least common denominator of $\dfrac{1}{3}$ and $\dfrac{2}{7}$.

Example 2

Find the least common denominator of $\dfrac{2}{5}$ and $\dfrac{7}{9}$.

Solution

The denominators of $\dfrac{2}{5}$ and $\dfrac{7}{9}$ are 5 and 9 .

The multiples of 5 are: $5 \times 1 = 5$, $5 \times 2 = 10$, $5 \times 3 = 15$, $5 \times 4 = 20$, $5 \times 5 = 25$, $5 \times 6 = 30$, $5 \times 7 = 35$, $5 \times 8 = 40$, $5 \times 9 = 45$, $5 \times 10 = 50$, . . .

Therefore, the multiples of 5 are: 5, 10, 15, 20, 25, 30, 35, 40, 45, 50, . . .

The multiples of 9 are: $9 \times 1 = 9$, $9 \times 2 = 18$, $9 \times 3 = 27$, $9 \times 4 = 36$, $9 \times 5 = 45$, . . .

Stop here because 45 is the smallest number which also appears as a multiple of 5. Therefore, 45 is the least common denominator of $\dfrac{2}{5}$ and $\dfrac{7}{9}$.

Example 3

Find the least common denominator of $\dfrac{2}{3}$, $\dfrac{3}{4}$, and $\dfrac{5}{9}$.

Solution

The denominators of $\frac{2}{3}$, $\frac{3}{4}$, and $\frac{5}{9}$ are 3, 4 and 9.

The multiples of 3 are: $3 \times 1 = 3$, $3 \times 2 = 6$, $3 \times 3 = 9$, $3 \times 4 = 12$, $3 \times 5 = 15$,

$\qquad$ $3 \times 6 = 18$, $3 \times 7 = 21$, $3 \times 8 = 24$, $3 \times 9 = 27$, $3 \times 10 = 30$,

$\qquad$ $3 \times 11 = 33$, $3 \times 12 = 36$, $3 \times 13 = 39$, . . .

Therefore the multiples of 3 are: 3, 6, 9, 12, 15, 18, 24, 27, 30, 33, (36), 39, . . .

The multiples of 4 are: $4 \times 1 = 4$, $4 \times 2 = 8$, $4 \times 3 = 12$, $4 \times 4 = 16$, $4 \times 5 = 20$,

$\qquad$ $4 \times 6 = 24$, $4 \times 7 = 28$, $4 \times 8 = 32$, $4 \times 9 = 36$, . . .

$\qquad$ $\uparrow$

Stop here because 36 is the smallest number that also appears as a multiple of 3 and the third denominator which is 9 can divide 36 evenly (without a remainder). Note also that 12 and 24 appear as multiples of both 3 and 4 but we cannot choose neither 12 nor 24 as the least common multiple of 3, 4 and 9 because 9 cannot divide neither 12 nor 24 evenly (without a remainder). Note that 12 and 24 are not multiples of 9. Therefore, the least common multiple of 3, 4, and 9 is 36 and the least common denominator of $\frac{2}{3}$, $\frac{3}{4}$,

and $\frac{5}{9}$ is 36.

Note 1: The best common denominator is the LCM of the denominator.

Note 2: Knowing the multiplication tables from 1 to 12 is very helpful in detecting quickly that $9 \times 4 = 36$ or 9 can divide into 36 evenly (without a remainder).

The notes and the generous worked examples have provided me with conceptual understanding and computational fluency to do my homework.

Exercises

1. What is the best common denominator?
2. Explain why knowing the multiplication tables from 1 to 12 is very helpful in determining the LCM and the LCD.
3. List the multiplication tables that you know.
4. Explain what is meant by the least common denominator (LCD).
5. Explain what is meant by the least common multiple (LCM).
6. Find the least common denominator of the following: Hint: See Examples **1** and **2**.

$\qquad$ **(a)** $\frac{1}{3}$ and $\frac{2}{5}$ $\qquad$ **(b)** $\frac{3}{4}$ and $\frac{5}{6}$ $\qquad$ **(c)** $\frac{1}{2}$ and $\frac{2}{5}$ $\qquad$ **(d)** $\frac{2}{3}$ and $\frac{1}{7}$

(e) $\dfrac{2}{7}$ and $\dfrac{2}{5}$ (f) $\dfrac{1}{4}$ and $\dfrac{3}{7}$ (g) $\dfrac{3}{5}$ and $\dfrac{3}{7}$ (h) $\dfrac{2}{3}$ and $\dfrac{5}{8}$

(i) $\dfrac{5}{8}$ and $\dfrac{5}{7}$ (j) $\dfrac{5}{6}$ and $\dfrac{5}{7}$ (k) $\dfrac{5}{6}$ and $\dfrac{5}{9}$ (l) $\dfrac{2}{9}$ and $\dfrac{5}{12}$

(m) $\dfrac{4}{9}$ and $\dfrac{1}{4}$ (n) $\dfrac{5}{7}$ and $\dfrac{4}{9}$ (o) $\dfrac{2}{11}$ and $\dfrac{7}{12}$ (p) $\dfrac{2}{3}$ and $\dfrac{3}{8}$

7. Find the least common denominator of the following. Hint: See Examples **1**, **2**, and **3**.

(a) $\dfrac{2}{3}$, $\dfrac{1}{4}$, and $\dfrac{1}{2}$ (b) $\dfrac{3}{4}$, $\dfrac{1}{5}$, and $\dfrac{3}{10}$ (c) $\dfrac{1}{3}$, $\dfrac{2}{7}$, and $\dfrac{2}{21}$

(d) $\dfrac{3}{4}$, $\dfrac{5}{6}$, and $\dfrac{1}{2}$ (e) $\dfrac{2}{7}$, $\dfrac{2}{9}$, and $\dfrac{2}{3}$ (f) $\dfrac{5}{6}$, $\dfrac{1}{3}$, and $\dfrac{5}{8}$

(g) $\dfrac{2}{9}$, $\dfrac{1}{6}$, and $\dfrac{1}{4}$ (h) $\dfrac{3}{5}$, $\dfrac{1}{2}$, and $\dfrac{3}{4}$ (i) $\dfrac{7}{8}$, $\dfrac{2}{9}$, and $\dfrac{1}{6}$

ADDITION OF FRACTIONS THAT HAVE UNLIKE DENOMINATORS

Rule 1

In order to add fractions, follow these three steps:

Step 1: First find a common denominator.

Step 2: Change each given fraction to an equivalent fraction that has the same denominator.

Step 3: Add the numerators of the equivalent fractions and write the sum of the numerators of the equivalent fraction over the common equivalent denominator.

Note: The larger or largest denominator in the question can be used as the equivalent common denominator which is the same as the least common denominator.

Example 1

Find $\dfrac{1}{2} + \dfrac{1}{4}$

Solution

Step 1: Find the common denominator. The common denominator is 4 because the denominator of $\dfrac{1}{2}$ which is 2 can divide evenly into the denominator of $\dfrac{1}{4}$ which is 4 (without a remainder). This is an example where the larger or largest denominator in the question can at times be used as the equivalent common denominator which is the same as the least common denominator.

$$\dfrac{1}{2} = \dfrac{?}{4} \quad \diagup \text{Equivalent common denominator}$$

$$\dfrac{1}{4} = \dfrac{1}{4} \quad \diagup \text{Equivalent common denominator}$$

Step 2: Write an equivalent fraction for $\dfrac{1}{2}$ by multiplying $\dfrac{1}{2}$ by $\dfrac{2}{2}$ as shown:

$$\dfrac{1}{2} \times \dfrac{2}{2} = \dfrac{2}{4} \rightarrow \text{Equivalent fraction.}$$

$$\dfrac{1}{4} \times \dfrac{1}{1} = \dfrac{1}{4} \rightarrow \text{Equivalent fraction.}$$

We do not need to find the equivalent of $\dfrac{1}{4}$ because the denominator of 4 is already being used as the equivalent common denominator. Now, $\dfrac{2}{4}$ and $\dfrac{1}{4}$ have a common denominator of 4.

Step 3: Add the numerators of the equivalent fractions and write the sum of the numerators over the common denominator.

$$\dfrac{2+1}{4} = \dfrac{3}{4} \quad \begin{array}{l} \diagup \text{Sum of the equivalent numerators} \\ \diagup \text{Common equivalent denominator (LCD).} \end{array}$$

Therefore, $\dfrac{1}{2} + \dfrac{1}{4} = \dfrac{3}{4}$

Example 2

Find $\dfrac{2}{3} + \dfrac{1}{4}$

Solution

Step 1: Find the least common denominator. Review the section on Least Common Denominator. The denominators are 3 and 4, but in this case, 4 cannot be the common factor because 3 cannot divide into 4 evenly (without a remainder). In this case, the least common denominator (LCD) is $3 \times 4 = 12$. Note that both 3 and 4 can divide into 12 evenly (without a remainder).

$$\frac{2}{3} = \frac{?}{12} \text{ ✓ Least common denominator.}$$

$$\frac{1}{4} = \frac{?}{12} \text{ ✓ Least common denominator.}$$

Step 2: Write equivalent fractions. Hint: Refer to the section on Equivalent Fractions.

$$\frac{2}{3} = \frac{2}{3} \times \frac{4}{4} = \frac{8}{12} \leftarrow \text{ Equivalent fraction.}$$

$$\frac{1}{4} = \frac{1}{4} \times \frac{3}{3} = \frac{3}{12} \leftarrow \text{ Equivalent fraction.}$$

Now, $\dfrac{8}{12}$ and $\dfrac{3}{12}$ have a common denominator of 12.

Step 3: Add the numerators of the equivalent fractions and write the sum of the numerators over the equivalent common denominator.

$$\frac{8 + 3}{12} = \frac{11}{12}$$

↗ Sum of the numerators of the equivalent fractions

↘ Common equivalent denominator (LCD).

Therefore, $\dfrac{2}{3} + \dfrac{1}{4} = \dfrac{11}{12}$

Example 3

Find $\dfrac{2}{5} + \dfrac{3}{7}$

Solution

Step 1: Find the least common denominator. Refer to the Least Common Denominator section. The denominators are 5 and 7, but in this case, 5 cannot divide evenly into seven (without a remainder). In this case, the common denominator is $5 \times 7 = 35$.
Note that both 5 and 7 can divide evenly into 35 (without a remainder).

$$\frac{2}{5} = \frac{?}{35} \quad \text{✓Least common denominator.}$$

$$\frac{3}{7} = \frac{?}{35} \quad \text{✓Least common denominator.}$$

Step 2: Write equivalent fractions. Hint: Refer to the section on Equivalent Fractions.

$$\frac{2}{5} \times \frac{7}{7} = \frac{14}{35} \quad \leftarrow \text{Equivalent fraction}$$

$$\frac{3}{7} \times \frac{5}{5} = \frac{15}{35} \quad \leftarrow \text{Equivalent fraction}$$

Now, $\dfrac{14}{35}$ and $\dfrac{15}{35}$ have a common denominator of 35.

Step 3: Add the numerators of the equivalent fractions and write the sum of the numerators over the common denominator.

$$\frac{14 + 15}{35} = \frac{29}{35}$$

✓Sum of the numerators of the equivalent fractions

↘Common equivalent denominator (LCD)

Therefore, $\dfrac{2}{5} + \dfrac{3}{7} = \dfrac{29}{35}$

Example 4

Find $\dfrac{3}{5} + \dfrac{2}{25}$

Solution

Step 1: Find the least common denominator. Review the section on Least Common Denominators. The denominators are 5 and 25. In this case, 5 can divide into 25 evenly (without any remainder), and therefore, the least common denominator is 25. Note that both 5 and 25 can divide evenly into 25 (without any remainder).

$$\frac{3}{5} = \frac{?}{25} \quad \text{✓Least common denominator}$$

$$\frac{2}{25} = \frac{?}{25} \quad \text{✓Least common denominator}$$

Step 2: Write the equivalent fractions. Hint: Review the section on Equivalent Fractions.

$$\frac{3}{5} \times \frac{5}{5} = \frac{15}{25} \leftarrow \text{Equivalent fraction}$$

$$\frac{2}{25} \times \frac{1}{1} = \frac{2}{25} \leftarrow \text{Equivalent fraction}$$

We do not have to write an equivalent fraction for $\frac{2}{25}$ because the denominator of 25 is already the common equivalent denominator for $\frac{3}{5}$.

Now, $\frac{15}{25}$ and $\frac{2}{25}$ have a common denominator of 25.

Step 3: Add the numerators of the equivalent fractions and write the sum of the numerators of the equivalent fraction over the equivalent common denominator.

$$\frac{15 + 2}{25} = \frac{17}{25} \quad \overset{\text{Sum of the numerators of equivalent fractions}}{}$$

$$\searrow \text{Common equivalent denominator (LCD)}$$

Therefore, $\dfrac{3}{5} + \dfrac{2}{25} = \dfrac{17}{25}$

Example 5

Find $\dfrac{2}{3} + \dfrac{2}{4} + \dfrac{2}{6}$

Solution

Step 1: Find the least common denominator. Review the section on the Least Common Denominator. The denominators are 3, 4, and 6. Although 3 can divide into 6 evenly (without a remainder), 4 cannot divide into 6 evenly (without a remainder), and therefore, 6 cannot be the common denominator. Look for the least number that can be divided by 3, 4, and 6 evenly (without a remainder) and that number is 12. Therefore, the common denominator is 12.

$$\frac{2}{3} = \frac{?}{12} \quad \diagup \text{Least common denominator}$$

$$\frac{2}{4} = \frac{?}{12} \quad \diagup \text{Least common denominator}$$

$$\frac{2}{6} = \frac{?}{12} \quad \diagup \text{Least common denominator}$$

Step 2: Write the equivalent fractions. Hint: Review the section on Equivalent fractions.

$$\frac{2}{3} \times \frac{4}{4} = \frac{8}{12} \leftarrow \text{Equivalent fraction}$$

$$\frac{2}{4} \times \frac{3}{3} = \frac{6}{12} \leftarrow \text{Equivalent fraction}$$

$$\frac{2}{6} \times \frac{2}{2} = \frac{4}{12} \leftarrow \text{Equivalent fraction}$$

Step 3: Add the numerators of the equivalent fractions and then write the sum of the numerators of the equivalent fractions over the equivalent common denominator.

$$\diagup \text{Sum of the numerators of the equivalent fractions.}$$

$$\frac{8+6+4}{12} = \frac{18}{12}$$

$$\diagdown \text{Common equivalent denominator (LCD).}$$

Therefore, $\dfrac{2}{4} + \dfrac{2}{6} = \dfrac{18}{12}$

The notes and the generous worked examples have provided me with conceptual understanding and computational fluency to do my homework.

Exercises
1. Find the sum. Hint: See Examples **1** and **4**.

a. $\dfrac{3}{10} + \dfrac{1}{5}$ **b.** $\dfrac{1}{4} + \dfrac{5}{16}$ **c.** $\dfrac{1}{3} + \dfrac{2}{9}$ **d.** $\dfrac{2}{4} + \dfrac{1}{8}$

2. Find the sum. Hint: See Examples **2** and **3**.

a. $\dfrac{3}{4} + \dfrac{1}{6}$ **b.** $\dfrac{2}{7} + \dfrac{1}{2}$ **c.** $\dfrac{1}{3} + \dfrac{2}{4}$ **d.** $\dfrac{2}{6} + \dfrac{3}{10}$

3. Find the sum. Hint: See Example **5**.

a. $\dfrac{3}{5} + \dfrac{1}{3} + \dfrac{2}{15}$ **b.** $\dfrac{1}{2} + \dfrac{3}{4} + \dfrac{2}{3}$ **c.** $\dfrac{1}{4} + \dfrac{3}{5} + \dfrac{3}{10}$ **d.** $\dfrac{3}{4} + \dfrac{1}{2} + \dfrac{5}{6}$

Challenge Questions

Find the sum.

4. $\dfrac{3}{4} + \dfrac{2}{3}$ **5.** $\dfrac{3}{5} + \dfrac{4}{3} + \dfrac{7}{30}$ **6.** $\dfrac{5}{18} + \dfrac{5}{6} + \dfrac{2}{3}$ **7.** $\dfrac{2}{7} + \dfrac{2}{3} + \dfrac{1}{21}$

Answers to Selected Questions

1a. $\dfrac{5}{10}$ or $\dfrac{1}{2}$ **2a.** $\dfrac{11}{12}$

REAL WORLD APPLICATIONS - WORD PROBLEMS
Addition of Fractions That Have Unlike Denominators

Example 6

Mary walked $\dfrac{3}{4}$ mile to the market and $\dfrac{1}{3}$ mile to school. How many miles did she walk?

Solution

Total miles walked $= \dfrac{3}{4} + \dfrac{1}{3}$

Step 1: Find the least common denominator. Review the section on Least Common Denominator. The denominators are 4 and 3. In this case, since 3 cannot divide into 4 evenly (without a remainder), 4 cannot be the common denominator. The least common denominator is $3 \times 4 = 12$. Note that the least number that both 4 and 3 can divide into evenly (without a remainder) is 12.

$$\dfrac{3}{4} = \dfrac{?}{12} \nearrow \text{Least common denominator}$$

$$\dfrac{1}{3} = \dfrac{?}{12} \nearrow \text{Least common denominator}$$

Step 2: Write equivalent fractions. Refer to the section under Equivalent Fractions.

$$\dfrac{3}{4} = \dfrac{3}{4} \times \dfrac{3}{3} = \dfrac{9}{12} \leftarrow \text{Equivalent fraction}$$

$$\dfrac{1}{3} = \dfrac{1}{3} \times \dfrac{4}{4} = \dfrac{4}{12} \leftarrow \text{Equivalent fraction}$$

Step 3: Add the numerators of the equivalent fractions and write the sum of the numerators of the equivalent fractions over the equivalent common denominator of 12.

$$\frac{9 + 4}{12} = \frac{13}{12}$$ ╱Sum of the numerators of the equivalent fractions

╱Equivalent common fraction (LCD)

Example 7

John needs $\frac{3}{8}$ yard, $\frac{1}{3}$ yard and $\frac{1}{6}$ yard of wood to do a school project. How many yards of wood is needed for the project?

Solution

Total yards needed for the project $= \frac{3}{8} + \frac{1}{3} + \frac{1}{6}$

Step 1: Find the least common denominator.

The denominators are 8, 3, and 6. The least common denominator (LCD) or the lowest number that can be divided by denominators 8, 3, and 6 evenly (without a remainder) is 24. Example: $8 \times 3 = 24$ and $6 \times 4 = 24$. Notice also that 8 is the largest denominator but 3 and 6 cannot divide into 8 evenly (without a reminder) and therefore the LCD is 24.

$$\frac{3}{8} = \frac{?}{24}$$ ╱ least common denominator

$$\frac{1}{3} = \frac{?}{24}$$ ╱ least common denominator

$$\frac{1}{6} = \frac{?}{24}$$ ╱least common denominator

Step 2: Write equivalent fractions. Review the section under Equivalent Fractions.

$$\frac{3}{8} \times \frac{3}{3} = \frac{9}{24} \leftarrow \text{Equivalent fraction.}$$

$$\frac{1}{3} \times \frac{8}{8} = \frac{8}{24} \leftarrow \text{Equivalent fraction.}$$

$$\frac{1}{6} \times \frac{4}{4} = \frac{4}{24} \leftarrow \text{Equivalent fraction.}$$

Step 3: Add the numerators of the equivalent fractions and write the sum of the numerators of the equivalent fractions over the equivalent common denominator as shown:

Sum of the numerators of the equivalent fractions.

$$\frac{9+8+4}{24} = \frac{21}{24}$$

Equivalent common denominator which is the same as the LCD.

The notes and the generous worked examples have provided me with conceptual understanding and computational fluency to do my homework.

Exercises

(**1**) John needs the following pieces of lumber to finish a project: $\frac{5}{7}$ foot, $\frac{3}{14}$ foot,

and $\frac{3}{7}$ foot. How many feet of lumber does he need? Hint: See Example **6**.

(**2**) Rose walked $\frac{3}{8}$ mile to the library, $\frac{3}{4}$ mile to school. How many miles did she

walk altogether? Hint: See Example **6**.

(**3**) Jane walked $\frac{3}{4}$ mile to school, $\frac{1}{6}$ mile to the market, and $\frac{2}{3}$ mile to the football

game. How many miles did she walk altogether? Hint: See Example **7**.

(**4**) A class needs the following lengths of fabric for an experiment: $\frac{2}{5}$ foot, $\frac{3}{10}$ foot,

and $\frac{17}{20}$ foot. How many feet of fabric are needed altogether? Hint: see Example 7.

Challenge Questions

(**5**) Nick would like to bake a cake by adding $\frac{3}{5}$ cup of milk, $\frac{2}{3}$ cup of chocolate, $\frac{1}{2}$

cup of flour, and $\frac{1}{4}$ cup of sugar. How many cups would he need? Hint: Review

how to find LCD.

Perform the following operations:

(**6**) $\frac{9}{16} + \frac{3}{8}$ (**7**) $\frac{15}{16} + \frac{1}{4}$ (**8**) $\frac{5}{7} + \frac{3}{14}$ (**9**) $\frac{5}{6} + \frac{1}{3}$ (**10**) $\frac{17}{21} + \frac{2}{7}$

(**11**) $\frac{3}{4} + \frac{2}{3}$ (**12**) $\frac{2}{3} + \frac{2}{9}$ (**13**) $\frac{2}{9} + \frac{7}{18}$ (**14**) $\frac{1}{5} + \frac{7}{15}$ (**15**) $\frac{2}{3} + \frac{1}{3}$

(16) $\dfrac{9}{28} + \dfrac{2}{7}$ **(17)** $\dfrac{3}{20} + \dfrac{2}{5}$ **(18)** $\dfrac{1}{5} + \dfrac{2}{10} + \dfrac{3}{20}$ **(19)** $\dfrac{2}{5} + \dfrac{3}{30} + \dfrac{11}{20}$

(20) $\dfrac{4}{5} + \dfrac{3}{20} + \dfrac{13}{20}$ **(21)** $\dfrac{3}{8} + \dfrac{3}{16} + \dfrac{7}{32}$ **(22)** $\dfrac{3}{4} + \dfrac{3}{8} + \dfrac{1}{5}$ **(23)** $\dfrac{3}{8} + \dfrac{2}{5}$

(24) $\dfrac{1}{3} + \dfrac{3}{8} + \dfrac{5}{12}$ **(25)** $\dfrac{1}{6} + \dfrac{2}{3} + \dfrac{5}{8}$ **(26)** $\dfrac{2}{7} + \dfrac{1}{4} + \dfrac{3}{14}$ **(27)** $\dfrac{5}{7} + \dfrac{3}{4}$

Answers to Selected Questions

1. $\dfrac{19}{14}$ **3.** $\dfrac{19}{12}$ **6.** $\dfrac{15}{16}$ **9.** $\dfrac{7}{6}$

(**Note**: We will learn how to change fractions to mixed fractions later.)

ADDITION OF MIXED FRACTIONS

Types of fractions are:
Proper fraction
Improper fraction
Mixed fraction

A proper fraction is a fraction that has a numerator which is less than the denominator.

Examples of proper fractions are: $\dfrac{1}{4}$, $\dfrac{2}{4}$, $\dfrac{2}{3}$, and $\dfrac{14}{15}$.

An improper fraction is a fraction that has a numerator which is greater than the denominator.

Examples of improper fractions are: $\dfrac{4}{3}$, $\dfrac{12}{9}$, $\dfrac{15}{12}$, and $\dfrac{38}{25}$.

A mixed fraction is a fraction that contains both a whole number and a fraction.
Examples of mixed fractions are:

whole number ↘   ↙ fraction
$$1\dfrac{1}{2}, \quad 2\dfrac{2}{5}, \quad 5\dfrac{7}{9}, \text{ and } 11\dfrac{7}{8}.$$

As stated above, a mixed fraction is a fraction that contains both a whole number and a fraction, and therefore, mixed fractions are added up in three steps as shown:

Step 1 : Add the whole numbers.
Step 2 : Add the fractions.
Step 3 : Combine the sum (addition) of the whole numbers in step 1 and the sum (addition) of the fractions in step 2 into a final sum.

Example 1

Add: $2\dfrac{1}{3} + 1\dfrac{1}{6}$

Solution

(**Notice** that in Step 1, an imaginary line | separates the whole numbers from the fractions so that we can work on the whole numbers and the fractions separately.)

Step 1: Add the whole numbers first.

$\downarrow$

Step 2: Add the fractions second.
(Review Addition of Fractions)
In order to add fractions, find the LCD.
$\swarrow$ Write equivalent fractions,
Determine LCD. and then add the fractions.

$$2|\ \frac{1}{3}$$
$$1|\ \frac{1}{6}$$
$$\overline{3}$$

$$2|\ \frac{1}{3} = \frac{}{6}\ \diagup LCD$$
$$1|\ \frac{1}{6} = \frac{}{6}\ \diagup LCD$$
$$\overline{3}$$

$$2|\ \frac{1}{3} \times \frac{2}{2} = \frac{2}{6}$$
$$1|\ \frac{1}{6} \times \frac{1}{1} = \frac{1}{6}$$
$$\overline{3} \qquad \overline{\dfrac{3}{6}}$$

addition of whole numbers

addition of fractions.

Step 2: Combine the sum (addition) of the whole numbers in Step 1 and the sum (addition) of the fractions in Step 2, into a final sum as shown:

From Step 1 $\diagup 3 + \dfrac{3}{6} = 3\dfrac{3}{6}$
$\diagup$ $\diagdown$Final sum
From Step 2

Example 2

Add: $4\dfrac{2}{3} + 10\dfrac{1}{4}$

Solution

(**Notice** that in Step 1, an imaginary line | separates the whole numbers from the fractions so that we can work on the whole numbers and the fractions separately.)

Step 1: Add the whole numbers first.

$\downarrow$

Step 2: Add fractions second.
(Review Addition of Fractions)
In order to add fractions, find the LCD.

Determine LCD.

Write equivalent fractions, and then add the fractions.

$$4\,|\ \dfrac{2}{3}$$
$$10\,|\ \dfrac{1}{4}$$
$$\overline{14}$$

Addition of whole numbers

$$4\,|\ \dfrac{2}{3} = \dfrac{}{12} \ \diagup \text{LCD}$$
$$10\,|\ \dfrac{1}{4} = \dfrac{}{12} \ \diagup \text{LCD}$$
$$\overline{14} \qquad \diagdown \text{LCD}$$

$$4\,|\ \dfrac{2}{3} \times \dfrac{4}{4} = \dfrac{8}{12}$$
$$10\,|\ \dfrac{1}{4} \times \dfrac{3}{3} = \dfrac{3}{12}$$
$$\overline{14} \qquad \qquad \overline{}$$
$$\dfrac{11}{12}$$

Addition of fractions

Step 3: Combine the sum (addition) of the whole numbers in Step 1 and the sum (addition) of the fractions in Step 2 into the final sum as shown:

From Step 1 $\diagup 14 + \dfrac{11}{12} = 14\dfrac{11}{12} \ \diagup$ Final sum

$\diagdown$ From Step 2

Example 3

Add: $11\dfrac{3}{4} + 4\dfrac{1}{8} + 2\dfrac{1}{2}$

Solution

(**Notice** that in Step 1, an imaginary line | separates the whole numbers from the fractions so that we can work on the whole numbers and the fractions separately.)

Step 1: Add the whole numbers first.
↓

Step 2: Add the fractions second.
(Review Addition of Fraction)
In order to add fractions, find the LCD.
↙
Determine LCD.

Write equivalent fractions, and then add the fractions.
↓

$$11 \mid \frac{3}{4}$$

$$4 \mid \frac{1}{8}$$

$$2 \mid \frac{1}{2}$$

$$\overline{17}$$

$$11 \mid \frac{3}{4} = \frac{}{8} \nearrow \text{LCD}$$

$$4 \mid \frac{1}{8} = \frac{}{8} \nearrow \text{LCD}$$

$$2 \mid \frac{1}{2} = \frac{}{8} \nearrow \text{LCD}$$

$$\overline{17}$$

$$11 \mid \frac{3}{4} = \frac{3}{4} \times \frac{2}{2} = \frac{6}{8}$$

$$4 \mid \frac{1}{8} = \frac{1}{8} \times \frac{1}{1} = \frac{1}{8}$$

$$2 \mid \frac{1}{2} = \frac{1}{2} \times \frac{4}{4} = \frac{4}{8}$$

$$\overline{17}$$

$$\overline{\frac{11}{8}}$$

↖ ↗

Addition of whole numbers

↗

Addition of fractions

Review how to change an improper fraction such as $\frac{11}{8}$ into a mixed number such as $1\frac{3}{8}$.

Step 3: Combine the sum (addition) of the whole numbers in Step 1 and the sum (addition) of the fractions in Step 2 into the final sum as shown:

From Step 1 $\nearrow 17 + 1\frac{3}{8} = 18\frac{3}{8}$

↗ ↖ Final sum

From Step 2

Example 4

Add: $\frac{2}{9} + 6\frac{2}{3} + 20\frac{8}{36}$

Solution

(**Notice** that in Step 1, an imaginary line | separates the whole numbers from the fractions so that we can work on the whole numbers and the fractions separately.)

Step 1: Add the whole numbers first.

$$\frac{2}{9}$$

$$6\Big|\ \frac{2}{3}$$

$$20\Big|\ \frac{8}{36}$$

$$\overline{26}$$

Addition of whole numbers

Step 2: Add the fractions second.
(Review Addition of Fractions)
In order to add fractions find the LCD.

Determine LCD.

$$\frac{2}{9} = \frac{\ }{36}\ \swarrow\text{LCD}$$

$$6\Big|\ \frac{2}{3} = \frac{\ }{36}\ \swarrow\text{LCD}$$

$$20\Big|\ \frac{8}{36} = \frac{\ }{36}\ \swarrow\text{LCD}$$

$$\overline{26}$$

Write equivalent fractions and then add the fractions.

$$\frac{2}{9} = \frac{2}{9} \times \frac{4}{4} = \frac{8}{36}$$

$$6\Big|\ \frac{2}{3} = \frac{2}{3} \times \frac{12}{12} = \frac{24}{36}$$

$$20\Big|\ \frac{8}{36} = \frac{8}{36} \times \frac{1}{1} = \frac{8}{36}$$

$$\overline{26}$$

$$\frac{40}{36}$$

Fraction addition.

(**Note**: Review how to change improper fractions such as $\frac{40}{36}$ into a mixed fraction such as $1\frac{4}{36}$).

Example: $\frac{40}{36} = 1\frac{4}{36}$

(**Note**: Review how to reduce fractions, $\frac{4}{36}$ can be reduced to $\frac{1}{9}$ by dividing both numerator and denominator by 4.

Step 3: Combine the sum (addition) of the whole numbers in Step 1 and the sum (addition) of the fractions in Step 2 into the final sum as shown:

Final sum

$$26 + 1\frac{1}{9} = 27\frac{1}{9}$$

From Step 1   From Step 2

Exercises

1. Add the following. Hint: See Example **1**

(a) $7\frac{2}{5} + 1\frac{3}{10}$ (b) $3\frac{1}{4} + 2\frac{3}{8}$ (c) $10\frac{5}{6} + 8\frac{2}{3}$ (d) $5\frac{5}{9} + 7\frac{2}{3}$

(e) $9\frac{1}{3} + 10\frac{2}{9}$ (f) $17\frac{2}{8} + 15\frac{2}{16}$ (g) $2\frac{11}{12} + 13\frac{1}{24}$ (h) $32\frac{3}{12} + 15\frac{1}{3}$

(i) $7\frac{5}{8} + 3\frac{1}{4}$ (j) $35\frac{7}{9} + 40\frac{5}{18}$ (k) $10\frac{3}{7} + 7\frac{3}{14}$ (l) $9\frac{3}{8} + 4\frac{7}{24}$

(m) $17\frac{2}{5} + 22\frac{16}{25}$ (n) $16\frac{3}{9} + 2\frac{5}{36}$ (o) $6\frac{2}{3} + 8\frac{5}{12}$ (p) $5\frac{3}{5} + 11\frac{2}{15}$

2. Add the following. Hint: See Examples **1** and **2**.

(a) $10\frac{3}{7}$ (b) $17\frac{3}{5}$ (c) $3\frac{3}{4}$ (d) $8\frac{3}{9}$

$7\frac{3}{14}$ $11\frac{2}{10}$ $27\frac{5}{12}$ $7\frac{4}{18}$

(e) $19\frac{4}{5} + 4\frac{2}{3}$ (f) $22\frac{3}{4} + 7\frac{1}{16}$ (g) $31\frac{5}{12} + 1\frac{3}{4}$ (h) $20\frac{2}{7} + 11\frac{2}{21}$

(i) $3\frac{3}{12} + 6\frac{2}{3}$ (j) $5\frac{3}{8} + 2\frac{2}{24}$ (k) $7\frac{5}{7} + \frac{11}{14}$ (l) $7\frac{5}{7} + 2\frac{2}{14}$

(m) $11\frac{9}{11} + 3\frac{15}{22}$ (n) $6\frac{7}{33} + 4\frac{10}{11}$ (o) $5\frac{3}{7} + 6\frac{4}{21}$ (p) $9\frac{3}{4} + 6\frac{4}{5}$

3. Add the following. Hint: See Examples **3** and **4**.

(a) $4\frac{2}{3} + 3\frac{3}{4} + 7\frac{5}{12}$ (b) $3\frac{4}{7} + 4\frac{4}{21} + 6\frac{5}{7}$ (c) $5\frac{3}{5} + 2\frac{7}{10} + 1\frac{7}{20}$

(d) $9\frac{5}{16} + 1\frac{7}{8} + 8\frac{3}{4}$ (e) $7\frac{2}{3} + 4\frac{4}{9} + 2\frac{5}{18}$ (f) $4\frac{7}{18} + 9\frac{5}{9} + 3\frac{2}{3}$

(g) $29\frac{1}{4} + 10\frac{5}{12} + 6\frac{3}{8}$ (h) $2\frac{3}{7} + 22\frac{11}{21} + 1\frac{1}{42}$ (i) $2\frac{3}{4} + 3\frac{3}{8} + 4\frac{1}{2}$

(j) $6\dfrac{2}{3} + 4\dfrac{1}{4} + 7\dfrac{5}{6}$ (k) $5\dfrac{2}{3} + 7\dfrac{1}{4} + 2\dfrac{5}{6}$ (l) $4\dfrac{5}{8} + 4\dfrac{9}{16} + 2\dfrac{27}{32}$

(m) $3\dfrac{1}{3} + 4\dfrac{5}{6} + 10\dfrac{5}{8}$ (n) $2\dfrac{11}{16} + 1\dfrac{21}{64} + 3\dfrac{3}{4}$ (o) $4\dfrac{6}{7} + \dfrac{3}{14} + 2\dfrac{5}{28}$

(p) $\dfrac{3}{5} + 7\dfrac{7}{25} + \dfrac{49}{50}$ (q) $2\dfrac{2}{5} + 2\dfrac{2}{3} + 1\dfrac{1}{5}$ (r) $1\dfrac{3}{4} + 2 + 2\dfrac{3}{5}$

4. Add the following. Hint: See Examples **3** and **4**.

(a) $3\dfrac{3}{4}$ (b) $5\dfrac{3}{4}$ (c) $9\dfrac{2}{3}$ (d) $7\dfrac{4}{5}$ (e) $5\dfrac{1}{3}$

   $4\dfrac{3}{8}$ $4\dfrac{4}{5}$ $1\dfrac{1}{4}$ $5\dfrac{12}{15}$ $30\dfrac{5}{8}$

   $7\dfrac{1}{2}$ $12\dfrac{1}{2}$ $5\dfrac{5}{6}$ $8\dfrac{5}{6}$ $7\dfrac{5}{6}$
   $\overline{}$ $\overline{}$ $\overline{}$ $\overline{}$ $\overline{}$

(f) $4\dfrac{19}{28}$ (g) $7\dfrac{2}{3}$ (h) $2\dfrac{3}{4}$ (i) $24\dfrac{31}{32}$ (j) $10\dfrac{1}{2}$

   $20\dfrac{5}{7}$ $8\dfrac{4}{5}$ $7\dfrac{5}{8}$ $7\dfrac{9}{16}$ $7\dfrac{3}{8}$

   $3\dfrac{9}{14}$ $5\dfrac{7}{10}$ $12\dfrac{3}{5}$ $12\dfrac{3}{8}$ $5\dfrac{3}{4}$
   $\overline{}$ $\overline{}$ $\overline{}$ $\overline{}$ $\overline{}$

(k) $4\dfrac{2}{3}$ (l) $7\dfrac{5}{6}$ (m) $4\dfrac{1}{3}$ (n) $22\dfrac{1}{2}$ (o) $5\dfrac{1}{7}$

   $6\dfrac{3}{4}$ $8\dfrac{7}{12}$ $5\dfrac{5}{6}$ $3\dfrac{2}{3}$ $6\dfrac{3}{14}$

   $7\dfrac{5}{6}$ $5\dfrac{3}{4}$ $3\dfrac{1}{4}$ $2\dfrac{5}{12}$ $4\dfrac{3}{4}$
   $\overline{}$ $\overline{}$ $\overline{}$ $\overline{}$ $\overline{}$

Answers to Selected Questions

1(a) $8\dfrac{7}{10}$ **2**(a) $17\dfrac{9}{14}$ **3**(a) $15\dfrac{5}{6}$ **3**(o) $7\dfrac{7}{28} = 7\dfrac{1}{4}$ **4**(a) $14\dfrac{13}{8} = 15\dfrac{5}{8}$

REAL WORLD APPLICATIONS - WORD PROBLEMS
Addition of Mixed Fractions

Example 1

If I traveled $40\frac{1}{4}$ miles, $13\frac{1}{8}$ miles, and $15\frac{7}{24}$ miles in one day, what is the total number of miles that I traveled?

Solution

The total number of miles traveled $= 40\frac{1}{4} + 13\frac{1}{8} + 15\frac{7}{24}$

(**Notice** that in Step 1, an imaginary line | separates the whole numbers from the fractions so that we can work on the whole numbers and fractions separately.)

Step 1: Add the whole numbers first.

Step 2: Add the fractions second.
  (Review Addition of Fractions)
  In order to add fractions, find the LCD.
  Determine LCD.
  Write the equivalent fractions, and then add the fractions.

$$40|\ \frac{1}{4}$$
$$13|\ \frac{1}{8}$$
$$15|\ \frac{7}{24}$$
$$\overline{68}$$

$$40|\ \frac{1}{4} = \frac{}{24}\ \diagup\text{LCM}$$
$$13|\ \frac{1}{8} = \frac{}{24}\ \diagup\text{LCM}$$
$$15|\ \frac{7}{24} = \frac{}{24}\ \diagup\text{LCM}$$
$$\overline{68}$$

$$40|\ \frac{1}{4} \times \frac{6}{6} = \frac{6}{24}$$
$$13|\ \frac{1}{8} \times \frac{3}{3} = \frac{3}{24}$$
$$15|\ \frac{7}{24} \times \frac{1}{1} = \frac{7}{24}$$
$$\overline{}$$
$$\frac{16}{24}$$

Addition of whole numbers

Addition of fractions

Notice that $\frac{16}{24}$ can be reduced to $\frac{2}{3}$ by dividing the numerator and the denominator of $\frac{16}{24}$ by 8.

Step 3: Combine the sum (addition) of the whole numbers in Step 1 and the sum (addition) of the fractions in Step 2 into the final sum as shown:

$$\text{From Step 1} \diagup 68 + \frac{2}{3} = 68\frac{2}{3} \text{ miles}$$

From Step 2   Final sum

Example 2:

Mary bought $8\frac{1}{2}$ pounds of pears, $3\frac{2}{3}$ pounds of apples, and $4\frac{5}{6}$ pounds of cherries. How many pounds of fruit did she buy?

Solution

The total number of pounds of fruit bought by Mary $= 8\frac{1}{2} + 3\frac{2}{3} + 4\frac{5}{6}$

(**Notice** that in Step 1, an imaginary line | separates the whole numbers from the fractions so that we can work on the whole numbers and the fractions separately.)

Step 1: Add the whole numbers first

Step 2: Add the fraction second. (Review fraction addition) In order to add fractions, find the LCD. Determine the LCD. Write the equivalent fractions, and then add the fractions.

$$8|\ \frac{1}{2}$$
$$3|\ \frac{2}{3}$$
$$4|\ \frac{5}{6}$$
$$\overline{15}$$

Addition of whole numbers.

$$8|\ \frac{1}{2} = \frac{}{6} \diagup \text{LCD}$$
$$3|\ \frac{2}{3} = \frac{}{6} \diagup \text{LCD}$$
$$4|\ \frac{5}{6} = \frac{}{6} \diagup \text{LCD}$$
$$\overline{15}$$

$$8|\ \frac{1}{2} \times \frac{3}{3} = \frac{3}{6}$$
$$3|\ \frac{2}{3} \times \frac{2}{2} = \frac{4}{6}$$
$$4|\ \frac{5}{6} \times \frac{1}{1} = \frac{5}{6}$$
$$\overline{15}$$
$$\frac{12}{6} = 2$$

Addition of fractions.

Step 3: Combine the sum (addition) of the whole numbers in Step 1 and the sum (addition) of the fractions in Step 2 into the final sum as shown:

$$\diagup \text{Final sum}$$
$$15 + 2 = 17$$

From step 1.   From step 2

Mary bought 17 pounds of fruits.

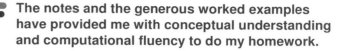

The notes and the generous worked examples have provided me with conceptual understanding and computational fluency to do my homework.

Exercises

1. A school project needs $6\dfrac{2}{3}$ inches, $8\dfrac{1}{2}$ inches and $4\dfrac{5}{12}$ inches of pipe. How many inches of pipe is needed? Hint: See Example **2**.

2. John needs $3\dfrac{2}{3}$ feet, $7\dfrac{1}{4}$ feet, and $2\dfrac{3}{4}$ feet of wood for a school project. How many feet of wood is needed by John for the total project? Hint: See Example **2**.

3. Rose walked $1\dfrac{1}{2}$ miles to the Post Office, $1\dfrac{5}{7}$ miles to the cinema, and $1\dfrac{3}{14}$ miles to the market. How many miles did she walk altogether? Hint: See Example **1**.

4. A baker used $3\dfrac{2}{3}$ dozen of eggs on Monday, $2\dfrac{3}{4}$ dozen on Tuesday, and $3\dfrac{1}{6}$ dozen on Wednesday for various mixes. How many dozen of eggs did the baker use? Hint: See Example **2**.

Challenge Questions

5. A plumber needs $8\dfrac{2}{3}$ inches, $6\dfrac{1}{6}$ inches, and $9\dfrac{1}{24}$ inches of pipe. What is the total length of the pipe that the plumber needs?

6. Rose bought three packages of meat weighing $6\dfrac{1}{5}$ pounds, 10 pounds, and $15\dfrac{2}{15}$ pounds. What was the total weight of the three packages of meat?

SUBTRACTION OF FRACTIONS

Rule 1: In order to subtract fractions, follow the three steps as follow:
Step 1: First find the least common denominator (LCD).
Step 2: Change each fraction to an equivalent fraction that has the same least common denominator (LCD).
Step 3: Subtract the numerators and write the difference of the numerators over the least common denominator (LCD).

Rule 2: The large or largest denominator in the question can, at times, be used as the least common denominator.

Rule 3: Knowing the multiplication tables from 1 to 12 will help to quickly identify the least common denominator (LCD).

Example 1

Subtract: $\dfrac{1}{2} - \dfrac{1}{4}$

Solution

Step 1: Find the least common denominator which is 4 because the denominator of $\dfrac{1}{2}$ which is 2 can divide evenly (without any remainder) the denominator of $\dfrac{1}{4}$ which is 4. Notice that rule 2 is being used.

$$\frac{1}{2} = \frac{\ }{4} \quad \checkmark \text{ least common denominator (LCD)}$$

$$\frac{1}{4} = \frac{\ }{4} \quad \checkmark \text{ least common denominator (LCD)}$$

Step 2: Write equivalent fractions. Review the section on Equivalent Fractions.

$$\frac{1}{2} = \frac{1}{2} \times \frac{2}{4} = \frac{2}{4} \leftarrow \text{Equivalent fraction}$$

$$-\frac{1}{4} = -\frac{1}{4} \times \frac{1}{1} = -\frac{1}{4} \leftarrow \text{Equivalent fraction}$$

Step 3: Subtract the numerators of the equivalent fractions and write the difference of the numerators of the equivalent fractions over the least common denominator (LCD) or over the common equivalent denominator to get the final difference as shown:

$$\overset{\nearrow \text{Difference of the numerators of the equivalent fraction}}{\frac{2 - 1}{4} = \frac{1}{4}}$$

$$\underset{\nwarrow \text{Common equivalent denominator or LCD}}{}$$

Example 2

Subtract: $\dfrac{3}{4} - \dfrac{2}{5}$

Solution

Step 1: Find the least common denominator. In order to find the LCD, we should find the least number that can be divided by both the denominators 4 and 5 evenly (without any remainder).

The multiples of 4 are:

$4 \times 1 = 4, 4 \times 2 = 8, 4 \times 3 = 12, 4 \times 4 = 16, 4 \times 5 = 20, 4 \times 6 = 24, \ldots$

Therefore the multiples of 4 are: 4, 8, 12, 16, 20, 24, . . .

The multiples of 5 are:

$5 \times 1 = 5, 5 \times 2 = 10, 5 \times 3 = 15, 5 \times 4 = 20, \ldots$

↑

Stop here because 20 appears as a multiple of 4. Since 20 is the smallest number that appears as the multiple of both 4 and 5, 20 is the LCD.

$\dfrac{3}{4} = \dfrac{}{20}$ ╱LCD Observe both sides of the equation, the denominator 4 must be multiplied by 5 in order to obtain the equivalent denominator of 20, and therefore, the numerator of 3 must also be multiplied by 5 to obtain 15 as shown in Step 2.

$-\dfrac{2}{5} = -\dfrac{}{20}$ ╱LCD Observe both sides of the equation, the denominator 5 must be multiplied by 4 in order to obtain the equivalent denominator of 20, and therefore, the numerator of 2 must also be multiplied by 4 to obtain an equivalent numerator of 8 as shown in Step 2.

Step 2: Write equivalent fractions. Review the section on Equivalent Fractions.

$$\dfrac{3}{4} = \dfrac{3}{4} \times \dfrac{5}{5} = \dfrac{15}{20} \leftarrow \text{Equivalent fraction}$$

$$-\dfrac{2}{5} = -\dfrac{2}{5} \times \dfrac{4}{4} = -\dfrac{8}{20} \leftarrow \text{Equivalent fraction}$$

Step 3: Subtract the numerators of the equivalent fractions and write the difference of the numerators of the equivalent fractions over the least common denominator (LCD) or over the common equivalent denominator of 20 to get the final difference as shown:

╱Difference of the numerators of the equivalent fractions

$$\dfrac{15 - 8}{20} = \dfrac{7}{20}$$

╲Denominator of the common equivalent fraction or LCD

Example 3

Subtract: $\dfrac{2}{3} - \dfrac{1}{7}$

Solution

Step 1: Find the LCD.

In order to find the LCD, we should find the least number that can be divided by both the denominators 3 and 7 evenly (without a remainder) by using multiples.

The multiples of 3 are:

$3 \times 1 = 3$, $3 \times 2 = 6$, $3 \times 3 = 9$, $3 \times 4 = 12$, $3 \times 5 = 15$, $3 \times 6 = 18$, $3 \times 7 = 21$, $3 \times 8 = 24$, . . .

Therefore, the multiples of 3 are: 3, 6, 9, 12, 15, 18, 21, 24, . . .

The multiples of 7 are:

$7 \times 1 = 7$, $7 \times 2 = 14$, $7 \times 3 = 21$, ...

↓

Stop here because 21 also appears as a multiple of 3. Since 21 appears as the smallest number that appears as a multiple of 3 and 7, 21 is the LCD.

$\dfrac{2}{3} = \dfrac{}{21}$ ⟋LCD

Observe both sides of the equation above. The denominator 3 must be multiplied by 7 in order to obtain the equivalent denominator (LCD) of 21, and the numerator of 2 must also be multiplied by 7 to obtain 14 as shown in Step 2.

$-\dfrac{1}{7} = -\dfrac{}{21}$ ⟋LCD

Observe both sides of the equation above. The denominator of 7 must be multiplied by 3 in order to obtain the equivalent denominator (LCD) of 21, and the numerator of 1 must also be multiplied by 3 in order to obtain the equivalent numerator of 3 as shown in Step 2.

Step 2: Write equivalent fractions. Review the section on Equivalent Fractions.

$\dfrac{2}{3} \times \dfrac{7}{7} = \dfrac{14}{21}$ ← Equivalent fraction

$-\dfrac{1}{7} \times \dfrac{3}{3} = -\dfrac{3}{21}$ ← Equivalent fraction

Step 3: Subtract the numerators of the equivalent fractions and write the difference of the numerators of the equivalent fractions over the least common equivalent denominator (LCD) to get the final difference as shown:

╱Difference of the numerators of the equivalent fractions

$$\frac{14-3}{21} = \frac{11}{21}$$ ╱Common equivalent denominator or the LCD

Example 4

Solve: $\dfrac{5}{6} - \dfrac{3}{8}$

Solution

Step 1: Find the LCD.

In order to find the LCD, we should find the least common number that can be divided by both 6 and 8 evenly (without a remainder) by using multiples. The multiples of 6 are:

$6 \times 1 = 6, 6 \times 2 = 12, 6 \times 3 = 18, 6 \times 4 = 24, 6 \times 5 = 30, \ldots$

Therefore, the multiples of 6 are: 6, 12, 18, 24, 30, . . .

The multiples of 8 are:

$8 \times 1 = 8, 8 \times 2 = 16, 8 \times 3 = 24, \ldots$

↑

Stop here because 24 also appears as a multiple of 6. Since 24 appears as the smallest number that appears as a multiple of both 6 and 8, 24 is the LCD.

$$\frac{5}{6} = \frac{}{24}$$ ╱LCD

Observe both sides of the equation above. The denominator 6 must be multiplied by 4 in order to obtain the equivalent denominator (LCD) of 24, and the numerator of 5 must also be multiplied by 4 to obtain 20 as shown in Step 2.

$$-\frac{3}{8} = -\frac{}{24}$$ ╱LCD

Observe both sides of the equation above. The denominator of 8 must be multiplied by 3 in order to obtain the equivalent denominator (LCD) of 24, and the numerator of 3 must also be multiplied by 3 in order to obtain the equivalent numerator of 9 as shown in Step 2.

Step 2: Write equivalent fractions. Review the topic on Equivalent Fractions.

$$\frac{5}{6} = \frac{5}{6} \times \frac{4}{4} = \frac{20}{24}$$ ← Equivalent fraction.

$$-\frac{3}{8} = -\frac{3}{8} \times \frac{3}{3} = -\frac{9}{24} \leftarrow \text{Equivalent fraction.}$$

Step 3: Subtract the numerators of the equivalent fractions and write the difference of the numerators of the equivalent fractions over the least common denominator (LCD) or over the common equivalent denominator to get the final difference as shown:

Difference of the numerators of the equivalent fractions

$$\frac{20 - 9}{24} = \frac{11}{24}$$

Common equivalent denominator or LCD

The notes and the generous worked examples have provided me with conceptual understanding and computational fluency to do my homework.

Exercises

1. State the three steps for doing subtraction.

2. What is meant by LCD?

3. Subtract the following. Hint: See Example **1**.

(a) $\dfrac{3}{4} - \dfrac{1}{8}$ (b) $\dfrac{7}{8} - \dfrac{3}{16}$ (c) $\dfrac{4}{5} - \dfrac{2}{10}$ (d) $\dfrac{5}{6} - \dfrac{3}{12}$ (e) $\dfrac{8}{9} - \dfrac{2}{3}$

4. Subtract the following. Hint: See Examples **2**, **3**, and **4**.

(a) $\dfrac{4}{5} - \dfrac{1}{4}$ (b) $\dfrac{5}{6} - \dfrac{1}{8}$ (c) $\dfrac{3}{5} - \dfrac{1}{3}$ (d) $\dfrac{4}{5} - \dfrac{3}{7}$ (e) $\dfrac{2}{3} - \dfrac{1}{7}$

(f) $\dfrac{2}{3} - \dfrac{2}{4}$ (g) $\dfrac{5}{7} - \dfrac{3}{8}$ (h) $\dfrac{4}{5} - \dfrac{2}{3}$ (i) $\dfrac{5}{6} - \dfrac{3}{8}$ (j) $\dfrac{3}{4} - \dfrac{1}{3}$

(k) $\dfrac{5}{8} - \dfrac{1}{3}$ (l) $\dfrac{2}{3} - \dfrac{1}{5}$ (m) $\dfrac{5}{6} - \dfrac{3}{4}$ (n) $\dfrac{4}{5} - \dfrac{3}{4}$ (o) $\dfrac{7}{8} - \dfrac{1}{5}$

Challenge Questions

(a) $\dfrac{10}{11} - \dfrac{2}{3}$ (b) $\dfrac{5}{7} - \dfrac{1}{6}$ (c) $\dfrac{5}{7} - \dfrac{4}{14}$ (d) $\dfrac{9}{10} - \dfrac{3}{5}$ (e) $\dfrac{1}{6} - \dfrac{3}{4}$

Answers to Selected Questions

3(a) $\dfrac{5}{8}$ **3(c)** $\dfrac{6}{10}$ or $\dfrac{3}{5}$ **4(a)** $\dfrac{11}{20}$ **4(c)** $\dfrac{4}{15}$

REAL WORLD APPLICATIONS - WORD PROBLEMS
Subtraction of Fractions

Example 1

Rose bought $\dfrac{3}{4}$ pound of sugar and she used $\dfrac{3}{16}$ pound for baking. How much sugar was left?

Solution

The amount of sugar left is $\dfrac{3}{4} - \dfrac{3}{16}$.

The subtraction is done just like the previous examples under the heading Subtraction of Fraction

Step 1: Find the LCD.

In order to find the LCD, we should find the least common number that can be divided by both the denominators of 4 and 16 evenly (without a remainder) by using multiples.

The multiples of 4 are:

$4 \times 1 = 4$, $4 \times 2 = 8$, $4 \times 3 = 12$, $4 \times 4 = 16$, $4 \times 5 = 20$, $4 \times 6 = 24$, . . .

Therefore, the multiples of 4 are:

4, 8, 12, 16, 20, 24, . . .

The multiples of 16 are:

$16 \times 1 = 16$, . . .

$\downarrow$

Stop here because 16 also appears as a multiple of 4. Since 16 appears as the smallest number that appears as the multiple of 4 and 16, 16 is the LCD. [Shortcut: By knowing the multiplication tables, $4 \times 4 = 16$ therefore, 4 can divide into 16 evenly (without any remainder), and therefore, we can know mentally that the LCD of 4 and 16 is 16.]

$$\frac{3}{4} = \frac{}{16}$$

$$\nwarrow$$

LCD

Observe both sides of the equation above. The denominator of 4 must be multiplied by 4 in order to obtain the equivalent denominator of 16, and the numerator of 3 must also be multiplied by 4 to obtain 12 as shown in

Step 2.

$$-\frac{3}{16} = -\frac{\quad}{16}$$

↖ LCD

Observe both sides of the equation above. The denominator of 16 at the left side of the equation is the same as the denominator of 16 at the right side of the equation, and he numerator of 3 on the left hand side of the equation must be the same (3) at the right side of the equation as shown in Step 2.

Step 2: Write equivalent fractions. Review the section on Equivalent Fractions.

$$\frac{3}{4} \times \frac{4}{4} = \frac{12}{16} \leftarrow \text{Equivalent fraction.}$$

$$-\frac{3}{16} \times \frac{1}{1} = -\frac{3}{16} \leftarrow \text{Equivalent fraction.}$$

Step 3: Subtract the numerators of the equivalent fractions and write the difference of the numerators of the equivalent fractions over the least common denominator (LCD) or over the common equivalent denominator to get the final difference as shown:

Difference of the numerators of the equivalent fraction

$$\frac{12-3}{16} = \frac{9}{16} \text{ pound of sugar}$$

↖ Common equivalent denominator or LCD

$\frac{9}{16}$ pound of sugar was left.

Example 2

A company bought $\frac{3}{4}$ ton of drinking water and used up $\frac{1}{2}$ ton. How much of the drinking water is left. (**Notice** that this problem is solved without detailed explanation as in Example 1. The student may see Example 1 for the similar detailed explanation.)

Solution

The amount of the drinking water left is $\frac{3}{4} - \frac{1}{2}$.

Step 1: Find the LCD.

Since the denominator 2 can divide 4 evenly (without a remainder), 4 is the

LCD of 2 and 4.

$$\frac{3}{4} = \frac{}{4} \;\nearrow\; LCD$$

$$-\frac{1}{2} = -\frac{}{4} \;\nearrow\; LCD$$

Step 2: Write equivalent fractions. Review the sections on Equivalent Fractions.

$$\frac{3}{4} \times \frac{1}{1} = \frac{3}{4} \;\leftarrow\; \text{Equivalent fraction}$$

$$-\frac{1}{2} \times \frac{2}{2} = -\frac{2}{4} \;\leftarrow\; \text{Equivalent fraction}$$

Step 3: Subtract the numerators of the equivalent fractions and write the difference of the numerators of the equivalent fractions over the least common denominator (LCD) to get the final difference as shown:

Difference of the numerators of the equivalent fractions

$$\frac{3-2}{4} = \frac{1}{4} \text{ ton of drinking water}$$

LCD or the common denominator of the equivalent fractions.

Example 3

Samuel bought $\frac{3}{4}$ pound of beef and ate $\frac{3}{8}$ pound for lunch. How much of the beef is left ?

Solution

(For similar detailed explanation, see Example 1.)

The amount of beef left is $\frac{3}{4} - \frac{3}{8}$

Step 1: Find the LCD.

Since denominator of 4 can divide the denominator of 8 evenly (without any remainder), 8 is the LCD of 4 and 8.

$$\frac{3}{4} = \frac{}{8} \;\nearrow\; LCD$$

$$-\frac{3}{8} = -\frac{}{8} \quad \diagup \text{LCD}$$

Step 2: Write equivalent fractions. Review the sections on Equivalent Fractions.

$$\frac{3}{4} \times \frac{2}{2} = \frac{6}{8} \quad \leftarrow \text{Equivalent fractions}$$

$$-\frac{3}{8} \times \frac{1}{1} = -\frac{3}{8} \quad \leftarrow \text{Equivalent fractions}$$

Step 3: Subtract the numerators of the equivalent fractions and write the difference over the least common denominator (LCD) or over the common denominator of the equivalent fraction to get the final difference as shown:

Difference of the numerators of the equivalent fractions

$$\frac{6-3}{8} = \frac{3}{8} \quad \text{pound of beef}$$

LCD or the common denominator of the equivalent fractions

$\frac{3}{8}$ pound of the beef is left.

Example 4

Joshua bought $\frac{7}{8}$ of a yard of material for a school project. If he only used $\frac{5}{6}$ of a yard, how much material was left?

Solution

(For similar detailed explanation, see Example 1.)

The material left is $\frac{7}{8} - \frac{5}{6}$.

Step 1: Find the LCD.

The denominators of the fractions are 8 and 6, however, 6 cannot divide 8 evenly (without any remainder), and therefore, 8 cannot be the LCD for 6 and 8.

Shortcut to find any LCD: Multiply the denominators together, then reduce the product of the denominators to the smallest number that can be divided by the denominators evenly (without any remainder), and **this smallest number is the LCD**. To find the LCD of 8 and 6, multiply 8 and 6 which is 48, then reduce 48 to the smallest number that can be divided by both 8 and 6 evenly (without a remainder) if possible. 48 can be reduced to

24 by dividing 48 by 2, and knowing from the " Multiplication Table" that $6 \times 4 = 24$ and $8 \times 3 = 24$, 24 is the least number that can be divided evenly (without a remainder), and therefore, 24 is the LCD.

$$\frac{7}{8} = \frac{}{24} \swarrow \text{LCD}$$

$$-\frac{5}{6} = -\frac{}{24} \swarrow \text{L CD}$$

Step 2: Write equivalent fractions. Review the sections on Equivalent Fractions.

$$\frac{7}{8} \times \frac{3}{3} = \frac{21}{24} \quad \leftarrow \text{Equivalent fractions}$$

$$-\frac{5}{6} \times \frac{4}{4} = -\frac{20}{24} \quad \leftarrow \text{Equivalent fractions}$$

Step 3: Subtract the numerators of the equivalent fractions and write the difference of the numerators of the equivalent fractions over the least common denominator (LCD) or over the common equivalent denominator to get the final difference shown:

$$\frac{21 - 20}{24} = \frac{1}{24} \text{ of a yard of material was left.}$$

The notes and the generous worked examples have provided me with conceptual understanding and computational fluency to do my homework.

Exercises

1. Samuel used $\frac{3}{4}$ cup of sugar and $\frac{1}{2}$ cup of milk to bake some cakes. How much more sugar than milk did he use? (Hint: Samuel used $\frac{3}{4} - \frac{1}{2}$ cup more of sugar than milk.) Hint: See Examples **1** to **4**.

2. John bought $\frac{6}{7}$ ton of coal and used up $\frac{1}{2}$ ton. How much coal was left? Hint: See Examples **1** to **4**.

3. Nick bought $\frac{3}{5}$ pound of beef and ate $\frac{1}{4}$ pound for lunch. How much of the beef was left? Hint: See Examples **1** to **4**.

4. John bought $\frac{7}{9}$ of a yard of material for a school project. If he only used $\frac{1}{4}$ of a yard, how much material was left? Hint: See Examples **1** to **4**.

5. Karen is $\dfrac{9}{10}$ meter tall and Mabel is $\dfrac{4}{5}$ meter tall. How much taller is Karen?

   Hint: See Examples **1** to **4**.

6. A bag contained $\dfrac{9}{10}$ pound of salt. If $\dfrac{2}{8}$ pound were used, how much of the salt

   remained? Hint: See Examples **1** to **4**.

7. Rose had $\dfrac{5}{6}$ yard of fabric. If she used $\dfrac{3}{4}$ yard, how much fabric is left?

   Hint: See Examples **1** to **4**.

SUBTRACTION OF MIXED NUMBERS

Subtraction often involves the technique known as **borrowing**. **Borrowing** is necessary when subtracting a larger digit number from a smaller digit number. You will learn about the technique of borrowing later in this chapter.

In the subtraction of mixed numbers, subtract the fractions first, and then subtract the whole numbers, see Example **3**.

The steps for subtracting mixed numbers are:
Step 1: Arrange the mixed numbers, one under the other and find the LCD.
Step 2: Write equivalent fractions.
Step 3: Subtract the equivalent fractions first by subtracting the numerators and put the difference over the equivalent denominator and if borrowing of a whole number is necessary, do so.
Step 4: Subtract the whole numbers and combine the subtraction of whole numbers and the subtraction of the equivalent fractions into the final answer.

Example 1
Subtract: $3\dfrac{5}{8} - 2\dfrac{5}{16}$
Solution
(**Notice** that in Step 1, an imaginary line | separates the whole numbers from the fractions so that we can work on the whole numbers and the fractions

258

separately.)

Step 1: Arrange the mixed numbers, one under the other and find the LCD. (Review the section on LCD)

$$3| \frac{5}{8} = \frac{}{16} \swarrow \text{LCD}$$

$$-2| \frac{5}{16} = -\frac{}{16} \swarrow \text{LCD}$$

8 can divide evenly into 16 (without any remainder) and therefore, 16 is the LCD of 8 and 16.

Step 2: Write equivalent fractions.

From Step 1, the denominator of $\frac{5}{8}$ which is 8 must have been multiplied by 2 to get the equivalent denominator of 16, and therefore, both the numerator and the denominator of $\frac{5}{8}$ in Step 2 should be multiplied by 2 as shown:

$$3| \frac{5}{8} \times \frac{2}{2} = \frac{10}{16} \leftarrow \text{Equivalent fraction}$$

From Step 1, the denominator of $\frac{5}{16}$ which is 16 must have been multiplied by 1 to get the equivalent denominator of 16 and therefore, both the numerator and the denominator of $\frac{5}{16}$ in Step 2 should be multiplied by 1 as shown:

$$2| \frac{5}{16} \times \frac{1}{1} = \frac{5}{16} \leftarrow \text{Equivalent fraction.}$$

Step 3: Subtract the equivalent fractions first by subtracting the numerators and put the difference over the equivalent denominator and if "borrowing" of a whole number is necessary, do so. (**Note**: "Borrowing" of a whole number is not needed in this case because $\frac{5}{16}$ is less than $\frac{10}{16}$.)

$$3| \frac{5}{8} \times \frac{2}{2} = \frac{10}{16} \leftarrow \text{Equivalent fraction}$$

$$-2| \frac{5}{16} \times \frac{1}{1} = -\frac{5}{16} \leftarrow \text{Equivalent fraction}$$

$$\frac{10-5}{16} = \frac{5}{16}$$

↗ Difference of the equivalent numerators

↖ Equivalent denominator

Step 4: Subtract the whole numbers and combine the subtraction of the whole numbers and the subtraction of the equivalent fractions into the final answer. (**Notice** that an imaginary line | separates the whole numbers from the fractions so that we can work on the whole numbers and fractions separately.)

$$3| \quad \frac{5}{8} \times \frac{2}{2} = \quad \frac{10}{16}$$

$$- 2| \quad \frac{5}{16} \times \frac{1}{1} = - \frac{5}{16}$$

$$\overline{1}$$

$$\frac{10 - 5}{16} = \frac{5}{16}$$ ↗ Difference of the equivalent numerators

↗ Subtraction of whole numbers.   ↘ Equivalent denominator

Combine the whole number which is 1 and the fraction which is $\frac{5}{16}$ into a

final answer of $1\frac{5}{16}$.

Therefore, $3\frac{5}{8} - 2\frac{5}{16} = 1\frac{5}{16}$

Example 2

Subtract: $7\frac{3}{4} - 5\frac{1}{5}$

Solution

Step 1: Arrange the mixed numbers, one under the other and find the LCD.

$$7| \quad \frac{3}{4} = \frac{}{20}$$ ↙ LCD

$$- 5| \quad \frac{1}{5} = - \frac{}{20}$$ ↙ LCD

Multiply the denominators 4 and 5 to obtain the LCD of 20. Note that 20 is the smallest number that can be divided by both 4 and 5 evenly (without any remainder).

Step 2: Write equivalent fractions.

From Step 1, the denominator of 4 must have been multiplied by 5 to get the equivalent denominator of 20, and therefore, both the numerator and the denominator of $\frac{3}{4}$ in Step 2 should be multiplied by 5 as shown:

$$7 \mid \frac{3}{4} \times \frac{5}{5} = \frac{15}{20} \quad \leftarrow \text{Equivalent fraction}$$

From Step 1, the denominator of $\frac{1}{5}$ which is 5 must have been multiplied by 4 to get the equivalent denominator of 20, and therefore, both the numerator and the denominator of $\frac{1}{5}$ in Step 2 should be multiplied by 4 as shown:

$$-5 \mid \frac{1}{5} \times \frac{4}{4} = -\frac{4}{20} \quad \leftarrow \text{Equivalent fraction}$$

Step 3: Subtract the equivalent fractions first by subtracting the numerators of the equivalent fractions and put the difference over the equivalent denominator, and if "borrowing" of a whole number is necessary, do so. (**Note** that borrowing of a whole number is not needed in this case because $\frac{4}{20}$ is less than $\frac{15}{20}$.)

$$7 \mid \frac{3}{4} \times \frac{5}{5} = \frac{15}{20} \quad \leftarrow \text{Equivalent fraction}$$

$$-5 \mid \frac{1}{5} \times \frac{4}{4} = -\frac{4}{20} \quad \leftarrow \text{Equivalent fraction}$$

$$\frac{15-4}{20} = \frac{11}{20} \quad \nearrow \text{Difference of the equivalent numerators}$$

$\nwarrow$ Equivalent denominator or the denominator of the equivalent fraction

Step 4: Subtract the whole numbers and combine the subtraction of the whole numbers and the subtraction of the equivalent fractions into the final answer as shown:

$$7 \mid \frac{3}{4} \times \frac{5}{5} = \frac{15}{20}$$

$$-5 \mid \frac{1}{5} \times \frac{4}{4} = -\frac{4}{20}$$

$$\overline{2}$$

$$\frac{15-4}{20} = \frac{11}{20} \quad \nearrow \text{Difference of the equivalent numerators.}$$

$\nearrow$

Subtraction of whole numbers (7 - 5 = 2.)

Combine the whole number 2 and the fraction $\dfrac{11}{20}$ into a final answer $2\dfrac{11}{20}$.

Therefore, $7\dfrac{3}{4} - 5\dfrac{1}{5} = 2\dfrac{11}{20}$.

Example 3

Subtract: $10\dfrac{2}{5} - 3\dfrac{5}{6}$

Solution

Step 1: Arrange the mixed numbers, one under the other and find the LCD.

$$10 \mid \dfrac{2}{5} = \dfrac{}{30} \swarrow \text{LCD}$$

(Multiply the denominators 5 and 6 to obtain the LCD of 30. Note that 30 is the smallest number that can

$$-3 \mid \dfrac{5}{6} = -\dfrac{}{30} \swarrow \text{LCD}$$

be divided by both 5 and 6 evenly (without remainder.)

Step 2: Write equivalent fractions.

From Step 1, the denominator 5 must have been multiplied by 6 to get the equivalent denominator of 30 and therefore, both the numerator and the denominator of $\dfrac{2}{5}$ in Step 2 should be multiplied by 6 as shown:

$$10 \mid \dfrac{2}{5} \times \dfrac{6}{6} = \dfrac{12}{30} \quad \leftarrow \text{Equivalent fraction}$$

From Step 1 the denominator of $\dfrac{5}{6}$ which is 6 must have been multiplied by 5 to get the equivalent denominator of 30, and therefore, both the numerator and the denominator of $\dfrac{5}{6}$ in Step 2 should be multiplied by 5 as shown:

$$-3 \mid \dfrac{5}{6} \times \dfrac{5}{5} = -\dfrac{25}{30} \quad \leftarrow \text{Equivalent fraction}$$

Step 3: Subtract the equivalent fraction first by subtracting the numerators and put the difference over the equivalent denominator, and if "**borrowing**" of a whole number is necessary, do so (Note that "borrowing" of a whole number from 10 is necessary because $\dfrac{23}{30}$ is greater than $\dfrac{12}{30}$.) Notice in Step 2 that the numerator of $\dfrac{25}{30}$ which is 25 is bigger than the numerator of $\dfrac{12}{30}$ which is 12. Since 25 cannot be taken from 12, borrow 1 from 10 and change 10 to 9.

Put the **borrowed** 1 in front of $\dfrac{12}{30}$, to get the mixed number $1\dfrac{12}{30}$ as shown:

$$\begin{aligned}
9&\\
10|\ \ \frac{2}{5}\times\frac{6}{6}&=1\frac{12}{30}\quad\leftarrow\text{Mixed number}\\[2mm]
-\,3|\ \ \frac{5}{6}\times\frac{5}{5}&=-\frac{25}{30}\quad\leftarrow\text{Equivalent fraction}
\end{aligned}$$

Change $1\dfrac{12}{30}$ to an improper fraction:

Rule: To change a mixed fraction to an improper fraction, multiply the denominator by the whole number, then add the numerator and put the addition over the denominator.

To change $1\dfrac{12}{30}$ to an improper fraction, multiply 30 by 1 and then add 12 and put the addition over 30. ($1\dfrac{12}{30}$ becomes $\dfrac{30\times1+12}{30}=\dfrac{42}{30}$.)

Replace $1\dfrac{12}{30}$ in Step 3 with $\dfrac{42}{30}$ in the problem and subtract $\dfrac{25}{30}$ from $\dfrac{42}{30}$. Then subtract the whole numbers and combine the two results into a final answer as shown:

$$\begin{aligned}
9&\\
10|\ \ \frac{2}{5}\times\frac{6}{6}=1\frac{12}{30}&\rightarrow\frac{42}{30}\\[2mm]
-\,3|\ \ \frac{5}{6}\times\frac{5}{5}=&\ -\frac{25}{30}\\[1mm]
\overline{9-3}&
\end{aligned}$$

$9-3=6$

$\diagup$Difference of equivalent numerators

$$\dfrac{42-25}{30}=\dfrac{17}{30}$$

$\diagdown$Difference of the whole number

Combine the whole number and the final fraction to obtain the final answer $6\dfrac{17}{30}$.

Therefore, $10\dfrac{2}{5}-3\dfrac{5}{6}=6\dfrac{17}{30}$

.

Special Note to the Student
The method for solving Example **3** is long, but Example **3** provides a logical detailed

method of solving the problem so that the students can understand the detailed logic of the mathematics. Once the detailed logic is understood, the student does not need to write detailed explanations during actual problem solving in class or during test. See Example **6** for a shortcut method involving "borrowing" to be used to solve problems and also Example **5** shows a shortcut method which does not involve "borrowing."

Example 4

Subtract: $10\dfrac{2}{5} - 3\dfrac{5}{6}$

Note that Example **4** is the same problem as Example **3**, however, Example **4** shows an alternate solution method to that of Example **3** where the whole number borrowed is changed to an equivalent fraction that has the common denominator as shown in Step 3.

Solution

Step 1: Find the LCD as in Step 1 of Example 3.

$$10 \mid \ \frac{2}{5} = \frac{}{30} \ \diagup \text{LCD}$$

$$-3 \mid \ \frac{5}{6} = -\frac{}{30} \ \diagup \text{LCD}$$

Step 2: Find the equivalent fraction as in Step 2 of Example 3.

$$10 \mid \ \frac{2}{5} \times \frac{6}{6} = \ \frac{12}{30} \ \leftarrow \text{Equivalent fraction}$$

$$-3 \mid \ \frac{5}{6} \times \frac{5}{5} = -\frac{25}{30} \ \leftarrow \text{Equivalent fraction}$$

Step 3: From Step 2, it can be seen that since $\dfrac{25}{30}$ is bigger than $\dfrac{12}{30}$, we cannot subtract the numerator of $\dfrac{25}{30}$ which is 25 from the numerator of $\dfrac{12}{30}$ which is 12. Therefore, as in Example **3**, we have to borrow 1 from the whole number of 10. The borrowed 1 should be written as an equivalent fraction that has a common denominator of 30. The borrowed 1 then becomes: $1 = \dfrac{30}{30}$. (Recall that the value of any fraction which has the same number as the numerator and the denominator is 1.) Add the borrowed $\dfrac{30}{30}$ to $\dfrac{12}{30}$ and then subtract as already done in Example **3** as shown:

$$9$$

$$10 \mid \quad \frac{2}{5} \times \frac{6}{6} = \frac{12}{30} + \frac{30}{30} \qquad \frac{42}{30}$$

↗ Addition of numerators

$$-3 \mid \quad \frac{5}{6} \times \frac{5}{5} = -\frac{25}{30} \quad \rightarrow \quad -\frac{25}{30}$$

$$\overline{9-3}$$

↗ Subtraction of numerators

$$9 - 3 = 6 \qquad \qquad \frac{42-25}{30} = \frac{17}{30} \leftarrow \text{Final fraction.}$$

↖ Whole number subtraction

Combine the whole number which is 6 and the final fraction which is $\frac{17}{30}$ to obtain the final answer $6\frac{17}{30}$.

Therefore, $10\frac{2}{5} - 3\frac{5}{6} = 6\frac{17}{30}$

Example 5

Subtract: $15\frac{3}{4} - 5\frac{5}{9}$ (See Examples **1** and **2** for sample detailed solutions.)

Solution

$$15 \mid \quad \frac{3}{4} \times \frac{9}{9} = \quad \frac{27}{36}$$

↘ LCD

$$-5 \mid \quad \frac{5}{9} \times \frac{4}{4} = -\frac{20}{36} \quad \text{↙ LCD}$$

$$\overline{10}$$

↗ Subtraction of the denominators

↗

Subtraction of whole numbers

$$\frac{27-20}{36} = \frac{7}{36} \leftarrow \text{Final fraction}$$

Combine the final fraction and the whole number to get the final answer $10\frac{7}{36}$.

Therefore, $15\frac{3}{4} - 5\frac{5}{9} = 10\frac{7}{36}$.

Note: It is recommended that the method of solution used for Example **5** should be used in solving homework problems without the detailed explanations.

Example 6

Subtract: $13\frac{1}{2} - 8\frac{5}{8}$ (See Example **4** for sample detailed solution method.)

Solution

$$13\,|\;\frac{1}{2} \times \frac{4}{4} = \frac{4}{8} \quad \diagup\text{LCD}$$

$$-8\,|\;\frac{5}{8} \times \frac{1}{1} = -\frac{5}{8} \quad \diagup\text{LCD}$$

$\frac{5}{8}$ is bigger than $\frac{4}{8}$, so we have to borrow 1 from 13 and the 1 is added to $\frac{4}{8}$ as $\frac{8}{8}$ as shown:

$$12 \qquad\qquad\qquad\qquad \diagup\text{This is the same as 1 added to } \frac{4}{8}$$

$$13\,|\;\frac{1}{2} \times \frac{4}{4} = \frac{4}{8} + \frac{8}{8} = \frac{12}{8}$$

$$-8\,|\;\frac{5}{8} \times \frac{1}{1} \qquad\qquad = -\frac{5}{8}$$

$$\overline{12 - 8} \qquad\qquad\qquad \overline{} \quad \diagup\text{Subtraction of numerators}$$

$$12 - 8 = 4 \qquad\qquad\qquad \frac{12 - 5}{8} = \frac{7}{8} \leftarrow \text{Final fraction}$$

$$\nwarrow$$

Whole number subtraction

Combine the whole number and the final fraction to obtain the final answer $4\frac{7}{8}$.

Therefore, $13\frac{1}{2} - 8\frac{5}{8} = 4\frac{7}{8}$

Note: It is recommended that the method of solution of Example 6 should be used in homework and tests without the detailed explanations.

Example 7

Subtract: $1 - \frac{2}{7}$

Solution

Step 1: Change the whole number 1 into an equivalent fraction that has the same denominator as that of $\frac{2}{7}$ which is 7. Therefore, $1 = \frac{7}{7}$. (Recall that any fraction which has the same number as both the numerator and the denominator has a value of 1.)

Therefore, $1 - \frac{2}{7}$ becomes $\frac{7}{7} - \frac{2}{7}$

Step 2: Subtract the numerators and put the difference over the common

266

denominator of 7 as shown:

$$\frac{7}{7} - \frac{2}{7} = \frac{7 - 2}{7} = \frac{5}{7}.$$

Example 8

Subtract: $1 - \dfrac{13}{49}$

Solution

Step 1: Change the whole number 1 into an equivalent fraction that has the same denominator as that of $\dfrac{13}{49}$ which is 49. Therefore, $1 = \dfrac{49}{49}$. (Recall that any fraction which has the same number as both the denominator and the numerator has a value of 1.)

Therefore, $1 - \dfrac{13}{49}$ becomes $\dfrac{49}{49} - \dfrac{13}{49} = \dfrac{36}{49}.$

Step 2: Subtract the numerators and put the difference over the common denominator of 49 as shown:

$$\frac{49}{49} - \frac{13}{49} = \frac{49 - 13}{49} = \frac{36}{49}.$$

The notes and the generous worked examples have provided me with conceptual understanding and computational fluency to do my homework.

Exercises

1. Subtract (Hint: See Examples **7** and **8**.)

(a) $1 - \dfrac{2}{5}$ (b) $1 - \dfrac{1}{4}$ (c) $1 - \dfrac{1}{10}$ (d) $1 - \dfrac{8}{9}$

(e) $1 - \dfrac{4}{7}$ (f) $1 - \dfrac{1}{6}$ (g) $1 - \dfrac{3}{11}$ (h) $1 - \dfrac{17}{18}$

(i) $1 - \dfrac{99}{100}$ (j) $1 - \dfrac{28}{44}$ (k) $1 - \dfrac{77}{78}$ (l) $1 - \dfrac{49}{74}$

(m) $1 - \dfrac{99}{200}$ (n) $1 - \dfrac{47}{64}$ (o) $1 - \dfrac{38}{65}$ (p) $1 - \dfrac{24}{37}$

2. Subtract (Hint: See Example **1**.)

(a) $3\dfrac{3}{4} - 1\dfrac{1}{8}$ (b) $7\dfrac{3}{4} - 5\dfrac{1}{6}$ (c) $5\dfrac{5}{6} - 3\dfrac{5}{12}$ (d) $8\dfrac{8}{9} - 2\dfrac{2}{9}$

(e) $4\dfrac{2}{3} - 2\dfrac{5}{12}$ (f) $10\dfrac{11}{12} - 3\dfrac{5}{6}$ (g) $3\dfrac{8}{9} - 1\dfrac{7}{9}$ (h) $6\dfrac{4}{5} - 2\dfrac{3}{10}$

(i) $8\dfrac{9}{12} - 3\dfrac{1}{3}$ (j) $12\dfrac{3}{4} - 7\dfrac{5}{16}$ (k) $6\dfrac{17}{18} - 2\dfrac{2}{9}$ (l) $28\dfrac{6}{7} - 2\dfrac{3}{14}$

(m) $9\dfrac{17}{21} - 3\dfrac{2}{7}$ (n) $13\dfrac{5}{6} - 4\dfrac{7}{18}$ (o) $56\dfrac{11}{15} - 6\dfrac{7}{30}$ (p) $10\dfrac{5}{6} - 2\dfrac{7}{24}$

(q) $110\dfrac{5}{8} - 90\dfrac{3}{64}$ (r) $94\dfrac{7}{9} - 64\dfrac{7}{36}$ (s) $32\dfrac{4}{5} - 19\dfrac{2}{15}$ (t) $6\dfrac{5}{6} - 2\dfrac{7}{24}$

3. Subtract (Hint: See Examples **2** and **5**.)

(a) $4\dfrac{2}{3} - 2\dfrac{1}{5}$ (b) $8\dfrac{4}{5} - 5\dfrac{1}{3}$ (c) $6\dfrac{3}{5} - 1\dfrac{1}{4}$ (d) $12\dfrac{1}{2} - 3\dfrac{2}{5}$

(e) $7\dfrac{2}{3} - 4\dfrac{1}{4}$ (f) $11\dfrac{7}{8} - 9\dfrac{1}{3}$ (g) $47\dfrac{4}{5} - 23\dfrac{2}{7}$ (h) $45\dfrac{2}{3} - 33\dfrac{3}{7}$

4. What is the rule for changing a mixed fraction into an improper fraction?

5. Subtract (Hint: See Example **1**).

(a) $10\dfrac{11}{12}$ (b) $4\dfrac{7}{8}$ (c) $12\dfrac{5}{6}$ (d) $9\dfrac{6}{7}$
$-\,3\dfrac{5}{6}$ $-\,2\dfrac{1}{4}$ $-\,6\dfrac{7}{12}$ $-\,6\dfrac{2}{7}$

(e) $11\dfrac{11}{12}$ (f) $28\dfrac{15}{16}$ (g) $5\dfrac{1}{2}$ (h) $29\dfrac{6}{7}$
$-\,6\dfrac{1}{6}$ $-\,17\dfrac{3}{8}$ $-\,2\dfrac{1}{4}$ $-\,3\dfrac{10}{21}$

6. Subtract (Hint: See Examples **2** and **5**.)

(a) $18\dfrac{2}{3}$ (b) $7\dfrac{4}{5}$ (c) $10\dfrac{11}{12}$ (d) $72\dfrac{3}{4}$
$-\,5\dfrac{1}{5}$ $-\,2\dfrac{2}{3}$ $-\,6\dfrac{3}{5}$ $-\,35\dfrac{2}{7}$

(e) $27\dfrac{4}{5}$ (f) $14\dfrac{6}{7}$ (g) $7\dfrac{7}{8}$ (h) $10\dfrac{3}{4}$
$-\,7\dfrac{1}{3}$ $-\,3\dfrac{2}{3}$ $-\,2\dfrac{4}{9}$ $-\,2\dfrac{1}{3}$

7. Subtract (Hint: See Examples **3**, **4**, and **6**.)

(a) $10\frac{2}{3} - 4\frac{4}{5}$　　(b) $4\frac{2}{7} - 2\frac{15}{21}$　　(c) $7\frac{1}{6} - 4\frac{2}{3}$　　(d) $11\frac{3}{5} - 2\frac{9}{10}$

(e) $15\frac{3}{11} - 7\frac{15}{22}$　　(f) $41\frac{1}{2} - 2\frac{7}{9}$　　(g) $7\frac{3}{7} - 5\frac{4}{5}$　　(h) $8\frac{1}{5} - 2\frac{2}{3}$

(i) $7\frac{2}{7} - 5\frac{2}{3}$　　(j) $8\frac{3}{11} - 5\frac{2}{3}$　　(k) $9\frac{2}{3} - 4\frac{7}{8}$　　(l) $15\frac{2}{5} - 4\frac{2}{3}$

(m) $9\frac{1}{6} - 7\frac{3}{4}$　　(n) $12\frac{2}{7} - 8\frac{16}{21}$　　(o) $25\frac{1}{16} - 5\frac{7}{8}$　　(p) $24\frac{2}{5} - 8\frac{14}{15}$

Challenge Questions

8. Subtract

(a) $14\frac{2}{9} - 2\frac{3}{4}$　　(b) $5\frac{7}{12} - 3\frac{5}{6}$　　(c) $7\frac{2}{3} - 2\frac{1}{8}$　　(d) $4\frac{5}{18} - 1\frac{1}{6}$

(e) $6\frac{23}{24} - 2\frac{1}{3}$　　(f) $14\frac{1}{4} - 6\frac{5}{8}$　　(g) $17\frac{4}{5} - 1\frac{3}{10}$　　(h) $29\frac{2}{9} - 9\frac{7}{18}$

Answers to Selected Questions

1(a) $\frac{3}{5}$　　2(a) $2\frac{5}{8}$　　3(a) $2\frac{7}{15}$　　5(a) $7\frac{1}{12}$　　7(a) $5\frac{13}{15}$

REAL WORLD APPLICATIONS - WORD PROBLEMS
SUBTRACTION OF MIXED NUMBERS

Example 1

After roasting $15\frac{1}{2}$ pounds of beef, the beef weighed $12\frac{7}{8}$ pounds. How much less did the beef weigh after roasting?

Solution

(**Notice** that in Step 1, an imaginary line | separates the whole numbers from the fractions so that we can work on the whole numbers and the fractions separately.)

The beef is $15\frac{1}{2} - 12\frac{7}{8}$ pounds less after roasting. (Refer to Examples **4** under the topic Subtraction of Mixed Numbers for a detailed sample solution.)

$15\frac{1}{2} - 12\frac{7}{8}$ is solved as shown:

$$15 \,\Big|\; \frac{1}{2} \times \frac{4}{4} = \frac{4}{8} \;\leftarrow \text{Equivalent fraction}$$

$$12 \,\Big|\; \frac{7}{8} \times \frac{1}{1} = \frac{7}{8} \;\leftarrow \text{Equivalent fraction}$$

$\frac{7}{8}$ is bigger than $\frac{4}{8}$, so we have to borrow 1 from 15 and add the 1 to $\frac{4}{8}$.

$$\overset{14}{\cancel{15}} \,\Big|\; \frac{1}{2} \times \frac{4}{4} = \frac{4}{8} + \frac{8}{8} \;\rightarrow\; \frac{12}{8}$$

This is adding the 1 borrowed from 15 here.

$$-12 \,\Big|\; \frac{7}{8} \times \frac{1}{1} = \frac{7}{8} \qquad\rightarrow\; \frac{7}{8}$$

$14 - 12 = 2$

$$\frac{12 - 7}{8} = \frac{5}{8}$$

Difference of the equivalent numerators.

Subtraction of whole numbers

Therefore $15\frac{1}{2} - 12\frac{7}{8} = 2\frac{5}{8}$ pounds.

Example 2

A painter had $12\frac{1}{4}$ gallons of paint. If he used $8\frac{2}{3}$ gallons of paint, how much paint is left?

Solution

The gallons of paint left $= 12\frac{1}{4} - 8\frac{2}{3}$. (Refer to Example **3**, under the topic Subtraction of Mixed Numbers for a detailed sample solution.)

$12\frac{1}{4} - 8\frac{2}{3}$ is solved as shown:

$$12 \mid \ \frac{1}{4} \times \frac{3}{3} = \frac{3}{12} \ \leftarrow \text{Equivalent fraction}$$

$$-8 \mid \ \frac{2}{3} \times \frac{4}{4} = \frac{8}{12} \ \leftarrow \text{Equivalent fraction}$$

$\dfrac{8}{12}$ is larger than $\dfrac{3}{12}$, so we have to borrow 1 from 12 and add the 1 to $\dfrac{3}{12}$ as shown:

1 which is borrowed from 12.

11　　　　　　　　↓

$$\overset{\not{12}}{} \mid \ \frac{1}{4} \times \frac{3}{3} = 1\frac{3}{12} \ \rightarrow \ \frac{15}{12} \ \leftarrow \text{Change mixed fraction to improper fraction.}$$

$$-8 \mid \ \frac{2}{3} \times \frac{4}{4} = \frac{8}{12} \ \rightarrow \ \frac{8}{12}$$

$$ \diagup \text{Difference in the numerators.}$$

$$11 - 8 = 3 \frac{15 - 8}{12} = \frac{7}{12}$$

$\nwarrow$

Subtraction of whole numbers

Therefore, $12\dfrac{1}{4} - 8\dfrac{2}{3} = 3\dfrac{7}{12}$ gallons.

(**Notice** that an imaginary line | separates the whole numbers from the fractions so that we can work on the whole numbers and the fractions separately.)

Example 3

John had $12\dfrac{1}{3}$ cups of flour and he used $5\dfrac{4}{5}$ cups to prepare food for his friends. How many cups of flour were left?

Solution

The cups of flour left $= 12\dfrac{1}{3} - 5\dfrac{4}{5}$. (Refer to the example under the topic Subtraction of Mixed Numbers for the detailed sample solution.)

$12\dfrac{1}{3} - 5\dfrac{4}{5}$ is solved as shown:

$$12 \mid \ \frac{1}{3} \times \frac{5}{5} = \frac{5}{15} \ \leftarrow \text{Equivalent fractions}$$

$$-5 \mid \ \frac{4}{5} \times \frac{3}{3} = -\frac{12}{15} \ \leftarrow \text{Equivalent fraction}$$

$\frac{12}{15}$ is larger than $\frac{5}{15}$, so we have to borrow 1 from 12 and add the 1 to $\frac{5}{15}$ as shown:

This is the 1 added to $\frac{5}{15}$

$$
\begin{array}{c}
11 \\
\cancel{12}\,| \quad \frac{1}{3} \times \frac{5}{5} = 1\frac{5}{15} \quad \rightarrow \quad \frac{20}{15} \quad \leftarrow \text{Change the mixed fraction to an improper fraction.} \\
-5\,| \quad \frac{4}{5} \times \frac{3}{3} = \frac{12}{15} \quad \rightarrow \quad -\frac{12}{15}
\end{array}
$$

11 − 5 = 6

$\frac{20 - 12}{15} = \frac{8}{15}$ ∕ Difference of the numerators

↖ Subtraction of whole numbers

Therefore, $12\frac{1}{3} - 5\frac{4}{5} = 6\frac{8}{15}$ cups of flour.

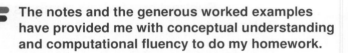

The notes and the generous worked examples have provided me with conceptual understanding and computational fluency to do my homework.

Exercises

1. After roasting $14\frac{1}{2}$ pounds of turkey, the turkey weighed $9\frac{2}{3}$ pounds. How much less did the turkey weigh after roasting? Hint: See Example **1**.

2. If a painter had $7\frac{1}{6}$ gallons of paint and he used up $3\frac{7}{8}$ gallons of the paint. How much paint is left? Hint: See Example **2**.

3. Nick had $15\frac{3}{4}$ cups of flour and if he used $2\frac{5}{6}$ cups to prepare cakes, how many cups of flour is left? Hint: See Example **3**.

Challenge Questions

4. John weighed $260\frac{2}{5}$ pounds. After going on a diet, he lost $70\frac{1}{2}$ pounds. What was John's weight after dieting?

5. Joshua had $6\frac{1}{2}$ dozen eggs and he used $2\frac{4}{5}$ dozen. How many dozen eggs were left?

6. Mary bought $20\frac{1}{2}$ feet of board for her school project. If she cut off $5\frac{5}{8}$ feet for the project, how many feet of board were left?

7. Joanna had $18\frac{2}{3}$ yards of ribbon. If she used $11\frac{7}{8}$ yards, how much ribbon did she have left?

Answers to Selected Questions

1. $4\frac{5}{6}$ pounds   **3**. $12\frac{11}{12}$ cups

SUBTRACTION OF A FRACTION FROM A WHOLE NUMBER

Example 1

Subtract: $1 - \frac{2}{3}$

Solution

Before a fraction can be subtracted from a whole number,

Step 1: Change the whole number 1 into an equivalent fraction that has the same denominator as that of $\frac{2}{3}$ which is 3. Therefore, $1 = \frac{3}{3}$. (Recall that any fraction which has the same number as both the numerator and the denominator has a value of 1.)

$$1 - \frac{2}{3} \text{ becomes } \frac{3}{3} - \frac{2}{3}$$

Step 2: Subtract the numerators and put the difference over the common denominator of 3.

$$\frac{3}{3} - \frac{2}{3} = \frac{1}{3}$$

Example 2

Subtract: $2 - \frac{2}{3}$

Solution

Step 1: Before a fraction can be subtracted from a whole number, 1 should be taken from the whole number and changed to an equivalent fraction that has the same denominator as the fraction which is being subtracted from the whole number. 2 can be written as $1 + 1$ and then, 1 can be changed to an equivalent fraction as follows:

$$2 - \frac{2}{3} = 1 + 1 - \frac{2}{3}$$

$$= 1 + \frac{3}{3} - \frac{2}{3} \quad \text{(Note: } \frac{3}{3} = 1)$$

$$\uparrow$$
Equivalent fraction

Step 2: Subtract the numerators of the fractions and put the difference over the common denominator of 3.

$$1 + \frac{3}{3} - \frac{2}{3} = 1 + \frac{3 - 2}{3}$$

$$= 1 + \frac{1}{3}$$

$$= 1\frac{1}{3} \quad \text{Combine the whole number and the fraction.}$$

Example 3

Subtract: $6 - \frac{3}{4}$

Solution

Step 1: Before a fraction can be subtracted from a whole number, 1 should be taken from the whole number and changed to an equivalent fraction that has the same denominator as the fraction which is being subtracted from the whole number. 6 can be written as $5 + 1$, and then, 1 can be changed to an equivalent fraction as shown:

$$6 - \frac{3}{4} = 5 + 1 - \frac{3}{4}$$

$$= 5 + \frac{4}{4} - \frac{3}{4} \qquad \text{(Note: } \frac{4}{4} = 1)$$

$$\uparrow$$
Equivalent fraction

Step 2: Subtract the numerators of the fractions and put the difference over the common denominator of 4.

$$5 + \frac{4}{4} - \frac{3}{4} = 5 + \frac{4-3}{4}$$

$$= 5 + \frac{1}{4}$$

$$= 5\frac{1}{4} \qquad \text{Combine the fraction and the whole number.}$$

The notes and the generous worked examples have provided me with conceptual understanding and computational fluency to do my homework.

Exercises

1. Subtract. Hint: See Example **1**.

(**a**) $1 - \frac{4}{8}$ (**b**) $1 - \frac{9}{10}$ (**c**) $1 - \frac{3}{6}$ (**d**) $1 - \frac{7}{8}$

(**e**) $1 - \frac{2}{9}$ (**f**) $1 - \frac{4}{11}$ (**g**) $1 - \frac{1}{12}$ (**h**) $1 - \frac{3}{5}$

(**i**) $1 - \frac{2}{19}$ (**j**) $1 - \frac{3}{4}$ (**k**) $1 - \frac{7}{12}$ (**l**) $1 - \frac{1}{99}$

(**m**) $1 - \frac{49}{50}$ (**n**) $1 - \frac{1}{39}$ (**o**) $1 - \frac{8}{9}$ (**p**) $1 - \frac{1}{64}$

(**q**) $1 - \frac{7}{49}$ (**r**) $1 - \frac{5}{16}$ (**s**) $1 - \frac{3}{25}$ (**t**) $1 - \frac{5}{6}$

(**u**) $1 - \frac{5}{14}$ (**v**) $1 - \frac{7}{11}$ (**w**) $1 - \frac{4}{7}$ (**x**) $1 - \frac{99}{200}$

2. Subtract. Hint: See Examples **2** and **3**.

(**a**) $7 - \frac{8}{9}$ (**b**) $2 - \frac{4}{11}$ (**c**) $8 - \frac{3}{5}$ (**d**) $10 - \frac{4}{9}$

(**e**) $12 - \frac{3}{7}$ (**f**) $4 - \frac{1}{9}$ (**g**) $9 - \frac{2}{7}$ (**h**) $3 - \frac{2}{11}$

(**i**) $10 - \frac{2}{5}$ (**j**) $5 - \frac{3}{8}$ (**k**) $6 - \frac{5}{12}$ (**l**) $10 - \frac{2}{5}$

(m) $90 - \dfrac{4}{5}$ **(n)** $64 - \dfrac{4}{9}$ **(o)** $3 - \dfrac{2}{9}$ **(p)** $28 - \dfrac{3}{7}$

(q) $12 - \dfrac{5}{12}$ **(r)** $15 - \dfrac{3}{5}$ **(s)** $11 - \dfrac{2}{30}$ **(t)** $9 - \dfrac{3}{16}$

(u) $8 - \dfrac{3}{7}$ **(v)** $15 - \dfrac{1}{15}$ **(w)** $12 - \dfrac{4}{9}$ **(x)** $14 - \dfrac{5}{8}$

Challenge Questions

3. Subtract:

(a) $200 - \dfrac{19}{20}$ **(b)** $4 - \dfrac{19}{100}$ **(c)** $1 - \dfrac{6}{7}$ **(d)** $1 - \dfrac{3}{8}$

Answers to Selected Questions

1(a) $\dfrac{4}{8}$ **2(a)** $6\dfrac{1}{9}$

(We will learn about how to reduce fractions to the lowest terms later.)

MULTIPLYING FRACTIONS

A fraction is made up of a numerator, a denominator, and a fraction bar as shown:

$\dfrac{2}{5}$ ⟋ numerator
    ← fraction bar
    ⟍ denominator

The fraction bar is a line that separates the numerator and the denominator.

Rule 1: To multiply fractions, multiply all the numerators together and multiply all the denominators together and then put the product of the numerators over the product of the denominators and if it is possible to reduce to the **lowest terms**, do so.

Example 1

Multiply: $\dfrac{2}{5} \times \dfrac{3}{4}$

Solution

Step 1: Multiply all the numerators together and multiply all the denominators together and then put the product of the numerators over the product of the denominators as shown:

$$\dfrac{2}{5} \times \dfrac{3}{4} = \dfrac{6}{20}$$

Step 2: Reduce $\dfrac{6}{20}$ to the lowest term by dividing both the numerator and the denominator of $\dfrac{6}{20}$ by the same number, and in this case 2 is the largest number that can divide evenly into 6 and 20 evenly without a remainder as shown:

$$\dfrac{\overset{3}{\cancel{6}}}{\underset{10}{\cancel{20}}} = \dfrac{3}{10} \qquad \text{Divide the numerator and the denominator by 2.}$$

Therefore, $\dfrac{2}{5} \times \dfrac{3}{4} = \dfrac{3}{10}$

Special Explanation

Note that Example **1** could have been solved differently by reducing $\dfrac{2}{5} \times \dfrac{3}{4}$ in Step 1 by dividing both the numerator and the denominator by 2 because 2 can divide the numerator 2 and the denominator 4.

Rule 2: In order to simplify the multiplication of fractions, divide any numerator and any denominator by the same number, and this is called canceling.

$$\dfrac{2}{5} \times \dfrac{3}{4} \text{ becomes } \dfrac{\overset{1}{\cancel{2}}}{5} \times \dfrac{3}{\underset{2}{\cancel{4}}} \qquad \text{Divide numerator and denominator by 2.}$$

$$\dfrac{1 \times 3}{5 \times 2} = \dfrac{3}{10} \qquad \text{This is the same answer for Example 1.}$$

Example 2

Multiply: $\dfrac{3}{7} \times \dfrac{5}{6}$

Solution

Step 1: Since 3 can divide evenly into the numerator 3 and the denominator 6 (without a remainder), divide the numerator and the denominator by 3. Rule 2 can be used here as shown:

$$\dfrac{3}{7} \times \dfrac{5}{6} = \dfrac{\overset{1}{3}}{7} \times \dfrac{5}{\underset{2}{6}}$$ Divide the numerator and the denominator by 3.

$$= \dfrac{1 \times 5}{7 \times 2} = \dfrac{5}{14}$$ Multiply the numerators and multiply the denominators and put the product of the numerator over the product of the denominator which is Rule 1.

Note: Since in Example 2, both the numerator and the denominator are divided by 3, and we can no more reduce $\dfrac{5}{14}$, Step 2 is not necessary in this case.

Recommendation

It is recommended that during the multiplication of fractions, the student should divide the numerators and the denominators by the same numbers if possible first before multiplying all the numerators and also multiplying all the denominators, and then put the product of the numerators over the product of the denominators.

Example 3

Multiply: $\dfrac{5}{12} \times \dfrac{4}{15}$

Solution

Step 1: Since 5 is the largest number that divides the numerator 5 and the denominator 15 evenly (without a remainder) and also, 4 is the largest number that divides the numerator 4 and the denominator 12 evenly (without a remainder), Rule 2 can be used here as shown:

$$\dfrac{\overset{1}{5}}{\underset{3}{12}} \times \dfrac{\overset{1}{4}}{\underset{3}{15}}$$ Divide both numerators and denominators by 5 and 4.

$(5 \div 5 = 1, 15 \div 5 = 3, 4 \div 4 = 1, 12 \div 4 = 3)$

$= \dfrac{1}{3} \times \dfrac{1}{3}$ Since we can no longer reduce $\dfrac{1}{3} \times \dfrac{1}{3}$, multiply the numerators and multiply the denominators and put the product of the numerators over the product of the denominators as shown:

$$= \dfrac{1 \times 1}{3 \times 3} = \dfrac{1}{9}$$

Example 4

Multiply: $\dfrac{5}{6} \times \dfrac{7}{9}$

Solution

Step 1: Since there is no number that can divide both the numerators and the denominators evenly (without a remainder), we can only multiply all the numerators, and then multiply all the denominators and put the product of the numerators over the denominators as shown:

$$\dfrac{5}{6} \times \dfrac{7}{9} = \dfrac{5 \times 7}{6 \times 9} \qquad \text{Rule 1 is used here.}$$

$$= \dfrac{35}{54}$$

Example 5

Multiply: $\dfrac{12}{15} \times \dfrac{3}{8} \times \dfrac{4}{9}$

Solution

Step 1: Since the numerators and the denominators can be divided by 2, 3, and 4, the fractions should be reduced by dividing by 2, 3, and 4 before the numerators should be multiplied together and the denominators multiplied together, and then put the product of the numerators over the product of the denominators as shown:

$$\overset{\overset{\displaystyle 1}{\overset{\displaystyle 4}{\cancel{12}}}}{\underset{5}{\cancel{15}}} \times \dfrac{\overset{1}{\cancel{3}}}{\underset{2}{\cancel{8}}} \times \dfrac{\overset{2}{\underset{1}{\cancel{4}}}}{\underset{3}{\cancel{9}}}$$

$(12 \div 3 = 4,\ 15 \div 3 = 5,\ 4 \div 4 = 1,\ 8 \div 4 = 2)$

$(2 \div 2 = 1,\ 4 \div 2 = 2)$
$(3 \div 3 = 1,\ 9 \div 3 = 3)$
Rule 2 is being used here.

279

$$= \frac{1}{5} \times \frac{1}{1} \times \frac{2}{3}$$

$$= \frac{1 \times 1 \times 2}{5 \times 1 \times 3} = \frac{2}{15} \qquad \text{Rule 1 is used here.}$$

The notes and the generous worked examples have provided me with conceptual understanding and computational fluency to do my homework.

Exercises

1. Multiply (Hint: See Example **2**.)

(a) $\frac{4}{7} \times \frac{5}{8}$ (b) $\frac{5}{7} \times \frac{2}{10}$ (c) $\frac{1}{3} \times \frac{3}{4}$ (d) $\frac{3}{5} \times \frac{5}{7}$

(e) $\frac{2}{5} \times \frac{1}{6}$ (f) $\frac{2}{3} \times \frac{1}{2}$ (g) $\frac{4}{7} \times \frac{14}{15}$ (h) $\frac{3}{4} \times \frac{5}{6}$

(i) $\frac{3}{49} \times \frac{7}{10}$ (j) $\frac{2}{9} \times \frac{27}{29}$ (k) $\frac{2}{12} \times \frac{7}{9}$ (l) $\frac{3}{11} \times \frac{22}{23}$

(m) $\frac{3}{7} \times \frac{77}{78}$ (n) $\frac{2}{3} \times \frac{3}{5}$ (o) $\frac{3}{4} \times \frac{4}{5}$ (p) $\frac{5}{6} \times \frac{7}{15}$

(q) $\frac{4}{5} \times \frac{7}{12}$ (r) $\frac{3}{7} \times \frac{4}{15}$ (s) $\frac{5}{7} \times \frac{21}{22}$ (t) $\frac{2}{33} \times \frac{11}{13}$

(u) $\frac{21}{22} \times \frac{3}{7}$ (v) $\frac{10}{18} \times \frac{6}{13}$ (w) $\frac{27}{30} \times \frac{7}{9}$ (x) $\frac{45}{46} \times \frac{1}{15}$

(y) $\frac{50}{51} \times \frac{7}{25}$ (z) $\frac{42}{50} \times \frac{3}{12}$ (a1) $\frac{7}{17} \times \frac{3}{14}$ (b1) $\frac{4}{9} \times \frac{12}{13}$

2. Multiply (Hint: See Example **3**.)

(a) $\frac{3}{4} \times \frac{2}{9}$ (b) $\frac{9}{10} \times \frac{2}{3}$ (c) $\frac{4}{5} \times \frac{5}{8}$ (d) $\frac{3}{7} \times \frac{14}{15}$

(e) $\frac{5}{6} \times \frac{3}{5}$ (f) $\frac{2}{5} \times \frac{5}{6}$ (g) $\frac{4}{7} \times \frac{7}{8}$ (h) $\frac{3}{8} \times \frac{4}{6}$

(i) $\dfrac{2}{5} \times \dfrac{10}{12}$ **(j)** $\dfrac{3}{5} \times \dfrac{10}{18}$ **(k)** $\dfrac{2}{3} \times \dfrac{24}{28}$ **(l)** $\dfrac{4}{5} \times \dfrac{15}{24}$

(m) $\dfrac{2}{9} \times \dfrac{3}{4}$ **(n)** $\dfrac{3}{16} \times \dfrac{4}{9}$ **(o)** $\dfrac{2}{5} \times \dfrac{15}{16}$ **(p)** $\dfrac{2}{5} \times \dfrac{20}{22}$

(q) $\dfrac{4}{11} \times \dfrac{22}{24}$ **(r)** $\dfrac{3}{4} \times \dfrac{8}{9}$ **(s)** $\dfrac{3}{4} \times \dfrac{12}{27}$ **(t)** $\dfrac{2}{11} \times \dfrac{33}{34}$

(u) $\dfrac{5}{7} \times \dfrac{14}{15}$ **(v)** $\dfrac{5}{6} \times \dfrac{12}{15}$ **(w)** $\dfrac{3}{8} \times \dfrac{24}{27}$ **(x)** $\dfrac{2}{9} \times \dfrac{18}{20}$

3. Multiply (Hint: See Example **4**.)

(a) $\dfrac{3}{4} \times \dfrac{3}{7}$ **(b)** $\dfrac{7}{22} \times \dfrac{5}{8}$ **(c)** $\dfrac{1}{4} \times \dfrac{5}{6}$ **(d)** $\dfrac{2}{5} \times \dfrac{3}{5}$

(e) $\dfrac{2}{7} \times \dfrac{3}{5}$ **(f)** $\dfrac{3}{7} \times \dfrac{2}{5}$ **(g)** $\dfrac{2}{9} \times \dfrac{11}{15}$ **(h)** $\dfrac{1}{8} \times \dfrac{5}{7}$

(i) $\dfrac{2}{3} \times \dfrac{3}{5}$ **(j)** $\dfrac{7}{8} \times \dfrac{9}{11}$ **(k)** $\dfrac{5}{6} \times \dfrac{5}{7}$ **(l)** $\dfrac{3}{4} \times \dfrac{5}{7}$

(m) $\dfrac{2}{5} \times \dfrac{3}{5}$ **(n)** $\dfrac{1}{7} \times \dfrac{3}{4}$ **(o)** $\dfrac{2}{11} \times \dfrac{2}{3}$ **(p)** $\dfrac{5}{6} \times \dfrac{7}{8}$

4. Multiply (Hint: See Example **5**.)

(a) $\dfrac{2}{3} \times \dfrac{6}{5} \times \dfrac{15}{18}$ **(b)** $\dfrac{2}{7} \times \dfrac{21}{22} \times \dfrac{11}{12}$ **(c)** $\dfrac{3}{4} \times \dfrac{4}{9} \times \dfrac{4}{16}$

(d) $\dfrac{5}{6} \times \dfrac{3}{15} \times \dfrac{2}{7}$ **(e)** $\dfrac{7}{9} \times \dfrac{18}{21} \times \dfrac{3}{4}$ **(f)** $\dfrac{4}{5} \times \dfrac{10}{12} \times \dfrac{3}{7}$

(g) $\dfrac{4}{5} \times \dfrac{15}{24} \times \dfrac{2}{3}$ **(h)** $\dfrac{1}{3} \times \dfrac{2}{3} \times \dfrac{9}{10}$ **(i)** $\dfrac{3}{4} \times \dfrac{16}{17} \times \dfrac{1}{6}$

(j) $\dfrac{2}{7} \times \dfrac{5}{6} \times \dfrac{14}{15}$ **(k)** $\dfrac{4}{7} \times \dfrac{14}{16} \times \dfrac{2}{3}$ **(l)** $\dfrac{4}{9} \times \dfrac{18}{19} \times \dfrac{19}{20}$

(m) $\dfrac{2}{3} \times \dfrac{4}{5} \times \dfrac{3}{8}$ **(n)** $\dfrac{5}{8} \times \dfrac{6}{7} \times \dfrac{14}{15}$ **(o)** $\dfrac{2}{3} \times \dfrac{9}{10} \times \dfrac{4}{9}$

Challenge Questions

5. Multiply:

(a) $\dfrac{3}{5} \times \dfrac{15}{16}$

(b) $\dfrac{3}{4} \times \dfrac{8}{9}$

(c) $\dfrac{1}{5} \times \dfrac{3}{5}$

(d) $\dfrac{3}{5} \times \dfrac{15}{18}$

(e) $\dfrac{4}{9} \times \dfrac{5}{8} \times \dfrac{3}{15}$

(f) $\dfrac{2}{11} \times \dfrac{3}{4} \times \dfrac{22}{24}$

(g) $\dfrac{3}{5} \times \dfrac{7}{12} \times \dfrac{5}{14}$

(h) $\dfrac{2}{7} \times \dfrac{3}{5} \times \dfrac{10}{9}$

(i) $\dfrac{4}{7} \times \dfrac{14}{15}$

(j) $\dfrac{2}{5} \times \dfrac{4}{7}$

(k) $\dfrac{2}{7} \times \dfrac{14}{15}$

(l) $\dfrac{5}{7} \times \dfrac{3}{4}$

(m) $\dfrac{2}{7} \times \dfrac{3}{7}$

(n) $\dfrac{2}{3} \times \dfrac{3}{4} \times \dfrac{4}{5}$

(o) $\dfrac{2}{5} \times \dfrac{2}{27} \times \dfrac{15}{16}$

(p) $\dfrac{3}{4} \times \dfrac{3}{4}$

Answers to Selected Questions

1(a) $\dfrac{5}{14}$ 2(a) $\dfrac{1}{6}$ 3(a) $\dfrac{9}{28}$ 4(a) $\dfrac{2}{3}$

REAL WORLD APPLICATIONS - WORD PROBLEMS
Multiplying Fractions

In mathematics "**of**" means to multiply.

Example 1

Mary won $\dfrac{3}{5}$ of a million dollars in a lottery. If she pays $\dfrac{1}{3}$ of the money in federal taxes, how much of her prize:
(**a**) is paid to the federal government?
(**b**) will remain after taxes?
Solution

(**a**) $\dfrac{1}{3}$ of the money is used to pay taxes.

$\dfrac{1}{3}$ of $\dfrac{3}{5}$ of a million dollars is used to pay taxes.

In mathematics "**of** " means to multiply.

Therefore, $\dfrac{1}{3}$ of $\dfrac{3}{5} = \dfrac{1}{3} \times \dfrac{3}{5}$

$$= \dfrac{1}{\overset{}{3}} \times \dfrac{\overset{1}{3}}{5} \quad \text{Divide the numerator and the denominator by 3.}$$
$$\phantom{= \dfrac{1}{3} \times \dfrac{3}{5}}_{1}$$

$$= \dfrac{1 \times 1}{1 \times 5}$$

$$= \dfrac{1}{5} \text{ of a million dollars is used to pay the taxes.}$$

(**b**) The total money won $= \dfrac{3}{5}$ of a million dollars.

The money used to pay taxes $= \dfrac{1}{5}$ of a million dollars.

Therefore, the money that remains $= \dfrac{3}{5} - \dfrac{1}{5}$

(Review topics on Subtraction of Fractions.)

$\dfrac{3}{5} - \dfrac{1}{5} = \dfrac{3-1}{5}$ Since the denominators of $\dfrac{3}{5}$ and $\dfrac{1}{5}$ are the same,

subtract the numerators and put the difference over 5.

$$= \dfrac{2}{5} \text{ of a million dollars remained.}$$

Example 2

A truck had a load of $\dfrac{11}{12}$ ton of goods. If $\dfrac{3}{11}$ of the goods were delivered,

(**a**) what part of a ton of the goods were delivered?
(**b**) what part of the ton of goods remained?

Solution

(**a**) Total load of goods $= \dfrac{11}{12}$ ton

$\dfrac{3}{11}$ of the goods were delivered.

283

Therefore, $\dfrac{3}{11}$ of $\dfrac{11}{12}$ ton of goods were delivered.

In mathematics "**of**" means to multiply.

$$\dfrac{3}{11} \text{ of } \dfrac{11}{12} = \dfrac{3}{11} \times \dfrac{11}{12}$$

$$= \dfrac{\overset{1}{\cancel{3}}}{\underset{1}{\cancel{11}}} \times \dfrac{\overset{1}{\cancel{11}}}{\underset{4}{\cancel{12}}}$$ (Divide the numerators and the denominators

by 3 and 11.)   ($3 \div 3 = 1, 12 \div 3 = 4, 11 \div 11 = 1$)

$$= \dfrac{1 \times 1}{1 \times 4}$$

$$= \dfrac{1}{4} \text{ ton of the goods were delivered.}$$

(**b**) Total load of the goods = $\dfrac{11}{12}$ ton

Load of goods delivered = $\dfrac{1}{4}$ ton

The remaining ton of goods = $\dfrac{11}{12} - \dfrac{1}{4}$

Step 1: Find the LCD of $\dfrac{11}{12}$ and $\dfrac{1}{4}$ (Review topics on Subtraction of Fractions.)

The LCD of $\dfrac{11}{12}$ and $\dfrac{1}{4}$ is 12 because it is the least number/denominator

that both 4 and 12 can divide evenly into (without a remainder).

$$\dfrac{11}{12} = \dfrac{}{12} \diagup \text{LCD}$$

$$-\dfrac{1}{4} = -\dfrac{}{12} \diagup \text{LCD}$$

Step 2: Write equivalent fractions.

284

$$\frac{11}{12} \times \frac{1}{1} = \frac{11}{12} \quad \leftarrow \text{Equivalent fractions}$$

$$-\frac{1}{4} \times \frac{3}{3} = -\frac{3}{12} \quad \leftarrow \text{Equivalent fractions}$$

Step 3: Subtract the numerators of the equivalent fractions and write the difference of the numerators over the least common denominator (LCD) to get the final difference.

$$\frac{11}{12} \times \frac{1}{1} = \frac{11}{12}$$

$$-\frac{1}{4} \times \frac{3}{3} = -\frac{3}{12}$$

$$\frac{11 - 3}{12} = \frac{8}{12} \quad \text{ton of goods remained.}$$

Note: $\dfrac{8}{12}$ should be reduced to the lowest term by dividing both the numerator and the denominator by 4 as shown:

$$\frac{8}{12} = \frac{\overset{2}{\cancel{8}}}{\underset{3}{\cancel{12}}} = \frac{2}{3} \quad \text{ton of goods remained.}$$

Example 3

Mary bought $\dfrac{9}{10}$ pound of beef and she used $\dfrac{1}{2}$ of the beef.

(**a**) What fraction of a pound did she use?
(**b**) What fraction of a pound remained?
Solution

(**a**) Total weight of the beef $= \dfrac{9}{10}$ pound.

$\dfrac{1}{2}$ pound of the beef was used.

Therefore, $\dfrac{1}{2}$ of $\dfrac{9}{10}$ of the beef was used.

In mathematics "**of** " means to multiply.

$$\frac{1}{2} \text{ of } \frac{9}{10} = \frac{1}{2} \times \frac{9}{10} \qquad \text{We cannot reduce to the lowest terms.}$$

$$= \frac{1 \times 9}{2 \times 10}$$

(The numerators are multiplied together and the denominators are multiplied together because there is no number that can divide both the numerator and the denominator evenly (without a remainder.)

$$= \frac{9}{20} \text{ pound of beef was used.}$$

(b) Total weight of the beef $= \dfrac{9}{10}$ pound

The weight of beef used $= \dfrac{9}{20}$ pound

Therefore the weight of beef that remains is equal to

$$\frac{9}{10} - \frac{9}{20} \qquad \text{(Review the topic on Subtraction of Fractions.)}$$

Step 1: Find the LCD.

The LCD for $\dfrac{9}{10}$ and $\dfrac{9}{20}$ is 20 because 20 is the least number that can be divided by 10 and 20 evenly (without a remainder).

$$\frac{9}{10} = \frac{}{20} \quad \checkmark \text{ LCD}$$

$$-\frac{9}{20} = -\frac{}{20} \quad \checkmark \text{ LCD}$$

Step 2: Write equivalent fractions.

$$\frac{9}{10} \times \frac{2}{2} = \frac{18}{20} \quad \leftarrow \text{ Equivalent fractions}$$

$$-\frac{9}{20} \times \frac{1}{1} = -\frac{9}{20} \quad \leftarrow \text{ Equivalent fractions}$$

Step 3: Subtract the numerators of the equivalent fractions and write the difference of the numerators over the least common denominator (LCD) to get the final difference.

$$\frac{9}{10} \times \frac{2}{2} = \frac{18}{20}$$

$$-\frac{9}{20} \times \frac{1}{1} = -\frac{9}{20}$$

$$\frac{18-9}{20} = \frac{9}{20} \text{ pound of the beef remained.}$$

Example 4

A boxer earned $\frac{8}{9}$ of a million dollars. If the agent of the boxer gets $\frac{3}{21}$ of the boxer's earnings, what fraction of a million did the agent get?

Solution

Total money earned by the boxer = $\frac{8}{9}$ of a million dollars.

$\frac{3}{21}$ of the boxer's earnings was received by the agent.

Therefore, $\frac{3}{21}$ of $\frac{8}{9}$ of a million dollars was received by the agent.

In mathematics, "**of**" means to multiply.

Therefore, $\frac{3}{21}$ of $\frac{8}{9} = \frac{3}{21} \times \frac{8}{9}$

$$= \frac{\overset{1}{\cancel{3}}}{21} \times \frac{8}{\underset{3}{\cancel{9}}} \qquad \text{Divide the numerator and denominator by 3.}$$
$$\qquad\qquad\qquad\qquad (3 \div 3 = 1,\ 9 \div 3 = 3)$$

$$= \frac{1 \times 8}{21 \times 3}$$

$$= \frac{8}{63} \text{ of a million was received by the agent.}$$

Example 5

Rose can mow her lawn in $\frac{8}{9}$ of an hour. How long will it take two people to do the same job assuming that each of the two people works at the same rate as Rose?

Solution

Time taken by 1 person (Rose) to mow the lawn = $\frac{8}{9}$ of an hour.

Time taken by 2 people to mow the lawn = $\frac{1}{2}$ of the time taken by 1 person.

$$= \frac{1}{2} \text{ of the time taken by Rose.}$$

In mathematics, "**of**" means multiplication

$$= \frac{1}{2} \text{ of } \frac{8}{9} = \frac{1}{2} \times \frac{8}{9}$$

$$= \frac{1}{2} \times \frac{\overset{4}{\cancel{8}}}{9} \qquad \text{(Divide numerator and the}$$
$$\qquad\qquad \underset{1}{} \qquad \text{denominator by 2.)}$$

$$= \frac{1 \times 4}{1 \times 9}$$

$$= \frac{4}{9} \text{ of an hour.}$$

The notes and the generous worked examples have provided me with conceptual understanding and computational fluency to do my homework.

Exercises

1. John won $\frac{6}{7}$ of a million dollars in a lottery. If he pays $\frac{1}{3}$ of the money in federal taxes, how much of his prize:

(**a**) Is paid to the federal government?
(**b**) Will remain?
Hint: See Example **1.**

2. Mary won $\frac{5}{6}$ of a million dollars in a lottery. Assume that she paid $\frac{4}{15}$ of the money in federal taxes, how much of her prize:

(**a**) Is paid to the federal government?
(**b**) Will remain?
Hint: See Example **1.**

3. A truck had a load of $\frac{9}{10}$ ton of goods. If $\frac{5}{6}$ of the goods were delivered,

(**a**) what part of a ton of the goods were delivered?
(**b**) what part of a ton of the goods remained?
Hint: See Example **2.**

4. A truck had a load of $\frac{7}{8}$ ton of sand. If $\frac{4}{21}$ of the sand was delivered,

(**a**) what part of a ton of the sand was delivered?
(**b**) what part of a ton of the sand remained?
Hint: See Example **2**.

5. Rose bought $\frac{3}{4}$ pound of ham and she used $\frac{1}{3}$ of the ham.

(**a**) What fraction of a pound did she use?
(**b**) What fraction of a pound remained?
Hint: See Example **3**.

6. Assume that a school district bought $\frac{3}{4}$ ton of rice for the year. If $\frac{1}{6}$ of the rice has been used,
(**a**) what fraction of a ton was used?
(**b**) what fraction of a ton remained?
Hint: See Example **3**.

7. A coach earned $\frac{5}{12}$ of a million dollars. If the trainer of the team gets $\frac{3}{10}$ of the coach's earnings, what fraction of a million did the trainer get?
Hint: See Example **4**

8. Frank can mow a lawn in $\frac{7}{9}$ of an hour. How long will it take 2 people to mow the same lawn, assuming that each of the two people works at the same rate as Frank? Hint: See Example **5**.

Challenge Questions

9. Nick can rake a lawn of leaves in $\frac{7}{12}$ of an hour. How long will it take three people to rake the same lawn, assuming that each of the three people works at the same rate as Nick?

MULTIPLICATION OF FRACTIONS AND WHOLE NUMBERS

Rule 1: To multiply fractions and whole numbers, write the whole numbers as fractions by dividing the whole numbers by 1. (Example: The fraction form of the whole number 9 is $\frac{9}{1}$.)

Rule 2: Before multiplying all the numerators and also multiplying all the denominators reduce the fractions to the lowest terms by dividing the numerators, and the denominators by the same number evenly (without a remainder) if possible.

Rule 3: Multiply the numerators and then multiply the denominators.

Rule 4: Change the answer (which is an improper fraction) to a mixed number by dividing the numerator by the denominator. (For example, the improper fraction $\dfrac{12}{5}$ can be written as $2\dfrac{2}{5}$ as a mixed number.)

Example 1

Multiply: $4 \times \dfrac{3}{4}$

Solution

Step 1: Change the whole number 4 to a fraction. See Rule 1.

$$4 = \frac{4}{1}$$

Therefore, $4 \times \dfrac{3}{4} = \dfrac{4}{1} \times \dfrac{3}{4}$

Step 2: Reduce the fractions to the lowest terms by dividing the numerators and the denominators by the same number evenly (without a remainder) if possible. See Rule 2.

$$\text{Therefore, } \frac{4}{1} \times \frac{3}{4} = \frac{\overset{1}{4}}{1} \times \frac{3}{\underset{1}{4}} \qquad (4 \div 4 = 1).$$

Step 3: Multiply the numerators and then multiply the denominators. See Rule 3.

$$\text{From Step 2, } \frac{1}{1} \times \frac{3}{1} = \frac{1 \times 3}{1 \times 1} = \frac{3}{1} = 3$$

$$\text{Therefore, } 4 \times \frac{3}{4} = 3$$

Example 2

Solve the question in Example 1 without showing the detailed explanations. Use a shortcut method.

Solution

$$\text{Shortcut: } \quad 4 \times \frac{3}{4} = \frac{4}{1} \times \frac{3}{4}$$

$$= \frac{\overset{1}{4}}{1} \times \frac{3}{\underset{1}{4}}$$

$$= \frac{1 \times 3}{1 \times 1} = \frac{3}{1} = 3$$

Example 3

Multiply: $12 \times \dfrac{3}{4}$

Solution

Step 1: Change the whole number 12 to a fraction. See Rule 1.

$$12 = \frac{12}{1}$$

Therefore, $12 \times \dfrac{3}{4} = \dfrac{12}{1} \times \dfrac{3}{4}$

Step 2: Reduce the fractions to the lowest terms by dividing the numerators and the denominators by the same number evenly (without a remainder), if possible. See Rule 2.

Therefore, $\dfrac{12}{1} \times \dfrac{3}{4} = \dfrac{\overset{3}{12}}{1} \times \dfrac{3}{\underset{1}{4}}$ $(12 \div 4 = 3, 4 \div 4 = 1)$.

Step 3: Multiply the numerators, and then multiply the denominators. See Rule 3.

From Step 2, $\dfrac{3}{1} \times \dfrac{3}{1} = \dfrac{3 \times 3}{1 \times 1} = \dfrac{9}{1} = 9$

Therefore, $12 \times \dfrac{3}{4} = 9$

Example 4

Solve the question in Example 3 without showing any detailed explanations. Use a shortcut method.

Solution

$$12 \times \frac{3}{4} = \frac{12}{1} \times \frac{3}{4}$$

$$= \frac{\overset{3}{12}}{1} \times \frac{3}{\underset{1}{4}}$$

$= 9$

Example 5

Use multiplication to explain what all the shaded areas of the models represent?

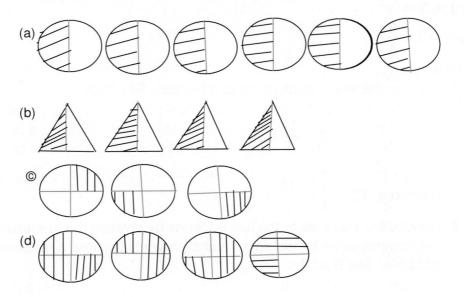

(a)

(b)

(c)

(d)

Solution

(**a**) Each shaded area shows $\dfrac{1}{2}$ of a circle.

There are 6 circles.

Therefore, the shaded area $= 6 \times \dfrac{1}{2}$ circles.

(**b**) Each shaded area shows $\dfrac{1}{2}$ of a triangle.

There are 4 triangles.

Therefore, the shaded area $= \dfrac{1}{2} \times 4$ triangles.

(**c**) Each shaded area shows $\dfrac{1}{4}$ of a circle.

There are 3 circles.

Therefore, the shaded area $= \dfrac{1}{4} \times 3$ circles.

(**d**) Each shaded area shows $\dfrac{3}{4}$ of a circle.

There are 4 circles.

Therefore, the shaded area $= 4 \times \dfrac{3}{4}$ circle.

Example 6

Multiply: $\dfrac{3}{5} \times 6$

Solution

Step 1: Change the whole number 6 to a fraction. See Rule 1.

$$6 = \dfrac{6}{1}$$

Therefore, $\dfrac{3}{5} \times 6 = \dfrac{3}{5} \times \dfrac{6}{1}$

Step 2: Reduce the fractions to the lowest terms by dividing the numerators and the denominators by the same number evenly (without a remainder) if possible. See Rule 2 . In this case, there is no number that can divide the numerators and the denominators of $\dfrac{3}{5} \times \dfrac{6}{1}$ evenly (without a remainder), therefore, go to Step 3.

Step 3: Multiply the numerators and then multiply the denominators. See Rule 3.

From Step 2, $\dfrac{3}{5} \times \dfrac{6}{1} = \dfrac{3 \times 6}{5 \times 1} = \dfrac{18}{5}$ ← Improper fraction

Step 4: Change the answer (which is an improper fraction) to a mixed number by dividing the numerator by the denominator. See Rule 4.

$$\dfrac{18}{5} = 3\dfrac{3}{5} \quad \text{(Note: } 18 \div 5 = 3 \text{ remainder 3, which is written as } 3\dfrac{3}{5}.)$$

Therefore, $\dfrac{3}{5} \times 6 = 3\dfrac{3}{5}$

Example 7

Solve the question in Example 6 without showing the detailed explanations. Use a shortcut method.

Solution

$$\dfrac{3}{5} \times 6 = \dfrac{3}{5} \times \dfrac{6}{1}$$

$$= \dfrac{3 \times 6}{5 \times 1}$$

$$= \dfrac{18}{5}$$

$$= 3\dfrac{3}{5}$$

Example 8

Find the product: $8 \times \dfrac{1}{3} \times 12 \times \dfrac{3}{4}$

Solution

Note: Find the product means to multiply.

Step 1: Change the whole numbers 8 and 12 to fractions. See Rule 1.

The fraction form of $8 = \dfrac{8}{1}$

The fraction form of $12 = \dfrac{12}{1}$

Therefore, $8 \times \dfrac{1}{3} \times 12 \times \dfrac{3}{4} = \dfrac{8}{1} \times \dfrac{1}{3} \times \dfrac{12}{1} \times \dfrac{3}{4}$

Step 2: Reduce the fractions to the lowest terms by dividing the numerators and the denominators by the same number evenly (without a remainder), if possible. See Rule 3.

$$\dfrac{\overset{2}{\cancel{8}}}{1} \times \dfrac{1}{\underset{1}{\cancel{3}}} \times \dfrac{\overset{1}{\cancel{12}}}{1} \times \dfrac{3}{\underset{1}{\cancel{4}}} \qquad (8 \div 4 = 2,\ 4 \div 4 = 1,\ 3 \div 3 = 1)$$

Step 3: Multiply the numerators, and then multiply the denominators. See Rule 3.

From Step 2, $\dfrac{2}{1} \times \dfrac{1}{1} \times \dfrac{12}{1} \times \dfrac{1}{1} = \dfrac{2 \times 1 \times 12 \times 1}{1 \times 1 \times 1 \times 1} = \dfrac{24}{1} = 24$

Example 9

Solve the question in Example 8 without showing the detailed explanations. Use the shortcut method.

Solution

Shortcut:

$$8 \times \dfrac{1}{3} \times 12 \times \dfrac{3}{4} = \dfrac{8}{1} \times \dfrac{1}{3} \times \dfrac{12}{1} \times \dfrac{3}{4}$$

$$= \dfrac{\overset{2}{\cancel{8}}}{1} \times \dfrac{1}{\underset{1}{\cancel{3}}} \times \dfrac{\overset{1}{\cancel{12}}}{1} \times \dfrac{3}{\underset{1}{\cancel{4}}}$$

$$= 24$$

> The notes and the generous worked examples have provided me with conceptual understanding and computational fluency to do my homework.

Exercises

1. Multiply the following. Hint: See Examples **1** and **3**.

(a) $12 \times \dfrac{1}{6}$

(b) $3 \times \dfrac{2}{3}$

(c) $15 \times \dfrac{2}{5}$

(d) $25 \times \dfrac{3}{5}$

(e) $14 \times \dfrac{2}{7}$

(f) $9 \times \dfrac{2}{3}$

(g) $6 \times \dfrac{2}{3}$

(h) $4 \times \dfrac{1}{4}$

(i) $16 \times \dfrac{3}{4}$

(j) $22 \times \dfrac{2}{11}$

(k) $21 \times \dfrac{3}{7}$

(l) $14 \times \dfrac{2}{7}$

(m) $18 \times \dfrac{5}{6}$

(n) $16 \times \dfrac{1}{4}$

(o) $12 \times \dfrac{1}{3}$

(p) $8 \times \dfrac{1}{4}$

(q) $18 \times \dfrac{2}{9}$

(r) $15 \times \dfrac{2}{3}$

(s) $12 \times \dfrac{3}{4}$

(t) $27 \times \dfrac{2}{3}$

(u) $36 \times \dfrac{5}{6}$

2. Solve questions **1(a)** to **1(u)** without showing detailed explanations. Use shortcut method. Hint: See Example **2** and **4**.

3. Multiply the following. Hint: See Example **6**.

(a) $\dfrac{3}{5} \times 6$

(b) $\dfrac{1}{4} \times 9$

(c) $\dfrac{3}{7} \times 3$

(d) $\dfrac{2}{3} \times 8$

(e) $\dfrac{2}{7} \times 4$

(f) $\dfrac{2}{9} \times 7$

(g) $\dfrac{1}{9} \times 14$

(h) $\dfrac{3}{7} \times 8$

(i) $\dfrac{2}{9} \times 11$

(j) $\dfrac{3}{5} \times 22$

(k) $\dfrac{3}{7} \times 5$

(l) $\dfrac{4}{5} \times 24$

(m) $\dfrac{3}{5} \times 24$

(n) $\dfrac{2}{7} \times 18$

(o) $\dfrac{3}{11} \times 30$

(p) $\dfrac{3}{4} \times 25$

4. Solve questions **3(a)** to **3(o)** without showing any detailed explanations. Use a shortcut method. Hint: See Example **7**.

5. Multiply: Hint: See Example **8**.

(a) $12 \times \dfrac{1}{4} \times 3 \times \dfrac{1}{3}$

(b) $\dfrac{2}{5} \times 15 \times \dfrac{2}{3}$

(c) $4 \times \dfrac{2}{5} \times \dfrac{5}{8}$

(d) $\dfrac{2}{7} \times 14 \times 2 \times \dfrac{3}{4}$

(e) $3 \times 4 \times \dfrac{2}{9} \times 6$

(f) $\dfrac{3}{4} \times 12 \times \dfrac{2}{5} \times 10$

(g) $\dfrac{3}{7} \times \dfrac{21}{27} \times 3 \times 2$

(h) $\dfrac{4}{5} \times \dfrac{2}{3} \times 6$

(i) $\dfrac{3}{5} \times \dfrac{2}{7} \times 35$

(j) $\dfrac{2}{9} \times 27 \times \dfrac{1}{4}$

(k) $\dfrac{2}{3} \times \dfrac{3}{4} \times \dfrac{6}{7} \times \dfrac{14}{18}$

(l) $\dfrac{3}{5} \times \dfrac{10}{12} \times \dfrac{3}{4}$

(m) $\dfrac{7}{8} \times \dfrac{3}{21} \times \dfrac{4}{9} \times 36$

(n) $\dfrac{3}{5} \times \dfrac{10}{11} \times \dfrac{22}{27}$

(o) $\dfrac{2}{7} \times \dfrac{5}{6} \times 14 \times \dfrac{2}{3}$

Challenge Questions

6. Find the product:

(a) $\dfrac{2}{3} \times 24$

(b) $24 \times \dfrac{5}{6}$

(c) $\dfrac{1}{3} \times 15$

(d) $\dfrac{2}{7} \times 5$

(e) $12 \times \dfrac{2}{3}$

(f) $14 \times \dfrac{3}{7}$

(g) $\dfrac{3}{5} \times 6$

(h) $3 \times \dfrac{7}{8}$

(i) $7 \times \dfrac{3}{21}$

(j) $\dfrac{2}{7} \times 10$

(k) $30 \times \dfrac{3}{5}$

(l) $\dfrac{3}{5} \times 20$

(m) $9 \times \dfrac{5}{8}$

(n) $\dfrac{4}{9} \times 7$

(o) $\dfrac{2}{5} \times 25$

(p) $\dfrac{4}{9} \times 27$

(q) $9 \times \dfrac{2}{3}$

(r) $16 \times \dfrac{3}{4}$

(s) $10 \times \dfrac{3}{4} \times \dfrac{2}{5} \times 6$

(t) $7 \times 3 \times \dfrac{5}{12} \times \dfrac{2}{21}$

(u) $\dfrac{2}{15} \times 8 \times \dfrac{5}{6} \times \dfrac{3}{4}$

(v) $\dfrac{2}{5} \times \dfrac{1}{3} \times \dfrac{2}{3}$

Answers to Selected Questions

1(a) 2   **3(a)** $\dfrac{18}{5}$ **5(a)** 3

REAL WORLD APPLICATIONS - WORD PROBLEMS
Multiplication of Fractions and Whole Numbers

Example 1

Given that $\dfrac{k}{3} \times 9 = 21$, find k.

Solution

Setup: Let us work on the left side of the equation which is $\dfrac{k}{3} \times 9$ to determine how 21 is obtained at the right side of the equation.

Step 1: Consider the left hand of the equation which is $\dfrac{k}{3} \times 9$ as the multiplication of a fraction by a whole number where $\dfrac{k}{3}$ is the fraction and 9 is the whole number. Recall that under the topic, Multiplication of Fractions and Whole Numbers, to multiply fractions by whole numbers, write the whole numbers as fractions by dividing the whole numbers by 1. Therefore, 9 can be written as the fraction $\dfrac{9}{1}$.

Therefore, the left side of the equation which is $\dfrac{k}{3} \times 9 = \dfrac{k}{3} \times \dfrac{9}{1}$

Step 2: Reduce the left side of the equation which is $\dfrac{k}{3} \times \dfrac{9}{1}$ to the lowest terms by dividing both the numerator and the denominator by the same number evenly (without remainder) if possible. In this case, both the numerator and the denominator can be divided by 3 as shown:

$$\dfrac{k}{3} \times \dfrac{9}{1} = \dfrac{k}{\underset{1}{\cancel{3}}} \times \dfrac{\overset{3}{\cancel{9}}}{1}$$

$$= \dfrac{k}{1} \times \dfrac{3}{1}$$

Step 3: Multiply all the numerators together, and then multiply all the denominators together as shown:

$$\frac{k}{1} \times \frac{3}{1} = \frac{3k}{1}$$

$$= 3k$$

Therefore, the left side of the equation which is $\frac{k}{3} \times 9$ is simplified to

become $3k$.

Step 4: Compare the simplified form of the left side of the equation, which is $3k$ to the right side of the equation which is 21.

Therefore:

$$3k = 21$$

We have to think of a number that can be multiplied by 3 to obtain 21, and that number is 7.

Therefore, $k = 7$.

Check your answer

$$3k = 21$$

$3 \times 7 = 21$ Substitute $k = 7$

$21 = 21$ Since the left side of the equation which is 21 is equal to the right side of the equation, which is 21, then $k = 7$ is a correct answer.

Example 2

Solve the question in Example 1 without showing detailed explanations. Use the shortcut method.

Solution

$$\frac{k}{3} \times 9 = 21$$

$$\frac{k}{\underset{1}{3}} \times \frac{\overset{3}{9}}{1} = 21$$

$$3k = 21$$
$$3 \times 7 = 21$$

Therefore, $k = 7$

Critical Thinking

The shortcut method is recommended for homework, class exercises and tests, however the detailed explanation method is to provide the students with the necessary mathematical logic for understanding the true concepts.

Example 3

Find the value of z in the equation $\frac{1}{3} \times z = 4$

Solution

Setup: Let us work on the left side of the equation which is $\frac{1}{3} \times z$ to determine how 4 is obtained at the right side of the equation.

Step 1: Consider the left side of the equation which is $\frac{1}{3} \times z$ as a multiplication of a fraction by a whole number where $\frac{1}{3}$ is a fraction and z is the whole number.

Recall that under the topic Multiplication of Fractions and Whole Numbers, to multiply fractions by whole numbers write the whole numbers as fractions by dividing the whole numbers by 1.

Therefore, z can be written as a fraction as $\frac{z}{1}$.

Therefore, the left side of the equation which is:

$$\frac{1}{3} \times z = \frac{1}{3} \times \frac{z}{1}$$

Step 2: Reduce the left side of the equation which is $\frac{1}{3} \times \frac{z}{1}$ to the lowest terms by dividing both the numerator and the denominator by the same number evenly (without a remainder) if possible.

In this case, both the numerator and the denominator cannot be divided by the same number evenly (Note: We do not know the value of z yet.) Go to Step 3.

Step 3: Multiply all the numerators together, and then multiply all the denominators together as shown:

$$\frac{1}{3} \times \frac{z}{1} = \frac{1 \times z}{3 \times 1}$$

$$= \frac{z}{3}$$

Therefore, the left side of the equation is simplified to become $\frac{z}{3}$.

Step 4: Compare the simplified form of the left side of the equation, which is $\frac{z}{3}$ to the right side of the equation, which is 4.

Therefore: $\frac{z}{3} = 4$

We have to think of a number that can be divided by 3 to obtain 4 and that number is 12. Therefore, $z = 12$.

Check your answer

$$\frac{z}{3} = 4$$

$$\frac{12}{3} = 4 \qquad \text{Substitute } z = 12$$

$$\frac{\overset{4}{\cancel{12}}}{\underset{1}{\cancel{3}}} = 4$$

$$4 = 4 \qquad \text{Since the left side of the equation is equal to 4 and the right side of the equation is also equal to 4, then, } z = 12 \text{ is a correct answer.}$$

Example 4

Solve the equation in Example 3 without showing detailed explanations. Use a shortcut method.

Solution

$$\frac{1}{3} \times z = 4$$

$$\frac{1}{3} \times \frac{z}{1} = 4$$

$$\frac{z}{3} = 4$$

$$\frac{12}{3} = 4$$

Therefore, $z = 12$

Check your answer

$$\frac{z}{3} = 4$$

$$\frac{12}{3} = 4 \qquad \text{Substitute } z = 12$$

$$4 = 4$$

Example 5

Find k in the equation $\dfrac{2}{k} \times 9 = 6$

Solution

Setup: Let us work on the left side of the equation, which is $\dfrac{2}{k} \times 9$ to determine how 6 on the right of the equation is obtained.

Step 1: Consider the left side of the equation, which is $\dfrac{2}{k} \times 9$ as a multiplication of a fraction by a whole number, where $\dfrac{2}{k}$ is the fraction and 9 is the whole number.

Recall that under the topic Multiplication of Fractions and Whole Numbers, to multiply fractions by whole numbers write the whole numbers as fractions by dividing the whole numbers by 1.

So, 9 can be written as a fraction as $\dfrac{9}{1}$.

Therefore, the left side of the equation which is:

$$\frac{2}{k} \times 9 = \frac{2}{k} \times \frac{9}{1}$$

Step 2: Reduce the left hand side of the equation which is $\dfrac{2}{k} \times \dfrac{9}{1}$ to the lowest terms by dividing the numerators and denominators by the same number evenly (without a remainder). Since we do not know the value of k yet, we cannot divide numerators and the denominators evenly (without a remainder.) Go to Step 3.

Step 3: Multiply all the numerators together and then multiply all the denominators together as shown:

$$\frac{2}{k} \times \frac{9}{1} = \frac{2 \times 9}{k \times 1}$$
$$= \frac{18}{k}$$

Therefore, the left side of the equation, which is $\dfrac{2}{k} \times \dfrac{9}{1}$ is simplified to become $\dfrac{18}{k}$.

Step 4: Compare the simplified form of the left side of the equation, which is $\dfrac{18}{k}$ to the right side of the equation, which is 6.

Therefore, $\dfrac{18}{k} = 6$

We have to think of a number that can divide 18 in order to obtain 6. The number is 3.

Therefore, k = 3.

Check your answer

$$\dfrac{18}{k} = 6$$

$$\dfrac{18}{3} = 6 \qquad \text{Substitute } k = 3$$

$$6 = 6 \qquad \text{Therefore, } k = 3 \text{ is a correct answer.}$$

Example 6

Solve the question in Example 5 without showing detailed information. Use a shortcut method.

Solution

$$\dfrac{2}{k} \times 9 = 6$$

$$\dfrac{2}{k} \times \dfrac{9}{1} = 6$$

$$\dfrac{18}{k} = 6, \qquad \dfrac{18}{3} = 6$$

Therefore, k = 3

The notes and the generous worked examples have provided me with conceptual understanding and computational fluency to do my homework.

Exercises

1. Solve for k in the following equations. (Hint: See Examples **1** and **2**.) Check your answer.

(a) $\dfrac{k}{2} \times 10 = 5$ (b) $\dfrac{k}{4} \times 12 = 9$ (c) $\dfrac{k}{5} \times 15 = 6$ (d) $\dfrac{k}{6} \times 24 = 20$

(e) $\dfrac{k}{3} \times 9 = 6$ (f) $\dfrac{k}{7} \times 21 = 12$ (g) $\dfrac{k}{8} \times 64 = 24$ (h) $\dfrac{k}{9} \times 18 = 10$

(i) $\dfrac{k}{10} \times 30 = 27$ (j) $\dfrac{k}{6} \times 60 = 20$ (k) $\dfrac{k}{5} \times 25 = 15$ (l) $\dfrac{k}{3} \times 24 = 16$

2. Solve for k in the following equations. (Hint: See Examples **3** and **4**.) Check your answer.

(a) $\dfrac{1}{3} \times k = 5$ (b) $\dfrac{2}{3} \times k = 4$ (c) $\dfrac{1}{4} \times k = 12$ (d) $\dfrac{2}{5} \times k = 4$

(e) $\dfrac{1}{5} \times k = 6$ (f) $\dfrac{1}{7} \times k = 6$ (g) $\dfrac{1}{6} \times k = 6$ (h) $\dfrac{1}{7} \times k = 2$

(i) $\dfrac{1}{10} \times k = 10$ (j) $\dfrac{1}{8} \times k = 2$ (k) $\dfrac{1}{6} \times k = 3$ (l) $\dfrac{1}{9} \times k = 9$

3. Solve for k in the following equations. (Hint: See Examples **5** and **6**.) Check your answer.

(a) $\dfrac{2}{k} \times 9 = 3$ (b) $\dfrac{2}{k} \times 6 = 2$ (c) $\dfrac{1}{k} \times 20 = 5$ (d) $\dfrac{1}{k} \times 28 = 4$

(e) $\dfrac{1}{k} \times 12 = 3$ (f) $\dfrac{1}{k} \times 12 = 4$ (g) $\dfrac{1}{k} \times 15 = 3$ (h) $\dfrac{1}{k} \times 15 = 5$

(i) $\dfrac{1}{k} \times 24 = 8$ (j) $\dfrac{3}{k} \times 6 = 3$ (k) $\dfrac{1}{k} \times 24 = 6$ (l) $\dfrac{1}{k} \times 24 = 4$

(m) $\dfrac{1}{k} \times 18 = 6$ (n) $\dfrac{1}{k} \times 18 = 3$ (o) $\dfrac{1}{k} \times 16 = 4$ (p) $\dfrac{1}{k} \times 6 = 2$

Challenge Questions

4. Solve for k in the following equations:

(a) $\dfrac{k}{5} \times 5 = 5$ (b) $\dfrac{2}{3} \times k = 6$ (c) $4 = \dfrac{2}{4} \times k$ (d) $\dfrac{1}{2k} \times 8 = 1$

5. Solve for w in the following equations:

(a). $w \times \dfrac{3}{4} = 9$ (b). $\dfrac{3}{5w} \times 15 = 27$ (c) $\dfrac{w}{7} = 11$ (d) $4w = 16$

Answers to Selected Questions.

1(a) 1   **1(d)** 5   **1(g)** 3   **2(b)** 6   **2(d)** 10   **3(a)** 6   **3(f)** 3   **3(n)** 6

Example 7

Solve for k in the equation:

$$\frac{3}{7} \times k = 3$$

Solution

Setup: Let us work on the left side of the equation, which is $\frac{3}{7} \times k$ to

determine how 3 on the right side of the equation is obtained.

Step 1: Consider the left side of the equation, which is $\frac{3}{7} \times k$ as a multiplication

of a fraction by a whole number where $\frac{3}{7}$ is the fraction and k is the whole

number. Recall that under the topic Multiplication of Fractions and Whole Numbers, to multiply fractions by whole numbers write the whole numbers as fractions by dividing the whole numbers by 1.

Therefore, k can be written as a fraction as: $\frac{k}{1}$.

Therefore, the left side of the equation, which is:

$$\frac{3}{7} \times 3 = \frac{3}{7} \times \frac{k}{1}$$

Step 2: Reduce the left side of the equation, which is $\frac{3}{7} \times \frac{k}{1}$ to the lowest

terms by dividing the numerators and the denominators by the same number evenly (without a remainder.) In this case, there is no number that can divide both the numerators and the denominators evenly (without a remainder) and the value of k is not known yet. Go to Step 3.

Step 3: Multiply all the numerators together, and then multiply all the denominators together as shown:

$$\frac{3}{7} \times \frac{k}{1} = \frac{3 \times k}{7 \times 1}$$

$$= \frac{3k}{7}$$

Therefore, $\frac{3k}{7} = 3$

We have to think of a number that can be divided by 7 in order to obtain 3 on the right side of the equation. The number is 21, because $21 \div 7 = 3$. (Note: Knowing the multiplication tables is very helpful in determining that $7 \times 3 = 21$ and, therefore, $21 \div 7 = 3$, Therefore, the number that can be divided by 7 in order to obtain 3 is 21.)

We can write $3k = 21$.

$$3k = 21 \text{ ————————— } [A]$$

Using equation $[A]$, the number that can be multiplied by 3 to obtain 21 is 7. Therefore,

$$k = 7 \ .$$

Check your answer

$$\frac{3}{7} \times k = 3$$

$$\frac{3}{7} \times 7 = 3 \qquad \text{Substitute } k = 7, \text{ then the numerator 7 can divide the}$$

denominator 7 such that $3 = 3$.

$$3 = 3 \qquad \text{Therefore, the answer } k = 7 \text{ is correct.}$$

Example 8

Solve the question in Example 7 without showing detailed explanations.
Solution

$$\frac{3}{7} \times k = 3$$

$$\frac{3k}{7} = 3$$

$$\frac{3 \times 7}{7} = 3 \qquad \text{Therefore, } k = 7$$

The notes and the generous worked examples have provided me with conceptual understanding and computational fluency to do my homework.

Exercises

1. Solve for k in the following equations. (Hint: See Examples **7** and **8**.) Check your answer.

(a) $\dfrac{4}{7} \times k = 4$ (b) $\dfrac{3}{9} \times k = 3$ (c) $\dfrac{2}{3} \times k = 6$ (d) $\dfrac{3}{4} \times k = 6$

(e) $\dfrac{3}{5} \times k = 6$ (f) $\dfrac{4}{7} \times k = 8$ (g) $\dfrac{3}{9} \times k = 6$ (h) $\dfrac{5}{6} \times k = 10$

Challenge Questions

2. Solve for p in the following equations.

(a) $\dfrac{3}{8} \times p = 9$ (b) $p \times \dfrac{3}{4} = 12$ (c) $21 = \dfrac{3}{7} \times p$ (d) $\dfrac{5}{4} \times p = 20$

REAL WORLD APPLICATIONS - WORD PROBLEMS
FINDING A NUMBER WHEN A FRACTIONAL PART OF IT IS KNOWN

Explanation

Given that there are 12 students in a science class, which represent $\frac{1}{4}$ of the number of the students in the class. Find the total number in the class.

This means 12 students $= \frac{1}{4} \times$ Total number of students

$$12 \text{ students} = \frac{1 \times \text{ Total number of students}}{4}$$

$$12 \text{ students} = \frac{\text{Total number of students}}{4}$$

Let us think of a number that can be divided by 4 to obtain 12. The number is 48. Therefore, the total number of students in the class is 48. Therefore, the multiplication problem involving 12 students $= \frac{1}{4} \times$ Total number of students can be changed to the division problem as shown:

$$12 \div \frac{1}{4} = ?$$

$$12 \div \frac{1}{4} = 12 \times \frac{4}{1} \quad \text{(To divide a number by a fraction, invert or flip}$$

the fraction and change the division sign to a multiplication sign. Review reciprocals.)

$$= 48 \text{ students}$$

We can therefore establish a rule to find a number when a fractional part of it is known as shown:

Rule: To find a number when a fractional part of the number is known, divide the known part by the fraction. The quotient is the unknown number.

Example 1

Given that 5 students in a class went to the zoo last week and this represents $\frac{1}{5}$ of

the students in the class. Find the total number of students in the class.

Solution

Using the rule, the total number of students in the class is:

$$5 \div \frac{1}{5}$$

$$5 \div \frac{1}{5} = 5 \times \frac{5}{1}$$ (When dividing by a fraction, invert or flip the fraction

and change the division sign to a multiplication sign. Review the section on Reciprocals.)

$$= \frac{5 \times 5}{1}$$

$$= 25$$

There are 25 students in the class.

Example 2

Mary saves $80 of her earnings each week. If this is $\frac{3}{5}$ of her earnings, what is her

weekly total earnings?

Solution

Using the rule, the total weekly earnings is:

$$80 \div \frac{3}{5}$$

$$80 \div \frac{3}{5} = 80 \times \frac{5}{3}$$ (When dividing by a fraction, invert or flip the

fraction and change the division sign to a multiplication sign. Review reciprocals.)

$$= \frac{80 \times 5}{3}$$

$$= \frac{400}{3}$$

$$= 133.33$$ You may use a calculator.

Therefore, the total weekly earnings is $133. 33.

Check your answer:

Savings per week $= \dfrac{3}{5} \times 133.33 = \dfrac{400}{5}$

$\qquad\qquad\qquad\qquad\qquad\quad = \$80$ which is given in the original question.

Therefore, the total weekly earnings of $133.33 is correct.

Example 3

If $\dfrac{3}{8}$ of a number is 24, find the number.

Solution

Using the rule, the number is:

$$24 \div \dfrac{3}{8}$$

$$24 \div \dfrac{3}{8} = 24 \times \dfrac{8}{3}$$ (When dividing by a fraction, invert or flip the

fraction and change the division sign to
a multiplication sign. Review reciprocals.)

$$= 24 \times \dfrac{\overset{8}{\cancel{24}}}{\underset{1}{\cancel{3}}}$$ Divide the numerator and the denominator by 3.

$$= 8 \times \dfrac{8}{1}$$

$$= 64$$

Therefore, the number is 64

Check your answer

$\dfrac{3}{8}$ of the unknown number $= 24$

$\dfrac{3}{8} \times 64 = 24$ Substitute 64 for the unknown number.

$\dfrac{3}{\underset{1}{\cancel{8}}} \times \overset{8}{\cancel{64}} = 24$ Divide the numerator and the denominator by 8.

$\dfrac{3}{1} \times 8 = 24$

$$24 = 24$$

The answer 64 is correct because the left side is equal to the right side of the equation.

Example 4

$\dfrac{5}{8}$ of what number is 40?

Solution

Using the Rule,

$\text{Number} = 40 \div \dfrac{5}{8}$

$40 \div \dfrac{5}{8} = 40 \times \dfrac{8}{5}$ Review the topic, Dividing a Number By a Fraction.

$= \overset{8}{40} \times \dfrac{8}{\underset{1}{5}}$ Divide the numerator and the denominator by 5.

$= 8 \times \dfrac{8}{1}$

$= 64$

The number is 64

Check your answer:

$\dfrac{5}{8}$ of an unknown number $= 40$

$\dfrac{5}{8}$ of $64 = 40$ Substitute 64 for the unknown number.

$\dfrac{5}{\underset{1}{8}} \times \overset{8}{64} = 40$

$\dfrac{5}{1} \times 8 = 40$

$40 = 40$

Since the left and the right sides of the equations are equal, the unknown number which is 64 is correct.

━━━━━━━━━━━━━━━━━━━━━━━━━━━━ The notes and the generous worked examples
━━━━━━━━━━━━━━━━━━━━━━━━━━━━ have provided me with conceptual understanding
and computational fluency to do my homework.

Exercises

1. Given that 5 students of a class visited the zoo last term, which is $\frac{1}{4}$ of the class, find the total number of students in the class. (Hint: See Example **1**.) Check your answer.

2. Nancy saved $10, 000.00 a year which represents $\frac{2}{5}$ of her salary. What is her total salary? (Hint: See Example **2**.) Check your answer.

3. $\frac{4}{7}$ of a number is 28. What is the number? (Hint: See Example **3**.) Check your answer.

4. Given that in a hospital, there are 64 female nurses. If the female nurses represent $\frac{4}{7}$ of the total nurses at the hospital, what is the total number of nurses at the hospital? (Hint: See Example **1**.). Check your answer.

5. John spent $30, 000. 00 last year, which represents $\frac{3}{4}$ of his salary. What is the salary of John? (Hint: See Example **2**). Check your answer.

6. 40 is $\frac{4}{7}$ of what number? (Hint: See Example **4**.) Check your answer.

Challenge Questions

7. Mary withdrew $20.00 from the bank and if this withdrawal represents $\frac{2}{5}$ of her total savings, how much money did she have at the bank?

8. 27 is $\frac{3}{4}$ of what number?

9. Ten members of a club went to see a football game. If the number of the club members that went to the football game represents $\frac{2}{5}$ of the total club members, what is the total number of club members?

Answers to Selected Questions
   (**1**) 20   (**3**) 49   (**6**) 70

MORE REAL WORLD APPLICATIONS - WORD PROBLEMS
FINDING A NUMBER WHEN A FRACTIONAL PART OF IT IS KNOWN

Example 1

A stadium has 40, 000 general admission seats. Find the total number of seats if this represents $\frac{2}{3}$ of the stadium seats.

Solution

Using the rule, the total number of seats is $40,000 \div \frac{2}{3}$.

$$40,000 \div \frac{2}{3} = 40,000 \times \frac{3}{2}$$ (When dividing by a fraction, invert or flip the fraction and change the division sign to a multiplication sign. Review the topic: Dividing a Number By a Fraction.)

$$= 4\cancel{0},000 \times \frac{3}{\cancel{2}}^{\,20,000}_{1}$$ Divide the numerator and denominator by 2.

$$= 20,000 \times \frac{3}{1}$$
$$= 60,000 \text{ seats.}$$

Example 2

The price of a shirt is reduced by $10.00. If the reduction was $\frac{5}{7}$ of the original price, what was the original price of the shirt?

Solution

Using the rule, the original price of the shirt is $10 \div \frac{5}{7}$

$$10 \div \frac{5}{7} = 10 \times \frac{7}{5}$$ (When dividing by a fraction, invert or flip the fraction and change the division sign to a multiplication sign. Review the topic: Dividing a

$$= 10 \times \frac{\overset{2}{\cancel{7}}}{\underset{1}{\cancel{5}}} \quad \text{Divide the numerator and the denominator by 5.}$$

$$= 2 \times \frac{7}{1}$$

$$= \$14.00$$

The original price of the shirt is $14.00.

Example 3

A school baseball team won 16 games. If they won $\frac{2}{3}$ of the games played,

what was the total number of games played?

Solution

Using the rule, the total number of games played is $16 \div \frac{2}{3}$

$$16 \div \frac{2}{3} = 16 \times \frac{3}{2} \quad \text{(When dividing by a fraction, invert or flip the}$$

fraction and change the division sign to a multiplication sign. Review the topic: Dividing a Number By a Fraction.)

$$= \overset{8}{\cancel{16}} \times \frac{3}{\underset{1}{\cancel{2}}} \quad \text{Divide the numerator and the denominator by 2.}$$

$$= 8 \times \frac{3}{1}$$

$$= 24$$

The total number of games won was 24.

_____

The notes and the generous worked examples have provided me with conceptual understanding and computational fluency to do my homework.

Exercises

1. A stadium has 25,000 general admission seats. Find the total number of seats
if this represents $\frac{5}{7}$ of the stadium seats. (Hint: See Example **1**.)

2. If the price of a shirt is reduced by $8.00 and if this reduction represents $\frac{2}{5}$ of the original price of the shirt, what was the original price of the shirt? (Hint: See Example **2**.)

3. A school baseball team won 20 games. If the school won $\frac{5}{7}$ of the games played, what was the total number of games played? (Hint: See Example **3**.)

Challenge Question

4. Regis received 450 votes for school president. If this represents $\frac{5}{8}$ of all the votes, how many students voted in the election?

FRACTIONAL PARTS

Rule: To find what fractional part one number is of another number, write a fraction with the partial amount as the numerator and the total amount as the denominator.

Example 1
What fractional part of 50 is 5?
Solution

Using the rule, the fractional part is $\dfrac{\text{partial amount}}{\text{Total amount}} = \dfrac{5}{50}$

$$\frac{5}{50} = \frac{\overset{1}{\cancel{5}}}{\underset{10}{\cancel{50}}} \quad \text{Divide the numerator and the denominator by 5.}$$

$$= \frac{1}{10} \quad .$$

The fractional part $= \dfrac{1}{10}$

Check your answer
Fractional part of 50 = 5

Therefore, $\frac{1}{10} \times 50 = 5$ (The fractional part is $\frac{1}{10}$ and "**of**" means multiplication.)

$$\frac{1}{\underset{1}{\cancel{10}}} \times \overset{5}{\cancel{50}} = 5$$

$$\frac{1}{1} \times 5 = 5$$

$$5 = 5$$

Since the left side and right side of the equation are the same (5), the fractional part $\frac{1}{10}$ is correct.

Example 2

James has $50.00 and if he spent $15.00, what fractional part of his money did he spend?

Solution

Using the rule, the fractional part of the money that he spent is $\dfrac{\text{Amount spent}}{\text{Total amount}} = \dfrac{15}{50}$

$$= \frac{\overset{3}{\cancel{15}}}{\underset{10}{\cancel{50}}}$$ (**Reduce the fraction to the lowest terms** by dividing the numerator and the denominator by 5.)

$$= \frac{3}{10}$$

Therefore, the fractional part which has been spent is $\frac{3}{10}$.

The notes and the generous worked examples have provided me with conceptual understanding and computational fluency to do my homework.

Exercises

1. Find the fractional part of the following: (Hint: See Example **1**.)
   (**a**) 6 is what part of 18?   (**b**) 3 is what part of 9?
   (**c**) 4 is what part of 12?   (**d**) 5 is what part of 15?
   (**e**) 11 is what part of 44?   (**f**) 8 is what part of 24?

314

(**g**) 4 is what part of 32?   (**h**) 7 is what part of 21?
(**i**) 7 is what part of 35?   (**j**) 9 is what part of 45?
(**k**) 5 is what part of 65?   (**l**) 8 is what part of 64?
(**m**) 3 is what part of 24?   (**n**) 4 is what part of 36?
(**o**) 15 is what part of 60?   (**p**) 10 is what part of 80?
(**q**) 30 is what part of 80?   (**r**) 25 is what part of 75?

2. If a student got 75 out of 100 questions correct, what fraction was correct? (Hint: See Example **2**.)
3. A student had $100.00 and he spent $75.00 on books. What fraction of the money was spent on books? (Hint: See Example **2**.)
4. There are 18 boys in a class of 34 students. What part of the class is boys? (Hint: See Example **2**.)

Challenge Questions.
5. If 4 students are absent in a class of 24 students, what fractional part of the class is absent?
6. If a 26 year old student spent 6 years in college, what part of the student's life was spent in college?
7. 100 is what part of 500?

Answers to Selected Questions

1(a) $\frac{1}{3}$ **1(g)** $\frac{1}{8}$ **1(p)** $\frac{1}{8}$ **(5)** $\frac{1}{6}$

CUMULATIVE REVIEW – FRACTIONS

1. Change the following improper fractions to mixed numbers.
(**a**) $\frac{12}{3}$ (**b**) $\frac{10}{4}$ (**c**) $\frac{11}{4}$ (**d**) $\frac{28}{7}$ (**e**) $\frac{32}{5}$ (**f**) $\frac{48}{5}$

2. Change the following mixed numbers to improper fractions.
(**a**) $1\frac{3}{5}$ (**b**) $2\frac{2}{7}$ (**c**) $4\frac{1}{7}$ (**d**) $7\frac{1}{9}$ (**e**) $5\frac{3}{4}$ (**f**) $8\frac{3}{5}$

3. Arrange each set of fractions in descending order of value.
(**a**) $\frac{4}{5}, \frac{6}{7}$ (**b**) $\frac{2}{3}, \frac{2}{5}$ (**c**) $\frac{2}{7}, \frac{3}{8}$ (**d**) $\frac{3}{4}, \frac{4}{5}$

(e) $\dfrac{2}{3}, \dfrac{4}{6}, \dfrac{3}{5}$ (f) $\dfrac{1}{5}, \dfrac{2}{7}, \dfrac{5}{14}$ (g) $\dfrac{2}{5}, \dfrac{3}{6}, \dfrac{2}{3}$ (h) $\dfrac{1}{4}, \dfrac{1}{5}$

4. Divide: Reduce the answer to the lowest terms.

(a) $\dfrac{2}{3} \div \dfrac{3}{8}$ (b) $\dfrac{4}{5} \div \dfrac{3}{5}$ (c) $\dfrac{5}{7} \div \dfrac{5}{14}$ (d) $\dfrac{2}{5} \div \dfrac{3}{10}$

5. Multiply: Reduce to the lowest terms.

(a) $\dfrac{2}{5} \times \dfrac{3}{4}$ (b) $\dfrac{3}{8} \times \dfrac{4}{9}$ (c) $\dfrac{3}{5} \times \dfrac{15}{21}$ (d) $\dfrac{2}{7} \times \dfrac{49}{50}$

(e) $\dfrac{2}{3} \times \dfrac{2}{5} \times \dfrac{3}{4}$ (f) $\dfrac{1}{4} \times \dfrac{2}{7} \times \dfrac{3}{4}$ (g) $\dfrac{2}{5} \times \dfrac{1}{5} \times \dfrac{2}{3}$ (h) $\dfrac{1}{5} \times \dfrac{2}{3} \times \dfrac{3}{4}$

6. Subtract: Reduce to the lowest terms.

(a) $\dfrac{3}{4} - \dfrac{1}{3}$ (b) $\dfrac{7}{9} - \dfrac{5}{18}$ (c) $\dfrac{7}{8} - \dfrac{5}{24}$ (d) $\dfrac{2}{3} - \dfrac{5}{15}$

7. Add and change the answers to mixed numbers.

(a) $\dfrac{2}{5} + \dfrac{1}{5} + \dfrac{4}{5} + \dfrac{3}{5}$ (b) $\dfrac{5}{8} + \dfrac{7}{8} + \dfrac{3}{8} + \dfrac{1}{8}$

(c) $\dfrac{5}{7} + \dfrac{4}{5}$ (d) $\dfrac{4}{8} + \dfrac{3}{4}$ (e) $\dfrac{1}{4} + \dfrac{5}{7}$

8. Change each fraction to a higher equivalent fraction that has the given denominator.

(a) $\dfrac{3}{10} = \dfrac{}{100}$ (b) $\dfrac{5}{25} = \dfrac{}{100}$ (c) $\dfrac{5}{8} = \dfrac{}{64}$

(d) $\dfrac{4}{7} = \dfrac{}{21}$ (e) $\dfrac{8}{9} = \dfrac{}{27}$ (f) $\dfrac{3}{7} = \dfrac{}{49}$

9. Add: Reduce to the lowest term.

(a) $\dfrac{2}{3}$ (b) $\dfrac{1}{4}$ (c) $\dfrac{2}{5}$ (d) $\dfrac{5}{12}$

   $\dfrac{4}{5}$ $\dfrac{3}{4}$ $\dfrac{2}{3}$ $\dfrac{2}{3}$

   $\dfrac{1}{2}$ $\dfrac{2}{3}$ $\dfrac{7}{15}$ $\dfrac{3}{4}$

10. Subtract: Reduce to the lowest term.

(a) $21 - 17\dfrac{2}{5}$ (b) $40 - 12\dfrac{1}{4}$ (c) $14 - 10\dfrac{5}{7}$

11. Add: Reduce to the lowest term.

(a) $2\dfrac{2}{3}$ (b) $3\dfrac{1}{3}$ (c) $4\dfrac{2}{3}$ (d) $\dfrac{2}{5}$

$$\begin{array}{c} 1\frac{1}{4} \\ 1\frac{1}{4} \\ \hline \end{array} \qquad \begin{array}{c} 4 \\ 2\frac{3}{4} \\ \hline \end{array} \qquad \begin{array}{c} 2\frac{1}{4} \\ 8 \\ \hline \end{array} \qquad \begin{array}{c} \frac{3}{4} \\ \frac{2}{20} \\ \hline \end{array}$$

12. Divide: Reduce to the lowest term.

(a) $\dfrac{3}{4} \div \dfrac{3}{4}$ (b) $6\dfrac{4}{5} \div \dfrac{2}{5}$ (c) $3\dfrac{1}{2} \div 1\dfrac{3}{4}$ (d) $\dfrac{3}{4} \div \dfrac{3}{8}$

(e) $7\dfrac{3}{6} \div 5$ (f) $10 \div 2\dfrac{2}{5}$

13. Find the unknown number.

(a) $\dfrac{2}{3}$ of what number is 90? (b) $\dfrac{1}{4}$ of what number is 24?

(c) $\dfrac{3}{7}$ of what number is 36? (d) $\dfrac{3}{5}$ of what number is 15?

14. Find the fractional parts.
(a) 3 is what part of 15? (b) 4 is what part of 24?
(c) 20 is what part of 60? (d) 5 is what part of 50?

15. Reduce the following to the lowest term

(a) $\dfrac{4}{12}$ (b) $\dfrac{5}{45}$ (c) $\dfrac{24}{60}$ (d) $\dfrac{36}{72}$ (e) $\dfrac{18}{72}$

MULTIPLICATION OF FRACTIONS, WHOLE NUMBERS, AND MIXED NUMBERS

Rule 1: To multiply whole numbers by mixed numbers or to multiply mixed numbers by whole numbers, change both the mixed numbers and the whole numbers to improper fractions.

Rule 2: To change a whole number to an improper fraction, write the whole number over the number 1 as the denominator.

Example 1
Write the following as improper fractions:

(**a**) 3   (**b**) 4   (**c**) 17   (**d**) 100

Solution

(**a**) The improper fraction of $3 = \dfrac{3}{1}$ (Use Rule 2)

(**b**) The improper fraction of $4 = \dfrac{4}{1}$ (Use Rule 2)

(**c**) The improper fraction of $17 = \dfrac{17}{1}$ (Use Rule 2)

(**d**) The improper fraction of $100 = \dfrac{100}{1}$ (Use Rule 2)

Rule 3: **To change a mixed number to an improper fraction, multiply the denominator by the whole number, add the numerator to the product, and then write the sum over the denominator.**

Example 2

Write the following mixed numbers as improper fractions:

(a) $4\dfrac{3}{11}$ (b) $3\dfrac{3}{4}$ (c) $10\dfrac{4}{7}$

Solution

(**a**) Using Rule 3, multiply 11 by 4, add 3 to the product (the product of 11 and 4) and write the sum over 11.

Therefore, $4\dfrac{3}{11} = \dfrac{11 \times 4 + 3}{11} = \dfrac{47}{11}$

The improper fraction of $4\dfrac{3}{11}$ is $\dfrac{47}{11}$.

(**b**) Using Rule 3, multiply 4 by 3, add 3 to the product (the product of 4 and 3) and write the sum over 4

Therefore, $3\dfrac{3}{4} = \dfrac{4 \times 3 + 3}{4} = \dfrac{15}{4}$

The improper fraction of $3\dfrac{3}{4}$ is $\dfrac{15}{4}$.

(**c**) Using Rule 3, multiply 7 by 10, add 4 to the product (the product of 7 and 10) and write the sum over 7.

Therefore, $10\dfrac{4}{7} = \dfrac{7 \times 10 + 4}{7} = \dfrac{74}{7}$

The improper fraction of $10\frac{4}{7}$ is $\frac{47}{7}$.

Example 3

Multiply: $4 \times 7\frac{3}{5}$

Solution

Step 1: Change both the whole number 4 and the mixed fraction $7\frac{3}{5}$ to improper

fractions and multiply the improper fractions. (See Rule 1)

The improper fraction of $4 = \frac{4}{1}$ (See Rule 2)

The improper fraction of $7\frac{3}{5} = \frac{7 \times 5 + 3}{5} = \frac{38}{5}$ (See Rule 3)

Write the multiplication of both improper fractions as shown:

$$\frac{4}{1} \times \frac{38}{5}$$

Step 2: Reduce the improper fractions to the lowest terms by dividing both the numerators and the denominators by the same numbers if possible.

Note that in this example, $\frac{4}{1} \times \frac{38}{5}$

there are no numbers that can divide both the numerators and the denominators evenly (without a remainder), go to Step 3.

Step 3: Multiply the numerators together and multiply the denominators together and put the product of the numerators over the product of the denominators.

$$\frac{4}{1} \times \frac{38}{5} = \frac{4 \times 38}{1 \times 5}$$

$$= \frac{152}{5}$$

Step 4: Change the improper fraction $\frac{152}{5}$ in Step 3 to mixed numbers by dividing

the numerator by the denominator.

$$\frac{152}{5} = 30\frac{2}{5} \qquad (152 \div 5 = 30 \text{ remainder } 2 = 30\frac{2}{5})$$

Therefore, $4 \times 7\dfrac{3}{5} = 30\dfrac{2}{5}$

Example 4

Multiply: $3 \times 4\dfrac{2}{3}$

Solution

Step 1: Change both the whole number 3 and the mixed fraction $4\dfrac{2}{3}$ to improper

fractions and multiply the improper fractions. (See Rule 1)

The improper fraction of $3 = \dfrac{3}{1}$ (See Rule 2)

The improper fraction of $4\dfrac{2}{3} = \dfrac{4 \times 3 + 2}{3}$ (See Rule 3)

$$= \dfrac{14}{3}$$

Write the multiplication of both improper fractions as shown:

$$\dfrac{3}{1} \times \dfrac{14}{3}$$

Step 2: Reduce the improper fractions to the lowest terms by dividing both the numerators and the denominators by the same number or numbers if possible.

$$\overset{1}{\underset{}{\dfrac{3}{1}}} \times \dfrac{14}{\underset{1}{3}}$$ Divide both the numerator and the denominator by 3.

                   Note: $3 \div 3 = 1$

Step 3: Multiply the numerators together and multiply the denominators together and put the product of the numerators over the product of the denominators.

From Step 2, $\dfrac{1}{1} \times \dfrac{14}{1} = \dfrac{1 \times 14}{1 \times 1}$

$$= \dfrac{14}{1}$$
$$= 14$$

Example 5

Multiply: $2\dfrac{2}{10} \times 5$

Solution

Step 1: Change both the fraction $2\frac{2}{10}$ and the whole number 5 to improper fractions and multiply the improper fractions.　　　(See Rule 1)

The improper fraction of $2\frac{2}{10} = \dfrac{10 \times 2 + 2}{10}$　　(See Rule 3)

$$= \frac{22}{10}$$

The improper fraction of $5 = \dfrac{5}{1}$　　　　(See Rule 2)

Write the multiplication of both improper fractions as shown:

$$\frac{22}{10} \times \frac{5}{1}$$

Step 2: Reduce the improper fractions to the lowest terms by dividing both the numerators and the denominators by the same number or numbers if possible.

$$\overset{\overset{11}{\cancel{22}}}{\underset{\underset{2}{\cancel{10}}}{}} \times \overset{1}{\underset{1}{\cancel{5}}} \quad (5 \div 5 = 1, \; 10 \div 5 = 2 , \; 2 \div 2 = 1, \; 22 \div 2 = 11)$$

$$= \frac{11}{1} \times \frac{1}{1}$$

Step 3: Multiply the numerators together and multiply the denominators together and put the product of the numerators over the product of the denominators.

From Step 2, $\dfrac{11}{1} \times \dfrac{1}{1} = \dfrac{11 \times 1}{1 \times 1}$

$$= \frac{11}{1}$$

$$= 11$$

Example 6

Multiply: $21 \times 2\frac{3}{14} \times 4$

Solution

Step 1: Change the whole number 21, the mixed number $2\dfrac{3}{14}$ and the whole number 4 to improper fractions and multiply all the improper fractions. (See Rule 1)

The improper fraction of $21 = \dfrac{21}{1}$ (See Rule 2)

The improper fraction of $2\dfrac{3}{14} = \dfrac{14 \times 2 + 3}{14}$ (See Rule 3)

$$= \dfrac{31}{14}$$

The improper fraction of $4 = \dfrac{4}{1}$ (See Rule 2)

Write the multiplication of all the improper fractions as shown:

$$\dfrac{21}{1} \times \dfrac{31}{14} \times \dfrac{4}{1}$$

Step 2: Reduce the improper fractions to the lowest terms by dividing the numerators and the denominators by the same number or numbers if possible.

$$\dfrac{\overset{3}{\cancel{21}}}{1} \times \dfrac{31}{\underset{2}{\cancel{14}}} \times \dfrac{\overset{2}{\cancel{4}}}{\underset{1}{}} \qquad (21 \div 7 = 3,\ 14 \div 7 = 2,\ 2 \div 2 = 1,\ 4 \div 2 = 2)$$

$$= \dfrac{3}{1} \times \dfrac{31}{1} \times \dfrac{2}{1}$$

Step 3: Multiply the numerators together and multiply the denominators together and put the product of the numerators over the product of the denominators.

From step 2, $\quad \dfrac{3}{1} \times \dfrac{31}{1} \times \dfrac{2}{1} = \dfrac{3 \times 31 \times 2}{1 \times 1 \times 1}$

$$= \dfrac{186}{1}$$

$$= 186$$

Example 7

Multiply: $2\dfrac{1}{2} \times 3\dfrac{1}{5}$

Solution

Step 1: Change the mixed number $2\dfrac{1}{2}$ and the mixed number $3\dfrac{1}{5}$ to improper fractions and multiply the improper fractions.   (See Rule 1)

The improper fraction of $2\dfrac{1}{2} = \dfrac{2 \times 2 + 1}{2}$ (See Rule 3)

$$= \dfrac{5}{2}$$

The improper fraction of $3\dfrac{1}{5} = \dfrac{5 \times 3 + 1}{5}$ (See Rule 3)

$$= \dfrac{16}{5}$$

Write the multiplication of the improper fractions as shown:

$$\dfrac{5}{2} \times \dfrac{16}{5}$$

Step 2: Reduce the improper fractions to the lowest terms by dividing the numerators and the denominators by the same number or numbers if possible.

$$\dfrac{\overset{1}{\cancel{5}}}{\underset{1}{\cancel{2}}} \times \dfrac{\overset{8}{\cancel{16}}}{\underset{1}{\cancel{5}}} \qquad (2 \div 2 = 1,\ 16 \div 2 = 8,\ 5 \div 5 = 1)$$

$$= \dfrac{1}{1} \times \dfrac{8}{1}$$

Step 3: Multiply the numerators together and multiply the denominators together and put the product of the numerators over the product of the denominators.

From step 2, $\dfrac{1}{1} \times \dfrac{8}{1} = \dfrac{1 \times 8}{1 \times 1}$

$$= \dfrac{8}{1}$$

$$= 8$$

Example 8

Multiply: $2\dfrac{3}{4} \times 3\dfrac{1}{6} \times 2\dfrac{2}{11}$

Solution

Step 1: Change the mixed numbers $2\dfrac{3}{4}$, $3\dfrac{1}{6}$ and $2\dfrac{2}{11}$ to improper fractions and multiply the improper fractions. (See Rule 1)

The improper fraction of $2\dfrac{3}{4} = \dfrac{4 \times 2 + 3}{4}$ (See Rule 3)

$$= \dfrac{11}{4}$$

The improper fraction of $3\dfrac{1}{6} = \dfrac{6 \times 3 + 1}{6}$ (See Rule 3)

$$= \dfrac{19}{6}$$

The improper fraction of $2\dfrac{2}{11} = \dfrac{11 \times 2 + 2}{11}$ (See Rule 3)

$$= \dfrac{24}{11}$$

Write the multiplication of the improper fractions as shown:

$$\dfrac{11}{4} \times \dfrac{19}{6} \times \dfrac{24}{11}$$

Step 2: Reduce the improper fractions to the lowest terms by dividing the numerators and the denominators by the same number or numbers if possible.

324

$$\begin{array}{ccc} & & 1 \\ 1 & & 6 \\ \frac{\cancel{11}}{4} \times \frac{19}{6} \times \frac{24}{\cancel{11}} & & \\ 1 & 1 & 1 \end{array} \quad (\ 11 \div 11 = 1,\ 4 \div 4 = 1,\ 24 \div 4 = 6,\ 6 \div 6 = 1)$$

Step 3: Multiply the numerators together and multiply the denominators together and put the product of the numerators over the product of the denominators.

From Step 2, $\dfrac{1}{1} \times \dfrac{19}{1} \times \dfrac{1}{1} = \dfrac{1 \times 19 \times 1}{1 \times 1 \times 1}$

$$= \frac{19}{1}$$

$$= 19$$

Example 9

Multiply: $2\dfrac{1}{6} \times 4\dfrac{3}{4} \times 1\dfrac{1}{19} \times 3\dfrac{1}{5}$

Solution

Step 1: Change the mixed numbers $2\dfrac{1}{6}$, $4\dfrac{3}{4}$, $1\dfrac{1}{19}$, and $3\dfrac{1}{5}$ to improper fractions.

(See Rule 1)

The improper fraction of $2\dfrac{1}{6} = \dfrac{6 \times 2 + 1}{6}$ (See Rule 3)

$$= \frac{13}{6}$$

The improper fraction of $4\dfrac{3}{4} = \dfrac{4 \times 4 + 3}{4}$ (See Rule 3)

$$= \frac{19}{4}$$

The improper fraction of $1\dfrac{1}{19} = \dfrac{19 \times 1 + 1}{19}$ (See Rule 3)

$$= \frac{20}{19}$$

325

The improper fraction of $3\dfrac{1}{5} = \dfrac{5 \times 3 + 1}{5}$ (See Rule 3)

$$= \dfrac{16}{5}$$

Write the multiplication of all the improper fractions as shown:

$$\dfrac{13}{6} \times \dfrac{19}{4} \times \dfrac{20}{19} \times \dfrac{16}{5}$$

Step 2: Reduce the improper fractions to the lowest terms by dividing the numerators and the denominators by the same numbers if possible.

$$\dfrac{\overset{1}{\cancel{13}}}{\underset{3}{\cancel{6}}} \times \dfrac{\overset{1}{\cancel{19}}}{\underset{1}{\cancel{4}}} \times \dfrac{\overset{\overset{2}{\cancel{10}}}{\cancel{20}}}{\underset{1}{\cancel{19}}} \times \dfrac{\overset{4}{\cancel{16}}}{\underset{1}{\cancel{5}}}$$
$(19 \div 19 = 1, 6 \div 2 = 3, 20 \div 2 = 10,)$

$(5 \div 5 = 1, 10 \div 5 = 2, 4 \div 4 = 1, 16 \div 4 = 4)$

$$= \dfrac{13}{3} \times \dfrac{1}{1} \times \dfrac{2}{1} \times \dfrac{4}{1}$$

Step 3: Multiply the numerators together and multiply the denominators together and put the product of the numerators over the product of the denominators.

From Step 2, $\dfrac{13}{3} \times \dfrac{1}{1} \times \dfrac{2}{1} \times \dfrac{4}{1} = \dfrac{13 \times 1 \times 2 \times 4}{3 \times 1 \times 1 \times 1}$

$$= \dfrac{104}{3}$$

Step 4: Change the improper fraction $\dfrac{104}{3}$ in Step 3 to mixed numbers by dividing the numerator by the denominator.

$$\dfrac{104}{3} = 34\dfrac{2}{3} \qquad (104 \div 3 = 34 \text{ remainder } 2 = 34\dfrac{2}{3})$$

Example 10

Multiply: $3\dfrac{1}{4} \times 4 \times 2\dfrac{2}{13} \times 2$

Solution

Step 1: Change the mixed number $3\dfrac{1}{4}$, the whole number 4, the mixed number $2\dfrac{2}{13}$

and the whole number 2 to improper fractions. (See Rule 1)

The improper fraction of $3\frac{1}{4} = \frac{4 \times 3 + 1}{4}$ (See Rule 3)

$$= \frac{13}{4}$$

The improper fraction of $4 = \frac{4}{1}$ (See Rule 2)

The improper fraction of $2\frac{2}{13} = \frac{13 \times 2 + 2}{13}$ (See Rule 3)

$$= \frac{28}{13}$$

The improper fraction of $2 = \frac{2}{1}$ (See Rule 2)

Write the multiplication of the improper fractions as shown:

$$\frac{13}{4} \times \frac{4}{1} \times \frac{28}{13} \times \frac{2}{1}$$

Step 2: Reduce the improper fractions to the lowest terms by dividing the numerators and the denominators by the same number or numbers if possible.

$$\frac{\overset{1}{\cancel{13}}}{\underset{1}{\cancel{4}}} \times \frac{\overset{1}{\cancel{4}}}{1} \times \frac{28}{\underset{1}{\cancel{13}}} \times \frac{2}{1} \qquad (13 \div 13 = 1,\ 4 \div 4 = 1)$$

$$= \frac{1}{1} \times \frac{1}{1} \times \frac{28}{1} \times \frac{2}{1}$$

Step 3: Multiply the numerators together and multiply the denominators together and put the product of the numerators over the product of the denominators.

From Step 2, $\frac{1}{1} \times \frac{1}{1} \times \frac{28}{1} \times \frac{2}{1} = \frac{1 \times 1 \times 28 \times 2}{1 \times 1 \times 1 \times 1}$

$$= \frac{56}{1}$$

$$= 56$$

Recommendation

Examples 1 to 10 show the detailed methods of solving the problems in order to provide the students with the logic needed in solving similar problems. Once the students master the skills of the problem solving, the detailed solution is not needed in doing homework, class exercises, or tests. The understanding of the logic of the problem solving is very important, and then the student can use shortcuts in solving similar problems.

It is recommended that after the students master the logic of the problem solving, during homework, class exercises or tests, the students should begin solving the problems starting from step 2, without showing detailed solutions as shown in Example 11.

Example 11

Multiply: $4\dfrac{1}{5} \times 1\dfrac{4}{11} \times 2\dfrac{3}{4} \times 2$

Solution

$$\dfrac{\cancel{21}}{\cancel{5}} \times \dfrac{\overset{3}{\cancel{15}}}{\cancel{11}} \times \dfrac{\overset{1}{\cancel{11}}}{\cancel{4}} \times \dfrac{\overset{1}{\cancel{2}}}{\cancel{1}} = \dfrac{63}{2} = 31\dfrac{1}{2}$$

The notes and the generous worked examples have provided me with conceptual understanding and computational fluency to do my homework.

Exercises

1. How do you change a whole number to an improper fraction? (Hint: See Rule 2)
2. How do you change a mixed number to an improper fraction? (Hint: See Rule 3)
3. Write the following as improper fractions: (a) 2, (b) 4, (c) 13 , (d) 200. (Hint: See Example **1**).
4. How do you change a mixed number to an improper fraction? (Hint: See Rule 3)
5. Write the following mixed numbers as improper fractions: (Hint: See Example **2**) Reduce to the lowest terms.

   (a) $2\dfrac{1}{2}$ (b) $7\dfrac{3}{4}$ (c) $10\dfrac{3}{4}$ (d) $4\dfrac{5}{6}$ (e) $7\dfrac{1}{7}$ (f) $5\dfrac{3}{5}$

6. Multiply the following whole numbers and mixed numbers: (Hint See Example **3**) Reduce to the lowest terms.

   (a) $6 \times 1\dfrac{7}{5}$ (b) $2 \times 2\dfrac{2}{3}$ (c) $3 \times 3\dfrac{2}{5}$ (d) $5 \times 2\dfrac{1}{4}$

(e) $4 \times 2\frac{2}{3}$ **(f)** $4 \times 3\frac{1}{7}$ **(g)** $6 \times 2\frac{2}{7}$ **(h)** $2 \times 2\frac{1}{9}$

7. Multiply the following whole numbers and mixed numbers: (Hint: See Example **4**)
   Reduce to the lowest terms.

   (a) $4 \times 3\frac{1}{4}$ **(b)** $6 \times 2\frac{1}{6}$ **(c)** $5 \times 3\frac{2}{5}$

   (d) $7 \times 2\frac{2}{7}$ **(e)** $3 \times 4\frac{1}{3}$ **(f)** $2 \times 3\frac{1}{2}$

   (g) $3 \times 4\frac{2}{3}$ **(h)** $8 \times 2\frac{3}{8}$ **(i)** $5 \times 2\frac{3}{5}$

8. Multiply the following whole numbers and mixed numbers: (Hint: See Example **5**).
   Reduce to the lowest terms.

   (a) $3\frac{1}{3} \times 3$ **(b)** $2\frac{1}{2} \times 2$ **(c)** $3\frac{1}{4} \times 4$ **(d)** $2\frac{2}{5} \times 5$

   (e) $4\frac{1}{2} \times 2$ **(f)** $3\frac{3}{4} \times 4$ **(g)** $5\frac{1}{5} \times 5$ **(h)** $2\frac{1}{6} \times 6$

9. Multiply the following whole numbers and a fraction: (Hint: See Example **6**)
   Reduce to the lowest terms.

   (a) $3 \times 4\frac{2}{3} \times 4$ **(b)** $2 \times 6\frac{1}{2} \times 3$ **(c)** $4 \times 2\frac{2}{3} \times 6$

   (d) $4 \times 3\frac{3}{4} \times 2$ **(e)** $5 \times 2\frac{2}{5} \times 3$ **(f)** $3 \times 4\frac{1}{3} \times 2$

   (g) $5 \times 3\frac{1}{5} \times 4$ **(h)** $7 \times 2\frac{5}{7} \times 3$ **(i)** $4 \times 3 \times 3\frac{3}{4}$

10. Multiply the following mixed numbers: (Hint: See Example **7**)
    Reduce to the lowest terms.

    (a) $3\frac{1}{3} \times 2\frac{1}{5}$ **(b)** $2\frac{2}{3} \times 1\frac{2}{4}$ **(c)** $3\frac{1}{3} \times 2\frac{2}{5}$

    (d) $2\frac{1}{4} \times 2\frac{2}{3}$ **(e)** $1\frac{2}{5} \times 2\frac{1}{7}$ **(f)** $2\frac{2}{3} \times 3\frac{3}{4}$

    (g) $4\frac{1}{2} \times 2\frac{2}{3}$ **(h)** $5\frac{3}{5} \times 4\frac{2}{7}$ **(i)** $1\frac{3}{4} \times 2\frac{2}{3}$

11. Multiply the following mixed numbers: (Hint: See Example **8**)
   Reduce to the lowest terms.

(a) $2\dfrac{1}{2} \times 4\dfrac{1}{6} \times 2\dfrac{2}{5}$

(b) $3\dfrac{2}{3} \times 2\dfrac{3}{11} \times 3\dfrac{1}{2}$

(c) $4\dfrac{2}{3} \times 2\dfrac{1}{7} \times 3\dfrac{1}{5}$

(d) $3\dfrac{1}{4} \times 2\dfrac{2}{7} \times 1\dfrac{1}{13}$

(e) $2\dfrac{1}{3} \times 4\dfrac{1}{2} \times 2\dfrac{1}{7}$

(f) $3\dfrac{1}{3} \times 1\dfrac{1}{2} \times 2\dfrac{4}{10}$

(g) $5\dfrac{3}{4} \times 2\dfrac{2}{5} \times 1\dfrac{1}{23}$

(h) $1\dfrac{3}{4} \times 2\dfrac{2}{7} \times 2\dfrac{2}{5}$

12. Multiply the following mixed numbers: (Hint: See Example **9**)
   Reduce to the lowest terms.

(a) $1\dfrac{1}{6} \times 2\dfrac{1}{5} \times 1\dfrac{1}{11} \times 2\dfrac{1}{7}$

(b) $2\dfrac{1}{7} \times 3\dfrac{1}{5} \times 4\dfrac{3}{4} \times 1\dfrac{1}{3}$

(c) $2\dfrac{1}{3} \times 6\dfrac{2}{5} \times 3\dfrac{1}{3} \times 2\dfrac{1}{2}$

(d) $4\dfrac{2}{3} \times 1\dfrac{3}{7} \times 2\dfrac{1}{6} \times 2\dfrac{2}{5}$

(e) $3\dfrac{2}{3} \times 4\dfrac{3}{4} \times 1\dfrac{1}{11} \times 2\dfrac{5}{6}$

(f) $7\dfrac{1}{7} \times 1\dfrac{4}{10} \times 3\dfrac{1}{5} \times 4\dfrac{3}{4}$

(g) $2\dfrac{2}{3} \times 3\dfrac{3}{5} \times 4\dfrac{1}{6} \times 7\dfrac{1}{3}$

(h) $4\dfrac{1}{2} \times 9\dfrac{2}{7} \times 4\dfrac{3}{5} \times 2\dfrac{3}{9}$

13. Multiply the following whole numbers and mixed numbers:
   (Hint: See Example **10**). Reduce your answers to the lowest terms if needed.

(a) $2\dfrac{1}{2} \times 3 \times 4\dfrac{4}{5} \times 2$

(b) $3\dfrac{1}{3} \times 3 \times 1\dfrac{1}{10} \times 4$

(c) $3\dfrac{1}{4} \times 9 \times 1\dfrac{1}{6} \times 2$

(d) $1\dfrac{3}{7} \times 14 \times 2\dfrac{2}{3} \times 3$

(e) $2 \times 4\dfrac{1}{3} \times 2\dfrac{1}{2} \times 3$

(f) $1\dfrac{1}{3} \times 4\dfrac{2}{7} \times 14 \times 2$

(g) $5 \times 2\dfrac{1}{2} \times 3\dfrac{1}{5} \times 2$

(h) $3\dfrac{1}{3} \times 2\dfrac{1}{7} \times 3 \times 2$

Challenge Questions
14. Multiply: Reduce to the lowest terms.

(a) $8 \times 3\frac{3}{4}$

(b) $1\frac{1}{3} \times 6\frac{1}{4} \times 1\frac{3}{5} \times 2\frac{1}{2}$

(c) $12 \times 5\frac{1}{6}$

(d) $4 \times 3\frac{2}{3} \times 3$

(e) $4\frac{2}{3} \times 5\frac{1}{7}$

(f) $3\frac{2}{3} \times 2\frac{1}{5} \times 2\frac{1}{7}$

(g) $2\frac{1}{2} \times 1\frac{3}{5} \times 6$

(h) $5\frac{1}{5} \times 1\frac{1}{13} \times 2 \times 2\frac{4}{7}$

(i) $3\frac{1}{3} \times 1\frac{1}{5} \times 4\frac{1}{6}$

(j) $5 \times 2\frac{2}{5} \times 2\frac{1}{4}$

Answers to Selected Questions

5(a) $\frac{5}{2}$　　**6(a)** $14\frac{2}{5}$　　**7(a)** 13　　**8(a)** 10　　**9(a)** 56

10(a) $7\frac{1}{3}$　　**11(a)** 25　　**12(a)** 6　　**13(a)** 72

Cumulative Review

1. Simplify:

　a. $32 \div 4 \times 2 =$　　**b.** $32 \times 4 \div 2 =$　　**c.** $7 + 3 \times 2 =$

　d. $2 - 1 + 2 =$　　**e.** $17 - 5 \times 3 =$　　**f.** $3.97 \times 3 =$

　g. $7.38 \times 2.3 =$　　**h.** $5^2 - 3^2 \times 2^2 =$　　**i.** $6^2 \times 2 =$

REAL WORLD APPLICATIONS - WORD PROBLEMS
MULTIPLICATION OF FRACTIONS, WHOLE NUMBERS, AND MIXED NUMBERS

Example 1

John needs $4\frac{3}{5}$ yards of material for a school project. How many yards of material will he need for 4 projects, assuming that each project requires the same amount of material?

Solution

1 school project needs $4\frac{3}{5}$ yards of material.

4 school projects will need $4 \times 4\frac{3}{5}$ yards of material.

We need to multiply 4 by $4\frac{3}{5}$ to obtain the amount of material needed.

Step 1: Change the whole number 4 and the mixed number $4\frac{3}{5}$ to improper fractions and multiply the improper fractions. (See Rule 1)

The improper fraction of $4 = \frac{4}{1}$ (See Rule 2)

The improper fraction of $4\frac{3}{5} = \frac{5 \times 4 + 3}{5}$ (See Rule 3)

$$= \frac{23}{5}$$

Write the multiplication of both of the improper fractions as shown:

$$\frac{4}{1} \times \frac{23}{5}$$

Step 2: Reduce the improper fractions to the lowest terms by dividing both the numerators and the denominators by the same number or numbers if possible.

Note that in this example, $\frac{4}{1} \times \frac{23}{5}$, there are no numbers that can divide both the numerators and the denominators evenly (without a remainder.)

Step 3: Multiply the numerators together and multiply the denominators together and put the product of the numerators over the product of the denominators.

$$\frac{4}{1} \times \frac{23}{5} = \frac{4 \times 23}{1 \times 5}$$

$$= \frac{92}{5}$$

Step 4: Change the improper fraction $\frac{92}{5}$ in Step 3 to mixed numbers by dividing the numerator by the denominator.

$$\frac{92}{5} = 18\frac{2}{5} \qquad (92 \div 5 = 18 \text{ remainder } 2 = 18\frac{2}{5})$$

Therefore, $18\frac{2}{5}$ yards of material will be needed for the 4 projects.

Example 2

A ground beef patty weighs $\frac{1}{3}$ pound. How many pounds will 24 ground beef patties weigh?

Solution

1 ground beef patty weighs $\frac{1}{3}$ pound.

24 ground beef patties will weigh $24 \times \frac{1}{3}$ pounds.

We have to multiply 24 by $\frac{1}{3}$ to obtain the weight of the 24 ground beef patties.

Step 1: Change the number 24 to an improper fraction and multiply the improper fraction by $\frac{1}{3}$. (See Rule 1)

The improper fraction of $24 = \frac{24}{1}$ (See Rule 2, under Multiplication of Fractions, Whole and Mixed Numbers.)

Write the multiplication of the improper fraction $\frac{24}{1}$ and $\frac{1}{3}$ as shown:

$$\frac{24}{1} \times \frac{1}{3}$$

Step 2: Reduce the improper fraction $\frac{24}{1}$ and the proper fraction $\frac{1}{3}$ to the lowest terms by dividing the numerators and the denominators by the same number or numbers if possible.

$$\overset{8}{\frac{24}{1}} \times \frac{1}{\underset{1}{3}} \qquad (24 \div 3 = 8, 3 \div 3 = 1)$$

$$= \frac{8}{1} \times \frac{1}{1}$$

Step 3: Multiply the numerators together and multiply the denominators together and put the product of the numerators over the product of the denominators.

From Step 2, $\dfrac{8}{1} \times \dfrac{1}{1} = \dfrac{8 \times 1}{1 \times 1}$

$$= \frac{8}{1}$$

$$= 8$$

Therefore, 24 patties will weigh 8 pounds.

Example 3

Karen's overtime pay is $10\dfrac{1}{2}$ dollars per hour. How much overtime pay did she earn

for $8\dfrac{3}{4}$ hours. (Note: $10\dfrac{1}{2}$ dollars = \$10.50)

Solution

Overtime pay for 1 hour = $10\dfrac{1}{2}$ dollars.

Overtime pay for $8\dfrac{3}{4}$ hours = $8\dfrac{3}{4} \times 10\dfrac{1}{2}$ dollars.

We have to multiply $8\dfrac{3}{4}$ by $10\dfrac{1}{2}$ to obtain the amount of overtime earned in $8\dfrac{3}{4}$ hours.

(See Rule 1)

Step 1: Change the mixed numbers $8\dfrac{3}{4}$ and $10\dfrac{1}{2}$ to improper fractions and multiply

the improper fractions.

$\qquad$ The improper fraction of $8\dfrac{3}{4} = \dfrac{4 \times 8 + 3}{4}$ $\quad$ (See Rule 3 under Multiplication

$\qquad\qquad\qquad\qquad\qquad = \dfrac{35}{4}$ $\qquad\qquad$ of Fractions, Whole and Mixed

$\qquad\qquad\qquad\qquad\qquad\qquad\qquad\qquad\qquad$ Numbers.)

$\qquad$ The improper fraction of $10\dfrac{1}{2} = \dfrac{2 \times 10 + 1}{2}$ $\quad$ (See Rule 3 under Multiplication

$\qquad\qquad\qquad\qquad\qquad\qquad\qquad\qquad$ of Fractions, Whole and Mixed

$\qquad\qquad\qquad\qquad\qquad = \dfrac{21}{2}$ $\qquad\qquad$ Numbers.)

$\qquad$ Write the multiplication of the improper fractions $\dfrac{35}{4}$ and $\dfrac{21}{2}$ as shown:

$$\dfrac{35}{4} \times \dfrac{21}{2}$$

Step 2: Reduce the improper fractions to the lowest terms by dividing the numerator and the denominator by the same number or numbers if possible.

$\qquad$ Note that in this example, $\dfrac{35}{4} \times \dfrac{21}{2}$, there are no numbers that can divide

both the numerators and the denominators evenly (without a remainder.)

Step 3: Multiply the numerators together and multiply the denominators together and put the product of the numerators over the product of the denominators.

$$\dfrac{35}{4} \times \dfrac{21}{2} = \dfrac{35 \times 21}{4 \times 2}$$

$$= \frac{735}{8}$$

Step 4: Change the improper fraction $\frac{735}{8}$ in Step 3 to mixed numbers by dividing the numerator by the denominator if needed.

$$\frac{735}{8} = 91\frac{7}{8} \qquad (735 \div 8 = 91 \text{ remainder } 7 = 91\frac{7}{8})$$

Therefore, Karen earned $91\frac{7}{8}$ dollars for $8\frac{3}{4}$ hours of overtime.

Example 4

Nick needs $12\frac{1}{4}$ feet of lumber for his school project. How many feet of lumber does Nick need in order to complete $10\frac{2}{5}$ of the same project? (Hint: The solution of this example does not show the detailed solution steps. It is recommended that after the student masters the logic of the detailed solution steps, the student should use shortcuts to solve homework, class exercises and tests as shown in this solution. It is recommended that the student should set up the solution initially, and then use Step 2 and Step 3 in solving the problem as shown in this example.

Solution

Initial setup:

1 school project requires $12\frac{1}{4}$ feet of lumber.

$10\frac{2}{5}$ school projects will require $10\frac{2}{5} \times 12\frac{1}{4}$ feet of lumber.

Shortcut Step:

$10\frac{2}{5}$ school projects will require $10\frac{2}{5} \times 12\frac{1}{4}$ feet of lumber.

$$10\frac{2}{5} \times 12\frac{1}{4} = \frac{52}{5} \times \frac{49}{4}$$

$$= \frac{\overset{13}{52}}{5} \times \frac{49}{\underset{1}{4}} \qquad (52 \div 4 = 13, 4 \div 4 = 1).$$

$$= \frac{13 \times 49}{5} = \frac{637}{5} = 127\frac{2}{5}$$

Therefore, $10\frac{2}{7}$ school projects will require $127\frac{2}{5}$ feet of lumber.

Example 5

A fabric material sells at \$3. 25 per yard. How much will $2\frac{2}{13}$ yards cost? (Hint: \$3.25 may be written as $3\frac{1}{4}$. Note that $0.25 = \frac{25}{100} = \frac{1}{4}$. $25 \div 25 = 1$, $100 \div 25 = 4$, hence $\frac{25}{100} = \frac{1}{4}$ and therefore, $3.25 = 3\frac{1}{4}$.) Solve this problem without showing the detailed solutions.

Solution

Initial setup:

1 yard of the fabric material sells at \$3.25.

$2\frac{2}{13}$ yards of the fabric material will cost $2\frac{2}{13} \times 3.25$ dollars.

Shortcut setup:

$2\frac{2}{13}$ yards of the fabric material will cost $2\frac{2}{13} \times 3.25$ dollars.

$$2\frac{2}{13} \times 3\frac{1}{4} = \frac{28}{13} \times \frac{13}{4}$$

$$= \frac{\overset{7}{\cancel{28}}}{\underset{1}{\cancel{13}}} \times \frac{\overset{1}{\cancel{13}}}{\underset{1}{\cancel{4}}}$$

$$= 7$$

Therefore, $2\frac{2}{13}$ yards of the fabric will cost \$7.00.

___

The notes and the generous worked examples have provided me with conceptual understanding and computational fluency to do my homework.

Exercises

1. If Rose, needs $6\frac{2}{5}$ yards of a material for a school project, how many yards of the material will she need for 15 projects assuming that each project requires the same amount of material? (Hint: See Example **1**)

2. Given that a ground beef patty weighs $\frac{2}{3}$ pounds, how many pounds will 30 ground beef patties weigh? (Hint: See Example **2**)

3. John's overtime pay is $12\frac{2}{3}$ dollars per hour. How much overtime pay did he earn for $4\frac{1}{2}$ hours? (Hint: See Example **3**)

4. Karen needs $16\frac{1}{4}$ feet of lumber for her school project. How many feet of lumber does she need to complete $3\frac{1}{5}$ of the same project? (Hint: See Example **4**, use shortcut method to solve this problem.)

5. If a fabric material sells at $5.75 per yard, how much will $2\frac{2}{23}$ yards cost? (Hint: See Example **5**, use the shortcut method to solve this problem. $5.75 may be written as $5\frac{3}{4}$. Note: $0.75 = \frac{75}{100} = \frac{3}{4}$)

Answers to Selected Questions
4. 52 feet.   **5.** $12.00

DIVISION OF FRACTIONS

New words: Divisor, Quotient, and Dividend

Quick Review
Invert: To invert is to turn upside down. Therefore, **to invert a fraction means that the numerator which is at the top will change to the bottom and the denominator which is at the bottom will change to the top.**

If $\frac{1}{4}$ is inverted, it becomes $\frac{4}{1}$. If $\frac{3}{5}$ is inverted, it becomes $\frac{5}{3}$.

If $\frac{99}{100}$ is inverted, it becomes $\frac{100}{99}$. If $\frac{25}{4}$ is inverted, it becomes $\frac{4}{25}$.

Reciprocal: To find the reciprocal of a number is the same as to invert the number.

Rule 1: To divide by fractions, invert the divisor which is the second

fraction and change the division sign to a multiplication sign.

The **reciprocal** of any number or fraction is the same as to divide 1 by the number or by the fraction.

Therefore, the reciprocal of $7 = \dfrac{1}{7}$, _____Case 1.

The **reciprocal** of $\dfrac{3}{5} = \dfrac{1}{\frac{3}{5}}$

$$= 1 \div \dfrac{3}{5} = 1 \times \dfrac{5}{3} \qquad\qquad \text{Using rule 1.}$$

$$= \dfrac{5}{3} \qquad\qquad \text{_____ Case 2.}$$

Considering cases 1 and 2, to invert a number or a fraction is the same as to find the reciprocal of the number.

Example 1

Divide: $\dfrac{3}{4} \div \dfrac{1}{8}$

Solution

Step 1: Use Rule 1, which states that " to divide fractions, invert the divisor which is the second fraction and change the division sign to a multiplication sign."

$\dfrac{3}{4} \div \dfrac{1}{8}$ then becomes $\dfrac{3}{4} \times \dfrac{8}{1}$ (Note that $\dfrac{1}{8}$ is inverted to become $\dfrac{8}{1}$ and the division sign changes to a multiplication sign.)

Step 2: Reduce the fractions to the lowest terms by dividing the numerators and the denominators by the same numbers if possible.

$$\dfrac{3}{4} \times \dfrac{8}{1} = \dfrac{3}{\underset{1}{4}} \times \dfrac{\overset{2}{8}}{1} \qquad\qquad (8 \div 4 = 2,\ 4 \div 4 = 1)$$

$$= \dfrac{3}{1} \times \dfrac{2}{1}$$

Step 3: Multiply the numerators together and multiply the denominators together and put the product of the numerator over the product of the denominator.

From Step 2, $\dfrac{3}{1} \times \dfrac{2}{1} = \dfrac{3 \times 2}{1 \times 1}$

$$= \dfrac{6}{1}$$

$$= 6$$

Example 2

Divide: $\dfrac{3}{8} \div \dfrac{3}{4}$.　　Check your answer.

Solution

Step 1: Use Rule 1

$\dfrac{3}{8} \div \dfrac{3}{4}$ then becomes $\dfrac{3}{8} \times \dfrac{4}{3}$　　(Note that $\dfrac{3}{4}$ is inverted to become $\dfrac{4}{3}$ and the $\div$ changes to $\times$.)

Step 2: Reduce the fractions to the lowest terms by dividing the numerators and the denominators by the same numbers if possible.

$$\dfrac{3}{8} \times \dfrac{4}{3} = \dfrac{\overset{1}{3}}{\underset{2}{8}} \times \dfrac{\overset{1}{4}}{\underset{1}{3}} \qquad (4 \div 4 = 1,\ 8 \div 4 = 2,\ 3 \div 3 = 1)$$

$$= \dfrac{1}{2} \times \dfrac{1}{1}$$

Step 3: Multiply the numerators together and multiply the denominators together and put the product of the numerators over the product of the denominators.

From Step 2, $\dfrac{1}{2} \times \dfrac{1}{1} = \dfrac{1 \times 1}{2 \times 1}$

$$= \dfrac{1}{2}$$

Check answer

From Example 2, $\dfrac{3}{8} \div \dfrac{3}{4} = \dfrac{1}{2}$

Dividend$\searrow$　　$\swarrow$Divisor

$$\dfrac{3}{8} \div \dfrac{3}{4} = \dfrac{1}{2}$$

$\nwarrow$Quotient

The quotient, which is the answer after the division, multiplied by the divisor should equal the dividend.

$$\textbf{Quotient} \times \textbf{Divisor} = \textbf{Dividend} \quad\rule{3cm}{0.4pt}\quad [A].$$

Substitute $\frac{1}{2}$ for Quotient, $\frac{3}{4}$ for Divisor and $\frac{3}{8}$ for Dividend in equation $[A]$.

Equation $[A]$ then becomes $\frac{1}{2} \times \frac{3}{4} = \frac{3}{8}$

$$\frac{1 \times 3}{2 \times 4} = \frac{3}{8}$$

$$\frac{3}{8} = \frac{3}{8} \quad\rule{3cm}{0.4pt}\quad [B]$$

Since the left side of the equation $[B]$ is the same as the right side of equation $[B]$ which is $\frac{3}{8}$, the answer $\frac{1}{2}$ in Step 3 is correct. We can create Rule 2.

Rule 2: **Quotient** $\times$ **Divisor** = **Dividend**

Divisor: For example, if $\frac{3}{4} \div \frac{1}{8}$, $\frac{1}{8}$ is the divisor.

If $\frac{7}{9} \div \frac{2}{5}$, $\frac{2}{5}$ is the divisor.

If $\frac{11}{12} \div \frac{3}{8}$, $\frac{3}{8}$ is the divisor.

Therefore, **the divisor is the number by which a dividend is divided**. The number to be divided is the **dividend**, as shown:

$$\frac{3}{4} \div \frac{1}{8}$$

Dividend   Divisor

Quotient is the number that results from the division of one number by another. Dividend is a quantity to be divided.

Relationship Among Dividend, Divisor, and Quotient
Let us investigate the relationship among the Dividend, Divisor and Quotient by

by using the fact that 8 ÷ 2 = 4 as shown:

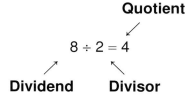

Quotient

$$8 \div 2 = 4$$

Dividend   **Divisor**

Therefore, (**a**) **Dividend ÷ Divisor = Quotient**

or

(**b**) **Quotient × Divisor = Dividend**. This statement will be useful in checking some answers to some questions later.

Example 3

Divide: $\dfrac{5}{8} \div \dfrac{3}{16}$. Check the answer.

Do not show any detailed method. Although the examples are intentionally designed to provide the students with detailed explanations including mathematical logic, it is recommended that the students use shortcuts in solving homework, class exercises and tests as much as possible as shown in Example **3**.

Solution

Shortcut:

$$\frac{5}{8} \div \frac{3}{16} = \frac{5}{8} \times \frac{16}{3}$$

$$= \frac{5}{\overset{}{8}} \times \frac{\overset{2}{16}}{\underset{1}{3}} \qquad \text{(Divide numerator and the denominator by 8.)}$$

$$= \frac{10}{3} \qquad (10 \div 3 = 3, \text{ remainder } 1, = 3\frac{1}{3})$$

$$= 3\frac{1}{3}$$

Check answer

Quotient × Divisor = Dividend

$$3\frac{1}{3} \times \frac{3}{16} = \frac{5}{8}$$

$$\frac{10}{3} \times \frac{3}{16} = \frac{5}{8} \qquad (3\frac{1}{3} = \frac{10}{3})$$

$$\frac{\overset{5}{\underset{1}{\cancel{\underset{3}{\cancel{10}}}}}}{3} \times \frac{\overset{1}{\cancel{3}}}{\underset{8}{\cancel{16}}} = \frac{5}{8}$$ (Divide the numerator and the denominator by 2 and 3).

$$\frac{5}{8} = \frac{5}{8} \hspace{2cm} [A]$$

Left side of equation $[A]$ is equal to the right side of equation $[A]$, therefore, the answer $3\frac{1}{3}$ is correct.

The notes and the generous worked examples have provided me with conceptual understanding and computational fluency to do my homework.

Exercises

1. How are fractions divided? (Hint: See Rule 1)
2. Explain the following:
   (a) Divisor
   (b) Quotient
   (c) Dividend.
   (d). State the relationship among the Divisor, Quotient, and Dividend.
3. Divide the following fractions: (Hint: See Example **1**)

   (a) $\frac{1}{4} \div \frac{3}{8}$ (b) $\frac{4}{5} \div \frac{4}{5}$ (c) $\frac{6}{7} \div \frac{3}{7}$ (d) $\frac{1}{3} \div \frac{5}{6}$

   (e) $\frac{2}{5} \div \frac{1}{5}$ (f) $\frac{5}{12} \div \frac{3}{4}$ (g) $\frac{2}{3} \div \frac{4}{5}$ (h) $\frac{5}{6} \div \frac{5}{6}$

4. Divide the following fractions and check your answer. (Hint: See Examples 2 and 3)

   (a) $\frac{4}{5} \div \frac{9}{10}$ (b) $\frac{2}{7} \div \frac{8}{21}$ (c) $\frac{11}{12} \div \frac{22}{24}$ (d) $\frac{3}{16} \div \frac{4}{9}$

   (e) $\frac{3}{7} \div \frac{6}{21}$ (f) $\frac{7}{15} \div \frac{7}{10}$ (g) $\frac{5}{64} \div \frac{5}{8}$ (h) $\frac{4}{9} \div \frac{5}{18}$

   (i) $\frac{5}{4} \div \frac{5}{16}$ (j) $\frac{5}{81} \div \frac{10}{9}$ (k) $\frac{3}{16} \div \frac{7}{8}$ (l) $\frac{9}{10} \div \frac{3}{5}$

(m) $\dfrac{3}{4} \div \dfrac{4}{5}$ **(n)** $\dfrac{11}{12} \div \dfrac{11}{24}$ **(o)** $\dfrac{3}{5} \div \dfrac{3}{10}$ **(p)** $\dfrac{3}{4} \div \dfrac{5}{6}$

Challenge Questions

5. (a) $\dfrac{1}{3} \div \dfrac{1}{24}$ **(b)** $\dfrac{11}{12} \div \dfrac{11}{24}$ **(c)** $\dfrac{4}{5} \div \dfrac{3}{10}$ **(d)** $\dfrac{6}{49} \div \dfrac{3}{7}$

(e) $\dfrac{5}{64} \div \dfrac{5}{8}$ **(f)** $\dfrac{16}{25} \div \dfrac{4}{15}$ **(g)** $\dfrac{3}{7} \div \dfrac{3}{14}$ **(h)** $\dfrac{2}{9} \div \dfrac{2}{3}$

Answers to Selected Questions

3(a) $\dfrac{2}{3}$ **4(a)** $\dfrac{8}{9}$ **5(a)** 8

REAL WORLD APPLICATIONS - WORD PROBLEMS
Division of Fractions

Example 1

How many $\dfrac{1}{8}$ yard pieces of pipe can be cut from a length of pipe measuring

$\dfrac{19}{24}$ yard? Check your answer.

Solution

Setup: The number of $\dfrac{1}{8}$ yard pieces of pipe that can be cut from a length of $\dfrac{19}{24}$

yard of pipe

$$= \dfrac{19}{24} \div \dfrac{1}{8}$$

Step 1: Use Rule 1, under Division of Fractions.

$$\dfrac{19}{24} \div \dfrac{1}{8} = \dfrac{19}{24} \times \dfrac{8}{1} \quad \text{(Note } \dfrac{1}{8} \text{ changes to } \dfrac{8}{1} \text{ and } \div \text{ changes to } \times.)$$

Step 2: Reduce the fractions to the lowest terms by dividing the numerators and the denominators by the same number or numbers if possible.

$$\dfrac{19}{24} \times \dfrac{8}{1} = \dfrac{19}{\underset{3}{24}} \times \dfrac{\overset{1}{8}}{1} \quad (24 \div 8 = 3, 8 \div 8 = 1)$$

$$= \frac{19}{3} \times \frac{1}{1}$$

Step 3: Multiply the numerators together and multiply the denominators together and put the product of the numerators over the product of the denominators.

From Step 2, $\frac{19}{3} \times \frac{1}{1} = \frac{19 \times 1}{3 \times 1}$

$$= \frac{19}{3}$$

Step 4: Change the improper fraction of $\frac{19}{3}$ to a mixed fraction by dividing the numerator by the denominator if needed.

$$\frac{19}{3} = 6\frac{1}{3} \qquad (19 \div 3 = 6 \text{ reminder } 1, \; = 6\frac{1}{3})$$

Therefore, $6\frac{1}{3}$ pieces of $\frac{1}{8}$ yard of pipe can be cut.

Check the answer

Quotient × Divisor = Dividend

$$6\frac{1}{3} \times \frac{1}{8} = \frac{19}{24}$$

$$\frac{19}{3} \times \frac{1}{8} = \frac{19}{24} \qquad (6\frac{1}{3} = \frac{19}{3})$$

$$\frac{19 \times 1}{3 \times 8} = \frac{19}{24}$$

$$\frac{19}{24} = \frac{19}{24} \qquad \text{———————— [A]}$$

Since the left side of the equation $[A]$ is equal to the right side of the equation $[A]$, the answer $6\frac{1}{3}$ is correct.

Example 2

How many $\frac{1}{8}$ hours are there in $\frac{17}{24}$ hours? Check your answer. Use the shortcut to solve this problem.

Solution

Setup: The number of $\frac{1}{8}$ hour $= \frac{17}{24} \div \frac{1}{8}$

Shortcut: $\frac{17}{24} \div \frac{1}{8} = \frac{17}{24} \times \frac{8}{1}$

$$= \frac{17}{\underset{3}{24}} \times \frac{\overset{1}{8}}{1} \qquad (24 \div 8 = 3, \ 8 \div 8 = 1)$$

$$= \frac{17}{3}$$

$$= 5\frac{2}{3} \qquad (17 \div 3 = 5 \text{ remainder } 2, \ = 5\frac{2}{3})$$

Therefore, there are $5\frac{2}{3}$ of $\frac{1}{8}$ hours in $\frac{17}{24}$ hours.

Check answer

Quotient $\times$ Divisor $=$ Dividend

$$5\frac{2}{3} \times \frac{1}{8} = \frac{17}{24}$$

$$\frac{17}{3} \times \frac{1}{8} = \frac{17}{24}$$

$$\frac{17 \times 1}{3 \times 8} = \frac{17}{24}$$

$$\frac{17}{24} = \frac{17}{24} \ \text{——————————} \ [A]$$

Since the left side of equation $[A]$ is equal to the right side of equation $[A]$ which is $\frac{17}{24}$, the answer is correct.

Example 3

How many periods of 10 minutes are there in $\frac{3}{4}$ of an hour? Use the shortcut method in solving the problem. (Hint: 10 minutes $= \frac{10}{60}$ hour $= \frac{1}{6}$ hour.)

Note: 60 minutes $=$ 1 hour.

Solution

Setup: The number of $\frac{1}{6}$ hour in $\frac{3}{4}$ hour

$$= \frac{3}{4} \div \frac{1}{6}$$

Shortcut:

$$\frac{3}{4} \div \frac{1}{6} = \frac{3}{4} \times \frac{6}{1}$$

$$= \frac{3}{4} \times \frac{\overset{3}{\cancel{6}}}{\underset{2}{1}} \qquad (6 \div 2 = 3, \ 4 \div 2 = 2)$$

$$= \frac{9}{2}$$

$$= 4\frac{1}{2} \qquad (9 \div 2 = 4 \text{ remainder } 1, = 4\frac{1}{2}).$$

Therefore, there are $4\frac{1}{2}$ of 10 minutes in $\frac{3}{4}$ hour.

Critical Thinking

Before any division is done, the unit of the dividend and the unit of the divisor must be the same. In Example 3 for example, we cannot divide $\frac{3}{4}$ hour by 10 minutes because we cannot divide hours by minutes, but we are able to divide $\frac{3}{4}$ hour by $\frac{1}{6}$ hour because both the unit of the dividend and the unit of the divisor are the same (hour.)

Example 4

Mary takes an average of 4 minutes to type a letter. How many similar letters can she type in $\frac{3}{4}$ hour? (Hint: Write 4 minutes as a fraction of an hour, and then reduce the fraction to the lowest terms.) Use the shortcut method to solve the problem.

Solution

Setup: First write 4 minutes as a fraction of an hour.

60 minutes = 1 hour

4 minutes $= \dfrac{4}{60}$ hour   (Reduce $\dfrac{4}{60}$ to the lowest terms, $4 \div 4 = 1$

$= \dfrac{1}{15}$ hour $60 \div 4 = 15$.)

In $\dfrac{1}{15}$ hour, 1 letter was typed.

In $\dfrac{3}{4}$ hour, she will type $\dfrac{3}{4} \div \dfrac{1}{15}$ letters.

Shortcut:

$$\dfrac{3}{4} \div \dfrac{1}{15} = \dfrac{3}{4} \times \dfrac{15}{1}$$

$$= \dfrac{3 \times 15}{4 \times 1}$$

$$= \dfrac{45}{4}$$

$$= 11\dfrac{1}{4}$$

Therefore, Mary will type $11\dfrac{1}{4}$ letters in $\dfrac{3}{4}$ hour.

Example 5

Anthony has $\dfrac{11}{12}$ gallon of drinking water. How many pint-size containers does he have? (Hint: 8 pints = 1 gallon)

Setup: Write 1 pint as a fraction of a gallon.

8 pints = 1 gallon

1 pint $= \dfrac{1}{8}$ gallon

The number of pint-size containers in $\dfrac{11}{12}$ gallons $= \dfrac{11}{12} \div \dfrac{1}{8}$

Shortcut: $\dfrac{11}{12} \div \dfrac{1}{8} = \dfrac{11}{12} \times \dfrac{8}{1}$

$$= \dfrac{11}{\underset{3}{12}} \times \dfrac{\overset{2}{8}}{1} \qquad (8 \div 4 = 2,\ 12 \div 4 = 3\,)$$

$$= \frac{11 \times 2}{3 \times 1}$$

$$= \frac{22}{3}$$

$$= 7\frac{1}{3}$$

Therefore, Anthony has $7\frac{1}{3}$ pint-size containers of drinking water.

━━━━━━━━━━━━━━━━━━━━━━━━ **The notes and the generous worked examples have provided me with conceptual understanding and computational fluency to do my homework.**

Exercises

1. How many $\frac{1}{6}$ yard pieces of wood can be cut from a length of wood measuring $\frac{5}{6}$ yard. Check your answer. (Hint: See Example **1**)

2. How many $\frac{1}{6}$ hours are there in $\frac{19}{24}$ hour? Check your answer.

(Hint: See Example **2**) Use the shortcut method to solve this problem.

3. How many periods of 15 minutes are there in $\frac{11}{12}$ of an hour? (Hint: 15 minutes

$= \frac{15}{60}$ hour $= \frac{1}{4}$ hour. Note that 60 minutes = 1 hour). Use the shortcut method to

solve this problem. (Hint: See Example **3**)

4. Nick takes an average of 5 minutes to type a letter. How many similar letters can

he type in $\frac{7}{12}$ hour? Check your answer. (Hint See Example **4**)

(Hint: 5 minutes $= \frac{5}{60}$ hour $= \frac{1}{12}$ hour. Note that 60 minutes = 1 hour).

Use the shortcut method to solve the problem.

5. Samuel has $\frac{7}{8}$ gallon of syrup. How many pint-size containers does he have?

(Hint: 8 pints = 1 gallon. See Example **5**) Use the shortcut method to solve the
problem.

Answers to Selected Questions
(1). 5 pieces of wood   **(4)**. 7 letters

DIVISION BY MIXED NUMBERS

Rule 1: To divide a mixed number by another mixed number, change the mixed numbers to improper fractions, invert the divisor and change the division sign to a multiplication sign.

Rule 2: To change a mixed number to an improper fraction, multiply the denominator by the whole number, add the numerator to the product and then write the sum over the denominator.

Example 1

Divide: $4\dfrac{1}{3} \div 1\dfrac{1}{6}$

Solution

Step 1: Change the mixed numbers $4\dfrac{1}{3}$ and $1\dfrac{1}{6}$ to improper fractions. (See Rule 1)

The improper fraction of the mixed number

$$4\frac{1}{3} = \frac{3 \times 4 + 1}{3} = \frac{13}{3}$$ (See Rule 2 and also Rule 3 under

Multiplication of Fractions, Whole and Mixed Numbers.)

The improper fraction of the mixed number

$$1\frac{1}{6} = \frac{6 \times 1 + 1}{6} = \frac{7}{6}$$ (See Rule 2 and also Rule 3 under

Multiplication of Fractions, Whole and Mixed Numbers,)

Therefore, $4\dfrac{1}{3} \div 1\dfrac{1}{6} = \dfrac{13}{3} \div \dfrac{7}{6}$

Step 2: Invert the divisor and change the ÷ sign to × sign. (Note: $\dfrac{7}{6}$ is the divisor)

$\dfrac{13}{3} \div \dfrac{7}{6}$ from Step 1 becomes $\dfrac{13}{3} \times \dfrac{6}{7}$ ($\dfrac{7}{6}$ is inverted to become $\dfrac{6}{7}$ and

÷ sign is changed to × sign.)
(See Rule 1)

Step 3: Reduce the fractions to the lowest terms by dividing the numerators and the denominators by the same number or numbers if possible.

$$\frac{13}{3} \times \frac{6}{7} = \frac{13}{\underset{1}{3}} \times \frac{\overset{2}{6}}{7} \qquad (6 \div 3 = 2,\ 3 \div 3 = 1)$$

Step 4: Multiply the numerators together and multiply the denominators together and put the product of the numerators over the product of the denominators.

$$\frac{13}{1} \times \frac{2}{7} = \frac{13 \times 2}{1 \times 7}$$

$$= \frac{26}{7} \qquad (26 \div 7 = 3 \text{ remainder } 5,\ = 3\frac{5}{7})$$

$$= 3\frac{5}{7}$$

Example 2

Solve the question in Example 1 without showing any detailed steps. (Hint: This is the shortcut method of problem solving. It is recommended that once the student understands the logic of the detailed solution, the students may use the shortcut method for homework, class exercises and tests.)

Solution

Divide: $4\frac{1}{3} \div 1\frac{1}{6}$ (Question from **Example 1**)

Shortcut

$$4\frac{1}{3} \div 1\frac{1}{6} = \frac{13}{\underset{1}{3}} \times \frac{\overset{2}{6}}{7}$$

$$= \frac{26}{7} = 3\frac{5}{7}$$

Example 3

Divide: $2\frac{2}{3} \div 7\frac{1}{2}$

Solution

Step 1: Change the mixed numbers $2\frac{2}{3}$ and $7\frac{1}{2}$ to improper fractions. (See Rule 1)

      The improper fraction of the mixed number

$$2\frac{2}{3} = \frac{3 \times 2 + 2}{3} = \frac{8}{3}$$ (See Rule 2 and also Rule 3 under

Multiplication of Fractions, Whole and Mixed Numbers.)

The improper fraction of the mixed number

$$7\frac{1}{2} = \frac{2 \times 7 + 1}{2} = \frac{15}{2}$$ (See Rule 2 and also Rule 3 under

Multiplication of Fractions, Whole and Mixed Numbers.)

Therefore, $2\frac{2}{3} \div 7\frac{1}{2} = \frac{8}{3} \div \frac{15}{2}$

Step 2: Invert the divisor and change the ÷ sign to × sign. (Note: $\frac{15}{2}$ is the divisor)

$\frac{8}{3} \div \frac{15}{2}$ from Step 1 becomes $\frac{8}{3} \times \frac{2}{15}$ ($\frac{15}{2}$ is inverted to become $\frac{2}{15}$

and ÷ sign is changed to × sign.)
(See Rule 1)

Step 3: Reduce the fractions to the lowest terms by dividing the numerators and the denominators by the same number or numbers if possible. In this case, there is no number that can divide both the numerators and denominators of $\frac{8}{3} \times \frac{2}{15}$ evenly (without a remainder.)

Step 4: Multiply the numerators together and multiply the denominators together and put the product of the numerators over the product of the denominators as the final answer.

$$\frac{8}{3} \times \frac{2}{15} = \frac{8 \times 2}{3 \times 15} = \frac{16}{45}$$

Example 4
Solve the question in Example **3** without showing any detailed explanations.
Solution

The question in Example **3** is to divide: $2\frac{2}{3} \div 7\frac{1}{2}$

Shortcut method:

$$2\frac{2}{3} \div 7\frac{1}{2} = \frac{8}{3} \times \frac{2}{15}$$

$$= \frac{16}{45}$$

Example 5

Divide: $6\frac{2}{3} \div 3\frac{1}{5}$

Solution

Step 1: Change the mixed numbers $6\frac{2}{3}$ and $3\frac{1}{5}$ to improper fractions.

(See Rule 1).
The improper fraction of the mixed number

$6\frac{2}{3} = \frac{3 \times 6 + 2}{3} = \frac{20}{3}$ (See Rule 2 and also Rule 3 under Multiplication

of Fractions, Whole and Mixed Numbers.)

The improper fraction of the mixed number

$3\frac{1}{5} = \frac{5 \times 3 + 1}{5} = \frac{16}{5}$ (See Rule 2 and also Rule 3 under Multiplication

of Fractions, Whole and Mixed Numbers.)

Therefore, $6\frac{2}{3} \div 3\frac{1}{5} = \frac{20}{3} \div \frac{16}{5}$

Step 2: Invert the divisor and change the ÷ sign to × sign. (Note: $\frac{16}{5}$ is the divisor.)

$\frac{20}{3} \div \frac{16}{5}$ from Step 1 becomes $\frac{20}{3} \times \frac{5}{16}$ ($\frac{16}{5}$ is inverted to become

$\frac{5}{16}$ and ÷ sign changes to × sign.)

(See Rule 1.)

Step 3: Reduce the fractions to the lowest terms by dividing the numerators and the denominators by the same number or numbers if possible.

$$\frac{20}{3} \times \frac{5}{16} = \frac{\overset{5}{20}}{3} \times \frac{5}{\underset{4}{16}}$$ (20 ÷ 4 = 5, 16 ÷ 4 = 4)

Step 4: Multiply the numerators together and multiply the denominators together and put the product of the numerators over the product of the denominators.

$$\frac{5}{3} \times \frac{5}{4} = \frac{5 \times 5}{3 \times 4}$$

$$= \frac{25}{12}$$

Step 5: Change the improper fraction $\frac{25}{12}$ to mixed numbers.

$$\frac{25}{12} = 2\frac{1}{12} \qquad (25 \div 12 = 2 \text{ remainder } 1, \ = 2\frac{1}{12})$$

Example 6

Solve the question in Example **5** without showing any detailed explanations.
(Hint: Use the shortcut method.)

Solution

The question in Example **5** is Divide: $6\frac{2}{3} \div 3\frac{1}{5}$

Solution

$$6\frac{2}{3} \div 3\frac{1}{5} = \frac{\overset{5}{\cancel{20}}}{3} \times \frac{5}{\underset{4}{\cancel{16}}}$$

$$= \frac{25}{12}$$

$$= 2\frac{1}{12}$$

Critical Link

When a fraction is being divided by another fraction, once the divisor is inverted and the ÷ sign changes to × sign, the question becomes multiplication of fractions. There are many examples of solutions of multiplications of fractions under the topic Multiplication of Fractions.

The notes and the generous worked examples have provided me with conceptual understanding and computational fluency to do my homework.

Exercises

1. Divide the following: Reduce to the lowest terms. (Hint: See Example 1.)

(a) $3\frac{1}{2} \div 1\frac{3}{4}$

(b) $2\frac{2}{5} \div 1\frac{1}{5}$

(c) $7\frac{1}{2} \div 2\frac{1}{2}$

(d) $4\frac{2}{3} \div 1\frac{5}{7}$

(e) $5\frac{1}{3} \div 1\frac{1}{3}$

(f) $6\frac{1}{2} \div 3\frac{1}{4}$

(g) What is the rule or the process for dividing a mixed number by another mixed number?

2. Divide the following using the shortcut method. (Hint: See Example **2**.)
Reduce to the lowest terms.

(a) $6\frac{2}{3} \div 1\frac{2}{3}$

(b) $3\frac{1}{3} \div 1\frac{2}{3}$

(c) $4\frac{1}{2} \div 1\frac{1}{2}$

(d) $4\frac{2}{3} \div 2\frac{1}{3}$

(e) $4\frac{2}{3} \div 2\frac{2}{6}$

(f) $3\frac{1}{2} \div 1\frac{3}{4}$

3. Divide the following: Reduce to the lowest terms. (Hint: See Example **3**.)

(a) $4\frac{1}{3} \div 10\frac{1}{2}$

(b) $2\frac{2}{7} \div 3\frac{3}{8}$

(c) $1\frac{1}{2} \div 2\frac{2}{3}$

(d) $3\frac{1}{4} \div 9\frac{3}{7}$

(e) $5\frac{1}{2} \div 6\frac{1}{5}$

(f) $4\frac{2}{5} \div 6\frac{1}{3}$

4. Divide the following using shortcut method. (Hint: See Example 4.)
Reduce to the lowest terms.

(a) $2\frac{1}{2} \div 3\frac{2}{3}$

(b) $1\frac{3}{7} \div 2\frac{3}{8}$

(c) $4\frac{2}{3} \div 5\frac{4}{5}$

(d) $2\frac{3}{5} \div 5\frac{1}{3}$

(e) $2\frac{1}{5} \div 4\frac{1}{3}$

(f) $3\frac{2}{3} \div 5\frac{2}{5}$

5. Divide the following: Reduce to the lowest terms. (Hint: See Example 5.)

(a) $4\frac{1}{2} \div 2\frac{1}{2}$

(b) $3\frac{3}{5} \div 1\frac{2}{3}$

(c) $5\frac{1}{3} \div 2\frac{2}{3}$

(d) $6\frac{2}{3} \div 1\frac{1}{4}$

(e) $8\frac{3}{4} \div 1\frac{2}{5}$

(f) $7\frac{1}{5} \div 2\frac{1}{4}$

6. Divide the following: (Hint: See Example 6.)
Solve Exercises **5(a)** to **5(f)** without showing any detailed explanations. Use the shortcut method. Reduce to the lowest terms.

Answers to Selected Questions

1(a) 2   **2(a)** 4   **3(a)** $\frac{26}{63}$ **3(b)** $\frac{128}{189}$ **3(f)** $\frac{66}{95}$

354

4(a) $\dfrac{15}{22}$ **4(c)** $\dfrac{70}{87}$ **5(a)** $1\dfrac{4}{5}$ **5(d)** $5\dfrac{1}{3}$

REAL WORLD APPLICATIONS - WORD PROBLEMS
DIVISION BY MIXED NUMBERS

Example 1

A rod is $8\dfrac{3}{4}$ meters long. How many pieces of rod measuring $1\dfrac{1}{4}$ meters can

the length of the $8\dfrac{3}{4}$ meters of rod be cut into?

Solution

Setup: The number of the pieces of rod measuring $1\dfrac{1}{4}$ meters that can be cut from

the $8\dfrac{3}{4}$ meters of rod $= 8\dfrac{3}{8} \div 1\dfrac{1}{4}$

(Note: We are required to find how many $1\dfrac{1}{4}$ meters are contained in $8\dfrac{3}{4}$

meters.)

Step 1: Change the mixed numbers $8\dfrac{3}{4}$ and $1\dfrac{1}{4}$ to improper fractions. (See Rule 1.)

The improper fraction of the mixed number

$8\dfrac{3}{4} = \dfrac{4 \times 8 + 3}{4} = \dfrac{35}{4}$ (See Rule 2 and also Rule 3 under Multiplication

of Fractions, Whole and Mixed Numbers.)

The improper fraction of the mixed number

$1\dfrac{1}{4} = \dfrac{4 \times 1 + 1}{4} = \dfrac{5}{4}$ (See Rule 2 and also Rule 3 under Multiplication

of Fractions, Whole and Mixed Numbers.)

Therefore, $8\dfrac{3}{4} \div 1\dfrac{1}{4} = \dfrac{35}{4} \div \dfrac{5}{4}$

Step 2: Invert the divisor and change the $\div$ sign to $\times$ sign (Note: $\dfrac{5}{4}$ is the divisor.)

$\dfrac{35}{4} \div \dfrac{5}{4}$ from Step 1 becomes $\dfrac{35}{4} \times \dfrac{4}{5}$ (Note: $\dfrac{5}{4}$ is inverted to become

$\dfrac{4}{5}$ and the ÷ sign is changed to × sign.) (See Rule 1.)

Step 3: Reduce the fractions in $\dfrac{35}{4} \times \dfrac{4}{5}$ to the lowest terms by dividing the numerators and the denominators by the same number or numbers if possible.

$$\dfrac{35}{4} \times \dfrac{4}{7} = \dfrac{\overset{7}{\cancel{35}}}{\underset{1}{\cancel{4}}} \times \dfrac{\overset{1}{\cancel{4}}}{\underset{1}{\cancel{5}}} \qquad (35 \div 5 = 7,\ 5 \div 5 = 1,\ 4 \div 4 = 1)$$

Step 4: Multiply the numerators together and multiply the denominators together and put the product of the numerators over the product of the denominators.

$$\dfrac{7}{1} \times \dfrac{1}{1} = \dfrac{7 \times 1}{1 \times 1}$$
$$= \dfrac{7}{1}$$
$$= 7$$

Therefore, 7 pieces of rod measuring $1\dfrac{1}{4}$ meters can be cut from $8\dfrac{3}{4}$ meters.

Example 2

Solve the question in Example **1** without showing any detailed explanations, and we refer to this as a shortcut method.

Solution

Setup: Number of $1\dfrac{1}{4}$ meters of rod $= 8\dfrac{3}{4} \div 1\dfrac{1}{4}$

Solve:
$$\dfrac{35}{4} \div \dfrac{5}{4} = \dfrac{35}{4} \times \dfrac{4}{5}$$

$$= \dfrac{\overset{7}{\cancel{35}}}{\underset{1}{\cancel{4}}} \times \dfrac{\overset{1}{\cancel{4}}}{\underset{1}{\cancel{5}}}$$

$$= 5$$

Therefore, 5 pieces of rod measuring $1\dfrac{1}{4}$ meters can be cut from the $8\dfrac{3}{4}$ meters of rod.

Example 3

Given that it takes $\frac{2}{3}$ yard of a fabric to make a baby's shirt, how many similar shirts can be made with $10\frac{2}{3}$ yards?

Solution

Setup: The number of $\frac{2}{3}$ yard of shirts that can be made with $10\frac{2}{3}$ yards of fabric is $10\frac{2}{3} \div \frac{2}{3}$ (Note: We are to find how many $\frac{2}{3}$ are contained in $10\frac{2}{3}$.)

Step 1: Change the mixed number $10\frac{2}{3}$ to an improper fraction. (See Rule 1.)

The improper fraction for the mixed number $10\frac{2}{3}$

$$= \frac{3 \times 10 + 2}{3} = \frac{32}{3}$$ (See Rule 2 and also rule 3 under Multiplication of Fractions, Whole, and Mixed Numbers.)

Therefore, $10\frac{2}{3} \div \frac{2}{3} = \frac{32}{3} \div \frac{2}{3}$

Step 2: Invert the divisor and change the $\div$ sign to $\times$ sign. (Note: $\frac{2}{3}$ is the divisor.)

$\frac{32}{3} \div \frac{2}{3}$ from Step 1 becomes $\frac{32}{3} \times \frac{3}{2}$ (Note: $\frac{2}{3}$ is inverted to become $\frac{3}{2}$ and the $\div$ sign changes to the $\times$ sign.) (See Rule 1.)

Step 3: Reduce the fractions in $\frac{32}{3} \times \frac{3}{2}$ to the lowest terms by dividing the numerators and the denominators by the same number or numbers if possible.

$$\frac{32}{3} \times \frac{3}{2} = \frac{\overset{16}{\cancel{32}}}{\underset{1}{\cancel{3}}} \times \frac{\overset{1}{\cancel{3}}}{\underset{1}{\cancel{2}}}$$ $(32 \div 2 = 16, 2 \div 2 = 1, 3 \div 3 = 1)$

Step 4: Multiply the numerators together and multiply the denominators together and put the product of the numerators over the product of the denominators.

$$\frac{16}{1} \times \frac{1}{1} = \frac{16 \times 1}{1 \times 1}$$

$$= \frac{16}{1}$$
$$= 16$$

Therefore, 16 of $\frac{2}{3}$ yard of shirts can be made from $10\frac{2}{3}$ yards of fabric.

Example 4

Solve the question in Example **3** without showing any detailed explanations.
(**Note**: We refer to this method of solution as the shortcut method.)

Solution

Setup: The number of $\frac{2}{3}$ yard of shirts that can be made with $10\frac{2}{3}$ yards of

fabric $= 10\frac{2}{3} \div \frac{2}{3}$

Solve:

$$10\frac{2}{3} \div \frac{2}{3} = \frac{\overset{16}{\cancel{32}}}{\underset{1}{\cancel{3}}} \times \frac{\overset{1}{\cancel{3}}}{\underset{1}{\cancel{2}}}$$ Divide by 3 and 2. $(32 \div 2 = 16$ and $3 \div 3 = 1)$

$$= \frac{16 \times 1}{1 \times 1}$$
$$= 16$$

Therefore, 16 of $\frac{2}{3}$ of shirts can be made with $10\frac{2}{3}$ yards of fabric.

The notes and the generous worked examples have provided me with conceptual understanding and computational fluency to do my homework.

Exercises

1. A pole is $9\frac{1}{3}$ feet long .How many pieces of the pole measuring $2\frac{1}{3}$ feet can be cut

   from the $9\frac{1}{3}$ feet long of the pole? (Hint: See Example **1**.)

2. Solve question 1 using the shortcut method. (Hint: See Example **2**.)

3. John bought a tape, which is $12\frac{4}{5}$ yards long. If he needs 8 pieces of tape

   measuring $1\frac{3}{5}$ yards for his school project, is $12\frac{4}{5}$ yards of tape enough for his

   project? (Hint: Find how many $1\frac{3}{5}$ are contained in $12\frac{4}{5}$. See Example **1**.)

4. Mrs. Aggor is making matching outfits for a school band. If a matching outfit

requires $1\frac{3}{5}$ yards of fabric, and she bought $11\frac{1}{5}$ yards of fabric, how many similar outfits could she make? (Hint: Find how many $1\frac{3}{5}$ are contained in $11\frac{1}{5}$. See Example **1**.)

5. Solve question 4 without showing any detailed explanations. (Hint: See Example **2**.)

6. Eric used $3\frac{1}{5}$ feet of wire for a school project. How many similar school projects could he make from $12\frac{4}{5}$ feet of wire? (See Example **1** or **2**.)

7. Solve question 6 without showing any detailed explanations. (Hint: See Example **2**.)

Challenge Questions

8. Given that it takes $\frac{9}{10}$ of a yard of fabric to make a baby's shirt, how many similar shirts can be made from $12\frac{3}{5}$ yards of fabric?

9. How many pieces of $2\frac{3}{4}$ meters of wire can be cut from $27\frac{1}{2}$ meters of wire?

Answer to Selected Questions

1. 4   **4.** 7   **8.** 14

DIVISION OF A WHOLE NUMBER BY A MIXED NUMBER AND DIVISION OF A MIXED NUMBER BY A WHOLE NUMBER

Rule 1: To divide a whole number by a mixed number or to divide a mixed number by a whole number, change both the mixed number and the whole number to improper fractions, invert the divisor and change the ÷ sign to × sign.

Rule 2: To change a mixed number to an improper fraction, multiply the denominator by the whole number, add the numerator to the product, and then write the sum over the denominator.

Rule 3: To change a whole number to an improper fraction, write the whole number over the number 1 as the denominator.

Example 1

Divide: $8 \div 1\frac{1}{3}$

Solution

Step 1: Change 8 and $1\frac{1}{3}$ to improper fractions. (See Rule 1.)

The improper fraction of $8 = \frac{8}{1}$ (See Rule 3 and also Rule 2 under Multiplication of Fractions, Whole, and Mixed Numbers.)

The improper fraction of $1\frac{1}{3} = \frac{3 \times 1 + 1}{3} = \frac{4}{3}$ (See Rule 2 and also Rule 3 under Multiplication of Fractions, Whole, and Mixed Numbers.)

Therefore, $8 \div 1\frac{1}{3} = \frac{8}{1} \div \frac{4}{3}$

Step 2: Invert the divisor and change the $\div$ sign to $\times$ sign. (Note: $\frac{4}{3}$ is the divisor.)

$\frac{8}{1} \div \frac{4}{3}$ from Step 1 becomes: $\frac{8}{1} \times \frac{3}{4}$ (Note: $\frac{4}{3}$ is inverted to become $\frac{3}{4}$ and $\div$ sign change to $\times$ sign.) (See Rule 1.)

Step 3: Reduce the fractions in $\frac{8}{1} \times \frac{3}{4}$ to the lowest terms by dividing the numerators and the denominators by the same number or numbers if possible.

$$\frac{8}{1} \times \frac{3}{4} = \frac{\overset{2}{\cancel{8}}}{1} \times \frac{3}{\underset{1}{\cancel{4}}} \quad\quad (8 \div 4 = 2, \; 4 \div 4 = 1)$$

$$= \frac{2}{1} \times \frac{3}{1}$$

Step 4: Multiply all the numerators and multiply all the denominators and put the product of the numerators over the product of the denominators.

$$\frac{2}{1} \times \frac{3}{1} = \frac{2 \times 3}{1} = \frac{6}{1}$$

$$= 6$$

Therefore, $8 \div 1\frac{1}{3} = 6$

Example 2
Solve the question in Example **1** without showing any detailed solution methods. Use

360

the shortcut method.

Solution

$$8 \div 1\frac{1}{3} = \frac{\overset{2}{\cancel{8}}}{1} \times \frac{3}{\cancel{4}_{1}}$$

$$= 6$$

Example 3

Divide: $3\frac{5}{8} \div 4$

Solution

Step 1: Change $3\frac{5}{8}$ and 4 to improper fractions. (See Rule 1.)

The improper fraction of $3\frac{5}{8} = \frac{8 \times 3 + 5}{8} = \frac{29}{8}$ (See Rule 2 and also Rule

3 under Multiplication of Fractions, Whole, and Mixed Numbers.)

The improper fraction of $4 = \frac{4}{1}$ (See Rule 3 and also Rule 2 under

Multiplication of Fractions, Whole, and Mixed Numbers.)

Therefore, $3\frac{5}{8} \div 4 = \frac{29}{8} \div \frac{4}{1}$

Step 2: Invert the divisor and change the ÷ sign to × sign. (Note: $\frac{4}{1}$ is the divisor.)

$\frac{29}{8} \div \frac{4}{1}$ from Step 1 becomes $\frac{29}{8} \times \frac{1}{4}$ (Note: $\frac{4}{1}$ is inverted to become $\frac{1}{4}$

and the ÷ sign changes to × sign.) (See Rule 1.)

Step 3: Reduce the fractions in $\frac{29}{8} \times \frac{1}{4}$ to the lowest terms by dividing the

numerators, and denominators by the same number or numbers if possible. In this case, there is no number that can divide the numerators and the denominators evenly (without a remainder.)

Step 4: Multiply all the numerators and multiply all the denominators and put the product of the numerators over the product of the denominators.

$$\frac{29}{8} \times \frac{1}{4} = \frac{29 \times 1}{8 \times 4} = \frac{29}{32}$$

Therefore, $3\frac{5}{8} \div 4 = \frac{29}{32}$

Example 4

Solve the question in Example 3 without showing any detailed explanations.
Use the shortcut method.

Solution

$$3\frac{5}{8} \div 4 = \frac{29}{8} \times \frac{1}{4} = \frac{29}{32}$$

Example 5

Divide: $7\frac{1}{7} \div 7$

Solution

Step 1: Change $7\frac{1}{7}$ and 7 to improper fractions. (See Rule 1.)

The improper fraction of $7\frac{1}{7} = \frac{7 \times 7 + 1}{7} = \frac{50}{7}$ (See Rule 2 and also Rule 3 under Multiplication of Fractions, Whole, and Mixed Numbers.)

The improper fraction of $7 = \frac{7}{1}$ (See Rule 3 and also Rule 2 under Multiplication of Fractions, Whole, and Mixed numbers.)

Therefore, $7\frac{1}{7} \div 7 = \frac{50}{7} \div \frac{7}{1}$

Step 2: Invert the divisor and change the ÷ sign to × sign.   (Note: $\frac{7}{1}$ is the divisor.)

$\frac{50}{7} \div \frac{7}{1}$ from Step 1 becomes $\frac{50}{7} \times \frac{1}{7}$ (Note: $\frac{7}{1}$ is inverted to become $\frac{1}{7}$ and ÷ sign changes to × sign.)
(See Rule 1.)

Step 3: Reduce the fraction in $\frac{50}{7} \times \frac{1}{7}$ to the lowest terms by dividing the numerators and the denominators by the same number or numbers if possible. In this case, there is no number that can divide the numerators and the denominators evenly (without a remainder.)

Step 4: Multiply all the numerators and multiply all the denominators and put the product of the numerators over the product of the denominators.

$$\frac{50}{7} \times \frac{1}{7} = \frac{50 \times 1}{7 \times 7} = \frac{50}{49}$$

Step 5: Change $\frac{50}{49}$ to a mixed fraction, by dividing the numerator by the denominator.

$$\frac{50}{49} = 1\frac{1}{49} \qquad (50 \div 49 = 1 \text{ remainder } 1, = 1\frac{1}{49}.)$$

Therefore, $7\frac{1}{7} \div 7 = 1\frac{1}{49}$

Example 6
Solve Example **5** without showing any detailed solutions.
Use the shortcut method.
Solution

$$7\frac{1}{7} \div 7 = \frac{50}{7} \times \frac{1}{7} = \frac{50}{49} = 1\frac{1}{49} \quad \text{(See Steps 4 and 5 in Example 5.)}$$

The notes and the generous worked examples have provided me with conceptual understanding and computational fluency to do my homework.

Exercises
1. Divide the following whole numbers by the mixed numbers. (Hint: See Example **1**.)

(a) $3 \div 1\frac{1}{2}$ (b) $16 \div 2\frac{2}{3}$ (c) $12 \div 2\frac{2}{3}$ (d) $10 \div 2\frac{1}{2}$

(e) $14 \div 2\frac{1}{3}$ (f) $18 \div 1\frac{2}{4}$ (g) $24 \div 1\frac{1}{3}$ (h) $18 \div 4\frac{1}{2}$

2. Solve question **1(a)** to **1(h)** using the shortcut method. (Hint: See Example **2**.)
3. Divide the following mixed numbers by the whole numbers. (Hint: See Examples **3** and **5**.)

(a) $4\frac{1}{2} \div 2$ (b) $9\frac{1}{3} \div 2$ (c) $4\frac{2}{3} \div 2$ (d) $10\frac{2}{3} \div 8$

(e) $5\frac{1}{3} \div 4$ (f) $12\frac{1}{2} \div 5$ (g) $3\frac{1}{2} \div 14$ (h) $4\frac{1}{2} \div 18$

4. Solve questions **3(a)** to **3(h)** using the shortcut method. (Hint: See Example **4**.)
5. Divide the following mixed numbers and whole numbers. (Hint: See Examples

1, 3, and **5**.)

(a) $4 \div 1\frac{1}{2}$ (b) $7\frac{1}{2} \div 5$ (c) $8 \div 3\frac{1}{3}$ (d) $64 \div 2\frac{2}{3}$

(e) $6\frac{2}{5} \div 8$ (f) $12 \div 2\frac{2}{4}$ (g) $9\frac{1}{3} \div 8$ (h) $27 \div 2\frac{1}{4}$

(i) $8\frac{1}{3} \div 5$ (j) $6 \div 1\frac{1}{3}$ (k) $3\frac{1}{3} \div 5$ (l) $4\frac{4}{5} \div 8$

6. Solve questions **5(a)** to **5(l)** using the shortcut methods. (Hint: See Examples **2**, **4**, and **6**.)

Challenge Questions

7. Divide the following mixed numbers and whole numbers.

(a) $5 \div 2\frac{1}{2}$ (b) $9\frac{1}{3} \div 7$ (c) $36 \div 2\frac{1}{2}$ (d) $17 \div 1\frac{1}{2}$

Answers to Selected Questions

1(a) 2   **1(c)** $4\frac{1}{2}$ **1(g)** 18   **2(b)** 6   **2(d)** 4

2(f) 12   **2(h)** 14   **5(a)** $2\frac{2}{3}$ **5(c)** $2\frac{2}{5}$ **5(h)** 12

REAL WORLD APPLICATIONS - WORD PROBLEMS

DIVISION OF A WHOLE NUMBER BY A MIXED NUMBER AND DIVISION OF A MIXED NUMBER BY A WHOLE NUMBER

Example 1

A store used $3\frac{3}{4}$ yards of material to make a dress. How many dresses can be made with 60 yards of material?

Solution

Setup: The number of $3\frac{3}{4}$ yards in 60 yards = $60 \div 3\frac{3}{4}$

Step 1: Change 60 and $3\frac{3}{4}$ to improper fractions. (See Rule 1.)

The improper fraction of $60 = \frac{60}{1}$. (See Rule 3.)

The improper fraction of $3\frac{3}{4} = \frac{4 \times 3 + 3}{4} = \frac{15}{4}$. (See Rule 2.)

Therefore, $60 \div 3\frac{3}{4}$ becomes $\frac{60}{1} \div \frac{15}{4}$.

Step 2: Invert the divisor and change ÷ sign to × sign. (Note: $\frac{15}{4}$ is the divisor.)

$\frac{60}{1} \div \frac{15}{4}$ from step 1 becomes: $\frac{60}{1} \times \frac{4}{15}$. (Note: $\frac{15}{4}$ is inverted to become $\frac{4}{15}$ and the ÷ sign changes to × sign.) (See Rule 1.)

Step 3: Reduce the fraction in $\frac{60}{1} \times \frac{4}{15}$ to the lowest terms by dividing the numerators and the denominators by the same number or numbers if possible.

$$\frac{60}{1} \times \frac{4}{15} = \frac{\overset{\overset{4}{\cancel{12}}}{\cancel{60}}}{1} \times \frac{4}{\underset{\underset{1}{\cancel{3}}}{\cancel{15}}} \qquad (60 \div 5 = 12,\ 15 \div 5 = 3,\ 12 \div 3 = 4,\ 3 \div 3 = 1)$$

Step 4: Multiply all the numerators together and multiply all the denominators together and put the product of the numerators over the product of the denominators.

$$\frac{4}{1} \times \frac{4}{1} = \frac{4 \times 4}{1 \times 1} = 16$$

Therefore, 16 dresses can be made from 60 yards of material.

Example 2

Solve Example **1** without showing detailed solution information. Use the shortcut method.

Solution

The number of $3\frac{3}{4}$ yards in 60 yards = $60 \div 3\frac{3}{4}$

$$= 60 \div 3\frac{3}{4} = \frac{\overset{12}{\cancel{60}}}{1} \times \frac{\overset{4}{\cancel{4}}}{\underset{1}{\cancel{15}}} \quad (60 \div 5 = 12,\ 15 \div 5 = 3,\ 12 \div 3 = 4,\ 3 \div 3 = 1)$$

$$= 4 \times 4 = 16$$

Therefore, 16 dresses can be made from 60 yards of material.

Exercises

1. Mary used $1\frac{2}{3}$ ounces of honey to make a loaf of bread. How many similar loaves can she make from a 60-ounce jar of honey? (Hint: See Example **1**.)

2. The Johnson family wants to know how many pieces of fence of length $3\frac{1}{3}$ yards is needed to fence around their garden, which has a total length of 200 yards. Is the Johnson's family correct by stating that 62 pieces of $3\frac{1}{3}$ yards are needed for the project? (Hint: See Example **1**.)

COMPARISON OF FRACTIONS

New Terms: Ascending Order and Descending Order

Two or more fractions can be compared to find their magnitude in ascending or descending order. **Ascending order** of magnitude means that the fractions are arranged from the lowest to the highest. **Descending order** of magnitude means that the fractions are arranged from the highest to the lowest.

Rule 1: To compare, write fractions in ascending or descending order of magnitude of two or more fractions, change all the fractions to equivalent fractions (with the same denominator.)

Once the equivalent fractions are written, the value of each numerator of the equivalent fraction determines how large or small each fraction is. The larger the numerator of the equivalent fraction, the larger that specific fraction and the smaller the numerator of the equivalent fraction, the smaller that specific fraction.

Critical Thinking
Two or more fractions can be compared by arranging the equivalent fractions in ascending or descending order.

Example 1

Which fraction is greater, $\dfrac{3}{5}$ or $\dfrac{3}{4}$?

Solution

Step 1: Using Rule 1, Change the fractions $\dfrac{3}{5}$ and $\dfrac{3}{4}$ to equivalent fractions. The

LCD of $\dfrac{3}{5}$ and $\dfrac{3}{4}$ is 20. Hint: See Examples under the topics Subtraction of Fractions or Addition of Fractions. For example, $5 \times 4 = 20$ and 5 and 4 can divide evenly into 20 (without a remainder.)

$$\frac{3}{5} = \frac{}{20} \quad \diagup\text{LCD}$$

$$\frac{3}{4} = \frac{}{20} \quad \diagup\text{LCD}$$

Step 2: Find the equivalent fractions. Review Equivalent Fractions.

$$\frac{3}{5} = \frac{3}{5} \times \frac{4}{4} = \frac{12}{20} \leftarrow \text{Equivalent fraction}$$

$$\frac{3}{4} = \frac{3}{4} \times \frac{5}{5} = \frac{15}{20} \leftarrow \text{Equivalent fraction}$$

Step 3: Compare the equivalent fractions.

Comparing the equivalent fractions $\dfrac{12}{20}$ and $\dfrac{15}{20}$, $\dfrac{15}{20} \succ \dfrac{12}{20}$ because the numerator 15 is greater than the numerator 12.

Therefore, $\dfrac{3}{4} > \dfrac{3}{5}$ The symbol > means greater than.

Example 2
Solve Example **1** without showing any detailed solutions.

Shortcut: The LCD of $\dfrac{3}{5}$ and $\dfrac{3}{4}$ is 20. Find the equivalent fractions.

$$\frac{3}{5} = \frac{3}{5} \times \frac{4}{4} = \frac{12}{20} \quad \leftarrow \text{Equivalent fraction}$$

$$\frac{3}{4} = \frac{3}{4} \times \frac{5}{5} = \frac{15}{20} \quad \leftarrow \text{Equivalent fraction}$$

By comparing equivalent fractions, $\frac{15}{20} > \frac{12}{20}$ because the numerator 15 is greater

than the numerator 12. Therefore, $\frac{3}{4} > \frac{3}{5}$.

Example 3
Arrange the fractions in ascending and descending order of magnitude.

$$\frac{2}{3}, \frac{3}{4}, \frac{4}{5}$$

Solution

Step 1: Using Rule 1, change the fractions $\frac{2}{3}$, $\frac{3}{4}$, and $\frac{4}{5}$ to equivalent fractions.

The LCD of the fractions $\frac{2}{3}$, $\frac{3}{4}$, and $\frac{4}{5}$ is 60. (For example, $3 \times 4 \times 5 = 60$.

Multiply all the denominators together to obtain the LCD.)

$$\frac{2}{3} = \frac{}{60} \quad \diagup \text{LCD}$$

$$\frac{3}{4} = \frac{}{60} \quad \diagup \text{LCD}$$

$$\frac{4}{5} = \frac{}{60} \quad \diagup \text{LCD}$$

Step 2: Find the equivalent fractions. (Review topics on Equivalent Fractions.)

$$\frac{2}{3} = \frac{2}{3} \times \frac{20}{20} = \frac{40}{60} \quad \leftarrow \text{Equivalent fraction}$$

$$\frac{3}{4} = \frac{3}{4} \times \frac{15}{15} = \frac{45}{60} \quad \leftarrow \text{Equivalent fraction}$$

$$\frac{4}{5} = \frac{4}{5} \times \frac{12}{12} = \frac{48}{60} \quad \leftarrow \text{Equivalent fraction}$$

Step 3: Compare the equivalent fractions

$$\frac{40}{60}, \frac{45}{60}, \text{ and } \frac{48}{60}$$

$$\frac{40}{60} < \frac{45}{60} < \frac{48}{60}$$ because the numerator 40 is

less than the numerator 45 and the numerator 45 is less than the numerator 48.)

Therefore, the ascending (increasing) order is: $\frac{2}{3}$, $\frac{3}{4}$, and $\frac{4}{5}$.

Therefore, the descending (decreasing) order is: $\frac{4}{5}$, $\frac{3}{4}$, and $\frac{2}{3}$.

Example 4

Solve Example **3**, without showing any detailed explanations. Use the shortcut method.

Solution

Shortcut:

The LCD for $\frac{2}{3}$, $\frac{3}{4}$ and $\frac{4}{5}$ is 60.

Write equivalent fractions:

$$\frac{2}{3} = \frac{2}{3} \times \frac{20}{20} = \frac{40}{60}$$ ← Equivalent fraction

$$\frac{3}{4} = \frac{3}{4} \times \frac{15}{15} = \frac{45}{60}$$ ← Equivalent fraction

$$\frac{4}{5} = \frac{4}{5} \times \frac{12}{12} = \frac{48}{60}$$ ← Equivalent fraction

By comparing equivalent fractions, the ascending order is $\frac{2}{3}$, $\frac{3}{4}$, and $\frac{4}{5}$ and the descending order is $\frac{4}{5}$, $\frac{3}{4}$, and $\frac{2}{3}$.

The notes and the generous worked examples have provided me with conceptual understanding and computational fluency to do my homework.

Exercise

1. Explain how fractions can be compared (Hint: See Rule 1.)
2. Which of the following pairs of fractions is greater?. (Hint: See Example **1**)

(a) $\frac{3}{7}$ and $\frac{2}{5}$ (b) $\frac{1}{4}$ and $\frac{2}{5}$ (c) $\frac{2}{5}$ and $\frac{3}{8}$

(d) $\dfrac{3}{5}$ and $\dfrac{4}{7}$ **(e)** $\dfrac{2}{7}$ and $\dfrac{1}{5}$ **(f)** $\dfrac{4}{5}$ and $\dfrac{3}{4}$

3. Solve questions **2(a)** to **2(f)** without showing a detailed solution method. Use the shortcut method. (Hint: See Example **2**.)
4. Arrange the following fractions in ascending and descending orders. (Hint: See Example **3**.)

   (a) $\dfrac{2}{3}, \dfrac{4}{7}, \dfrac{8}{21}$ **(b)** $\dfrac{2}{5}, \dfrac{3}{8}, \dfrac{3}{4}$ **(c)** $\dfrac{4}{9}, \dfrac{1}{3}, \dfrac{1}{4}$

   (d) $\dfrac{1}{5}, \dfrac{2}{7}, \dfrac{8}{35}$ **(e)** $\dfrac{1}{3}, \dfrac{2}{5}, \dfrac{4}{15}$ **(f)** $\dfrac{2}{3}, \dfrac{3}{4}, \dfrac{4}{5}$

5. Solve questions **4(a)** to **4(f)** without showing a detailed solution method. Use the shortcut method. (Hint: See Example **4**.)

Challenge Questions

6. Arrange the following fractions in ascending and descending orders.

   (a) $\dfrac{1}{4}, \dfrac{2}{3}, \dfrac{5}{6}$ **(b)** $\dfrac{3}{5}, \dfrac{4}{7}$ **(c)** $\dfrac{3}{5}, \dfrac{2}{3}$ **(d)** $\dfrac{4}{7}, \dfrac{8}{14}, \dfrac{5}{7}$

Answers to Selected Questions

2(a) $\dfrac{3}{7}$ **4(a)** Ascending order is $\dfrac{8}{21}, \dfrac{4}{7}, \dfrac{2}{3}$ Descending order is $\dfrac{2}{3}, \dfrac{4}{7}, \dfrac{8}{21}$

DECIMAL FRACTIONS

Cumulative Review
Solve:

(1). $2\dfrac{2}{3} \div 4 =$ **(2)**. $4 \times 3\dfrac{3}{4} =$ **(3)**. $6\dfrac{1}{4} \div 1\dfrac{2}{3} =$ **(4)**. $17 - 8 \div 2 \times 2 =$

New Terms
Common fractions – Common fractions are fractions with fraction bars such as

$$\dfrac{1}{2} \longleftarrow \textbf{Fraction bar}$$

Decimal fractions – Decimal fractions are numbers to the right of the decimal point as shown below. See also Fig. 1.

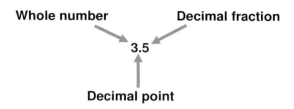

Decimal point – The decimal point in a number separates the whole number part from the fractional part such as shown above. See also fig. 1.

Mixed decimals – A mixed decimal is made of a whole number and a decimal fraction such as 3.5, where 3 is the whole number and .5 is a decimal fraction.

Digits – **The numbers 0**, **1**, **2**, **3**, **4**, **5**, **6**, **7**, **8**, **and 9 are called digits**.
The number 3.5 has a total of two digits which are 3 and 5. The number 3.56 has a total of 3 digits which are 3, 5 and 6.

Decimal place – The decimal place is the number of the digits after the decimal point. For example, 3.5 has one decimal place because 3.5 has one digit after the decimal point and the digit is 5, and 3.56 has two decimal places because 3.56 has two digits after the decimal point and these two digits are 5 and 6.

Fig.1 shows whole numbers, a decimal point, fractions such as $\dfrac{1}{10}$, and decimal fractions such as .1. Note that Fig. 1 shows that the whole numbers are at the left side of the decimal point and the fractions are at the right side of the decimal point.

Fig. 1

Words	Ten thousands	Thousands	Hundreds	Tens	Units		Tenths	Hundredths	Thousandths
Numbers	10,000	1000	100	10	1	.	$\frac{1}{10}$ or .1	$\frac{1}{100}$ or .01	$\frac{1}{1000}$ or .001

Whole numbers ◄————————► Fractions or decimals

Decimal point

Note: From Fig.1,

    1). the names of the decimal fractions end with **–ths** such as ten**ths**, hundred**ths**, and thousand**ths**.

    2). the names of the whole numbers end in -**s** such as ten-thousand**s**, thousand**s**, hundred**s**, ten**s**, and unit**s**.

    3). it can be seen that the decimal fraction is based on 10 because as you move from left to right, each column (digit) is divided by 10, or as you move from right to left, each column (digit) is multiplied by 10. For example, as we move to the right of the decimal point, the value of the tenths is divided by 10 to get the value of the hundredths, the value of the hundredths is divided by 10 to get the value of the thousandths.

    4). It can be seen that a number can be written in words, fractional and decimal forms. For example, tenths, specifically one tenth, $\dfrac{1}{10}$, and .1 have the same value as shown:

$$.1 = \text{one tenth} = \dfrac{1}{10} \leftarrow \text{Fractional form}$$

Decimal form ↗   ↖ Word form

Group Exercise

Using Fig. 1, complete the following statements. Hint: See the **note from Fig. 1, item 3**.

1. Starting at the ones or units place, and as you move left one place or one column, the number in the column is multiplied by _____. (Select the correct answer: 10, 20, 30, or 100.)
2. Now starting from the thousands place, and as you move right one place or one column, the number in the column is div_____ by 10.
3. Now starting from the tenths place, and as you move right one place or one column, the number in the column is divided by ____. (Select the correct answer: 10, 20, 30, or 100.)
4. Now starting from the thousandths place, and as you move left two places or two columns, the number in the final column is multip_____ by 100.

Place Value of the Digits

Place value of the digits chart.

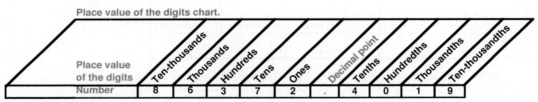

Place value of the digits	Ten-thousands	Thousands	Hundreds	Tens	Ones	Decimal point	Tenths	Hundredths	Thousandths	Ten-thousandths
Number	8	6	3	7	2	.	4	0	1	9

Place value of digits **is the value given to the place a digit has in a number.** By looking at the "**Place Value of the Digits**" chart, we can find out that:

a. 2 has a place value of ones or we can simply say **2 ones** or 2 ×1 = 2 because the first digit before the decimal point (or the first whole number just before the decimal point) has the place value of one**s**. We may say that 2 is in the one**s** place.

b. 7 has a place value of ten**s** or we can simply say "**7 tens**" or 7 × 10 = 70 because the second digit before the decimal point (or the second whole number before the decimal point) has the place value of ten**s**. We may say that 7 is in the ten**s** place.

c. 3 has a place value of hundred**s** or we can simply say "**3 hundreds**" or 3 × 100 = 300 because the third digit before the decimal point (or the third whole number before the decimal point) has the place value of hundred**s**. We may say that 3 is in the hundred**s** place.

d. 6 has a place value of thousand**s** or we can simply say "**6 thousands**" or 6 ×1000 = 6000 because the fourth digit before the decimal point (or the fourth whole number before the decimal point) has the place value of thousand**s**. We may say that 6 is in the thousand**s** place.

e. 8 has a place value of ten-thousand**s** or we can simply say "**8 ten-thousands**" or 8 × 10,000 = 80,000 because the fifth digit before the decimal point (or the fifth whole number before the decimal point) has a place value of ten-thousand**s**. We may say that 8 is in the ten-thousand**s** place.

f. 4 has a place value of ten**ths** or we can simply say "**4 tenths**" or $\dfrac{4}{10}$ = .4 because the first digit after the decimal point has a place value of ten**ths**. We say that 4 is in the ten**ths** place.

g. 0 has a place value of hundred**ths** or we can simply say "**0 hundredths**" or $\dfrac{0}{100}$ = 0 because the second digit after the decimal point has a place value of hundred**ths**. We say that 0 is in the hundred**ths** place.

h. 1 has a place value of thousand**ths** or we can simply say "**1 thousandths**" or $\dfrac{1}{1000}$ = .001 because the third digit after the decimal point has a place value of thousand**ths**. We say that 1 is in the thousand**ths** place.

i. 9 has a place value of ten-thousand**ths** or we can simply say "**9 ten-thousandths**" or $\dfrac{9}{10,000}$ = .0009 because the fourth digit after the decimal point has a place value of ten-thousand**ths**. We say that 9 is in the ten-thousand**ths** place.

j. To determine the value of each digit, **look at its place in the number**.

Group Exercise or Class Exercise
1. Explain what is meant by place value of digits.
2. Using the similar idea of the "**place value of digits**" chart, make a place value chart for (**a**) 2543.691   (**b**) 901.21   (**c**) 127.0458   (**d**) 67.9352   (**e**) 9824.375
3. What is meant by digits?
4. What is meant by a decimal point?
5. Using the similar idea of the "**place value of digits**" chart, state the value of each digit in the bold face.
   (**a**) 234.00**2**   (**b**) **7**78.923   (**c**) 7.2**3**4   (**d**) 4.5**6**   (**e**) 19.2**0**6

Group Exercise
Using Fig. 1, complete the following statements:
1. Starting from the place value of ones and as you move right one place, the place

value is divided by _____. (Select the correct answer: 10, 20, 30, or 100).

2. Now starting from the place value of thousands and you move left one place, the place value is multiplied by _____.

3. Now starting from the place value of tenths and you move right one place, the place value is divided by ___. (Select the correct answer: 10, 20, 30, or 100).

4. Now starting from the place value of thousandths and you move left two places, the place value is multip_____ by 100

Names of Decimal Fractions

Name	Place values	Example	Number of digits to the right of the decimal point	Denominator as a power of 10
Two tenths	tenths	0.2	1 digit	10^1
Fifteen hudredths	hundredths	0.15	2 digits	10^2
One hundred eight thousandths	thousandths	0.108	3 digits	10^3
Six ten-thousandths	ten-thousands	0.0006	4 digits	10^4
Twenty-eight hundred-thousandths	hundred-thousandths	0.00028	5 digits	10^5
Two million	millionths	0.000002	6 digits	10^6

Fig. 2

DENOMINATOR OF A POWER OF 10

Compare the column ("Number of digits to the right of the decimal point ") to the column ("Denominator as a power of 10 ") in fig. 2, it can be seen that the number of the digits of the zeros corresponds to the value of the exponents. For example, 10^1 has an exponent of 1, 10^2 has 2 as the exponent, 10^4 has 4 as the exponent and so on.

In summary, recall that while a common fraction can have any number as the denominator, a decimal fraction must have a denominator which is a power of 10 such as $10^1 = 10$

$$10^2 = 10 \times 10 = 100$$
$$10^3 = 10 \times 10 \times 10 = 1,000$$
$$10^4 = 10 \times 10 \times 10 \times 10 = 10,000$$
$$10^5 = 10 \times 10 \times 10 \times 10 \times 10 = 100,000$$
$$10^6 = 10 \times 10 \times 10 \times 10 \times 10 \times 10 = 1,000,000$$

When a decimal fraction is written, the denominator is never written. The denominator is determined by the number of digits to the right side of the decimal point. For example, using the column "**Example** " in Fig. 2,

One digit

$$.2 = \frac{2}{10} \quad \text{Denominator (with one zero)}$$

Two digits

$$.15 = \frac{15}{100} \quad \text{Denominator (with two zeros)}$$

Three digits

$$.108 = \frac{108}{1,000} \quad \text{Denominator (with three zeros)}$$

Four digits

$$.0006 = \frac{6}{10,000} \quad \text{Denominator (with four zeros)}$$

Five digits

$$.00028 = \frac{28}{100,000} \quad \text{Denominator (with five zeros)}$$

Six digits

$$.000002 = \frac{2}{1,000,000} \quad \text{Denominator (with six digits)}$$

Decimal $\qquad$ Fractions

Group Exercise

Recall that the decimal fraction .2 can be written as the common fraction $\frac{2}{10}$.

Using similar idea, write the common fractions for the following decimal fractions:
(**1**) .4 $\qquad$ (**2**) .82 $\qquad$ (**3**) .496 $\qquad$ (**4**) .9 $\qquad$ (**5**) .005

How to Read Mixed Decimal Fractions

A mixed number is made up of a whole number and a common fraction. Similarly, a mixed decimal consists of a whole number and a decimal fraction.

Mixed decimals are read by saying the name of the whole numbers, **replacing the decimal point with** "**and** " then adding the names of the decimal fractions.

Example 1

How is 8.09 read?

Solution

"**And**" is used for the decimal point. Therefore, 8.09 is read as eight and nine hundredths.

Example 2

(**a**). How is " 98.64" read?

(**b**). Write the mixed decimal of 460.237 in word phrase. Hint: See the chart of fig. 2.

(**c**). Write the mixed decimal for the word phrase two hundred forty and three hundred sixty four ten thousandths. Hint: See the chart of fig. 2.

Solution

(**a**). "And " is used for the decimal point. Therefore, 98.64 is read as ninety-eight and sixty-four hundredths.

(**b**). Mixed decimals are read by saying the name of the whole numbers, replacing the decimal point with "and" then adding the names of the decimal fraction as shown:

The name for the whole number 460 is four hundred sixty.

The name for the decimal fraction .237 is two hundred thirty seven thousandths. (Note that .237 has three digits after the decimal point and therefore, the decimal fraction of .237 must have three zeros in the denominator, and therefore, .237 has a place value of two hundred thirty seven thousandths.)

Therefore, the word phrase for 460.237 is four hundred sixty **and** two hundred thirty seven thousandths.

(**c**). The mixed decimal for the word phrase two hundred forty and three hundred sixty four ten thousandths is written as shown:

Two hundred forty is written as 240. "**and**" stands for a decimal point.

Three hundred sixty four ten thousandths is written as .0364. (Note that the "ten thousandths" suggests four digits after the decimal point in the "place value chart" or the "ten thousandths suggests that there are four zeros in the denominator of the decimal fraction three hundred sixty four ten thousandths, and therefore, the three hundred sixty four ten thousandths must have four digits and this is achieved by adding a zero at the front as follows, .0364.

Therefore, the mixed decimal for the word phrase two hundred forty and three hundred sixty four ten thousandths is 240.0364.

> The notes and the generous worked examples
> have provided me with conceptual understanding
> and computational fluency to do my homework.

Exercises

1. How are the following decimal fractions read? Hint: See Example 1.
   a. 24.01   **b.** 5.09   **c.** 100.01   **d.** 15.07   **e.** 20.044   **f.** 4.017

2. How are the following decimal fractions read? Hint: See Example 2.
   a. 14.55   **b.** 67.94   **c.** 112.99   **d.** 23.144   **e.** 2.432   **f.** 106.4002

3. State the value of each digit in the bold face. Hint: See the topic under "Place Value of the Digits."
   a. 33.8**4**   **b.** 2**1**3.123   **c.** 74.95**2**2   **d.** 256.8**4**5   **e.** 9356.09**3**4   **f.** 321.45**7**

4. Write the following decimal fractions and mixed decimals as word phrases. Hint: See fig. 2, Examples 1 and 2.

a. 4.46	**b.** .9	**c.** .6	**d.** .064	**e.** 12.16
f. 201.611	**g.** 2.0049	**h.** .04	**i.** .752	**j.** 475.281
k. .0001	**l.** .0401	**m.** 341.781	**n.** 75.38	**o.** 570.01
p. 63.417	**q.** .0067	**r.** .777	**s.** 88.888	**t.** 250.394

5. Write the decimal fraction for each of the following word phrases. Hint: See fig. 2, Examples 1 and 2.
   a. Forty hundredths
   b. One hundred and fifty thousandths
   c. Two thousand four hundred twenty-one ten-thousandths
   d. Twenty-four hundredths
   e. Twenty-eight hundredths
   f. Six hundred twenty-four ten-thousandths seventy-four hundredths
   g. Nine tenths
   h. Two and eighth thousandths
   i. Ten and twenty-four ten-thousandths
   j. Two and seven thousandths.

Challenge Questions

6. How are the following decimal fractions read?
   a. 99.241   **b.** 679.057   **c.** 3.001   **d.** .956   **e.** 48.039   **f.** 5431.3456

7. State the value of each digit in the bold face.
   a. 41.2**2**4   **b.** 678.**9**09   **c.** 56.000**2**   **d.** **5**43.214   **e.** 321.0**6**62   **f.** 2.1**4**

How to Convert Common Fractions to Decimal Fractions

Rule: To convert common fractions to decimal fractions, the number of the zeros in the denominator is the number of the decimal places and also the number of the digits in the decimal fraction is the number of the decimal places.

Example 3

Convert $\dfrac{3}{10}$ to a decimal fraction.

Solution

The common fraction $\dfrac{3}{10}$ has a denominator of 10. The 10 has one zero. The number of the zeros in the denominator is the number of the decimal places and also provides the number of the digits.

Therefore, $\dfrac{3}{10}$ has one decimal place and also 1 digit.

So, the decimal fraction of the common fraction $\dfrac{3}{10}$ is .3 and this is the required answer.

$$.3$$

Decimal point ↗   ↖3 is just one number on the right hand side of the decimal point, and therefore, has one decimal place and one digit.

Note that the decimal point in .3 is located by counting from right to left one decimal place from behind the numerator of 3 as shown:

Count one decimal place from right to left starting from behind the numerator.

0.3

Decimal point location

One decimal place (one digit).

This example is solved showing a detailed explanations just for the students' understanding. When solving homework or doing a test, it is not necessary to show the detailed explanations. This example can easily be solved as shown:

$$\dfrac{3}{10} = .3$$

Example 4

What is the decimal fraction of $\dfrac{17}{100}$?

Solution

The common fraction $\dfrac{17}{100}$ has 100 as the denominator and 100 has two zeros.

The number of zeros in the denominator is the number of the decimal places and also provides the number of the digits of the decimal fraction.

Therefore, the common fraction $\dfrac{17}{100}$ is the decimal fraction .17

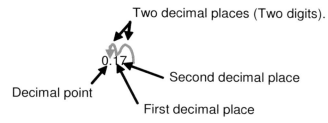

Two decimal places (Two digits).

0.17

Second decimal place

Decimal point

First decimal place

The combination of the first decimal place and the second decimal place make the two decimal places which is determined by the two zeros of the denominator 100. Note that the decimal point in .17 is located by counting from right to left two decimal places starting from behind the numerator of 17 as shown:

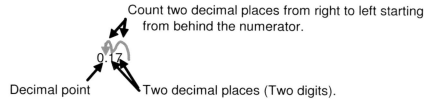

Count two decimal places from right to left starting from behind the numerator.

0.17

Decimal point

Two decimal places (Two digits).

The solution to this question is simply $\dfrac{17}{100} = .17$

Example 5

Write $\dfrac{138}{1000}$ as a decimal fraction.

Solution

The common fraction $\dfrac{138}{1000}$ has 1000 as the denominator and 1000 has three zeros. The number of zeros in the denominator is the number of the decimal places and also provides the number of the digits of the decimal fraction. So, the decimal fraction of the common fraction $\dfrac{138}{1000}$ is .138

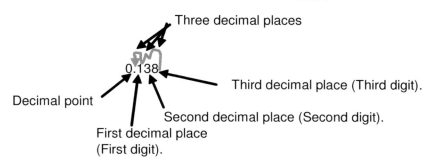

Three decimal places

0.138

Third decimal place (Third digit).

Decimal point

Second decimal place (Second digit).

First decimal place (First digit).

The combination of the first, second and the third decimal places make the three decimals which is determined by three zeros of the denominator 1000.
Note that the decimal point in .138 is located by counting from right to left three decimal places from behind the numerator of 138 as shown:

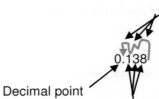

Count three decimal places from right to left starting from behind the numerator 138.

0.138

Decimal point

Three decimal places (Three digits).

When doing a homework or a test, it is not necessary to give detailed explanations, but rather solve the problem directly as shown:

$$\frac{138}{1000} = .138$$

Example 6

Express $\dfrac{2748}{10,000}$ as a decimal fraction.

Solution

The decimal fraction of the common fraction

$$\frac{2748}{10,000} = .2748$$

Note that the denominator 10,000 has four zeros, and therefore, the decimal fraction needs four decimal places.

Example 7

What is the decimal fraction of $\dfrac{99848}{100,000}$?

Solution

The decimal fraction of the common fraction

$$\frac{99848}{100,000} = .99848$$

Note that the denominator 100,000 has five zeros, and therefore, the decimal fraction needs five decimal places.

Example 8

Express $\dfrac{6}{10,000}$ as a decimal fraction.

Solution

The decimal fraction of the common fraction

$$\frac{6}{10,000} \text{ is } .0006$$

Note that in this case, the denominator of 10,000 has 4 zeros, and therefore, the required decimal fraction should have four decimal places, but the numerator has only the number 6. Therefore, count four decimal places from right to left starting from behind the numerator 6 as shown:

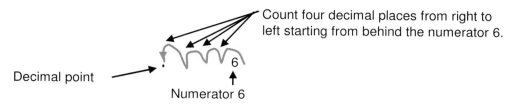

Count four decimal places from right to left starting from behind the numerator 6.

Decimal point → Numerator 6

Put zeros in the places of the decimal places which have no numbers as follows:

Four decimal places.

0.0006

Put zeros in place of the decimal places which have no numbers.

Therefore, the decimal fraction of the common fraction

$\dfrac{6}{10,000}$ is .0006

Example 9

Write the decimal fraction of $\dfrac{28}{100,000}$.

Solution

The decimal fraction of the common fraction

$\dfrac{28}{100,000}$ is .00028

Note that in this case, the denominator 100,000 has 5 zeros, and therefore, the required decimal fraction should have 5 decimal places, but the numerator has only the number 28. Count 5 decimal places from right to left starting from behind the numerator 28 as shown:

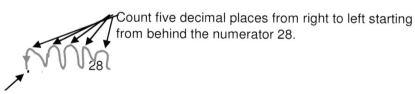

Count five decimal places from right to left starting from behind the numerator 28.

28

Put zeros in the places of the decimal places which have no numbers as shown:

Five decimal places (Five digits).

0.00028

Put zeros in places of the decimal places
which have no numbers.

Therefore, the decimal fraction of the common fraction,

$$\frac{28}{100,000} \text{ is } .00028$$

Example 10

Write $\dfrac{2}{100}$ as a decimal fraction.

Solution

The decimal fraction of the common fraction

$$\frac{2}{100} \text{ is } .02$$

Note that in this case, the denominator 100 has two zeros, and therefore, the
required decimal fraction should have two decimal places, but the numerator has
only the number 2. Count two decimal places from right to left starting from
behind the numerator 2 as shown:

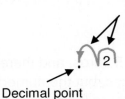

Count two decimal places from right to left
starting from behind the numerator 2.

2

Decimal point

Put a zero in place of the decimal place which has no number as shown:

Two decimal places (Two digits).

0.02

Decimal point

Put a zero in place of the decimal place
which has no numbers.

Therefore, the decimal fraction of the common fraction

$$\frac{2}{100} \text{ is } .02$$

382

The notes and the generous worked examples have provided me with conceptual understanding and computational fluency to do my homework.

Exercises

1. Change the following common fractions to decimal fractions.
Hint: See Example 3.

(a) $\dfrac{9}{10}$ (b) $\dfrac{7}{10}$ (c) $\dfrac{1}{10}$ (d) $\dfrac{5}{10}$ (e) $\dfrac{6}{10}$

2. Change the following common fractions to decimal fractions.
Hint: See Example 4

(a) $\dfrac{98}{100}$ (b) $\dfrac{1}{100}$ (c) $\dfrac{16}{100}$ d) $\dfrac{57}{100}$ (e) $\dfrac{39}{100}$

3. Change the following common fractions to decimal fractions.
Hint: See Example 5

(a) $\dfrac{798}{1,000}$ (b) $\dfrac{201}{1,000}$ (c) $\dfrac{157}{1,000}$ (d) $\dfrac{911}{1,000}$ (e) $\dfrac{401}{1,000}$

4. Change the following common fractions to decimal fractions.
Hint: See Example 6.

(a) $\dfrac{6749}{10,000}$ (b) $\dfrac{9461}{10,000}$ (c) $\dfrac{2008}{10,000}$ (d) $\dfrac{1781}{10,000}$ (e) $\dfrac{6223}{10,000}$

5. Change the following common fractions to decimal fractions.
Hint: See Example 7.

(a) $\dfrac{33245}{100,000}$ (b) $\dfrac{73205}{100,000}$ (c) $\dfrac{90045}{100,000}$ (d) $\dfrac{39245}{100,000}$ (e) $\dfrac{178245}{100,000}$

6. Change the following common fractions to decimal fractions.
Hint: See Example 8.

(a) $\dfrac{1}{10,000}$ (b) $\dfrac{9}{10,000}$ (c) $\dfrac{3}{10,000}$ (d) $\dfrac{6}{10,000}$ (e) $\dfrac{8}{10,000}$

7. Change the following common fractions to decimal fractions.
Hint: See Example 9.

(a) $\dfrac{13}{100,000}$ (b) $\dfrac{49}{100,000}$ (c) $\dfrac{11}{100,000}$ (d) $\dfrac{13}{100,000}$ (e) $\dfrac{13}{100,000}$

8. Change the following common fractions to decimal fractions.
Hint: See Example 10

(a) $\dfrac{9}{100}$ (b). $\dfrac{1}{100}$ (c) $\dfrac{7}{100}$ (d) $\dfrac{5}{100}$ (e) $\dfrac{8}{100}$

Challenge Questions

9. Change the following common fractions to decimal fractions.

(a) $\dfrac{17}{100}$ (b) $\dfrac{17}{10,000}$ (c) $\dfrac{967}{1,000}$ (d) $\dfrac{8}{10}$ (e) $\dfrac{1}{10,000}$

REAL WORLD APPLICATIONS - WORD PROBLEM
How to Convert Common Fractions to Decimal Fractions

Example 1

A computer selling for $1,000.00 was reduced by $100.00. Write the reduction as a decimal fraction of the price.

Solution

The reduction   = $100.00
Total selling price = $1,000.00

The reduction as a decimal fraction $= \dfrac{\text{Reduction}}{\text{Total Selling Price}}$

$$= \dfrac{100}{1000}$$

The denominator 1000 has three zeros, and therefore, the required decimal fraction should have three decimal places as shown:

Move three decimal places from right to left starting from behind the numerator 100.

.100

Decimal point

The reduction as a decimal fraction is .100 or just .1 because the zeros at the end of the decimal fractions have no values.

Example 2

Mary has $10.00. If she spent $3.00, write as a decimal the part of the money

384

she spent.

Solution

The common fraction of the amount she spent $= \dfrac{\text{Amount spent}}{\text{Total amount}}$

Amount spent = $3.00
Total amount = $10.00

The common fraction of the amount she spent $= \dfrac{3}{10}$

The decimal fraction of $\dfrac{3}{10}$ is .3 because the denominator 10 has one zero and

so, the decimal fraction has one decimal place as shown:

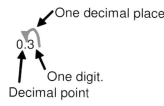

One decimal place

0.3

One digit.
Decimal point

She spent .3 of the total money.

Example 3

John bought a house for $100,000 and made a down payment of $15,250.
Write the down payment as a decimal fraction of the cost of the house.

Solution

The common fraction of the down payment $= \dfrac{\text{Down payment}}{\text{Total Amount}}$

Down payment = $15,250
Total Amount = $100,000

The common fraction of $\dfrac{15,250}{100,000}$ is equal to the decimal fraction of .15250

because the denominator 100,000 has five zeros and therefore the decimal
fraction should have five decimal places or five digits as shown:

Five decimal places.

. 15250

Decimal point

The required decimal fraction is .15250

**The notes and the generous worked examples
have provided me with conceptual understanding
and computational fluency to do my homework.**

Exercises
1. A computer selling for $1,000.00 was reduced by $108.00. Write the reduction as a decimal fraction of the price. Hint: See Example 1.
2. Eric had $10.00. If he spent $8.00, write the part of the money he spent as a decimal fraction. Hint: See Example 2.
3. Rose bought a special car for $10,000.00 and made a down payment of $1,528.00. Write the down payment as a decimal fraction of the cost of the car. Hint: See Example 3.

Challenge Questions
4. A book selling for $100.00 was reduced by $32.00. Write the reduction as a decimal fraction of the price.
5. Given that a sale tax in a certain year was $0.05 for every $1.00 of purchase, write the sales tax as a decimal fraction of the purchase. (Hint: $0.05 = 5 cents and $1.00 = 100 cents).
6. Given that a salesman earns $12.00 for every $100.00 of sales, write his earnings as a decimal fraction of the sales.
7. A sweater selling for $100.00 was reduced by $8.00. Write the reduction as a decimal fraction of the price.
8. An electrical equipment which was selling at $10,000.00 was reduced by $234.00. Write the reduction as a decimal fraction of the selling price.

Compare Common Fractions and Decimal Fraction

Common fraction	Equivalent decimal fraction	Decimal fraction name	Number of digits to the right of the decimal point	Denominator
$\frac{3}{10}$	0.3	Three tenths	1 digit	10
$\frac{17}{100}$	0.17	Seventeen hundredths	2 digits	100
$\frac{138}{1000}$	0.138	One hundred thirty-eight thousandths	3 digits	1000

Mixed Fraction and Mixed Decimals
A mixed fraction is made up of a whole number and a common fraction such as $7\frac{1}{2}$ where 7 is the whole number and $\frac{1}{2}$ is the common fraction.

A mixed decimal is made up of a whole number and a decimal fraction such as 3.68 where 3 is the whole number and .68 is the decimal fraction.

Summary of Types of Fractions

Types	Example	Comments
Common fraction	$\dfrac{1}{10}$	It has no whole numbers.
Decimal fraction	0.1	It has no whole numbers.
Mixed common fraction	$1\dfrac{1}{10}$	It has a whole number and a common fraction.
Mixed decimal fraction	1.1	It has both a whole number and a decimal fraction.

Exercise

1. (a) Compare a mixed fraction and a mixed decimal. Hint: See the notes under "Mixed Fractions and Mixed Decimals".

(b) Given 9.48 and $9\dfrac{48}{100}$, state which number is a mixed fraction and which number is a mixed decimal. Give reasons for your answer. Hint: See the notes under "Mixed Fractions and Mixed Decimals".

How to Convert Decimal Fractions to Common Fractions

Rule 1: Although decimal fractions do not show their denominators, decimal fractions have denominators of powers of 10. So, simply maintain the numbers of the decimal fraction as the numerator and put this numerator over the denominator that is determined by the number of digits in the decimal fraction using the power of 10.

New phrase:

Powers of 10 means $10 \times 10 \times 10 \times \ldots = \mathbf{10^n}$ where n is the power.
For example,
(a).

$$.2 = \frac{2}{10}$$

One digit　　One zero　　↑　Denominator of the power of 10

(b).

Numerator

$$.03 = \frac{03}{100} = \frac{3}{100}$$　Note: $03 = 3$, the 0 has no value.

Two zeros　　Denominator of the power of 10 ($100 = 10 \times 10 = 10^2$).

Similarly, for an example, $.93 = \dfrac{93}{100}$ and the denominator has a power of 10.

387

(c).

/Numerator

$$.007 = \frac{007}{1000} = \frac{7}{1000}$$ Note: 007 = 7, 00 in front of 7 has no value.

/// ↑↑↑ \Denominator of the power of 10. (1000 = 10 × 10

Three digits   Three zeros   × 10 = 10^3.)

Similarly, for an example .561 = $\dfrac{561}{1000}$ and the denominator has a power of 10.

(d).

/Numerator

$$.0009 = \frac{0009}{10,000} = \frac{9}{10,000}$$ Note: 0009 = 9, 000 in front of 9 has no value.

//// ↑↑↑↑   \Denominator of the power of 10 (10,000 = 10 × 10

Four digits   Four zeros   × 10 × 10 = 10^4.)

Similarly, for an example, .643 = $\dfrac{643}{1000}$ and the denominator is of the power of 10.

See Rules 2 and 3 for further explanations.

Rule 2: To convert a decimal fraction to a common fraction, rewrite the decimal fraction as a fraction that has the equivalent denominator in a power of 10, and then reduce the common fraction to the lowest terms.

Rule 3: The number of digits in the decimal fraction is the same as the number of zeros in the denominator.

Example 1
Change .2 to a common fraction.
Solution
Using Rule 3, the number of digits in the decimal fraction is the same as the number of zeros in the denominator. The .2 has one digit, and therefore, has one zero in the denominator as shown: (use Rules 1 and 2)

.2

↑

One digit (one decimal place).

/Numerator

$$.2 = \frac{2}{10}$$

One digit ↗   \One zero in the denominator

Note that one-digit decimal fraction changes to a fraction with one zero in the denominator. Note also that the decimal fraction two tenths is rewritten as the common fraction $\frac{2}{10}$.

$.2 = \frac{2}{10}$, we can reduce $\frac{2}{10}$ to the lowest terms by dividing the numerator and

the denominator of $\frac{2}{10}$ by 2 as shown:

$$\frac{\overset{1}{\cancel{2}}}{\underset{5}{\cancel{10}}} = \frac{1}{5} \ . \quad \text{Therefore, } .2 = \frac{1}{5}$$

Example 2

Change .36 to a common fraction.

Solution

Using Rule 3, the number of digits in the decimal fraction is the same as the number of zeros in the denominator.

.36 has two digits, and therefore, .36 has two zeros in the denominator as shown: (use Rules 1 and 2)

$$0.36$$

Two digits(two decimal places).

$$.36 = \frac{36}{100} \quad \text{Numerator}$$

Two digits   Two zeros in the denominator

Note that a two-digit decimal fraction changes to a common fraction with two zeros in the denominator. Note also that the decimal fraction thirty six hundredths is rewritten as a common fraction $\frac{36}{100}$.

$.36 = \frac{36}{100}$, we can reduce $\frac{36}{100}$ to the lowest term by dividing both 36 and 100 by 4 as shown:

$$\frac{\overset{9}{\cancel{36}}}{\underset{25}{\cancel{100}}} = \frac{9}{25}$$

Therefore, $.36 = \dfrac{9}{25}$

Example 3
Convert .613 to a common fraction.
Solution
Using Rule 3, the number of digits in the decimal fraction is the same as the number of zeros in the denominator.

.613 has three digits, and therefore, has three zeros in the denominator as follows: (use Rules 1 and 2)

0.613

Three digits (three decimal places).

Numerator

$$.613 = \dfrac{613}{1000}$$

Three digits   Three zeros in the denominator

Note that a three-digit decimal fraction changes to a common fraction with three zeros in the denominator. Note also that the decimal fraction six hundred thirteen thousandths is rewritten as common fraction $\dfrac{613}{1000}$.

$.613 = \dfrac{613}{1000}$, and $\dfrac{613}{1000}$ cannot be reduced to the lowest terms because, there is no number that can divide both 613 and 1000 evenly (without a remainder.)

The required answer is $.613 = \dfrac{613}{1000}$

Example 4
Convert .0891 to a common fraction
Solution
Using Rule 3, the number of digits in the decimal fraction is the same as the number of zeros in the denominator.

.0891 has four digits, and therefore, has four zeros in the denominator as shown: (Use Rules 1 and 2)

0.0891

Four digits (four decimal places).

Numerator has four digits.

$$.0891 = \frac{0891}{10,000} = \frac{891}{10,000}$$ Note: 0891 = 891 because the 0 has no value.

Four digits   Four zeros in the denominator

Note that a four-digit decimal fraction changes to a common fraction with four zeros in the denominator. Note also that the decimal fraction eight hundred ninety one ten-thousandths is rewritten as a common fraction $\frac{891}{10,000}$.

$$.0891 = \frac{891}{10,000}$$ and $\frac{891}{10,000}$ cannot be reduced to the lowest terms because there is no number that can divide both 891 and 10,000 evenly (without a remainder).

The required answer is $.0891 = \frac{891}{10,000}$

Example 5

Change .009 to a common fraction.

Solution

Using Rule 3, the number of digits in the decimal fraction is the same as the number of zeros in the denominator.

.009 has three digits, and therefore, has three zeros in the denominator as shown: (use Rule 1 and 2)

0.009

Three digits (three decimal places).

Numerator

$$.009 = \frac{009}{1000} = \frac{9}{1000}$$ Note: 009 = 9 because the 00 has no value.

Three digits   Three zeros in the denominator

Note that a three-digit decimal fraction changes to a common fraction with three zeros in the denominator. Note also that the decimal fraction nine thousandths is rewritten as the common fraction $\frac{9}{1000}$ and $\frac{9}{1000}$ cannot be reduced to the lowest term because there is no number that can divide both 9 and 1000 evenly (without a remainder.)

The required answer is .009 = $\dfrac{9}{1000}$

The notes and the generous worked examples have provided me with conceptual understanding and computational fluency to do my homework.

Exercises
1. Explain how you can change a decimal fraction to a common fraction.
2. Change the following decimal fractions to common fractions: (Hint: See Example 1.) Reduce your answers to the lowest terms.
   (a) .1　　(b) .4　　(c) .6　　(d) .7　　(e) .9
3. Change the following decimal fractions to common fractions: (Hint: See Example 2.) Reduce your answers to the lowest terms.
   (a) .12　　(b) .24　　(c) .99　　(d) .55　　(e) .79

   (f) .27　　(g) .07　　(h) .06　　(i) .08　　(j) .09
4. Convert the following decimal fractions to common fractions: (Hint: See Example 3.) Reduce your answers to the lowest terms.
   (a) .137　　(b) .322　　(c) .111　　(d) .222

   (e) .631　　(f) .412　　(g) .225　　(h) .362

   (i) .844　　(j) .255　　(k) .245　　(l) .842
5. Change the following decimal fractions to common fractions: (Hint: See Example 4.) Reduce your answers to the lowest terms.
   (a) .0148　　(b) .0946　　(c) .0777　　(d) .0581

   (e) .0419　　(f) .0762　　(g) .0518　　(h) .0255

   (i) .0733　　(j) .0650　　(k) .0205　　(l) .0914
6. Change the following decimal fractions to common fractions: (Hint: See Example 5.) Reduce your answers to the lowest terms.
   (a) .006　　(b) .007　　(c) .003　　(d) .001

   (e) .002　　(f) .004　　(g) .084　　(h) .002

   (i) .033　　(j) .096　　(k) .026　　(l) .071

Challenge Questions.

7. Change the following decimal fractions to common fractions. Reduce your answers to the lowest terms.

(a) .29   (b) .008   (c) .05   (d) .239

(e) .2250   (f) .0431   (g) .0001   (h) .9854

(i) .33   (j) .7   (k) .06   (l) .225

(m) .3   (n) .090   (o) .90   (p) .117

(q) .0535   (r) .72   (s) .781   (t) .060

(u) .84   (v) .9   (w) .1114   (x) .3892

Answers to Selected Questions

2(a) $\dfrac{1}{10}$ 2(b) $\dfrac{2}{5}$ 3(d) $\dfrac{11}{20}$ 4(b) $\dfrac{161}{500}$

4(g) $\dfrac{9}{40}$ 5(a) $\dfrac{37}{2500}$ 5(i) $\dfrac{733}{10,000}$ 6(a) $\dfrac{3}{500}$

REAL WORLD APPLICATIONS - WORD PROBLEMS
HOW TO CONVERT DECIMAL FRACTIONS TO COMMON FRACTIONS

Example 1

Given that John walks .28 miles to school every day, write the distance as a common fraction of a mile. Hint: See Rules 1, 2, and 3 and Example 3 under the topic, "Converting Decimal Fractions to Common Fractions."

Solution

Using Rules 1, 2, and 3,

$$.28 = \frac{28}{100} \quad \text{See Rules 1, 2 and 3.}$$

Two digits   Two zeros

Reduce $\dfrac{28}{100}$ to the lowest terms by dividing both 28 and 100 by 4 as follows:

$$\frac{\overset{7}{\cancel{28}}}{\underset{25}{\cancel{100}}} = \frac{7}{25}$$

Therefore, $.28 = \dfrac{7}{25}$

Example 2

Write $.97 as a common fraction of a dollar. (Hint: See Rule 1, 2, and 3 and Example 1.)

Solution

Using Rules 1, 2, and 3,

$$.97 = \dfrac{97}{100}$$

Two digits   Two zeros

Therefore, $.97 = \dfrac{97}{100}$

Example 3

Given that a certain pencil has a thickness of .31 of an inch. Write the thickness as a common fraction. Hint: See Rules 1, 2, and 3 under the topic "Converting Decimal Fractions to Common Fraction."

Solution

Using Rules 1, 2, and 3:

$$.31 = \dfrac{31}{100}$$

Two digits   Two zeros

Therefore, $.31 = \dfrac{31}{100}$.

Example 4

The decimal fraction .75 of a mile is equal to what common fraction of a mile? Hint: See Rules 1, 2 and 3 under the topic "Converting Decimal Fractions to Common Fractions."

Solution

Using Rules 1, 2 and 3:

$$.75 = \dfrac{75}{100}$$

Two digits   Two zeros

Reduce $\dfrac{75}{100}$ to the lowest term by dividing both 75 and 100 by 5 as shown:

$$\frac{\overset{15}{\cancel{75}}}{\underset{20}{\cancel{100}}} = \frac{15}{20}$$

Still reduce $\frac{15}{20}$ to the lowest term by dividing 15 and 20 by 5 as shown:

$$\frac{\overset{3}{\cancel{15}}}{\underset{4}{\cancel{20}}} = \frac{3}{4}$$

Therefore, .75 mile $= \frac{3}{4}$ mile.

The notes and the generous worked examples have provided me with conceptual understanding and computational fluency to do my homework.

Exercises

1. Given that Eric walks .95 miles to school, write the distance as a common fraction of a mile. Hint: See Example 1.

2. Write $.92 as a common fraction of a dollar. Hint: See Example 2.

3. Given that a certain pen has a thickness of .28 of an inch. Write the thickness as a common fraction of an inch. Hint: See Example 3.

Challenge Questions

4. Write $.90 as a common fraction of a dollar.

5. Eric walks .65 miles to school, write the distance as a common fraction of a mile.

6. Given that a shoe lace is .125 inches thick, write the thickness as a common fraction of an inch.

MIXED REVIEW - SIMILAR EXTERNAL TEST
Exercises

1. Write the word phrase for each decimal fraction.

(a) .1	(b) .07	(c) .002	(d) .45
(e) .0007	(f) .120	(g) .945	(h) .114
(i) .0013	(j) .725	(k) .421	(l) 3.333

2. Write the decimal fraction for each word phrase.

(a) One tenths

(b) Seventy–eight thousandths

(c) Nine ten–thousandths

(d) Forty–two hundredths

(e) Two and five hundredths

COMPARING DECIMAL FRACTIONS

Mixed Review
How are common fractions compared? Common fractions are compared by converting the denominators to a common denominator (same denominator) and then we compare the numerators. The bigger the numerator, the bigger is the common fraction and the smaller the numerator the less is the common fraction. Review the topic under Comparing Fractions.

Comparing Decimal Fractions
Rule 1: To compare decimal fractions, change all the decimal fractions to decimal fractions that have the same number of decimal places by putting zeros behind the last digit until the desired number of the decimal places is achieved, and then compare the numbers of these decimal fractions with the common number of decimal places. The bigger the common fraction with the common number of decimal places, the bigger the value of the number.

Another way to compare or order decimal fractions is by using the number line such that the decimal fractions to the right of the number line are greater than the decimal fractions to the left of the number line. Review the section on number line.

Critical Thinking
Why can decimal fractions be compared by changing the decimal fractions to decimal fractions that have the same (common) number of decimal places? The answer is, it is easier to compare decimal fractions when the decimal fractions belong to the same tenths, hundredths, thousandths, ten-thousandths, or hundred thousands. For example, it is easier to compare two tenths (.2) to five tenths (.5) than to compare two tenths (.2) to fifteen hundredths (.15).

Example 1
Compare .9 and .85, which number is bigger?
Solution
Using Rule 1, change .9 and .85 to the same or common decimal places.
.85 has the higher number of decimal places of 2, and therefore change .9 which has 1 decimal place also to 2 decimal places by putting a zero behind .9 as follows:

/Put zero behind .9

.9 = .90

One decimal place   Two decimal places.

We can now compare .90 and .85 because .90 and .85 have the same (common) number of decimal places of 2 as shown:
The bigger decimal fraction is .90 (90 hundredths), followed by .85 (85 hundredths). Therefore, .9 is bigger than .85 or .9 > .85

Example 2
Which number is bigger, .65 or .7?
Solution
Using Rule 1, change .65 and .7 to the same (common) number of decimal places. .65 has the higher number of decimal places of 2, and therefore, change .7 which has one decimal place also to 2 decimal places by putting zero behind .7 as shown

/Put a zero behind .7

.7 = .70

One decimal place ↗   ↖↖

Two decimal places

We can now compare .65 and .70 because both .65 and .70 have the same (common) number of decimal places of 2 as follows:
The bigger decimal fraction is .70 (70 hundredths), followed by .65 (65 hundredths). Therefore, .7 is bigger than .65 or .7 > .65

Example 3
Arrange .5, .005, .05, and .0005 in order of the (a) biggest values first, (b) smallest values first.
Solution
Using Rule 1, change .5, .005, .05, and .0005 to the same (common) number of decimal places. Note that .0005 has the highest number of decimal places of 4, and therefore, change .5, .005, and .05 also to 4 decimal places by putting zero/zeros behind .5, .005, and .05 as shown:
Changing .5 to four decimal places becomes:

Put 3 zeros behind .5

.5000

Four decimal places

Changing .005 to four decimal places becomes

/Put a zero behind .005

.0050

4 decimal places.

Changing .05 to four decimal places becomes

Put two zeros behind .05

.0500

Four decimal places

We can now compare .5000 , .0050 , .0500, and .0005 because all the decimal fractions have the same (common) number of decimal places of 4 as shown: The biggest decimal fraction is .5000 (five thousand ten-thousandths , followed by .0500 (five hundred ten–thousandths), followed by .0050 (fifty ten–thousandths), followed by .0005 (five ten–thousandths).

(a) Therefore, the required order showing the biggest number first is .5, .05, .005, .0005, or .5 > .05 > .005 > .0005

(b) The required order showing the smallest numbers first is .0005, .005, .05, .05, .5, or .0005 < .005 < .05 < .5

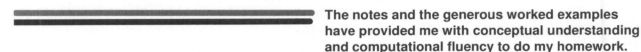

The notes and the generous worked examples have provided me with conceptual understanding and computational fluency to do my homework.

Exercises

1. Explain how you could compare two or more decimal fractions.

2. Which decimal fraction is bigger? Hint: See Examples 1 and 2.

   (a) .3, .314   (b) .6, .61   (c) .41, .39

   (d) .25, .35   (e) .07, .7   (f) .8, .85

3. Which decimal fraction is smaller? Hint: See Example 1 and 2.

   (a) .21, .20   (b) .3, .34   (c) .68, .60

   (d) .01, .10   (e) .9, .09   (f) .5 , .55

4. Arrange the following decimal fractions in order with the biggest values first. Hint: See Example 3(a).

   (a) .606, .066, .0066   (b) .1, .001, .010

   (c) .250, .205, .025   (d) .35, .305, .351

   (e) .75, .705, .751   (f) .202, .220, .022

   (g) .743, .734, .704, .741   (h) .404, .414, .441, .399

   (i) .81, .811, .801, .081   (j) .371, .47, .407, .372

   (k) .734, .704, .747, .774   (l) .505, .550, .005, .500

5. Arrange the decimal fractions in order with the smallest values first. Hint: See Example 3(b).

   (a) .03, .303, .003   (b) .4, .4001, .404, .0404

(c) .489, .561, .67, .067   (d) .250, .025, .25
(e) .140, .104, .110, .141   (f) .871, .666, .737
(g) .999, .099, .909, .919   (h) .550, .0519, .005

6. Select the decimals that have the same value. Hint: Apply Example 3.
   (a) .001, .100, .101, .0010   (b) .0040, .04, .004
   (c) .2 , .202, .20   (d) .90, .9, .901
   (e) .5, .500, .505   (f) .08, .008, .0800
   (g) .7, .07, .70   (h) .18, .180, .0180
   (i) .0300, .03, .003   (k) .101, .0110, .011

Answers to Selected Questions

2(a) .314   **3(a)** .20   **4(a)** .606, .066, .0066

5(a) .003, .03, .303   **6(a)** .001 and .0010

REAL WORLD APPLICATIONS – WORD PROBLEMS
Comparing Decimal Fractions

Exercises
1. John is 6.5 feet tall and Nick is 5.8 feet tall. Who is taller?
   Hint: See Example 2. Compare 6.5 to 5.8.
2. Frank walks .18 miles to school and Jamal walks .2 miles to school. Who
   walks further? Hint: See Example 2, compare .18 to .2.
3. Robin jogs 2.8 miles every day and Diana jogs 3 miles every day. Who jogs
   more? Hint: See Example 2, compare 2.8 to 3.
4. Five lengths of rods are 6.58 feet, 6.56 feet, 5.68 feet, 5.98 feet and 6.01 feet.
   (a) Arrange the lengths of the rods from the longest to the shortest.
       Hint: See Example 3(a).
   (b) Arrange the lengths of the rods from the shortest to the longest.
       Hint: See Example 3(b).

ROUNDING OFF DECIMAL FRACTIONS
Decimals are rounded in the same way that whole numbers are rounded.
When a decimal fraction is rounded off, its true value is changed to an
approximate value by limiting the number of the digits such as to the nearest
tenth, hundredth or thousandth.
Rule 1:
If the digit to the right side of the required place is 5 or greater than 5,
then the digit to the right of the required place is rounded up to 1 and the 1
should be added to the digit at the required place, but if the digit to the right of
the required place is less than 5 then the digit to the right side of the required

place remains the same.

Rule 2:

From Rule 1, if the digit to the right of the required place is 5 or greater than 5, then the digit to the right of the required place is rounded up to 1 and this 1 should be added to the digit at the required place, but the true value of the 1 when:

(a) we round off to the nearest tenth is .1

(b) we round off to the nearest hundredth is .01

(c) we round off to the nearest thousandth is .001

(d) we round off to the nearest ten thousandth is .0001

(e) and so on.

Rule 3:

To round off decimal fractions, omit all the digits at the right side of the required place.

Special Note:

(a) To round off to the nearest tenth, the digit in the tenths place is the digit that 1 should be added to if the digit at the right side of the tenths place is 5 or greater than 5.

(b) To round off to the nearest hundredth, the digit in the hundredths place is the digit that 1 should be added to if the digit at the right side of the hundredths place is 5 or greater than 5.

(c) To round off to the nearest thousandth, the digit in the thousandths place is the digit that 1 should be added to if the digit at the right side of the thousandths place is 5 or greater than 5.

(d) To round off to the nearest ten-thousandth, the digit in the ten-thousandths place is the digit that 1 should be added to if the digit at the right side of the ten-thousandths place is 5 or greater than 5.

Summary of How to Round off Decimal Fractions

Step 1: Locate the position of the digit and the digit in the question such as the tenths place for the nearest tenth, the hundredths place for the nearest hundredth, the thousandths place for the nearest thousandth, or the ten-thousandths place for the nearest ten-thousandth.

Step 2: Consider the digit at the right side of the required place in Step 1 to determine if this digit is 5 or greater than 5 or not, and if this digit is 5 or greater than 5, then add 1 to the digit at the required place in Step 1, and if the digit at the right side of the required place is less than 5, then just round off the decimal fraction to the required place without adding 1 to the digit at the required place. See the examples for detailed explanations.

Step 3: Omit all the digits after the required place digits such as the tenths place digit, the hundredths place digit, the thousandths place digit, or the ten-thousandths place digit.

Example 1

Round off .6891 to the nearest tenth.

Solution

Step 1: The digit at the tenths place is .6 as shown:

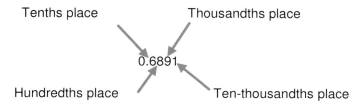

Tenths place   Thousandths place

0.6891

Hundredths place   Ten-thousandths place

Step 2: Using Rule 1, if the digit at the right side of the tenths place is 5 or greater than 5, then round up the digit to the right of the tenths place to 1 and add this 1 to the digit at the tenths place.

$$8 > 5, \text{ therefore, add 1 to .6}$$

$$\text{Using Rule 2, in this case } 1 = \text{one tenth} = \frac{1}{10} = .1$$

$$\text{Therefore,} \qquad \begin{array}{r} .6 \\ + .1 \\ \hline .7 \end{array}$$

Step 3: The last three digits of .6891 which are 891 are omitted by using Rule 3 as shown:

.6891   becomes .6 + .1 = .7

↑↑↑

Omitted

Answer: .6891 = .7 to the nearest tenth.

Example 2

Round off .3418 to the nearest tenth.

Solution

Step 1: The digit at the tenths place is .3 as shown:

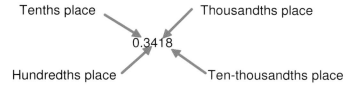

Tenths place   Thousandths place

0.3418

Hundredths place   Ten-thousandths place

Step 2: Using Rule 1, if the digit at the right side of tenths place is less than 5, then the digit to the right side of the tenths place is rounded down to 0 such that 0 should be added to the digit in the tenths place. Since 4 is the digit at the right side of the tenths place, and 4 is less than 5, add 0 to .3 as shown:

$$\begin{array}{r} .3 \\ + \ 0 \\ \hline .3 \end{array}$$

Step 3: The last three digits of .3418 which are 418 are omitted by Rule 3 as shown:

$$.3418 = .3 \text{ to the nearest tenth.}$$
$$\uparrow\uparrow\uparrow$$
Omitted

The required answer: .3418 = .3 to the nearest tenth.

Example 3
Round off .7643 to the nearest hundredth.
Solution
Step 1: The digit at the hundredths place is 6 as shown:

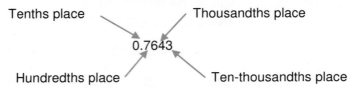

Step 2: Using Rule 1, if the digit at the right side of the hundredths place is less than 5, then round down the digit at the right side of the hundredths place to 0 such that 0 is added to the digit at the hundredths place. Since 4 is the digit at the right side of the hundredths place, and 4 is less than 5, add 0 to .76 as shown:

$$
\begin{array}{r}
.76 \\
+\ \ 0 \\
\hline
.76
\end{array}
$$

Step 3: The last two digits of .7643 which are 43 are omitted by Rule 3 as shown:

$$.7643 = .76 \text{ to the nearest hundredth.}$$
$$\uparrow\uparrow$$
Omitted

The required answer: .7643 = .76 to the nearest hundredth.

Example 4
Round off .2952 to the nearest hundredth.
Solution
Step 1: The digit at the hundredths place is 9 as shown:

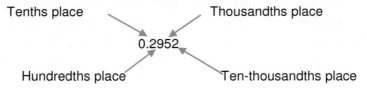

Step 2: Using Rule 1, if the digit at the right side of the hundredths place is 5 or

greater than 5, then add 1 to the digit at the hundredths place. Since the digit at the right side of the hundredths place is 5 and 5 is equal to 5 add 1 to 9.

Using Rule 2, in this case, 1 = one hundredth = $\dfrac{1}{100}$ = .01.

Adding:
$$
\begin{array}{r}
.29 \\
+\ .01 \\
\hline
.30
\end{array}
$$

Step 3: The last two digits of .2952 which are 52 are omitted in the final answer by using Rule 3 as shown:

.2952 = .29 + .01 = .30 to the nearest hundredth.

↑↑
Omitted

The required answer: .2952 = .29 + .01 = .30 to the nearest hundredth.

Example 5

Round off .1687 to the nearest thousandth.
Solution
Step 1: The digit at the thousandths place is 8 as shown:

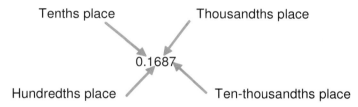

Step 2: Using Rule 1, if the digit at the right side of the thousandths place is 5 or greater than 5, then add 1 to the digit at the thousandths place. Since 7 is at the right side of the thousandths place, and 7 is greater than 5, add 1 to 8. Using Rule 2, in this case, 1 = one thousandth = $\dfrac{1}{1000}$ = .001

Adding:
$$
\begin{array}{r}
.168 \\
+\ .001 \\
\hline
.169
\end{array}
$$

Step 3: The last digit of .1687 which is 7 is omitted in the final answer by using Rule 3 as shown:

.1687 = .168 + .001 = .169 to the nearest thousandth.

↑
Omitted
The required answer is .1687 = .168 + .001 = .169 to the nearest thousandth.

Note: Detailed explanations in Example 1 to 5 are provided to give the student the vital understanding of the concept; however, the detailed explanations are not recommended for homework and tests.

Example 6
Round off the following numbers to the nearest tenths without showing the detailed explanations.

(a) 2.68   (b) 3.41   (c) .761   (d) .4678   (e) .841

Solution

(a) 2.68 = 2.7 because 8 > 5, and therefore, 1 should be added to 6 to make 7 which is expressed in tenths as .7

(b) 3.41 = 3.4 because 1 < 5, and therefore, 0 is added to 4 which is expressed in tenths as .4.

(c) .761 = .8 because 6 > 5, and therefore, 1 should be added to 7 to make 8 which is expressed in tenths as .8

(d) .4678 = .5 because 6 > 5, and therefore, 1 should be added to 4 to make 5 which is expressed in tenths as .5

(e) .841 = .8 because 4 < 5, and therefore, 0 is added to 8 which is expressed in tenths as .8.

Example 7
Round off the following numbers to the nearest hundredths without showing detailed explanations.

(a) 2.86514   (b) 3.640641   (c) .01841   (d) .00941   (e) .00392

Solution

(a) 2.86514 = 2.87 because 5 = 5, and therefore, 1 is added to 6 to make 7.

(b) 3.640641 = 3.64 because 0 < 5, and therefore, 0 is added to 4 to make 4.

(c) .01841 = .02 because 8 > 5, and therefore, 1 is added to 1 to make 2.

(d) .00941 = .01 because 9 > 5, and therefore, 1 is added to 0 to make 1.

(e) .00392 = .00 = 0 because 3 < 5, and therefore, 0 is added to zero to make 0.

Example 8
Round off the followings numbers to the nearest thousandths without detailed explanations.

(a) .11580   (b) .9642   (c) .0027   (d) .4119   (e) .42238

Solution

(a) .11580 = .116 because 8 > 5, and therefore, 1 is added to 5 to make 6.

(b) .9642 = .964 because 2 < 5, and therefore, 0 is added 4 to make 4.

(c) .0027 = .003 because 7 > 5, and therefore, 1 is added to 2 to make 3.

(d) .4119 = .412 because 9 > 5, and therefore, 1 is added to 1 to make 2.

(e) .42238 = .422 because 3 < 5, and therefore, 0 is added to 2 to make 2.

The notes and the generous worked examples have provided me with conceptual understanding and computational fluency to do my homework.

Exercises

1. Round off the following to the nearest tenths. Hint: See Examples 1, 2, and 6.

(a) .17	(b) .31	(c) .55	(d) .74	(e) .774
(f) .4893	(g) .0918	(h) .861	(k) .418	(l) .064
(m) .731	(n) .83416	(o) .306	(p) .0109	(q) .3689

2. Round off the following to the nearest hundredths. Hint: See Examples 3, 4, and 7.

(a) .114	(b) .9165	(c) .6582	(d) .78941	(e) .74562
(f) .41184	(g) .9678	(h) .09092	(i) .01901	(j) .94561
(k) .84119	(l) .60918	(m) .76009	(n) .04766	(o) .57618
(p) .8488	(q) .8422	(r) .25841	(s) .66991	(t) .88654

Answers to Selected Questions

1(a) .2   **1(h)** .9   **2(a)** .11   **2(h)** .09   **3(a)** .009   **3(h)** .091

REAL WORLD APPLICATIONS - WORD PROBLEMS
(See similar Examples 1 to 8)

The notes and the generous worked examples have provided me with conceptual understanding and computational fluency to do my homework.

Exercises

1. What is the approximate weight of .834 pounds of a metal rounded off to the nearest tenth?

2. The diameter of a rod measures 2.4610. Round off the measurement to the nearest hundredth.

3. A package of beef weighs 4.8126 pounds. Round off the weight to the nearest thousandth.

4. John weighs 155.468 pounds. What is the approximate weight of John rounded to the nearest hundredth?

REVIEW — SIMILAR EXTERNAL TEST, CHALLENGE QUESTIONS

1. Round off the following numbers to the nearest hundredths.

    (a) .008   (b) .1096   (c) 4.236   (d) .211361

    (e) 2.0491   (f) 9.9999   (g) .289   (h) .9895

2. Round off the following to the nearest tenths.

    (a) .09   (b) .68   (c) .0995   (d) 7.894
    (e) 9.9511   (f) .2861   (g) .0095   (h) 29.097

3. Round off the following to the nearest thousandths.

    (a) .0009   (b) 1.0007   (c) .68989   (d) .41148

    (e) .4891   (f) 2.6789   (g) 4.3811   (h) 3.8971

4. Which is the greatest decimal fraction?

    (a) .090, .909, .9909, .9, .990   (b) .5, .005, .5505, .5601

    (c) .6, .0606, .606, .6606   (d) 1.1, 1.01, .1100, 11.01

Answers to Selected Questions
1(a) .01   **1(c)** 4.24   **2(a)** .1   2(d) 7.9   **3(b)** 1.001   **3(g)** 4.381   **4(b)** .5601

DECIMAL PLACES

The decimal places are the positions of the digits to the right of the decimal point as shown:

First decimal place   Third decimal place

3.4184

Second decimal place   Fourth decimal place

Decimal places can be compared to the tenths, hundredths and the thousandths places or positions as shown:

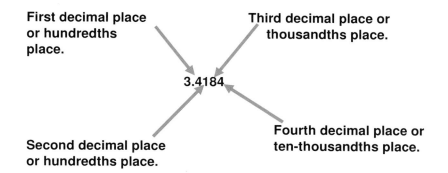

Locating Decimal Places

Decimal places are located as shown:

two decimal places.
↓↓
3.4184
↑
One decimal place.

three decimal places.
↓↓↓
3.4184
↑↑↑↑
four decimal places.

Note: How are decimal fractions rounded to a number of decimal places? Decimal fractions can be rounded to the nearest tenths, hundredths and thousandths, and similarly, decimal fractions can be rounded to 1, 2, 3, 4, . . . decimal places by considering the digits to the right of the decimal point, such that if the digit to the right of the required decimal place is 5 or greater than 5, then 1 is added to the digit at the required decimal place and if the digit to the right of the required decimal place is less than 5, then 0 is added to the digit at the required decimal place.

Example 1

Convert 8.23678 to 3 decimal places.

Solution

We should first find the number in the 3rd decimal place position. In 8.23678, 6 is in the third decimal place, and the number after 6 is 7 which is greater than 5. Therefore, 1 is added to 6 to give 7. Therefore, the required answer is 8.237.

Example 2

Round off each of the following numbers to the nearest unit.
(a) 2.58   (b) 6.96   (c) 8.75   (d) 6.01   (e) .95

Solution

Hint: This question means that each number should be converted to the nearest whole number.

(a) $2.58 = 3$ because $5 = 5$, so .5 is converted to 1 or simply add 1 to 2 such that $2 + 1 = 3$.

(b) $6.96 = 7$ because $9 > 5$, so .9 is converted to 1 or simply 1 is added to 6 such that $6 + 1 = 7$.

(c) $8.75 = 9$ because $7 > 5$, so .7 is converted to 1 or simply 1 is added to 8 such that $8 + 1 = 9$.

(d) $6.01 = 6$ because $0 < 5$, so 0 is added to 6 to make 6.

(e) $.95 = 1$ because $9 > 5$, so .9 is converted to 1 or simply 1 is added to 0 such that $.95 = 0.95 = 0 + 1 = 1$

$$\downarrow \quad \searrow$$
$$0 \;+\; 1 = 1$$

Example 3

Round off each of the following numbers to 1 decimal place. Hint: "to 1 decimal place" is the same as the nearest tenth.

(a) 1.46   (b) 2.894   (c) 6.63   (d).942

Solution

(a) $1.46 = 1.5$ because $6 > 5$, 1 is added to 4 to make 5.

(b) $2.894 = 2.9$ because $9 > 5$, 1 is added to 8 to make 9.

(c) $6.63 = 6.6$ because $3 < 5$, 0 is added to 6 to make 6.

(d) $.942 = .9$ because $4 < 5$, 0 is added to 9 to make 9.

Example 4

Round each of the following numbers to 3 decimal places. Hint: "to 3 decimal places" is the same as to the nearest thousandth.

(a) 5.0847   (b) 94.14274   (c) 12.2418   (d) 3.48214   (e) .2346

Solution

(a) $5.0847 = 5.085$ because $7 > 5$, 1 is added to 4 to make 5.

(b) $94.14274 = 94.143$ because $7 > 5$, 1 is added to 2 to make 3.

(c) $12.2418 = 12.242$ because $8 > 5$, 1 is added to 1 to make 2.

(d) $3.48214 = 3.482$ because $1 < 5$, 0 is added to 1 to make 1.

(e) $.2346 = .235$ because $6 > 5$, 1 is added to 4 to make 5.

The notes and the generous worked examples have provided me with conceptual understanding and computational fluency to do my homework.

Exercises

1. Round off the following numbers to 3 decimal places. Hint: See Example 4.

(a) 2.0148   (b) 4.2984   (c) .4289   (d) 12.4814

(e) 5.6899   (f) .98718   (g) 1.4889   (h) 9.0089

2. How are decimal fractions rounded off to a number of decimal places?

3. Round off each of the following numbers to the nearest unit.
Hint: See Example 2.

(a) 9.01   (b) 10.82   (c) 2.11   (d) .944

(e) 12.78   (f) 11.09   (g) 14.840   (h) .65091

4. Round off each of the following numbers to 1 decimal place.
Hint: See Example 3.

(a) .941   (b) .o814   (c) 2.129   (d) 6.089

(e) 4.85   (f) 8.774   (g) .848   (h) 5.050

Challenge Question

5. Round off each of the following numbers to 2 decimal places.

(a) .874   (b) 2.0998   (c) .908   (d) 3.145

(e) 2.919   (f) 3.048   (g) 4.6185   (h) 4.1346

Answers Selected Questions

1(a) 2.015   1(f) .987   3(b) 11   3(d) 1.0 4(b) .1   4(f) 8.8 5   5(c) .91   5(g) 4.62

NEAREST WHOLE NUMBER

To write a number to the nearest whole number means that the number should consist of whole numbers only. This means that the decimal part of the number should either be rounded up to 1 if the decimal is .5 or greater than .5, or if the decimal part is less than .5, the decimal part is rounded down to 0. If the decimal part is .5 or greater than .5, the decimal part is rounded up to 1 and this 1 is then added to the last digit in the whole number.

Example 1

Round off these numbers to the nearest whole number.

(a) .3   (b) .5   (c) .8   (d) 4.6

(e) 5.5   (f) 5.8   (g) 48.9   (h) 400.7

Solution

(a) .3 = 0 (to the nearest whole number because .3 < .5, so .3 is rounded down to 0).

(b) .5 = 1 (to the nearest whole number because .5 = .5, so .5 is rounded up to 1.)

(c) .8 = 1 (to the nearest whole number because .8 > .5, so .8 is rounded up to 1.)

(d) 4.6 = 5 (to the nearest whole number because .6 > .5, so .6 is rounded up to 1 and the 1 is added to 4 to make 5; 4 + 1 = 5.)

(e) 5.5 = 6 (to the nearest whole number because .5 = .5, so .5 is rounded up to 1 and the 1 is added to 5 to make 6; 5 + 1 = 6.)

(f) 5.8 = 6 (to the nearest whole number because .8 > .5, so .8 is rounded up to 1 and the 1 is added to 5 to make 6; 5 + 1 = 6.)

(g) 48.9 = 49 (to the nearest whole number because .9 > .5, so .9 is rounded up to 1 and the 1 is added to 48 to make 49; 48 + 1 = 49.)

(h) 400.7 = 401 (to the nearest whole number because .7 > .5, so .7 is rounded up to 1 and the 1 is added to 400 to make 401; 400 + 1 = 401.)

The notes and the generous worked examples have provided me with conceptual understanding and computational fluency to do my homework.

Exercises

1. Round off the following numbers to the nearest whole number. Hint: See Example 1 and compare how similar problems are solved.

(a) 5.14	(b) 100.2	(c) 55.8	(d) 16.5	(e) .8
(f) .01	(g) .75	(h) 1.04	(i) .005	(j) .0009
(k) 1.994	(l) 2.491	(m) .09	(n) .91	(0) 1.85
(p) 4.004	(q) 1.45	(r) 1.50	(s) 2.61	(t) 2.29
(u) .90	(v) 18.85	(w) 6.61	(x) 5.51	(y) 9.014

Challenge Questions

2. Round the following numbers to the nearest whole number.

(a) 25.09   (b). 99.9   (c) 200.61   (d) .1   (e) .69

Answers to Selected Questions

1(a) 5   **1(h)** 1   **1(i)** 0

NEAREST TEN

Numbers may be written to the nearest ten and this means that the last digit of the number should be a zero. In this case, if the last digit of a number is 5 or greater than 5, then add 1 to the tens digit and replace the last digit of the number by 0, and if the last digit of the number is less than 5 do not add 1 to the tens digit, but replace the last digit of the number by 0.

Example 2
Round off the following numbers to the nearest ten.

(a) 2   (b) 8   (c) 23   (d) 48

(e) 81   (f) 182   (g) 103.2   (h) 108

Solution

(a) $2 = 0$ (to the nearest ten because $2 < 5$, so 2 is rounded down to 0.)

(b) $8 = 10$ (to the nearest ten because $8 > 5$, so 8 is rounded up to 10.)

(c) $23 = 20$ (to the nearest ten because $3 < 5$, so replace the last digit of the number by 0.)

(d) $48 = 50$ (to the nearest ten because $8 > 5$, so add 1 to the tens digit and replace the number at the last digit by 0.)

Further Explanation

48

$\diagup \diagdown$

$40 \ + \ \ 8$

$\downarrow \qquad \downarrow$ 8 is rounded up to 10.

$40 \ \ + \ 10 \ = 50$

(e) $81 = 80$ (to the nearest ten because $1 < 5$, so replace the last digit by 0.)

Further explanation

81

$\diagup \diagdown$

$80 \ + \ \ 1$

$\downarrow \qquad \downarrow$ 1 is rounded down to 0.

$80 \ \ + \ \ 0 = 80$

(f) $182 = 180$ (to the nearest ten because $2 < 5$, so replace the last digit by 0.)

(g) $103.2 = 100$ (to the nearest ten because $3 < 5$, so replace the last digit of the whole number by 0.)

(h) $108 = 110$ (to the nearest ten because $8 > 5$, so add 1 to the tens digit and replace the last digit by 0.)

Further Explanation

108

$\diagup \diagdown$

$100 \ + \ 8$

$\downarrow \qquad \downarrow$ 8 is rounded up to 10.

$100 \ + \ 10 \ = 110$

Exercises

1. Round off the following numbers to the nearest ten. Hint: See Example 2(a).

(a) 3   (b) 1   (c) 4

2. Round off the following numbers to the nearest ten. Hint: See Example 2(b).

(a) 9   (b) 7   (c) 6

3. Round off the following numbers to the nearest ten. Hint; See Example 2(c) 2(e) and 2(f)..

(a) 52   (b) 14   (c) 33   (d) 201   (e) 94

4. Round the following numbers to the nearest ten. Hint: See Example 2(d) and 2(h).

(a) 78   (b). 36   (c) 69   (d) 306   (e) 155

5. Round the following numbers to the nearest ten. Hint: See Example 2(g).

(a) 44.3   (b) 167.1   (c) 94.4   (d) 29.26   (e) 208.5

Challenge Questions

6. Round the following numbers to the nearest ten.

(a) 43.57   (b) 48   (c) 277   (d) 1   (e) 111

Answers to Selected Questions

1(a) 0   **2(a)** 10   **3(a)** 50   **4(a)** 80   **5(e)** 210

NEAREST HUNDRED

Numbers may be written to the nearest hundred and this means that the last two digits of the number should be zeros. If the last two digits of a number are 50 or greater than 50, then this last two digits are rounded up to 100, and then added to the number. If the last two digits of the number are less than 50, then the last two digits are rounded down to zero. It may also be stated in a different way that if the last two digits of the number are 50 or greater than 50, then 1 should be added to the hundreds digit, and then replace the last two digits of the number with two zeros.

Example 3

Round off the following numbers to the nearest hundred.

(a) 10   (b) 48   (c) 51   (d) 95   (e) 154

(f) 199   (g) 201   (h) 265   (i) 762   (j) 865

Solution

(a) 10 = 0 (to the nearest hundred because the last two digits, 10, are less than 50, so 10 is rounded down to 0.)

(b) 48 = 0 (to the nearest hundred because the last two digits, 48, are less than 50, so 48 is rounded down to 0.)

(c) 51 = 100 (to the nearest hundred because the last two digits, 51, are greater than 50, and the 51 is rounded up to 100.)

(d) 95 = 100 (to the nearest hundred because the last two digits, 95, are greater than 50, and therefore, 95 is rounded up to 100.)

(e) 154 = 200 (to the nearest hundred because the last two digits, 54, are greater than 50, therefore, 54 is rounded up to 100 so that 100 + 100 = 200.)

Further Explanation

154

100 + 54

↓   ↓54 is rounded up to 100.

100 + 100 = 200

(f) 199 = 200 (to the nearest hundred because the last two digits, 99, is greater than 50, and therefore, 99 is rounded up to 100, so that 100 + 100 = 200.)

(g) 201 = 200 (to the nearest hundred because the last two digits, 01, are less than 50, and therefore, 1 is rounded down to 0.)

(h) 265 = 300 (to the nearest hundred because the last two digits, 65, are greater than 50, and therefore, 65 is rounded up to 100 so that 200 + 100 = 300.)

Further Explanation

265

200 + 65

↓   ↓ 65 is rounded up to 100.

200 + 100 = 300

(i) 762 = 800 (to the nearest hundred because the last two digits, 62, are greater than 50, and therefore, 62 is rounded up to 100, so that 700 + 100 = 800.)

Further Explanation

762

700 + 62

↓   ↓ 62 is rounded up to 100.

700 + 100 = 800

(j) 865 = 900 (to the nearest hundred because the last two digits, 65, are greater than

50, and therefore, 65 is rounded up to 100, so that 800 + 100 = 900.)

Further Explanation

865

↙ ↘

800 + 65

↓   ↓ 65 is rounded up to 100.

800 + 100 = 900

The notes and the generous worked examples have provided me with conceptual understanding and computational fluency to do my homework.

Exercises

1. Round the following numbers to the nearest hundred. Hint: See Examples 3(a) and 3(b).
   (a) 35   (b) 49   (c) 25   (d) 1   (e) 17

2. Round the following numbers to the nearest hundred. Hint: See Examples 3(c) and 3(d).
   (a) 55   (b) 88   (c) 73   (d) 94   (e) 69

3. Round the following numbers to the nearest hundred. Hint: See Example 3(e) 3(f), 3(h) and (i).
   (a). 177   (b) 175   (c) 263   (d) 399   (e) 381

4. Round the following numbers to the nearest hundred. Hint: See Examples 3(g).
   (a) 401   (b) 125   (c) 202   (d) 738   (e) 849

Challenge Questions

5. Round the following numbers to the nearest hundred.
   (a) 94   (b) 999   (c) 25   (d) 510   (e) 678

Answers to Selected Questions

1(a) 0   2(a) 100   3(a) 200   4(a) 400

NEAREST THOUSAND

Numbers may be written to the nearest thousand and this means that the last three digits should be zeros. If the last three digits of the number are equal to 500 or greater than 500, then the last three digits are rounded up to 1000 and the 1000 is added to the number. If the last three digits of the number are less than 500, then the last three digits are rounded down to 0. It can also be stated that when the last three digits of a number are 500 or greater than 500, then 1 is added to the thousands digit and the last three digits of the number are replaced by zeros.

Example 4.

Round off the following numbers to the nearest thousand:

(a) 7   (b) 502   (c) 998   (d) 1,395

(e) 1,750   (f) 2,200   (g) 4,900   (h) 8,502

Solution

(a) 7 = 0   (to the nearest thousand because 7 is less than 500, so 7 is rounded down to 0.)

(b) 502 = 1000 (to the nearest thousand because the last three digits, 502, are greater than 500, so, 502 is rounded up to 1000.)

(c) 998 = 1000 (to the nearest thousand because the last three digits, 998, are greater than 500, so 998 is rounded up to 1000.)

(d) 1,395 = 1000 (to the nearest thousand because the last three digits, 395, are less than 500, so, 395 is rounded down to 0.)

(e) 1750 = 2000 (to the nearest thousand because the last three digits, 750, are greater than 500, so 750 is rounded up to 1000 so that: 1000 + 1000 = 2000.)

Further Explanation

1,750

1000 + 750

↓   ↓ 750 is rounded up to 1000.

1000 + 1000 = 2000

(f) 2,200 = 2000 (to the nearest thousand because the last three digits, 200, are than 500, and therefore, the 200 is rounded down to zero.)

Further explanation

2,200

2000 + 200

↓   ↓ 200 is rounded down to zero.

2000 + 0 = 2000

(g) 4,900 = 5000 (to the nearest 1000 because the last three digits, 900, are greater than 500, so 900 is rounded up to 1000).

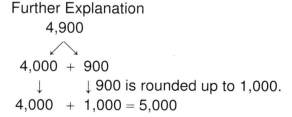

Further Explanation

4,900

4,000 + 900

↓   ↓ 900 is rounded up to 1,000.

4,000 + 1,000 = 5,000

(h) 8,502 = 9,000 (to the nearest 1000 because the last three digits, 502, are greater than 500, and therefore, 502 is rounded up to 1,000.

Further Explanation

8,502

8000 + 502

↓ ↓ 502 is rounded up to 1,000.

8000 + 1000 = 9000

The notes and the generous worked examples have provided me with conceptual understanding and computational fluency to do my homework.

Exercises

1. Round off the following numbers to the nearest thousand. Hint: See Example 4(a).
   (a) 90   (b) 2   (c) 479   (d) 249
2. Round off the following numbers to the nearest thousand. Hint: See Examples 4(b) and 4(c).
   (a) 570   (b) 904   (c) 744   (d). 666
3. Round off the following numbers to the nearest thousand. Hint: See Examples 4(d) and 4(f).
   (a) 1001   (b) 3,250   (c) 7073   (d) 5499

Challenge Questions

4. Round the following numbers to the nearest thousand.
   (a). 7002   (b) 1678   (c) 92   (d) 4590

Answers to Selected Questions

   1(a) 0   2(a) 1000   3(a) 1000

ADDITION OF DECIMAL FRACTIONS

Rule 1:
Line up all the decimal points.
Rule 2:
Line up all the digits to the right and left of each decimal point according to their

values such that hundredths should be under the hundredths column, the tenths should be under the tenths column and the ones should be under the ones column, and so on.

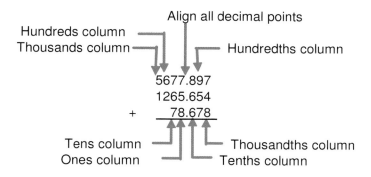

Rule 3:

Follow the procedure for adding whole numbers. (Regroup if necessary. You may review regrouping under the chapter, "Multiplication of Whole Numbers.")

Example 1

Add: 2.87 + .95

Solution

Step 1: Line up all the decimal points.

Decimal points should be lined up in a straight line.

$$\begin{array}{r} \downarrow \\ 2.87 \\ + \ \ .95 \\ \hline \end{array}$$

Step 2: Add the hundredths column first. Regroup if necessary.

Hundredths column

$$\begin{array}{r} 2.87 \\ + \ 0.95 \\ \hline 2 \end{array}$$

Step 3: Add the tenths column second. Regroup if necessary.

Tenths column
Hundredths column

$$\begin{array}{r} 2.87 \\ + \ 0.95 \\ \hline 82 \end{array}$$

Step 4: Add the ones column third while the decimal point should be in line with the other decimal points.

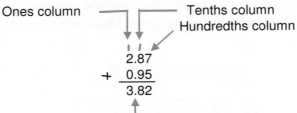

Therefore, 2.87 + .95 = 3.82

Example 2

Add: 4.78 + 9.68

Solution

Step 1: Line up all the decimal points.

Decimal points should be lined up in a straight line.

```
      ↓
   4.78
 + 9.68
```

Step 2: Add the hundredths column first. Regroup if necessary.

```
                    ┌── Hundredths column
              ı     ▼
           4.78
         + 9.68
         ─────
              6
```

Step 3: Add the tenths column second. Regroup if necessary.

```
  Tenths column ──┐ ┌── Hundredths column
              ı ı ▼ ▼
           4.78
         + 9.68
         ─────
             46
```

Step 4: Add the ones column third and place the decimal point in line with the other decimal points.

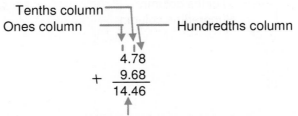

Put the decimal point to be in line with the other decimal points.

Therefore, 4.78 + 9.68 = 14.46

Example 3

Add: 4.5 + 19.25 + .241

Step 1: Line up all the decimal points.

Decimal points should be lined up in a straight line.

$$
\begin{array}{r}
\downarrow \\
4.5 \\
19.25 \\
+\quad .241 \\
\hline
\end{array}
$$

Step 2: Add the thousandths column first. Regroup if necessary.

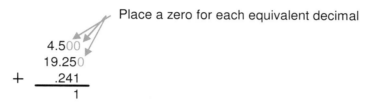

Place a zero for each equivalent decimal

$$
\begin{array}{r}
4.500 \\
19.250 \\
+\quad .241 \\
\hline
1
\end{array}
$$

Note: Zeros placed to the right of the last digit in a decimal fraction does not change its value.

Step 3: Add the hundredths column second. Regroup if necessary.

Hundredths column
$$
\begin{array}{r}
\downarrow \\
4.500 \\
19.250 \\
+\quad .241 \\
\hline
91
\end{array}
$$

Step 4: Add the tenths column third. Regroup if necessary.

Tenths column
$$
\begin{array}{r}
\downarrow \\
4.500 \\
19.250 \\
+\quad .241 \\
\hline
991
\end{array}
$$

Step 5: Add the ones column fourth, and write the decimal point. Regroup if necessary.

Ones column
$$
\begin{array}{r}
\downarrow \\
4.500 \\
19.250 \\
+\quad .241 \\
\hline
3.991
\end{array}
$$

Put the decimal point to be in line with the other decimal points.

Step 6: Add the tens column fifth.

Tens column
↓

$$\begin{array}{r} 4.500 \\ 19.250 \\ +\ \ \underline{.241} \\ 23.991 \end{array}$$

Therefore, $4.5 + 19.25 + .241 = 23.991$

Example 4

Find the sum: $9.37 + 814.64 + 200 + 25.114$

Solution

Step 1: Line up all the decimal points. Note that 200 is a whole number, so it should be written on the left side of the decimal point.

Line up all the decimal points

$$\begin{array}{r} 9.37 \\ 814.64 \\ 200. \\ +\ \ \underline{25.114} \end{array}$$

Step 2: Add the thousandths column first. Regroup if necessary.

Thousandths column

$$\begin{array}{r} 9.370 \\ 814.640 \\ 200.000 \\ +\ \ \underline{25.114} \\ 4 \end{array}$$ Place a zero for each equivalent decimal.

Step 3: Add the hundredths column second. Regroup if necessary.

Hundredths column

$$\begin{array}{r} 9.370 \\ 814.640 \\ 200.000 \\ +\ \ \underline{25.114} \\ 24 \end{array}$$

Step 4: Add the tenths column third. Regroup if necessary.

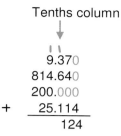

Tenths column
↓

9.37**0**
814.64**0**
200.**000**
+   25.114
_____
124

Step 5: Add the ones column fourth and write the decimal point. Regroup if necessary.

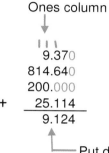

Ones column
↓

9.37**0**
814.64**0**
200.**000**
+   25.114
_____
9.124

Put decimal point to be in line with the other decimal points.

Step 6: Add the tens column fifth. Regroup if necessary.

Tens column
↓

9.37**0**
814.64**0**
200.**000**
+   25.114
_____
49.124

Step 7: Add the hundreds column sixth.

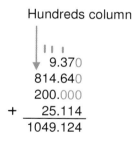

Hundreds column
↓

9.37**0**
814.64**0**
200.**000**
+   25.114
_____
1049.124

The answer is 1049.124

The notes and the generous worked examples have provided me with conceptual understanding and computational fluency to do my homework.

Exercises

1. Find the sum. Hint: See Examples 1 and 2.

(a) $\begin{array}{r} 0.8 \\ + 0.7 \\ \hline \end{array}$
(b) $\begin{array}{r} 4.5 \\ + 0.9 \\ \hline \end{array}$
(c) $\begin{array}{r} 15.48 \\ + 6.93 \\ \hline \end{array}$
(d) $\begin{array}{r} 14.04 \\ + 7.2 \\ \hline \end{array}$

(d) $\begin{array}{r} 7.6 \\ + 9.3 \\ \hline \end{array}$
(e) $\begin{array}{r} 8.36 \\ + 6.68 \\ \hline \end{array}$
(f) $\begin{array}{r} 9.5 \\ + 2.74 \\ \hline \end{array}$
(g) $\begin{array}{r} 3.7 \\ + 4.5 \\ \hline \end{array}$

(h) $\begin{array}{r} 0.36 \\ + 5.38 \\ \hline \end{array}$
(i) $\begin{array}{r} 23.04 \\ + 9.15 \\ \hline \end{array}$
(j) $\begin{array}{r} 3.86 \\ + 4.7 \\ \hline \end{array}$
(k) $\begin{array}{r} 7.05 \\ + 8.88 \\ \hline \end{array}$

2. Find the sum. Hint: See Examples 3 and 4.

(a) $\begin{array}{r} 11.0 \\ 13.01 \\ + 7.24 \\ \hline \end{array}$
(b) $\begin{array}{r} 6.14 \\ 2.846 \\ + 1.23 \\ \hline \end{array}$
(c) $\begin{array}{r} 5.1 \\ 12.24 \\ 6.08 \\ + 1.41 \\ \hline \end{array}$
(d) $\begin{array}{r} 51.23 \\ 6.2 \\ 35.321 \\ + 4.0 \\ \hline \end{array}$

(e) $\begin{array}{r} 2.3 \\ 4.2 \\ 3.7 \\ + 4.4 \\ \hline \end{array}$
(f) $\begin{array}{r} 6.34 \\ 5.11 \\ + 7.7 \\ \hline \end{array}$
(g) $\begin{array}{r} 4.45 \\ 1.88 \\ + 0.22 \\ \hline \end{array}$
(h) $\begin{array}{r} 33.56 \\ 69.79 \\ + 88.45 \\ \hline \end{array}$

3. Find the sum. Hint: See Examples 3 and 4.

(a) 22.4 + 7 + 478.607 =   (b) 14.83 + 28.466 + 59.5 =
(c) 19.93 + 44.095 + 147.2 =   (d) 124.3 + 284.641 + 786.1482 =
(e) 431.2 + 648.2361 + 248.69 = (f) 644.38 + 11 + 738.8291 =
(g) 99.468 + 158.735 + 731 =   (h) 539.348 + 624.84 + 2.9841 =
(i) 8.4 + 7.5 =   (j) 12.45 + 13.44 =   (k) 77.32 + 15.20 + 1.7 =
(l) 6.6 + 1.07 =   (m) 15.22 + 13.44 =   (n) 4.08 + 1.204 + 3.8 =

Answers to Selected Questions

1(a) 1.5   **1(c)** 22.41   **2(a)** 31.25   **2(c)** 24.83

Challenge Questions

4. Add.

(a) 1.41 + 2.91 =   (b) 1.39 + 6.76 =

(c) 1.63 + 1.04 + 8 + 2.01 =   (d) 2.9 + 3.641 + 4.09 =

(e) 4.374 + 2.1 + 3.07 =   (f) 7.7 + 3.001 + 14 + 25.34 =

(g) 24.978 + 37.694 + 104.799 =   (h) 84.39 +78.84 + 99.189 =

(i)   7.37   (j)   43.62   (k)   3.86   (l)   7.05
     + 5.38   + 7.15   + 9.7   + 4.44

REAL WORLD APPLICATIONS – WORD PROBLEMS
Addition of Decimal Fractions

Example 1
John is a student at Peki High School in Ghana. His expenses for the week are shown in the table.

Expense Item	Monday	Tuesday	Wednesday	Thursday	Friday
Breakfast	$2.10	$1.98	$2.58	$2.25	$1.95
Lunch	$3.45	$2.95	$4.10	$3.98	$3.35
Dinner	$5.20	$4.65	$4.50	$4.30	$4.25

(a) Find his total expenses for breakfast.
(b) Find his total expenses on Thursday.
Solution
(a) Add all the money that John spent on breakfast.

$$\begin{array}{r} \overset{2\ 2}{\$2.10} \\ \$1.98 \\ \$2.58 \\ \$2.25 \\ + \quad \$1.95 \\ \hline \$10.86 \end{array} \quad \text{Answer}$$

(b) Add all the money that John spent on Thursday.

$$\begin{array}{r} \overset{1\ 1}{\$2.25} \\ \$3.98 \\ \$4.30 \\ \hline \$10.53 \end{array} \quad \text{Answer}$$

Example 2
Mary recorded that she traveled the following distances last December: 10.6 miles, 34.8 miles, 155.8 miles, 65.5 miles and 25.6 miles. What is the total miles that Mary traveled?
Solution
Add all the distances traveled by Mary. Regroup if necessary.

$$
\begin{array}{r}
|23\\
10.6\\
34.8\\
155.8\\
65.5\\
\underline{25.6}\\
292.3
\end{array}
$$ miles   Answer

Exercises

1. Alice is a student at the Hohoe Secondary School in Ghana. Her expenses for the week are shown in the table. Hint: See Example 1.

Expense Item	Monday	Tuesday	Wednesday	Thursday	Friday
Breakfast	$1.98	$2.25	$2.24	$1.85	$1.90
Lunch	$2.95	$3.30	$3.10	$3.25	$3.15
Dinner	$4.10	$43.95	$3.85	$4.15	$3.89

(a) What is the total amount that Alice spent on dinner?

(b) What is the total amount that Alice spent on breakfast?

(c) What is the total amount that Alice spent on lunch?

(d) Using your answers for (a), (b), and (c), what is the total amount that Alice spent on food?

(e) What is the total amount spent on Wednesday?

(f) What is the total amount spent on Friday?

2. Group exercise: Make an expense account table for an average student's breakfast, lunch, and dinner for a week at your school.

3. Nick bought a shirt for $18.25, a coat for $65.95 and a pair of shoes for $55.65. How much money did he spend?

4. A man saved $505.48 and $695.37 in two different banks. What is the total amount that he saved?

Mixed Review

1. Solve the following operations using the Order of Operations:

(a) $2 + 3 \times 4 =$

(b) $4 - 4 \div 2 =$

(c) $2^3 + 4 \div 2 =$

(d) $3^2 \div 3 - 2 =$

(e) $81 \div 9 \times 3 =$

(f) $12 + 6 - 4^2 =$

2. Change the following decimal fractions to common fractions:

(a) .007   (b) .28   (c) .0421   (d) .01

3. Round off the following to 3 decimal places :

(a) .4985   (b) 2.0174   (c) 1.9096   (d) 2.8901

4. Write each fraction as a mixed number.

(a) $\dfrac{9}{2}$ (b) $\dfrac{12}{7}$ (c) $\dfrac{17}{5}$ (d) $\dfrac{15}{2}$ (e) $\dfrac{23}{7}$

5. Write the mixed numbers as a fraction.

(a) $2\dfrac{1}{4}$ (b) $3\dfrac{1}{3}$ (c) $4\dfrac{1}{2}$ (d) $4\dfrac{6}{7}$

SUBTRACTION OF DECIMAL FRACTIONS

The method for adding decimal fractions is similar to the method for subtracting decimal fractions because both methods require you to:

(a) Line up all the decimal points.

(b) Line up all the digits to the right and left of each decimal point according to their values such that hundredths should be under the hundredths column, the tenths should be under the tenths column and the ones should be under the ones column and so on. Then, follow the procedure for subtracting whole numbers.

(c) Regroup if necessary. Note that during subtraction, borrowing is the process for regrouping.

Example 1

Subtract: .94 − .68

Solution

Step 1: Line up all the decimal points.

Decimal points should be lined up in a straight line.

$$
\begin{array}{r}
.94 \\
- \ .68 \\
\hline
\end{array}
$$

Step 2: Regroup if necessary. Subtract the hundredths column first.

Hundredths column

Note: We cannot subtract 8 from 4, so we borrow 1 from 9 to be added to 4 to make 14 because the 1 we borrowed from 9 has a value of 10, and therefore 10 + 4 = 14. We can now subtract 8 from 14 to obtain 6. (All the digits at the hundredths column have values of hundredths. For example, when we subtracted 8 from 14 to obtain 6, we actually subtracted 8 hundredths from 14 hundredths to obtain 6 hundredths.)

Step 3: Subtract the tenths column second.

Tenths column

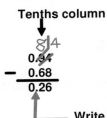

Note: 8 - 6 = 2 (All digits at the tenths column have values of tenths. For example, 8 - 6 = 2 is actually 6 tenths subtracted from 8 tenths to obtain 2 tenths.)

Write the decimal point to align with the other decimal points.

Therefore, .94 − .68 = .26

Notice that the zeros before the decimal points do not change the values of the decimal fractions.

Example 2

Subtract: .632 − .346

Solution

Step 1: Line up all the decimal points.

Decimal points should be lined up in a straight line.

$$\begin{array}{r} \downarrow \\ .632 \\ - \ .346 \\ \hline \end{array}$$

Step 2: Regroup if necessary. Subtract the thousandths column first.

Thousandths column

Note: We cannot subtract 6 from 2, so we borrow 1 from 3 to be added to 2 to make 12 because the 1 we borrowed from 3 has a value of 10, and therefore, 10 + 2 = 12. We can now subtract 6 from 12 to obtain 6. When we borrowed 1 from 3, it leaves 2 and this 2 is written immediately above the 3. (All digits in the thousandths column have values of thousandths. For example, when we subtracted 6 from 12 to obtain 6, we actually subtracted 6 thousandths from 12 thousandths to obtain 6 thousandths.)

Step 3: Regroup if necessary. Subtract the hundredths column second.

Hundredths column

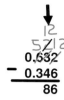

$$\begin{array}{r} 0.632 \\ -\ 0.346 \\ \hline 86 \end{array}$$

Note: From Step 2, we borrowed 1 from 3, leaving 2, but we cannot subtract 4 from 2, and therefore, we borrow 1 from 6 and this 1 is added to 2 to make 12. The 1 we borrowed from 6 has a value of 10, and therefore, 10 + 2 = 12 and the 12 is written above the 2 in the hundredths column. We can now subtract 4 from 12 to obtain 8. (All digits in the hundredths column have values of hundredths. For example, when we subtracted 4 from 12 to obtain 8, we were actually subtracting 4 hundredths from 12 hundredths to obtain 8 hundredths.)

Step 4: Subtract the tenths column third.

Tenths column

$$\begin{array}{r} 0.632 \\ -\ 0.346 \\ \hline 0.286 \end{array}$$

Note: From Step 3, we borrowed 1 from 6, leaving 5 remaining. Subtract 3 from 5 to obtain 2. (All digits at the tenths column have values of tenths. For example, when we subtracted 3 from 5 to obtain 2, we actually subtracted 3 tenths from 5 tenths to obtain 2 tenths Write the decimal point to align with the other decimal points.)

Therefore, .632 − .346 = 0.286

Example 3
Subtract without showing a detailed solution method:
(a) 4.4 − 1.261   (b) 58.48 − 12.8
Solution

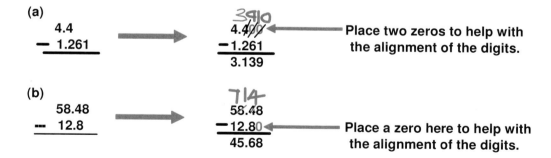

The notes and the generous worked examples have provided me with conceptual understanding and computational fluency to do my homework.

Exercises

1. Subtract the following. Hint: See Examples 1 to 3, match questions with similar examples.

(a) .9 − .5	(b) 2.69 − 1.79	(c) 4.84 − .95	(d) .948 − .269

(e) .7 − .5 =   (f) 34.4 − 10.231 =   (g) .731 − .584 =

(h) .247 − .125 =   (i) 6.341 − 2.321 =   (j) 1.444 − .611 =

(k) 8.3 − 5.59 =   (l) 15.94 − 11.83 =   (m) 44.91 − 4.82 =

(n) 7.001 − 5.348 =   (o) 4.531 − 2.9 =   (p) 82.08 − 4.69 =

(q) 58.969 − 50.446 =   (r) 36.78 − 16.36   (s) 1.5 − .641 =

(t) $2.96 − $1.50 =   (u) $18.05 − $9.86 =   (v) 66.3 − 41.8 =

(w) 20.05 − 9.48 =   (x) 9 − .289 =   (y) 5 - 1.946 =

2. Subtract. Hint: See Examples 1 to 3, match questions with similar examples.

(a) 74.32 − 14.44	(b) .49 − .28	(c) .38 − .09	(d) .358 − .147
(e) .74 − .52	(f) .649 − .438	(g) 6.891 − 1.982	(h) 5.69 − 1.78
(i) 37.06 − 24.67	(j) 3.618 − 1.729	(k) 55.7 − 13.941	(l) 4.77 − 2.894
(m) .66 − .38	(n) .523 − .334	(o) 29.01 − 4.674	(p) 3.001 − 1.982

Challenge Questions

3. Subtract.

(a) .56 − .38	(b) 1.004 − .846	(s) 57.8 − 22.976 =	(t) 18.02 − 9.866 =

(u) 6.641
− 2.230   (v) 1.2 − .648 =   (w) .64 − .2782 =   (x) 4.6 − 2.2 =

REAL WORLD APPLICATIONS — WORD PROBLEMS
Subtraction of Decimal Fractions

Example 1

John went to the store with $100.00. If he bought a shirt for $18.95, how much money is left?

Solution

Total money that John took to the store = $100.00

Amount of money spent on the shirt   = $18.95

Amount left = Total money taken to the store − Amount spent

$\quad\quad$ = $100.00 − $18.95

$$
\begin{array}{r}
\overset{\text{99 910}}{100.00} \\
-\ \ 18.95 \\
\hline
81.05
\end{array}
$$

Therefore, the amount left = $81.05

Example 2

Charles earns $20,000.00 per year and his brother earns $2,394.86 less, how much does his brother earn per year?

Solution

Charles' brother earns $20,000.00 − $2,394.86 which can be written as:

$$
\begin{array}{r}
\overset{\text{199999 910}}{\$20,000.00} \\
-\ \ \ 2,394.86 \\
\hline
\$17,605.14
\end{array}
$$

Therefore, Charles' brother earns $17,605.14.

Example 3

Eric took the bus to the store which is 4 miles from his house. He had a ride home which covered 3.725 miles, and he then walked the remainder of the distance home. How many miles did he walk home?

Solution

Total distance from Eric's house to the store = 4 miles.

Distance covered by the ride   = 3.725 miles.

Distance walked home =

Total distance to the store − Distance covered by the ride
= 4 − 3.725 miles.

$$
\begin{array}{r}
3\,{}^{9}\!9\,{}^{9}\!1\,0 \\
4.0\,\cancel{0}\,\cancel{0} \\
3.725 \\
\hline
0.275
\end{array}
$$

Therefore, Eric walked 0.275 miles home.

Example 4

If George withdrew $245.36 from the bank, and he spent $50.30 on food, $46.01 on clothes, $18.95 on medicine and $32.58 on books, find how much money is left.

Solution

Add all the amounts that George spent and subtract the sum from the money that he withdrew from the bank in order to obtain the amount left.

Total amount spent is:

$$
\begin{array}{r}
{}^{1}\ {}^{1}\ {}^{1} \\
\$50.30 \\
\$46.01 \\
\$18.95 \\
+\ \$32.58 \\
\hline
\$147.84
\end{array}
$$

Therefore, total amount spent = $147.84
Amount of money left = Amount withdrew from bank − Total amount spent
= $245.36 − 147.84

$$
\begin{array}{r}
{}^{1}\,{}^{13}\!/\!4\ {}^{13} \\
\$245.36 \\
\$147.84 \\
\hline
\$97.52
\end{array}
$$

Therefore, the amount of money left = $97.52

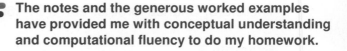

The notes and the generous worked examples have provided me with conceptual understanding and computational fluency to do my homework.

Exercises

1. Isabel went to the store with $200.00. She spent a total of $175.88 on food. How much is left? Hint: See Example 1.

2. Mary earns $30,000.00 per year and her brother earns $5,984.6 less, how much does her brother earn? Hint: See Example 2.

3. Sara was given 2.5 hours to play outside. If she used .2 hours to get to the play ground, .35 hours to play basket ball, .18 hours to talk to Ellen, and .58 hours to play soccer, how much of the time is left? Hint: See Example 4.

4. If Evans puts a television set which cost $584.78 on a layaway plan and he made the following two payments, $64.35 and $78.98. How much does Evans still owe for the television? Hint: See Example 4.

Challenge Questions

5. Ellen bought a computer for $945.58. If she made a down payment of $120.65 and an installment payment of $60.47, how much does she still owe?

6. A computer selling for $895.12 was reduced to $796.43. What is the amount of the reduction?

7. If Rebecca ran 150 yards in 56.48 seconds and a week later, she ran the same distance in 47.59 seconds, how much did she improve her time?

Mixed Review

1. 431 + 679

2. 911 − 799

3. 300 − 177

4. 294 + 189

5. $\frac{1}{2} \times \frac{2}{9}$

6. $\frac{4}{9} \div \frac{3}{8}$

7. $2\frac{3}{4} \times \frac{4}{11}$

8. $1\frac{3}{5} \div \frac{5}{6}$

9. 2.41 − 1.84

10. 7.348 + 1.412

11. $22 - 4 \div 2 =$

12. $14 \div 2 - 1 =$

13. $3 \times 4 \div 2 =$

14. $10 + 4 \div 2 =$

15. $10 + 4^2 \div 4 =$

16. $22 \times (12 - 2) + 1 =$

17. $2 - .584 =$

18. $14.34 - 2 =$

19. Arrange the following numbers with the smallest values first (arrange the numbers in ascending order.)

(a) .3, 3.03, .33, .303, 3.33   b) 5.55, .51, .505, 5.5, .55

20. Use the pattern to find the next two numbers:

(a) 3, 6, 12, 24, 48, ___, ____.   (b) 18, 16, 14, 12, 10, ____, _____.

(c) 4, 6, 8, 10, ____, ____.   (d) 1.1, 3.3, 9.9, 29.7, ____, _____.

21. Write each number as a common fraction, mixed number and in words.

(a) .75   (b) 6.2   (c) 37.001   (d) 181.08

(e) .99   (f) 1.84   (g) .0001   (h) 1.1

22. Write each number as a decimal.

(a) Nine and three tenths   (b) twenty-five and three thousandths

(c) $\frac{1}{10}$ (d) $\frac{7}{100}$ (e) $\frac{31}{100}$ (f) $\frac{51}{1,000}$

(g) $\dfrac{731}{1,000}$　　　(h) $\dfrac{1}{10,000}$　　　(i) $\dfrac{9899}{10,000}$　　　(j) $2\dfrac{1}{4}$

23. Write each decimal in words.
    (a) 1.101　　　(b) 1.001　　　(c) .002　　　(d) .026
    (f) 5.78　　　(g) 12.709　　　(h) 628.2　　　(i) 628.264

24. What is the value of each bold digit?
    (a) 2.**2**4　　　(b) .0**9**4　　　(c) 4.2**8**1　　　(d) 349.78
    (e) .000**1**　　　(f) .00**9**　　　(g) .00**8**　　　(h) 6784.01

25. Replace each ? with $<$, $>$, or $=$.
    (a) 2.78 ? 2.87　　　(b) .75 ? .750　　　(c) 4.80 ? 48.08
    (d) 39.70 ? 39.700　　　(e) 2.99 ? 2.909　　　(f) 50.002 ? 50.0009

26. Write each list of numbers from the least to the greatest (write the numbers in ascending order.)
    (a) 12.728, 12.827, 12.782　　　(b) .2406, .2046, .2604
    (c) 2.984, 29.84, 2.998, 2.909　　　(d) 431.211, 43.1211, 43.099

27. Write each list of numbers from the greatest to the least (write the numbers in descending order.)
    (a) 2.77, 2.707, 2.077, 2.771,　　　(b) 14.241, 1.424, 142.4, 14.074
    (c) 38.44, 3.844, 384.44, 38.994　　　(d) .48, .498, 4.001, 4.9

Answers to Selected Questions

21(g) $\dfrac{1}{10,000}$ $=$ one ten-thousandth

MULTIPLICATION OF DECIMALS

New Words:
1. Multiplicand — The number that is to be multiplied by another.
2. Multiplier — A number by which another number is multiplied.
3. Product — The product is the answer to a multiplication problem.

　　　　　.7　← Multiplicand
　　　×. .2　← Multiplier
　　　　　?　← Product (the answer to the multiplication problem).

The method of multiplication of decimal fractions by whole numbers is similar to the multiplication of whole numbers by whole numbers. The only difference is to remember to insert the decimal point at the correct position in the answer. The two rules involving all types of decimal multiplication are:

Rule 1.

First follow the procedure for multiplying whole numbers. (See MathMasters Series, "Elementary Mathematics for Students and Parents", Grades 4 and 5).

Rule 2.

Determine the correct position of the decimal point in the product by counting the total number of the digits to the right of the decimal points in the problem (considering both the multiplier and the multiplicand), and insert the decimal point in the product by counting as many digits of the product from right to left as there are in the problem.

Note: The number of digits to the right of the decimal point is equal to the number of the decimal places.

Example 1

Multiply: $.9 \times .8 =$

Solution

Step 1: Follow the procedure for multiplying whole numbers. This is Rule 1.

$$.9 \times .8 = 72 \qquad\qquad (9 \times 8 = 72)$$

Step 2: Determine the correct position of the decimal point in the product of 72 above. This is Rule 2.

One digit after the
decimal point.   Count two digits from right to left of the product and
      ↓   ╱╱ insert the decimal point because the problem has a
$.9 \times .8 = .72$ total of 2 digits after the decimal point in the problem.
    ↑
One digit after the decimal point.

Therefore, $.9 \times .8 = .72$

Example 2

Multiply: $.2 \times 4 =$

Solution

Step 1: Follow the procedure for multiplying whole numbers. This is Rule 1.

$$.2 \times 4 = 8 \qquad\qquad (2 \times 4 = 8)$$

. **Step 2**: Determine the correct position of the decimal point in the product of 8 above. This is Rule 2.

One digit after the
decimal point.

⟍   ⟋Count one digit from right to left of the product and then
.2 × 4 = .8   insert the decimal point because the problem has a total
↑   of one digit after the decimal point in the problem.
There is no
decimal point.

Therefore, .2 × 4 = .8

Example 3
Multiply: .842 × 2 =
Solution
Step 1: Follow the procedure of multiplying whole numbers. This is Rule 1.

$$\begin{array}{r} .842 \\ \times \quad 2 \\ \hline 1684 \end{array}$$ (842 × 2 = 1684)

Step 2: Determine the correct position of the decimal point in the product of 1684. This is Rule 2.

3 digits after the
decimal point.
↓↓↓
$$\begin{array}{r} .842 \\ \times \quad 2 \\ \hline 1.684 \end{array}$$ ← There is no decimal point.
       ← Product
↑

Count 3 digits from right to left of the product and then insert the
decimal point because the problem has a total of 3 digits after
the decimal point.

Therefore, .842 × 2 = 1.684

Example 4
Multiply: .842 × .2 =
Solution
Step 1: Follow the procedure for multiplying whole numbers, this is Rule 1.

$$\begin{array}{r} .842 \\ \times \quad .2 \\ \hline 1684 \end{array}$$ (842 × 2 = 1684)

Step 2: Determine the correct position of the decimal point in the product of 1684. This is Rule 2.

.842 → There are 3 digits after the decimal point.
×   .2 → There is 1 digit after the decimal point.
.1684 ← Product
↑
Count 4 digits from right to left of the product and then insert the decimal point because the problem has a total of 4 digits after the decimal points.

Example 5.

Multiply: 78.949
×   0.31

Solution

Step 1: Follow the procedure for multiplying whole numbers. This is Rule 1.

```
    ² ¹²
  78.949  ◄──────── There are three digits after the decimal point.
×    0.31  ◄──────── There are two digits after the decimal point.
   78949
+ 2368470  ◄──────      Add this zero here in order to align the numbers.
  0000000    Add the last two zeros in order to align the numbers or place value.
  2447419  ◄──────────  Product
```

Step 2: Determine the correct position of the decimal point in the product 2447419. This is Rule 2.

```
    ² ¹²
  78.949  ◄──────── There are three digits after the decimal point.
×    0.31  ◄──────── There are two digits after the decimal point.
   78949
+ 2368470  ◄──────      Add this zero here in order to align the numbers.
  0000000    Add the last two zeros in order to align the numbers or place value.
  24.47419  ◄──────────  Product
     ↑
```

Count 5 digits from right to left of the product 2447419 and then insert the decimal point in the product because the problem has a total of 5 digits after the decimal points.

Therefore, the answer is 24.47419

Example 6

Multiply: 3.74 × 4.83
Solution
Step 1: Follow the procedure for multiplying whole numbers. This is Rule 1.

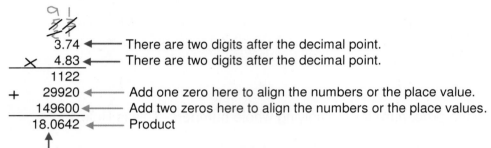

$$\begin{array}{r} 3.74 \\ \times \quad 4.83 \\ \hline 1122 \\ + \quad 29920 \quad \longleftarrow \text{Add one zero here to align the numbers or the place value.} \\ \underline{149600} \quad \longleftarrow \text{Add two zeros here to align the numbers or the place values.} \\ 180642 \quad \longleftarrow \text{Product} \end{array}$$

Step 2: Determine the correct position of the decimal point in the product 180642. This is Rule 2.

$$\begin{array}{r} 3.74 \quad \longleftarrow \text{There are two digits after the decimal point.} \\ \times \quad 4.83 \quad \longleftarrow \text{There are two digits after the decimal point.} \\ \hline 1122 \\ + \quad 29920 \quad \longleftarrow \text{Add one zero here to align the numbers or the place value.} \\ \underline{149600} \quad \longleftarrow \text{Add two zeros here to align the numbers or the place values.} \\ 18.0642 \quad \longleftarrow \text{Product} \end{array}$$

Count 4 digits from right to left of the product 180642 and then insert the decimal point because the problem has a total of 4 digits after the decimal points.

The answer is 18.0642

The notes and the generous worked examples have provided me with conceptual understanding and computational fluency to do my homework.

Exercises

1. What two major steps or rules should you follow when doing multiplication involving decimals?

2. Multiply. Hint: See Example 1.

(a) $.4 \times .4 =$	(b) $.3 \times .5 =$	(c) $.7 \times .7 =$
(d) $.9 \times .2 =$	(e) $.10 \times .4 =$	(f) $.9 \times .5 =$
(g) $.6 \times .7 =$	(h) $.7 \times .6 =$	(i) $.5 \times .5 =$
(j) $.12 \times .1 =$	(k) $.3 \times .4 =$	(l) $.16 \times .4 =$

3. Multiply. Hint: See Examples 2 and 3.

(a) $.421 \times 3 =$	(b) $764 \times .3 =$	(c) $.148 \times 2 =$
(d) $.52 \times 4 =$	(e) $.981 \times 5 =$	(f) $8 \times .431 =$
(g) $.641 \times 6 =$	(h) $.251 \times 2 =$	(i) $734 \times .2 =$
(j) $841 \times .4 =$	(k) $232 \times .9 =$	(l) $.24 \times 3 =$
(m) $4.06 \times 16 =$	(n) $631 \times .016 =$	(o) $.07 \times 9 =$
(p) $.013 \times 4 =$	(q) $.72 \times 7 =$	(r) $2.11 \times 6 =$

4. Solve. Hint: See Example 4.

  (a) $.93 \times .5 =$ (b) $.416 \times .9 =$ (c) $.627 \times .8 =$

5. Solve. Hint: See Example 5.

(a)	24.41 $\times\ .22$	(b)	3.64 $\times\ \ .2$	(c)	5.04 $\times\ \ .01$	(d)	2.982 $\times\ \ .44$

(e)	4.21 $\times\ .61$	(f)	71.4 $\times\ \ .23$	(g)	48.08 $\times\ \ .91$	(h)	.05 $\times\ .27$

6. Solve. See Example 6.

(a)	4.37 $\times\ 2.08$	(b)	4.9 $\times\ 2.9$	(c)	34.71 $\times\ 3.2$	(d)	73.2 $\times\ 3.7$

(e)	9.48 $\times\ 2.41$	(f)	2.6 $\times\ 5.7$	(g)	9.19 $\times\ 8.12$	(h)	34.62 $\times\ 2.03$

Challenge Questions

7. Solve.

  (a) $28.041 \times .08 =$ (b) $.8 \times .9 =$ (c) $946 \times .7 =$

  (d) $7.04 \times 3.41 =$ (e) $.7 \times 6 =$ (f) $.741 \times .24 =$

  (g) $.4 \times 3 =$ (h) $.009 \times .45 =$ (i) $30.64 \times .09 =$

  (j) $.07 \times 1.09 =$ (k) $7.04 \times 1.08 =$ (l) $36.6 \times 29 =$

Answers to Selected Questions

2(a) .16   **3(a)** 1.263   **4(a)** .465   **5(a)** 5.3702   **6(a)** 9.0896

Special Cases

Example 1

Solve: $.4 \times .1 =$

Solution

Step 1: Follow the procedure for multiplying whole numbers, this is Rule 1.

$$\begin{array}{r} .4 \\ \times\ \underline{.1} \\ 4 \end{array} \leftarrow \text{ Product} \qquad (4 \times 1 = 4)$$

Step 2: Determine the correct position of the decimal point in the product of 4.

This is Rule 2.

$$.4 \leftarrow \text{There is 1 digit after the decimal point.}$$
$$\times \ \underline{.1} \leftarrow \text{There is 1 digit after the decimal point.}$$
$$4 \ \leftarrow \text{Product}$$

There are a total of 2 digits after the decimal points in the problem, but the product has only one digit of 4.

We have to count two digits from right to left in the product and then insert the decimal point, but the product has one digit of 4 after the decimal point and therefore, we have to put 0 in front of 4 to make 04 before inserting the decimal point as shown:

$$.4$$
$$\times \ \underline{.1}$$
$$.04 \leftarrow \text{The product has 2 decimal places or 2 digits after the}$$
$$\uparrow \qquad \text{decimal point.}$$

Add zero in order to make 2 digits after the decimal point.

Therefore, $.4 \times .1 = .04$

Example 2

Multiply: $\qquad .44 \times .2 =$

Solution

Step 1: Follow the procedure for multiplying whole numbers. This is Rule 1.

$$.44$$
$$\times \ \underline{.2}$$
$$88 \qquad\qquad (44 \times 2 = 88)$$

Step 2: Determine the correct position of the decimal point in the product of 88. This is Rule 2.

$$.44 \leftarrow \text{There are 2 digits after the decimal point.}$$
$$\times \ \underline{.2} \leftarrow \text{There is 1 digit after the decimal point.}$$
$$88 \leftarrow \text{Product.}$$

There are a total of 3 digits after the decimal points in the problem, but the product has only 2 digits of 88 . We have to count 3 digits from right to left at the product, but the product has only two digits of 88, and therefore, place 0 in front of 88 to make 088. This makes the 3 digits in the product. Insert the decimal point after the 3 digits (after counting 3 digits from right to left) as shown:

$$\begin{array}{r} .44 \\ \times\ \ .2 \\ \hline .088 \end{array}$$ ← The product has 3 digits after the decimal point.

↑

Attach a zero in order to make 3 digits after the decimal point.

Therefore, .44 × .2 = .088

The notes and the generous worked examples have provided me with conceptual understanding and computational fluency to do my homework.

Exercises
1. Multiply. Hint: See Examples 1 and 2.

(a) .11 × .1 =

(b) .62 × .1 =

(c) .42 × .2 =

(d) .222 × .2 =

(e) .414 × .2 =

(f) .3 × .3 =

(g) .411 × .2 =

(h) .3211 × .2 =

(i) .243 × .3 =

Challenge Questions
2. Multiply:

(a) .99 × .1

(b) .24 × .21

(c) 24.34 × .102

(d) .021 × .04

(e) 2.03 × 1.041

(f) .421 × 2.41

Answers to Selected Questions
1(a) .011

1(h) .06422

Cumulative Review
1. Mary said that $7^2 + 2^2 = 52$. Is her statement correct? Explain your answer.

2. John said that 6 - 2 × 5 = 20. Is his statement correct? Explain your answer.

4. What is the formula for finding the area of:

    a. a triangle?   **b**. a rectangle?   **c**. a circle?

    Hint: Read the chapter/sections of the MathMasters Series on areas of triangles, rectangles, and circles.

REAL WORLD APPLICATIONS — WORD PROBLEMS
Special Cases

Example 1
Eric bought a box of pencils for $3.48. If John wants to buy 5 boxes of the same pencils that Eric bought, how much will John pay for the 5 boxes of the pencils?
Solution
Setup:

Cost of 1 box of pencils = $3.48
Cost of 5 boxes of pencils = $3.48 × 5

Step 1: Follow the procedure for multiplying whole numbers, this is Rule 1.

$$
\begin{array}{r}
{\scriptstyle 2\ 4} \\
\$3.48 \\
\times \quad 5 \\
\hline
\$1,740
\end{array}
$$
◄——— Product

Step 2: Determine the correct position of the decimal point in the product of 1740. This is Rule 2.

$$
\begin{array}{r}
{\scriptstyle 2\ 4} \\
\$3.48 \\
\times \quad 5 \\
\hline
\$17.40
\end{array}
$$

$3.48 ◄——— There are 2 digits after the decimal point.
5 ◄——— There is no decimal point.
$17.40 ◄——— Product

Count 2 digits from right to left of the product and then insert the decimal point because the problem has a total of 2 digits after the decimal point.

Therefore, John paid $17.40 for 5 boxes of the pencils.

Example 2
How much will 112 erasers cost at $.28 each?
Solution
Setup: Cost of 1 eraser   = $.28
        Cost of 112 erasers   = $.28 × 112
Step 1: Follow the procedure for multiplying whole numbers. This is Rule 1.

Ignore this zero ——┐

$$
\begin{array}{r}
\$0.28 \\
\times \quad 112 \\
\hline
56 \\
280 \\
+ \quad 2800 \\
\hline
\$3,136
\end{array}
$$

56
280 ◄——— Inser a zero here to align the numbers or place values.
2800 ◄——— Insert two zeros here to align the numbers or the place values.
$3,136 ◄——— Product

Step 2: Determine the correct position of the decimal point in the product 3136.

This is Rule 2.

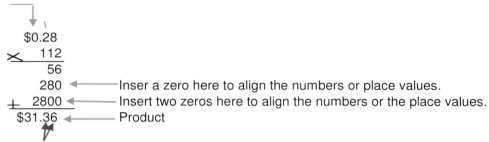

Ignore this zero

$0.28
×   112
――――――
     56
    280 ←――――― Inser a zero here to align the numbers or place values.
+ 2800 ←――――― Insert two zeros here to align the numbers or the place values.
――――――
$31.36 ←――――― Product

Count 2 digits from right to left of the product 3136 and then insert the decimal point because the problem has a total of 2 digits after the decimal point.

Therefore, 112 erasers cost $31.36

Example 3
Given that a box of tile weighs 24.68 pounds, how much would 4 boxes of the tile weigh?

Solution

Setup: Weight of 1 box of tile   = 24.68 pounds
          Weight of 4 boxes of tile   = 24.68 × 4 pounds

Step 1: Follow the procedure for multiplying whole numbers. This is Rule 1.

24.68
×   4
――――――
 9872 ←――――― Product

Step 2: Determine the correct position of the decimal point in the product 9872. This is Rule 2.

24.68 ←――――― There are 2 digits after the decimal point
×   4 ←――――― There is no decimal.
――――――
98.72 ←――――― Product

Count 2 digits from right to left of the product 9872 and then insert the decimal point because the problem has a total of 2 digits after the decimal point.

Example 4:
Nick bought a computer set by paying 7 installment payments of $75.68 each. What is the total cost of the computer set?

Solution

Setup: 1 installment payment = $75.68
          7 installment payments = $75.68 × 7

Step 1: Follow the procedure for multiplying whole numbers. This is Rule 1.

441

$$\overset{34\ 5}{\$75.68}$$
$$\times\ \ \ \ \ 7$$
$$\overline{\$52{,}976}\ \longleftarrow\ \text{Product}$$

Step 2: Determine the correct position of the decimal point in the product of 52976. This is Rule 2.

$$\overset{34\ 5}{\$75.68}\ \longleftarrow\ \text{There are 2 digits after the decimal point.}$$
$$\times\ \ \ \ \ 7\ \longleftarrow\ \text{There is no decimal point.}$$
$$\overline{\$529.76}\ \longleftarrow\ \text{Product}$$

Count 2 digits from right to left of the product 52976 and then insert the decimal point because the problem has a total of 2 digits after the decimal point.

Therefore, the total cost of the computer set is $529.76

The notes and the generous worked examples have provided me with conceptual understanding and computational fluency to do my homework.

Exercises

1. A box of pens costs $4.98. If Jones bought 4 boxes of the same type of the pens, how much did he pay for them? Hint: See Example 1.
2. One eraser costs $.38, how much will 98 erasers cost? Hint: See Example 2.
3. A science book costs $75.59. How much will 35 of the same science books cost? Hint: See Example 2.
4. A box of nails weighs 24.94 pounds. How much will 9 boxes of the same type of nails cost? Hint: See Example 3.
5. Given that a car can be bought by paying 39 equal installments of $125.97, how much does the car cost? Hint: See Example 4.

Challenge Questions

6. If a mathematics book weighs 2.48 pounds, what is the weight of 27 of the same mathematics books?
7. If Beatrice can pay her school fees by making 9 equal installments of $48.79, how much is the total cost of her school fees?
8. Insert the decimal point in each product. Hint: Count the total number of digits after the decimal point in the problems.
   (a) $.8 \times .75 = 600$
   (b) $24.84 \times .23 = 57132$

   (c) $.001 \times .075 = 000075$
   (d) $4.09 \times .15 = 6135$

DIVIDING DECIMALS

New Terms
Dividend — A number to be divided.
Divisor   — The number by which a dividend is divided.
Quotient — The number obtained by dividing one number by another.

Dividend, divisor, and quotient are shown as:

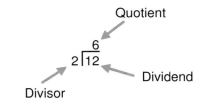

or

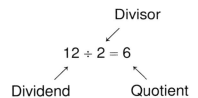

Dividing When the Dividend is a Decimal
In order to perform division involving decimals, follow the procedure for the division of whole numbers, but you should be careful to know where to insert the decimal point in the answer.
Rule 1
Use the long division symbol and insert a decimal point directly above the decimal point in the dividend.

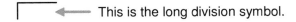

Rule 2
Then follow the procedure for the division of whole numbers.

Example 1
Divide: $4.2 \div 2$
Solution
Step 1: Follow Rule 1 by using the long division symbol and inserting a decimal

point directly above the decimal point in the dividend as shown:

Insert a decimal point directly above the decimal point in the dividend

$$2\overline{)4.2}$$ ←——Dividend

Step 2: Follow Rule 2 by following the procedure for the division of whole numbers.

$$
\begin{array}{r}
2.1 \\
2\overline{)4.2} \\
-4 \\
\hline
0\,2 \\
-2 \\
\hline
0
\end{array}
$$

Therefore, $4.2 \div 2 = 2.1$

Example 2
Divide: $.42 \div 2$
Solution
Step 1: Follow Rule 1 by inserting a decimal point directly above the decimal point in the dividend.

Insert a decimal point directly above the decimal point in the dividend.

$$2\overline{)0.42}$$ ←———— Dividend

Step 2: Follow Rule 2 by following the procedure for the division of whole numbers.

$$
\begin{array}{r}
.21 \\
2\overline{)0.42} \\
-4 \\
\hline
0\,2 \\
-2 \\
\hline
0
\end{array}
$$

Therefore, $.42 \div 2 = .21$

Example 3
Divide: $.425 \div 5$
Solution
Step 1: Follow Rule 1 by inserting a decimal point directly above the decimal point in the dividend.

Insert a decimal point directly above the decimal point in the dividend.

$$5\overline{)0.425}$$ ←———— Dividend

Step 2: Follow Rule 2 by following the procedure for the division of whole numbers.

Write 0 here because 4 < 5 and therefore, 5 cannot divide 4 easily.

$$
\begin{array}{r}
.085 \\
5\overline{\smash{)}\,0.425} \\
-\underline{40} \\
025 \\
-\underline{25} \\
00
\end{array}
$$

Therefore, $.425 \div 5 = .085$

Example 4

Divide: $.0425 \div 5$

Solution

Step 1: Follow Rule 1 by inserting a decimal point directly above the decimal point in the dividend.

Insert a decimal point directly above the decimal point in the dividend.

$$
5\overline{\smash{)}\,0.0425}
$$
— Dividend

Step 2: Follow Rule 2 by following the procedure for the division of whole numbers.

Write 0 here because the 0 after the decimal point is < 5, which is the divisor.
Write 0 here because 4 < 5, which is the divisor.

$$
\begin{array}{r}
.0085 \\
5\overline{\smash{)}\,0.0425} \\
-\underline{040} \\
0025 \\
-\underline{25} \\
00
\end{array}
$$

Therefore, $.0425 \div 5 = .0085$

Example 5

Divide: $2.52 \div 6$

Solution

Step 1: Follow Rule 1 by inserting a decimal point directly above the decimal point in the dividend.

Insert a decimal point directly above the decimal point in the dividend.

$$
6\overline{\smash{)}\,2.52}
$$
—Dividend

Step 2: Follow Rule 2 by following the procedure for the division of whole numbers.

$$\begin{array}{r} .42 \\ 6\,\overline{\smash{)}2.52} \\ -\underline{24} \\ 12 \\ -\underline{12} \\ 00 \end{array}$$

Therefore, $2.52 \div 6 = .42$

Example 6
Divide:

$42\,\overline{)136.78}$ Give your answer to 2 decimal places.

Solution
Step 1: Follow Rule 1 by inserting a decimal point directly above the decimal point in the dividend.

Insert a decimal point directly above the decimal point in the dividend.

$42\,\overline{)136.78}$ ←——— Dividend

Step 2: Follow Rule 1 by following the procedure for the division of whole numbers.

$$\begin{array}{r} 3.256 \\ 42\,\overline{)136.78} \\ -\underline{126} \\ 0107 \\ -\underline{84} \\ 238 \\ -\underline{210} \\ 0280 \\ -\underline{252} \\ 028 \end{array}$$

Write this 0 here because $28 < 42$, which is the divisor.

Note: It is required in the problem to give the answer to 2 decimal places, but we have to work to three decimal places, and then round up the second digit to the right of the decimal point, if the third digit is > 5, then 1 is added to the second digit to the right of the decimal point, but if the third digit is < 5, then 1 will not be added to the second digit to the right of the decimal point. In this particular case, the answer is 3.256 to three decimal places, and since the third digit to the right of the decimal point is 6 and $6 > 5$, 1 is added to the second digit to the right of the decimal point as follows:

$$\begin{array}{r} 3.25 \\ +\underline{1} \\ 3.26 \end{array}$$

Therefore, the answer is 3.26 to 2 decimal places.

The notes and the generous worked examples have provided me with conceptual understanding and computational fluency to do my homework.

Exercises

1. Divide. Hint: See Example 1.

(a) 9.3 ÷ 3   (b) 2.2 ÷ 2   (c) 8.2 ÷ 2
(d) 5.5 ÷ 5   (e) 6.2 ÷ 2   (f) 4.8 ÷ 4
(g) 8.4 ÷ 4   (h) 2.8 ÷ 2   (i) 6.3 ÷ 3

2. Divide. Hint: See Example 2.

(a) .93 ÷ 3   (b) .82 ÷ 2   (c) .42 ÷ 2
(d) .62 ÷ 2   (e) .48 ÷ 4   (f) .84 ÷ 4

3. Divide. Hint: See Example 3.

(a) .435 ÷ 5   (b) .246 ÷ 6   (c) .324 ÷ 4
(d) .332 ÷ 4   (e) .656 ÷ 8   (f) .365 ÷ 5

4. Divide. Hint: See Example 4.

(a) .0324 ÷ 4   (b) .0365 ÷ 5   (c) .0435 ÷ 5
(d) .0246 ÷ 6   (e) .0656 ÷ 8   (f) .0332 ÷ 4

5. Divide. Hint: See Example 5.

(a) 3.55 ÷ 5   (b) 2.64 ÷ 4   (c) 6.44 ÷ 7
(d) 7.44 ÷ 8   (e) 8.37 ÷ 9   (f) 5.52 ÷ 6

6. Divide. Hint: See Example 6. Give your answer to 2 decimal places.

(a) 44 ⟌ 144.38   (b) 36 ⟌ 241.58   © 26 ⟌ 48.42

(d) 46 ⟌ 228.64   (e) 24 ⟌ 138.84   (f) 27 ⟌ 46.23

Answers to Selected Questions

1(h) 1.4   **2(a)** .31   **3(b)** .041
4(a) .0081   **5(a)** .71   **6(d)** 4.970

Challenge Questions

Divide.

(a) .64 ÷ 4   (b) .048 ÷ 12   (c) 6. 64 ÷ 8
(d) .00081 ÷ 3   (e) 9.2 ÷ 4   (f) 12.84 ÷ 32

REAL WORLD APPLICATIONS — WORD PROBLEMS
Dividing When the Dividend is a Decimal

Example 1

In a week, Nick spent $13.45 for his lunch at school. If he goes to school 5
days in a week, how much does he spend on his lunch daily. Assume that
he spent an equal amount of money for his lunch every day.

Solution

Setup: In 5 days, Nick spent $13.45

In 1 day, Nick spent $ $13.45 \div 5$

Step 1: Follow Rule 1 by inserting a decimal point directly above the decimal
point in the dividend.

Insert a decimal point directly above the decimal point
in the dividend.

5 ⟌ 13.45 ◄————Dividend

Step 2: Follow Rule 1 by following the procedure for the division of whole numbers.

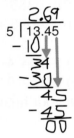

Therefore, Nick spent $2.69 daily on lunch.

_____

The notes and the generous worked examples
have provided me with conceptual understanding
and computational fluency to do my homework.

Exercises

1. Edward spent $14.75 weekly on his lunch at school. If he went to school five
   days in a week and he spent an equal amount of money daily on his lunch, how
   much did he spend daily on his lunch? Hint: See Example 1.
2. The Aggor's family paid $4,806.6 for rent last year. What was the monthly rent?
   Hint: 1 year = 12 months. Hint: See Example 1.
3. A man bought 5 boxes of the same type of tile for $61.65. How much did he
   pay for a box of tile? Hint: See Example 1.

Challenge Question

4. A lady paid $135.96 for 11 of the same type of shirts. How much did she pay for

one shirt?

Answers to Selected Questions
(**3**) $12.33

Division When the Divisor has a Decimal Point

Rule 1
The divisor must always be a whole number before dividing.

How to Change a Decimal Divisor to a Whole Number
The decimal point in the divisor must be removed before dividing. The decimal point in the divisor is removed by moving the decimal point towards the right of the decimal point such that the number of the movements of the decimal point should be equal to the number of digits after the decimal point. Since the decimal point in the divisor is moved towards the right of the decimal point so that the number of the movements of the decimal point is equal to the number of digits after the decimal point, the decimal point in the dividend should also be moved the same number of digits or places to the right. Each time a decimal point is moved one place to the right, it is the same as multiplying by 10. Review the section on "Place Values."

How to Divide With a Decimal Point in the Divisor
After changing the decimal divisor to a whole number, follow the procedure for dividing whole numbers.

Example 1
Divide. 4.2 ÷ .2 =   Check your answer.
Solution
Step 1: Make the divisor a whole number, and this is Rule 1.
The divisor .2 has one digit after the decimal point, and therefore, the decimal point should be moved one unit or one place to the right such that .2 becomes 2 which is a whole number as shown:

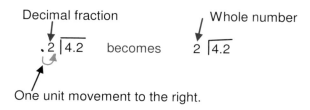

One unit movement to the right.

449

Step 2: Since the decimal point in the divisor is moved one unit or one place to the right, the decimal point in the dividend should also be moved one unit or one place to the right as shown:

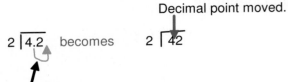

Decimal point moved.

$2\overline{)4.2}$ becomes $2\overline{)42}$

One unit movement to the right.

Step 3: Follow the procedure for dividing whole numbers.

$$
\begin{array}{r}
21 \\
2\overline{)42} \\
-4 \\
\hline
2 \\
-2 \\
\hline
0
\end{array}
$$

Therefore, 4.2 ÷ 2 = 21 Answer

Check your answer: Quotient × Initial Divisor = Initial Dividend

Quotient = 21, initial divisor = .2 and the initial dividend = 4.2

$$
\begin{array}{r}
21 \\
\times\ .2 \\
\hline
4.2
\end{array}
$$
← This is the initial dividend, and therefore, the answer is correct.

Example 2

Divide. 34.1 ÷ .11   Check your answer.

Solution

Step 1: Make the divisor a whole number.

The divisor .11 has two digits after the decimal point, and therefore, the decimal point should be moved two units or two places to the right such that .11 becomes 11 which is a whole number as shown:

Decimal fraction   Whole number

$.11\overline{)34.1}$ becomes $11\overline{)34.1}$

Two units of movements to the right.

Step 2: Since the decimal point in the divisor is moved two units to the right, the decimal point in the dividend should also be moved two units to the right as shown:

450

Write 0 here to obtain 2 units of the movement of the decimal point.

11 |34.1 becomes 11 |3410

Two units of movements to the right.

Step 3: Follow the procedure for dividing whole numbers.

$$
\begin{array}{r}
310 \\
11\overline{)3410} \\
-33 \\
\hline
11 \\
-11 \\
\hline
0 \\
-0 \\
\hline
0
\end{array}
$$

Therefore, $34.1 \div .11 = 310$ Answer

Check your answer: Quotient × Initial Divisor = Initial Dividend

Quotient = 310, Initial divisor = .11 and the initial dividend = 34.1.

$$310 \times .11 = ?$$

$$
\begin{array}{r}
310 \\
\times \quad .11 \\
\hline
310 \\
+3100 \\
\hline
34.10
\end{array}
$$

310 — Write this zero to align the numbers or place values.

34.10 ⟵ This is the initial dividend and therefore the answer is correct.

Note that 34.10 is the same as 34.1.

Example 3

Divide. $24.36 \div 1.2$ Check your answer,

Solution

Step 1: Make the divisor a whole number.

The divisor 1.2 has one digit after the decimal point, and therefore, the decimal point should be moved one unit to the right such that 1.2 becomes 12 which is a whole number as shown:

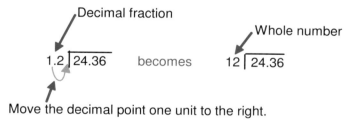

Decimal fraction

Whole number

1.2 |24.36 becomes 12 |24.36

Move the decimal point one unit to the right.

Step 2: Since the decimal point in the divisor is moved one unit to the right,

451

the dividend should also be moved one unit to the right as shown:

$$12\,\overline{)24.36} \quad \text{becomes} \quad 12\,\overline{)243.6}$$

Move the decimal point one unit to the right.

Step 3: Follow the procedure for dividing whole numbers.

Write this 0 here because the 3 in the quotient is < 12, and 12 is the divisor.

$$
\begin{array}{r}
20.3 \\
12\,\overline{)243.6} \\
-24 \\
\hline
36 \\
-36 \\
\hline
00
\end{array}
$$

This 3 is < 12.

Check your answer: Quotient × Initial Divisor = Initial Dividend
Quotient = 20.3, Initial Divisor = 1.2, and the initial dividend = 24.36
20.3 × 1.2 = ?

$$
\begin{array}{r}
20.3 \\
\times \quad 1.2 \\
\hline
406 \\
+ \quad 2030 \\
\hline
24.36
\end{array}
$$

← Write this 0 to align the numbers or place values.

← This is the initial dividend, and therefore, the answer is correct.

Example 4
Divide. 0.3042 ÷ .13 =   Check your answer.
Solution
Step 1: Make the divisor a whole number.
The divisor .13 has two digits after the decimal point, and therefore, the decimal point should be moved two units to the right such that .13 becomes 13, which is a whole number as shown:

Decimal fraction   Whole number

$$.13\,\overline{)0.3042} \quad \text{becomes} \quad 13\,\overline{)0.3042}$$

Move the decimal point two units to the right.

Step 2: Since the decimal point in the divisor .13 has been moved two units to the right, the decimal point in the dividend should also be moved two units to the right.

$$13\overline{)0.3042} \quad \text{becomes} \quad 13\overline{)30.42}$$

Move the decimal point two places to the right.

Step 3: Follow the procedure for dividing whole numbers.

$$
\begin{array}{r}
2.34 \\
13\overline{)30.42} \\
-26\downarrow \\
\hline
44 \\
-39\downarrow \\
\hline
52 \\
-52 \\
\hline
00
\end{array}
$$

Therefore, $0.3042 \div .13 = 2.34$ Answer.

Check your answer: Quotient × Initial Divisor = Initial Dividend

Quotient = 2.34, Initial Divisor = .13, Initial Dividend = 0.3042

$$2.34 \times .13 = ?$$

$$
\begin{array}{r}
2.34 \\
\times \quad .13 \\
\hline
702 \\
+ \quad 2340 \\
\hline
.3042
\end{array}
$$

← This is the initial dividend, therefore, the answer is correct.

Note that .3042 is the same as 0.3042.

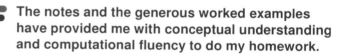

The notes and the generous worked examples have provided me with conceptual understanding and computational fluency to do my homework.

Exercises

1. Divide. Check your answer. Hint: See Example 1.

(a) $9.3 \div .3 =$ (b) $8.2 \div .2 =$ (c) $6.2 \div .2 =$

(d) $4.4 \div .4 =$ (e) $7.7 \div .7 =$ (f) $5.5 \div .5 =$

(g) $6.3 \div .3 =$ (h) $3.3 \div .3 =$ (i) $8.8 \div .4 =$

2. Divide. Hint: See Example 2. Check your answer.

(a) $25.2 \div .12 =$ (b) $89.1 \div .11 =$ (c) $27.3 \div .13 =$

(d) $15.4 \div .14 =$ (e) $13.2 \div .12 =$ (f) $16.5 \div .15 =$

(g) $33.6 \div .16 =$ (h) $29.4 \div 14 =$ (i) $45.1 \div .11 =$

3. Divide. Hint: See Example 3. Check your answer.

(a) $24.24 \div 1.2 =$ (b) $26.13 \div 1.3 =$ (c) $36.12 \div 1.2 =$

(d) $11.11 \div 1.1 =$ (e) $28.14 \div 1.4 =$ (f) $30.30 \div 1.5 =$

(g) $15.15 \div 1.5 =$ (h) $13.13 \div 1.3 =$ (i) $32.32 \div 1.6 =$

4. Divide. Hint: See Example 4. Check your answer.

(a) $.12\overline{)0.4092}$ (b) $.14\overline{)0.2982}$ (c) $.13\overline{)0.2769}$

(d) $.9\overline{)0.4068}$ (e) $.11\overline{)0.6204}$ (f) $.8\overline{)0.2736}$

(g) $.12\overline{)0.3216}$ (h) $.9\overline{)0.3078}$ (i) $.14\overline{)0.3402}$

Challenge Questions

5. Divide. Check your answer.

(a) $2.1 \div .3 =$ (b) $3.6 \div .4 =$ (c) $2.55 \div .5 =$ (d) $1.44 \div 1.2 =$

(f) $15.075 \div 2.5 =$ (g) $38.4 \div 1.2 =$ (h) $.605 \div .5 =$ (i) $38.4 \div .6 =$

Answer to Selected Questions

1(a) 31   **2(a)** 210   **3(a)** 20.2   **4(a)** 3.41

REAL WORLD APPLICATIONS — WORD PROBLEMS
Division When the Divisor has a Decimal Point

Example 1

If a pen costs $.23, how many pens of the same type can be bought with $3.45?

Solution

Setup: $.23 can buy one pen.

$3.45 can buy $3.45 ÷ .23 pens.

Step 1: Make the divisor a whole number.

The divisor .23 has two digits after the decimal point, and therefore, the decimal point should be moved two units to the right such that .23 becomes 23 which is a whole number as shown:

Decimal fraction   Whole number

$.23\overline{)3.45}$ becomes $23\overline{)3.45}$

Move the decimal point two units to the right.

Step 2: Since the decimal point in the divisor is moved two units to the right, the decimal point in the dividend 3.45 should also be moved two units to the right as shown:

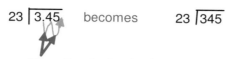

23 | 3.45   becomes   23 | 345

Move the decimal point two units to the right.

Step 3: Follow the procedure for dividing whole numbers.

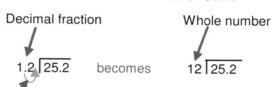

Therefore, 15 pens can be bought with $3.45.

Example 2

Eric drove 25.2 miles in 1.2 hours. What is his speed per hour?
(Hint: Speed per hour = Distance traveled ÷ Time taken to travel.)

Solution

Setup: Speed per hour = Distance traveled ÷ Time taken to travel the distance.

$$= 25.2 ÷ 1.2$$

Step 1: Make the divisor a whole number.

The divisor 1.2 has one digit after the decimal point, and therefore, the decimal point should be moved one unit to the right such that 1.2 becomes 12 which is a whole number as shown:

Decimal fraction   Whole number

1.2 | 25.2   becomes   12 | 25.2

Move the decimal point one unit to the right.

Step 2: Since the decimal point in the divisor has been moved one unit to the right, the decimal point in the dividend should also be moved one unit to the right. Move the decimal point in the dividend also one unit to the right as shown:

12 | 25.2   becomes   12 | 252

Move the decimal point one unit to the right.

Step 3: Follow the procedure for dividing whole numbers.

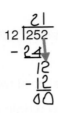

Therefore, the speed per hour = 21 miles per hour.

Example 3

Alice bought a computer set on an installment plan for $413.76. If her monthly payment is $34.48, how many months will she be making the payment?

Solution

Setup: $34.48 is the payment for 1 month.

$413.76 is the payment for $413.76 ÷ $34.48 months.

Step 1: Make the divisor a whole number.

The divisor 34.48 has two digits after the decimal point, and therefore, the decimal point should be moved two units to the right such that 34.48 becomes 3448 which is a whole number as shown:

Move the decimal point two units to the right.

Step 2: Since the decimal point in the divisor is moved two units to the right, the decimal point in the dividend should also be moved two units to the right as shown:

$$3448 \overline{)413.76} \quad \text{becomes} \quad 3448 \overline{)41376}$$

Move the decimal point two units to the right.

Step 3: Follow the procedure for dividing whole numbers.

$$
\begin{array}{r}
12 \\
3448 \overline{)41376} \\
-3448 \downarrow \\
\hline
6896 \\
-6896 \\
\hline
0000
\end{array}
$$

Therefore, Alice will use 12 months in making the payments.

The notes and the generous worked examples have provided me with conceptual understanding and computational fluency to do my homework.

Exercises

1. If an eraser costs $.61, how many similar erasers can be bought with $6.71? Hint: See Example 1.

2. Grace travelled 18.2 miles in 1.4 hours on her bicycle. What is her speed per hour? Hint: See Example 2.

3. George bought a camera for $19.36 on an installment plan. If he paid $1.21 monthly, how many months did he take to finish paying for the camera? Hint: See Example 3.

Challenge Questions

4. If a special pen costs $.27, how many similar pens can be bought for $3.24?

5. Alice bought a telephone for $47.79 on an installment plan. If she paid $5.31 monthly, how many months did she take to finish paying for the telephone?

6. Nick travelled 36.3 miles in 1.1 hour. What is his speed per hour?

Mixed Questions — Review

(1) $2.46 \div 6$ **(2)** $2.46 \div .6$ **(3)** $\dfrac{3}{4} \div \dfrac{3}{5} =$ **(4)** $\dfrac{4}{25} \times \dfrac{5}{16} =$

(5) $11.24 + .46 + 1.4 + 2 =$ **(6)** $\dfrac{1}{4} + \dfrac{2}{3}$ **(7)** $\dfrac{3}{4} - \dfrac{1}{3}$ **(8)** $4^2 - 10 =$

Dividing a Smaller Whole Number by a Bigger Whole Number

If one apple is shared by two students, each student will receive a fraction of the apple and similarly, after dividing a smaller whole number by a bigger whole number, the answer (quotient) will be a common fraction or a decimal fraction.

Rule 1: In order to divide a smaller number by a bigger number, put a decimal point and a zero behind the smaller number (dividend), and then put another decimal point directly above the decimal point in the dividend, and then divide as in whole numbers.

Rule 2: While dividing, continue to put zeros behind the dividend until the answer with the required number of the decimal places or digits after the decimal point such as the nearest tenth, nearest hundredth, nearest thousandth, or nearest ten-thousandth is obtained.

Example 1

Divide: $2 \div 3$, give your answer to the nearest tenth.

Solution

Step 1: Follow Rule 1, which is to put a decimal point and a zero behind the smaller number (dividend), and then put another decimal point directly above the decimal point in the dividend. Then, divide as in whole numbers.

Put a decimal point directly above the decimal point in the dividend.

$$3\,\overline{)2.0}$$

Note that 2 is the dividend.

Put a decimal point and a zero behind the dividend.

Step 2: Follow Rule 2, which is to continue to put zeros behind the dividend during division until the answer with the required number of the decimal places or the number of the digits after the decimal point such as the nearest tenth, hundredth, thousandth or ten-thousandth, is obtained.

$$
\begin{array}{r}
.66 \\
3\,\overline{)2.0} \\
-18 \\
\hline
20 \\
-18 \\
\hline
2
\end{array}
$$

← Write this zero in order to continue the division.

Note: To work to the nearest tenths, we have to work to the nearest hundredths and if the hundredths position digit is 5 or greater than 5, then 1 is added to the tenths digit (we round up the tenths digit), and if the hundredths digit is less than 5, nothing is added to the tenths digit (we round down the tenths digit.)

Since the quotient is .66, the 6 in the hundredths position is greater than 5 and therefore, 1 is added to the 6 at the tenths position to become 7 (we round up 6 to become 7.)

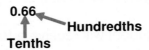

0.66

Hundredths

Tenths

Therefore, the final answer is .7 to the nearest tenths.

How many digits after the decimal point are required to round to the nearest tenth, hundredth, thousandth or ten-thousandth?

After reviewing the section on place values, the following table can be made.

To the nearest position	Number of digits after the decimal point
Nearest tenth	1
Nearest hundredth	2
Nearest thousandth	3
Nearest ten-thousandth	4

Example 2

Divide: 3 ÷ 8, round off your answer to the nearest hundredth.

Solution

Step 1: Follow Rule 1, which is to put a decimal point and a zero behind the smaller number (dividend), and then put another decimal point directly above the decimal point in the dividend. Then, divide as in whole numbers.

Put a decimal point directly above the decimal point in the dividend.

$$8\overline{)3.0}$$

Put a decimal point and a zero behind the dividend.

Step 2: Follow Rule 2, which during division, is continue to put zeros behind the dividend until the answer with the required number of the decimal places or the number of the digits after the decimal point, such as the nearest tenth, hundredth, thousandth, or ten-thousandth, is obtained.

```
      .375
  8 | 3.0
    -24
      6 0    ←——Write this zero in order to continue the division.
     -5 6
       40    ←—— Write this zero in order to continue the division.
      -40
       00
```

Note: To work to the nearest hundredths, we have to work to the nearest thousandths and if the thousandths position digit is 5 or greater than 5, 1 is added to the digit at the hundredths position, but if the digit at the thousandths position is less than 5, nothing is added to the hundredths position. Since the quotient is .375, the digit at the thousandths position is 5, and therefore, 1 is added to 7 to make 8.

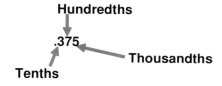

Hundredths

.375

Tenths   **Thousandths**

Therefore, the final answer is .38 to the nearest hundredth.

Example 3

Divide: 1 ÷ 12. Round off your answer to the nearest thousandth.

Solution

Step 1: Follow Rule 1, which is to put a decimal point and a zero behind the smaller number (dividend), and then put another decimal point directly above the decimal point in the dividend. Then, divide as in whole numbers.

Put a decimal point directly above the decimal point in the dividend.

$$12\overline{)1.0}$$

Put a decimal point and a zero behind the dividend.

Step 2: Follow Rule 2, which during division, is continue to put zeros behind the dividend until the answer with the required number of the decimal places or the number of the digits after the decimal point such as the nearest tenth, hundredth, thousandth, or ten-thousandth, is obtained.

$$12\overline{)1.0}$$

Critical Thinking: From Step 2 above, 1.0 which is read as ten cannot be divided by 12, and therefore, a 0 is written after the decimal point in the quotient, and another zero is added to the dividend of 1.0 to make 1.00. (1.00 is read as one hundred). Note carefully that whenever two zeros are placed in the dividend before a division can take place, then a zero is placed in the quotient as a place holder as shown:

Place a 0 in the quotient as a place holder when the second 0 is placed in the dividend.

$$12\overline{)1.00}$$

Place the second 0 in the dividend.

Continue the division.

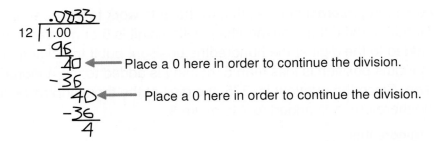

Place a 0 here in order to continue the division.

Place a 0 here in order to continue the division.

Note: To work to the nearest thousandths, we have to work to the nearest ten-thousandths, and then if the ten-thousandths position digit is 5 or greater than 5, 1 is added to the digit at the thousandths position, but if the digit at the ten-thousandth position is less than 5, nothing is added to the thousandths position digit. Since the quotient is .0833, the 3 at the ten-thousandths position is less than

5, and therefore, nothing is added to the thousandths position digit. Therefore, the final answer is .083 to the nearest thousandth.

The notes and the generous worked examples have provided me with conceptual understanding and computational fluency to do my homework.

Exercises

1. Divide and round your answer to the nearest tenth. Hint: See Example 1.

(a) $2 \div 6 =$ (b) $2 \div 7 =$ (c) $3 \div 4 =$ (d) $3 \div 7 =$ (e) $4 \div 6 =$

(f) $7\overline{)5}$ (g) $8\overline{)5}$ (h) $11\overline{)8}$ (i) $12\overline{)9}$ (j) $13\overline{)2}$

(k) $9\overline{)8}$ (l) $9\overline{)2}$ (m) $7\overline{)6}$ (n) $13\overline{)4}$ (o) $12\overline{)10}$

2. Divide and round your answer to the nearest hundredth. Hint: See Example 2.

(a) $8\overline{)3}$ (b) $6\overline{)1}$ (c) $12\overline{)3}$ (d) $11\overline{)2}$ (e) $9\overline{)4}$

(f) $14\overline{)7}$ (g) $13\overline{)9}$ (h) $12\overline{)3}$ (i) $15\overline{)2}$ (j) $8\overline{)7}$

(k) $3 \div 5 =$ (l) $3 \div 7 =$ (m) $2 \div 12 =$ (n) $9 \div 11 =$ (o) $5 \div 12 =$

3. Divide and round your answer to the nearest thousandth. Hint: See Example 3.

(a) $1 \div 11$ (b) $2 \div 21$ (c) $1 \div 14$ (d) $2 \div 22$ (e) $2 \div 25$

(f) $15\overline{)1}$ (g) $31\overline{)3}$ (h) $16\overline{)1}$ (i) $20\overline{)1}$ (j) $25\overline{)2}$

Challenge Questions

4. Divide, $1 \div 13$, round your answer to the nearest hundredth.

5. Solve, round your answer to the nearest thousandth.

(a) $8\overline{)16}$ (b) $24\overline{)2}$ (c) $9\overline{)2}$ di) $30\overline{)1}$ (j) $22\overline{)2}$

REAL WORLD APPLICATIONS — WORD PROBLEMS
Dividing a Small Whole Number by a Bigger Whole Number

Example 1

If 3 oranges sell for $2, what is the cost of 1 orange? Solve the problem without showing a detailed explanation.

Solution

Setup: 3 oranges cost $2

       1 orange cost $2 ÷ 3

Solve the problem without showing a detailed explanation.

$$3 \overline{) 2.0} = .666$$

$$\begin{array}{r} .666 \\ 3\overline{)2.0} \\ -18 \\ \hline 20 \\ -18 \\ \hline 20 \\ -18 \\ \hline 2 \end{array}$$

1 orange will cost $.67

Example 2

If a package of 5 pencils sells for $2, what is the cost of 1 pencil? Solve the problem without showing a detailed explanation.

Solution

Setup: 5 pencils cost $2

       1 pencil costs $2 ÷ 5

Solve the problem without showing a detailed explanations.

$$\begin{array}{r} .40 \\ 5\overline{)2.0} \\ -20 \\ \hline 000 \\ -0 \\ \hline 0 \end{array}$$

1 pencil costs $.40

Example 3

A mechanic took 4 hours to repair 9 cars. Given that it takes the same amount of time to repair each car, find the time needed to repair 1 car. The answer should be in decimal fraction of an hour. Do not show a detailed solution method.

Solution

Setup: 9 cars were repaired in 4 hours.

       1 car will be required in 4 ÷ 9 hours.

Solve the problem without showing a detailed solution method.

$$
9\overline{)4.0}^{.444}
$$
$$
\begin{array}{r}
-36 \\
\hline
40 \\
-36 \\
\hline
40 \\
-36 \\
\hline
4
\end{array}
$$

The time needed to repair 1 car is .44 hours.

The notes and the generous worked examples have provided me with conceptual understanding and computational fluency to do my homework.

Exercises

1. If 7 oranges cost $3, what is the price of 1 orange? Hint: See Example 1.

2. A package of 12 pencils sells for $3. What is the cost of 1 pencil? Hint: See Example 2.

3. A technician can assemble 12 toys in 5 hours. How long does it take the technician to assemble 1 toy? Hint: See Example 3.

Challenge Questions

1. A man can assemble 15 similar toys in 7 hours. How long does it take the man to assemble 1 toy? Round your answer to the nearest hundredth of an hour.

Cumulative Review

(**1**) $4.348 - 1.2 =$

(**2**) $7.689 - 2 =$

(**3**) $\dfrac{3}{4} \div \dfrac{3}{2} =$

(**4**) $\dfrac{6}{7} \div \dfrac{14}{24} =$

(**5**) $1 \div 8 =$

(**6**) $22 - 17\dfrac{2}{5} =$

(**7**) $41 - 13\dfrac{1}{4} =$

(**8**) $2\dfrac{4}{5}$
  $1\dfrac{1}{4}$
  $+\ 2\dfrac{3}{4}$

(**9**) $2\dfrac{1}{3}$
  6
  $+\ 2\dfrac{3}{4}$

(10) $9^2 - 2^4 =$ **(11)** $12 - 8 \div 2 \times 3 =$ **(12)** $.041 \times 2.64 =$

(13) $2.67 \times .102 =$ **(14)** Given that $\dfrac{k}{3} \times 9 = 21$, find the value of k .

(15) Find each quotient and write each answer in the lowest terms.

(a) $6\dfrac{3}{4} \div 6 =$ (b) $9 \div 5\dfrac{3}{4} =$ (c) $4 \div \dfrac{2}{3} =$ (d) $\dfrac{6}{16} \div \dfrac{3}{8} =$

(e) $1 \div \dfrac{1}{9} =$ (f) $2 \div \dfrac{5}{8} =$ (g) $14 \div \dfrac{7}{11} =$ (h) $4\dfrac{1}{4} \div \dfrac{1}{2} =$

(16) Find each sum and write each sum in the lowest terms.

(a) $\dfrac{3}{7} + \dfrac{6}{7} =$ (b) $\dfrac{3}{5} + \dfrac{2}{3} =$ (c) $4\dfrac{3}{4} + 2\dfrac{1}{4} =$

(d) $3\dfrac{1}{5} + \dfrac{14}{8} =$ (e) $1\dfrac{1}{2} + 2\dfrac{1}{3} + 6\dfrac{1}{4} =$ (f) $\dfrac{1}{4} + \dfrac{5}{8} + \dfrac{1}{2} + \dfrac{3}{8} =$

(17) A lady paid $120.25 for 13 shirts. How much did 1 shirt cost?

Change Common Fractions to Decimal Fractions

To change common fractions to decimal fractions is the same as dividing a smaller whole number, by a bigger whole number, which was discussed in the preceding section.

Rule 1

In order to change a common fraction to a decimal fraction divide the numerator by the denominator.

Example 1

Change $\dfrac{3}{4}$ to a decimal fraction.

Solution

Follow Rule 1 and Rule 2 under the topic "Dividing a Smaller Number by a Bigger Whole Number."

$$
\begin{array}{r}
.75 \\
4\overline{)30} \\
-28 \\
\hline
20 \\
-20 \\
\hline
00
\end{array}
$$

The decimal fraction of $\frac{3}{4}$ is .75

The notes and the generous worked examples have provided me with conceptual understanding and computational fluency to do my homework.

Exercises

Change the following common fractions to decimal fractions and round your answers to the nearest hundredths. Hint: See Example 1.

(a) $\frac{1}{4}$ (b) $\frac{2}{3}$ (c) $\frac{3}{5}$ (d) $\frac{7}{20}$ (e) $\frac{4}{17}$ (f) $\frac{1}{12}$

(g) $\frac{2}{9}$ (h) $\frac{4}{11}$ (i) $\frac{9}{15}$ (j) $\frac{13}{17}$ (k) $\frac{23}{28}$ (l) $\frac{49}{50}$

(m) $\frac{14}{40}$ (n) $\frac{23}{30}$ (o) $\frac{3}{13}$ (p) $\frac{4}{14}$ (q) $\frac{2}{17}$ (r) $\frac{5}{12}$

Answers to Selected Questions

(a) .25   (k) .82

Cumulative Review

1. A side of a square object is 6 ft.
    a. Find the perimeter of the object.
    b. Find the area of the object.
2. What is the formula for finding the area of a triangle?
3. What is the formula for finding the area and the perimeter of a rectangle?
    Hint: Review the Math Teaching Series for grade 5 or grade 6.
4. Test each number to see if it is divisible be by 2, 3, 5, 9, or 10.
    a. 100   b. 162   c. 39
    d. 25   e. 746   f. 49
    Hint: Use Divisibility Rules. Review the Math Teaching Series for Grade 5 on Divisibility.
5. Find the mean, mode, and the median of the set of each data.
    a. 4, 7, 2, 3, 4   b. 10, 1, 4, 1   c. 3, 1, 3. 5, 3
6. Mary said that the mean is the same as the average. Is her statement correct?
    Review your Math Teaching Series on Average and Mean.

PERCENT

Percent Concept
The word **percent** means per one hundred. Percent may also be explained as a certain number out of 100. For example, 40 out of 100 students went to the zoo, means 40 percent went to the zoo and the 40 percent can be written as 40%. The 40% or 40 out of 100 can also be expressed as the fraction $\frac{40}{100}$.

The word percent is replaced by the symbol %. Note also that any common fraction that has a denominator of 100 can be expressed as a percent as follows:

(a) $\frac{12}{100} = 12\%$ (b) $\frac{8}{100} = 8\%$ (c) $\frac{99.9}{100} = 99.9\%$

(d) $\frac{300}{100} = 300\%$ (e) $\frac{100}{100} = 100\%$ (f) $\frac{2\frac{1}{2}}{100} = 2\frac{1}{2}\%$

(g) $\frac{\frac{1}{2}}{100} = \frac{1}{2}\%$ (h). $\frac{.8}{100} = .8\%$ (i) $\frac{1}{100} = 1\%$

Let us use the grid that has 100 squares to explain the concept of percent.

(a). Each square represents 1 out of 100 squares of the grid which can be expressed as one percent or 1%.

(b). There are 10 squares that contain the letter A, out of the 100 squares of the grid, and this can be expressed as 10 percent (10%) of the squares of the grid contain the letter A.

(**c**). There are 4 squares that contain the letter B, out of the 100 squares of the grid. This can be expressed as 4 percent (4%) of the squares of the grid contain the letter B.

Team Exercise

The class should be divided into four groups. Each group should use the grid to answer the following questions, and then report the answers to the class. The grid has a total of 100 squares.

What percent of the squares contain:

(**a**). Q   (**b**). P   (**c**). X   (**d**). M   (**e**). K

K		Q	X	K	P				P
	M						M		
P		Q					Q		
P			K						
				P					
	K		K					Q	
P									
P			X		P		M		Q

Example 1

70 out of 100 is what percent?

Solution

Step 1: Express 70 out of 100 as a percent.

$$70 \text{ out of } 100 = \frac{70}{100} = 70\%$$

Therefore, 70 out of 100 is 70% .

Exercises

Express the following as a percent. Hint: See Example 1.

(**1**) 2 out of 100   (**2**) 28 out of 100   (**3**) 23 out of 100

(**4**) 100 out of 100   (**5**) $78\frac{1}{2}$ out of 100   (**9**) 48.5 out of 100

Answers to Selected Questions

(**1**) 2%   (**2**) 28%

Express Percent as a Fraction

1. If we count 33 squares out of 100 squares of a grid, then we can represent the 33 squares out of the 100 squares as 33% or $\dfrac{33}{100}$.

2. **Team Exercise**: Each team should sketch a grid that contains 100 squares. The grid should have a total of ten columns and ten rows. Each column and each row should contain ten squares. Each team should shade five columns which are joined together from one edge of the grid blue. Compare the five columns which are shaded blue, to the whole grid. Is the size of the five columns which are shaded blue about half the size of the whole grid? The five columns which are shaded blue contain 50 squares out of the 100 squares of the grid, and this can be expressed as $\dfrac{50}{100}$ or 50%, but the five columns which are shaded blue are half of the whole grid, so we can say:

$$\frac{50}{100} = 50\% = \frac{1}{2}$$

Rule: To express a percent as a fraction, put the percent number as a numerator over 100, and then reduce the fraction to the lowest term if possible.

Example 1
Change 37% to a fraction.
Solution
Using the rule to express a percent as a fraction, put the percent number as the numerator over 100, and then reduce the fraction to the lowest term if possible.

$$37\% = \frac{37}{100}$$

Example 2
Change 25% to a fraction.
Solution
Using the rule to express a percent as a fraction, put the percent number as the numerator over 100, and then reduce the fraction to the lowest term if possible.

$$25\% = \frac{25}{100} = \frac{\overset{1}{\cancel{25}}}{\underset{4}{\cancel{100}}} \quad \text{Reduce to the lowest term by dividing by 5.}$$

$$= \frac{1}{4}$$

Example 3

Change 125% to a fraction.

Solution

Using the rule to express a percent as a fraction, put the percent number as the numerator over 100, and then reduce the fraction to the lowest term if possible.

$$125\% = \frac{125}{100}$$

$$= \frac{\overset{5}{\overset{25}{\cancel{125}}}}{\underset{4}{\underset{20}{\cancel{100}}}} \qquad \text{Reduce to the lowest term by dividing by 5.}$$

$$= \frac{5}{4} \qquad \text{(This can be changed to a mixed number as } 1\frac{1}{4}.\text{)}$$

Example 4

Express $22\frac{1}{2}$ % as a fraction.

Solution

Using the rule to express a percent as a fraction, put the percent number as the numerator over 100, and then reduce to the lowest term if possible.

$$22\frac{1}{2}\% = \frac{22\frac{1}{2}}{100}$$

$\dfrac{22\frac{1}{2}}{100}$ can be written as $22\frac{1}{2} \div 100$

$$= \frac{45}{2} \div \frac{100}{1} \quad (\textbf{Note}: 22\frac{1}{2} = \frac{45}{2} \text{ and } 100 = \frac{100}{1}. \text{ Refer to the chapter on fractions).}$$

$$= \frac{45}{2} \times \frac{1}{100} \quad (\textbf{Note}: 100 \text{ is inverted which is the reciprocal of 100 and the division symbol changes to a multiplication symbol because to divide by a fraction is the same as to multiply by the reciprocal of the fraction. Review the chapter on the Division of Fractions).}$$

$$= \frac{\overset{9}{\cancel{45}}}{2} \times \frac{1}{\underset{20}{\cancel{100}}} \qquad \text{Reduce to the lowest terms by dividing by 5.}$$

$$= \frac{9}{2} \times \frac{1}{20} = \frac{9}{40}$$

Example 5

Change .4% to a fraction.

Solution

Using the rule to express a percent as a fraction, put the percent number as the numerator over 100, and then reduce the fraction to the lowest term if possible.

$$4\% = \frac{.4}{100}$$

$$= .4 \times \frac{1}{100} \qquad \text{Rearrange } \frac{.4}{100} \text{ as } .4 \times \frac{1}{100}.$$

$$= \frac{4}{10} \times \frac{1}{100} \qquad .4 = \frac{4}{10}, \text{ review the chapter on decimals.}$$

$$\qquad\qquad\qquad .4 \text{ is in a decimal form, and } \frac{4}{10} \text{ is in a fraction form.}$$

$$= \frac{\overset{1}{\cancel{4}}}{10} \times \frac{1}{\underset{25}{\cancel{100}}} \qquad \text{Divide by 4.}$$

$$= \frac{1}{10} \times \frac{1}{25}$$

$$= \frac{1}{250} \qquad\qquad 25 \times 10 = 250$$

The required fraction is $\frac{1}{250}$.

Example 6

Change .12% to a fraction.

Solution

Using the rule to express a percent as a fraction, put the percent number as the numerator over 100, and then reduce to the lowest term if possible.

$$.12\% = \frac{.12}{100}$$

$$= .12 \times \frac{1}{100}$$ Rearrange $\frac{.12}{100}$ as $.12 \times \frac{1}{100}$.

$$= \frac{12}{100} \times \frac{1}{100}$$ $.12 = \frac{12}{100}$, review the chapter on decimals.

$.12$ is in a decimal form, and $\frac{12}{100}$ is in a fraction form.

$$= \frac{\overset{3}{\cancel{12}}}{\underset{25}{\cancel{100}}} \times \frac{1}{100}$$ Divide by 4.

$$= \frac{3}{25} \times \frac{1}{100}$$

$$= \frac{3}{2500}$$ $25 \times 100 = 2500$

The required fraction is $\frac{3}{2500}$.

Example 7
Change $.124\%$ to a fraction.
Solution
Using the rule to express a percent as a fraction, put the percent number as the numerator over 100, and then reduce to the lowest term if possible.

$$.124\% = \frac{.124}{100}$$

$$= .124 \times \frac{1}{100}$$ Rearrange $\frac{.124}{100}$ as $.124 \times \frac{1}{100}$.

$$= \frac{124}{1000} \times \frac{1}{100}$$ $.124 = \frac{124}{1000}$, review the chapter on decimals.

$.124$ is in a decimal form, and $\frac{124}{1000}$ is in a fraction form.

$$= \frac{\overset{31}{\cancel{124}}}{1000} \times \frac{1}{\underset{25}{\cancel{100}}}$$ Divide by 4.

$$= \frac{31}{1000} \times \frac{1}{25}$$

$$= \frac{31}{2500} \qquad 25 \times 100 = 2500$$

The required fraction is $\frac{31}{2500}$.

Exercises

1. Express the following percents as fractions and reduce the answers to the lowest terms if possible. Hint: See Examples 1, 2, and 3.

   (**a**) 27%   (**b**) 20%   (**c**) 135%   (**d**) 90%   (**e**) 110%

2. Express the following percents as fractions and reduce the answers to the lowest terms if possible. Hint: See Example 4.

   (**a**) $32\frac{1}{2}$%   (**b**) $4\frac{2}{3}$%   (**c**) $6\frac{3}{4}$%   (**d**) $17\frac{1}{3}$%   (**e**) $1\frac{1}{9}$%

3. Express the following percents as fractions and reduce the answers to the lowest terms if possible. Hint: See Example 5.

   (**a**) .2%   (**b**) .7%   (**c**) .5%   (**d**) .3%   (**e**) .8%

4. Express the following percents as fractions and reduce the answers to the lowest terms if possible. Hint: See Example 6.

   (**a**) .14%   (**b**) .11%   (**c**) .15%   (**d**) .31%   (**e**) .70%

5. Express the following percents as fractions and reduce the answers to the lowest terms if possible. Hint: See Example 7.

   (**a**) .114%   (**b**) .133%   (**c**) .115%   (**d**) .131%   (**e**) .105%

Challenge Exercises

6. Express the following percents as fractions and reduce the answers to the lowest terms if possible.

   (**a**) .6%   (**b**) 75%   (**c**) $7\frac{3}{5}$%   (**d**) .215%   (**e**) 135%

   (**f**) 10%   (**g**) 6%   (**h**) .12%   (**i**) $6\frac{1}{2}$%   (**j**) 110%

Answers to Selected Exercises

1(a) $\frac{27}{100}$ **1(b)** $\frac{1}{5}$ **2(a)** $\frac{13}{40}$ **2(b)** $\frac{7}{150}$

3(a) $\frac{1}{500}$ **3(b)** $\frac{7}{1000}$ **4(a)** $\frac{7}{5000}$ **4(b)** $\frac{11}{10,000}$

5(a) $\dfrac{57}{50,000}$ **5(b)** $\dfrac{133}{100,000}$

REAL WORLD APPLICATIONS - WORD PROBLEMS
Express Percent as Fraction

Example 1
Yesterday, 2% of the students in a school were absent. What fraction of the students were absent?
Solution
Using the rule to express a percent as a fraction, write the percent number as the numerator over 100 and then reduce to the lowest term if possible.

$$2\% = \frac{2}{100}$$

$$= \frac{\overset{1}{\cancel{2}}}{\underset{50}{\cancel{100}}} \qquad \text{Reduce to the lowest term by dividing by 2.}$$

$$= \frac{1}{50}$$

The fraction of the students that were absent was $\dfrac{1}{50}$.

Example 2
A television set was reduced by 15%. What fraction of the price is the reduction?
Solution
Using the rule to express a percent as a fraction, write the percent number as the numerator over 100 and then reduce the fraction to the lowest term if possible.

$$15\% = \frac{15}{100}$$

$$= \frac{\overset{3}{\cancel{15}}}{\underset{20}{\cancel{100}}} \qquad \text{Reduce to the lowest term by dividing by 5.}$$

$$= \frac{3}{20}$$

The fraction of the price that was the reduction is $\frac{3}{20}$

Example 3

In a school, 65% of the students like soccer, what fraction of the students like soccer?

Solution

Using the rule to express a percent as a fraction, write the percent number as the numerator over 100, and then reduce the fraction to the lowest term if possible.

$$65\% = \frac{65}{100}$$

$$= \frac{\overset{13}{\cancel{65}}}{\underset{20}{\cancel{100}}} \qquad \text{Reduce to the lowest term by dividing by 5.}$$

$$= \frac{13}{20}$$

The fraction of the students that like soccer is $\frac{13}{20}$.

Example 4

A computer system was on sale at 10% off the regular price. What fraction of the regular price was the reduction?

Solution

Using the rule to express a percent as a fraction, write the percent number as the numerator over 100 and then reduce to the lowest term if possible.

$$10\% = \frac{10}{100} \qquad \text{The reduction was 10\%.}$$

$$= \frac{\overset{1}{\cancel{10}}}{\underset{10}{\cancel{100}}} \qquad \text{Reduce to the lowest term by dividing by 10.}$$

$$= \frac{1}{10}$$

The fraction of the regular price that was on sale is $\frac{1}{10}$.

Exercises

1. 25% of the students in a class went to the zoo. What fraction of the students went to the zoo? Hint: See Example 1.

2. A television set was reduced by 10%. What fraction of the price is the reduction? Hint: See Example 2.

3. 75% of the students in a class like science. What fraction of the students like science? Hint: See Example 3.

4. A car is on sale at 6% off the regular price. What fraction of the regular price is the the reduction? Hint: See Example 4.

5. A house was sold at 8% off the original selling price. What is the fraction of the reduction of the price of the house? Hint: See Example 4.

6. 16% of the students in a class went to medical schools. What is the fraction of the students that went to medical schools? Hint: See Example 3.

Challenge Questions

7. 55% of the students at the Peki Secondary School are girls. What is the fraction of the girls in the school?

8. A printer was sold at 25% off the original price. What is the fraction of the reduction of the price of the computer?

Answers to Selected Exercises

1. $\dfrac{1}{4}$ **2.** $\dfrac{1}{10}$ **3.** $\dfrac{3}{4}$

Express Fractions as Percents

Recall that we already discussed the grid at the beginning of this chapter (Percent). One square out of the 100 squares in the grid can be written as 1% and this can be expressed as $\dfrac{1}{100}$. This means that if we have a fraction such as $\dfrac{1}{100}$ and we want to change the fraction which is $\dfrac{1}{100}$ to a percent, we have to multiply the fraction by 100, and then attach the % sign.

$$\dfrac{1}{100} \times 100$$

$$= \dfrac{1}{\underset{1}{\cancel{100}}} \times \overset{1}{\cancel{100}} \qquad \text{Do the division.}$$

$$= 1\%$$

Rule: To express a fraction as a percent multiply the fraction by 100, and then attach the % sign to the answer.

Example 1

Express $\frac{1}{10}$ as a percent.

Solution

Using the rule express the fraction as a percent by multiplying the fraction by 100, and then attach the % sign to the answer.

$$\frac{1}{10} \text{ as a percent} = \frac{1}{10} \times 100$$

$$= \frac{\overset{10}{\cancel{100}}}{\underset{1}{\cancel{10}}} \quad \text{Reduce to the lowest term by dividing by 10.}$$

$$= 10\%$$

Example 2

Change $\frac{2}{15}$ to a percent.

Solution

Using the rule express the fraction as a percent by multiplying the fraction by 100, and then attach the % sign to the answer.

$$\frac{2}{15} \text{ as percent} = \frac{2}{15} \times 100$$

$$= \frac{2}{\underset{3}{\cancel{15}}} \times \overset{20}{\cancel{100}} \quad \text{Reduce to the lowest term by dividing by 5.}$$

$$= \frac{40}{3} = 13\frac{1}{3}\% \quad \text{Review the section on mixed numbers.}$$

Example 3

Change $\frac{3}{7}$ to a percent.

Solution

Using the rule express the fraction as a percent by multiplying the fraction by 100, and then attach the % sign to the answer.

$$\frac{3}{7} \text{ as a percent} = \frac{3}{7} \times 100$$

$$= \frac{300}{7}$$

$$= 42\frac{6}{7} \qquad \text{Review the section on Mixed Numbers.}$$

$$\frac{3}{7} \text{ as a percent} = 42\frac{6}{7}\%.$$

Exercises

1. Express the following fractions as percents. Hint: See Example 1.

    a) $\frac{1}{2}$ **b)** $\frac{1}{4}$ **c)** $\frac{1}{5}$ **d)** $\frac{1}{15}$ **e)** $\frac{1}{25}$ **f)** $\frac{1}{50}$

2. Express the following fractions as percents. Hint: See Example 2.

    a) $\frac{2}{5}$ **b)** $\frac{3}{10}$ **c)** $\frac{4}{5}$ **d)** $\frac{4}{15}$ **e)** $\frac{1}{25}$ **f)** $\frac{7}{25}$

3. Change the following fractions to percents. Hint: See Example 3.

    a). $\frac{2}{3}$ **b)**. $\frac{2}{7}$ **c)**. $\frac{2}{9}$ **d)**. $\frac{3}{8}$ **e)**. $\frac{3}{11}$ **f)**. $\frac{5}{12}$

Challenge Questions

4. Change the following fractions to percents.

    a) $\frac{4}{15}$ **b)**. $\frac{1}{3}$ **c)**. $\frac{1}{20}$ **d)**. $\frac{7}{30}$ **e)**. $\frac{7}{8}$ **f)**. $\frac{4}{9}$

Answers to Selected Exercises

    1(a) 50%   **1(b)** 25%   **2(a)** 40%   **2(b)** 30%

    3(a) $66\frac{2}{3}\%$ **3(b)** $28\frac{4}{7}\%$

REAL WORLD APPLICATIONS – WORD PROBLEMS
Express Fractions as Percents

Example 1

Given that $\frac{4}{5}$ of the students in a high school like soccer. What percent of the students like soccer?

Solution

Using the rule express the fraction as a percent by multiplying the fraction by 100, and then attach the % sign to the answer.

Percent of the student population = 100%

Percent of $\frac{4}{5}$ of the students like soccer = $\frac{4}{5}$ of 100%

$$= \frac{4}{5} \times 100\% \quad \text{"of" becomes a multiplication sign.}$$

$$= \frac{4}{\underset{1}{5}} \times \overset{20\%}{100\%} \quad \text{Divide by 5.}$$

$$= 4 \times 20\% = 80\%$$

Therefore, 80% of the students like soccer.

Example 2

A television set was reduced by $\frac{1}{5}$ off the regular price. What was the percent of reduction in the price?

Solution

Using the rule express the fraction as a percent by multiplying the fraction by 100, and then attach the % sign to the answer.

The percent of the original price of the television set = 100%

The percent of $\frac{1}{5}$ off the original price = $\frac{1}{5}$ of 100%

$$= \frac{1}{5} \times 100\% \quad \text{"of" becomes a multiplication sign.}$$

$$= \frac{1}{\underset{1}{5}} \times \overset{20}{100\%} \quad \text{Reduce to the lowest term by dividing by 5.}$$

$$= 20\%$$

The percent of reduction in the price = 20%

Exercises

1. Given that $\dfrac{1}{25}$ of the workers in a plant are engineers, what percent of the workers are engineers? Hint: See Example 1.

2. A computer set was reduced by $\dfrac{1}{15}$ off the regular price. What was the percentage of reduction in price? Hint: See Example 2.

Challenge Questions

3. In 1990, the population of the Peki High School was 950 students. In 1991, the students population increased by $\dfrac{1}{10}$.

    a. What is the increase of the population of the students in 1991?

      Hint: The increase of the population of the students $= \dfrac{1}{10} \times 950$

    b. What is the percent increase of the population of the students?

    c. What is the population of the students in 1991?

    Hint: Population of the students in 1991

                 = Population in 1990 + Increase in population.

4. A television set was increased by $\dfrac{3}{50}$ of the regular price. What was the percent increase in price?

Express Percent as a Decimal

Recall that we already discussed the grid at the beginning of this chapter (percent). One square out of the 100 squares in the grid can be written as 1% and this can be expressed as $\dfrac{1}{100}$. Recall from the chapter on decimal fractions that the fraction $\dfrac{1}{100}$ can be changed to a decimal by dividing 1 by 100 as shown:

$$100\overline{)1} = 100\overline{)100}\ \ \overset{.01}{}$$
$$-\underline{100}$$
$$000$$

Therefore, $1\% = \dfrac{1}{100} = .01$. Note that 1% is changed to the decimal fraction .01 by dividing 1 by 100 or simply moving the decimal point in the percent number two places or two digits to the left.

Decimal point

Write 0 here to hold the place value.

$1\% = .01 = .01$

Move the imaginary decimal point behind 1 two places or two digits to the left.

Note: There is an imaginary decimal point behind the last digit of all whole numbers. (Review the chapter on decimal fractions).

Rule: To express a percent as a decimal fraction, move the decimal point in the percent number two places or two digits to the left of the decimal point, and ignore the percent sign.

Example 1
Express 25.5% as a decimal fraction.
Solution
Using the rule, to express a percent as a decimal fraction, move the decimal point in the percent number two places or two digits to the left of the decimal point, and ignore the percent sign as shown:

$$25.5\% = 25.5 = .255$$

Move the decimal point two places or two digits to the left.

Therefore, 25.5% = .255

Example 2
Express 25% as a decimal fraction.
Solution
Using the rule, to express a percent as a decimal fraction, move the decimal point in the percent number two places or two digits to the left of the decimal point, and ignore the percent sign as shown:

$$25\% = .25 = .25$$

Move the imaginary decimal point behind 25 two places or two digits to the left.

Therefore, 25% = .25
Note: There is an imaginary decimal point behind the last digit of every whole number.

Example 3
Express 2.55% as a decimal fraction.

Solution

Using the rule, to express a percent as a decimal fraction, move the decimal point in the percent number two places or two digits to the left of the decimal point, and ignore the percent sign.

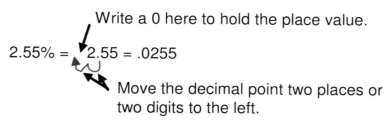

Write a 0 here to hold the place value.

2.55% = 2.55 = .0255

Move the decimal point two places or two digits to the left.

Therefore, 2.55% = .0255

Example 4

Express .255% as a decimal fraction.

Solution

Using the rule, to express a percent as a decimal fraction, move the decimal point in the percent number two places or two digits to the left of the decimal point, and ignore the percent sign.

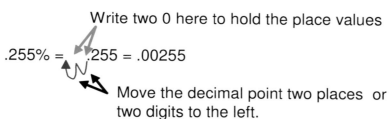

Write two 0 here to hold the place values

.255% = .255 = .00255

Move the decimal point two places or two digits to the left.

Therefore, .255% = .00255

Exercises

1. Express the following percents as decimals. Hint: See Example 1.

(a) 28.1%	(b) 95.5%	(c) 64.9%	(d) 75.5%	(e) 95.3%
(f) 12.4%	(g) 17.7%	(h) 55.6%	(i) 49.9%	(j) 99.9%
(k) 39.8%	(l) 16.6%	(m) 11.1%	(n) 36.7%	(o) 57.8%

2. Express the following percents as decimals. Hint: See Example 2.

(a) 26%	(b) 27%	(c) 99%	(d) 35%	(e) 64%
(f) 75%	(g) 38%	(h) 45%	(i) 17%	(j) 19%
(k) 11%	(l) 34%	(m) 17%	(n) 88%	(o) 96%

3. Express the following percents as decimals. Hint: See Example 3.

(a) 3.22%	(b) 4.45%	(c) 7.1%	(d) 9.61	(e) 1.1%
(f) 2.1%	(g) 9.9%	(h) 8.5%	(i) 6.25%	(j) 7.9%

4. Express the following percents as decimals. Hint: See Example 4.

(a) .234%	(b) .641%	(c) .111%	(d) .2%	(e) .12%
(f) .75%	(g) .35%	(h) .99%	(i) .1%	(j) .4%

Challenge Questions

5. Express the following percents as decimal fractions.

(**a**) 72%   (**b**) 33.4%   (**c**) .01%   (**d**) 1.71%   (**e**) .09%

(**f**) .3%   (**g**) 4.2%   (**h**) 13.1%   (**i**) 95%   (**j**) .88%

Answers to Selected Questions.

(**1**)(**a**) .281   **2**(**a**) .26   **3**(**a**) .0322   **4**(**a**) .00234

REAL WORLD APPLICATIONS – WORD PROBLEMS
PERCENT TO DECIMAL FRACTIONS

Example 1
Given that 12.32% of the items in a store are on sale, what decimal fraction of the items is on sale?

Solution

Using the rule to express a percent as a decimal fraction, move the decimal point in the percent number two places or two digits to the left of the decimal point, and ignore the percent sign.

$$12.32\% = 12.32 = .1232$$

Move the decimal point two places or two digits to the left.

The decimal fraction of the items on sale = .1232

Example 2
There are 7% of the boys at the Peki High School who work at the Peki Super Market. What is the decimal fraction of the boys that work at the Peki Super Market?

Solution

Using the rule to express a percent as a decimal fraction, move the decimal point in the percent number two places or two digits to the left of the decimal point, and ignore the percent sign.

Write a 0 here to hold the place value.

$$7\% = 7 = .07$$

Move the imaginary decimal point behind 7 to two places or two digits to the left.

Therefore, .07 is the decimal fraction of the boys.

Example 3

.64% of a certain concentration of orange drink is water. What is the decimal fraction of the concentration made of water?

Solution

Hint: Orange drink is made by mixing pure orange juice with water.

Using the rule to express a percent as a decimal fraction, move the decimal point in the percent number two places or two digits to the left of the decimal point, and ignore the percent sign.

Write two 0 here to hold the place value.

.64% = .64 = .0064

Move the decimal point two places or two digits to the left.

The decimal fraction of the concentration of the orange drink is .0064.

Exercises

1. Given that 17.2% of the computers in a certain store are on sale, what decimal fraction of the computers are on sale? Hint: See Example 1.
2. In a certain elementary school, 3% of the girls like soccer. What is the decimal fraction of the girls that like soccer? Hint: See Example 2.
3. The concentration of a certain orange drink is made up of .95% water. What is the decimal fraction of the concentration of water in the orange drink? Hint: See Example 3.

Challenge Questions

4. Given that the concentration of a certain drink is .5% water, what is the decimal fraction of the concentration of the water in the drink?
5. If 1% of the employees in a certain company prefer to take their vacation in the summer, what is the decimal fraction of the employees that prefer to take their vacation in the summer?
6. Mrs. Aggor went to the store to buy a shirt because 46.8% of the shirts were on sale. What is the decimal fraction of the shirts that are on sale?

Express Decimal Fractions as Percents

Note that expressing decimal fractions as percents is the opposite of expressing percents as decimal fractions, and therefore, the method of expressing decimal fractions as percents is the opposite of the method of expressing the percents as decimal fractions. Review the rule for expressing percents as decimal fractions in the preceding rule.

Rule: **To express decimal fractions as percent, move the decimal point two places or two digits to the right, and then attach the % sign.**

Example 1
Express .92 as a percent.
Solution
Using the rule to express decimal fractions as percents, move the decimal point two places or two digits to the right, and then attach the % sign.

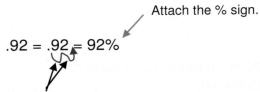

Attach the % sign.

$$.92 = .92 = 92\%$$

Move the decimal point two places or two digits to the right.

Therefore, .92 = 92%

Example 2
Change the following decimal fractions to percents:
(**a**) 1.87   (**b**) 1.8
Solution
(**a**). Using the rule to express decimal fractions as percents, move the decimal point two places or two digits to the right, and then attach the % sign:

Attach the % sign.

$$1.87 = 1.87 = 187\%$$

Move the decimal point two places or two digits to the right.

Therefore, 1.87 = 187%
(**b**). Using the rule to express decimal fractions as percents, move the decimal point two places or two digits to the right, and then attach the % sign.

Write a 0 here to hold the place value.

$$1.8 = 1.8 = 180\%$$ ◄──── Attach the % sign.

Move the decimal point two places or two digits to the right.

Example 3

Change the following decimal fractions to percents.

(a) .001   **(b)** .275   **(c)** 1.00

Solution

(a). Using the rule to express decimal fractions as percents, move the decimal point two places or two digits to the right, and then attach the % sign.

Attach the % sign.

.001 = .001 = .1%

Move the decimal point two places or two digits to the right.

Therefore, .001 = .1%

(b). Using the rule to express decimal fractions as percents, move the decimal point two places or two digits to the right, and then attach the % sign.

Attach the % sign.

.275 = .275 = 27.5%

Move the decimal point two places or two digits to the right.

Therefore, .275 = 27.5%

(c). Using the rule to express decimal fractions as percents, move the decimal point two places or two digits to the right, and then attach the % sign.

Attach the % sign.

1.00 = 1.00 = 100%

Move the decimal point two places or two digits to the right.

Therefore, 1.00 = 100%

Exercises

1. Change the following decimal fractions to percents. Hint: See Example **1**.
   (a) .79   **(b)** .34   **(c)** .07   **(d)** .12   **(e)** .11

2. Change the following decimal fractions to percents. Hint: See Example **2(a)**.
   (a) 2.94   **(b)** 9.99   **(c)** 3.40   **(d)** 7.75   **(e)** 1.25

3. Change the following decimal fractions to percents. Hint: See Example **3(a)**.
   (a) 3.9   **(b)** 9.9   **(c)** 28.1   **(d)** 44.6   **(e)** 7.8

4. Change the following decimal fractions to percents. Hint : See Example **3(a)**.
   (a) .002   **(b)** .009   **(c)** .004   **(d)** 2.001   **(e)** 10.002

5. Change the following decimal fractions to percents. Hint: See Example **3(b)**.
   (**a**) .298   (**b**) .444   (**c**) .891   (**d**) .658   (**e**) .481
6. Change the following decimal fractions to percents. Hint: See Example 3(c).
   (**a**) 9.00   (**b**) 6.00   (**c**) 4.00   (**d**) 8.00   (**e**) 2.00

Challenge questions
7. Express the following decimal fractions as percents.
   (**a**) .3   (**b**) 4.2   (**c**) 13.1   (**d**) 95   (**e**) .88
8. Express the following decimal fractions as percents.
   (**a**) 1.1   (**b**) .001   (**c**) 1.78   (**d**) 7.0   (**e**) .09
   (**f**) .90   (**g**) 3.0   (**h**) 1   (**i**) .21   (**j**) .01

Answers to Selected Exercises
1(a) 79%   **2(a)** 294%   **3(a)** 390%
4(a) 0.2%   **5(a)** 29.8%   **6(a)** 900%

REAL WORLD APPLICATIONS – WORD PROBLEMS
EXPRESS DECIMAL FRACTIONS AS PERCENTS

Example 1
Given that .65 of the students in a certain school are girls, what percent of the students are girls?
Solution
Using the rule to express decimal fractions as percents, move the decimal point two places or two digits to the right, and then attach the % sign.

Attach the % sign.

$$.65 = .65 = 65\%$$

Move the decimal point two places or two digits to the right.

The percent of the girls $= 65\%$.

Example 2
John will make 1.9 profit on his investment.
Express his profit as a percent.
Solution
Using the rule to express decimal fractions as percents, move the decimal point two places or two digits to the right, and then attach the % sign.

Write a 0 here to hold the place value.

$1.9 = 1.9 = 190\%$ ←——— Attach the % sign.

Move the decimal point two places or two digits to the right.

The percent profit = 190%.

Example 3

Given that .268 of the computers in a certain store were sold at a discount. What percent of the computers were sold at a discount ?

Solution

Using the rule to express decimal fractions as percents, move the decimal point two places or two digits to the right, and then attach the % sign:

Attach the % sign.

$.268 = .268 = 26.8\%$

Move the decimal point two places or two digits to the right.

The percent of the computers sold at a discount was 26.8%

Example 4

Given that .022 of the students in a certain class study history, what is the percent of the students that study history?

Solution

Using the rule, to express decimal fractions as percents, move the decimal point two places or two digits to the right, and then attach the % sign.

Attach the % sign.

$.022 = .022 = 2.2\%$

Move the decimal point two places or two digits to the right.

The percent of the students that study history is 2.2%

Exercises

1. Given that .75 of the students in a certain class are boys, what percent of the students are boys ? Hint: See Example 1.

2. Eric made .078 profit on his investment. What is his percent profit? Hint: See Example 2 .

3. Given that .289 of the people who go to the zoo are children, what percent of the people who go to the zoo are children? Hint: See Example 3.

4. Given that .501 of the students in a certain class study chemistry, what percent of the students study chemistry? Hint: See Example 4.

Challenge Questions
5. Given that .018 of the animals in a certain zoo are lions, what percent of the animals are lions?

6. Given that .684 of the books in a certain library involve science, what is the percent of the books that involves science?

Key Facts - Summary
a. To change a percent to a common fraction, put the percent number over 100 as a denominator, and then reduce to the lowest terms if possible.

b. To change a common fraction to decimal fraction, move the decimal point in the numerator two places or two digits to the left if the denominator is 100, otherwise, just divide the numerator by the denominator.

c. To change a decimal fraction to a common fraction, count the number of the decimal places or the number of digits after the decimal point and this number of decimal places or the number of digits after the decimal point is equal to the number of zeros which form the denominator of the common fraction, and the actual number of the decimal fraction becomes the numerator as shown:

(1) .5 has one decimal place or one digit after the decimal point, so the denominator has one zero and the denominator is 10 and the numerator is 5 and the common fraction is $\dfrac{5}{10}$.

(2) .05 has two decimal places or two digits after the decimal point, so the denominator has two zeros and the denominator is 100 and the numerator is 5 and the common fraction is $\dfrac{5}{100}$.

(3) .005 has three decimal places or three digits after the decimal point, so the denominator has three zeros and the denominator is 1000, and the numerator is 5 and the common fraction is $\dfrac{5}{1000}$.

(4) .523 has three decimal places or three digits after the decimal point, therefore the denominator has three zeros and the denominator is 1000 and the numerator is 523 and the common fraction is $\dfrac{523}{1000}$.

The table below summarizes how to change decimal fractions to common fractions.

Decimal Fraction	No. of decimal places	No. of zeros in denominator	Common fraction
.5	1	1	$\dfrac{5}{10}$
.05	2	2	$\dfrac{5}{100}$
.005	3	3	$\dfrac{5}{1,000}$
.523	3	3	$\dfrac{523}{1,000}$
.0931	4	4	$\dfrac{931}{10,000}$
.74895	5	5	$\dfrac{74895}{100,000}$

d. To change a common fraction to a percent, multiply the common fraction by 100, and then attach the % sign. For example,

$\dfrac{5}{100}$ is:

$$\dfrac{5}{100} \times 100$$

$$\dfrac{5}{\cancel{100}} \times \cancel{100}^{\,1} = 5\%$$

e. To change a percent to a decimal fraction, move the decimal point in the percent to two decimal places or two digits to the left, or just express the percent as a common fraction with 100 as the denominator and divide.

Exercises

1. Complete the table by filling in the columns for percents, fractions and decimal fractions. Hint: See examples in the sections under percents, fractions and decimals. See also the example in the second row of the table in this question.

Percents (%)	Fractions	Decimals or Decimal Fractions
5%	$\dfrac{5}{100}$	.05
65%		
16%		
	$\dfrac{17}{100}$	
	$\dfrac{73}{100}$	
		.008
		.08
		.8
2.1%		
.33%		

2. Complete the table by filling in the columns for decimal fractions, percents and fractions. Hint: See examples under the sections in decimal fractions, percents, common fractions, and also see the two examples in the second and the third rows of the table in this question.

> The table for Exercise 2 is on the next page.
>
> (Are you having fun with mathematics?)

490

Decimal fractions	Percent (%)	Common fractions
.8	$\frac{8}{10} \times 100 = 80\%$	$\frac{8}{10} = \frac{4}{5}$
.004	$\frac{4}{1000} \times 100 = .4\%$	$\frac{4}{1000} = \frac{1}{250}$
2.67		
85.8		
.561		
.018		
.o8		
.7		
9.49		
72.004		
.47		
.15		
$\frac{35}{100} = .35$	35%	$\frac{35}{100} = \frac{7}{20}$
	60%	
	160%	
	74.5%	
	9.8%	
	2%	
	13.11%	
12.5% = .125	$\frac{1}{8} \times 100 = 12.5\%$	$\frac{1}{8}$
		$\frac{272}{100}$
		$\frac{6}{12}$
		$\frac{9.7}{100}$
		$\frac{24\frac{1}{3}}{60}$
		$\frac{100}{100}$

3. Copy and complete the table by filling in the columns for common fractions,

491

decimal fractions, and percents. Hint: See separate examples under the sections on decimal fractions, percents, and common fractions.

Common fraction	Decimal fraction	%
$\frac{57}{100}$		
$\frac{8}{24}$		
$\frac{7}{9}$		
$\frac{9.7}{100}$		
$\frac{5645}{100}$		
$\frac{18}{65}$		
	.358	
	.019	
	75.45	
	38.01	
	3.2	
	.6	
		2.5%
		275%
		1%
		60%
		4700.8%
		26.15%

Understanding 100%

(**1**) 100% means $\frac{100}{100} = \frac{1}{1} = 1$. 100% therefore means one whole of anything or the total of anything.

(**2**) If 100% of the employees at a certain company are women, it means that no men work at the company.

(**3**) If 100% of the students in grade 5B are boys, it means that all the students in grade 5B are boys.

(**4**) If 100% of the students visited the zoo yesterday, it means that all the students visited the zoo.

Understanding Percent

(**1**) If 70% of the students in a certain school are girls, it means that 100% – 70% = 30% are boys since the whole student population should be 100%.

(**2**) If 55% of the doctors in a certain hospital are women, then the percent of the male doctors is 100% – 55% = 45% since the whole doctor population in the hospital should be 100%.

(**3**) If 5% of a class is absent, it means that 100% – 5% = 95% of the students are present since the whole class should be 100%.

REAL WORLD APPLICATIONS – WORD PROBLEMS
UNDERSTANDING PERCENT

Example 1

There are 48% of boys in a school. What is the percent of the girls?

Solution

The percent of the girls = 100% – 48% = 52%

Example 2

An advance school consists of students studying chemistry, physics and biology. A student may study only one subject. Given that 25% of the students study chemistry and 30% of the students study biology, what is the percent of the students that study physics?

Solution

Total student population = 100%

Percent of students that study chemistry and biology = 25% + 30% = 55%.

Percent of students that study physics = 100% – 55% = 45%.

Example 3

A school has 800 students. If 55% of the student population are boys,

(**a**) what is the percent of girls in the school?

(**b**) how many girls are in the school?

Solution

(**a**) Total student population = 100%

　　Percent of the boys　= 55%

　　Percent of the girls = 100% - 55% = 45%

(**b**) From solution (a), the percent of the girls = 45%

　　The number of the girls in the school = 45% of 800

$$= \frac{45}{100} \times 800 \qquad \text{Note: } 45\% = \frac{45}{100}, \text{ "of" is } \times.$$

$$= \frac{45}{\underset{1}{100}} \times \overset{8}{800} \qquad \text{Divide by 100.}$$

$$= 45 \times 8$$
$$= 360 \text{ girls}$$

Therefore, the number of the girls in the school is 360.

Example 4

A school has a population of 1,200 students. If 5 percent of the students are absent,
(**a**) what is the percent of the students present?
(**b**) what is the number of the students present?
(**c**) what is the number of the students absent?

Solution

(**a**) The percent of the whole student population $= 100\%$
    The percent of the students that are absent $= 5\%$
    The percent of the students that are present $= 100\% - 5\% = 95\%$

(**b**) From the solution of (**a**), the percent of the students that are present $= 95\%$
    Student population of the school $= 1,200$
    The number of the students present $= 95\%$ of the student population.
$$= 95\% \text{ of } 1,200$$
$$\downarrow \quad \downarrow \quad \downarrow$$
$$= \frac{95}{100} \times 1,200 \quad \text{Note: } 95\% = \frac{95}{100}, \text{ "of" is} \times.$$

$$= \frac{95}{\underset{1}{100}} \times \overset{12}{1,200} \qquad \text{Divide by 100.}$$

$$= 95 \times 12$$
$$= 1140 \text{ students.}$$

Therefore, 1140 students were present.

(**c**) The number of students absent
      $=$ Student population $-$ Number of students present.
      $= 1,200 - 1140$
      $= 60 \text{ students.}$

Therefore, 60 students were absent.

Fractional Parts of Percents

The fractional part of a percent such as $\frac{1}{5}$% means $\frac{1}{5}$ out of 100. Recall that,

for example, 2% means 2 out of 100. Recall that $2\% = \frac{2}{100}$ and therefore $\frac{1}{5}\% = \frac{\frac{1}{5}}{100}$.

Rule: To express a fraction of a percent as a decimal fraction, write the fraction over 100 and then divide, ignoring the % sign.

Example 1

Express $\frac{1}{5}$% as a decimal fraction

Solution

Using the rule to express a fraction of a percent as a decimal fraction, write the fraction over 100 and then divide, ignoring the % sign.

$$\frac{1}{5}\% = \frac{\frac{1}{5}}{100}$$

$$= \frac{\frac{1}{5}}{\frac{100}{1}} \qquad \text{Change 100 to a fraction by writing 100 as } \frac{100}{1} = 100.$$

$$= \frac{1}{5} \times \frac{1}{100} \qquad \text{Recall that to divide a fraction by another fraction, the}$$

top fraction $(\frac{1}{5})$ is multiplied by the inverted bottom

fraction $(\frac{1}{100})$. The inverted bottom fraction is called the

reciprocal.

$$= \frac{1 \times 1}{5 \times 100} = \frac{1}{500}$$

$$500\overline{)1} \quad = 500\overline{)1.000} \begin{array}{r} .002 \\ \phantom{500\overline{)}} \\ -\underline{1000} \\ 0000 \end{array}$$

(Review the chapter on dividing a smaller number by a bigger number).

Therefore, $\frac{1}{5}\% = .002$

Example 2

Change $\frac{6}{8}$% to a decimal fraction.

Solution

Using the rule to express a fraction of a percent as a decimal fraction, write the fraction over 100, and then divide, ignoring the % sign.

$$\frac{6}{8}\% = \frac{\frac{6}{8}}{100}$$

$$= \frac{\frac{6}{8}}{\frac{100}{1}} \qquad \text{Change 100 to a fraction by writing 100 as } \frac{100}{1} = 100.$$

$$= \frac{6}{8} \times \frac{1}{100} \qquad \text{Recall that to divide a fraction by another fraction, the top}$$

fraction ($\frac{6}{8}$) is multiplied by the inverted bottom

fraction ($\frac{1}{100}$). The inverted bottom fraction is called the

reciprocal.

$$= \frac{\overset{3}{6}}{\underset{4}{8}} \times \frac{1}{100} \qquad \text{Divide the numerator and the denominator by 2.}$$

$$= \frac{3}{4} \times \frac{1}{100} = \frac{3 \times 1}{4 \times 100} = \frac{3}{400}$$

$$400\overline{)3} = 400\overline{)3.0000} \quad \begin{array}{r} .0075 \\ \hline \end{array}$$
$$\begin{array}{r} -2800\!\downarrow \\ \hline 2000 \\ -2000 \\ \hline 0000 \end{array}$$

(Review the chapter on dividing a smaller number by a bigger number).

Therefore, $\frac{6}{8}\% = .0075$

Example 3

Change $2\frac{1}{2}\%$ to decimal fraction.

Solution

Using the rule to express a fraction of a percent as a decimal fraction, write the fraction over 100, and then divide, ignoring the % sign.

$$2\frac{1}{2}\% = \frac{2\frac{1}{2}}{100}$$

$$= \frac{\frac{5}{2}}{100} \qquad \text{Change } 2\frac{1}{2} \text{ to an improper fraction of } \frac{5}{2}.$$

$$= \frac{\frac{5}{2}}{\frac{100}{1}} \qquad \text{Change 100 to a fraction by writing 100 as } \frac{100}{1} = 100.$$

$$= \frac{5}{2} \times \frac{1}{100} \qquad \text{Recall that to divide a fraction by another fraction,}$$

$$\text{the top fraction } (\frac{5}{2}) \text{ is multiplied by the inverted}$$

$$\text{bottom fraction } (\frac{1}{100}), \text{ which is the reciprocal.}$$

$$= \frac{\overset{1}{\cancel{5}}}{2} \times \frac{1}{\underset{20}{\cancel{100}}} \qquad \text{Divide numerator and denominator by 5.}$$

$$= \frac{1}{2} \times \frac{1}{20} = \frac{1 \times 1}{2 \times 20} = \frac{1}{40}$$

$$40\overline{)1} \quad = \quad 40\overline{)1.000} \begin{array}{l} .025 \\ \underline{-80}\downarrow \\ 200 \\ \underline{-200} \\ 000 \end{array}$$

(Review the chapter on dividing a smaller number by a bigger number.)

Therefore, $2\frac{1}{2}\% = .025$

Exercises

1. Express the following fractions of percents as decimals. Round your answer to 3 decimal places. Hint: See Example 1.

(a) $\frac{1}{2}\%$ (b) $\frac{1}{4}\%$ (c) $\frac{1}{3}\%$ (d) $\frac{1}{10}\%$ (e) $\frac{1}{12}\%$

(f) $\frac{1}{7}\%$ (g) $\frac{1}{9}\%$ (h) $\frac{1}{15}\%$ (i) $\frac{1}{11}\%$ (j) $\frac{1}{20}\%$

2. Change the following fractions of percents to decimals. Round your answer to 3 decimal places. Hint: See Example 2.

(a) $\frac{2}{10}\%$ (b) $\frac{2}{5}\%$ (c) $\frac{3}{7}\%$ (d) $\frac{2}{7}\%$ (e) $\frac{3}{5}\%$

(f) $\frac{3}{5}\%$ (g) $\frac{3}{11}\%$ (h) $\frac{4}{15}\%$ (i) $\frac{5}{8}\%$ (j) $\frac{9}{10}\%$

3. Change the following mixed numbers of percents to decimals. Round your answer to 3 decimal places, Hint: See Example 3.

(a) $2\frac{1}{4}\%$ (b) $1\frac{1}{2}\%$ (c) $2\frac{2}{5}\%$ (d) $1\frac{3}{5}\%$ (e) $4\frac{3}{4}\%$

(f) $5\frac{2}{5}\%$ (g) $6\frac{5}{6}\%$ (h) $10\frac{2}{3}\%$ (i) $8\frac{2}{5}\%$ (j) $3\frac{3}{4}\%$

Challenge Questions

4. Change the following mixed numbers and fractions from percents to decimals.

(a) $2\frac{3}{4}\%$ (b) $\frac{1}{6}\%$ (c) $\frac{2}{9}\%$ (d) $2\frac{3}{5}\%$ (e) $\frac{1}{10}\%$

(f) $\frac{3}{8}\%$ (g) $5\frac{5}{6}\%$ (h) $\frac{1}{8}\%$ (i) $7\frac{1}{7}\%$ (j) $\frac{5}{7}\%$

Answers to Selected Exercises

1(a) 0.005   **2(a)** 0.002   **3(a)** 0.023

REAL WORLD APPLICATIONS - WORD PROBLEMS
EXPRESS FRACTIONS OF PERCENTS AS DECIMALS

Example 1

Given that $\frac{3}{4}\%$ of the goods in a certain store are on sale, what is the decimal fraction of the goods that are on sale?

Solution

Using the rule, to express a fraction of a percent as a decimal fraction, write the fraction over 100, and then divide, ignoring the % sign.

$$\frac{3}{4}\% = \frac{\frac{3}{4}}{100}$$

$$= \frac{\frac{3}{4}}{\frac{100}{1}} \qquad \text{Change 100 to a fraction by writing 100 as } \frac{100}{1} = 100.$$

$$= \frac{3}{4} \times \frac{1}{100} \qquad \text{Recall that to divide a fraction by another fraction, the top fraction } (\frac{3}{4}) \text{ is multiplied by the inverted bottom fraction } (\frac{1}{100}). \text{ The inverted bottom fraction is called the reciprocal.}$$

$$= \frac{3 \times 1}{4 \times 100} = \frac{3}{400}$$

$$400\overline{)3} = 400\overline{)3.0000} \\ \quad\quad\quad\; .0075$$
$$\quad\quad -2800 \\ \quad\quad\quad 2000 \\ \quad\quad -2000 \\ \quad\quad\quad 0000$$

(Review the chapter on dividing a smaller number by a bigger number).

Therefore, $\frac{3}{4}\% = .0075$.

Example 2

Agbeko Fish Pond has a lot of fish. Mr. Johnson owns $22\frac{1}{2}$% of the fish in the pond. What is the decimal fraction of the fish that is owned by Mr. Johnson?

Solution

Using the rule, to express a fraction of a percent as a decimal fraction, write the fraction over 100, and then divide, ignoring the % sign.

$$22\frac{1}{2}\% = \frac{22\frac{1}{2}}{100}$$

$$= \frac{\frac{45}{2}}{100} \qquad \text{Change } 22\frac{1}{2} \text{ to an improper fraction } (\frac{45}{2}).$$

$$= \frac{\frac{45}{2}}{\frac{100}{1}} \qquad \text{Change 100 to fraction by writing 100 as } \frac{100}{1} = 100.$$

$$= \frac{45}{2} \div \frac{100}{1} \qquad \text{Review Division of Fractions.}$$

$$= \frac{45}{2} \times \frac{1}{100} \qquad \text{Recall that to divide a fraction by another fraction,}$$

the top fraction is multiplied by the inverted

bottom fraction $(\frac{1}{100})$. The inverted bottom fraction

is called the reciprocal.

$$= \frac{\overset{9}{\cancel{45}}}{2} \times \frac{1}{\underset{20}{\cancel{100}}} \qquad \text{Divide the numerator and the denominator by 5.}$$

$$= \frac{9 \times 1}{2 \times 20} = \frac{9}{40}$$

$$40\overline{)9} \quad = \quad 40\overline{)9.000}$$

(division work shown: .225 quotient, with subtractions of 80, 100, −80, 200, −200, 000)

(Review the chapter on dividing a smaller number by a bigger number).

Therefore, $22\frac{1}{2}\% = .225$.

Exercises

1. A bank rate was increased by $\frac{3}{10}\%$, what is the decimal fraction of the increase? Hint: See Example 1.

2. The population of a certain country increased by $8\frac{1}{3}\%$ last year. What is the decimal fraction of the increase? Hint: See Example 2.

Challenge Questions.

3. Eric's academic performance has improved by $5\frac{1}{3}\%$. What is the decimal fraction of his improvement?

4. The number of books at the library has been reduced by $\frac{7}{10}\%$. What is the decimal fraction of the reduction of the books?

FRACTIONAL PARTS OF PERCENTS - Alternative Method

The preceding sections show how to change the fractional parts of percents to decimals. This section shows an alternative method of changing the fractional parts of percents to decimals.

Rule: To express a fraction of a percent as a decimal, change the common fraction to a decimal fraction by dividing the numerator by the denominator, and then dividing the result by 100 by moving the decimal point two places or digits to the left and then ignore the % sign.

Example 1

Express $\frac{2}{5}\%$ as a decimal.

Solution

Use the rule which states, to express a fraction of a percent as a decimal, change the common fraction to a decimal fraction by dividing the numerator by the denominator, and then divide the result by 100 by moving the decimal point two places or two digits to the left, and then ignore the % sign.

Step 1: Change the common fraction to a decimal fraction by dividing the numerator by the denominator.

$$\frac{2}{5} = 5\overline{\smash{)}2.0} \quad \begin{array}{r} .4 \\ -20 \\ \hline 00 \end{array}$$

$$\frac{2}{5}\% = .4\%$$

Step 2: Divide the result in Step 1 by 100 by moving the decimal point two places or two digits to the left.

Write two 0 here to hold the place value.

$$.4\% = \frac{.4}{100} = .4 = .004$$

Move the decimal point two places or two digits to the left.

Therefore, $\frac{2}{5}\% = .004$

Exercises
Use the preceding alternative method in Example 1 for "changing a fractional part of a percent to a decimal" to solve the exercises under the section, "Fractional Parts of Percent."

Find the Percent of a Number
Rule 1: **To find the percent of a number, multiply the given percent by the given number.**

Example 1
Find 5% of 80
Solution
Using the rule to find the percent of a number, multiply the given percent by the given number.

$$5\% \text{ of } 80 = 5\% \times 80 \qquad \textbf{Note}: \text{"of" means to multiply.}$$

$$= \frac{5}{100} \times 80 \qquad \textbf{Note}: 5\% = \frac{5}{100}.$$

$$= \frac{\overset{1}{\cancel{5}}}{\underset{20}{\cancel{100}}} \times 80 \qquad \text{Divide by 5.}$$

$$= \frac{1}{\underset{1}{\cancel{20}}} \times \overset{4}{\cancel{80}} \qquad \text{Divide by 20.}$$

$$= \frac{4}{1} = 4$$

Therefore, 5% of 80 = 4

Rule 2: **To find the percent of a number, change the percent to a decimal fraction and then multiply the decimal fraction equivalent of the percent by the number.**

Note: Rule 2 is an alternative method of finding the percent of a number.

Example 2
Find 5% of 80. Hint: Use Rule 2 in solving this problem. This problem is the same as Example 1.
Solution
Using Rule 2 to find the percent of a number, change the percent to a decimal fraction, and then multiply the decimal fraction equivalent of the percent by the number as shown:
Step 1: Change the percent to a decimal fraction.

Write a 0 here as a place holder.

$$5\% = \frac{5}{100} = .05$$

Move the imaginary decimal point behind 5 two places or two digits to the left.

Note: There is an imaginary decimal point behind the last digit of any whole number. (Review the chapter on Decimals).
Step 2: Multiply the decimal fraction equivalent of the percent by the number as shown:

$$\begin{array}{r} 80 \\ \times\ \underline{.05} \\ 400 \\ +\ \underline{000} \leftarrow \\ 4.00 \end{array}$$ Review Decimal Multiplication.

Write this 0 as a place holder.

Therefore, 5% of 80 is 4.

Note that the methods used in Example 1 and 2 give the same answer of 4.

Example 3

What is 1.7% of $50?

Solution

Using Rule 2 to find the percent of a number, change the percent to a decimal fraction, and then multiply the decimal fraction equivalent of the percent by the number as shown:

Step 1: Change the percent to a decimal fraction.

Write a 0 here as a place holder.

$$1.7\% = \frac{1.7}{100} = 1.7 = .017$$

Move the decimal point two places or .

Step 2: Multiply the decimal fraction equivalent of the percent by the number ($50) as shown:

$$\begin{array}{r} \$50 \times \\ \underline{.017} \\ 350 \\ 500 \leftarrow \\ +\ \underline{0000} \leftarrow \\ 0.850 \end{array}$$

Write a 0 here as a place holder.

Write two 0s here as a place holder

Move the decimal point three decimal places or 3 digits to the left. Review Decimal Multiplication.

Therefore, 1.7% of $50 is $.85

Example 4

Find $6\frac{1}{4}\%$ of $28.14.

Solution

Using Rule 2 to find the percent of a number, change the percent to a decimal fraction, and then multiply the decimal fraction equivalent of the percent by the number as shown:

Step 1: Change the percent to a decimal fraction.

$$\frac{1}{4} = 4\overline{)1} = 4\overline{)1.00}$$

Write a 0 here as a place holder.
↓

$$6\frac{1}{4}\% = \frac{6\frac{1}{4}}{100} = \frac{6.25}{100} = .\ 6.25 = .0625 \qquad \text{Note: } 6\frac{1}{4} = 6.25$$

↑

Move the decimal point two decimal places
or two digits to the left.

Step 2: Multiply the decimal fraction equivalent of the percent by the number ($28.14) as shown:

$$
\begin{array}{r}
\$28.14 \\
\times\ .0625 \\
\hline
14070 \\
56280 \\
+\ 1688400 \\
\hline
1.758750
\end{array}
$$

← Write a 0 here as a place holder.
← Write two 0s here as a place holder.

↑

Move the decimal point 6 decimal places or 6 digits
to the left.

Therefore, $6\frac{1}{4}$ of $28.14 is $1.76 to the nearest hundredths or cent.

Exercises

1. Find 7% of the following numbers. Hint: See Example 1. Give your answer to three decimal places.

(**a**) 160   (**b**) 16.4   (**c**) 58.2   (**d**) 142.1

2. Find 15% of the following numbers. Hint: See Example 2. Give your answer to 3 decimal places.

(**a**) 35   (**b**) 46.2   (**c**) 10   (**d**) 242

3. Find 26% of the following numbers. Hint See Example 2. Give your answer to 3 decimal places.

(**a**) 24 (**b**) 78.51 (**c**) .01 (**d**) .8

4. Find 3.8% of the following amounts. Hint: See Example 3.
   (**a**) $70 (**b**) $75 (**c**) $115 (**d**) $275

5. Find 35.8% of the following amounts. Hint: See Example 3.
   (**a**) $48 (**b**) $12 (**c**) 28 (**d**) $36

6. Find $8\frac{1}{2}$% of the following amounts. Hint: See Example 4.

   (**a**) $50.25 (**b**) $12.78 (**c**) $78.17 (**d**) 124.48

7. Find $16\frac{1}{4}$% of the following amounts. Hint: See Example 4.

   (**a**) $24.25 (**b**) 47.34 (**c**) $66.48 (**d**) $164.28

8. Find $12\frac{1}{5}$% of the following numbers. Hint: See Example 4. Give your answer

   to 3 decimal places.
   (**a**) 72 (**b**) 36.3 (**c**) 46.32 (**d**) 147.18

Challenge Questions

9. Find $\frac{1}{4}$% of 100. Hint : Review the section on "fractional parts of percent." Give

   your answer to 3 decimal places.

10. Find .8% of 64.12. Hint: Review the section on "Fractional parts of percentages."
    Round your answer to 3 decimal places.

11. Find 7.8% of $36.87.

12. Find 8% of 1348. Round your answer to 3 decimal places.

13. Find $\frac{4}{5}$% of 125. Hint: Review the section on "Fractional parts of percentages."

    Round your answer to 3 decimal places.

14. Find $24\frac{1}{4}$% of $78.36

Answers to Selected Questions

1(a) 11.200 **4(a)** $2.66 **6(a)** $4.27

REAL WORLD APPLICATIONS – WORD PROBLEMS
To Find the Percent of a Number

Example 1
There are 20 students in a class. If 45% of the students are boys, how many boys are in the class?
Solution

Using Rule 2 to find the percent of a number, change the percent to a decimal fraction, and then multiply the decimal fraction equivalent of the percent by the number as follows:

Step 1: Change the percent to a decimal fraction

$$45\% = \frac{45}{100} = .45 = .45$$

↑
Move the imaginary decimal point
2 decimal places to the left.

Step 2: Multiply the decimal fraction equivalent of the percent by the number (20) as shown:

$$
\begin{array}{r}
20 \\
\times\ .45 \\
\hline
100 \\
+\ 800 \\
\hline
9.00
\end{array}
$$
← Write a 0 here as a place holder.

↑
Move the decimal point two decimal or
two digits to the left. Review the section on decimal multiplication.

The number of boys in the class is 9.

Example 2

An employee earns $9\frac{1}{2}$% commission. What is the commission earned on a sale of $3,580.28?

Solution

Using Rule 2 to find the percent of a number, change the percent to a decimal fraction, and then multiply the decimal fraction equivalent of the percent by the number as shown:

Step 1: Change the percent to a decimal fraction.

Need to fill this digit position with
a zero as a place holder.
↓

$$9\frac{1}{2}\% = 9.5\% = \frac{9.5}{100} = 9.5 = .095$$

↑↑
Move the decimal point two decimal places or two digits
to the left.

Step 2: Multiply the decimal fraction equivalent of the percent by the number (3,580.28) as shown:

$$\begin{array}{r}
\$3{,}580.28 \\
\times \quad\quad .095 \\
\hline
1790140 \\
32222520 \\
+\ 00000000 \\
\hline
\$340.12660
\end{array}$$

← Write a 0 here as a place holder
← Write two 0s here as place holders

Move the decimal point 5 places to the left.
Review the section on Decimal Multiplication.

Therefore $9\frac{1}{2}$% of $3,580.28 is $340.13 to the nearest cent.

Example 3

George's salary was $45,200. If his salary is increased by 12%,
(**a**) what is the increase in his salary?
(**b**) what is his new salary?

Solution

Using Rule 2 to find the percent of a number, change the percent to a decimal fraction, and then multiply the decimal fraction equivalent of the percent by the number as shown:

(**a**) **Step 1**: Change the percent to a decimal fraction.

$$12\% = \frac{12}{100} = .12 = .12$$

Move the decimal point two decimal or
two digits to the left.

Step 2: Multiply the decimal fraction equivalent of the percent by the number (45,200) as shown:

$$\begin{array}{r}
\$45{,}200 \\
\times \quad\quad .12 \\
\hline
90400 \\
+\ 452000 \\
\hline
\$5424.00
\end{array}$$

← Write a 0 here as a place holder.

Move the decimal point two
places or digits to the left.

Therefore, the increase in George's salary is $5424.00

(b) George's new salary = current salary + Increase in salary
$$= \$45,200.00 + \$5,424.00$$
$$= \$50,624.00$$

Example 4

Mr. Benson needs a 15% down payment on a new house. If the new house costs $200,000, how much of a down payment does Mr. Benson need?

Solution

Using Rule 2 to find the percent of a number, change the percent to a decimal fraction, and then multiply the decimal fraction equivalent of the percent by the number.

Step 1: Change the percent to a decimal fraction.

$$15\% = \frac{15}{100} = .15 = .15$$

$\uparrow\uparrow$

Move the decimal point two decimal places or two digits to the left.

Step 2: Multiply the decimal fraction equivalent of the percent by the number (200,000).

```
        $200,000
   ×          .15
        1000000
    +   2000000   ← Write a 0 here as a place holder
      $30,000.00
```
$\uparrow\uparrow$

Move two decimal places or two digits to the left.

Therefore, the down payment is $30,000.00.

Exercises

1. In a school, 55% of the students are boys. If there are 500 students in the school,
   (**a**) how many boys are in the school?
   (**b**) how many girls are in the school? Hint: See Example 1.

2. An employee earns $13\frac{1}{4}\%$ commission. What is the commission earned on a sale of $6,258? Hint: See Example 2.

3. Ama's salary was $55,436.19. If her salary is increased by 5%,
   (**a**) what is the increase in her salary?
   (**b**) what is her new salary?
   Hint: See Example 3.

4. Seth bought a new house for $175,000. If he paid 8% down payment on the new

house, how much did he pay for the new house? Hint: See Example 4.

Challenge Questions

1. Mr. Albert has to pay 14% down payment on a new house. If the new house cost $225,000, what is the down payment of Mr. Albert?

2. Elizabeth's current salary is increased by $12\frac{1}{2}\%$. If her current salary is $55,200.78, what is the increment in her salary?

3. An employee earns $8\frac{1}{2}\%$ commission. What is the commission earned on a sale of $3,648.37?

4. The population of a school is 650 students. If 40% of the students are girls,
   (**a**) how many girls are in the school?
   (**b**) how many boys are in the school?

Percent of One Number Compared to Another Number

In mathematics, it is possible to find what percent a number is of another number, and this is really a ratio expressed in percent.

Rule: To find what percent a number is of another number, divide the first number by the second number, and then move the decimal point two places or two digits to the right in the quotient, and then attach the % sign.

Special note: Some students who may find it difficult in setting up the solution of the percent problems can use the "is of" ($\frac{is}{of}$) method. The facts in the rule can be stated as "a number is what percent of another number?", and this can be expressed generally as:

$$\frac{is}{of} = \frac{a\ number}{another\ number}$$

Example 1

Express 3 as a percent of 5.

Solution

The facts in the question can be stated as: "3 **is** what percent **of** 5?" and this can be expressed as:

$$\frac{is}{of} = \frac{3}{5}$$

Using the rule to find what percent of a number is of another number, divide 3 by 5 and then move the decimal point two places or two digits to the right in the quotient, and then attach the % sign.

Step 1: Divide the first number by the second number as shown:

$$\frac{3}{5} = 5\overline{\smash{)}3} = 5\overline{\smash{)}3.0} \quad \begin{array}{r} .6 \\ -30 \\ \hline 00 \end{array}$$

Step 2: Change the .6 to a percent by moving the decimal point two places or two digits to the right, and then adding the percent sign, which is the same as multiplying .6 by 100.

Write a 0 here as a place holder.
↓
.6 = .6 = 60%
↑↑

Move the decimal point two places or two digits to the right.
(Review the chapter on decimal fraction and percent.)
Therefore, 3 is 60% of 5.

Example 2

Express the ratio 2 out of 10 as a percent to the nearest whole number.
Solution
The facts in the question can be stated as: "2 **is** what percent **of** 10?" and this can be expressed as:

$$\frac{\text{is}}{\text{of}} = \frac{2}{10}$$

Using the rule to find what percent a number is of another number, divide 2 by 10, and then move the decimal point two places or two digits to the right in the quotient, and then attach the % sign.

Step 1: " 2 out of 10 " is $\frac{2}{10}$ or simply divide 2 by 10.

$$\frac{2}{10} = 10\overline{\smash{)}2} = 10\overline{\smash{)}2.0} \quad \begin{array}{r} .2 \\ -20 \\ \hline 00 \end{array}$$

Step 2: Change .2 to a percent by moving the decimal point two places or two digits to the right, and then attach the percent sign.

Write a 0 here as a place holder.

.2 = .2 = 20%

Move the decimal point two places or two digits to the right.

Therefore, 2 is 20% of 10.

Exercises. Round all answers to the nearest whole number.
1. Express the following ratios as percents. Hint: See Example 2.

(**a**) 1 out of 5	(**b**) 3 out of 10	(**c**) 3 out of 20
(**d**) 4 out of 12	(**e**) 3 out of 9	(**f**) 2 out of 8
(**g**) 2 out of 20	(**h**) 4 out of 100	(**i**) 20 out of 50
(**j**) 12 out of 60	(**k**) 3 out of 15	(**l**) 8 out of 64

2. Express 2 as a percent of 8. Hint: See Example 1.
3. Express 10 as a percent of 100. Hint: See Example 1.
4. Express 5 as a percent of 25. Hint: See Example 1.
5. Express 6 as a percent of 24. Hint: See Example 1.
6. Express 40 as a percent of 90. Hint: See Example 1.
7. 15 is what percent of 125? Hint: See Example 1.

Challenge Questions
8. Express the following ratios as percents. Round your answers to the nearest whole number.

(**a**) 25 out of 75	(**b**) 5 out of 65	(**c**) 6 out of 36
(**d**) 35 out of 100	(**e**) 15 out of 100	(**f**) 50 out of 150

9. 25 is what percent of 125? Round your answer to the nearest whole number.
10. Express 4 as a percent of 48. Round your answer to the nearest whole number.

REAL WORLD APPLICATIONS – WORD PROBLEMS
Percent of One Number Compared to Another Number

Example 1
There are 8 girls and 12 boys in a class. What percent of the class is boys?
Solution
Total number of the students = 8 + 12 = 20 students.
The facts in the question can be stated as: "12 **is** what percent **of** 20?" and this can be expressed as:
$$\frac{is}{of} = \frac{12}{20}$$
Using the rule to find what percent a number is of another number, divide the number of boys by the total number of the students, and then move the decimal point two places or two digits to the right in the quotient, and then attach the % sign.
Step 1: Divide the number of boys by the total number of students as shown:

$$\frac{\text{Number of boys}}{\text{Total number of students}} = \frac{12}{20}$$

$$= \frac{\overset{3}{\cancel{12}}}{\underset{5}{\cancel{20}}} \qquad \text{Reduce to the lowest term by dividing by 4.}$$

$$= \frac{3}{5}$$

$$\frac{3}{5} = 5\overline{)3} = 5\overline{)3.0} \atop \begin{array}{r} .6 \\ \hline -30 \\ \hline 0 \end{array}$$

Step 2: Change .6 to a percent by moving the decimal point 2 places to the right and then attach the percent sign which is the same as multiplying by 100.

Write a 0 here as a place holder.

.6 = .6 = 60%

Move the decimal point two places or two digits to the right.

Therefore, 60% of the class are boys.

Example 2
In a class of 24 students, 8 students like biology. What is the percent of the students that like biology?

Solution

The facts in the question can be stated as: "8 **is** what percent **of** 24?" and this can be expressed as:

$$\frac{\text{is}}{\text{of}} = \frac{8}{24}$$

Using the rule to find what percent a number is of another number, divide the number of students that like biology by the total number of the students, and then move the decimal point two places or two digits to the right in the quotient, and then attach the % sign.

Step1: Divide the number of students who like biology by the total number of students as shown:

$$\frac{\text{Number of students that like biology}}{\text{Total number of students}} = \frac{8}{24}$$

513

$$= \frac{\overset{1}{\cancel{8}}}{\underset{3}{\cancel{24}}}$$ Reduce to the lowest term by dividing by 8.

$$= \frac{1}{3}$$

$$\frac{1}{3} = 3\overline{)1} = 3\overline{)1.000} \quad .333$$

Step 2: Change .333 to a percent by moving the decimal point 2 places to the right and then attach the percent sign as shown:

$$.333 = .333 = 33.3\%$$

Move the decimal point two places or two digits to the right.

Therefore, 33.3% of the students like biology.

Example 3

Judith earned $10.25 for baby-sitting. If she spent $2.50, what percent of the money did she spend?

Solution

The facts in the question can be stated as: "$2.50 **is** what percent **of** $10.25?" and this can be expressed as:

$$\frac{\text{is}}{\text{of}} = \frac{\$2.50}{\$10.25}$$

Using the rule to find what percent a number is of another number, divide the amount spent by the total amount earned, and then move the decimal point two places or two digits to the right in the quotient, and then attach the % sign.

Step 1: Divide the amount that she spent by the total amount that she earned.

$$\frac{\text{Amount spent}}{\text{Total amount earned}} = \frac{\$2.50}{\$10.25}$$

$$= .244 \quad \text{You may use a calculator to divide.}$$

Step 2: Change .244 to a percent by moving the decimal point two places to the right, and then adding the percent sign.

$$.244 = .244 = 24.4\%$$

Move the decimal point two places or two digits to the right.

Therefore, Judith spent 24.4% of her money.

Example 4

Helen earned $25,600 last year. If she saved $5,000, what percent of her income did she save?

Solution

The facts in the question can be stated as: "$5,000 **is** what percent **of** $25,600?" and this can be expressed as:

$$\frac{\text{is}}{\text{of}} = \frac{\$5,000}{\$25,600}$$

Using the rule to find what percent a number is of another number, divide the amount saved by the total amount earned, and then move the decimal point two places or two digits to the right in the quotient, and then attach the % sign.

Step 1: Divide the amount saved by the total amount earned.

$$\frac{\text{Amount saved}}{\text{Total Amount earned}} = \frac{\$5,000}{25,600}$$

$$= .195 \qquad \text{You may use a calculator to divide.}$$

Step 2: Change .195 to a percent by moving the decimal point two places to the right, and then attach the % sign.

$$.195 = .195 = 19.5\%$$

Move the decimal point two places or two digits to the right.

Therefore, Helen saved 19.5% of what she earned last year.

Exercises

1. There are 10 boys and 15 girls in a certain class. What is the percent of the girls in the class? Hint: See Example 1.
2. In a class of 30 students, 5 of them like Chemistry. What is the percent of the students that like chemistry? Hint: See Example 2.
3. George earned $15 for baby-sitting. If he spent $5, what is the percent of the money that he spent? Hint: See Example 3.

515

4. If Hope made a down payment of $12 on a television set that cost $224, what is the percent of her down payment? Hint: See Example 4.

Challenge Questions
5. If Grace earned $8 for baby-sitting and she spent $2.50 of it, what is the percent of the money that she spent?
6. Robert made a down payment of $20 on a computer that cost $350. What is the percent of his down payment?
7. There are 26 students in a class. If 10 of the students like history, what is the percent of the students that like history?
8. A certain class consists of 6 girls and 14 boys. What percent of the class is boys?

Cumulative Review
1. Find: (Round your answer to 2 decimal places).
  (**a**) 2 out of 125   (**b**) 5% of 100   (**c**) 15% of 52.50
2. Change each percent to a decimal. Round the answer to 2 decimal places.
  (**a**) 1%   (**b**) $8\frac{1}{2}$%   (**c**) 120%
  (**d**) 15%   (**e**) 12%   (**f**) 45%
3. Write the following ratios as percents. Round your answer to 2 decimal places.
  (**a**) 2 out of 5   (**b**) 9 out of 10   (**c**) 8 out of 20
  (**d**) 7 out of 49   (**e**) 15 out of 125   (**f**) 3 out of 12
4. Change each decimal to a percent. Round your answer to 2 decimal places.
  (**a**) .5   (**b**) .48   (**c**) .34
  (**d**) 4.98   (**e**) .08   (**f**) .002
  (**g**) .7   (**h**) 1.25   (**i**) .041
5. Change the following to decimal fractions. Round off each answer to the nearest hundredth.
  (**a**) $\frac{1}{5}$ (**b**) $\frac{9}{10}$ (**c**) $\frac{4}{7}$ (**d**) $\frac{3}{8}$ (**e**) $\frac{5}{12}$
  (**f**) $\frac{4}{9}$ (**g**) $\frac{5}{14}$ (**h**) $\frac{5}{9}$ (**i**) $\frac{2}{7}$ (**j**) $\frac{13}{15}$

6. 120 ÷ .24 =   **7.** 5.04 × .09 =   **8.** .91 + 784.1 =

9. 91 − 7.989 =   **10.** 45.381 − 2.492 =   **11.** .41 × .98 =

12. $\frac{1}{2} \div \frac{1}{2}$ =   **13.** $\frac{3}{4} \div \frac{3}{8}$ =   **14.** $\frac{5}{7} \times \frac{14}{2}$ =

15. .4 ÷ 10 =   **16.** 18.7 × 100 =   **17.** 78 × 10 =

18. $\$24.64 \times .23 =$ 　　　　**19.** $36.93 \div 3 =$ 　　　　**20.** $56 \div 1{,}000 =$

21. $2\dfrac{1}{2} \div 3\dfrac{1}{3}$ 　　　　**22.** $3\dfrac{2}{4} \div 4\dfrac{2}{3}$ 　　　　**23.** $4\dfrac{3}{4} \times 2\dfrac{1}{2}$

24. Change each percent to a decimal.

(**a**) 12% 　　　(**b**) 15.5% 　　　(**c**) $4\dfrac{1}{2}\%$ 　　　(**d**) 9%

25. Change each decimal to a percent.

(**a**) .002 　　　(**b**) .7 　　　(**c**) .95 　　　(**d**) 4.12

26. Write each decimal as a word phrase:

(**a**) 4.44 　　　(**b**) 5.09 　　　(**c**) .038 　　　(**d**) 2.009

27. Write each word phrase as a decimal:

(**a**) Nine tenths. 　　　(**b**) Fourteen thousandths.

(**c**) Eight and three hundred fifteen ten–thousandths.

(**d**) Twelve thousandths.

28. (**a**) $8 \div \dfrac{1}{4} =$ 　　　(**b**) $\dfrac{3}{4} \div 12 =$ 　　　(**c**) $\dfrac{7}{8} \div \dfrac{21}{24} =$

CHAPTER 16

METRIC AND CUSTOMARY SYSTEMS OF UNITS

Understanding Measures

When the early humans changed from hunters to farmers, they needed to measure the size of their farms. The first units of length were based on the human body parts such as the length of the palm and the length of a finger. For example, the people of Ghana in West Africa use the distance from the tip of the left middle finger to the tip of the right middle finger of an adult as approximately 6 feet or 2 yards. (3 feet = 1 yard). People do not have the same body size, and therefore each of the measures using body parts differed considerably. In order to avoid confusion, measures were made standard so that everybody would use the same standards.

　　The National Bureau of Standards in Washington D.C. determines the units on rulers or measuring tapes. When you measure something with a ruler or a tape measure, you are actually comparing it with these standard units.

　　The two main systems of measurements are the Customary and the Metric systems. The Customary system is also known as the English system. The metric system is used in most countries and the metric system is also known as SI which stands for System International.

METRIC SYSTEM

Metric Length

The metric unit is named after the unit of length, the meter, because the metric units of length are based on the meter. The diagram shows a part of the metric length of a ruler in centimeters. The distance between any small division = 1 millimeter (mm) and 10 millimeters (mm) = 1 centimeter (cm). Note carefully that when you take a ruler, the type of the units at any edge of the ruler is indicated such as centimeter (cm) or inch (in.).

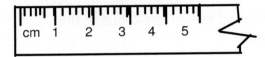

Let us measure the length of an eraser as shown in the diagram.

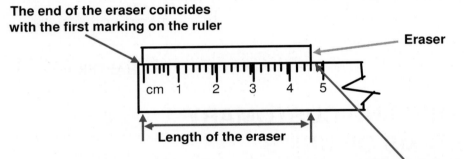

The length of the ruler is **4 centimeters and 6 millimeters**.

To measure the length of an eraser or any object, one of the edges of the eraser or the object should coincide with the first marking on the ruler, and then read the marking on the ruler that coincides with the other edge of the eraser or the object. This method of measuring the length of any object is very useful in solving many exercises later.

Benchmark

A benchmark is an object whose measure is already known and we can then use the object to estimate the lengths of other objects. For example if we know the length of your mathematics textbook, we can then use the textbook as a benchmark to measure the length of the top of your desk at school. We should then record the length of your desk in "mathematics textbook lengths."

Team Exercise

1. Use a ruler to measure the length of your mathematics textbook to the nearest millimeter (for example, the measurement could be 10 centimeters and 4 millimeters.)

2. Now use the length of the mathematics textbook to estimate the length of the top of your desk.

3. Record the length of the top of your desk in "mathematics textbook lengths."

   For example, your record could be $3\frac{1}{3}$ mathematics textbook lengths.

4. Now use a ruler to measure the length of the top of your desk.

5. Which unit is more convenient to use in measuring the length of the top of your desk? (Length of the mathematics textbook or using a ruler.) Explain your answer.

Team Exercise

Each team should measure the following objects and then select the most appropriate measure. (Hint: It is more convenient to use a measuring tape to measure longer distances or objects.)

Object to be measured.	Measurements
1. The length of your classroom door.	**a.** 1 meter **b.** $2\frac{1}{2}$ meters **c.** 50 meters
2. The thickness of a quarter.	**a.** 2 centimeters **b.** 35 cm **c.** 1 millimeters
3. The length of a new pencil.	**a.** 1 meter **b.** 35 cm **c.** 19 cm
4. The length of a dollar bill.	**a.** $15\frac{1}{2}$ cm **b.** 2 cm **c.** 1 m
5. The width of a dollar bill.	**a.** $2\frac{1}{2}$ m **b.** $6\frac{1}{2}$ cm **c.** 12 cm

6. Track events are measured in meters. Each team should record two track events in meters.

7. Each team should use a measuring tape to measure the length and width of the classroom. What unit would be the most appropriate for measuring the length and the width of the classroom? (a) meters (b) centimeters (c) millimeters.
   Hint: The largest feasible unit is the correct answer.

8. What unit would be the most appropriate for measuring the length of a postage stamp?
   (a) meters (b) centimeters (c) millimeters. Hint: The largest feasible unit is the correct answer.

9. Explain why the length of the chalkboard should be expressed in meters instead of millimeters?

10. Select the correct answer
    a. Your classroom door is about 92 cm, 92 m, or 92 km wide.
    b. The thickness of a dime is about 1 kg, 1 cm, or 1 mm.

c. The width of an index fingernail is about 1 mm, or 1 cm or 1 km.

d. The height of a kitchen counter is about 90 km, 90 m, or 90 cm.

e. The width of a quarter is about 1 mm, 1 cm, or 1 m

Each team should report their answers to the whole class.

The notes and the generous worked examples have provided me with conceptual understanding and computational fluency to do my homework.

Group Exercises/Exercises

Use the method of measuring the length of the eraser to measure the length of each line with a ruler. Record your answers in centimeters and milliliters. (Group Exercises: 1 - 4, Exercises: 5 - 10)

1 ——————————— = ? cm and ? mm

2 ——————— = ? cm and ? mm

3 ————————————— = ? cm and ? mm

4 ——— = ? cm and ? mm

5 ————— = ? cm and ? mm

6 —————————— = ? cm and ? mm

7 ———————————————— = ? cm ? mm

8 ——————————————————— = ? cm and ? mm

9 ————————————————— = ? cm and ? mm

10 ————————————— = ? cm and ? mm

Metric Units of Length

10 millimeters (mm) = 1 centimeter (cm)
100 centimeters (cm) = 1 meter (m)
1,000 meters (m) = 1 kilometer (km)

Look at the metric equations involving millimeters, centimeters, meters, and kilometers. **Note** that the metric system is easy to use because the units of measurements are related by the powers of 10. For example, to change different size units you just divide or multiply by 10, 100, or 1,000. The prefixes **milli**-, **centi**-, **deci**-, **deka**-, **hecto**-, and **Kilo**- shows how the measures are related to the basic unit which is the meter. For example;

a. **milli** - means "thousandth" therefore, 1 **milli**meter is .001 or $\dfrac{1}{1000}$ of a meter.

b. **Centi** - means "hundredth" therefore, 1 **centi**meter is .01 or $\dfrac{1}{100}$ of a meter.

c. **Kilo** - means "one thousand " and therefore, 1 Kilometer means 1000 meters.

Table of Metric Prefixes - Based on the meter

Prefix	Meaning
milli-	one thousandth or .001 or $\dfrac{1}{1000}$
centi-	one hundredth or .01 or $\dfrac{1}{100}$
deci-	one tenth or .1 or $\dfrac{1}{10}$
basic unit (meter)	1
deka	ten or 10
hecto-	one hundred or 100
kilo-	one thousand or 1000

The prefixes that are in the bold type are most commonly used units of measurement.

Table of Metric Units

Unit	Abbreviation	Equivalent
millimeter	**mm**	.001 m, .01 dm, **.1 cm**
centimeter	**cm**	**.01 m**, .1 dm, **10 mm**
decimeter	dm	.1m, 10 cm, 100 mm
meter	**m**	10 dm, **100 cm**, **1,000 mm**, .1 dam, .01 hm, .001 km
dekameter	dam	10 m, .1 hm, .01 km
hectometer	hm	100 m, 10 dam, .1 km
kilometer	**km**	**1,000 m**, 100 dam, 10 hm

The prefixes that are in the bold type are most commonly used units of measurement.

Converting Between the Metric Units

There are two ways to convert between the metric units as shown:
(a). by multiplying by .001, .01, .1, 10, 100, or 1,000 as applicable.
(b). by multiplying or dividing by 10, 100, or 1000 as applicable.

Rule 1: To change a smaller unit to a larger unit follow the following two steps:

Step 1: Find how many smaller units are contained in one unit of the larger unit.

Step 2: **Divide** the given number of smaller units by the number you have determined in step 1.

Rule 2: To change a larger unit to a smaller unit follow the following two steps:

Step 1: Find how many smaller units are **contained** in one unit of the larger unit.

Step 2: **Multiply** the given number of larger units by the number you have determined in Step 1.

Example 1

How many centimeters are there in 200 millimeters?

Solution

We are converting from millimeters to centimeters and therefore, we are converting from a smaller unit to a larger unit. Therefore, we can use **Rule 1** as shown:

Step 1: 10 mm = 1 cm

Step 2: Therefore, 200 mm = 200 mm ÷ 10 mm = $\dfrac{200}{10} = \dfrac{\overset{20}{\cancel{200}}}{\underset{1}{\cancel{10}}} = 20$ cm.

Example 2

Solve: 25 cm = ? mm

Solution

We are converting from centimeters to millimeters, and therefore, we are converting from a larger unit to a smaller unit. Therefore, we can use **Rule 2** as follows:

Step 1: I cm = 10 mm

Step 2: Therefore, 25 cm = 25 × 10 mm = 250 mm.

Example 3

Solve:15 m = ? cm.

Solution

We are converting from meters to centimeters, and therefore, we are converting from a larger unit to a smaller unit. Therefore, we can use **Rule 2** as shown:

Step 1: 1 m = 100 cm.

Step 2: Therefore, 15 m = 15 × 100 cm = 1500 cm.

Example 4

Solve: ? m = 250 cm.

Solution

We are converting from centimeters to meters, and therefore, we are converting from a smaller unit to a larger unit. Therefore, we can use **Rule 1** as shown:

Step 1: 1m = 100 cm

Step 2: Therefore, $\dfrac{250}{100}$ m = 250 cm.

$$\dfrac{250}{100} \text{ m} = 250 \text{ cm.}$$

$$\dfrac{250}{100} \text{ m} = 250 \text{ cm.}$$

2.5m = 250 cm.　　　　$\dfrac{250}{100} = 2.5$ by moving the decimal

point two places to the left.

Example 5
Solve: 8 km = ? m.
Solution
We are converting from kilometers to meters, and therefore, we are converting from a larger unit to a smaller unit. Therefore, we can use **Rule 2** as shown:
Step 1: 1 km = 1000 m.
Step 2: Therefore, 8 km = 8 × 1000 m = 8,000 m.

Example 6
Solve: 300 m = ? km.
Solution
We are converting from meters to kilometers and therefore, we are converting from a smaller unit to a larger unit. Therefore, we can use **Rule 1** as shown:
Step 1: 1 km = 1000 m.

Step 2: Therefore, 300 m = $\dfrac{300}{1000}$ km.

$$= \dfrac{300}{1000} \text{ km.}$$

$$= \dfrac{3}{10} \text{ km.} \qquad (\dfrac{300}{1000} = \dfrac{3}{10} \text{ by dividing by 100)}$$

$$= .3 \text{ km.}$$

Example 7
Solve: 5 km = ? cm.
Solution
We are converting kilometers to centimeters, and therefore, we are converting from a

larger unit to a smaller unit. Therefore, we can use **Rule 2** as shown:

Step 1: 1 km = 100,000 cm.

Step 2: Therefore, 5 km = 5 × 100,000 cm = 500,000 cm.

Example 8

Solve: 250,000 cm = ? km.

Solution

We are converting centimeters to kilometers and therefore we are converting from a smaller unit to a larger unit. Therefore, we can use **Rule 1** as shown:

Step 1: 1 km = 100,000 cm.

Step 2: Therefore, 250,000 cm = $\dfrac{250,000}{100,000}$ km.

$$= \dfrac{25}{10} \text{ km.} \qquad (\dfrac{250,000}{100,000} = \dfrac{25}{10} \text{ by dividing by 10,000.})$$

$$= 2.5 \text{ km.} \qquad (\dfrac{25}{10} = 2.5 \text{ by moving the decimal point}$$

one place to the left.)

Summary

1. In order to convert a smaller unit to a larger unit, **divide** by moving the decimal point to the **left** as needed.
2. In order to convert a larger unit to a smaller unit, **multiply** by moving the decimal point to the **right** as needed.

The notes and the generous worked examples have provided me with conceptual understanding and computational fluency to do my homework.

Exercises

1. How many centimeters are there in 300 millimeters? Hint: See Example 1.
2. How many centimeters are there in the following? Hint: See Example 1.

   a. 150 mm   **b**. 500 mm   **c**. 520 mm   **d**. 80 mm

3. Solve the following: Hint: See Example 2.

   a. 100 cm = ? mm   **b**. 60 cm. = ? mm   **c**. 15 cm. = ? mm

   d. 5 cm. = ? mm   **e**. 8 cm = ? mm   **f**. 18 cm = ? mm

4. Solve the following: Hint :See Example 3.

   a. 10 m = ? cm   **b**. 13 m = ? cm   **c**. 18 m = ? mm

   d. 5 m. = ? cm   **e**. 17 m. = ? cm   **f**. 22 m = ? mm

5. Solve the following: Hint: See Example 4.

    a. ? m = 270 cm   **b**. ? m = 300 cm   **c**. ? m = 150 cm
    d. ? m = 200 cm   **e**. ? m = 90 cm   **f**. ? m = 180 cm

6. Solve the following: Hint: See Example 5.
    a. 10 km = ? m   **b**. 5 km = ? m   **c**. 20 km = ? m
    d. 6 km = ? m   **e**. 2 km = ? m   **f**. 11 km = ? m

7. Solve the following: Hint: See Example 6.
    a. 200 m = ? km   **b**. 2500 m = ? km   **c**. 20 km = ? km
    d. 900 m = ? m   **e**. 2 km = ? m   **f**. 560 m = ? km

8. Solve the following: Hint: See Example 7.
    a. 6 km = ? cm   **b**. 12 km = ? cm   **c**. 16 km = ? cm
    d. 2 km = ? cm   **e**. 8 km = ? cm   **f**. 3 km = ? cm

9. Solve the following: Hint: See Example 8.
    a. 150,000 cm = ? km   **b**. 200,000 cm = ? km   **c**. 100,000 cm = ? km

Challenge Questions

10. Solve the following:
    a. 9 m = ? cm   **b**. 3 km = ? m   **c**. 95 cm = ? mm
    d. 450 mm = ? cm   **e** 1500 m = ? km   **f**. 160,000 cm = ? km

Answers to Selected Questions

1. 30 cm   **2a**. 15 cm   **3a**. 1000 mm   **4a**. 1000 cm

REAL WORLD APPLICATIONS - WORD PROBLEMS
Metric Units of Length

Example 1

John runs 4.2 kilometers every day. How many meters does he run in a week?

Solution

Setup: There are 7 days in a week, therefore, multiply 4.2 kilometers by 7 to obtain the total number of kilometers that John runs in a week. Then, change the total number of kilometers that John runs in a week to meters.

Step 1: Find the total number of kilometers that John runs every week as shown:
    In 1 day John runs 4.2 km.
    In 7 days (1 week) John will run 7 × 4.2 km = 29.4 km.

Step 2: Change the 29.4 km into meters as shown:
    1 km = 1000 m (See the section on "Metric units of Length,")
    therefore, 29.4 km = 29.4 × 1000 m = 29,400 m.   Review Decimal Multiplication.
    Therefore, John runs 29,400 m. in a week.

Example 2

How many meters are in $\frac{4}{5}$ kilometer?

Solution

Setup: Change the common fraction $\frac{4}{5}$ to a decimal fraction. Then find the number of meters that are contained in the decimal fraction of the kilometer.

Step 1: Change the common fraction $\frac{4}{5}$ to a decimal fraction as shown:

$$\frac{4}{5} = 5\overline{\smash)40} = .8$$
$$\begin{array}{r} 0.8 \\ 5\overline{\smash)40} \\ -\underline{40} \\ 00 \end{array}$$

Step 2: Find the number of meters that are contained in .8 km as shown:
   1 km = 1000 m (See the section on "Metric units of Length")
   Therefore, .8 × 1000 m = 800 m.   (Review Decimal Multiplication).

Example 3

Mary has a wire that measures .8 meters long. If her school project requires many lengths of a wire measuring 20 millimeters, how many lengths of 20 millimeters can she cut from the .8 meter long wire?

Solution

Setup: Change the .8 meters to millimeters, and then **divide** by 20 millimeters.

Step 1: Change the .8 meters to millimeters as shown:
   1 m = 1000 mm (See the section on "Metric units of Length.")
   Therefore, .8 m = .8 × 1000 mm = 800 mm. (Review decimal multiplication.)

Step 2: Find the number of 20 mm that are contain in 800 mm as shown:
   Divide 800 mm by 20 mm to obtain the number of 20 mm that are contained in 800 mm as shown:

$$800 \div 20 = \frac{800}{20}$$

$$= \frac{800\!\!\!/}{20\!\!\!/}$$ Cancel out the zero by dividing by 10.

$$= \frac{\overset{40}{\cancel{80}}}{\underset{1}{\cancel{2}}}$$ Divide by 2.

$$= 40$$

Therefore, 40 lengths of 20 mm can be cut from the .8 m of the wire.

Example 4

Given that the scale on a map is 10 mm = 78 km, how many kilometers are represented by 5.5 cm?

Solution

Setup: Change 5.5 cm to millimeters, and then find how many 10 mm (10 mm = 1 cm) are contained in 5.5 cm. Finally, multiply 78 km by the number of 10 mm in 5.5 cm.

Step 1: Change the 5.5 cm to millimeters as shown:

1 cm =10 mm (See the section on "Metric units of Length.")

Therefore, 5.5 cm = 5.5 × 10 mm = 55 mm.   (Review decimal multiplication.)

Step 2: Find the number of 10 mm that are contained in the 55 mm as shown:

Divide 55 mm by 10 = 55 ÷ 10 = $\dfrac{55}{10}$ = 5.5

Step 3: Find the kilometers represented by 5.5 cm on the map as shown:

Multiply 78 km by 55 = 78 km × 55 = 429 km.

Therefore, 5.5 cm on the map represents 429 km.

The notes and the generous worked examples have provided me with conceptual understanding and computational fluency to do my homework.

Exercises

1. Eric runs 3.8 kilometers every day. How many meters does he run in a week? Hint: See Example 1.

2. How many meters are contained in $\dfrac{3}{5}$ kilometers? Hint: See Example 2.

3. Susan has a wire that measures .95 meters long. If her school project requires many lengths of the wire measuring 30 millimeters, how many lengths can she cut from the .95 meter long wire. Hint: See Example 3.

4. Given that the scale on a certain map is 5 mm = 74 km, how many kilometers are represented by 7.2 cm? Hint: See Example 3.

Challenge Question

5. How many meters are contained in $\dfrac{2}{5}$ km?

Add and Subtract Measurements
Example 1

Copy and complete.

2 m + 150 cm = ? cm

Solution

Change the 2 m to centimeters by multiplying 2 m by 100 because 1 m = 100 cm (See the section on "Metric Units of Length") and then add as shown:

2 m × 100 + 150 cm = ? cm

200 cm + 150 cm = 350 cm

Example 2

Copy and complete.

3 m + 400 cm = ? m

Solution

Change the 400 cm to meters by dividing 400 cm by 100 because 1 m = 100 cm (See the section on "Metric units of Length") and then add as shown:

$$3 \text{ m} + \frac{400}{100} \text{ m} = ? \text{ m}$$

$$3 \text{ m} + \frac{\overset{4}{400}}{\underset{1}{100}} \text{ m} = ? \text{ m}$$

3 m + 4 m = 7 m

Example 3

Copy and complete.

2 cm + 8 mm + 7 mm + 1 cm =

Solution

Step 1: Add the like units together as shown:

2 cm + 1 cm + 8 mm + 7 mm =

3 cm + 15 mm =

Step 2: Change 15 mm to centimeters and millimeters by dividing 15 mm by 10 because 1 cm = 10 mm (See the section on "Metric units of Length,") such that 15 mm ÷ 10 = 1 remainder 5 and the 1 has a unit of cm and the 5 has a unit of mm as shown:

3 cm + 1 cm + 5 mm = 4 cm + 5 mm

= 4 cm 5 mm

Example 4

Solve: 10 km   600 m

           - 2 km   900 m

           _____

Solution

Step 1: We cannot subtract 900 m from 600 m, therefore, we have to borrow 1 km from the 10 km. The borrowed 1 km = 1000 m (See the section on "Metric units of Length") and add the 1000 m to the 600 m to obtain 1600 m as shown:

```
     9      1600
    10 km   600 m
  - 2 km    900 m
```

Step 2: Do the subtraction now as shown:

```
     9      1600
    10 km   600 m
  - 2 km    900 m
    7 km    700 m
```

Example 5
Solve: 6 cm 3 mm - 2 cm 8 mm =
Solution
Step 1: Rewrite the question as shown:

```
    6 cm  3 mm
  - 2 cm  8 mm
```

Step 2: We cannot subtract 8 mm from 3 mm, and therefore, we have to borrow 1 cm from 6 cm and then change the 1 cm to millimeters, 1 cm = 10 mm (See the section on "Metric units of Length,") then add the 10 mm to the 3 mm to obtain 13 mm as shown:

```
    5     13
    6 cm  3 mm
  - 2 cm  8 mm
```

Step 3: Do the subtraction now as shown:

```
    5     13
    6 cm  3 mm
  - 2 cm  8 mm
    3 cm  5 mm
```

Example 6
Solve: 12 m 9 cm
        - 8 m 5 cm

Solution

Do the subtraction as shown:

```
  12 m   9 cm
-  8 m   5 cm
─────────────
   4 m   4 cm
```

The notes and the generous worked examples have provided me with conceptual understanding and computational fluency to do my homework.

Exercises

1. Copy and complete. Hint: See Example 1.

    a. 4 m + 125 cm =? cm   **b.** 1 m + 85 cm = ? cm

    c. 6 m + 201 cm = ? cm   **d.** 3 m + 111 cm = ? cm

2. Copy and complete. Hint: See Example 2.

    a. 4 m + 300 cm = ? m   **b.** 1 m + 100 cm = ? m

    c. 2 m + 500 cm = ? m   **d.** 3 m + 200 cm = ? m

3. Copy and complete. Hint: See Example 3.

    a. 3 cm + 4 mm + 12 mm + 2 cm =

    b. 7 mm + 1 cm + 3 mm + 4 cm =

    c. 10 cm + 6 mm + 4 cm + 12 mm =

    d. 12 mm + 5 cm + 5 mm + 2 cm =

4. Solve: See Example 4.

    a.   4 km   200 m   **b.**   3 km   700 m   **c.**   5 km   98 m

       -1 km   400 m   - 2 km   800 m   - 3 km   100 m

5. Solve: Hint: See Example 5.

    a. 3 cm 4 mm - 1 cm 6 mm =

    b. 2 cm 5 mm - 1 cm 7 mm =

    c. 6 cm 8 mm - 2 cm 9 mm =

    d. 12 cm 6 mm - 9 cm 7 mm =

6. Solve: Hint: See Example 6.

    a.   10 m   8 cm   **b.**   2 m   5 cm   **c.**   4 m   7 cm

       - 5 m   3 cm   - 1 m   2 cm   - 2 m   5 cm

Challenge Questions

7. Copy and complete.

    a. 9 cm + 4 mm + 2 cm + 8 mm =

    b. 4 cm 3 mm - 2 cm 9 mm =

c. 6 cm 7 mm - 5 cm 5 mm =

d. 3 m + 600 cm = ? m

e. 10 m + 150 cm = ? cm

8. Solve:

a.	12 km 700 m	**b.**	2 cm 9 mm	**c.**	6 m + 700 cm = ? m
	- 2 km 800 m		+ 5 cm 5 mm		

Answers to Selected Questions

1a. 525 cm   **2a.** 7 m   **3a.** 6 cm 6 mm   **4a.** 2 km 800 m

CUSTOMARY UNITS OF LENGTH

The Customary unit of length are the inch, foot, yard, and mile.

12 inches (in.) = 1 foot (ft)

3 feet (ft) = 1 yard (yd)

5,280 feet (ft) = 1 mile (mi)

1,760 yards = 1 mile

Detailed Customary Units of Length table

Unit	Abbreviation	Equivalence
inch	in.	12 in. = 1 foot
foot	ft	1 ft = 12 in., 3 ft = 1 yard, 5,280 ft = 1 mile
yard	yd	1 yd = 3 ft, 1 yd = 36 in., 1,760 yd = 1 mile

Example 1

How many inches are in 5 feet?

Solution

We are to find 5 feet = how many inches.

Note: To change from a larger unit (for example feet) to a smaller unit, (for example inches), multiply as shown:

Number of feet × Number of inches in 1 foot = Number of inches.

Number of feet × Number of inches in 1 foot = Number of inches

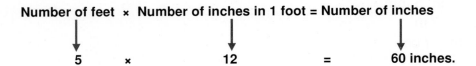

| 5 | × | 12 | = | 60 inches. |

There are 60 inches in 5 feet.

Example 2

How many feet are in 48 inches?

Solution

We are to find 48 inches = how many feet.

Note: To change from a smaller unit (such as inches) to a larger unit (such as feet), divide.

Number of inches ÷ Number of inches in 1 foot = Number of feet.

Number of inches ÷ Number of inches in 1 foot = Number of feet.

| 48 | ÷ | 12 | = | 4 feet |

There are 4 feet in 48 inches.

Example 3

An electric wire is 72 yards long. How many feet does the wire contain?

Solution

We are to find 72 yards = how many feet.

Note: To change from a larger unit (yard) to a smaller unit (feet), multiply.

Number of yards × Number of feet in 1 yard = Number of feet.

Number of yards × Number of feet in 1 yard = Number of feet.

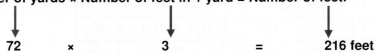

| 72 | × | 3 | = | 216 feet |

There are 216 feet in 72 yards.

Example 4

One of the school's hallways is 99 feet long. How long is the hallway in yards?

Solution

We are to find 99 feet = how many yards.

Note: To change from a smaller unit (feet) to a larger unit (yard), divide.

Number of feet ÷ Number of feet in 1 yard = Number of yards.

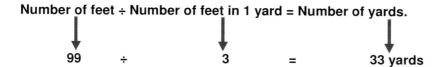

Number of feet ÷ Number of feet in 1 yard = Number of yards.

99 ÷ 3 = 33 yards

There are 33 yards in 99 feet.

Example 5

Find 3 ft 5 in + 6ft 11 in.

Solution

Step 1: Rewrite the question and add the like units as shown:

$$
\begin{array}{r}
3\ \text{ft} \quad 5\ \text{in.} \\
+\ 6\ \text{ft} \quad 11\ \text{in.} \\
\hline
9\ \text{ft} \quad 16\ \text{in.}
\end{array}
$$

Step 2: Change 16 in. into feet and inches as shown:

16 in. is more than 1 foot because 12 in. = 1 ft, therefore, rename 16 in. as 1 ft + 4 in (16 in. ÷ 12 =1 ft remainder 4 in.).

(Note that from the customary unit of length, 12 inches = 1 foot).

Therefore, the 9 ft 16 in. = 9 ft + (1 ft + 4 in.).

Step 3: Combine the like units as shown:

$$
\begin{aligned}
9\ \text{ft} + (1\ \text{ft} + 4\ \text{in.}) &= 9\ \text{ft} + 1\ \text{ft} + 4\ \text{in.} \\
&= 10\ \text{ft}\ 4\ \text{in.}
\end{aligned}
$$

Example 6

Solve:
$$
\begin{array}{r}
8\ \text{yd} \quad 1\ \text{ft} \\
-\ 3\ \text{yd} \quad 2\ \text{ft} \\
\hline
\end{array}
$$

Solution

Step 1: 2 ft cannot be subtracted from 1 ft because 2 ft is greater than 1 ft and therefore, we have to borrow 1 yd from 8 yd and this 1 yd = 3 ft (See customary unit of length.) Add the 3 ft to 1 ft to become 4 ft and rewrite the question as shown:

$$
\begin{array}{cc}
7 & 4 \\
8\ \text{yd} & 1\ \text{ft} \\
-\ 3\ \text{yd} & 2\ \text{ft} \\
\hline
\end{array}
$$

Step 2: Do the subtraction as shown:

$$
\begin{array}{cc}
7 & 4 \\
8\ \text{yd} & 1\ \text{ft} \\
-\ 3\ \text{yd} & 2\ \text{ft} \\
\hline
4\ \text{yd} & 2\ \text{ft}
\end{array}
$$

Example 7

Solve: 5 yd   2 ft
          - 2 yd   1 ft

Solution

Do the subtraction as shown:

          5 yd   2 ft
        - 2 yd   1 ft
        _____
          3 yd   1 ft

The notes and the generous worked examples have provided me with conceptual understanding and computational fluency to do my homework.

Exercises

1. What are the customary units of length?
2. How many inches are in the following lengths? Hint: See Example 1.
   a. 10 ft   **b**. 4 ft   **c**. 8 ft   **d**. 2 ft
3. How many feet are in the following lengths? Hint See Example 2.
   a. 24 in.   **b**. 60 in.   **c**. 36 in.   **d**. 72 in.
4. A fence is 144 yards long. How long is the fence in feet?
   Hint: See Example 3.
5. A swimming pool is 39 ft long. How long is the swimming pool in yards?
   Hint: See Example 4.
6. Solve: Hint: See Example 5.
   a. 4 ft 8 in. + 7 ft 6 in. =   **b**. 2 ft 7 in. + 3 ft 8 in. =
   c. 12 ft 5 in. + 2 ft 8 in. =   **c**. 1 f 9 in. + 8 ft 6 in. =
7. Solve: Hint: See Example 6.
   a. 6 yd   1 ft   **b**. 9 yd   1 ft   **c**. 5 yd   0 ft
          - 4 yd   2 ft   - 6 yd   2 ft   - 3 yd   1 ft

Challenge Questions

8. Copy and complete
   a. 72 in. = ? ft   **b**. 6 yd = ? ft   **c**. 9 ft = ? in.
   d. 36 ft = ? yd   **e**. 15 yd = ? ft   **f**. 9ft = ? yd

Answers to Selected Questions

2a. 120 in.   **3a**. 2 ft   **6a**. 12 ft 2 in.

CUSTOMARY UNITS OF SQUARE MEASURE

The basic customary units of square measures are square inches, square foot, square yard, acre and square miles. These basic customary units of square measure are shown in the table.

Table

Unit	Equivalence	Abbreviation
Square inch (in.²)	144 in.² = 1 ft² 1,296 in.² = 1 yd²	in.²
Square foot (ft²)	1 ft² = 144 in.² 9 ft² = 1 yd²	ft²
Square yard (yd²)	1 yd² = 9 ft² 1 yd² = 1,296 in² 4,840 yd² = 1 A.	yd²
Acre	1 A. = 43,560 ft² 1 A. = 4,840 yd² 640 A. = 1 mi.²	A.
Square mile (mi.²)	1 mi.² = 640 A.	mi.²

Although the basic customary units of the square measure are given in the table, we will only discuss two most important ones as shown:

$$1 \text{ ft}^2 = 144 \text{ in.}^2$$
$$1 \text{ yd}^2 = 9 \text{ ft}^2$$

It is important to know that the rules for changing units of square measurement are the same as the rules for the linear measurements as shown:
First, find how many smaller units are contained in one unit of the bigger unit, and then;
1. **To change a smaller unit to a bigger unit, divide by the number that you have found.**
2. **To change a bigger unit to a smaller unit, multiply by the number that you have found.**

Example 1
Change 288 in.² to square feet.
Solution
When we compare inches to feet, the smaller unit is inches. Using the rule, to change from smaller unit to bigger unit, we must divide.

$144 \text{ in.}^2 = 1 \text{ ft}^2$ See the table

Therefore, $288 \text{ in.}^2 = 288 \text{ in.}^2 \div 144 \text{ in.}^2 = 2 \text{ ft}^2$ Using the rule, we must divide.

$$144 \overline{\smash)288} \atop \begin{array}{r} 2 \\ -288 \\ \hline 000 \end{array}$$

Example 2

Change 2 ft^2 to square inches.

Solution

When we compare feet to inches, the feet is a bigger unit. Using the rule, to change a bigger unit to a smaller unit, we must multiply.

1 ft^2 = 144 in.^{2}	See table
Therefore, 2 ft^2 = 2 × 144	Using the rule, we must multiply.
= 288 in^2.	

Example 3

Change 4 yd^2 to square feet.

Solution

When we compare yards to feet, the yard is a bigger unit. Using the rule, to change a bigger unit to a smaller unit, we must multiply.

1 yd^2 = 9 ft^2	See the table.
Therefore, 4 yd^2 = 4 × 9	Using the rule, we must multiply.
= 36 ft^2	

Example 4

Change $5\frac{2}{3}$ yd^2 to square feet

Solution

When we compare yards to feet, the yard is a bigger unit. Using the rule, to change a bigger unit to a smaller unit, we must multiply.

$$1 \text{ yd}^2 = 9 \text{ ft}^2 \qquad \text{See the table}$$

$$\text{Therefore, } 5\frac{2}{3} \text{ yd}^2 = 5\frac{2}{3} \times 9 \text{ ft}^2 \qquad \text{Using the rule, must multiply}$$

$$= \frac{17}{3} \times 9 \text{ ft}^2 \qquad \text{Review fractions}$$

$$= \frac{17}{\underset{1}{3}} \times \overset{3}{9} \text{ ft}^2 \qquad \text{Divide by 3}$$

$$= 17 \times 3 \text{ ft}^2$$

$$= 51 \text{ ft}^2$$

Example 5

Change 63 square feet to square yards.

Solution

When we compare feet and yard, feet is the smaller unit. Using the rule, changing from the smaller unit to the bigger unit, we must divide.

$9 \text{ ft}^2 = 1 \text{ yd}^2$ See the table.

Therefore, $63 \text{ ft}^2 = 63 \div 9$ Using the rule, we must divide.

$= 7 \text{ yd}^2$

Exercises

1. Change the following square inches to square feet. Hint: See Example 1.
   a. 432 in.^{2} **b**. 720 in.^{2}

2. Change the following square feet to square inches. Hint: See Example 2.
   a. 3 ft^2 **b**. 8 ft^2 **c**. 10 ft^2 **d**. 12 ft^2

3. Change the following square yards to square feet. Hint: See Example 3.
   a. 3 yd^2 **b**. 7 yd^2 **c**. 10 yd^2 **d**. 6 yd^2

4. Change the following square yards to square feet. Hint: See Example 4.
   a. $4\frac{1}{3}$ yd^2 **b**. $6\frac{2}{3}$ yd^2 **c**. $7\frac{1}{3}$ yd^2 **d**. $3\frac{2}{3}$ yd^2

5. Change the following square feet to square yards. Hint: See Example 5.
   a. 18 ft^2 **b**. 90 ft^2 **c**. 45 ft^2 **d**. 72 ft^2

Challenge Questions

5. Change the following square yards to square feet
   a. $2\frac{2}{3}$ yd^2 **b**. 1 yd^2 **c**. 11 yd^2

6. Change the following square inches to square feet.
   a. 144 in^2 **b**. 576 in^2

7. Change the following square feet to square inches.
   a. 4 ft^2 **b**. 7 ft^2 **c**. 8 ft^2

8. Change the following square feet to square yards.
   a. 27 ft^2 **b**. 36 ft^2 **c**. 45 ft^2 **d**. 9 ft^2

Answers to Selected Questions

1a. 3 ft^2 **2a**. 432 in^2 **3a**. 27 ft^2

REAL WORLD APPLICATIONS - WORD PROBLEMS
Customary Units of Square Measures

Example 1
A room has 99 square feet of floor space. How many square yards of tiles is needed for the floor assuming that there will be no waste of the tiles.

Solution
When we compare feet to yard, the yard is a bigger unit. Using the rule, to change from smaller unit to bigger unit, we must divide.

$$9 \text{ ft}^2 = 1 \text{ yd}^2 \qquad \text{See the table.}$$

Therefore, $99 \text{ ft}^2 = 99 \div 9 \qquad \text{Using the rule, we must divide.}$

$$= 11 \text{ yd}^2$$

Exercise
A room has 72 square feet of floor space. How many square yards of tiles is needed for the floor assuming that there will be no waste of the tiles.
Hint: See Example 1.

METRIC MASS AND CUSTOMARY WEIGHT

Metric Mass
Recall that the units of the metric length are based on the meter, similarly the units of the metric mass are based on the gram. A benchmark for 1 gram is the mass of a large paper clip.

Team Work
Each team should do a research at a super market and list the names and the weights of 4 different packages of cookies in grams. The weights are already written on the packages. Can you compare the mass of a large paper clip, which is 1 gram to the mass of each package of cookie?

Metric Prefixes

Prefix	Meaning	Abbreviations
milli-	one thousandth, (0.001) or $\dfrac{1}{1000}$	mg for milligram
kilo-	one thousand, (1,000)	kg for kilogram

The prefix for gram is g.

Metric Mass Units

1 milligram (mg) = .001 g or $\dfrac{1}{1000}$ g

1 gram (g) = 1,000 mg, .001 kg or $\dfrac{1}{1000}$ kg

1 kilogram (kg) = 1,000, .001 metric ton or $\dfrac{1}{1000}$ metric tons.

1 metric ton (t) = 1,000 kg, 1,000,000 g.

Rule 1: To change smaller units to larger units **divide**.

Rule 2: To change larger units to smaller units **multiply**.

Example 1

How many grams are there in 5 kilograms?

Solution

The question may be rewritten as shown:

5 kilograms = ? grams.

To change larger units to smaller units multiply.

Number of kilograms × Number of grams in 1 kilogram = Number of grams.

5	×	1,000	=	5,000 gram.

There are 5,000 grams in 5 kilograms.

Example 2

If glucophage 1000 mg tablet is one of the medications that Nick takes daily, what is the mass of 1 tablet of the glucophage in grams?

Solution

The question may be rewritten as follows:

1000 mg = ? g

To change from smaller units (for example mg) to larger units (for example g) divide as shown:

Number of mg ÷ Number of mg in 1 g = Number of grams.

1,000	÷	1,000	=	1 gram

Therefore the mass of 1 tablet of glucophage is 1 gram.

Example 3

Replace ? with the number that makes the statement true.

6 g = ? mg

Solution

To change from larger units (for example g) to smaller units (for example mg) multiply as shown:

Number of grams × Number of milligrams in 1 gram = Number of milligrams.

| 6 | × | 1,000 | = | 6,000 milligrams |

Therefore, 6 g = 6,000 mg.

Example 4

Solve: 3.6 kg = ? g.

Solution

To change from larger units (for example kg) to smaller units (for example g) multiply as follows:

Number of kilograms × Number of grams in 1 kilogram = Number of grams.

| 3.6 | × | 1,000 | = | 3,600 |

Therefore, 3.6 kg = 3, 600 grams.   **(Review decimal multiplication).**

Example 5

Solve: 7500 kg = ? metric ton

Solution

To change from smaller units (for example kg) to larger units (for example metric tons) divide as shown:

Number of kilograms ÷ Number of kilograms in 1 metric ton = Number of metric tons.

$$7,500 \quad ÷ \quad 1,000 \quad = \quad \frac{7500}{1000}$$

$$= \quad \frac{75\cancel{0}\cancel{0}}{10\cancel{0}\cancel{0}}$$

$$= \quad 7.5$$

Therefore, 7,500 kg = 7.5 metric tons

Example 6

Compare and write =, < or > for ?

3 metric tons ? 2,500,000 g

Solution

Setup: The first step in comparing numbers is to change the numbers to the same units before comparing.

Step 1: Change 3 metric tons to grams. To change from larger units (for example metric tons) to smaller units (for example grams) multiply as shown:

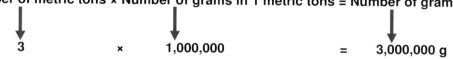

Number of metric tons × Number of grams in 1 metric tons = Number of grams.

| 3 | × | 1,000,000 | = | 3,000,000 g |

Therefore, 3 metric tons = 3,000,000 g.

But 3,000,000 g is greater than 2,500,00 g. Therefore, 3 metric tons > 2,500,000 g.

The notes and the generous worked examples have provided me with conceptual understanding and computational fluency to do my homework.

Exercises

1. Select the correct answer. The metric mass is based on:

    a. inches   **b**. meter   **c**. gram   **d**. kilogram

2. How many grams are there in the following? Hint: See Example 1.

    a. 6 kg   **b**. 2 kg   **c**. 1.5 kg   **d**. 3 kg

3. If the mass of 1 tablet of a medication is 500 mg, what is the weight of the tablet in grams? Hint: See Example 2.

4. Replace ? with the number that makes the statement true. Hint: See Example 3.

    a. 2 g = ? mg   **b**. 4 g = ? mg   **c**. 3 g = ? mg

5. Solve the following: Hint: See Example 4.

    a. 4.2 kg = ? g   **b**. 2.3 kg = ? g   **c**. 1.5 kg = ? g

6. Solve: Hint: See Example 5.

    a. 2,500 kg = ? metric tons   **b**. 3,300 kg = ? metric tons

    c. 1,100 kg = ? metric tons   **d**. 6,200 kg = ? metric tons

7. Compare and write =, < or > for ? Hint: See Example 6.

    a. 2 metric tons ? 2,000,000 g   **b**. 4 metric tons ? 3,900,000 g

    c. 3 metric tons ? 3,100,000 g   **d**. 5 kg ? 4,900 g

Challenge Questions

8. Solve:

    a. 4 metric tons = ? kg   **b**. 8 g = ? mg   **c**. 5000 g = ? kg.

    d. 3,000,000g =? metric tons   **e**. 4,500 mg = ? g.

CUSTOMARY UNITS OF WEIGHT

The basic unit of mass in the Customary System is the pound.

16 ounces (oz) =1 pound (lb)
2,000 pounds =1 ton (T)

Example 1

Solve: 40 oz = ? lb

To change from smaller units (for example, ounces) to larger units (for example pound), divide as shown:

Number of ounces ÷ Number of ounces in 1 pound = Number of pounds.

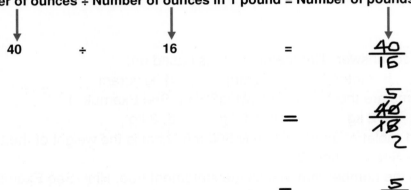

Therefore, 40 oz $= 2\frac{1}{2}$ lb.

Example 2

Solve: 4lb = ? oz.

Solution

To change from larger units (for example, pounds) to smaller units (for example ounces), multiply as shown:

Number of pounds × Number of ounces in 1 pound = Number of ounces.

| 4 | X | 16 | = | 64 ounces. |

Therefore, 4 lb = 64 oz.

Example 3

Solve: 6,000 lb = ? T
Solution
To change from smaller units (for example, pounds) to larger units (for example tons), divide as shown:

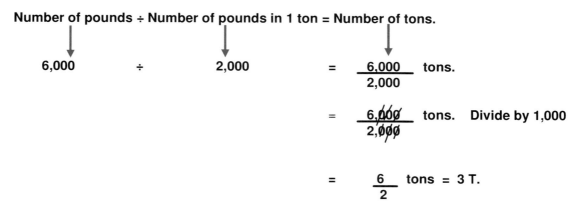

Number of pounds ÷ Number of pounds in 1 ton = Number of tons.

$$6,000 \div 2,000 = \frac{6,000}{2,000} \text{ tons.}$$

$$= \frac{6,\cancel{000}}{2,\cancel{000}} \text{ tons.} \quad \text{Divide by 1,000}$$

$$= \frac{6}{2} \text{ tons} = 3 \text{ T.}$$

Therefore, 6,000 lb = 3 T

Example 4

Solve: 4 T = ? lb
Solution
To change from larger units (for example, tons) to smaller units (for example pounds), multiply as shown:

Number of tons × Number of pounds in 1 ton = Number of pounds.

$$4 \times 2,000 = 8,000 \text{ pounds}$$

Therefore, 4 T = 8,000 lb.

REAL WORLD APPLICATION - WORD PROBLEMS
Customary Units of Weight

Example 5

How many 100-pound bags of potatoes can be obtained from a ton of potatoes?
Solution
Setup: Change a ton of potatoes to pounds of potatoes and then divide by 100 pounds.
To change from larger units (for example, tons) to smaller units (for example pounds), multiply as shown:

Number of tons × Number of pounds in 1 ton = Number of pounds.

$$1 \quad \times \quad 2{,}000 \quad = \quad 2{,}000 \text{ pounds.}$$

Therefore, there are 2000 lb in 1 ton.

To find how many 100-pound bags of potatoes are contained in the 2000 lb of potatoes, divide 2000 lb by 100 lb as shown:

$$\frac{2{,}000 \text{ lb}}{100 \text{ lb}} = \frac{2{,}000 \text{ lb}}{100 \text{ lb}} \qquad \text{Divide by 100.}$$

$$= 20$$

Therefore, there are 20-pound bags of potatoes in a ton of the potatoes.

Example 6

How much would 48 ounces of candy cost at $4.00 per pound?

Solution

Setup: Let us find how many pounds are there in 48 ounces, and then multiply the number of pounds in 48 ounces by $4.00 to obtain the cost of 48 ounces of the candy as shown:

To change from smaller units (for example, ounces) to larger units (for example pounds), divide as shown:

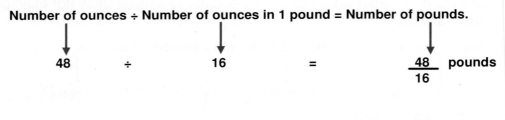

Number of ounces ÷ Number of ounces in 1 pound = Number of pounds.

$$48 \quad \div \quad 16 \quad = \quad \frac{48}{16} \text{ pounds}$$

$$= 3 \text{ (Divide by 4 and by 4 again).}$$

Therefore, there are 3 pounds in 48 ounces.

If 1 lb of the candy costs $4.00, then 3 lb of the candy will cost 3 × $4.00 = $12.00.

The notes and the generous worked examples have provided me with conceptual understanding and computational fluency to do my homework.

Exercises

1. The basic unit of mass in the Customary System is the_____.

2. Solve: Hint: See Example 1.

   a. 32 oz = ? lb   **b**. 24 oz = ? lb   **c**. 8 oz = ? lb   **d**. 48 oz = ? lb

3. Solve: Hit: See Example 2.

   a. 2 lb = ? oz   **b**. 5 lb = ? oz   **c**.10 lb = ? oz   **d**. 7 lb = ? oz

4. Solve: Hint: See Example 3.

   a. 2000 lb = ? T   **b**. 1000 lb = ? T   **c**. 4000lb = ? T   **d**. 8000 lb = ? T

5. Solve: Hint: See Example 6.

   a. 2 T = ? lb   **b**. 6 T = ? lb   **c**. 3 T = ? lb   **d**. 5 T = ? lb

6. Solve: Hint: See Example 5.

   How many 50-pound bags of rice can be obtained from 2 tons of rice?

7. Solve: Hint: See Example 6.

   How much would 32 ounces of candy cost at $3.00 per pound?

Challenge Questions

8. Solve: **a**. 6 lb = ? oz   **b**. 40 oz = ? lb   **c**. 10 T = ? lb   **d**. 5000 lb = ? t

Answers to Selected Questions

2a. 2 lb   **3a**. 32 oz   **4a**. 1 T   **5a**. 4000 lb

METRIC CAPACITY AND CUSTOMARY CAPACITY

METRIC CAPACITY

The basic unit in measuring liquid is the liter. The metric units of capacity are:

1,000 millimeters (ml) = 1 liter (L)

250 milliliters = 1 metric cup

4 metric cups = 1 liter

1,000 liters = 1 kilometer (KL)

Team Project

The class should be divided into four teams. (Each team should bring the big, bigger and the biggest empty containers of milk, orange juice and soda drink from the super market to the class.) Each team should sketch and complete the chart using the labels on the containers.

Table 1

Product Name	Big size/Sketch	Bigger size/Sketch	Biggest size/Sketch
Milk containers	Capacity = ?	Capacity = ?	capacity = 3.78 L
Orange juice container	Sketch = ? Capacity = ?	Sketch = ? Capacity = ?	Sketch = ? Capacity = ?
Soda drink container	Sketch = ? Capacity = ?	Sketch = ? Capacity = ?	Sketch = ? Capacity = ?

a. What size and what capacity of milk is used most in each team member's family?

b. What size and what capacity of orange juice is used the least in each member's family?

c. What size and what capacity of the soda drink is used the most in each team member's family?

Example 1
Explain when you would multiply or divide in order to change one unit to another unit.
Solution
In order to change from lower units such as milliliters to higher units such as liters we should **divide** because the final answer we are looking for should be less than the number of the lower unit. For example, 1,000 milliliters = 1 liter. Therefore, to change 1,000 milliliters to liters, we have to **divide** 1,000 milliliters by 1,000 to obtain the number of liters that are contained in 1,000 milliliters.

In order to change from higher units such as liters to metric cups, we should **multiply** because the final answer that we are looking for should be more than the number of the higher units. For example, 4 metric cups = 1 liter and to change 1 liter to metric cups we have to **multiply** the 1 liter by 4.

Example 2
Solve: 8 metric cups = ? liters.
Solution
To change smaller units (metric cups) to bigger units (liters) we **divide** as shown:

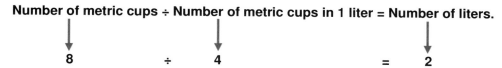

Number of metric cups ÷ Number of metric cups in 1 liter = Number of liters.

| 8 | ÷ | 4 | | = | 2 |

There are 2 liters in 8 metric cups.

Example 3

a. Change 22 liters to milliliters.

b. Change 164 milliliters to liters.

Solution

a. To change from larger units (such as liters) to smaller units (such as milliliters), we should **multiply** as shown:

Number of liters × Number of milliliters in 1 liter = Number of milliliters.

| 22 | × | 1,000 | = | 22,000 milliliters. |

Therefore, there are 22,000 milliliters in 22 liters.

b. To change from smaller units (such as milliliters) to larger units (such as liters), we should **divide** as shown:

Number of milliliters ÷ Number of milliliters in 1 liter = Number of liters

| 164 | ÷ | 1,000 | = | $\dfrac{164}{1,000}$ |

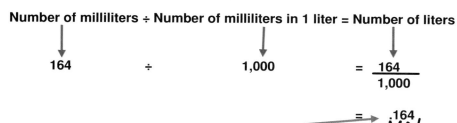

$$= \quad .164$$

We are dividing by 1,000 which has three zeros and therefore, we have to move the decimal point three places or three digits to the left.

Therefore, there are .164 liters in 164 milliliters.

Example 4

Solve: ? milliliters = 10 metric cups

Solution

To change from larger units (such as metric cups) to smaller units (such as milliliters) we multiply as shown:

Number of metric cups × Number of milliliters in 1 mtric cup = Number of milliliters.

| 10 | × | 250 | = | 2,500 milliliters |

Therefore, there are 2500 milliliters in 10 metric cups.

Example 5

Compare: Write <, >, or = for ? in the question.

a. 4,000 L ? 3 kL

b. 2 L ? 9 metric cups

Solution

a. In order to compare two quantities, we must change both quantities to the **same units** first before comparing. In this case, let us change kL to L first as shown:
To change from larger units (such as kL) to smaller units (such as L), multiply as shown:

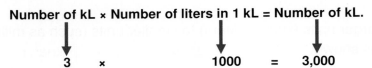

Number of kL × Number of liters in 1 kL = Number of kL.

　　3　×　　　　1000　　=　　3,000

Therefore, there are 3,000 liters in 3 kL.

We can now compare the 4,000 L and the 3,000 L because 3,000 L and 4,000 L have the same units. Since 4,000 L is greater than 3,000 L, we can write:
4,000 L > 3,000 L, and therefore, 4,000 L > 3 kL.
(Note: We have already showed that 3kL = 3,000 L.)

b. In order to compare two quantities, we must change both quantities to the same units first before comparing them. In this case, let us change 2L to metric cups first as shown:

To change from larger units (such as liters) to smaller units (such as metric cups) we multiply as shown:

Number of liters × Number of metric cups in 1 liter = Number of metric cups.

　　2　×　　　　4　　　=　　　　8 metric cups.

Therefore, there are 8 metric cups in 2 L.

Now, we can compare the 8 metric cups and the 9 metric cups because the 8 metric cups and the 9 metric cups have the same units. Since 8 metric cups is less than 9 metric cups we can write:
8 metric cups < 9 metric cups. Therefore, we can write:
2 L < 9 metric cups (Note: We have already showed that 2 L = 8 metric cups).

REAL WORLD APPLICATIONS - WORD PROBLEMS
Metric Capacity

Example 6

How many bottles each holding 150 milliliters of orange juice can be filled from a plastic container that holds 4.5 liters of the orange juice?

Solution

Change the 150 milliliters and 4.5 liters to the same unit, and then divide 4.5 liters by 150 milliliters. Let us change 4.5 liters to milliliters as shown:

Number of liters × Number of milliliters in 1 liter = Number of milliliters.

$$4.5 \quad \times \quad 1{,}000 \quad = \quad 4500.0 \text{ milliliters.}$$

Therefore, there are 4,500 milliliters in 4.5 liters.
Let us find how many 150 milliliters are contained in 4,500 milliliters by dividing 4,500 milliliters by 150 milliliters as shown:

$$\frac{4{,}500}{150} = \frac{4{,}500}{150} \qquad \text{Divide the numerator and the denominator by 10.}$$

$$= \frac{\overset{90}{450}}{\underset{3}{15}} \qquad \text{Divide the numerator and the denominator by 5.}$$

$$= \frac{\overset{30}{90}}{\underset{1}{3}} \qquad \text{Divide the numerator and the denominator by 3.}$$

$$= 30$$

Therefore, 30 bottles each holding 150 milliliters of orange juice can be filled from a plastic container that holds 4.5 liters of orange juice.

Example 7

Five engineers drank a total of 4 L of water. If each engineer drank an equal amount of water, how many milliliters did each engineer drink?

Solution

Step 1: Change 4 L to milliliters as shown:

To change from larger units (such as liters) to smaller units (such as milliliters) we should multiply as shown:

Number of liters × Number of milliliters in 1 liter = Number of milliliters.

$$4 \quad \times \quad 1{,}000 \quad = \quad 4000 \text{ milliliters.}$$

Therefore, there are 4000 milliliters in 4 liters.

Step 2: To find the amount of water that each engineer drank, find the average amount of water that each engineer drank by dividing 4000 milliliters by 5 engineers as shown:

$$\frac{4,000}{5} = \frac{\overset{800}{\cancel{4,000}}}{\underset{1}{\cancel{5}}}$$

= 800 milliliters of water.

Therefore, each engineer drank 800 milliliters of water.

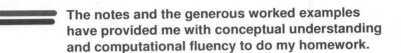

The notes and the generous worked examples have provided me with conceptual understanding and computational fluency to do my homework.

Exercises

1. When do we divide and when do we multiply if we want to convert one unit to another? Hint: See Example 1.

2. Solve: (Hint: See Example 2).
    a. 12 metric cups = ? liters   **b**. 4 metric cups = ? liters
    c. 16 metric cups = ? liters   **d**. 2 metric cups = ? liters

3a. Change 8 liters to milliliters. Hint: See Example **3a**.

3b. Change 158 milliliters to liters. Hint: See Example **3b**.

4. Solve: Hint: See example 4.
    a. ? milliliters = 8 metric cups.   **b**. ? milliliters = 5 metric cups.
    c. ? milliliters = 3 metric cups.   **d**. ? milliliters = 4 metric cups

5. Compare. Write <, > or = for ? in the questions. Hint: See example **5a**.
    a. 2000 L ? 4 kL   **b**. 2500 L ? 2 kL   **c**. 3000 L ? 3 kL   **d**. 5000 L ? 4 kL

6. Compare. Write <, > or = for ? in the questions. Hint: See Example **5b**.
    a. 2 L ? 8 metric cups   **b**. 3L ? 12 metric cups
    c. 16 metric cups ? 4 L   **d**. 8 metric cups ? 3 L

7. How many bottles each holding 100 milliliters can be filled from a plastic container that holds:
    a. 1 liter?   **b**. 2 liters?   **c**. 3 liters?   (Hint: See Example **6**.)

8. How many bottles each holding 250 milliliters of apple juice can be filled from a plastic container that holds:
    a. 1 liter of the apple juice?   **b**. 2 liters of the apple juice?
    c. 3 liters of the apple juice?
Hint: See Example 6.

9. Four nurses drank a total of 2 L of water. If each nurse drank an equal amount of water, how many milliliters did each nurse drink? Hint: See Example **7**.

Challenge Questions

10. Solve: **a.** ? milliliters = 6 metric cups   **b.** ? milliliters = 7 metric cups
11. Solve: **a.** 6 metric cups = ? liters   **b.** 10 metric cups = ? liters
12. How many bottles each holding 200 milliliters can be filled from a plastic container
that holds:
   a. 1 liter?   **b.** 4 liters?
14. Compare. Write <, > or = for ? in the questions.
   a. 3 L ? 12 metric cups   **b.** 5000 L ? 4 kL

Answers to Selected Questions

2a. 3 L   **3a.** 8,000 ml   **4a.** 2000 ml   **5a.** <

CUSTOMARY CAPACITY

The basic unit in measuring liquids in the Customary system is the gallon.
The Customary units of capacity are as shown:

8 fluid ounces (fl oz) = 1 cup (c)
2 cups = 1 pint (pt)
2 pints = 1 quart (qt)
4 cups = 1 quart (qt)
4 quarts = 1 gallon (gal)

Group Exercise
The class should be divided into four groups.
a. Each group should list four liquid products that can be seen at the supermarket
with their corresponding measurements involving capacity. For example, a
container of milk at the supermarket may have a capacity of one gallon or half
a gallon.
b. Sketch the container of each product.
c. Compare the lists with the corresponding capacities from the other groups and
list the products in increasing order of their capacity.

Example 1
In the Customary system the basic unit in measuring liquids is the gallon, true or
false? Hint: See notes.
Solution
The student is to find the answer to example 1 by reading the notes/text in this book.

Example 2
Solve: 12 quarts = ? pints

Solution

To change larger units (such as quarts) to smaller units (such as pints) **multiply** as shown:

Number of quarts × Number of pints in 1 quart = Number of pints.

$$12 \quad \times \quad 2 \quad = \quad 24 \text{ pints}$$

Example 3

Solve: 20 quarts = ? gal

Solution

To change smaller units (such as quarts) to larger units (such as gallons) **divide** as shown:

Number of quarts ÷ Number of quarts in 1 gallon = Number of gallons.

$$20 \quad \div \quad 4 \quad = \quad 5 \text{ gallons.}$$

Example 4

Solve: 16 c = ? qt

Solution

To change smaller units (such as cups) to larger units (such as quarts) **divide** as shown:

Number of cups ÷ Number of cups in 1 quart = Number of quarts.

$$16 \quad \div \quad 4 \quad = \quad 4 \text{ quarts}$$

Example 5

Solve: 6 gal = ? c

Solution

Setup: This is a two step solution.

Step 1: Change the gallons to quarts.

To change from larger units (such as gallons) to smaller units (such as quarts), **multiply** as shown:

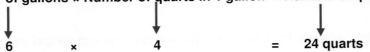

Number of gallons × Number of quarts in 1 gallon = Number of quarts.

$$6 \quad \times \quad 4 \quad = \quad 24 \text{ quarts}$$

Step 2: Change the 24 quarts to cups.

To change from larger units (such as quarts) to smaller units (such as cups), **multiply** as shown:

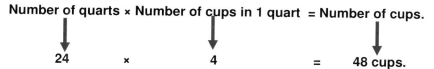

Number of quarts × Number of cups in 1 quart = Number of cups.

$$24 \quad \times \quad 4 \quad = \quad 48 \text{ cups.}$$

Example 6

Solve: 7 c = ? ft oz

To change larger units (such as cups) to smaller units (such as fluid ounces) **multiply** as shown:

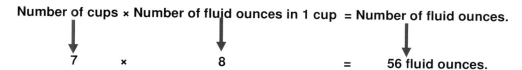

Number of cups × Number of fluid ounces in 1 cup = Number of fluid ounces.

$$7 \quad \times \quad 8 \quad = \quad 56 \text{ fluid ounces.}$$

Therefore, there are 56 fluid ounces in 7 cups.

REAL WORLD APPLICATIONS - WORD PROBLEMS
Customary Capacity

Example 7

Given that 1 gallon of a certain ice cream is on sale for $3.95 and two 1-quart containers of the same ice cream are on sale for $2.25. If Mary needs 1 gallon of ice cream for her birthday party, which is a better buy?

Solution

Setup: The better buy will be the least expensive buy. One choice is to buy the 1 gallon ice cream for $3.95 and the other choice is to buy four 1-quart containers of the same ice cream because 4 quarts makes 1 gallon.

Step 1: Find the cost of four 1-quart containers of the same ice cream.
Two 1–quart containers of ice cream = $2.25
Four 1–quart containers of ice cream = 2.25 × 2 = $4.50.

Step 2: Decide which size of the ice cream is a better buy.
Since $3.95 < $4.50, the 1 gallon of ice cream which is on sale for $3.95 is a better buy.

The notes and the generous worked examples have provided me with conceptual understanding and computational fluency to do my homework.

Exercises

1. In the customary system the basic unit for measuring liquid is _____
   Hint: See Example 1

2. Solve: (See Example 2).

   a. 10 quarts = ? pints
   c. 2 quarts = ? pints

   b. 4 quarts = ? pints
   d. 12 quarts = ? pints

3. Solve: (See Example 3).

   a. 12 quarts = ? gal
   c. 16 quarts = ? gal

   b. 8 quarts = ? gal
   d. 4 quarts = ? gal

4. Solve: (See Example 4).

   a. 4 c = ? qt
   c. 20 c = ? qt

   b. 12 c = ? qt
   d. 10 c = ? qt

5. Solve: (See Example 5).

   a. 4 gal = ? c
   c. 8 gal = ? c

   b. 10 gal = ? c
   d. 3 gal = ? c

6. Solve: (See Example 6).

   a. 6 c = ? ft oz
   c. 2 c = ? ft oz

   b. 3 c = ? ft oz
   d. 5 c = ? ft oz

7. If 1 gallon of type A ice cream costs $2.85 and 4 cups of type B ice cream costs $.50, which type of the ice cream is cheaper? Hint: See Example 7.

Challenge Questions

8. Solve:
   a. 7 gal = ? c
   d. 10 quarts = ? gal

   b. 16 c = ? qt
   e. 6 qt = ? qt

   c. 24 c = ? qt
   f. 4 gal = ? c

Cumulative Review

1. 15 ÷ (-3) =

2. -15 ÷ (-3) =

3. -24 ÷ 6 =

4. $\dfrac{3}{4} \div \dfrac{3}{8} =$

TIME

Review of How to Tell the Time

The time is 12: 20

The time is 9:55

Measuring time is measuring the interval of time between two separate events. An example of two separate events is when John started to eat and when John finished eating. We should be able to determine the length of the interval between two given times. There are 24 hours that make up a day and this 24 hours is divided into two periods, the A.M. (which is before noon) hours from 12 o'clock midnight to 12 o'clock noon and the P.M. (which is after noon) hours from 12 o'clock noon to 12 o'clock midnight.

Rule 1: To find the length of the time interval between two given times that are both A.M. or both P.M., subtract the hours and the minutes of the earlier time from the later time.

Rule 2: To find the length of the time interval between two given times when one is A.M. and the other is P.M., use the fact that 12:00 o'clock is the time that separates A.M. from P.M. hours, and therefore, we first find how far each of the given times is from 12:00 o'clock and secondly, we add the two results.

Table 1

The units of time are as follows:	
60 seconds (sec) = 1 minute (min)	
60 minutes	= 1 hour (hr)
24 hours	= 1 day (da)
7 days	= 1 week (wk)
4 weeks	= 1 month (mo)
52 weeks	= 1 year (yr)
365 days	= 1 year (yr)
366 days	= 1 leap year
10 years	= 1 decade
100 years	= 1 century
1,000 years	= 1 millennium

Example 1
What is the length of time between 7:15 A.M. and 10:50 A.M.?
Solution
Use Rule 1 to solve the question as shown:

$$
\begin{array}{ll}
10\ \text{hr} & 50\ \text{min} \\
-\ 7\ \text{hr} & 15\ \text{min} \\
\hline
3\ \text{hr} & 35\ \text{min}
\end{array}
$$

Therefore, the length of time between 7:15 A.M. and 10:50 A.M. is 3 hr and 35 minutes.

Example 2
Find the length of time between 2:50 P.M. and 10:23 P.M.
Solution
Use Rule 1 to solve the question as shown:

$$
\begin{array}{ll}
10\ \text{hr} & 23\ \text{min} \\
-\ 2\ \text{hr} & 50\ \text{min} \\
\hline
\end{array}
$$

We cannot subtract 50 minutes from 23 minutes, and therefore, we have to borrow 1 hr from 10 hr and this 1 hr becomes 60 minutes (see Table 1), and we then add the 60 minutes to the 23 minutes to obtain 83 minutes, and the 10 hours is therefore reduced to 9 hours, and then subtract as shown:

$$
\begin{array}{ll}
9 & 83 \\
\cancel{10}\ \text{hr} & \cancel{23}\ \text{min} \\
-\ 2\ \text{hr} & 50\ \text{min} \\
\hline
7\ \text{hr} & 33\ \text{min}
\end{array}
$$

Therefore, the length of the time between 2:50 P.M. and 10:23 P.M. is 7 hr 33 min.

Example 3
The school day of the Accra Middle School starts at 8:10 A.M and ends at 2:51 P.M. How long is the school day?
Solution
Use Rule 2 to solve the question as shown:
Step 1: Subtract to find the length of the time from 8:10 A.M. to 12:00 noon.

$$
\begin{array}{ll}
12\ \text{hr} & 00\ \text{min} \\
-\ 8\ \text{hr} & 10\ \text{min} \\
\hline
\end{array}
$$

We cannot subtract 10 minutes from 00 minutes, and therefore, we have to borrow 1 hour from 12 hours, and this 1 hr is 60 minutes (see Table 1), and we then add the 60 minutes to the 00 minutes to become 60 minutes and the 12 hours is therefore, reduced to 11 hours, and then we subtract as shown:

```
      11      60
      12 hr   00 min
    - 8 hr    10 min
    _____
      3 hr    50 min
```

Step 2: 2:51 P.M. is 2 hours and 51 minutes after 12:00 noon.

Step 3: Add the two intervals found in Steps 1 and 2 as shown:

```
      3 hr    50 min
    + 2 hr    51 min
    _____
      5 hr   101 min
```

Note that 101 minutes is more than 60 minutes and 60 minutes is equal to one hour. Divide 101 minutes by 60 to obtain the hours and minutes that are contained in 101 minutes as shown:

```
        1 hr remainder 41 minutes
    60 | 101 minutes
      - 60
       ____
        41
```

Therefore, 5 hr 101 min can be written as:

```
      5 hr
    + 1 hr    41 min
    _____
      6 hr    41 min
```

Therefore, the school day is 6 hours and 41 minutes.

Example 4

Find the length of the interval between 9:45 P.M and 4:10 A.M.

Solution

Use Rule 2 to solve the question as shown:

Step 1: Subtract to find the length of the time from 9:45 P.M to 12:00 midnight.

```
      12 hr    00 min
    -  9 hr    45 min
```

We cannot subtract 45 minutes from 00 minutes, and therefore, we borrow 1 hour from 12 hours and this 1 hour is 60 minutes and we add the 60 minutes to 00 minutes to obtain 60 minutes and the 12 hours is reduced to 11 hours and we then subtract as shown:

$$
\begin{array}{cc}
11 & 60 \\
\cancel{12}\ \text{hr} & \cancel{00}\ \text{min} \\
-\ \ 9\ \text{hr} & 45\ \text{min} \\
\hline
2\ \text{hr} & 15\ \text{min}
\end{array}
$$

Step 2: 4:10 A.M. is 4 hours and 10 minutes after 12 midnight.
Step 3: Add the two intervals found in steps 1 and 2 as shown:

$$
\begin{array}{cc}
2\ \text{hr} & 15\ \text{min} \\
+\ 4\ \text{hr} & 10\ \text{min} \\
\hline
6\ \text{hr} & 25\ \text{min}
\end{array}
$$

Therefore, the interval between 9:45 P.M and 4:10 A.M is 6 hr 25 min.

Example 5
How many hours are in 3 days?
Solution
To change from larger units such as days to smaller units such as hours, multiply as shown:

Number of days × Number of hours in 1 day = Number of hours.

3   ×   24   =   72 hours

Therefore, there are 72 hours in 3 days.

Example 6
How many weeks are in 28 days?
Solution
To change from smaller units such as days to larger units such as weeks, divide as shown:

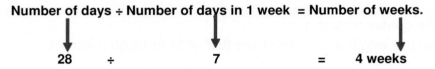

Number of days ÷ Number of days in 1 week = Number of weeks.

28   ÷   7   =   4 weeks

Therefore, there are 4 weeks in 28 days.

The notes and the generous worked examples have provided me with conceptual understanding and computational fluency to do my homework.

Exercises

1. State the rule that is used in finding the length of the time interval between two given times that are both A.M. or both P.M. Hint:See Rule 1.
2. State the rule that is used in finding the length of the time interval between two given times when one is A.M. and the other is P.M. Hint: See Rule 2.
3. Find the length of the interval between the two given times. Hint: See Example 1.
    a. 7:30 A.M. to 11:46 A.M.   **b**. 6:14 A.M. to 10:34 A.M.
    c. 9:47 A.M. to 10:59 A.M.   **d**. 10:01 A.M. to 11:09 A.M.
4. Find the length of the interval between the two given times. Hint: See Example 2.
    a. 6:30 P.M. to 9:40 P.M   **b**. 4:10 P.M. to 8:30 P.M.
    c. 7:20 A.M. to 10:45 A.M   **d**. 8:15 A.M. to 11:35 A.M
5. Find the length of the interval between the two given times. Hint: See Example 3.
    a. 10:30 A.M to 3:15 P.M   **b**. 9:00 A.M. to 2:30 P.M.
    c. 7:40 A.M. to 2:45 P.M.   **d**. 8:07 A.M. to 5:45 P.M.
6. Find the length of the interval between the two given times. Hint: See Example 4.
    a. 10:30 P.M to 2:30 A.M   **b**. 7:00 P.M. to 4:00 A.M
    c. 8:18 P.M. to 8:19 A.M   **d**. 11:20 P.M. to 1:40 A.M
7. Solve: (Hint: See Example 5).
    a. How many hours are in 6 days?   **b**. How many hours are in 2 days?
8. Solve: (Hint: See Example 6).
    a. How many weeks are in 21 days?   **b**. How many weeks are in 35 days?

Challenge Questions

9. Find the length of the interval between the two given times.
    a. 11:15 P.M. to 3:00 A.M.   **b**. 5:20 A.M. to 10:30 A.M.
    c. 7:48 A.M. to 11:57 A.M.   **d**. 1:31 P.M. to 9:20 P.M.
    e. 7:25 A.M. to 4:15 P.M.   **f**. 9:00 A.M. to 11:30 A.M.
    g. 6:18 A.M. to 11:30 A.M.   **h**. 2:40 P.M. to 3:15 A.M.

Answers to Selected Questions

3a. 4 hr 16 min   **4a**. 3 hr 10 min   **5a**. 4 hr 45 min.   **6a**. 4 hr 0 min

PROBABILITY

Cumulative Review

1. $8 + 9 =$ 2. $12 + 9 =$ 3. $11 - 8 =$ 4. $7 \times 2 =$
5. $12 \div 3 =$ 6. $23 - 14 =$ 7. $24 \div 6 =$ 8. $13 - 7 =$

9. $\begin{array}{r} 11 \\ \times\ 2 \\ \hline \end{array}$ 10. $\begin{array}{r} 26 \\ +\ 25 \\ \hline \end{array}$ 11. $\begin{array}{r} 31 \\ -\ 13 \\ \hline \end{array}$ 12. $\begin{array}{r} 8 \\ \times\ 4 \\ \hline \end{array}$

13. $18 \div 6 =$ 14. $24 \div 3 =$ 15. $12 + 8 =$ 16. $19 - 12 =$

17. $\begin{array}{r} 27 \\ \times\ 3 \\ \hline \end{array}$ 18. $\begin{array}{r} 17 \\ +\ 18 \\ \hline \end{array}$ 19. $\begin{array}{r} 39 \\ -\ 13 \\ \hline \end{array}$ 20. $\begin{array}{r} 18 \\ \times\ 4 \\ \hline \end{array}$

21. $48 \div 3 =$ 22. $24 \div 8 =$ 23. $12 + 38 =$ 24. $36 - 17 =$

25. $\begin{array}{r} 14 \\ \times\ 5 \\ \hline \end{array}$ 26. $\begin{array}{r} 23 \\ +\ 27 \\ \hline \end{array}$ 27. $\begin{array}{r} 19 \\ -\ 15 \\ \hline \end{array}$ 28. $\begin{array}{r} 12 \\ \times\ 3 \\ \hline \end{array}$

29. $48 - 17 =$ 30. $20 \div 4 =$ 31. $16 + 38 =$ 32. $28 - 16 =$

New Terms: probability, outcome, experiment

Probability is sometimes used in decision making. For example, if two friends
want to go to either a movie or a football game together, but they are not sure if they
should go to the movie first or the football game, then they may use coin flipping for
decision making. There must be established rules before the coin is flipped, such as,
if a head appears, they should go to the movie first and if a tail appears, they
should go to the football game first.

Class Exercise
1. Give reasons why you think that coin flipping for decision making is not fair.
2. Give reasons why you think that coin flipping for decision making is fair.
.

Group Exercise
In a soccer game, a coin toss is used to decide which team gets to select on which
direction of the field it wants to play towards on the first play of the game.
Let us divide the class into two soccer teams of Team A and Team B. Each
team should toss a coin 10 times and record the results using the tally table as

shown:

Team A and Team B Sample Chart

Trials	Heads tally	Tails tally
1st trial		
2nd trial		
3rd trial		
4th trial		
5th trial		
6th trial		
7th trial		
8th trial		
9th trial		
10th trial		
Total trials		
Fraction	$\dfrac{\text{Number of Heads}}{\text{Sum of total trials of heads and tails}} = \dfrac{?}{10}$	

Add up the results for the heads and tails. Find the fraction of the heads by using the formula :

$$\text{Fraction of the heads} = \frac{\text{Number of heads}}{\text{Number of trials}} = \frac{?}{10}$$

Find the fraction of the tails by using the formula:

$$\text{Fraction of the tails} = \frac{\text{Number of tails}}{\text{Number of trials}} = \frac{?}{10}$$

Conclusions of the Group Exercise

1. The group exercise is an example of an **experiment**. Therefore, the toss of a coin is an experiment.
2. The result of the experiment is the **outcome**. Therefore, the results of the number of heads and tails during the toss of the coin is the outcome.
3. The fraction of heads is actually the chances of obtaining a head when the coin is tossed 10 times, and this is known as the **probability** of obtaining a head.
4. The fraction of tails is actually the chances of obtaining a tail when the coin is tossed 10 times, and this is known as the **probability** of obtaining a tail.
5. From the group exercise, what is the fraction of heads? What is the probability of obtaining a head?
6. From the group exercise, what is the fraction of tails? What is the probability of obtaining a tail?
7. The outcomes of Team A and Team B should not necessarily be the same.

8. Note that the probability that Team A and Team B have found are fractions, for example, $\frac{?}{10}$. However, the probability can be expressed in **decimal** and **percent** also. Each group should change the fractional probability to decimal and percent probability (review the section on Decimal and Percent.)

9. When a coin was tossed, it was equally likely for either a head or a tail to occur. When outcomes have the same chance of occurring, they are said to be **equally likely**.

10. In the group exercise, we tossed the coin 10 times. It is possible to toss the coin more than 10 times, such as 20, 40, 100, or 200 times. Note that **the more we repeat the experiment, the closer we are to the true value of the probability**.

Experimental Probability

Experimental probability can be found by repeating an experiment many times and observing the results, as we did with the group exercise.

The formula for finding the experimental probability is given as shown:

$$\text{Experimental probability (outcome)} = \frac{\text{number of outcomes}}{\text{number of times the experiment was repeated}}$$

The experimental probability is sometimes called the **relative frequency**.

Example 1

A coin was tossed 45 times and 25 heads occurred.

(a) What is the experimental probability of obtaining heads? Express your answer as a fraction, a decimal, and a percent. Round your answer to the nearest hundredth.

(b) What is the experimental probability of obtaining tails? Express your answer as a fraction, a decimal, and a percent. Round your answer to two decimal places.

Solution

The number of times the coin was tossed = 45
The number of times the heads occurred = 25

$$\text{Experimental probability of heads} = \frac{\text{number of times heads occurred}}{\text{number of times the coin was tossed}}$$

$$= \frac{25}{45} \quad \text{This is the fractional form.}$$

$$= \frac{\overset{5}{25}}{\underset{9}{45}} \quad \text{Reduce to the lowest term by dividing by 5.}$$

$$= \frac{5}{9} \quad \text{This is the probability in the fractional form,}$$

reduced to the lowest term.

To change the probability of $\frac{5}{9}$ to decimal, divide 5 by 9 as shown:

$$
\begin{array}{r}
.555 \\
9\overline{\smash{)}50} \\
-\ 45 \\
\hline
050 \\
-\ 45 \\
\hline
050 \\
-\ 45 \\
\hline
05
\end{array}
$$

The decimal probability is .56 to the nearest hundredth. (Review the section on decimal fractions.)

The decimal probability of .56 can be changed to a percent form by moving the decimal point in .56 two decimal places or two digits to the right which is the same as multiplying .56 by 100 as shown:

$$.56 = .56 = 56\%$$

Move the decimal point two decimal places to the right.

Decimal
↓

Therefore, the probability of $\frac{5}{9}$ = .56 = 56%.

↑   ↑

Fraction   Percent

(b) The coin was tossed 45 times and the outcome in each toss was either a head or a tail. Since the heads occurred 25 times, then the number of tails is 45 − 25 = 20.

$$\text{Experimental probability of tails} = \frac{\text{Number of times tails occurred}}{\text{Number of times the coin was tossed.}}$$

$$= \frac{20}{45} \quad \text{This is the fractional form.}$$

$$= \frac{\overset{4}{\cancel{20}}}{\underset{9}{\cancel{45}}}$$ Reducing to the lowest term by dividing by 5.

$$= \frac{4}{9}$$ This is the probability in the fractional form,

reduced to the lowest term.

To change the probability of $\frac{4}{9}$ to a decimal form, divide 4 by 9 as shown:

$$
\begin{array}{r}
.444 \\
9\overline{)40} \\
\underline{36} \\
40 \\
\underline{36} \\
40 \\
\underline{36} \\
4
\end{array}
$$

The decimal probability = .44 to the nearest hundredth.

The decimal probability of .44 can be changed to a percent by moving the decimal point in .44 two decimal places or two digits to the right which is the same as multiplying .44 by 100 as shown:

$$.44 = .44 = 44\%$$

Move the decimal point two places to the right.

Decimal
↓

Therefore, the probability of $\frac{4}{9}$ = .44 = 44%

↑   ↑
Fraction   Percent

Example 2

What is the probability of getting a tail when a coin is tossed?

Solution

We can use the tree diagram to solve the problem as follows with H representing a head and T representing a tail when a coin is tossed once.

a head and T representing a tail when a coin is tossed once.

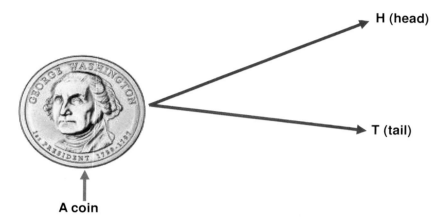

A coin

There is one successful outcome of a tail or a T out of two possible outcomes of H or T as shown in the diagram. There are two possible outcomes, which are a head or a tail when a coin is tossed.

The probability of getting a tail when a coin is tossed

$$= \frac{\text{Number of successful outcomes}}{\text{Number of possible outcomes}} = \frac{1}{2}$$

Special Note: The probability of getting a tail is $\frac{1}{2}$ and this can also be expressed in a decimal form as .5 and in percent form as 50%. This means that the probability of getting a head $= 100\% - 50\% = 50\%$ (The total probability $= 100\%$ or 1). We can then say that there is a **fifty-fifty chance** of getting a head or a tail when a coin is tossed.

Example 3
(a) Using T_1 and T_2 for tails and H_1 and H_2 for heads, show all the possible outcomes of tossing a coin twice by drawing a tree diagram.
(b) How is the tree diagram read? Write the possible outcomes.
(c) Explain the possible outcomes in terms of probability.
Solution
(a) The tree diagram is shown as shown:

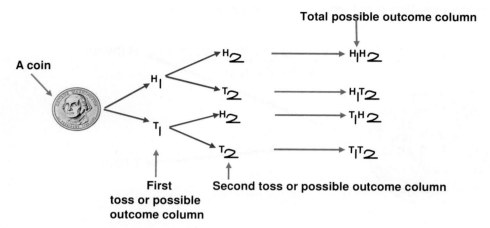

Total possible outcome column

A coin

H_1

$H_2 \longrightarrow H_1H_2$

$T_2 \longrightarrow H_1T_2$

T_1

$H_2 \longrightarrow T_1H_2$

$T_2 \longrightarrow T_1T_2$

First toss or possible outcome column

Second toss or possible outcome column

(b) The tree diagram is read by following each branch from left to right. Using this idea and starting from the top of the tree diagram, the possible outcomes are: H_1H_2, H_1T_2, T_1H_2, and T_1T_2.

(c) There are 4 possible outcomes which are H_1H_2, H_1T_2, T_1H_2, and T_1T_2. Exactly two heads or H_1H_2 occurred one time out of the 4 outcomes, and therefore the probability of obtaining exactly two heads

$$= \frac{\text{Number of times } H_1H_2 \text{ occurred}}{\text{Total possible outcomes}}$$

$$= \frac{1}{4}$$

The probability that at least one head occurred is 3 times in H_1H_2, H_1T_2, and T_1H_2 out of 4 possible outcomes of H_1H_2, H_1T_2, T_1H_2, and T_1T_2 is:

$$= \frac{\text{Number of times that at least one head occurred}}{\text{Total possible outcomes}}$$

$$= \frac{3}{4} \quad \text{(At least one head occurred 3 times in } H_1H_2, H_1T_2, \text{ and } T_1H_2\text{).}$$

The probability that at least one tail occurred 3 times in H_1T_2, T_1H_2, and T_1T_2 out of 4 possible outcomes of H_1H_2, H_1T_2, T_1H_2, and T_1T_2

$$= \frac{\text{Number of times at least one tail occurred}}{\text{Total possible outcomes}}$$

$$= \frac{3}{4}$$

The probability of exactly two tails or T_1T_2 occurred one time out of the 4 possible outcomes of H_1H_2, H_1T_2, T_1H_2, and T_1T_2

$$= \frac{\text{Number of times exactly two tails occurred}}{\text{Total possible outcomes}}$$

$$= \frac{1}{4}$$

The probability of no tails occurring is the same as the probability of exactly two heads occurring because there is no T_1 or T_2 in H_1H_2.

The probability of no heads occurring is the same as the probability of exactly two tails occurring because there is no H_1 or H_2 in T_1T_2.

Special Note: Tossing two coins once is the same as tossing one coin twice.

Group Exercise

Recall that experimental probability is sometimes called relative frequency. Let us find out how we can use relative frequency to find the probability. The class should select one person as the recorder to record the month in which every student in the class was born on a frequency table as shown:

Months	Jan	Feb	Mar	Apr	May	June	July	Aug	Sept	Oct	Nov	Dec
Frequency												

Frequency here means how many students are born in each month.
Sum of the frequencies = Total number of students in the class.
Let us answer a few questions.
(a) What is the fraction of the students who were born in January?

$$\text{The fraction of the students who were born in January} = \frac{\text{Frequency for January}}{\text{Sum of the frequencies}}$$

$$= \frac{\text{No. of students born in January}}{\text{Total number of students}}$$

Using your frequency table, find the fraction of the students who were born in January. How do you think that we can interpret this fraction? We can interpret this fraction by stating that the probability of selecting a student at random from the class that was born in January.

(b) Similarly, we can find the probability of selecting a student at random that was born in August as shown:

Probability of selecting a student at random that was born in August =

$$\frac{\text{Frequency of students born in August}}{\text{Sum of the frequencies}} = \frac{\text{No. of students born in August}}{\text{Total number of students in the class}}$$

Using your frequency table, find the probability that if a student is selected at random from the class, that student was born in August.

(c) Similarly using your frequency table, find the probability that if a student is selected at random, the student was born in: (1) June, (2) December, (3) April, (4) October.

Note: **Random** selection means that the selection is from a population without being biased. Population means a group , such as a group of students in a class or the total number of students is a population of students.

Exercises

1. Explain what is meant by probability.
2. Explain what is meant by an experiment and an outcome of an experiment.
3. Explain what is meant by the probability of obtaining a head.
4. Explain what is meant by "an outcome is equally likely."
5. The more we repeat the experiment, the closer we are to the true value of the probability. True or False?
6. What is the formula for finding experimental probability?.
7. The experimental probability is sometimes called relative frequency. True or False?
8. A coin was tossed 10 times and 3 heads occurred.
   (a) What is the experimental probability of obtaining a head. Express your answer in a fraction, a decimal, and a percent. Hint: See Example **1**.
   (b) What is the experimental probability of obtaining a tail? Express your answer in a fraction, a decimal, and a percent. Hint: See Example 1.
9. A coin was tossed 15 times and 5 tails occurred.
   (a) What is the probability of obtaining a tail? Express your answer in a fraction, a decimal, and a percent. Hint: See Example **1**.
   (b) What is the probability of obtaining a head? Express your answer in a fraction, a decimal, and a percent. Hint: See Example **1**.
10. Explain why a coin is tossed, there is a fifty-fifty chance of obtaining a head or a tail? Hint: See Example **2**.
11. Draw a tree diagram when a coin is tossed twice.
   (a) From your diagram, what are the possible outcomes?
   (b) What is the probability of obtaining exactly 2 tails?
   (c) What is the probability of obtaining exactly 2 heads?
   Hint: See Example **3**.

THEORETICAL PROBABILITY

Theoretical probability is when the probability of an event is found without doing an experiment.
A set of outcomes for a particular experiment is known as an **event**.

$$\text{Theoretical probability of an event} = \frac{\text{Number of outcomes in the event}}{\text{Total number of possible outcomes}}$$

Example 1
What is the theoretical probability that in the spinner below, the pointer will:
(a) land on 2?   (b) land on an even number?
(c) land on an odd number?   (d) land on a prime number?

Solution
(a) There is one outcome of 2 out of a total of 4 possible outcomes of 1, 2, 3, and 4
   when the pointer lands on 2. Therefore, the theoretical probability that the spinner

   $$\text{will land on 2} = \frac{\text{Number of the number 2 outcomes}}{\text{Total number of possible outcomes}}$$

   $$= \frac{1}{4}$$

(b) The even numbers on the spinner are 2 and 4, and that means, there will be two
   outcomes of even numbers out of a possible of 4 outcomes of 1, 2, 3, and 4.
   Therefore, the theoretical probability that the spinner will land on an even number

   $$= \frac{\text{Number of even number outcomes}}{\text{Total number of possible outcomes}}$$

   $$= \frac{2}{4}$$

   $$= \frac{\overset{1}{2}}{\underset{2}{4}} \quad \text{Reduce to the lowest term by dividing by 2.}$$

569

$$= \frac{1}{2}$$

(c) The odd numbers on the spinner are 1 and 3, that means, there will be two outcomes of odd numbers out of a total of 4 possible outcomes of 1,2,3, and 4. Therefore, the theoretical probability that the spinner will land on an odd number

$$= \frac{\text{Number of odd number outcomes}}{\text{Total number of possible outcomes}}$$

$$= \frac{2}{4}$$

$$= \frac{\frac{1}{2}}{\frac{4}{2}} \quad \text{Reduce to the lowest term by dividing by 2.}$$

$$= \frac{1}{2}$$

(d) A prime number is a number that has exactly two factors, which are 1 and the number itself. Out of the numbers 1, 2, 3, and 4 on the spinner, only 2 and 3 are prime numbers. Therefore, two out of four numbers are prime numbers. Therefore, there will be two outcomes of prime numbers out of the possible 4 outcomes of 1, 2, 3, and 4.

Theoretical probability of a prime number $= \dfrac{\text{Number of prime number outcomes}}{\text{Total number of possible outcomes}}$

$$= \frac{2}{4}$$

$$= \frac{\frac{1}{2}}{\frac{4}{2}} \quad \text{Reduce to the lowest term by dividing by 2}$$

$$= \frac{1}{2}$$

Example 2

Find the theoretical probability of each event .

(a) The spinner stops on C.

(b) The spinner stops on a vowel.

Solution

(a) There is one letter which is C out of a possible 8 letters.

$$\text{The theoretical probability of event C} = \frac{\text{Number of outcomes of C}}{\text{Total number of possible outcomes}}$$

$$= \frac{1}{8}$$

(b) All the vowels in the English language are a, e, i, o, and u. The vowels on the spinner are A, O and U, therefore, there are 3 vowels out of the 8 possible letters on the spinner.

The theoretical probability that the spinner stops on a vowel

$$= \frac{\text{Number of outcomes of a vowel}}{\text{Total number of possible outcomes}}$$

$$= \frac{3}{8}$$

0 and 1 Probability Values

A probability of 0 is an event that cannot happen, and it is, therefore, an **impossible event**. A probability of 1 is an event that must happen, and it is, therefore a **certain event**. Some events are either impossible or certain. For example if, a bag contains only 10 green apples, the probability of drawing a green apple is $\frac{10}{10}$ which is 1.

The event of drawing a green apple is certain to occur because no other types of apples are in the bag and therefore, no other result is possible. An event which is certain to occur has a probability of 1.

Using the same bag of green apples, the event of drawing a red apple is impossible because the bag contains no red apples. Therefore, the probability of drawing a red apple is $\frac{0}{10} = 0$. An **impossible event has a probability of 0**.

Some more examples of impossible events are:

(a) obtaining an outcome of 7 from a single roll of a die because the maximum number on a die is 6, and so the outcome of a 7 will never occur. The number of outcomes of a 7 is 0 out of the possible outcomes of 6. Therefore, the probability of obtaining a 7 is $\dfrac{0}{6} = 0$. Obtaining an outcome of a 7 is impossible.

(b) A spinner has the numbers 1, 2, 3, 4, and 5. The probability of obtaining an outcome of a 9 out of 5 possible outcomes is 0 because there is no 9 on the spinner. Obtaining an outcome of a 9 is impossible.

Group Exercise
Decide if the following events are impossible or certain:
(a) A spinner has the numbers 1, 2, 3, 4, 5, 6, 7, and 8. What is the probability of the pointer stopping on 10?
(b) A bag has 6 black pens. What is the probability of drawing a red pen? What is the probability of drawing a black pen?
(c) The probability of obtaining a 10 from the roll of a single die.

Extreme Values of Probability
The extreme values of probability are 0 and 1 where an impossible event is 0 and an event certain to happen is 1. The probability of all other events is between 0 and 1. The extreme values of probability means the minimum and the maximum values of probability.

Example 3
Plot the probability of an impossible event, certain event, a 50-50 chance event, an equally likely event, 0% chance of an event and 100% chance of an event.
Solution
Since the extreme values of probability are 0 and 1, probabilities can be plotted on the part of a number line between 0 and 1 as shown:

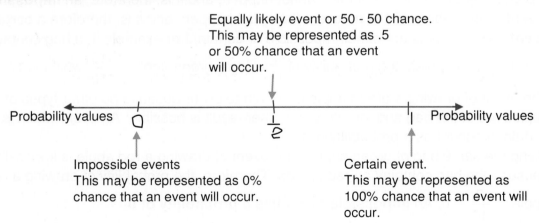

Comparing the Values of Probability
Since an event which is certain to happen has a probability of 1 and an impossible event has a probability of 0, an event which has a probability value close to 1 has a better chance of occurring than an event that has a probability value that is close to 0.

Rule: Given the probability values of many events, the event that has the highest probability value has the best chance of occurring and the event that has the lowest probability value has the least chance of occurring.

If the value of an event is close to 0, it is likely that the **event will not occur.** If the value of an event is close to 1, it is likely that the **event will occur.**

Group Exercise

1. Using the rule, select the event which has the best chance of occurring and the least chance of occurring and explain your choices.
(a) Event A has the probability of .4 of occurring, event B has the probability of .2 of occurring and event C has the probability of .9 of occurring.

(b) Event A has the probability of $\frac{3}{4}$ of occurring, event B has the probability of $\frac{1}{4}$ of occurring and event C has the probability of $\frac{4}{4}$ of occurring.

(c) Event A has the probability of $\frac{1}{2}$ of occurring, event B has the probability of $\frac{1}{4}$ of occurring and event C has the probability of $\frac{1}{3}$ of occurring. Hint: Change all the fractions of the probabilities to have the **same** least common denominator (LCD), and then you will be able to compare the fractions (numerators). (Hint: Refer to the sections/chapter on fractions.) You may also change all the fractions to decimals and then compare the decimals. (Hint: Refer to the section/chapter on decimals.)

(d) Event A has an 80% chance of occurring, event B has a 20% chance of occurring, and event C has a 100% chance of occurring.

2. Discuss five examples of impossible events and five examples of certain events in everyday life. The class should be divided into 8 groups for the discussion and each group should record their five examples and report them to the class.

Example 4

A spinner is divided into 8 sections. If the pointer is spun, find the theoretical probability that it will land on:

(a) a number 3   (b) an even number   (c) an odd number
(d) a prime number   (e) a number 9   (f) a number greater than 8
(g) a number which is not a 6   (h) a number less than 5
(i) a number greater than 3

Indicate the probabilities of the events on a number line.

Solution

These solutions may be considered by some students to be long, but this example is designed to show the students various ways to solve the problem and also to enable the students to logically compare many solution methods.

(a) There is only one number 3 out of the total number of 8. Therefore, the probability of landing on the number 3 out of 8 numbers can be represented as shown:

$$\text{The the theoretical probability of landing on 3} = \frac{\text{Number of outcomes of 3}}{\text{Total number of possible outcomes}}$$

$$= \frac{1}{8}$$

(b) An even number is a number that can be divided by 2. The spinner has 4 even numbers which are 2, 4, 6, and 8 out of a total of 8 numbers on the spinner. Therefore, the probability of landing on an even number can be represented as shown:

The theoretical probability of landing on an even number

$$= \frac{\text{Number of even number outcomes}}{\text{Total number of possible outcomes}}$$

$$= \frac{4}{8}$$

$$= \frac{\overset{1}{\cancel{4}}}{\underset{2}{\cancel{8}}} \quad \text{Reduce to the lowest term by dividing by 4}$$

$$= \frac{1}{2}$$

(c) An odd number is a number that cannot be divided by 2. The spinner has 4 odd numbers which are 1, 3, 5, and 7 out of a total of 8 numbers on the spinner. Therefore, the probability of landing on an odd number can be represented as shown:

The theoretical probability of landing on an odd number

$$= \frac{\text{Number of odd number outcomes}}{\text{Total number of possible outcomes}}$$

$$= \frac{4}{8}$$

$$= \frac{\overset{1}{\cancel{4}}}{\underset{2}{\cancel{8}}} \quad \text{Reducing to lowest term by dividing by 4.}$$

$$= \frac{1}{2}$$

(d) A prime number is a number that has exactly two factors, which are 1 and the number itself. There are four prime numbers on the spinner, which are 2, 3, 5, and 7 out of the total of 8 numbers on the spinner. Therefore, the probability of landing on a prime number can be represented as shown:

Theoretical probability of landing on a prime number

$$= \frac{\text{Number of outcomes of a prime number}}{\text{Total number of possible outcomes}}$$

$$= \frac{4}{8}$$

$$= \frac{\overset{1}{\cancel{4}}}{\underset{2}{\cancel{8}}} \quad \text{Reduce to the lowest term by dividing by 4.}$$

$$= \frac{1}{2}$$

(e) There is no number 9 on the spinner, so it is impossible for the pointer to land on number 9. The impossible events have the probability of 0.

(f) There is no number greater than 8, so it is impossible for the pointer to land on a number greater than 8. The impossible events have the probability of 0.

(g) The total number of numbers on the spinner is 8. If the pointer will not land on 6, then the pointer will land on the other 7 remaining numbers of 1, 2, 3, 4, 5, 7, and 8 out of the total number of 8 on the spinner. The probability that the pointer will not land on the number 6 can be represented as:

$$\text{Theoretical probability of not landing on 6} = \frac{\text{Number of outcomes of not landing on 6}}{\text{Total possible outcomes}}$$

$$= \frac{7}{8}$$

(h) The numbers on the spinner which are less than 5 are 1, 2, 3, and 4. Therefore, there are 4 numbers that are less than 5 out of the total number of 8 numbers on the spinner. The probability that the pointer will land on a number less than 5 can be represented as:

Theoretical probability of landing on a number less than 5

$$= \frac{\text{Number of outcomes that are less than 5}}{\text{Total possible outcomes}}$$

$$= \frac{4}{8}$$

$$= \frac{\overset{1}{\cancel{4}}}{\underset{2}{\cancel{8}}} \quad \text{Reduce to the lowest term by dividing by 4.}$$

$$= \frac{1}{2}$$

(i) The numbers on the spinner which are greater than 3 are 4, 5, 6, 7, and 8. There are a total of five numbers that are greater than 3 out of the total number of 8 on the spinner.
Theoretical probability of landing on a number which is greater than 3

$$= \frac{\text{Number of outcomes} > 3}{\text{Total possible outcomes}}$$

$$= \frac{5}{8}$$

The probabilities of the events are indicated on the number line using assigned solution numbers.

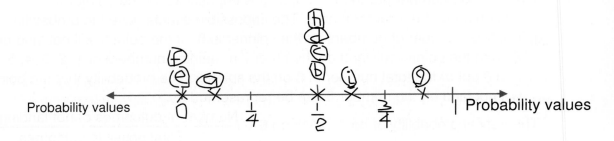

Example 5
(a) Find the theoretical probability of the outcome of B. Give your answer in a
fraction, a decimal, and a percent form.
(b) Find the experimental probability of the outcome of B.
(c) Find the experimental probability of the outcome of A.
(d) Find the experimental probability of the outcome of C.
(e) Find the experimental probability of the outcome of D.

This diagram is used to find the theoretical
probability because the data on the spinner
is obtained without conducting any
experiment.

Outcome	Number of spins
A	8
B	2
C	7
D	3
Total	20

This diagram is used to find the
experimental probability because
the data in the diagram is got
from conducting the experiment.

Solution
(a) The spinner is divided into 4 equal sections labelled A, B, C, and D. Section B is 1
out of the 4 equal parts of the spinner.

$$\text{Theoretical probability of outcome of B} = \frac{\text{Number of outcomes of B}}{\text{Total number of possible outcomes}}$$

$$= \frac{1}{4} \text{ (Fraction form of the probability).}$$

The decimal form of the theoretical probability of $\frac{1}{4}$ can be obtained by dividing 1

by 4 as shown:

$$
\begin{array}{r}
.25 \\
4\overline{)10} \\
-8 \\
\overline{20} \\
-20 \\
\overline{00}
\end{array}
$$

The decimal form of the theoretical probability of $\frac{1}{4}$ = .25

The decimal form of the theoretical probability of .25 can be changed to a percent by
moving the decimal point 2 places or two digits to the right, and attaching the
percent sign (%), which is the same as multiplying by 100 as shown:

577

$$.25 = .25. = 25\%$$

Therefore, the theoretical probability of $\dfrac{1}{4} = .25 = 25\%$

(b) The number of spins that give the outcomes of B are 2 out of the total of 20 spins.

Experimental probability of outcome of B $= \dfrac{\text{Number of spins that give outcomes of B}}{\text{Total number of possible spins}}$

$$= \dfrac{2}{20}$$

$$= \dfrac{\overset{1}{2}}{\underset{10}{20}} \quad \text{Reduce to the lowest term by dividing by 2.}$$

$$= \dfrac{1}{10}$$

(c) The number of spins that give the outcomes of A are 8 out of the total of 20 spins.

Experimental probability of outcome of A $= \dfrac{\text{Number of spins that give outcomes of A}}{\text{Total number of possible spins}}$

$$= \dfrac{8}{20}$$

$$= \dfrac{\overset{2}{8}}{\underset{5}{20}} \quad \text{Reduce to the lowest term by dividing by 4.}$$

$$= \dfrac{2}{5}$$

(d) The number of spins that give the outcomes of C are 7 out of the total of 20 spins.

Experimental probability of outcome of C $= \dfrac{\text{Number of spins that give outcomes of C}}{\text{Total number of possible spins}}$

$$= \dfrac{7}{20}$$

(e) The number of spins that give the outcomes of D are 3 out of the total of 20 spins.

Experimental probability of outcome of D = $\dfrac{\text{Number of spins that give outcomes of D}}{\text{Total number of possible spins}}$

$$= \frac{3}{20}$$

Example 6
A die is a small solid cube marked on each face from one to six spots or dots.

 ←———This is a die.

A die was rolled 10 times. On 2 of the rolls, the outcome was three dots on the die.
(a) What is the experimental probability of rolling a three?
   Give your answer as a fraction, a decimal, and a percent.
(b) How many rolls was the outcome not showing the side with three dots? What is the experimental probability of not rolling the side with three dots?
(c) Based on the experimental probabilities that you have found, and suppose the die is rolled 100 times, about how many times do you expect to roll a side:
   (i) with three dots?
   (ii) without three dots?

Solution
Note that this is an experimental probability because the event was repeated, for example, it was repeated 10 times.
(a) The outcome of the three dots on the die is 2 out of 10 total possible rolls.
   Experimental probability of the outcome of rolling a three

$$= \frac{\text{Number of outcomes of rolling a three on a side}}{\text{Total number of possible rolls or outcomes}}$$

$$= \frac{2}{10}$$

$$= \frac{\overset{1}{\cancel{2}}}{\underset{5}{\cancel{10}}} \qquad \text{Reduce to the lowest term by dividing by 2.}$$

$$= \frac{1}{5}$$

The experimental probability of $\dfrac{1}{5}$ can be expressed as a decimal by dividing 1 by 5 as shown:

$$\begin{array}{r} .2 \\ 5\overline{)10} \\ -\underline{10} \\ 00 \end{array}$$

Therefore, the decimal form of the experimental probability of $\frac{1}{5}$ = .2

The decimal form of the experimental probability of .2 can be expressed as a percent by moving the decimal point two places or two digits to the right and attaching the percent sign (%) which is the same as multiplying by 100 as shown:

Write a zero here as a place holder.

$.2 = .20 = 20\%$

Therefore, the experimental probability of $\frac{1}{5}$ = .2 = 20%

(b) The die was rolled 10 times. The outcome of the side with three dots was 2 and therefore, the number of rolls that the outcomes were not the side with three dots

= 10 rolls - 2 rolls

= 8 rolls

Experimental probability of not rolling the side with three dots

$$= \frac{\text{Number of outcomes without rolling a three}}{\text{Total number of possible rolls or outcomes}}$$

$$= \frac{8}{10}$$

$$= \frac{\overset{4}{\cancel{8}}}{\underset{5}{\cancel{10}}} \qquad \text{Reduce to the lowest term by dividing by 2.}$$

$$= \frac{4}{5}$$

(c)(i) From Example 6(c), the number of possible rolls = 100.

Let the number of outcomes with three dots when the die is rolled 100 times = x. The experimental probability of the outcomes with the three dots when the die is rolled 100 times

$$= \frac{\text{Number of outcomes with a three when the die is rolled 100 times}}{\text{Number of possible rolls}}$$

$$= \frac{x}{100} \text{————————————————————}[A]$$

From the solution of Example 6(a), the experimental probability of the outcome of the side with the three dots $= \frac{1}{5}$ ————————————$[B]$

Equation $[A]$ and equation $[B]$ are equal because $\frac{x}{100}$ and $\frac{1}{5}$ are equivalent fractions or equivalent ratios, therefore,

$$\frac{x}{100} = \frac{1}{5} \text{————————————————}[C]$$

(Review the section on Equivalent Fractions or Equivalent Ratios).
The cross products of equivalent fractions or ratios are equal, so

$$\frac{x}{100} \bowtie \frac{1}{5}$$

Therefore, $5 \times x = 100 \times 1$

$$5x = 100 \text{————————————————}[D]$$

Divide each side of equation $[D]$ by 5 in order to obtain the value of x as shown:

$$\frac{\overset{x}{\cancel{5x}}}{\underset{1}{\cancel{5}}} = \frac{\overset{20}{\cancel{100}}}{\underset{1}{\cancel{5}}}$$

$$x = 20 \text{ outcomes of three dots.}$$

(ii) From Example 6(c), the number of possible rolls = 100.

Let $y = $ "the number of times of outcomes with no side with three dots out of 100 possible rolls."

The experimental probability of not rolling the side with three dots out of 100 possible outcomes

$$= \frac{\text{Number of outcomes with no three dots when the die is rolled 100 times}}{\text{Total number of possible rolls}}$$

$$= \frac{y}{100} \text{————————————————————}[E]$$

From solution of Example 6(b), the experimental probability of not rolling the side with three dots $= \frac{4}{5}$ ————————————$[F]$

Equation $[E]$ and equation $[F]$ are equal because $\dfrac{y}{100}$ and $\dfrac{4}{5}$ are equivalent fractions or ratios, and therefore,

$$\dfrac{y}{100} = \dfrac{4}{5}$$

(Review the section on Equivalent Fractions and Equivalent Ratios).
The cross products of equivalent fractions or ratios are equal, so

$$\dfrac{y}{100} \times \dfrac{4}{5}$$

Therefore, $= 5 \times y = 4 \times 100$

$$5y = 400 \text{———————————————}[G]$$

Divide each side of equation $[G]$ by 5 in order to obtain the value of y as shown:

$$\dfrac{5y}{5} = \dfrac{400}{5}$$

$$\dfrac{\overset{y}{\cancel{5y}}}{\underset{1}{\cancel{5}}} = \dfrac{\overset{80}{\cancel{400}}}{\underset{1}{\cancel{5}}} \quad \text{Divide each side of the equation by 5.}$$

$y = 80$ outcomes of not rolling a side with three dots.

Example 7
(Example 7 is intentionally designed to be long to provide the student with critical and logical methods of solving diverse problems.)
A die was thrown once.
(a) List the possible outcomes.
　　From your possible outcomes in (a), what is the theoretical probability of rolling:
(b) an even number.　　　　(c) an odd number.　　(d) a number greater than 2.
(e) a number between 2 and 5.　(f) a multiple of 3.　　(g) not a multiple of 3.
(h) a prime number.　　　　(i) not a prime number.

Solution
(a) A die has six sides and the sides are numbered from 1 to 6. When the die is thrown, any of the six sides can show up, so there are six possible outcomes, which are 1, 2, 3, 4, 5, and 6.
(b) The even numbers out of the total possible outcomes of 1, 2, 3, 4, 5 and 6 are 2, 4, and 6. There are three even numbers out of the total of 6 possible outcomes. The theoretical probability of obtaining an even number

$$= \frac{\text{Number of outcomes of an even number}}{\text{Total number of possible outcomes}}$$

$$= \frac{3}{6}$$

$$= \frac{\overset{1}{\cancel{3}}}{\underset{2}{\cancel{6}}} \qquad \text{Reduce to the lowest term by dividing by 3.}$$

$$= \frac{1}{2}$$

(c) The odd numbers out of the total possible outcomes of 1, 2, 3, 4, 5, and 6 are 1, 3, and 5. Therefore, there are three odd numbers out of the total of 6 possible outcomes.

The theoretical probability of obtaining an odd number

$$= \frac{\text{Number of outcomes of an odd number}}{\text{Total number of possible outcomes}}$$

$$= \frac{3}{6}$$

$$= \frac{\overset{1}{\cancel{3}}}{\underset{3}{\cancel{6}}} \qquad \text{Reduce to the lowest term by dividing by 3.}$$

$$= \frac{1}{2}$$

(d) The outcome of the numbers that are greater than 2 out of the total possible outcomes of 1, 2, 3, 4, 5, and 6 are 3, 4, 5, and 6. There are four numbers, which are greater than 2 out of the total possible outcome of 6 numbers. The theoretical probability of obtaining a number greater than 2

$$= \frac{\text{Number of outcomes greater than 2}}{\text{Total number of possible outcomes}}$$

$$= \frac{4}{6}$$

$$= \frac{\overset{2}{4}}{\underset{3}{6}} \qquad \text{Reduce to the lowest term by dividing by 2.}$$

$$= \frac{2}{3}$$

(e) The numbers between 2 and 5 are 3 and 4 out of the total possible outcomes of 1, 2, 3, 4, 5, and 6. There are two numbers between 2 and 5 out of the total possible outcome of 6 numbers.

The theoretical probability of obtaining a number between 2 and 5

$$= \frac{\text{Number of outcomes of a number between 2 and 5}}{\text{Total number of possible outcomes}}$$

$$= \frac{2}{6}$$

$$= \frac{\overset{1}{2}}{\underset{3}{6}} \qquad \text{Reduce to the lowest term by dividing by 2.}$$

$$= \frac{1}{3}$$

(f) The multiples of 3 out of the total numbers of possible outcomes of 1, 2, 3, 4, 5, and 6 are 3 and 6. There are two numbers (3 and 6) that are multiples of 3 out of the total of the 6 possible outcomes of 1, 2, 3, 4, 5, and 6.

The theoretical probability of obtaining a multiple of 3

$$= \frac{\text{Number of outcomes of a multiple of 3}}{\text{Total number of possible outcomes}}$$

$$= \frac{2}{6}$$

$$= \frac{\overset{1}{2}}{\underset{3}{6}} \quad \text{Reduce to the lowest term by dividing by 2.}$$

$$= \frac{1}{3}$$

(g) The numbers that are not multiples of 3 out of the total outcomes of 1, 2, 3, 4, 5, and 6 are 1, 2, 4, and 5. There are 4 numbers (1, 2, 4, and 5) that are not multiples of 3 out of a total of 6 possible outcomes.

The theoretical probability of obtaining a number that is not a multiple of 3

$$= \frac{\text{Number of outcomes that are not multiples of 3}}{\text{Total number of possible outcomes}}$$

$$= \frac{4}{6}$$

$$= \frac{\overset{2}{\cancel{4}}}{\underset{3}{\cancel{6}}} \qquad \text{Reduce to the lowest term by dividing by 2}$$

$$= \frac{2}{3}$$

(h) A prime number has exactly two factors which are 1 and the number itself. The prime numbers out of the total possible outcomes of 1, 2, 3, 4, 5, and 6 are 2, 3, and 5. There are 3 prime numbers (2, 3, and 5) out of the total possible outcomes of 6 numbers.

The theoretical probability of obtaining a prime number

$$= \frac{\text{Number of outcomes of a prime number}}{\text{Total number of possible outcomes}}$$

$$= \frac{3}{6}$$

$$= \frac{\overset{1}{\cancel{3}}}{\underset{2}{\cancel{6}}} \qquad \text{Reduce to the lowest term by dividing by 3.}$$

$$= \frac{1}{2}$$

(i) The numbers which are not prime numbers out of the total possible outcome of

1, 2, 3, 4, 5, and 6 are 1, 4, and 6. There are 3 numbers (1, 4, and 6), which are not prime numbers out of a total possible outcomes of 6 numbers.

The theoretical probability of not getting a prime number

$$= \frac{\text{Number of outcomes which are not a prime number}}{\text{Total number of possible outcomes}}$$

$$= \frac{3}{6}$$

$$= \frac{\overset{1}{\cancel{3}}}{\underset{2}{\cancel{6}}} \qquad \text{Reduce to the lowest term by dividing by 3.}$$

$$= \frac{1}{2}$$

Exercises

1. Explain what is meant by (a) theoretical probability, (b) an event.
2. How do you find the theoretical probability of an event?
3. What is the theoretical probability that if you spin the spinner:

   (a). The pointer will land on 3?
   (b). The pointer will land on an even number?
   (c). The pointer will land on an odd number?
   (d). The pointer will land on a prime number?
   Hint: See Example 1.

4. Find the theoretical probability of each event:

   (a). The spinner will stop on E.
   (b). The spinner will stop on a vowel.
   Hint: See example 2.

5. Explain (a) an impossible event, (b) equally likely event, (c) certain event.
   Hint: See Example 3.
6. The probability of an event A occurring is .6, B occurring is .9, C occurring is .5, and D occurring is .2. By comparing the probability values, which event is most likely to occur and which event is least likely to occur? Hint: See the section under "Comparing the Values of Probability."
7. Find the theoretical probability that the pointer will land on:

(a). a number 10.
(b). a number 0.
(c). an odd number.
(d). an even number.
(e). a number less than 3.
(f). a prime number.
Indicate the probabilities on a number line.
Hint: See example 4.

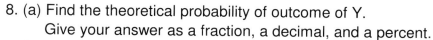

8. (a) Find the theoretical probability of outcome of Y.
   Give your answer as a fraction, a decimal, and a percent.
   (b) Find the experimental probability of the outcome of W.
   (c) Find the experimental probability of the outcome of Z.
   (d) Find the experimental probability of the outcome of Y.
   (e) Find the experimental probability of the outcome of X.
   Hint: See Example **5**.

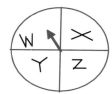

Outcome	Number of spins
W	3
X	6
Y	8
X	4

9. A die was rolled 20 times. On 4 of the rolls the outcome was a 2.
   (a) What is the experimental probability of rolling a 2?
   Give your answer as a fraction, a decimal, and a percent.
   (b) How many rolls was the outcome not showing a 2? What is the experimental probability of not rolling a 2?
   (c) Based on the experimental probabilities that you have found and suppose the die is rolled 100 times, about how many times do you expect to roll a side:
   (i) with a 2?
   (ii) without a 2?
   Hint: See Example **6**.

10. A die was thrown once.
    (a) List the possible outcomes.
    From your possible outcomes in (a), what is the theoretical probability of obtaining:
    (b) an odd number?   (c) an even number?
    (d) a number greater than 4?   (e) a number between 3 and 6?
    (f) a multiple of 2?   (g) not a multiple of 2?
    (h) a prime number?   (i) not a prime number?
    Hint: See Example **7**.

Challenge Questions

11. Using the spinner, what is the probability in fractions, decimals and percent of:

      (a). Obtaining a number less than 30.
      (b). Obtaining a number between 15 and 35.
      (c). Obtaining an even number?
      (d). Obtaining an odd number?
      (e). Obtaining a number greater than 60.

12. A bag contains 3 green balls and 7 yellow balls. If a ball is selected at random, what is the probability that the ball is: (a) green, (b) yellow, (c) not green, (d) not yellow?

Answers to Selected Questions

3a. $\dfrac{1}{3}$ **4a.** $\dfrac{1}{4}$ **7a.** 0

GRAPHS

Cumulative Review

1. $13 + 8 =$ **2.** $12 \div 4 =$ **3.** $16 - 8 =$ **4.** $8 \times 3 =$

5. $25 \div 5 =$ **6.** $21 - 12 =$ **7.** $30 \div 6 =$ **8.** $17 - 8 =$

9. $\begin{array}{r} 24 \\ \times\ 3 \\ \hline \end{array}$ **10.** $\begin{array}{r} 14 \\ +\ 19 \\ \hline \end{array}$ **11.** $\begin{array}{r} 35 \\ -\ 13 \\ \hline \end{array}$ **12.** $\begin{array}{r} 19 \\ \times\ 4 \\ \hline \end{array}$

13. $48 \div 3 =$ **14.** $24 \div 8 =$ **15.** $12 + 38 =$ **16.** $36 - 17 =$

17. $2.9 + 3.7 =$ **18.** $5.6 \times 4 =$ **19.** $2.5 \times 3.4 =$ **20.** $24.7 - 1.6 =$

21. $\dfrac{2}{3} \times \dfrac{1}{5} =$ **22.** $\dfrac{2}{3} \div \dfrac{2}{5} =$ **23.** $\dfrac{3}{4} - \dfrac{1}{5} =$ **24.** $2\dfrac{1}{3} + 3\dfrac{3}{4} =$

New Terms: frequency table, at least, at most, fewer than, relative frequency

Interpreting Data

Frequency Table
A **frequency table** is a table that shows the number of times each event occurs.

Note that in the tally column in example 1, the 5th time of an event is indicated by crossing the previous 4 events as follows: ~~1111~~ .

Example 1

The frequency table shows the number of subjects studied by students in grade 11 at the Peki Secondary school in Ghana.

Number of subjects studied by students		
Number of subjects studied	Number of students. Tally	Number of students. Frequency
9	1111	4
8	~~1111~~ ~~1111~~ 11	12
7	~~1111~~ 1	6
6	111	3
5	11	2

a. How many students studied 8 subjects?

b. How many students studied at least 7 subjects?

c. How many students studied 6 or more subjects?

d. How many students studied at most 7 subjects?

e. How many students were in the survey?

f. What percent of the students studied 6 subjects?

g. What percent of the students studied fewer than 6 subjects?

h. What percent of the students studied at least 7 subjects?

i. What percent of the students studied at most 7 subjects?

j. What is the relative frequency of the students that studied 5 subjects?

k. If a student is selected at random, what is the probability that the student studied 9 subjects?

Solution

a. The frequency column shows that 12 students studied 8 subjects.

b. "**At least 7 subjects**" means 7 or more subjects. Therefore, the number of students that studied at least 7 subjects is the sum of the frequencies of the students that studied 7, 8, and 9 subjects which = 6 + 12 + 4 = 22 students.

c. The number of students that studied 6 or more subjects is the sum of the frequencies of the students that studied 6, 7, 8, and 9 subjects which = 3 + 6 + 12 + 4 = 25 students.

d. "**At most 7 subjects**" means 7 or less subjects. Therefore, the number of students that studied at most 7 subjects is the sum of the frequencies of the students that studied 7, 6, and 5 subjects which = 6 + 3 + 2 = 11 students.

e. The number of the students in the survey is the sum of the total frequency which
$$= 4 + 12 + 6 + 3 + 2 = 27 \text{ students.}$$

f. Percent of students that studied 6 subjects

$$= \frac{\text{Number that studied 6 subjects}}{\text{Total number of students}} \times 100 \quad \text{(Hint: Review the section on Percent.)}$$

$$= \frac{3}{27} \times 100 \qquad\qquad (\frac{\text{Part}}{\text{Total}} \times 100 = \text{Percent of the total.})$$

$$= \frac{\overset{1}{\cancel{3}}}{\underset{9}{\cancel{27}}} \times 100 \qquad\qquad \text{Divide by 3.}$$

$$= \frac{100}{9} = 11\frac{1}{9}\% \qquad\qquad \text{Divide by 9.}$$

g. Those who studied **fewer than** 6 subjects means those who studied 5 subjects. The number of students that studied 5 subjects = 2

h. Percent of the students that studied **at least** 7 subjects

$$= \frac{\text{Number that studied at least 7 subjects}}{\text{Total number of students}} \times 100 \quad \text{(Review the section on percent).}$$

$$= \frac{22}{27} \times 100 \qquad\qquad \text{(From solution (b) 22 students studied at least 7 subjects)}$$

$$(\frac{\text{part}}{\text{Total}} \times 100 = \text{percent of total}).$$

$$= 81.48\% \qquad\qquad \text{You many use a calender.}$$

i. Percent of students that studied **at most** 7 subjects

$$= \frac{\text{Number of students that studied at most 7 subjects}}{\text{Total number of students}} \times 100$$

Review the section on Percent.

$$= \frac{11}{27} \times 100 \qquad\qquad (\frac{\text{Part}}{\text{Total}} \times 100 = \text{Percent of the total}).$$

(From solution **d**, the number of the students that studied at most 7 subjects is 11).

$$= 40.74\% \qquad\qquad \text{You may use a calculator.}$$

j. The relative frequency of an event

$$= \frac{\text{Frequency of the event.}}{\text{Total frequencies}}, \text{ therefore,}$$

the **relative frequency** of the students that studied 5 subjects

$$= \frac{\text{Frequency of the students that studied 5 subjects}}{\text{Total frequencies}}$$

$$= \frac{2}{27}$$

k. Probability that a student selected studied 9 subjects

$$= \frac{\text{Number of students that studied 9 subjects}}{\text{Total number of students}}$$

(Review the section on Probability).

$$= \frac{4}{27}$$

Bar Graph

A bar graph is a graph in which the height of the vertical bars represent the frequencies or values assigned to each activity. The bars are spaced evenly and they may be drawn vertically or horizontally. A bar graph is drawn from a frequency table.

Example 2

Use the bar graph to answer the following question:

(The bar graph is located on the next page.)

Students' test scores in percent.

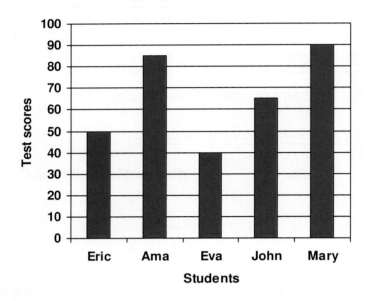

a. Who did the best in the test?

b. Who did the poorest in the test?

c. How many more marks did Mary have than Erica?

d. Who scored 10% more marks than Eva?

e. What is the range of the scores?

Solution

a. Mary had the highest score of 90%, and therefore, Mary did the best in the test.

b. Eva had the lowest score of 40%, and therefore Eva did poorest in the test.

c. Mary's score was 90%, and Eric's score was 50%, and therefore, Mary has 40% or (90% - 50%) more marks than Eric.

d. Eric scored 50%, and Eva scored 40%, and therefore, Eric scored 10% or (50% - 40%) more marks than Eva.

e. The range of the scores:

$$= \text{Greatest score - Least score}$$
$$= 90\% - 40\%$$
$$= 50\%$$

Example 3

Use the frequency table to draw a bar graph on graph paper. Hint: Recall that the bar graph is spaced evenly and may be drawn vertically or horizontally.

Number of movies attended in 3 months by students		
Number of movies	Number of students. Tally	Number of students. Frequency
3	~~1111~~ ~~1111~~ 1	11
2	~~1111~~ 111	8
1	111	3
0	1111	4

Solution

The horizontal bar graph is drawn as shown below. Hint: You may draw the vertical bar graph as shown in Example **2** if you want.

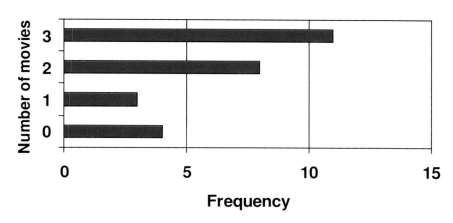

Hint: It is best to draw graphs on a graph or grid paper.

Multiple Bar Graph
A multiple bar graph consists of two or more component bar columns or graphs which are evenly spaced and the heights of the component bars represent the frequencies or values assigned to each activity. Like a bar graph, the multiple bar graph can be vertical or horizontal.

Test scores of two schools in percent		
Year	School A	School B
2000	95	80
2001	85	90
2002	95	95

a. Which school had the better score in 2000?
b. In which year were the performance of schools A and B the same?
Solution

Test scores of two schools in percent.

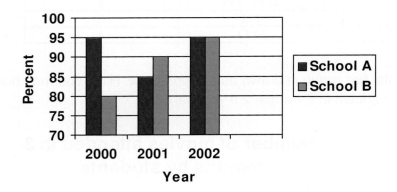

The graph shows a vertical multiple bar graph. The component bar column or graph are evenly spaced and the heights of the component bar columns represent the frequencies or values assigned to each activity.

a. School A had a better score than school B because school A had a higher score of 95% in 2000 whereas school B has a score of 80%.

b. The performance of the schools A and B were the same in 2002 because both schools had the same score of 95%. Hint: It is best to draw graphs on graph paper or grid paper.

Histogram

A histogram is a bar graph which does not have any space between the bars.
Like the bar graph, a histogram can be vertical or horizontal.

Example 5

Some school districts in Ghana were surveyed to find the number of goals scored by the soccer teams during the year. A frequency table is made with intervals of 10 goals.

Goals	Frequency of the school district
0 - 9	3
10 - 19	4
20 - 29	2
30 - 39	0
40 - 49	1
50 - 59	3

a. Draw a histogram of the frequency table.

b. From the survey, how many school districts scored the highest number of goals?

c. How many school districts took part in the survey?

d. How many school districts scored the least number of goals?

e. If a school district is selected at random,

    (i) what is the probability that its goals are between 10 - 19?

    (ii) what is the probability that its goals are between 30 -39?

  Hint: Review the section on probability.

Solution

a. The histogram of the frequency table is drawn. Hint: It is best to draw a graph on a paper or grid paper.

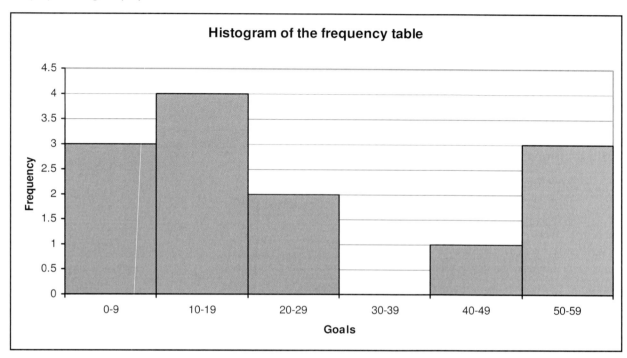

b. Three schools scored the highest number of goals between 50 - 59 goals.

c. The number of the school districts that took part in the survey

$$= \text{sum of the frequencies}$$
$$= 3 + 4 + 2 + 0 + 1 + 3$$
$$= 13 \text{ school districts.}$$

d. Three schools scored the least goals in the interval of 0 - 9 goals.

e(i). The number of school districts that have goals between 10 - 19 is 4. The total number of school districts that took part in the survey is the sum of the frequencies which is $(3 + 4 + 2 + 0 + 1 + 3 = 13)$.

The probability of selecting a school district that has goals between 10 - 19

$$\frac{\text{Number of school districts that have goals between 10 - 19}}{\text{Total number of schools}}$$

$$= \frac{4}{13}$$

e(ii). The number of school districts that have goals between 30 - 39 is 0. The total number of school districts that took part in the survey is the sum of the frequencies which is $(3 + 4 + 2 + 0 + 1 + 3 = 13)$. Therefore, the number of school districts that has goals between 30 - 39

$$= \frac{\text{Number of school districts that have goals between 30 - 39}}{\text{Total number of school districts}}$$

$$= \frac{0}{13} = 0$$

Example 6
Use the frequency table to draw a histogram.

Students	Joe	Mary	Eric	Ben	Eli
Ages in years	6	7	10	9	8

Solution
The histogram of the frequency table is drawn. Hint: It is best to draw graphs on graph paper or grid paper.

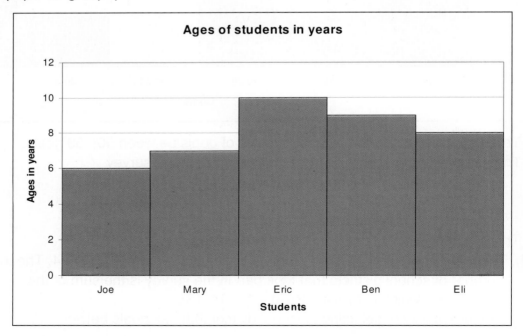

Line Graphs
Line graphs are ordered pairs from a data in a table and the ordered pairs are plotted on a grid or graph paper and the points of the plotted ordered pairs are

connected with lines. What is the line graph used for? **The line graph is used to find or estimate one of the ordered pairs if the other ordered pair is known.**

Example 7

Make a line graph of the given data.

Months	1	2	3	4	5	6	7
Savings in dollars	10	15	10	8	5	20	30

Solution

Use the ordered pairs of the data to plot each point, for example, the first set of the data is the savings in the first month which is $10 which may be written as a pair of data as (months, dollars) or (1,10) where 1 is the first month's savings and 10 is $10 saved in the first month. Similarly, the other sets of data or ordered pairs of data are (2, 15), (3, 10), (4, 8), (5, 5), (6, 20), and (7, 30). To plot the points using the ordered pairs of data, first draw the axis for the savings for the months horizontally and draw the axis for the savings vertically and then for the first ordered pair of data (1,10), locate 1 which represents the first month on the horizontal axis and locate the 10 which represent the $10 on the vertical axis. Where (1,10) meet is the required point to be plotted. Similarly, you can plot the points of the remaining ordered pairs of data. (Hint: See how to plot points under the chapter on "Coordinate Geometry.") Connect the points with lines to form a line graph as shown.

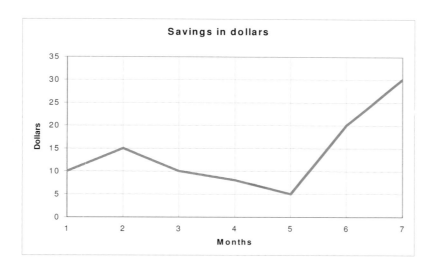

When a line in a line graph goes up from left to right, it shows that there is **an increase in the data**. When a line in a line graph goes down from left to right, it shows that there is **a decrease in the data**. When a line in a line graph is horizontal (for example between two points,) it shows that there is **no change in the data**. The **trend** in the data is the increase or decrease in the data.

Example 8

Use the line graph to answer each question (**a** to **d**.)

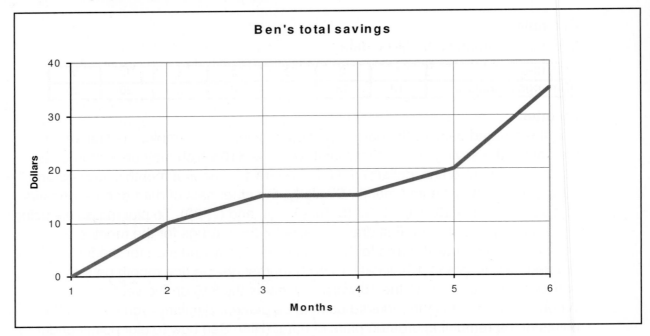

Ben's total savings

a. During which month did Ben not save any money? Explain your answer.
b. During which month did Ben save most? Give reasons for your answer.
c. If Ben is saving his money to buy a calculator which costs $70, what percent of the money did he save at the end of the fifth week?
d. Did the savings increase from the first month to the second month? Explain your answer.
e. In Example 7, did the savings increase or decrease from the second month to the third month? Explain your answer.

Solution

a. Ben did not save any money during the third month because the line graph during the third month is horizontal which means that there was no increment of savings in the third month.
b. Ben saved most in the fifth month because the line graph during the fifth month is the steepest which shows the greatest savings of $35 - $20 = $15.
c. The total money saved at the end of the fifth month is $35. Therefore, the percent of the amount saved is:

$$= \frac{35}{70} \times 100 \qquad (\frac{\text{Part}}{\text{Total}} \times 100 = \text{Percent of the total}).$$

$$= \frac{\overset{5}{\cancel{35}}}{\underset{7}{\cancel{70}}} \times \overset{}{\cancel{100}} \qquad \text{Divide by 10 and 7.}$$

598

$$= 5 \times 10 = 50\%$$

d. Yes, the savings has increased from the first month to the second month because, the line of the line graph between the first and second months went up from left to right.

e. The savings has decreased from the second month to the third month because the line of the line graph between the second and the third months went down from left to right.

Circle Graph

A circle graph is data shown in a circle using the sectors of the circle proportionally.

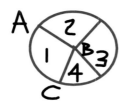

In this circle graph, the area 1, 2, 3, and 4 represent sectors. For example, the sector ABC is represented by area 1.

Example 9

If Mary spends her monthly income according to the circle graph, find:

a. How much she spends on rent?

b. How much she spends on food?

c. How much more does she spend on the rent than food monthly?

d. On which item does she spend the least amount of money?

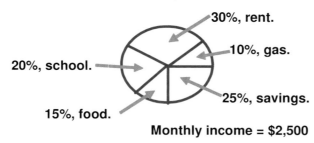

Monthly income = $2,500

Solution

a. She spent 30% of $2,500 on rent,

$$= \frac{30}{100} \times \$2,500 \quad \text{(Express 30\% as } \frac{30}{100} \text{ and "of" is the same as}$$

multiplication). Hint: Review the section on percent.

599

$$= \dfrac{\overset{25}{\cancel{30}}}{\cancel{100}} \times \$2,500 \qquad \text{Divide by 100 by canceling the two zeros.}$$

$$= 30 \times \$25$$
$$= \$750.$$

b. She spends 15% of $2,500 on food,

$$= \dfrac{15}{100} \times \$2,500 \qquad \left(\text{Express 15\% as } \dfrac{15}{100} \text{ and "of" is the same as}\right.$$

multiplication.) Hint: Review the section on Percent.

$$= \dfrac{15}{\cancel{100}} \times \$2,5\cancel{00} \qquad \text{Divide by 100 by canceling the zeros}$$

$$= 15 \times \$25 = \$375$$

c. From the solution of **a**, she spends $750 on rent, from the solution of **b**, she spends $375 on food, and therefore, she spends

$750 - $375 more on rent than food.

$$= \$375$$

d. She spends the least amount of money on gas because the percent of gas is the lowest percent among the items that she spends money on.

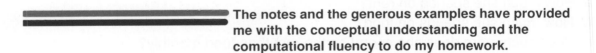 The notes and the generous examples have provided me with the conceptual understanding and the computational fluency to do my homework.

Exercises

1. Answer the questions by using the frequency table. Hint: See Example 1.
   a. How many students were surveyed?
   b. How many students had their driving lessons at least by the age of 18 years?
   c. How many students had their driving lessons at most by the age of 17 years?
   d. What percent of the students had their driving license at the age of 18 years?
   e. What percent of the students had their driving license at the age less than 18 years?
   f. What percent of the students had their driving license at the age of at least 17 least?
   g. What is the relative frequency of the students who had their driving license at the age of 19 years.
   h. If a student is selected at random, what is the probability that the student is

16 years old?

Student's age of obtaining a license.		
Age	Tally	Frequency
16	~~1111~~ ~~1111~~ 11	12
17	~~1111~~ 111	8
18	~~1111~~	5
19	111	3

2. Describe a bar graph.

3. Use the bar graph to answer the following questions:

   a. Who did the best in the test?

   b. Who did the poorest on the test?

   c. How many more marks did student D have than student A?

   d. Which student had 25% more marks than student A?

   e. What is the range of scores?

  Hint: See Example **2**.

Test scores of students A, B, C, and D in percent.

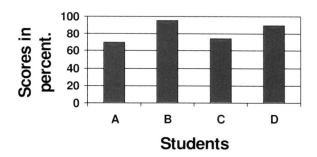

4. Use the frequency table to draw a bar graph on a graph paper.
   Hint: See Example **3**.

Number of movies attended in 3 months by students		
Number of movies.	Number of students. Tally	Number of students. Frequency
4	~~1111~~ 11	7
3	1111	4
2	~~1111~~ 111	8
1	~~1111~~	5
0	11	2

5. Describe a multiple bar graph.

6. Use the table to draw a multiple bar graph.

Year	Test scores of two schools A and B in percent.	
	School A	School B
2002	88	92
2003	79	80
2004	95	95
2005	98	97

(**a**) Which school had the better score in 2004?

(**b**) In which year were the scores of schools A and B the same?

Hint: See Example **4**.

7. Describe a histogram.

8. Use the data in the table to draw a histogram.

Goals (soccer)	Frequency of schools.
0 - 9	2
10 - 19	5
20 - 29	3
30 - 39	0
40 - 49	4
50 - 59	7
60 - 69	1

a. How many schools scored the highest number of goals?

b. How many schools took part in the survey?

c. How many schools scored the least number of goals?

d. If a school is selected at random, what is the probability that the school's goals were between 50 - 59?

e. If a school is selected at random, what is the probability that the school's goals were between 20 - 29?

f. If a school is selected at random, what is the probability that the school's goals were between 30 - 39?

Hint: See Example **5**.

9. Use the frequency table to draw a histogram.

Students	Nick	Rose	Josh	Sam	Eric
Ages in years.	12	14	10	15	8

Hint: See Example **6**.

10. Describe a line graph. What is a **trend** in a line graph?

11. Make a line graph of the given data.

Weeks	1	2	3	4	5	6
Savings in dollars.	12	8	13	9	10	11

Hint: See Example **7**.

12. Use the line graph to answer each question.

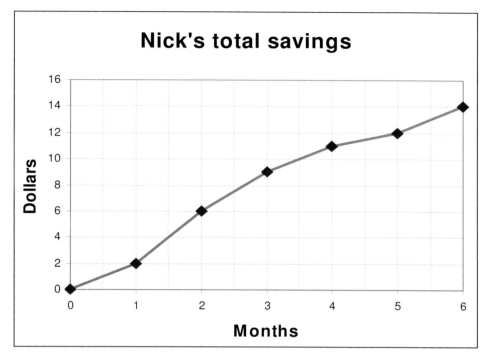

Nick's total savings

a. During which month did Nick not save any money? Explain your answer.

b. During which month did Nick save the most?
Explain you answer.

c. If Nick is saving his money to buy a calculator which costs $21, what percent of the money did he save by the end of the sixth month?
Hint: See Example **8**.

13. Describe a circle graph.

14. If Nick spends his monthly income according to the circle graph, find:

a. How much he spent on insurance?

b. How much he spent on school?

c. How much more does he spend on school than on insurance monthly?

d. On which item does he spend the least amount of money?

Hint: See Example **9**.

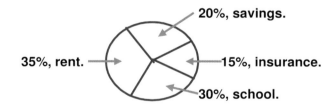

35%, rent.   20%, savings.   15%, insurance.   30%, school.

Challenge Questions

15. Use the line graph to answer each question.

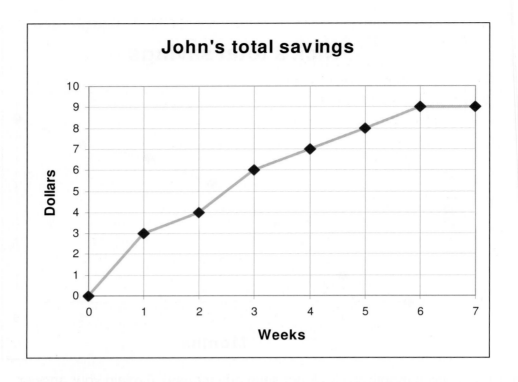

John's total savings

(**a**) If John is saving his money to buy a toy that costs $12.00, what percent of the money did he save by the end of the seventh week?

(**b**) During which week did he save most?
Explain your answer.

(**c**) During which week did he not save any money? Explain your answer?

16. Make a line graph of the given data.

Weeks	1	2	3	4	5	6	7
Savings in dollars.	5	8	4	10	9	7	5

17. Use the data in the table to draw a histogram.

Goals (soccer)	Frequency of schools.
0 - 9	7
10 - 19	5
20 - 29	6
30 - 39	4
40 - 49	0
50 - 59	3
60 - 69	8
70 - 79	4

a. If a school is selected at random, what is the probability that the school scored between 50 - 59 goals?

b. How many schools scored the most goals?

c. If a school is selected at random, what is the probability that the school scored between 40 - 49 goals?

18. If the circle graph shows how a bookstore spent $2000 on books for specific subjects, find:

a. the amount spent on math books.

b. the amount spent on history books.

c. the greatest amount spent on history books.

d. which subject is the least money spent on?

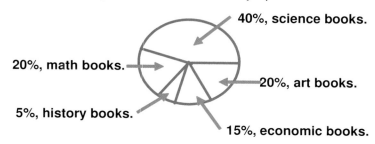

19. Use the bar graph to answer the following questions.

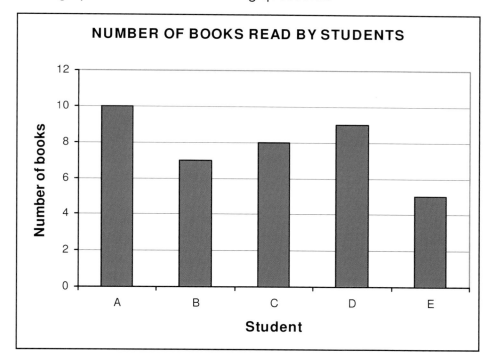

a. Which student read the most books?

b. What is the range of the number of books read?

c. How many more books did student A read than student E?

d. What fraction of the total books in the survey was read by student D?

Hint: Fraction of books read by student D = $\dfrac{\text{Number of books read by student D}}{\text{Total number of books}}$

e. What percent of the books was read by student D?

Hint: Percent of books read by student D = $\dfrac{\text{Number of books read by student D}}{\text{Total number of books.}} \times 100$

Answers to Selected Questions.

1a. 28 students   **1h**. $\dfrac{3}{7}$ **6b**. 2004

8f. 0   **12c**. $66\dfrac{2}{3}\%$ **14d**. Insurance

MISLEADING GRAPHS AND STATISTICS

Cumulative Review
Solve or simplify:

1. $3x = 18$ **2**. $\dfrac{3x}{4} = 9$ **3**. $27 = 9y$ **4**. $6w - 2(2w - 8) = -4$

5. Simplify **a**. $\dfrac{3}{4} - \dfrac{3}{8} =$ **b**. $4\dfrac{1}{3} \div \dfrac{2}{13} =$ **c**. $\dfrac{5}{7} \times \dfrac{14}{15} =$ **d**. $\dfrac{2}{3} + 3\dfrac{2}{5} =$

Identifying Misleading Graphs
Sometimes graphs such as bar graphs and histograms can give a misleading impression of the data they display if the height of the bars are not proportional to the values they represent.

Example 1
Draw a line graph of the data in the table using:
a. a vertical scale of 5 units.
b. a vertical scale of 1 unit, and then, go to **c**.
c. compare line graph **a** and **b**. What is your conclusion?
    The savings is in dollars.

Week	1	2	3	4	5
Savings	2	3	5	8	9

Solution
a. A line graph with a vertical scale of 5 units is shown below.

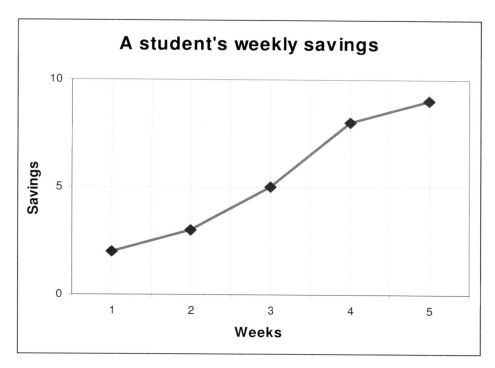

b. A line graph with a vertical scale of 1 unit is shown below.

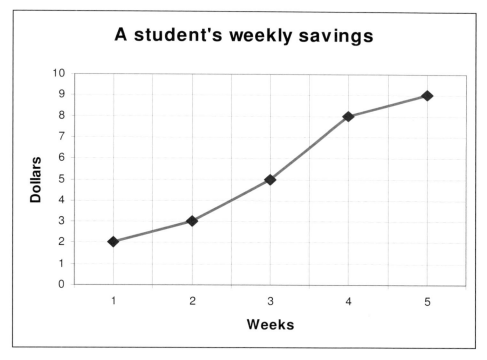

c. By changing the vertical scale of the line graph from 5 units as in **a**, to 1 unit as in **b**, the data values seem large in **b**. It can be concluded that the vertical scale of a line graph can be changed or adjusted to make the data values seem larger or smaller.

Statistics

Example 2

Some of the factors of misleading statistics are: **a**. small sample size,
b. period of the sample, and **c**. average.
Explain the factors of misleading statistics as listed in **a**, **b**, and **c**.

Solution

a. Small sample size: The bigger the sample size, the closer we are to the true value of the statistics. For example, if two students are selected randomly, and both of them had an A in chemistry, it does not necessarily mean that every student in the school had an A in chemistry, because the school has over 800 students whose grades we do not know.

b. The period of the sample: For example, the weather may affect the outcome of a sampling if one sampling is done in the Winter and the other is done in the Summer. Another example is when one sampling is done during the low sale season and the other sampling is done during the high sale season. The period or season of certain sampling can be misleading.

c. When average is used: An average does not show the true picture of the individual data that form the sample. For example, the sample of the ages of 5 people are 10 years, 12 years, 11 years, 10 years, and 95 years. The average age of the five people is

$$= \frac{\text{Sum of ages}}{\text{Total ages}}$$

$$= \frac{10 + 12 + 11 + 10 + 95}{5}$$

$$= \frac{138}{5} = 27\frac{2}{5} \text{ years.}$$

Although the average age is $27\frac{2}{5}$ years, only one person out of five whose age is greater than $27\frac{2}{5}$ years. Note that although the average is high, the age of the majority of the people is rather low and this can be misleading.

The samples in **a**, **b**, and **c** are **biased because they are not representative of each population**. A **biased sampling** is one of the **causes of misleading statistics**.

Example 3

A business had 6 employees with the following salaries: $14,000, $15,000, $13,000, $14,000, $120,000 (owner), $10,000. "Employment available, average salary

$31,000" was the owner's advertisement . It is therefore, not likely that the salary of a new employee would be $31,000. The advertisement is misleading noting that only the owner had a huge salary of $120, 000.

Example 4

If the total revenue of market A during the three months in the summer was $400,000 and the total revenue of market B in the winter was $800,000,

a. Will it be misleading to compare the revenues of markets A and B?

b. What is the correct method of comparing the revenues of markets A and B?

Solution

a. Yes, it is misleading to compare the revenues of markets A and B because the revenues were measured at two different seasons of the year which are winter and summer and that during the busy shopping season of winter, the revenue of market B is greater than the revenue of market A in the summer.

b. The correct method of comparing the revenues of markets A and B is to measure the revenue for both markets at the same season.

Example 5

a. If a car dealership claims that out of a survey of 10 customers, 5 of them are satisfied with their cars, and the dealership's ad states: "5 out of 10 customers are satisfied with their cars", is this ad misleading?

b. What is the correct way of doing the survey?

Solution

a. Yes, the ad is misleading because the sample size of 10 customers is too small. The sample size of 10 customers is not representative of the population of the customers who bought cars from the dealership. The dealership has many more customers than 10.

b. The correct method of doing the survey is to include all the customers who bought vehicles from the dealership in the survey and that will enable the dealership to know the total number of people who are satisfied with their vehicles.

Exercises

1. It can be concluded that the vertical scale of a line graph can be changed or adjusted to make changes in the data values seem larger or smaller. True or false? Explain. Hint: See Example 1.

2. "Five out of seven students scored 90% in the math test".

a. How many students are in the sample?

b. Can you say that the number of students in the sample is representative of the student population?

c. Is the statement misleading? Hint: See Examples **2a** and **5**.

3. A school newspaper is comparing the total revenue of two stores, P-mart and J-Mart. If the total revenue of P-Mart from May 1st to August 1st is compared to the total revenue for J-Mart from October 1st to January 1st, do you think that the comparison is misleading? Explain your answer. Hint: See Examples 2b and 4.

Challenge Questions

4. A biased sampling is one of the causes of misleading statistics. True or false? Explain.

5. Comparing the total summer revenue of one super market to the total winter revenue of another super market is misleading statistics. True or false? Explain.

6. Explain how the average revenue for twelve months of a supermarket could be misleading statistics.

7. Explain how a vertical scale of a line graph can be adjusted to make changes in a data value seem larger or smaller.

TWO OR THREE LINE GRAPHS ON THE SAME AXES

Examples of "Two or Three Line Graphs on the Same Axes" are shown to provide the logic in solving similar problems. "Two or Three Line Graphs on the Same Axes" are used to compare two or three events, such as the populations of two or three cities.

Example 1
The graph shows the basketball scores of schools A and B.
The games were played six times (2000, 2001, 2002, 2003, 2004, and 2005.)
a. How many times did schools A and B have a tie? Explain your answer.
b. What is the highest point scored by school B? Explain your answer.
c. Between what two years did school A score the same points? Explain your answer.
d. What were the scores in 2002 for both school?
e. What was the difference in scores in 2002 between schools A and B?

Basketball scores

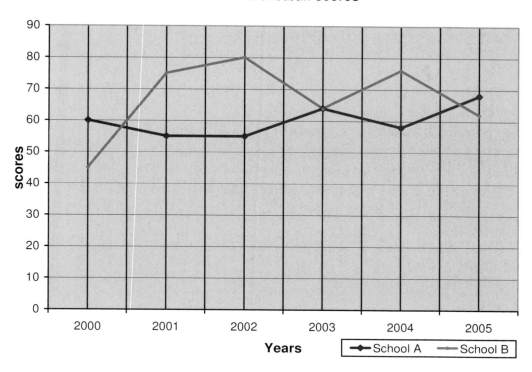

Solution

a. Schools A and B had a draw once, because the line graphs of schools A and B intersect or cross each other at one point (in 2003) where there was a game. (Notice that the scores of both teams are the same at the point of intersection where there was a game.) Hint: We have to determine in which year there was a draw.

b. The highest points scored by school B is 80 because 80 is the highest point on the graph for school B.

c. School A scored the same points in 2001 and 2002 because the line graph for school A was horizontal between 2001 and 2002. A horizontal line graph shows that there has been no increase or decrease in the scores between 2001 and 2002. So, the scores in 2001 and 2002 must be the same.

d. From the graph, school A scored 55 points and school B scored 80 points in 2002.

e. From the solution **d**, school A scored 55 points and school B scored 80 points in 2002. So, the difference in scores in 2002 is 80 - 55 = 25.

Example 2

The graph shows the math test scores for Kent School and Rosa School.
The tests were given six times (2001, 2002, 2003, 2004, 2005, and 2006.)

a. What was the test score in 2001 of Kent School?

b. What was the difference in scores in 2001 between the two schools?

c. In which year did the Kent School and Rosa School have the same math test scores? Explain your answer.

Math Test Scores

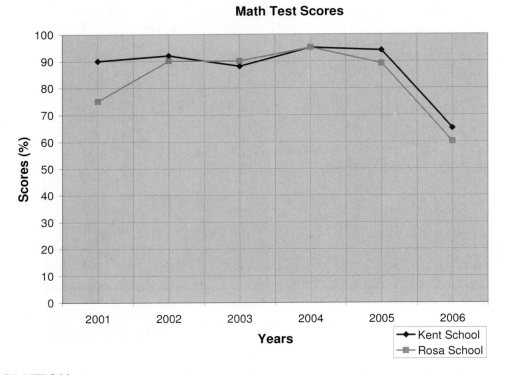

SOLUTION

a. In 2001, Kent School scored 90% and Rosa School scored 75%. (Notice that the scores can be read at the point on the graph where each line graph crosses or intersects the year 2001 line.)

b. From solution **a**, Kent School scored 90% and Rosa School scored 75%. So,the difference in scores in 2001 is 90% - 75% = 15%.

c. Kent School and Rosa School had the same math test scores in 2004 because the line graphs of the test scores of both schools intersect in 2004. (Notice that at the point of intersection, where there were actual tests, both line graphs (test scores) have the same value.) Hint: We have to determine in which year the scores were the same.

Example 3

The two line graphs show the basketball scores of James School and Rox Schools from 2002 to 2006. Five games were played (2002, 2003, 2004, 2005, and 2006.)

a. In which year did James School have the highest score? Explain your answer.

b. What were the highest and the lowest scores of James school? Explain your answer?

c. What is the range of the scores of James School? Explain your answer.

d. How many times did James School and Rox School have a tie?

612

Basketball Scores

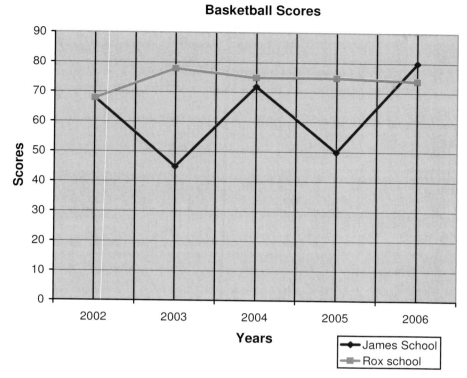

Solution

a. James School scored the highest goals in 2006 because 2006 indicates the highest point on the graph for James School.

b. The highest score of the James School was 80 because 80 was the highest point on the graph for James School. The lowest score of the James School was 45, because 45 was the lowest point on the graph.

c. The range is the difference between the greatest score and the least score. (Hint: Review the chapter on "Median, Mode, and Range.) From the solution of **b**, the highest score was 80 and the lowest score was 45. So, the range of the scores was:

Range = Highest score - Lowest score
   = 80 - 45
   = 35

d. James School and Rox School had a draw once because the line graphs of the James School and the Rox School intersect or cross each other at one point (2002) where there was a game. Hint: We should find the year the tie occurred. Notice that the scores at the point of each intersection where actual games took place are the same.

Example 4

The line graph shows the savings of Nick, Tom, and Mary.

a. In which month did Mary save the most money? Explain your answer.

b. What was the most money that Mary saved? Explain your answer.

c. Describe the savings of Nick, Tom, and Mary in March.

d. What was the highest amount of money saved by Tom? Explain your answer.

e. In which month did Nick save the most money? Explain your answer.

f. What is the range of Mary's savings? Explain your answer.

g. Who saved the least amount of money in May? Explain your answer.

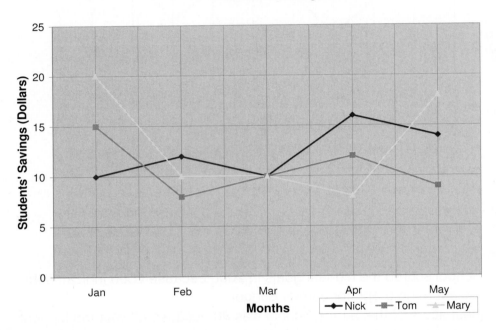

Students' Savings

Solution

a. Mary saved the most money in January because the line graph of her savings indicates the highest point in January.

b. The most money that Mary saved was $20.00 because the highest point on the line graph for Mary indicates $20.00.

c. Nick, Tom, and Mary saved the same amount of money ($10.00) in March, because the three line graphs for Nick, Tom, and Mary intersect at a point that indicates or corresponds to $10.00.

d. The highest amount of money saved by Tom was $15.00, because the highest point on Tom's line graph indicates or corresponds to $15.00.

e. Nick saved the highest money in April because the highest point of Nick's line graph occurs in April.

f. The highest amount of money saved by Mary was $20.00, because the $20.00 corresponds to the highest point on Mary's line graph. The least amount of money saved by Mary corresponds to the amount that corresponds to the lowest point on Mary's line graph. This lowest point corresponds to about $7.50. The range of the money saved by Mary is the difference between the most money saved and the least money saved. So:

Range = Most money saved - Least money saved

= $20.00 - $7.50

= $12.50

g. Tom saved the least amount of money in May because Tom's line graph shows the lowest point in May compared to that of Nick's and Mary's line graphs.

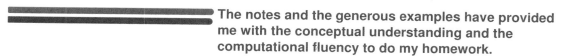 The notes and the generous examples have provided me with the conceptual understanding and the computational fluency to do my homework.

Exercises

1. The graph shows the basketball scores of Peki School and Mawul School.

a. What was the highest score of Peki School? Explain your answer.

b. What is the highest point scored by the Peki School? Explain your answer.

c. Between what two months are the scores of the two schools the same? Explain your answer.

d. What were the scores in January for both schools?

e. What was the difference in scores in January?

f. Explain why there was not a tie between the two schools. (Hint: Did the lines of the line graph intersect or cross each other during a game? The games occur at the locations where the points are plotted on the line graph.)

Hint: See Examples 1 and 3.

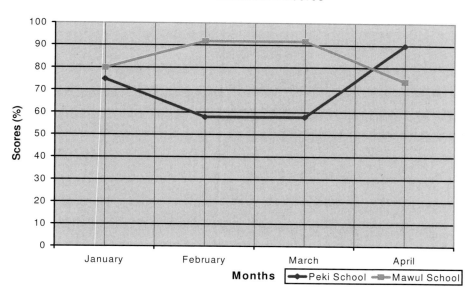

Basketball Scores

2. The graph shows the basketball scores of Team A and Team B.

  a. What were the scores in April of both teams? Explain your answer.

  b. What was the difference in the scores in April between the two teams? Explain your answer.

  c. What was the highest score of Team B? Explain your answer.

Hint: See Examples 1 and 3.

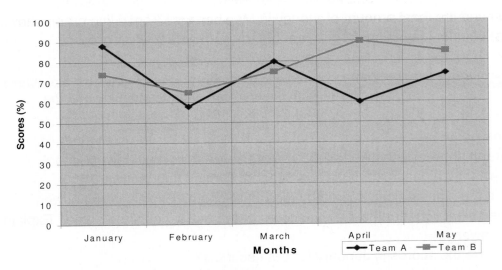

Basketball Scores

3. The graph shows the test scores of Rose and Amanda.
   a. What was the highest score of Amanda? Explain your answer.
   b. How many times did they score the same points? (Hint: "To score the same points is similar to a draw.") Explain your answer.
   c. What were the scores in June for both girls? Explain your answer.
   d. What were the scores in January for both girls?
   e. What was the difference in scores in January between Rose and Amanda?
   Hint: See Example 2.

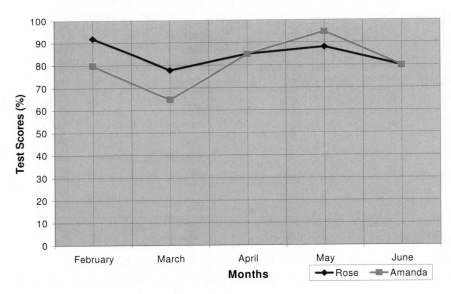

Test Scores

4. The line graph shows the savings of three students.

a. In which month did all the students save the same amount of money? Explain your answer.

b. What was the highest amount of money saved? Explain your answer.

c. What was the lowest amount of money saved in April? Explain your answer.

d. What was the lowest amount of money saved in January? Explain your answer.

e. Who saved the most money in May? Explain your answer.

f. Who saved the least money in April? Explain your answer.

g. What is the range of the savings of Mary? Explain your answer.

h. What is the difference between the savings of Nick and Tom in January? Hint: See Example 4.

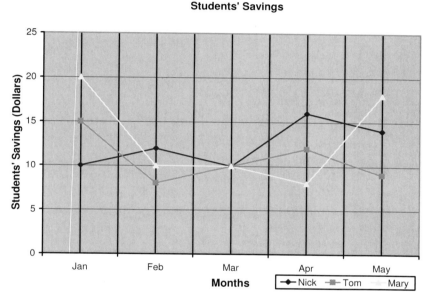

Challenge Questions

5. The graph shows Sam's and Josh's science test scores.

   a. In which months did Sam and Josh have the same score?

   b. Who had the lowest test score?

   c. What is the difference between Sam's and Josh's test scores in February?

   d. What is the difference between Sam's and Josh's test scores in May?

Science Test Scores

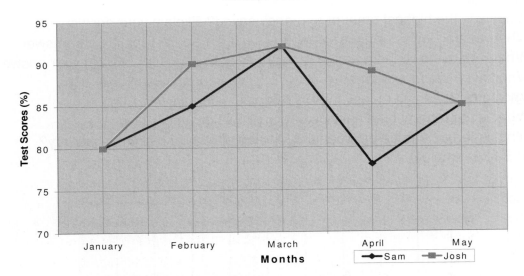

6. The graph shows the savings of Nick, John, and Mark.
   a. In which two months were their savings the same? How much did they save?
   b. What is the range of the savings of Nick?
   c. What is the range of the savings of John?
   d. What is the range of the savings of Mike?

Savings

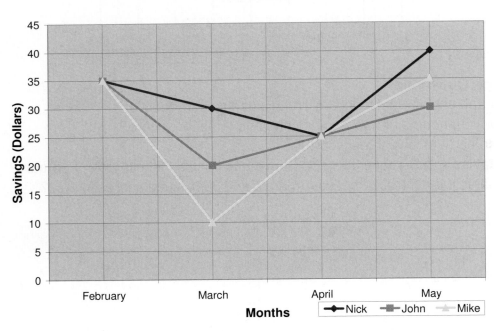

Answers to Selected Questions

5c. 90% - 85% = 5%   **6b**. $40 - $25 = $15

COORDINATE SYSTEM

INTRODUCTION

New Terms: coordinate system, coordinate plane, x-axis, y-axis, origin, quadrants, ordered pair, x-coordinate, y-coordinate.

The **coordinate system** or the **coordinate plane** is formed by two perpendicular and intersecting number lines called the x-axis and the y-axis. The horizontal number line is called the x-axis and the vertical number line is called the y-axis. The point where the two number lines intersect is called the **origin** and the origin has a coordinate of (**0, 0**). The coordinate of a point is an **ordered pair of numbers** such that the first number is related to a point on the x-axis and the second number is related to a point on the y-axis. The x-axis, y-axis, and the origin are shown in the diagram.

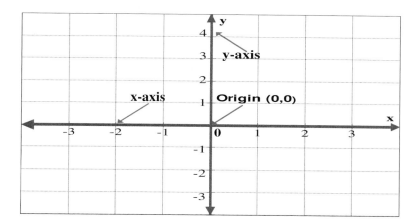

Example 1
Describe how to find the coordinates of the ordered pair of point A.

(The graph showing point A is located on the next page.)

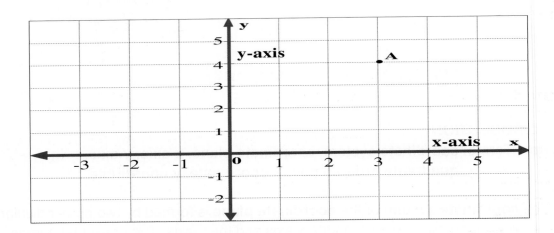

Solution

Step 1: Find the x-coordinate first. From point A, imagine a perpendicular line on the x-axis and this imaginary perpendicular line meets the x-axis at point 3, and therefore, the first coordinate of the ordered pair is 3.

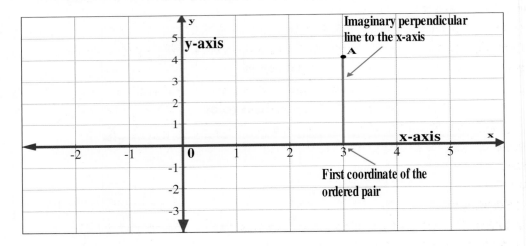

Step 2: Find the y-coordinate second. From point A, imagine a perpendicular line on the y-axis and this imaginary perpendicular line meets the y-axis at point 4, and therefore, the second coordinate of the ordered pair is point 4.

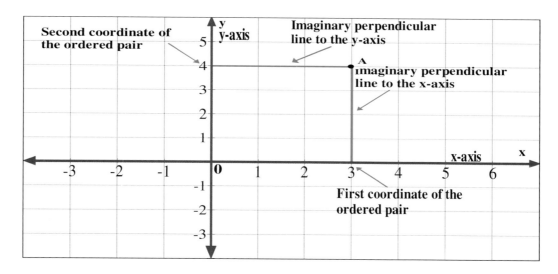

Step 3: Combine the first coordinate of the ordered pair which is 3 with the second coordinate of the ordered pair which is 4 to form the **coordinates of the ordered pair of the point A as** (**3**, **4**).

Special Notes
1. In general, the coordinates of the ordered pair of any point may be written as (x, y) where x, which is always the first pair refers to a number on the x-axis and y which is always the second pair refers to a number on the y-axis.
2. How can the coordinates of a point be read? The coordinates of a point can be read by moving along the x-axis to read the first coordinate and then moving along the y-axis to read the second coordinate.

Exercises
1. Find the coordinates of the ordered pair of point B in the diagram.
   Hint: See Example **1**.

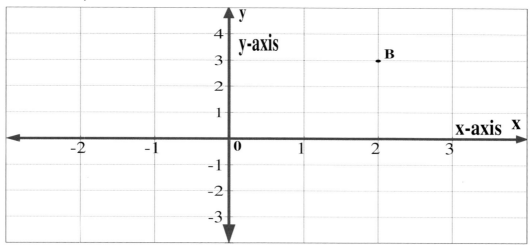

2. Find the coordinates of the ordered pair of the point C in the diagram.
   Hint: See Example 1.

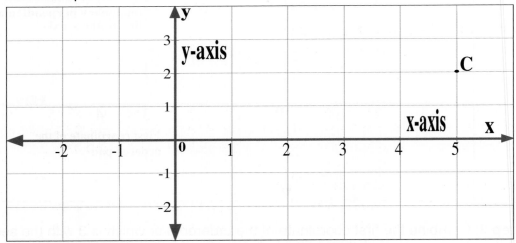

3. Using the diagram, copy and complete the sentences.
   Hint: See Examples **1**, Step **3**.

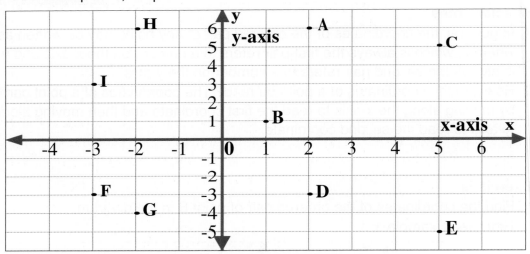

   a. (2, 6) are the coordinates of the ordered pair of the point _____.
   b. (-2, 6) are the coordinates of the ordered pair of the point _____.
      Hint: The negative x-coordinates are at the left side of the origin.
   c. (_, _) are the coordinates of the ordered pair of point C.
   d. The coordinates of the ordered pair of the point E is (5, -5) and (_, _) are the
      coordinates of the ordered pair of the point D.
      Hint: The negative y-coordinates are below the origin.
   e. The coordinates of the ordered pair of the point G is (-2, -4) and (_, _) are the
      coordinates of the ordered pair of the point F.
   f. (1, 1) are the coordinates of the ordered pair of point B.
4. What is meant by the coordinate system or the coordinate plane?
5. What is meant by the origin?

6. What is meant by the coordinate plane.

Answers to Selected Questions
1. (2, 3)   **3b.** point H

Critical thinking: What is the importance of the coordinates of a point? The coordinates of a point show how far and in which direction to move horizontally along the x-axis, and then vertically along the y-axis on the coordinate plane.

Graphing on the Coordinate Plane
We can graph the coordinates of the ordered pair of any point by moving along the x-axis until we are at the x-coordinate of the required ordered pair. Then we continue by moving perpendicularly to the x-axis until we meet the imaginary perpendicular line from the y-coordinate of the ordered pair which is on the y-axis. The point where the imaginary perpendicular line from the x-coordinate of the ordered pair meets the imaginary perpendicular line from the y-coordinate of the ordered pair is the point or the graph of the point.

Example 1
Graph the point (3, 5).
Solution
Move along the x-axis from the origin (0, 0) until you are at the coordinate of the first required ordered pair which is 3, then you move perpendicular to the x-axis (imaginary) until you meet the imaginary perpendicular line from point 5 on the y-axis. Where the imaginary perpendicular line from the x-axis coincide with the imaginary perpendicular line from the y-axis is the point (3, 5).

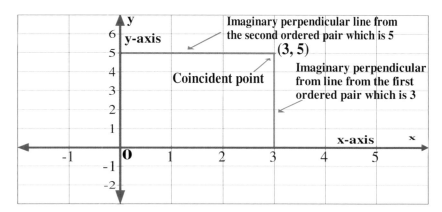

Importance of the Sign of the Coordinates
1. If the first coordinate is negative, then move along the x-axis towards the left side

of the origin (0, 0), but if the sign is positive, then move towards the right of the origin (0, 0).

2. If the second coordinate is negative, then move along the y-axis below the origin (0, 0), but if the sign is positive, then move along the y-axis above the origin (0, 0).

Example 2
Graph the point (-3, 4).
Solution
Move along the x-axis from the origin (0, 0) until you are at the x-coordinate of -3 and then move perpendicularly to the x-axis until you coincide with the imaginary perpendicular line from the point 4 on the y-axis. Where the imaginary perpendicular lines from the x-coordinate of -3 and the y-coordinate of 4 meet is the coordinate of the ordered pair of the point (-3, 4) or the graph of the point.

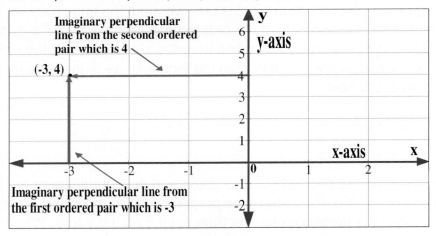

Example 3
a. Graph the points B and C with the coordinates (0, -3) and (2, 0) respectively on the same diagram.
b. Draw a line through points B and C.
Solution
a. To graph the point B(0, -3), from the x-coordinate of 0 on the x-axis, move perpendicularly to the x-axis until you come to the y-coordinate of -3 and this point will have the coordinates of (0, -3) as shown in the diagram.

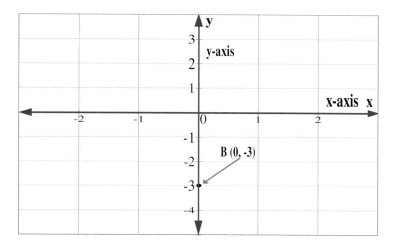

To graph the point C(2, 0), move along the x-axis from the origin (0, 0) until you are at the x-coordinates of 2 but y = 0 on the x-axis and this means that the y-coordinate of 0 is on the x-axis therefore, the point (2, 0) is the graph of point C as shown in the diagram.

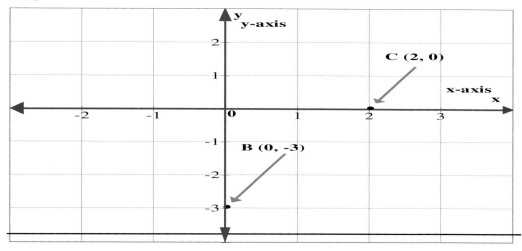

b. Draw a line through the points B(0, -3) and C(2, 0).

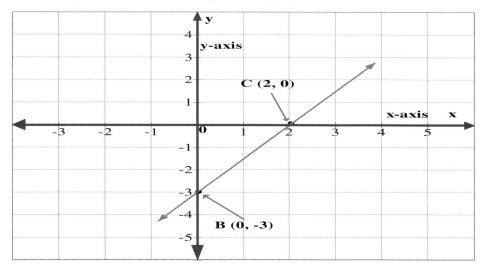

Example 4

Graph the point A with coordinates (-3, -2).

Solution

Move along the x-axis from the origin (0, 0) until you are at the x-coordinate of the ordered pair which is -3 and then move perpendicularly to the x-axis until you meet the imaginary perpendicular line from the point -2 on the y-axis. This meeting point are the coordinates of the ordered pair (-3, -2) or the graph of the point (-3, -2).

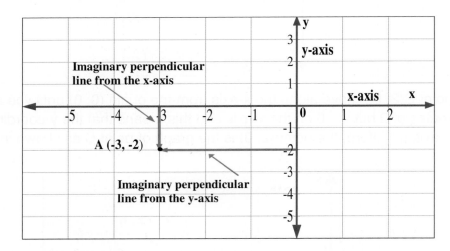

Exercises

1. Graph the following points. Hint: See Example **1**.

   a. A(2, 1)   **b.** B(3, 1)   **c.** C(4, 1)   **d.** D(2, 1)

   e. E(2, 2)   **f.** F(-1, 1)   **g.** G(4, 4)   **h.** H(2, 4)

2. Graph the following points. Hint: See Example **2**.

   a. A(-2, 1)   **b.** B(-3, 4)   **c.** C(-1, 2)   **d.** D(-4, 1)

   e. E(-2, 2)   **f.** F(-1, 1)   **g.** G(-2, 3)   **h.** H(-3, 1)

3. Graph the following points. Hint: See Example **3a**.

   a. A(0, -2)   **b.** B(0, -1)   **c.** C(0, -4)   **d.** D(0, -5)

   e. E(1, 0)   **f.** F(3, 0)   **g.** G(5, 0)   **h.** H(6, 0)

4. Using question 3, join the following points with a line. Hint: See Example **3b**.

   a. A and E   **b.** B and F   **c.** C and G   **d.** D and H

5. Graph the following points. Hint: See Example **4**.

   a. A(-1, -1)   **b.** B(-3, -2)   **c.** C(-2, -3)   **d.** D(-1, -4)

Challenge Questions

6. Graph the following points.

   a. A(0, 4)   **b.** B(1, 4)   **c.** C(0, -6)   **d.** D(-3, -3)

7. Graph the three points (1, 2), (3, 1), and (1, 3).

   Join the three points to form a triangle.

Quadrants

Quadrants are the four areas that the x-axis and the y-axis divide the coordinate system into as shown in Figure 1.

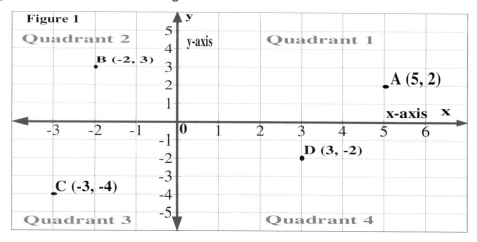

Critical Thinking

Using Figure 1:

1. The coordinates of the point A are (5, 2) which are positive and the point A is located in the quadrant 1, and therefore, any point that has both positive x-coordinate and y-coordinate is in quadrant 1.

2. The coordinates of the point B are (-2, 3) which shows that the x-coordinate is negative and the y-coordinate is positive and the point B is located in the quadrant 2. Therefore, any point that has a negative x-coordinate and a positive y-coordinate is located in the quadrant 2.

3. The coordinates of the point C are (-3, -4) which shows that both the x-coordinate and the y-coordinate are negative and the point C is located in the quadrant 3. Therefore, any point that has a negative x-coordinate and a negative y-coordinate is located in the quadrant 3.

4. The coordinates of the point D are (3, -2) which shows that the x-coordinate is positive and the y-coordinate is negative and the point D is located in the quadrant 4. Therefore, any point that has a positive x-coordinate and a negative y-coordinate is located in the quadrant 4.

Team Exercises

Using the notes under "Critical Thinking,"

1. in which quadrant is the graph of the following ordered pairs located?

    a. (-1, -3)   **b.** (3, -1)   **c.** (-2, 3)   **d.** (4, 3).

2. in which quadrant is a graph of the ordered pair located when both coordinates are negative?

3. in which quadrant is a graph of the ordered pair located when both coordinates are positive?

1. Draw a number line and use dots to locate the integers on it. Then list the integers from the greatest to the smallest.

10, 2, -3, -8, 6, 0, and -1

2. Simplify:

a. $\dfrac{2}{3} \div \dfrac{1}{6} =$ **b.** $2\dfrac{1}{4} - 1\dfrac{1}{2} =$ **c.** $\dfrac{7}{9} \times \dfrac{12}{4} =$ **d.** $\dfrac{3}{4} + \dfrac{2}{3} =$

REAL WORLD APPLICATIONS - WORD PROBLEMS
COORDINATE SYSTEM

Example 1

Mary started walking from the origin (0, 0). If she went 4 units to the right on the x-axis, and then went 3 units down what are the coordinates of the final location of Mary?

Solution

Mary walked 4 units from the origin (0, 0) to the right on the x-axis and therefore her location is 4 units to the right. She then went 3 units down and her position on the y-axis is -3. The coordinates of her location are (4, -3) as shown in the diagram.

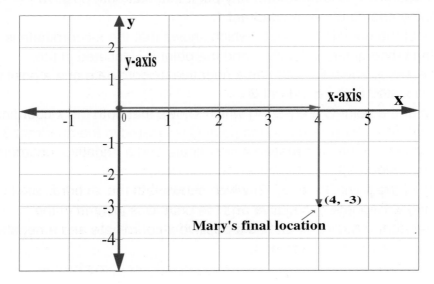

Example 2

John started walking from the origin. If he moved 6 units to the left and then 5 units up what are the coordinates of John?

Solution

John moved 6 units to the left from the origin, and therefore the x-coordinate of his location is -6. He then moved 5 units up, and therefore his y-coordinate is 5. The coordinates of his location are (-6, 5) as shown in the diagram.

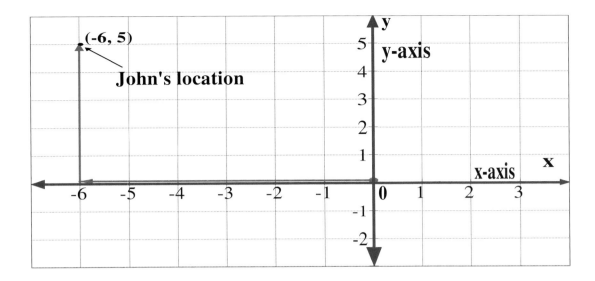

Exercises

1. Eric started at the origin and moved 5 units to the right and then 5 units down. What are the coordinates of Eric? Hint: See Example 1.
2. Start at the origin, move 1 unit to the left and then 4 units up. What are the coordinates of the location? Hint: See Example 2.

Graphing of Equations

An equation is a mathematics statement which indicates that one expression is equivalent to another expression. An example of an equation is y = 2x + 2.

How Can We Graph An Equation?

1. In the previous section under "Graphing on the coordinate plane" we learned that we can graph a point if we know the x and the y coordinates.
2. Similarly in order to graph an equation of a line, we need to find at least two sets of the values of the x and y coordinates of the equation by giving a value to x (usually starting from 0 and finding the corresponding value of y as shown in example 1.
3. Using the values of the x and y coordinates, we can write the ordered pairs to be graphed.
4. Make the graph by:
   a. Plotting each ordered pair on a coordinate plane
   b. Connect all the points by using a straight line
   c. Put arrows at both ends of the line to show that the line continues in both directions.

Example 1

Graph the equation y = x on a coordinate plane.

Solution

Step 1: Pick values for x (usually starting from 0) and then find the corresponding values for y by substituting the value for x into the given equation y = x.

when x = 0, y = 0   Note, when you put x = 0 into the equation y = x, then the equation becomes y = 0.

when x = 1, y = 1   Note, when you put x = 1 into the equation y = x, then the equation becomes y = 1.

when x = 2, y = 2   Note, when you put x = 2 into the equation y= x, then the equation becomes y = 2.

Therefore the ordered pairs of the coordinates are (0, 0), (1, 1), and (2, 2).

Step 2: Plot the ordered pairs of the coordinates on a coordinate plane and draw a line through the points.

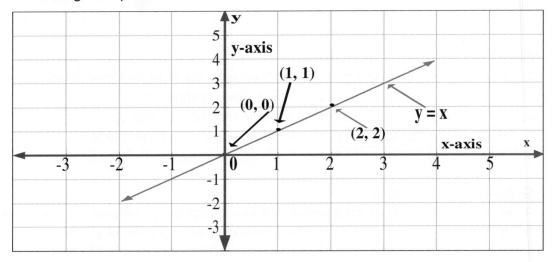

The graph shows the equation y = x.

Example 2

Graph the equation y = x + 1 on a coordinate plane.

Solution

Step 1: Pick values for x (usually starting from 0) and then find the corresponding values for y by substituting the values for x in the given equation y = x + 1.

When x = 0, y = 0 + 1 = 1.   Note, when you put x = 0 into the equation y = x + 1, the equation becomes y = 0 + 1 = 1. Therefore, when x = 0, y = 1.

When x = 1, y = 1 + 1 = 2   Note, when you put x = 1 into the equation y = x + 1, the equation becomes y = 1 + 1 = 2. Therefore, when x = 1, y = 2.

When x = 2, y = 2 + 1 = 3   Note, when you put x = 2 into the equation y = x + 1, the equation becomes y = 2 + 1 = 3. Therefore, when x = 1, y = 3.

Therefore, the ordered pairs of the coordinates are (0, 1), (1, 2), and (2, 3).

Step 2: Plot the ordered pairs on a coordinate plane and draw a line through the points.

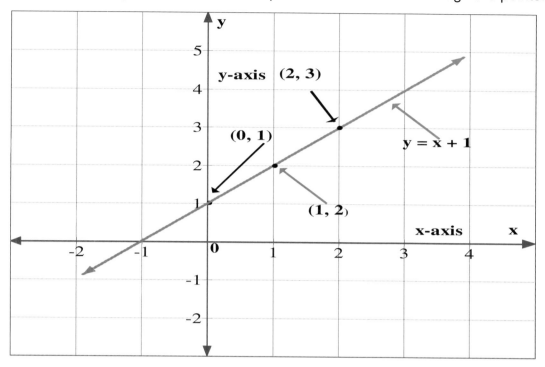

The graph shows the equation y = x + 1.

Example 3
Graph the equation y = 2x + 3.
Solution
Step 1: Pick values for x (usually starting from 0), and then find the corresponding values for y.

When x = 0, y = 2 × 0 + 3 = 3   Note, when you put x = 0 into the equation y = 2x + 3, the equation becomes y = 2 × 0 + 3 = 3. Therefore, when x = 0, y = 3.

When x = 1, y = 2 × 1 + 3 = 5   Note, when you put x = 1 into the equation y = 2x + 3, the equation becomes y = 2 × 1 + 3 = 5. So, when x = 1, y = 5.

When x = 2, y = 2 × 2 + 3 = 7   Note, when you put x = 2 into the equation y = 2x + 3, the equation becomes y = 2 × 2 + 3 = 7. Therefore, when x = 2, y = 7.

Therefore, the ordered pair of the coordinates are (0, 3), (1, 5), and (2, 7).

Step 2: Plot the ordered pairs of the coordinates on a coordinate plane and draw a line through the points.

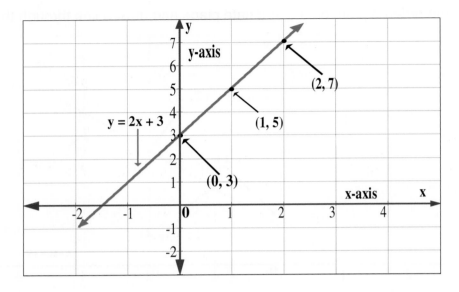

The graph shows the equation $y = 2x + 3$

Exercises

1 Graph the following equations Hint: See Example **1**.

   a. $y = 2x$ **b**. $y = 3x$ **c**. $y = 4x$ **d**. $y = 5x$

2. Graph the following equations. Hint: See Example **2**.

   a. $y = x + 2$ **b**. $y = x + 3$ **c**. $y = x + 5$ **d**. $y = x + 4$

3. Graph the following equations. Hint: See Example **3**.

   a. $y = 2x + 2$ **b**. $y = 3x + 1$ **c**. $y = 4x + 1$ **d**. $y = 2x - 1$

Challenge Questions

4. Graph the following equations.

   a. $y = 3x - 1$ **b**. $y = 2x + 3$ **c**. $y = 3x + 2$ **d**. $y = 2x - 2$

5. A real world application of the ordered pair of numbers may be the temperature corresponding to each day as shown in the table.

Day	1	2	3	4	5	6
Temperature (°F)	4	-2	6	0	-3	2

Let the day be on the x-coordinate and the temperature be on the y-coordinate and graph each ordered point. Hint: the first coordinate may be written as (1, 4).

Mixed Review

1. The sum of the measures of two angles of a triangle is 101^0. What is the measure of the third angle?

2. The sum of the measures of three angles of a quadrilateral is 300^0. What is the measure of the fourth angle?

3. The sum of the angles on a line except an angle labelled A is 155^0. What is the measure of angle A?

4. Solve for x:

    a. $5x - 3 = 3x + 7$ **b.** $\dfrac{3x}{8} = \dfrac{3}{4}$ **c.** $90^0 + 3x = 180^0$

5. Find 20% of $200

6. What is the reciprocal of $\dfrac{2}{5}$?

7. A square swimming pool has an area of 100 m². Find the perimeter of the swimming pool.

8. Simplify:

    a. $\dfrac{4}{5} \div \dfrac{3}{20}$ **b.** $\dfrac{5 \times 3 \times 4 \times 2}{3 \times 20 \times 2 \times 3}$ **c.** $20 \div 4 - 2$ **d.** $20 - 4 \div 2$

SLOPE OF A LINE

The slope of a line is the ratio: $\dfrac{\text{Vertical change}}{\text{Horizontal change}} = \dfrac{\text{Change in y distance}}{\text{Change in x distance}} = \dfrac{\text{rise}}{\text{run}}$,

where the "rise" is the number of units moved up or down and the "run" is the number of units moved to the left or right.

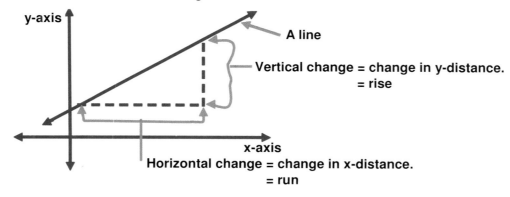

Types of Slopes

The four types of slopes are positive, zero, negative, and undefined slopes.

The four types of slopes may be described as follows:

a. An upward slope (↗) has a positive slope.

b. A horizontal slope (→) has a zero slope.

c. A downward slope (↘) has a negative slope.

d. A vertical slope (↓) has an undefined slope.

Students may be able to remember the four types of slopes if they can recall the slopes sketch below. Let us call these slopes sketch the "Aggor slopes sketch."

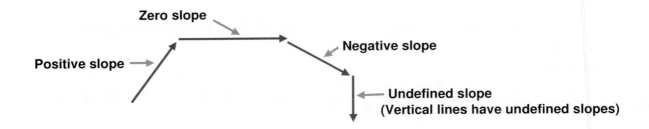

Hint: Example 1 explained positive, zero, negative, and undefined slopes.

Example 1

a. Name the four types of slopes.

b. Sketch the four types of slopes on a coordinate plane.

c. Describe a line with a positive slope.

d. Describe a line with a negative slope.

e. Describe a line with a zero slope.

f. Describe a line with an undefined slope.

Solution

a. The four types of slopes are positive slope, zero slope, negative slope, and undefined slopes.

b. The four types of slopes on the coordinate plane are as shown:

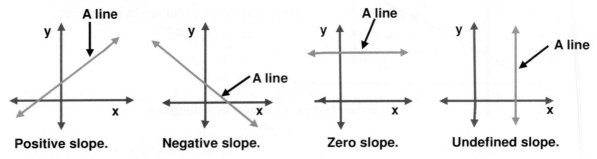

Positive slope. Negative slope. Zero slope. Undefined slope.

c. A line with a positive slope goes up in the direction from left to right. Hint: See the positive slope diagram in the solution **b**.

d. A line with a negative slope goes down from the direction of left to right. Hint: See the negative slope diagram in the solution **b**.

e. A line with a zero slope is parallel to the horizontal or the x axis. Hint: See the diagram of the line with a zero slope in the solution **b**.

f. A line with an undefined slope is parallel to the y axis or it is vertical. Hint: See the diagram of the line with the undefined slope in the solution **b**.

Example 2

What is the slope of the line that passes through the points (x_1, y_1) and (x_2, y_2).

Solution

The line is sketched with the points as shown below.

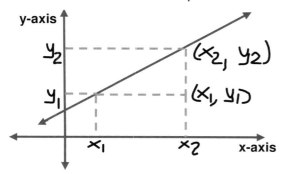

The slope of a line is the ratio: $\dfrac{\text{Vertical change}}{\text{Horizontal change}} = \dfrac{\text{change in y-distance}}{\text{change in x-distance}}$

$$= \dfrac{\text{rise}}{\text{run}} = \dfrac{y_2 - y_1}{x_2 - x_1}$$

Note: The formula for finding the slope of a line is:

$$\textbf{Slope} = \dfrac{\textbf{Vertical change}}{\textbf{Horizontal change}} = \dfrac{\textbf{change in y-distance}}{\textbf{change in x-distance}} = \dfrac{\textbf{rise}}{\textbf{run}} = \dfrac{y_2 - y_1}{x_2 - x_1}$$

Exercises

1. What is the slope of a line? Hint: See the notes.

2. What are the four types of slopes?   Hint: See Example **1**.

3a. Sketch the four types of slopes. Hint: See Example **1**.

3b. Label each slope of the line as undefined, zero, positive and negative.
   Hint: See the notes.

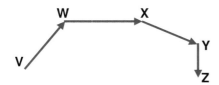

4. The slope of a line $= \dfrac{y_2 - y_1}{x_2 - x_1}$. Is this true or false? Hint: See Example **2**

5. a. Vertical change = change in y distance = rise. True or false?

b. Horizontal change = change in x distance = run. True or false?

c. Rise is the number of units moved up or d_____.

d. Run is the number of units moved to the left or r_____.

e The slope of a line is the ratio:

$$\frac{\text{Vertical change}}{\text{horizontal change}} = \frac{\text{Change in y distance}}{\text{Change in x distance}} = \frac{\text{rise}}{\text{run}}, \text{true or false?}$$

Hint: See the notes.

6. Describe the slope of the line x at the top of the mountain and the slopes of the two lines Y and Z at the sides of the mountain. Hint: See the notes.

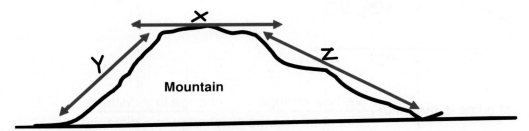

Mountain

7. Do the following slopes appear to be zero, positive, negative, or undefined? Hint: See Example **1.**

a.   b.    c.    d.

AREA AND PERIMETER

Cumulative Review

1. 14 + 17 =   **2.** 15 ÷ 3 =   **3.** 25 - 8 =   **4.** 7 × 7 =

5. 45 ÷ 5 =   **6.** 31 - 12 =   **7.** 36 ÷ 6 =   **8.** 33 - 8 =

9.   28   **10.**   35   **11.**   34   **12.**   27
    × 4   + 19   - 19   × 6

13. 42 ÷ 6 =   **14.** 45 ÷ 9 =   **15.** 14 + 37 =   **16.** 31 - 17 =

17. 2.5 + 3.9 =   **18.** 5.7 × 5 =   **19.** 3.6 × 3.5 =   **20.** 21.7 - 1.4 =

21. $\dfrac{2}{3} \times \dfrac{2}{5} =$ **22.** $\dfrac{2}{3} \div \dfrac{4}{3} =$ **23.** $\dfrac{3}{4} - \dfrac{2}{3} =$ **24.** $1\dfrac{1}{3} + 4\dfrac{3}{4} =$

AREA

Rectangle and Square

The area of a figure is the number of the square units that covers it. For example, in the diagram, the area colored yellow is 8 square units because 8 units are colored yellow.

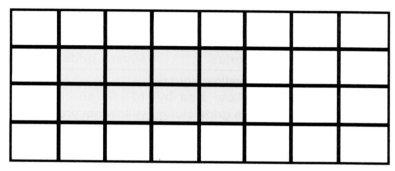

Example 1

What is the area of the region colored yellow in the diagram? Give a reason to justify your answer.

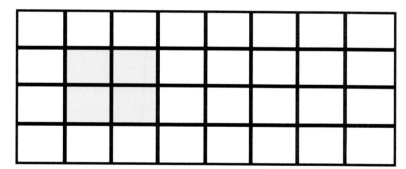

Solution

The area of the region colored yellow is 4 units because there are 4 squares that are colored yellow.

Team Work

1. Each team should draw a rectangle which consists of 10 squares by 6 squares and color the squares as shown in Figure 1. Count the number of the colored grid squares.
2. Each team should draw a square which consists of 6 squares by 6 squares and shade the squares as shown in Figure 2.

Figure 1

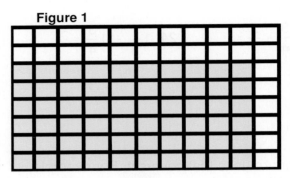

Figure 2

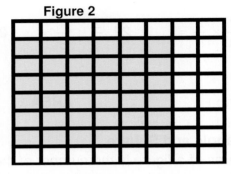

3. Observe the yellow square grids in the Figures 1 and 2 and complete the chart.

Activities	Figure 1	Figure 2
(a). Count the number of the yellow grids which is the area of the yellow grids.	60 yellow square grids.	36 yellow square grids.
(b). Multiply the number of the yellow square grids along the length of the yellow area by the number of the yellow square grids along the width of the yellow area.	10 × 6 = 60 yellow square grids.	6 × 6 = 36 yellow square grids.

4. Comparing 3(a) and 3(b), Figure 1 shows that if we multiply the number of the yellow square grids along the length of the yellow grid area by the number of the yellow square grids along the width of the yellow grid area will give the area of the yellow square grids. Therefore, in general, the formula for finding the area of a rectangular Figure is:

   Length × Width = L × W

   (The area covered by the yellow square grids in figure 1 is in the shape of a rectangle).

5. Observe that the area of the yellow square grids in figure 2 is obtained by multiplying the number of the yellow square grids along one side of the square by the number of the yellow square grids along the other side of the square. Therefore, in general, the formula for finding the area of a square is:

   Side × Side = S × S

   (The area covered by the yellow square grids in figure 2 is in the shape of a square).

   Observe that the area is a measurement of two dimensions (such as **length × width** or **side × side**), and therefore, it is expressed in square units such as centimeter square or **cm × cm = cm²**.

Example 2

The length of a rectangle is 4 cm and the width is 3 cm. Find the area of the rectangle.

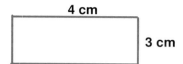

Solution

The formula for finding the area of a rectangle is:

$$\textbf{Area} = \textbf{Length} \times \textbf{Width}$$
$$= L \times W$$
$$= 4 \text{ cm} \times 3 \text{ cm}$$
$$= 12 \text{ square cm}$$
$$= 12 \text{ cm}^2$$

Example 3

The side of a square is 5 ft. What is the area of the square?

Solution

Area of a square = Side × Side
$$= S \times S$$
$$= 5 \text{ ft} \times 5 \text{ ft}$$
$$= 25 \text{ square ft}$$
$$= 25 \text{ ft}^2$$

Example 4

Find the area of the figure.

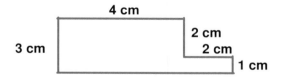

Solution

Step 1: Divide the polygon into **two parts**.

The area of some polygons can be found by dividing them into two or more different polygons. Divide the figure/polygon into two rectangles B and C by the broken line as shown:

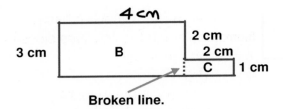

Broken line.

Step 2: Find the areas of the rectangles B and C.

Considering area B;

L = 4 cm, W = 3 cm

Area = L × W

= 4 cm × 3 cm

= 12 cm²

Considering area C;

L = 2 cm, W = 1 cm

Area = L × W

= 2 cm × 1 cm

= 2 cm²

Step 3: Combine the areas of the rectangles B and C.

Total area = Area of rectangle B + Area of rectangle C.

= 12 cm² + 2 cm²

= 14 cm²

Example 5

Find the area of the figure.

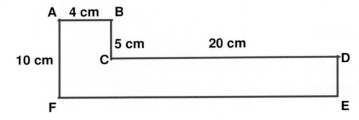

Solution

Step 1: Divide the polygon into two rectangles X and Y by the dotted lines.

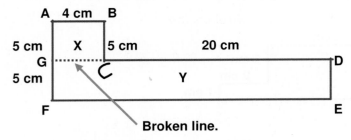

Broken line.

Step 2: Find the areas of the rectangles X and Y.

Considering rectangles X

L = 5 cm, W = 4 cm

Area = L × W

= 5 cm × 4 cm

= 20 cm²

Considering area Y.

L = $\overline{GC}$ + $\overline{CD}$

= 4 cm + 20 cm = 24 cm

W = GF = $\overline{AF}$ - $\overline{AG}$

= 10 cm - 5 cm

$$= 5 \text{ cm}$$

Note that $\overline{AG} = \overline{BC} = 5$ cm because ABCG is a rectangle and the opposite sides of a rectangle are equal.

$$\text{Area} = L \times w$$
$$= 24 \text{ cm} \times 5 \text{ cm} \quad (L = 24 \text{ cm}, W = 5 \text{ cm}).$$
$$= 100 \text{ cm}^2$$

Step 3: Combine the areas of rectangles X and Y.

Total area = Area of rectangle X + Area of rectangle Y.
$$= 20 \text{ cm}^2 + 100 \text{ cm}^2$$
$$= 120 \text{ cm}^2$$

Example 6

Find the area of the figure given that AFGH forms a rectangle, and also BCDE forms a rectangle.

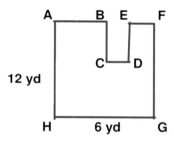

$\overline{AB}$ = 4 yd
$\overline{ED}$ = 5 yd
$\overline{CD}$ = 1 yd

Solution

Step 1: Divide the figure into 3 rectangles X, Y, and Z by the broken lines.

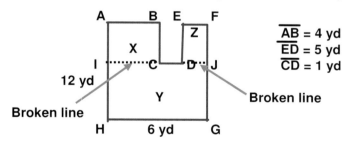

$\overline{AB}$ = 4 yd
$\overline{ED}$ = 5 yd
$\overline{CD}$ = 1 yd

Step 2: Find the areas of the rectangles X, Y, and Z.

Considering the area of rectangle X.

$L = \overline{BC} = 5$ yd because $\overline{BC}$ and $\overline{ED}$ have the same lengths.
$W = \overline{AB} = 4$ yd.
Therefore, the area of the rectangle $X = L \times W$
$$= 5 \text{ yd} \times 4 \text{ yd}$$
$$= 20 \text{ yd}^2$$

Considering the area of the rectangle Y

$L = \overline{AH} - \overline{AI}$ and $\overline{AI}$ has the same length as $\overline{BC}$ because the $\overline{AI}$ and the $\overline{BC}$ are the opposite sides of the rectangle ABCI and the opposite sides of a rectangle are congruent (equal).

$L = \overline{AH} - \overline{AI}$

$\quad = 12 \text{ yd} - 5 \text{ yd}$

$\quad = 7 \text{ yd}$

$W = \overline{HG} = 6 \text{ yd}$

Area of rectangle $Y = L \times W$

$\qquad\qquad\qquad = 7 \text{ yd} \times 6 \text{ yd}$

$\qquad\qquad\qquad = 42 \text{ yd}^2$

Considering the area of the rectangle Z

$L = \overline{DE} = 5 \text{ yd.}$

$W = \overline{HG} - \overline{AB} - \overline{CD}$ because $\overline{HG} = \overline{AF}$ (AFGH is a rectangle, and the opposite sides of a rectangle are equal).

$W = 6 \text{ yd} - 4 \text{ yd} - 1 \text{ yd.}$

$\quad = 6 \text{ yd} - 5 \text{ yd}$

$\quad = 1 \text{ yd}$

Area of rectangle $Z = L \times W$

$\qquad\qquad\qquad = 5 \text{ yd} \times 1 \text{ yd}$

$\qquad\qquad\qquad = 5 \text{ yd}^2$

Step 3: Combine the areas of the rectangles X, Y and Z.

Total area = Area of rectangle X + Area of rectangle Y + Area of rectangle Z.

$\qquad\qquad = 20 \text{ yd}^2 + 42 \text{ yd}^2 + 5 \text{ yd}^2$

$\qquad\qquad = 67 \text{ yd}^2$

Example 7

The area of a rectangle is 24 ft^2 . If the length is 6 ft, find the width of the rectangle.

Solution

Step 1: Setup using the formula for finding the area of a rectangle.

Using the formula for finding the area of a rectangle;

$\qquad\qquad A = L \times W \qquad\qquad\qquad$ A = Area, L = Length, and W = Width.

From the question, A = 24 ft^2 and L = 6 ft.

Substitute A = 24 ft^2 and L = 6 ft into the equation $A = L \times W$ as shown:

$\qquad A = L \times W$

$24 \text{ ft}^2 = 6 \text{ ft} \times W$

Step 2: Find the width of the rectangle.

Divide both sides of the equation (24 ft^2 = 6 ft $\times$ W) by 6 ft in order to obtain the value for W as shown:

$$\frac{24 \text{ ft}^2}{6 \text{ ft}} = \frac{6 \text{ ft} \times W}{6 \text{ ft}}$$

$$\begin{array}{cc} \overset{\displaystyle 4\text{ ft}}{\cancel{24 \text{ ft}^2}} & \overset{\displaystyle 1}{} \\ \dfrac{\cancel{24 \text{ ft}^2}}{\underset{1}{\cancel{6 \text{ ft}}}} = \dfrac{\cancel{6 \text{ ft}} \times W}{\underset{1}{\cancel{6 \text{ ft}}}} \end{array}$$

4 ft $=$ W

Therefore, the width of the rectangle is 4 ft.

Example 8 - Real World Application

The area of a special rectangular classroom is 200 yd². If the width of the classroom is 10 yd, how long is the classroom?

Solution

Step 1: Setup using the formula for finding the area of a rectangle.

Using the formula for finding the area of a rectangle;

$A = L \times W$ $\qquad\qquad$ A = Area, L = Length, and W = Width

From the question, A $=$ 200 yd² and W $=$ 10 yd.

Substitute A $=$ 200 ft² and W $=$ 10 ft into the equation A $=$ L $\times$ W as shown:

$A = L \times W$

200 yd² $=$ L $\times$ 10 yd

Step 2: Find the length of the rectangle (classroom)

Divide both sides of the equation (200 yd² $=$ L $\times$ 10 yd) by 10 yd in order to obtain the value for L as shown:

$$\dfrac{200 \text{ yd}^2}{10 \text{ yd}} = \dfrac{L \times 10 \text{ yd}}{10 \text{ yd}}$$

$$\begin{array}{cc} \overset{\displaystyle 20\text{ yd}}{} & \overset{\displaystyle 1}{} \\ \dfrac{\cancel{200 \text{ yd}^2}}{\underset{1}{\cancel{10 \text{ yd}}}} = \dfrac{L \times \cancel{10 \text{ yd}}}{\underset{1}{\cancel{10 \text{ yd}}}} \end{array}$$

20 yd $=$ L

Therefore, the length of the rectangle (classroom) is 20 yd.

PERIMETER

Example 9
a. What is the perimeter of an object?
b. Find the perimeter of the following figures:

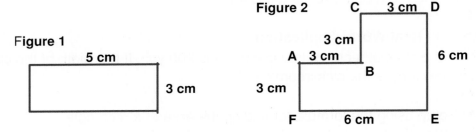

Figure 1

Figure 2

c. One side of a square is 3 ft. What is the area and the perimeter of the square?

Solution
a. The perimeter of an object is the distance around the object.
b. Figure 1 is a rectangle and recall from the "geometric figures" that the opposite
   sides of a rectangle are equal. Therefore, the dimensions of Figure 1 are shown
   in the diagram as shown:

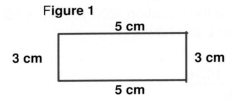

Figure 1

The perimeter of Figure 1 is:

$$5 \text{ cm} + 3 \text{ cm} + 5 \text{ cm} + 3 \text{ cm} = 16 \text{ cm.}$$

Alternative solution
The formula for finding the perimeter of a rectangle can also be used to find the
perimeter of figure 1 as follows:

Perimeter = 2L + 2W   (where L = length and W = width).
= 2 · 5 cm + 2 · 3 cm   (where L = 5 cm and W = 3 cm).
= 10 cm + 6 cm
= 16 cm.

The perimeter of figure 2 is the distance around figure 2 as shown:

Perimeter = $\overline{AB} + \overline{BC} + \overline{CD} + \overline{DE} + \overline{EF} + \overline{FA}$
= 3 cm + 3 cm + 3 cm + 6 cm + 6 cm + 3 cm
= 24 cm

c. It is given that one side of a square is 3 ft, and therefore all the other sides of
   the square are also 3 ft because all the sides of a square are equal. The perimeter
   of the square is:

Perimeter = S + S + S + S   (S = dimension of a side of the square).

       = 3 ft + 3 ft + 3 ft + 3 ft

       = 12 ft.

The formula for finding the area of a square is S × S.

Area of a square = S × S   (S = dimension of a side of the square).

       = 3 ft × 3 ft

       = 9 ft^2

Example 10

Given that the perimeter of a rectangle is 24 ft and the length is 8ft,

a. find the width.

b. find the area.

Solution

a. The formula for finding the perimeter of a rectangle is:

   Perimeter = 2L + 2W   [A]

   Substitute perimeter = 24ft and L = 8ft into equation [A] as shown:

      24 ft = 2·8 ft + 2W

      24 ft = 16 ft + 2W   [B]

Subtract 16 ft from both sides of the equation [B] in order to obtain 2W only on the right side of the equation [B] as shown:

    24 ft - 16 ft = 16 ft - 16 ft + 2W

         8 ft = 0 + 2W

         8 ft = 2W   [C]

Divide both sides of equation [C] by 2 to obtain the value for W as shown:

$$\frac{8 \text{ ft}}{2} = \frac{2W}{2}$$

$$\frac{\overset{4 \text{ ft}}{\cancel{8 \text{ ft}}}}{\underset{1}{2}} = \frac{\overset{W}{\cancel{2W}}}{\underset{1}{2}}$$

      4 ft = W

Therefore, the width of the rectangle is 4 ft.

b. The formula for the area of the rectangle is:

     Area = L × W

        = 8 ft × 4 ft

        = 32 ft^2

Therefore, the area is 32 ft.

Exercises

1. Explain what is meant by the area of a figure? Hint: See notes in this book.

2. What is the formula for finding the area of a rectangle? Hint: See the notes in this chapter.

3. What is the formula for finding the area of a square? Hint: See the notes in this chapter.

4. What is the area of the yellow square grids in the diagrams. Hint: See Example **1**.

a.

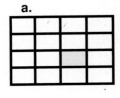

b.

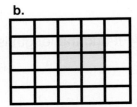

c.

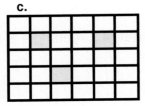

5. Find the area of each rectangle. Hint: See Example **2**.

   a. L = 2ft   **b.** L = 4 in.   **c.** L = 6 cm
       W = 1 ft   W = 3 in.   W = 3 cm

   d. L = 4.2 yd   **e.** L = 5 cm   **f.** $L = 5\frac{1}{2}$ ft

       W = 3 yd   W = 4 cm   W = 3 ft

6. Find the area of each square figure with the following sides. Hint: See Example **3**.

   a. 6 cm   **b.** 10 ft   **c.** 7 in   **d.** 5 cm   **e.** 8 m

7. Find the area of the following figures. Hint: See Example **4**.

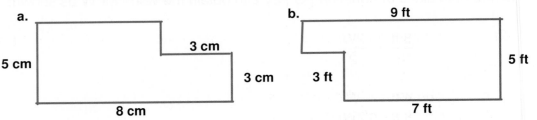

8. Find the area of the following figures. Hint: See Example **5**.

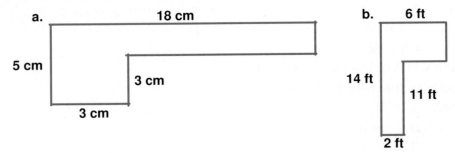

9. Find the area of each figure. Hint: See Example **6**.

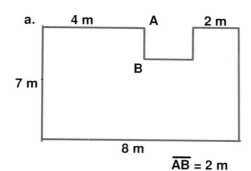

a.

4 m   A   2 m

B

7 m

8 m

$\overline{AB}$ = 2 m

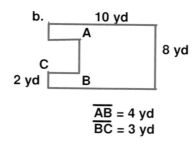

b.

10 yd

A

C

2 yd   B

8 yd

$\overline{AB}$ = 4 yd
$\overline{BC}$ = 3 yd

10. Find the missing measurement of each rectangle. Hint: See Example **7**.

a. A = 16 cm²
   L = 8 cm
   W = ?

b. A = 20 ft²
   L = 5 ft
   W = ?

c. A = 36 m²
   L = 9 m
   W = ?

11. Find the missing measurement of each rectangle. Hint: See Example **8**.

a. A = 100 in.²
   W = 5 in
   L = ?

b. A = 48 cm²
   W = 6 cm
   L = ?

c. A = 27 m²
   W = 3 m
   L = ?

12a. Find the perimeter of the following figures. Hint: See Example **9b**.

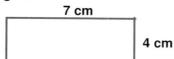

Figure 1

7 cm

4 cm

Figure 2   C   5 cm   D

5 cm

A   5 cm

B

7 cm

5 cm

F   7 cm   E

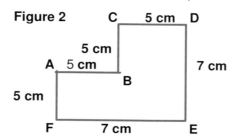

12b. Find the area and the perimeter of a square given that one side of the square is 6 m long. Hint: See Example **9b**.

13. The perimeter of a rectangle is 26 m and the length is 9 m.

  a. Find the width of the rectangle.

  b. Find the area of the rectangle .

  Hint: See Example **10**.

14. Find the missing measurements of the rectangles. Hint: See Example **10**.

  a. Perimeter = 12 cm
        L = 4 cm
      W = ?
      A = ?

  b. Perimeter = 36 m
       W = 4 m
       L = ?
       A = ?

Challenge Questions

15. Find the missing measurement of each rectangle.

  a. A = 18 m²
     L = 6 m
    W = ?
Perimeter =?

  b. L = 5 ft
     W = 3 ft
    A = ?
Perimeter = ?

  c. A = 28 cm²
     W = 4 cm
    L = ?
Perimeter = ?

d. L = 7 ft
W = 3 ft
A = ?
Perimeter = ?

e. Perimeter = 36 cm
L = 12 cm
W = ?
A = ?

f. Perimeter = 16 ft
W = 2 ft
L = ?
A = ?

16. The area of a square is 100 cm². Find the measure of the sides of the square. Hint: The formula for the area of the square is **Side** × **Side** therefore find a number that can be multiplied by itself to obtain 100.

Answer to Selected Questions

4a 1 square unit.

5a. 2 ft²

6a. 36 cm²

7a. 34 cm²

10a. 2 cm

11a 20 in.

AREA AND PERIMETER

AREA AND PERIMETER OF A TRIANGLE

New Terms: **base**, **height**

Area of a Triangle
Example 1
Show that the area of a triangle is half the area of a rectangle and also show that the

area of a triangle $= \dfrac{1}{2}$ **base** × **height**.

Solution

Step 1: Sketch a rectangle ABCD with the length 10 cm and the width 6 cm.

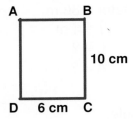

Step 2: Find the area of the rectangle ABCD.
Length of the rectangle ABCD = 10 cm.
Width of the rectangle ABCD = 6 cm.

648

The formula for finding the **area of a rectangle is Length × Width**.
Area of rectangle ABCD = 10 cm × 6 cm

$$= 60 \text{ cm}^2$$

Step 3: Let us divide the rectangle ABCD into two equal halves by drawing a line
from B to D.

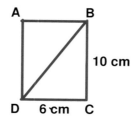

Step 4: Notice that the area of triangle BCD is half the area of the rectangle ABCD
and this can be written as shown:

$$\text{Area of triangle ABC} = \frac{1}{2} \times (\text{Area of rectangle ABCD})$$

$$= \frac{1}{2} \times \text{Length} \times \text{Width} \qquad (\text{Note: Area of a rectangle} = \mathbf{L} \times \mathbf{W})$$

$$= \frac{1}{2} \times \text{L} \times \text{W}$$

Step 5: In the triangle BCD we can replace the length BC by "height" and the width
DC by "base," and therefore, the area of the triangle BCD

$$= \frac{1}{2} \times \text{base} \times \text{height}$$

$$= \frac{1}{2} \times \text{b} \times \text{h} \qquad \text{b} = \text{base and h} = \text{height.}$$

$$= \frac{1}{2} \times 6 \text{ cm.} \times 10 \text{ cm} \qquad \text{b} = 6 \text{ cm and h} = 10 \text{ cm}$$

$$= \frac{1}{\cancel{2}_{1}} \times \overset{3}{\cancel{6}} \text{ cm} \times 10 \text{ cm} \qquad \text{Divide by 2}$$

$$= 3 \text{ cm} \times 10 \text{ cm} = 30 \text{ cm}^2$$

The **height** of a triangle is the perpendicular segment to the base of
the triangle. The **base** of the triangle is the perpendicular segment to the height
of the triangle.

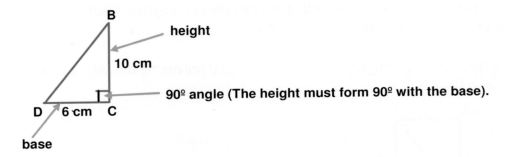

B

height

10 cm

90º angle (The height must form 90º with the base).

D 6 cm C

base

Team Project
The class may be divided into four teams.
1. Sketch the rectangle ABCD in Example 1, Step 1 on a grid paper where each unit of length is 1 cm.
2. Do step 3 in Example 1.
3. Use a pair of scissors to cut out the rectangle ABCD.
4. Use a pair of scissors to cut along the segment BD.
5. Place the triangle BCD over the triangle DAB.
6. Could you say that triangle BCD has the same area as triangle DAB? Why?
7. Could you say that the area of a triangle is half the area of a rectangle? Why?

Example 2
Find the area of the following triangles:

a.

4 cm

2 cm

b.

7 cm

3 cm

Solution
a. The height of the triangle = 4 cm
   The width of the triangle = 2 cm

The formula for finding the area of a triangle $= \dfrac{1}{2} \times b \times h$

Therefore, the area of the triangle $= \dfrac{1}{2} \times 2 \text{ cm} \times 4 \text{ cm}$

$$= \dfrac{1}{\cancel{2}} \times \cancel{2} \text{ cm} \times 4 \text{ cm} \qquad \text{Divide by 2.}$$

$$= 4 \text{ cm}^2$$

b. The height of the triangle = 4 cm.
The width of the triangle = 2 cm.

The formula for finding the area of a triangle $= \dfrac{1}{2} \times b \times h$

Therefore, the area of the triangle $= \dfrac{1}{2} \times 3 \text{ cm} \times 7 \text{ cm} =$

$$= \dfrac{21}{2} \text{ cm}^2 = 10\dfrac{1}{2} \text{ cm}^2$$

Note: Some triangles are not right triangles and in order to find the height of such triangles, draw a perpendicular line from a vertex of the triangle to the base of the triangle as shown:

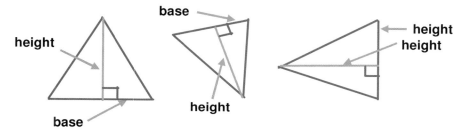

Example 3
Find the area of the following triangles:

a. 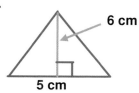 6 cm
5 cm

b. 8 cm 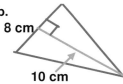 10 cm

c. 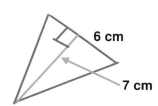 6 cm
7 cm

Solution
a. The height of the triangle = 6 cm.
The base of the triangle = 5 cm.

The formula for finding the area of a triangle is $\dfrac{1}{2} \times b \times h$

Therefore, the area of the triangle $= \dfrac{1}{2} \times 5 \text{ cm} \times 6 \text{ cm}$

$$= \dfrac{1}{\underset{1}{2}} \times 5 \text{ cm} \times \overset{3}{6} \text{ cm}$$

$$= 5 \text{ cm} \times 3 \text{ cm}$$
$$= 15 \text{ cm}^2$$

b. The height of the triangle = 10 cm.
The base of the triangle = 8 cm.

The formula for finding the area of a triangle is $\frac{1}{2} \times b \times h$

Therefore, the area of the triangle $= \frac{1}{2} \times 8 \text{ cm} \times 10 \text{ cm}$

$$= \frac{1}{\overset{}{2}_{1}} \times \overset{4}{8} \text{ cm} \times 10 \text{ cm}$$

$$= 4 \text{ cm} \times 10 \text{ cm}$$
$$= 40 \text{ cm}^2$$

c. The height of the triangle = 7 cm
The base of the triangle = 6 cm

The formula for finding the area of a triangle is $\frac{1}{2} \times b \times h$

Therefore, the area of a triangle $= \frac{1}{2} \times 6 \text{ cm} \times 7 \text{ cm}$

$$= \frac{1}{\overset{}{2}_{1}} \times \overset{3}{6} \text{ cm} \times 7 \text{ cm}$$

$$= 3 \text{ cm} \times 7 \text{ cm}$$
$$= 21 \text{ cm}^2$$

Example 4
A triangle has an area of 50 cm² and if the base of the triangle is 5 cm, find the height of the triangle.

Solution
The area of the triangle = 50 cm².
The base of the triangle = 5 cm.
Let the height of the triangle = h.

The formula for finding the area of a triangle is $\frac{1}{2} \times b \times h$.

Therefore, 50 cm^2 = $\dfrac{1}{2}$ × 5 cm × h

50 cm^2 = $\dfrac{5h}{2}$ cm _____[A]

Multiply both sides of the equation [A] by 2 in order to eliminate the 2 at the right side of the equation as a denominator as shown:

$$50 \text{ cm}^2 \times 2 = \dfrac{5h}{2} \times 2 \text{ cm}$$

$$100 \text{ cm}^2 = \dfrac{5h}{\overset{}{\underset{1}{2}}} \times \overset{1}{2} \text{ cm}$$

100 cm^2 = 5h cm ——————————————————————————[B]

Divide both sides of the equation [B] by 5 cm in order to obtain the value of h as shown:

$$\dfrac{\overset{20}{\cancel{100}}}{\underset{1}{5 \text{ cm}}} \text{ cm}^2 = \dfrac{\overset{h}{\cancel{5h}}}{\underset{1}{5 \text{ cm}}} \text{ cm}$$

20 cm = h   (Note: cm^2 ÷ cm = cm, and cm ÷ cm = 1)

Therefore, the height of the triangle = 20 cm.

Example 5

Find the length of the base of each triangle.

a.
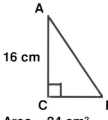
16 cm

A

C   B

Area = 24 cm²

b.
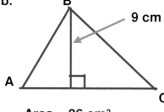
9 cm

B

A

C

Area = 36 cm²

c.
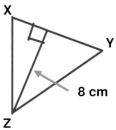
X

Y

Z

8 cm

Area = 18 cm²

Solution

a. The area of the triangle = 24 cm^2.

The height of the triangle = 16 cm.

Let the length of the base of the triangle = b. The base is $\overline{BC}$.

The formula for finding the area of a triangle is:

$$\text{Area} = \frac{1}{2} \times b \times h$$

Therefore, $24 \text{ cm}^2 = \frac{1}{2} \times b \times 16 \text{ cm}$ (Substitute 24 cm² = area, and 16 cm = h.)

$$= \frac{1}{\underset{1}{2}} \times b \times \overset{8}{16} \text{ cm}$$ (Dividing by 2)

$$= 8b \text{ cm} \rule{6cm}{0.4pt}[A]$$

Divide both sides of the equation [A] by 8 cm in order to eliminate the 8 at the right side of equation [A], and then obtain the value of b as shown:

$$\frac{24}{8} \text{ cm}^2 = \frac{8b}{8} \text{ cm}$$

$$\frac{\overset{3}{24}}{\underset{1}{8 \text{ cm}}} \text{ cm}^2 = \frac{\overset{b}{8b}}{\underset{1}{8 \text{ cm}}} \text{ cm}$$

3 cm = b.   (Note: cm² ÷ cm = cm, and cm ÷ cm = 1)

The base is 3 cm.

b. The area of the triangle = 36 cm²

The height of the triangle = 9 cm

Let the length of the base = b. The base is $\overline{AC}$.

The formula for finding the area of a triangle is:

$$\text{Area} = \frac{1}{2} \times b \times h$$

Therefore, $36 \text{ cm}^2 = \frac{1}{2} \times b \times 9 \text{ cm}$ (Substitute area = 36 cm², and h = 9 cm)

$$36 \text{ cm}^2 = \frac{9b}{2} \text{ cm} \rule{5cm}{0.4pt}[B]$$

Multiply both sides of the equation [B] by 2 in order to eliminate the 2 at the right side of the equation [B] as shown:

$$36 \text{ cm}^2 \times 2 = \frac{9b}{2} \text{ cm} \times 2$$ Notice that the 2s on the right side will cancel out.

$$36 \text{ cm}^2 \times 2 = \frac{9b}{\overset{1}{\underset{1}{2}}} \text{ cm} \times \overset{1}{2} \qquad \text{Divide the 2s on the right side by canceling.}$$

$$72 \text{ cm}^2 = 9b \text{ cm} \underline{\hspace{6cm}} [\text{C}]$$

Divide each side of equation $[\text{C}]$ by 9 cm in order to obtain the value of b as shown:

$$\frac{72 \text{ cm}^2}{9 \text{ cm}} = \frac{9b \text{ cm}}{9 \text{ cm}}$$

$$\frac{\overset{8 \text{ cm}}{72 \text{ cm}^2}}{\underset{1}{9 \text{ cm}}} = \frac{\overset{b}{9b \cancel{\text{ cm}}}}{\underset{1}{9 \cancel{\text{ cm}}}} \qquad (\text{Note: cm}^2 \div \text{cm} = \text{cm, and cm} \div \text{cm} = 1)$$

$$8 \text{ cm} = b.$$

The length of the base = 8 cm

c. The area of the triangle = 18 cm²

The height of the triangle = 8 cm

Let the length of the base = b. The base is $\overline{\text{XY}}$.

The formula for finding the area of a triangle is:

$$\text{Area} = \frac{1}{2} \times b \times h$$

Therefore, $18 \text{ cm}^2 = \frac{1}{2} \times b \times 8 \text{ cm}$ (Substitute 18 cm² = area, and 8 cm = h)

$$= \frac{1}{\underset{1}{2}} \times b \times \overset{4}{8} \text{ cm} \qquad (\text{Dividing by 2})$$

$$18 \text{ cm}^2 = 4b \text{ cm} \underline{\hspace{6cm}} [\text{D}]$$

Divide both sides of equation $[\text{D}]$ by 4 cm in order to eliminate the 4 at the right side of equation $[\text{D}]$, and then to obtain the value of b as shown:

$$\frac{18 \text{ cm}^2}{4 \text{ cm}} = \frac{4b \text{ cm}}{4 \text{ cm}}$$

$$\frac{18 \text{ cm}^2}{4 \text{ cm}} = \frac{\overset{1}{\cancel{4}b \cancel{\text{cm}}}}{\underset{1}{\cancel{4} \cancel{\text{cm}}}}$$

$4\dfrac{2}{4}$ cm = b $18 \div 4 = 4\dfrac{2}{4}$, cm² ÷ cm = cm, and cm ÷ cm = 1

$4\dfrac{\overset{1}{\cancel{2}}}{\underset{2}{\cancel{4}}}$ cm = b   Reduce to the lowest term by dividing by 2

$4\dfrac{1}{2}$ cm = b.

The base of the triangle is $4\dfrac{1}{2}$ cm.

Exercises

1. The area of a triangle is half the area of a rec_____. Hint: See the notes in Example **1**.

2. Find the area of the following triangles. Hint: See Example **2**.

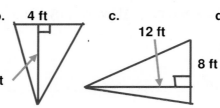

a. 5 cm 2 cm   **b.** 6 ft 4 ft   **c.** 8 cm 6 cm   **d.** 6 cm 3 cm

3. Find the area of each triangle. Hint: See Example **3**.

a. 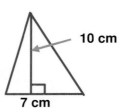 10 cm 7 cm   **b.** 4 ft 6 ft   **c.** 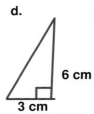 12 ft 8 ft   **d.** 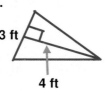 3 ft 4 ft

4. Find the height of each triangle. Hint: See Example **4**.

  a. Area = 12 cm²   **b**. Area = 16 ft²   **c**. Area = 24 cm²
     Base = 4 cm   Base = 3 ft   Base = 3 cm

5. Find the base of each triangle. Hint: See Example **5**.

  a. Area = 16ft²   **b**. Area = 9 cm²   **c**. Area =18 cm²
     Height = 4ft   Height = 2 cm   Height = 6 cm

Challenge Questions

6. Find the missing measurement for each triangle.

a. Base = 3 cm
Height = 5 cm
Area = ?

b. Base = ?
Height = 6ft
Area = 28 ft²

c. Base = 5 cm
Height = ?
Area = 25 cm²

7. Find the area of each triangle.

a.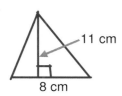

b.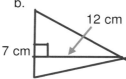

c.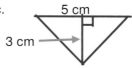

8. Find the base of each triangle.

a.

Area = 10 cm²

b.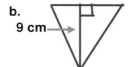

Area = 36 cm²

c.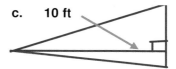

Area = 25 ft²

9. Find the height of each triangle.

a.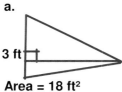

Area = 18 ft²

b.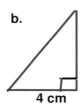

4 cm
Area = 28 cm²

c.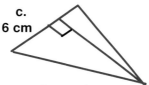

Area = 24 cm²

Answers to Selected Questions

2a. 5 cm²   **3a.** 35 cm²   **4a.** 6 cm   **5a.** 8 ft

Cumulative Review

1. Solve:

a. $\dfrac{5}{12} \div \dfrac{2}{3}$

b. $\dfrac{4}{7} \div 8$

c. $1\dfrac{3}{4} \div \dfrac{3}{4}$

d. $\dfrac{2}{5} \times \dfrac{15}{16}$

e. $\dfrac{3}{4} - \dfrac{1}{2}$

f. $1\dfrac{1}{2} - \dfrac{3}{4}$

g. $3 \div \dfrac{3}{4}$

h. $1\dfrac{3}{4} + \dfrac{1}{2}$

2. What is the reciprocal of each of the following:

a. 5   **b.** $\dfrac{1}{7}$ **c.** $\dfrac{9}{10}$ **d.** $2\dfrac{1}{2}$

PERIMETER OF A TRIANGLE

The perimeter of any object is the distance around the object and therefore, the perimeter of a triangle is the distance around the triangle. The formula for finding the perimeter of a triangle is:

Perimeter = Side + Side + Side

$$= \mathbf{S_1 + S_2 + S_3} \quad (\mathbf{S_1, S_2, \text{ and } S_3} \text{ represent the length of the}$$

sides of the triangle)

Example 1
The measure of the sides of a triangle are 2 cm, 5 cm, and 6 cm. Find the perimeter of the triangle.

Solution
The formula for finding the perimeter of a triangle is:

Perimeter = Side + Side + S ide

$$= \mathbf{S_1 + S_2 + S_3} \underline{\hspace{5cm}} [A]$$

Therefore, substitute $S_1 = 2$ cm, $S_2 = 5$ cm, and $S_3 = 6$ cm into equation $[A]$.

Equation $[A]$ then becomes:

Perimeter = 2 cm + 5 cm + 6 cm

$$= 13 \text{ cm}$$

Example 2
The perimeter of a triangle is 25 cm. If the sum of the two sides of the triangle is 15, what is the measure of the third side of the triangle?

Solution
The formula for finding the perimeter of a triangle is:

Perimeter $= \mathbf{S_1 + S_2 + S_3}$ $\underline{\hspace{5cm}} [B]$.

Since the perimeter of the triangle = 25 cm and the sum of the two sides

= 15 cm, let $S_1 + S_2 = 15$ cm. Substitute perimeter = 25 cm and the sum of the two sides of the triangle = 15 cm into equation $[B]$ as shown:

25 cm = 15 + S_3 $\underline{\hspace{5cm}} [C]$

Subtract 15 from both sides of equation $[C]$ in order to eliminate the 15 at the right side of equation $[C]$ and then isolate S_3 as shown:

25 cm - 15 cm = 15 cm - 15 cm + S_3

10 cm = S_3

The third side of the triangle is 10 cm.

Example 3

One side of an equilateral triangle is 8 ft. Find the perimeter of the triangle.

Recall that an equilateral triangle is a triangle which has all the three sides equal, and therefore, each side of the triangle is 8 ft. The formula for finding the perimeter of a triangle is:

$$\textbf{Perimeter} = \textbf{S}_1 + \textbf{S}_2 + \textbf{S}_3 \underline{\hspace{6cm}} [D]$$

Substitute $S_1 = 8$ ft, $S_2 = 8$ ft and $S_3 = 8$ ft into equation $[D]$ in order to find the perimeter of the triangle as shown:

$$\text{Perimeter} = 8 \text{ ft} + 8 \text{ ft} + 8 \text{ft}$$
$$= 24 \text{ ft}$$

Therefore, the perimeter of the triangle is 24 ft.

Example 4

The area of a triangle is 12 cm² and the height of the triangle is $3\frac{1}{2}$ cm.

a. Find the base of the triangle.

b. Assume that the triangle is an equilateral triangle, find the perimeter of the triangle.

Solution

a. The formula for finding the area of a triangle is:

$$\textbf{Area} = \frac{1}{2}\textbf{base} \times \textbf{height} \underline{\hspace{5cm}} [E]$$

Substitute the area $= 12$ cm² and the height of the triangle $= 3\frac{1}{2}$ cm into equation $[E]$

as shown:

$$12 \text{ cm}^2 = \frac{1}{2}\text{base} \times 3\frac{1}{2} \text{ cm} \underline{\hspace{5cm}} [F].$$

Multiply both sides of the equation $[F]$ by 2 in order to eliminate the $\frac{1}{2}$ at the right side

of equation $[F]$ as shown:

$$12 \text{ cm}^2 \times 2 = \frac{1}{2} \times 2 \times \text{base} \times 3\frac{1}{2} \text{ cm}$$

$$24 \text{ cm}^2 = \frac{1}{\cancel{2}} \times \cancel{2} \times \text{base} \times 3\frac{1}{2} \text{ cm}$$

$$24 \text{ cm}^2 = \text{base} \times 3\frac{1}{2} \text{ cm} \underline{\hspace{5cm}} [G].$$

Divide both sides of the equation $[G]$ by $3\frac{1}{2}$ cm in order to eliminate the $3\frac{1}{2}$ cm from the right side of the equation so that we can obtain the value of the base as shown:

$$\frac{24 \text{ cm}^2}{3\frac{1}{2} \text{ cm}} = \frac{\text{base} \times 3\frac{1}{2} \text{ cm}}{3\frac{1}{2} \text{ cm}}$$

$$\frac{24 \text{ cm}}{3\frac{1}{2}} = \text{base}$$

$3\frac{1}{2}$ cm $\div$ $3\frac{1}{2}$ cm = 1 and cm^2 $\div$ cm = cm

$$\frac{24 \text{ cm}}{\frac{7}{2}} = \text{base}$$

$3\frac{1}{2} = \frac{7}{2}$ (Review Improper Fractions).

$$24 \text{ cm} \times \frac{2}{7} = \text{base}$$

To divide by a fraction is the same as to multiply by the reciprocal of the fraction.

$$\frac{48}{7} \text{ cm} = \text{base}$$

6.86 cm = base

You may use a calculator and round your answer to two decimal places.

Therefore, the base of the triangle is 6.86 cm.

b. If we assume that the triangle is an equilateral triangle, then all the sides are equal. The formula for finding the perimeter of a triangle is:

Perimeter = $S_1 \times S_2 \times S_3$ _____[H]

Substitute S_1 = 6.86 cm, S_2 = 6.86 cm, and S_3 = 6.86 cm into equation [H] as shown:

Perimeter = 6.86 cm + 6.86 cm + 6.86 cm

           = 20.58 cm   You may use a calculator.

Exercises

1. The measure of the three sides of each triangle is given. Find the perimeter of each triangle. Hint: See Example **1**.
     a. 3 m, 8 m, and 7 m   **b**. 9 ft, 2 ft, and 6 ft   **c**. 5 in., 8 in., and 11 in.
     d. 9 cm, 12 cm, and 5 cm   **e**. 6 m, 17 m, and 4 m   **f**. 7 ft, 4 ft, and 9 ft
     g. 8 m, 12 m, and 10 m   **h**. 7 ft, 13 ft, and 5 ft   **i**. 10 cm, 5 cm, and 9 cm

2. The perimeter and the sum of the two sides of each triangle are given. Find the measure of the third side of the triangle. Hint: See Example **2**.

a. Perimeter = 28 cm and the sum of the two sides = 17 cm.

b. Perimeter = 15 ft and the sum of the two sides = 9 ft.

c. Perimeter = 30 in. and the sum of the two sides = 19 in.

d. Perimeter = 25 cm and the sum of the two sides = 19 cm.

3. One side of each equilateral triangle is given. Find the perimeter of each equilateral triangle. Hint: See Example **3**.

a. 10 cm	**b.** 5 ft	**c.** 8 in.	**d.** 7 m	**e.** 4 cm
f. 11 m	**g.** 9 cm	**h.** 6 m	**i.** 12 in.	**j.** 3 ft

4. The area of a triangle is 7 m² and the height of the triangle is $3\frac{1}{2}$ m.

   a. Find the measure of the base triangle.

   b. Find the perimeter of the triangle given that the triangle is an equilateral triangle. Hint: See Example 4.

Challenge Questions

5. The sum of the measure of the two sides of a triangle is 19 cm. If the perimeter of the triangle is 27 cm, find the measure of the third side of the triangle.

6. The measure of the sides of a triangle are 8 ft, 6 ft, and 5 ft. Find the perimeter of the triangle.

7. The measure of one side of an equilateral triangle is 12 cm. Find the perimeter of the triangle.

Answers to Selected Questions

1a. 18 m   **2a.** 11 cm   **3a.** 30 cm

AREA AND PERIMETER OF PARALLELOGRAMS

What is a parallelogram? Recall that a parallelogram is a quadrilateral which has parallel and congruent opposite sides. The height and the base of a parallelogram is shown below.

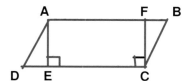

$\overline{AE} = \overline{FC}$ = **Height**
$\overline{DC}$ = **Base**

The height of a parallelogram is the perpendicular segment to the base of the parallelogram. The base of a parallelogram is a side of the parallelogram that the height of the parallelogram is perpendicular to.

Example 1

Show that the area of a parallelogram is equal to the area of a rectangle that has the same base (length) and height (width).

Solution

Step 1: Sketch the parallelogram ABCD on a grid paper with height $\overline{AE}$.

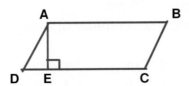

Step 2: Cut out the left triangle AED, and then paste the left triangle AED at the right side of the parallelogram to form a rectangle ABEE as shown:

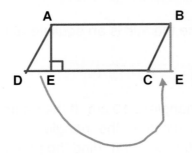

Step 3: Conclude that the same area that forms the parallelogram ABCD also forms the rectangle ABEE as shown:

Team Project
1. The class should be divided into four teams and each team should do steps 1, 2 and 3 of example 1.
2. From your project, do you agree with the question in Example 1? Explain.

Formula for finding the area of a parallelogram
Since the area of a parallelogram is equal to the area of a rectangle that has the same base (length) and height (width), the formula for finding the area of a parallelogram is similar to the formula for finding the area of a rectangle as shown:
Area of a rectangle = **Length** × **Width**
Area of a parallelogram = **Base** × **Height**

Example 2
Find the area of each parallelogram.

a.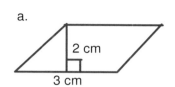

b.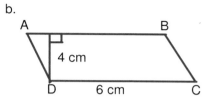

c.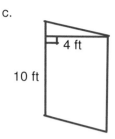

Solution

a. Height of the parallelogram = 2 m

Base of the parallelogram = 3 m

The formula for finding the area of a parallelogram is:

Area = Base × Height.

Therefore, the area of the parallelogram is:

Area = 3 m × 2 m

= 6 m^2

b. Height of the parallelogram = 4 cm.

Base of the parallelogram = $\overline{AB}$

But $\overline{AB} = \overline{DC}$ because the opposite sides of a parallelogram are equal.

Therefore, the base of the parallelogram = 6 cm.

The formula for finding the area of a parallelogram is

Area = **Base** × **Height**.

Therefore, the area of the parallelogram = 6 cm × 4 cm = 24 cm^2

c. Height of the parallelogram = 4 ft

Base of the parallelogram = 10 ft

The formula for finding the area of a parallelogram = Base × Height.

Therefore, the area of the parallelogram = 10 ft × 4 ft = 40 ft^2

Example 3

Find the missing dimension for each parallelogram.

a. Base = 6 cm   **b.** Base = ?

Height = ?   Height = 8 cm

Area = 32 cm^2 Area = 24 cm^2

Solution

a. Let the height of the parallelogram = H

The formula for finding the area of a parallelogram is:

Area = Base × Height.

Therefore, the area of the parallelogram is:

32 cm^2 = 6 cm × H _____[A]

Divide both sides of equation [A] by 6 cm in order to eliminate the 6 cm from the right side of the equation, and then to obtain the value of H as shown:

663

$$\frac{32 \text{ cm}^2}{6 \text{ cm}} = \frac{6 \text{ cm}}{6 \text{ cm}} \times H$$

$$\frac{32 \text{ cm}^2}{6 \text{ cm}} = \frac{\overset{1}{\cancel{6 \text{ cm}}}}{\underset{1}{\cancel{6 \text{ cm}}}} \times H$$

$5\dfrac{2}{6} = H$ $\qquad$ $32 \div 6 = 5$ remainder 2 or $5\dfrac{2}{6}$.

$5\dfrac{1}{3} = H$ $\qquad$ Reduce $\dfrac{2}{6}$ to the lowest term by dividing the numerator and the denominator by 2.

b. Let the base of the parallelogram = B

The formula for finding the area of the parallelogram is:

Area = Base × Height.

Therefore, the area of the parallelogram is:

$24 \text{ cm}^2 = B \times 8 \text{ cm}$ _____[Y]

Divide both sides of equation [Y] by 8 cm in order to eliminate the 8 cm at the right side of equation [Y], and then to obtain the value of B as shown:

$$\frac{24 \text{ cm}^2}{8 \text{ cm}} = B \times \frac{8 \text{ cm}}{8 \text{ cm}}$$

$$\frac{\overset{3}{\cancel{24 \text{ cm}^2}}}{\underset{1}{\cancel{8 \text{ cm}}}} = B \times \frac{\overset{1}{\cancel{8 \text{ cm}}}}{\underset{1}{\cancel{8 \text{ cm}}}}$$

$3 \text{ cm} = B$ $\qquad$ **Note**: $\text{cm}^2 \div \text{cm} = \text{cm}$, and $\text{cm} \div \text{cm} = 1$.

The base of the parallelogram is 3 cm.

Exercises

1. What is the formula for finding the area of a parallelogram? Hint: See Example **1**.
2. Find the area of each of the parallelograms. Hint: See Example **2**.

a.

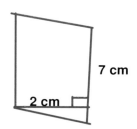

7 cm

2 cm

b.

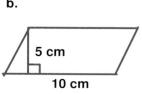

5 cm

10 cm

c.

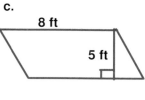

8 ft

5 ft

3. Find the missing dimension for each parallelogram. Hint: See Example **3**.
   a. Base = 5 m   **b.** Base = ?   **c.** Base = 7 ft   **d.** Base = ?
   Height = ?   Height = 9 cm   Height = ?   Height = 4 in.
   Area = 30 cm^2 Area = 36 cm^2 Area = 63 ft^2 Area = 32 in^2

Challenge Questions

4. Find the missing dimension for each parallelogram.
   a. Base = 6 cm   **b.** Base = ?   **c.** Base = 5 ft   **d.** Base = ?
   Height = 8 cm   Height = 2 ft   Height = ?   Height = 3 m
   Area = ?   Area = 24 m^2 Area = 35 ft^2 Area = 30 m^2

5. Find the area of each parallelogram.

a.

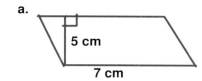

5 cm

7 cm

b.

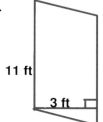

11 ft

3 ft

c.

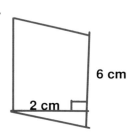

6 cm

2 cm

Answers to Selected Questions

2a. 14 cm^2 **3a.** 6 m

PERIMETER OF A PARALLELOGRAM

Recall that a parallelogram is a quadrilateral that has parallel and congruent opposite sides. Since the opposite sides of a parallelogram are congruent, the opposite sides of a parallelogram are equal. The perimeter of the parallelogram is the distance around the parallelogram. Therefore, the perimeter of the parallelogram in figure 1 is:

Perimeter = L + L + W + W   (L represents length and W represents width)
= 2L + 2W

Therefore, the formula for finding the perimeter of a parallelogram is:

Perimeter = 2L + 2W

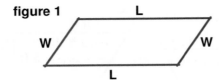

figure 1

Example 1

The length of a parallelogram is 7 cm and the width is 4 cm. Find the perimeter of the parallelogram.

Solution

The formula for finding the perimeter of a parallelogram is:

$$\text{Perimeter} = 2L + 2W \underline{\hspace{10cm}}[B]$$

Substitute L = 7 cm and W = 4 cm into equation $[B]$ as shown:

$$\begin{aligned}\text{Perimeter} &= 2 \cdot 7 \text{ cm} + 2 \cdot 4 \text{ cm}\\ &= 14 \text{ cm} + 8 \text{ cm}\\ &= 22 \text{ cm}\end{aligned}$$

Therefore, the perimeter of the triangle is 22 cm.

Example 2

The perimeter of a parallelogram is 24 cm. If the width of the parallelogram is 3 cm, find the length of the parallelogram.

Solution

The formula for finding the perimeter of a parallelogram is:

$$\text{Perimeter} = 2L + 2W \underline{\hspace{10cm}}[C].$$

Substitute the perimeter = 24 cm and W = 3 cm into equation $[C]$ as shown:

$$\begin{aligned}24 \text{ cm} &= 2L + 2 \cdot 3 \text{ cm}\\ 24 \text{ cm} &= 2L + 6 \text{ cm} \underline{\hspace{7cm}}[D]\end{aligned}$$

Subtract 6 cm from both sides of the equation $[D]$ in order to eliminate the 6 cm at the right side of the equation $[D]$ and then to isolate the 2L as shown:

$$\begin{aligned}24 \text{ cm - 6 cm} &= 2L + 6 \text{ cm - 6 cm}\\ 18 \text{ cm} &= 2L \underline{\hspace{7cm}}[E]\end{aligned}$$

Note: 6 cm - 6 cm = 0

Divide both sides of the equation $[E]$ by 2 in order to eliminate the 2 at the right side of the equation $[E]$ and then to isolate L as shown:

$$\frac{18}{2} \text{ cm} = \frac{2L}{2}$$

$$\frac{\overset{9}{\cancel{18}}}{\underset{1}{\cancel{2}}} \text{ cm} = \frac{\overset{L}{\cancel{2L}}}{\underset{1}{\cancel{2}}}$$

9 cm = L

Therefore, the length of the perimeter is 9 cm.

Note: The method for the solution of example 2 can also be used to find the width of the parallelogram when the length and the perimeter of the parallelogram are given.

Exercises

1. Find the perimeter of each of the parallelograms with the given length and width.
   Hint: See Example **1**.
   a. L = 10 m and W = 4 m   **b.** L = 6 ft and W = 2 ft
   c. L = 12 cm and W = 6 cm   **d.** L = 6 cm and W = 3 cm
2. The perimeter of a parallelogram is 36 cm and the width is 4 cm. Find the length of the parallelogram. Hint: See Example **2**
3. The length of a side of a parallelogram is 14 cm and the perimeter is 48 cm. Find the width of the parallelogram. Hint: See Example **2**.

Challenge Questions

4. Find the missing dimension in each of the parallelograms.
   a. Perimeter = 16 m, L = ?, and W = 2 cm.
   b. Perimeter = ? , L = 9 m, and W = 3 m.
   c. Perimeter = 26 ft, L = 9 ft, and W = ?
   d. Perimeter = 33 m, L = 10 m, and W = ?
   e. Perimeter = 29 cm, L = ?, and W = 4 cm.

Cumulative Review

1. Solve:

   a. 2% of 50 = ?   **b.** $\dfrac{3}{7} \times 21 = ?$ **c.** $3^2 - \sqrt{16} = ?$

2. Solve for n:

   a. 3n = 12   **b.** $\dfrac{3n}{4} = \dfrac{3}{2}$ **c.** $\dfrac{3}{4} = \dfrac{3}{2n}$

   Hint: See the chapter on Equations.

3. Divide, subtract, or multiply:

   a. $\dfrac{2}{3} \div \dfrac{4}{3} =$ **b.** $\dfrac{4}{3} - \dfrac{2}{3}$ **c.** $\dfrac{2}{3} \times \dfrac{4}{3} =$

4. Divide, subtract, or multiply:
   a. 6.66 - 2.77   **b.** 666 - 277   **c.** 12.4 ÷ 4 =

Summary of Perimeter and Area

Shape	Sketch	Perimeter	Area
Square		Perimeter = S + S + S + S Perimeter = 4S	Area = S × S Area = S^2
Rectangle		Perimeter = L + W + L + W Perimeter = 2L + 2W Perimeter = 2(L + W)	Area = L × W
Parallelogram		Perimeter = b + s + b + s Perimeter = 2b + 2s Perimeter = 2(b + s)	Area = b × h
Triangle		Perimeter = a + b + c	Area = $\frac{1}{2}$b × h

Cumulative Review

1. What is an equilateral triangle?

2. Explain what is meant by parallel lines.

3. Solve for n:

  a. 3n + 1 = 10   **b.** 4n = 16   **c.** 8 = 2 + 3n

CHAPTER 24

NETS FOR SOLID FIGURES

What is a **net**? A net is **a two-dimensional pattern** that can be folded into a **three-dimensional object** or polyhedron.

A **Polyhedron** is a solid formed by plane faces that are polygons.

Table showing the sketches of nets.

Name	Nets	Number of faces	Three-dimensional polyhedron
Rectangular prism	base top	6	
Square prism	top bottom	6	
Rectangular pyramid	bottom	5	
Square pyramid	base	5	
Triangular pyramid	base	4	
Pentagonal prism	base	6	
Hexagonal prism	top bottom	8	

Team Project

1. Each team should sketch the nets in the table containing nets.

2. Cut out the nets.

3. Fold and tape each net to form the object.

4. Confirm the number of faces that each object has.

Exercises

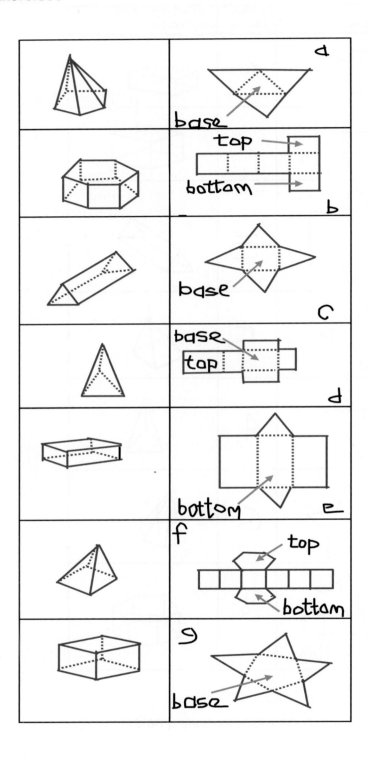

Match each solid figure with its net by writing a, b, c, d, e, or f. Hint: See the table of nets.

SURFACE AREA

The **surface area** of a solid figure is the **sum of the areas of the faces of the solid figure**.

How to Find the Surface Area of a Solid Figure

To find the surface area of a solid figure, use the net of each solid figure to determine the number of faces that is contained in each solid figure, find the area of each face and then add up the areas of all the faces to obtain the total surface area of the solid figure. Refer to the chapter on net to determine the number of faces contained in each solid figure.

Example 1

Find the surface area of the rectangular prism.

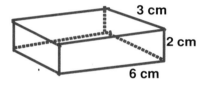

Solution

Step 1: Sketch the net of the rectangular prism with dimensions as shown:

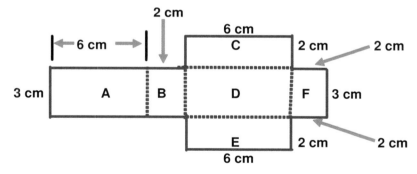

Step 2: Find the area of each face as shown:

Face	Length (L)	Width (W)	Area = L × W
A	6 cm	3 cm	18 cm^2
B	2 cm	3 cm	6 cm^2
C	6 cm	2 cm	12 cm^2
D	6 cm	3 cm	18 cm^2
E	6 cm	2 cm	12 cm^2
F	2 cm	3 cm	6 cm^2

Step 3: Add the area of each face together in order to obtain the surface area as shown:

$$\text{Surface Area} = 18 \text{ cm}^2 + 6 \text{ cm}^2 + 12 \text{ cm}^2 + 18 \text{ cm}^2 + 12 \text{ cm}^2 + 6 \text{ cm}^2$$
$$= 72 \text{ cm}^2$$

Alternate Method

Example 1 can be solved by noting that the opposite faces of a rectangular prism are congruent, and therefore, the opposite areas of a rectangular prism are congruent.
(**Note**: Congruent simply means "is equal to".)
Therefore; Face A is congruent to face D.

              Face B is congruent to face F.

              Face C is congruent to face E

Therefore, we can find the surface area by multiplying the sum of the areas of faces A, B and C by 2 as shown:

From step 2:

The area of face A = 18 cm^2

The area of face B = 6 cm^2

The area of face C = 12 cm

The sum of the surface area of the faces A, B, and C

$$= 18 \text{ cm}^2 + 6 \text{ cm}^2 + 12 \text{ cm}^2 = 36 \text{ cm}^2$$

(Area of faces A, B, and C) × 2 = 36 cm^2 × 2 = 72 cm^2

Therefore the surface area = 72 cm^2

Or from step 2:

The area of face D = 18 cm^2

The area of face E = 6 cm^2

The area of face F = 12 cm^2

The sum of the surface area of faces D, F, and E = 18 cm^2 + 6 cm^2 + 12 cm^2 = 36 cm^2

(Area of faces A, B, and C) × 2 = 36 cm^2 × 2 = 72 cm^2

Therefore, the surface area = 72 cm^2

Special Note

It is not always necessary to sketch the nets before solving the surface area problems of solid figures. However, the knowledge of nets will help the student to determine the number of faces and the associated dimensions mentally.

Example 2
Find the surface area of the square pyramid.

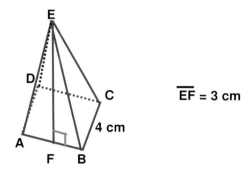

$\overline{EF}$ = 3 cm

Solution
Setup:
From the chapter on nets, we know that a square pyramid has 5 faces consisting of four congruent triangles and one square base as shown:

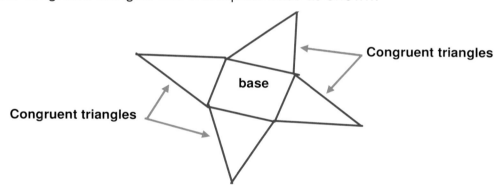

Congruent triangles

base

Congruent triangles

Step 1: Find the area of the four congruent triangles.

The height of the triangle = EF = 3 cm.   Note that $\overline{EF}$ is 90° to $\overline{AB}$
The base of each triangle = 4 cm.

The formula for finding the area of a triangle = $\frac{1}{2}$ base × height.

Therefore, the area of each triangle = $\frac{1}{2}$ × 4 cm × 3 cm

$$= \frac{1}{\cancel{2}} \times \overset{2}{\cancel{4}} \text{ cm} \times 3 \text{ cm} \qquad \text{Divide by 2.}$$

$$= 2 \text{ cm} \times 3 \text{ cm}$$
$$= 6 \text{ cm}^2$$

Therefore the area of the 4 congruent triangles $= 6 \text{ cm}^2 \times 4$
$$= 24 \text{ cm}^2$$

Step 2: Find the area of the square base. The length of the side of the
square base $= 4$ cm
The formula for finding the area of the square base = **Side** $\times$ **Side**.
Therefore, the area of the square base $= 4 \text{ cm} \times 4 \text{ cm}$
$$= 16 \text{ cm}^2$$

Step 3: Find the surface area of the square pyramid.
The surface area of the pyramid
$$= \text{Area of the 4 congruent triangles} + \text{Area of the square base.}$$
$$= 24 \text{ cm}^2 + 16 \text{ cm}^2$$
$$= 40 \text{ cm}^2$$

Exercises

1. What is meant by the surface area?
2. Explain how you would find the surface area of a rectangular prism.
3. Find the surface area of each prism. Hint: See Example **1**.

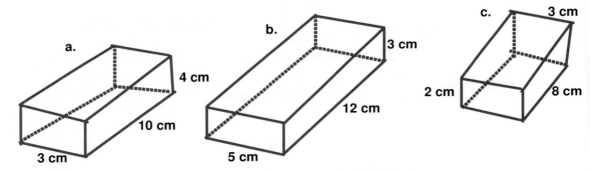

4. Find the surface area of each square pyramid. Hint: See Example **2**.

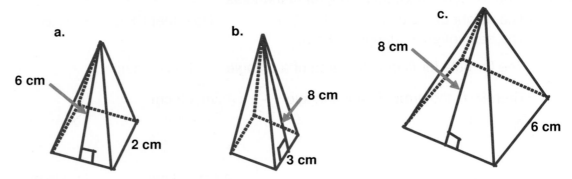

Example 3

What is the surface area of a box 4 cm long, 2 cm wide, and 3 cm high?
Solution
Step 1: Sketch the box with the associated dimensions.

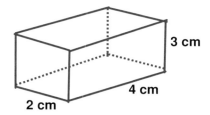

The area of the opposite sides or opposite faces of the box are congruent.
Step 2: Find the area of each face as shown:

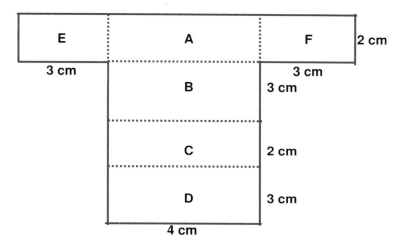

Step 3: Find the surface area of each face as shown:

Face	Length	Width	Area = L × W
A	4 cm	2 cm	4 cm × 2 cm = 8 cm²
B	4 cm	3 cm	4 cm × 3 cm = 12 cm²
C	4 cm	2 cm	4 cm × 2 cm = 8 cm²
D	4 cm	3 cm	4 cm × 3 cm = 12 cm²
E	3 cm	2 cm	3 cm × 2 cm = 6 cm²
F	3 cm	2 cm	3 cm × 2 cm = 6 cm²

The surface area = The sum of the areas of all the faces of the box.
The surface area = 8 cm² + 12 cm² + 8 cm² + 12 cm² + 6 cm² + 6 cm² = 52 cm²

Exercises
1. What is the surface area of a rectangular box which is 10 cm long, 9 cm wide and 4 cm high. Hint: See Example **3**.
2. Find the surface area of a rectangular block which is 8ft long, 6 ft wide and 5ft high.

Hint: See Example **3**.

Challenge Questions

3. Find the surface area of each solid figure.

a.

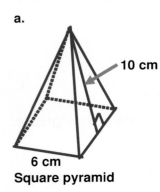

10 cm

6 cm
Square pyramid

b.

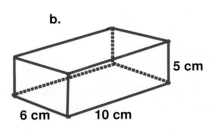

5 cm

6 cm   **10 cm**

4. What is the surface area of a cube-shaped box which has a side of 5 ft.
    Hint: A cube-shaped box has equal sides.

CHAPTER 26

VOLUME

What is volume? **Volume** is the amount of space occupied by any object. Volume is measured in cubic units because the volume is a measurement of three dimensions (such as Length × Width × Height) and therefore it is expressed in cubic units such as centimeter cube or cm × cm × = cm^3. Note: cm^3 is called centimeter cube. We can therefore estimate or find the volume of a rectangular prism by visualizing how many cubes will fill it.

VOLUME OF RECTANGULAR PRISM

Team Project
Goal of the project: Whether we can use cubes to estimate or find the volume of a rectangular prism?
Material: 1 transparent rectangular prism or container and 60 plastic cubes of the same size.
Method:
Step 1
Make a row of 5 cubes along the length of the container.

676

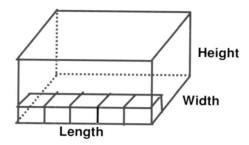

Step 2: Make 3 rows of 5 cubes along the width to make 1 layer.

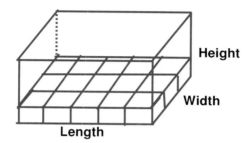

Step 3: Make 4 layers of 15 cubes to fill the container or to complete the rectangular prism.

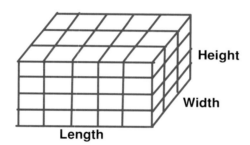

Step 4: Count the total number of the cubes that fill up the container or that makes the prism = 60 cubes or 5 × 3 × 4 = 60 cubes

Step 5: The space occupied by the total number of the cubes is the volume of the container occupied by the cubes.

Since the cubes are placed closely together so that there is no gap between the cubes, the total space occupied by the cubes is the space contained in the container and this space is known as the volume. The number of cubes that occupy the space/container is obtained by multiplying the Length by Width by Height to obtain 60 cubes as shown:

Number of the cubes that occupy the space/container.

= Length × Width × Height

= 5 × 3 × 4

= 60

Therefore, the volume of the container/prism.

= 60 cubes

= Length × Width × Height

Special note: Some schools may not have the exact size of the plastic cubes and the transparent container for this experiment, however, any size of the cubes and the container may be used. The logic of the project will be the same.

Formula for Finding the Volume of a Rectangular Prism

From the team project, we know that we can find the volume of a rectangular prism or a container by counting cubes. However, instead of counting cubes, we can use a formula to find the volume of a rectangular prism as shown:

1. Volume = Length × Width × Height

$\qquad$ = L × W × H

2. Volume = Area × Height $\qquad$ (Note: L × W = Area. Review the topic on Area).

$\qquad$ = A × H $\qquad\qquad$ (A = Area and H = Height).

Example 1

The length of a rectangular prism is 6 cm, the width is 5 cm, and the height is 2 cm. What is the volume of the rectangular prism?

Solution

L = 6 cm, W = 5 cm, and H = 2 cm.

The formula for finding the volume of a rectangular prism is:

V = L × W × H $\qquad\qquad\qquad\qquad\qquad\qquad\qquad\qquad\qquad\qquad$ [A]

$\qquad$ = 6 cm × 5 cm × 2 cm $\qquad$ (Substitute L = 6 cm, W = 5 cm
$\qquad\qquad\qquad\qquad\qquad\qquad\qquad$ and H = 2 cm into equation [A].)

$\qquad$ = 60 cm^3

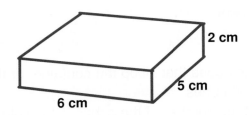

Example 2

A rectangular tank has all the sides equal. If one side of the tank is 5 cm, what is the volume of the tank?

Solution

Since all the sides of the rectangular tank are equal,

L = 5 cm, W = 5 cm, and H = 5 cm.

The formula for finding the volume of a rectangular tank or object is:

V = L × W × H $\qquad\qquad\qquad\qquad\qquad\qquad\qquad\qquad\qquad\qquad$ [B]

$\qquad$ = 5 cm × 5 cm × 5 cm $\quad$ (Substitute L = 5 cm, W = 5 cm, and H = 5 cm into
$\qquad\qquad\qquad\qquad\qquad\qquad$ equation [B]).

$\qquad$ =125 cm^3

Example 3

The volume of a water tank is 36 m³. If the length of the water tank is 6 m, the width is 3 m, what is the height of the water tank?

Solution

V =36 m³, L = 6m, W = 3 m, and H = ?

The formula for finding the volume of a water tank is:

V = L × W × H _____[C]

Substitute V = 36 m³, L = 6 m, and W = 3 m into equation [C] as shown:

$$36 \text{ m}^3 = 6 \text{ m} \times 3 \text{ m} \times H$$
$$36 \text{ m}^3 = 18 \text{ m}^2 \times H \text{ _____[D]}$$

(6 m × 3 m =18 m² because m × m = m².)

Divide both sides of the equation [D] by 18 m² in order to isolate and to obtain the value of H as shown:

$$\frac{36 \text{ m}^3}{18 \text{ m}^2} = \frac{18 \text{ m}^2}{18 \text{ m}^2} \times H$$

$$\frac{\overset{2\,m}{\cancel{36}\,\cancel{m}^3}}{\underset{1}{\cancel{18}\,\cancel{m}^2}} = \frac{\overset{1}{\cancel{18}\,\cancel{m}^2}}{\underset{1}{\cancel{18}\,\cancel{m}^2}} \times H \qquad \text{(Note: } \frac{m^3}{m^2} = \frac{\overset{1}{\cancel{m}} \times \overset{1}{\cancel{m}} \times m}{\underset{1}{\cancel{m}} \times \underset{1}{\cancel{m}}} = m)$$

$$2 \text{ m} = H$$

Therefore, the height of the water tank is 2 m.

Example 4

A gasoline tank is 10 m long and 3 m high. If the volume of the gasoline tank is 90 m³, how wide is the gasoline tank?

Solution

V = 90 m³, L = 10 m, H = 3 m, and W = ?

The formula for finding the volume of the tank is:

V = L × W × H _____[E]

Substitute V = 90 m³, L = 10 m, and H = 3 m, into equation [E] as shown:

$$90 \text{ m}^3 = 10 \text{ m} \times W \times 3 \text{ m}$$
$$90 \text{ m}^3 = 30 \text{ m}^2 \times W \text{ _____[F]}$$

(Note: 10 m × 3 m = 30 m² because m × m = m²).

Divide both sides of the equation [F] in order to isolate and to obtain the value of W as shown:

$$\frac{90 \text{ m}^3}{30 \text{ m}^2} = \frac{30 \text{ m}^2}{30 \text{ m}^2} \times W$$

$$\frac{\overset{3 \text{ m}}{\cancel{90 \text{ m}^3}}}{\underset{1}{\cancel{30 \text{ m}^2}}} = \frac{\overset{1}{\cancel{30 \text{ m}^2}}}{\underset{1}{\cancel{30 \text{ m}^2}}} \times W \qquad \left(\textbf{Note: } \frac{m^3}{m^2} = \frac{\overset{1}{\cancel{m}} \times \overset{1}{\cancel{m}} \times m}{\underset{1}{\cancel{m}} \times \underset{1}{\cancel{m}}} = m\right).$$

$$3 \text{ m} = W$$

Therefore, the width of the gasoline tank is 3 m.

Example 5

A new milk tank is installed in a chocolate factory. If the tank is 3 yd wide, 4yd high and has a volume of 60 yd³, what is the length of the milk tank?

Solution

$V = 60$ yd³, $L = ?$, $W = 3$ yd, and $H = 4$ yd

The formula for finding the volume of the milk tank is:

$V = L \times W \times H$ _____[G]

Substitute $V = 60$ yd³, $W = 3$ yd, and $H = 4$ yd into equation [G] as shown:

$$60 \text{ yd}^3 = L \times 3 \text{ yd} \times 4 \text{ yd}$$
$$60 \text{ yd}^3 = 12 \text{ yd}^2 \times L \text{ _____[H]}$$

(**Note**: 3 yd × 4 yd = 12 yd² because yd × yd = yd²).

Divide both sides of equation [H] by 12 yd² in order to isolate and obtain the value of H as shown:

$$\frac{60 \text{ yd}^3}{12 \text{ yd}^2} = \frac{12 \text{ yd}^2}{12 \text{ yd}^2} \times L$$

$$\frac{\overset{5 \text{ yd}}{\cancel{60 \text{ yd}^3}}}{\underset{1}{\cancel{12 \text{ yd}^2}}} = \frac{\overset{1}{\cancel{12 \text{ yd}^2}}}{\underset{1}{\cancel{12 \text{ yd}^2}}} \times L \qquad \left(\textbf{Note: } \frac{yd^3}{yd^2} = \frac{\overset{1}{\cancel{yd}} \times \overset{1}{\cancel{yd}} \times yd}{\underset{1}{\cancel{yd}} \times \underset{1}{\cancel{yd}}} = yd\right).$$

$$5 \text{ yd} = L$$

Therefore, the length of the milk tank = 5 yd.

Exercises

1. Explain what is meant by volume?
2. Which of the following is a correct unit of volume?
   a. cm   **b.** cm²   **c.** cm³
3. What is the formula for finding the volume of a rectangular prism?
4. Find the volume of each rectangular prism. Hint: See Example **1**.

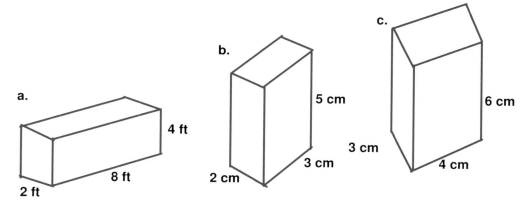

a.

4 ft

8 ft

2 ft

b.

5 cm

3 cm

2 cm

c.

6 cm

3 cm

4 cm

5. Find the height of each rectangular prism. Hint: See Example **3**.

   a. $V = 24$ cm^3 **b**. $V = 36$ ft^3 **c**. $V = 48$ in^3 **d**. $V = 28$ cm^3

    L = 6 cm   L = 9 ft   L = 6 in   L = 7 cm

    W = 2 cm   W = 2 ft   W = 4 in   W = 2 cm

    H = ?   H = ?   H = ?   H = ?

6. Find the width of each rectangular prism. Hint: See Example **4**.

   a. $V = 36$ cm^3 **b**. $V = 40$ yd^3 **c**. $V = 45$ cm^3 **d**. $V = 16$ cm^3

    L = 4 cm   L = 5 yd   L = 5 cm   L = 4 cm

    W = ?   W = ?   W = ?   W = ?

    H = 3 cm   H = 4 yd   H = 3 cm   H = 2 cm

7. Find the length of each rectangular object. Hint: See Example **5**.

   a. $V = 24$ ft^3 **b**. $V = 16$ yd^3 **c**. $V = 45$ m^3 **d**. $V = 18$ m^3

    L = ?   L = ?   L = ?   L = ?

    W = 3 ft   W = 2 yd   W = 5 m   W = 1 m

    H = 2 ft   H = 2 yd   H = 1 m   H = 2 m

Challenge Questions

8. Find the unknown measure in each rectangular block.

   a. L = 3 ft   **b**. $V = 15$ m^3 **c**. $V = 50$ ft^3 **d**. $V = 60$ m^3

    W = 2 ft   L = 5 m   L = ?   L = 5 m^3

    H = 1ft   W = 1 m   W = 2 ft   W = ?

    V = ?   H = ?   H = 1 ft   H = 4 m

9. Mary is using construction paper to cover a box 4 ft long, 3 ft wide and 1 ft high. What is the volume of the construction paper? Hint: This question is the same as asking for the volume of the box.

Answers to Selected Questions

   4a. 64 ft   **5a**. 2 cm   **6a**. 3 cm   **7a**. 4 ft

More on Volume - **Real World Applications**

The formula for finding the volume of a rectangular prism is:

$$\text{Volume} = \text{Length} \times \text{Width} \times \text{Height}$$

$V = L \times W \times H$ (V = Volume, L = Length, W = Width, H = Height)

$= \text{Area} \times H$ (Note: L × W = Area). Review lessons on area.

$= A \times H$ Where A = Area

Example 6

A rectangular box has a volume of 120 cm^3. If the area of the bottom of the rectangular box is 30 cm^2, how high is the box?

Solution

V = 60 cm^3, A = 30 cm^2 and H = ?

The formula for finding the volume of a rectangular prism or box is:

$V = L \times W \times H$

$V = \text{Area} \times H$ Note: Area = L × W

$V = A \times H$ _____[A]

Substitute V = 120 cm^3 and A = 30 cm^2 into equation [A] as shown:

120 cm^3 = 30 cm^2 × H   _____[B]

Divide both sides of the equation [B] by 30 cm^2 in order to isolate H in order to obtain the value of H as shown:

$$\frac{120\ \text{cm}^3}{30\ \text{cm}^2} = \frac{30\ \text{cm}^2}{30\ \text{cm}^2} \times H$$

$$\frac{\overset{4\ \text{cm}}{\cancel{120\ \text{cm}^3}}}{\underset{1}{\cancel{30\ \text{cm}^2}}} = \frac{\overset{1}{\cancel{30\ \text{cm}^2}}}{\underset{1}{\cancel{30\ \text{cm}^2}}} \times H$$

$$\left(\text{Note: } \frac{\text{cm}^3}{\text{cm}^2} = \frac{\overset{1}{\cancel{\text{cm}}} \times \overset{1}{\cancel{\text{cm}}} \times \text{cm}}{\underset{1}{\cancel{\text{cm}}} \times \underset{1}{\cancel{\text{cm}}}} = m\right).$$

$$4\ \text{cm} = H$$

Therefore, the box is 4 cm high.

Example 7

A rectangular swimming pool is 6 ft deep and the volume of the water in the pool is 240 ft^3. What is the area of the bottom of the swimming pool? Hint: 6 ft deep is the same as 6 ft high which is the same as the height of the pool.

Solution

The formula for finding the volume of a rectangular object is:

$V = L \times W \times H$

$V = \text{Area} \times H$ Note: Area = L × W

$V = A \times H$ _____[A]

Substitute V = 240 ft^3 and H = 6 ft into equation [A] as shown:

240 ft = A × 6 ft _____[B]

Divide both sides of the equation [B] by 6 ft in order to isolate A which is the area and also to obtain the value of A as shown:

$$\frac{240 \text{ ft}^3}{6 \text{ ft}} = A \times \frac{6 \text{ ft}}{6 \text{ ft}}$$

$$\frac{\overset{40 \text{ ft}^2}{\cancel{240 \text{ ft}^3}}}{\underset{1}{\cancel{6 \text{ ft}}}} = A \times \frac{\overset{1}{\cancel{6 \text{ ft}}}}{\underset{1}{\cancel{6 \text{ ft}}}} \qquad \text{(Note: } \frac{\text{ft}^3}{\text{ft}} = \frac{\text{ft} \times \text{ft} \times \text{ft}}{\cancel{\text{ft}}} = \text{ft} \times \text{ft} = \text{ft}^2\text{).}$$

40 ft² = A

Therefore, the area of the bottom of the swimming pool is 40 ft²

Example 8

The bottom area of a rectangular swimming pool is 180 yd². If the swimming pool is 4 yd deep what is the volume of the water that the swimming pool can hold?
Hint: 4 yd deep is the same as 4 yd high which is the same as the height of the swimming pool.

Solution

A = 180 yd², H = 4 yd, and V = ?
The formula for finding the volume of any rectangular object is.

$\quad$ V = L × W × H

$\quad$ V = Area × H $\qquad$ Note: Area = L × W

$\quad$ V = A × H $\quad$ _____[L]

Substitute A = 180 yd² and h = 4 yd into the equation [L] as shown:

$\quad$ V = 180 yd² × 4 yd

$\quad$ V = 720 yd³ $\;$ (**Note**: yd² × yd = yd × yd × yd = yd³). Review the power of numbers.

Therefore, the volume of the water that the swimming pool can hold is 720 yd³.

Exercises

1. What is the formula for finding the volume of a rectangular object if only the bottom area and the height of the object is known?

2. A rectangular swimming pool has a volume of 360 ft³ and if the bottom of the swimming pool has an area of 40 ft² how deep is the swimming pool? Hint: See Example **6**. Hint: How deep is the pool is the same as how high is the pool and it is also the same as what is the height of the swimming pool?

3. A rectangular swimming pool is 3 yd deep and the volume of the water in the swimming pool is 180 yd³. What is the area of the bottom of the swimming pool? Hint: See Example **7**.

4. If the bottom area of a rectangular block is 9 in² and the block is 10 in high. What is

the volume of the block? Hint: See Example **8**.

Challenge Questions
5. Find the unknown measure in each rectangular object.

    a. $V = 24 \text{ m}^3$ **b.** $V = 16 \text{ ft}^3$ **c.** $V = ?$ **d.** $V = 45 \text{ cm}^3$

      $A = 8 \text{ m}^2$ $A = ?$ $A = 5 \text{ cm}^2$ $A = 15 \text{ cm}^2$

      $H = ?$ $H = 4 \text{ ft}$ $H = 4 \text{ cm}$ $H = ?$

6. A rectangular object has a volume of 36 cm² and if the area of the bottom of the object is 9 cm² how high is the object?
7. If the bottom area of a rectangular fish tank is 12 ft² and the tank is 10 ft high, what is the volume of the tank?
8. The volume of water in a swimming pool is 160 yd³. If the swimming pool is 2 yd deep what is the area of the bottom of the swimming pool?

Cumulative Review
1. What is the formula for finding the area of a triangle?
2. What is meant by perpendicular lines?

3. 5 m = ? cm   **4.** $4^2 \div 2 =$ **5.** $\dfrac{3}{4} \div \dfrac{3}{4} =$ **6.** $1\dfrac{1}{2} \times 2\dfrac{1}{4} =$ **7.** 2 yd = ? ft

8. An equilateral triangle is a_____.   **9.** Parallel lines are_____. **10.** A trapezoid is a_____.

VOLUME OF A CUBE

New Term: **Cube**
What is a cube? **A cube is a rectangular prism that has all sides equal**.
We can use the method of the team project under the chapter on the "Volume of Rectangular Prisms" to find or estimate the volume of a cube by using cubes (Hint: See the team project under the chapter "Volume of Rectangular Prisms.")

The formula for finding the volume of a rectangular prism is:

    $V = L \times W \times H$, but since the length of the sides of a cube are all equal, the **formula for finding the volume of a cube is**:

    $V = S \times S \times S$, where S is the length of a side of the cube.
The **formula for finding the volume of a cube can also be represented as**:
    $V = S^3$, since $S \times S \times S = S^3$.

Example 1
Find the volume of the cube.

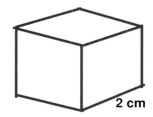

2 cm

Solution

Length of a side of the cube $= 2$ cm.

Formula for the volume of a cube is:

$V = S \times S \times S$, where S is the length of a side of the cube.

$V = 2$ cm $\times 2$ cm $\times 2$ cm.   All the sides of a cube are equal.

$V = 8$ cm^3

Therefore, the volume of the cube is 8 cm^3.

Example 2

The length of a side of a cube is 5 ft. What is the volume of the cube?

Solution

Length of a side of the cube $= 5$ ft.

Formula for the volume of a cube is:

$V = S \times S \times S$, where S is the length of a side of the cube.

$V = 5$ ft $\times 5$ ft $\times 5$ ft.   All the sides of a cube are equal.

$V = 125$ ft^3

Example 3

The volume of a cube is 8 cm^3. What is the length of a side of the cube?

Solution

The formula for finding the volume of a cube is

$V = S \times S \times S$, where S is the length of a side of the cube.

The side of the cube is multiplied by itself 3 times to obtain the volume of the cube. Therefore, let us find a number that can be multiplied by itself 3 times to obtain 8 cm^3 which is the volume. If we select the dimension 4 cm as the length of a side of the cube and we multiply the 4 cm by itself 3 times, we obtain 64 cm^3 as shown:

4 cm $\times 4$ cm $\times 4$ cm $= 64$ cm^3

But 64 cm^3 is greater than the volume of the cube which is 8 cm^3. Let us try 3 cm which is a less dimension than 4 cm as the length of the side of the cube by multiplying 3 cm by itself for 3 times to see if the result will be 8 cm^3 as shown:

3 cm $\times 3$ cm $\times 3$ cm $= 27$ cm^3

But 27 cm^3 is greater than the volume of the cube which is 8 cm^3. Let us try 2 cm which is a less dimension than 3 cm as the length of the side of the cube by multiplying 2 cm by itself for 3 times to see if the result will be 8 cm^3 as shown:

$$2 \text{ cm} \times 2 \text{ cm} \times 2 \text{ cm} = 8 \text{ cm}^3$$

Since 2 cm × 2 cm × 2 cm = 8 cm³ and 8 cm³ is the volume of the cube, **then 2 cm is the correct dimension of the cube**.

Note: You can find the dimension of the side of the cube to be 2 cm directly, if you know that 2 cm × 2 cm × 2 cm = 8 cm³ without trying 4 cm and 3 cm first.

Exercises

1. What is a cube?

2. What is the formula for finding the volume of a cube?

3. Find the volume of each cube. Hint: See Example 1.

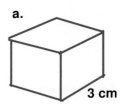 **a.**

3 cm

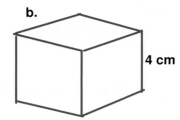 **b.**

4 cm

4. The length of a side of each cube is given. What is the volume of each cube? Hint: See example 2, and also **the unit of a volume could be cm³, m³, in³, ft³, or yd³**.

   a. 1 m   **b**. 3 ft   **c**. 4 yd   **d**. 5 cm

5. The volume of each cube is given. What is the length of a side of each cube? Hint: See example 3.

   a. 27 cm³   **b**. 125 ft³   **c**. 64 in³

Review - Comparing the Dimensions of Perimeter, Area, and Volume

Let us compare the dimension of the measures of perimeter, area, and volume. Geometric figures are measured in one, two, or three dimensions. The units of perimeter area and volume depends upon the number of the dimensions being used.

Perimeter: What is a perimeter? A perimeter is the distance around any figure. For example the distance around a rectangular block is the perimeter. Since the perimeter is measured in **one dimension** which is the **length** the unit of measure is **linear** such as ft, yd, cm, or m.

Area: What is an area? An area of a figure is the number of the square units needed to cover the figure. For example, the number of the square units needed to cover a football field is the area of the football field. Since an area is measured in two dimensions which are **length** and **width**, the unit of measure is **square units** such as in², ft², yd², cm², or m².

Volume: What is meant by volume? The volume is the amount of space occupied by a solid figure. For example the number of cubic units that can fill a space or a container is the volume of that space or container. Since volume is measured in three dimensions which are **length**, **width**, and **height**, the unit of measure is cubic such as cm³, m³, in³, ft³, and yd³.

Cumulative Review
1. Explain regular polygon
2. About 52 weeks = ? year/s
3. -7 + 2 =   **4**. -8 - 3 =   5. The factors of 36 are _____

SCALE DRAWING

What is a **scale drawing**? A **scale drawing** shows a real distance smaller than or longer than the real distance. When a scale drawing shows a real distance that is smaller than the real distance, is called a **reduction**. When a scale drawing shows a real distance that is longer than the real distance, is called an **enlargement**. A **map scale** is the ratio that compares the distance on a map to the actual distance.

Team Project 1
Goal of the project: To use a scale drawing and a map scale to find the actual distance between Peki and Hoe by using equivalent ratios.
Method:

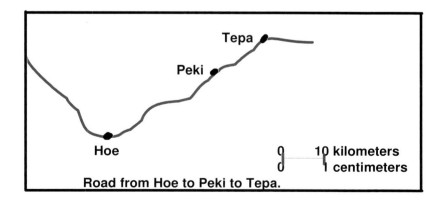

Step 1: **Read the map scale.**

687

The map shows the scale of 1 cm = 10 km, or $\dfrac{1 \text{ cm}}{10 \text{ km}}$.

Step 2: **Use a string to measure the distance from Peki to Hoe on the map**.

The distance between Peki and Hoe is marked on the string.

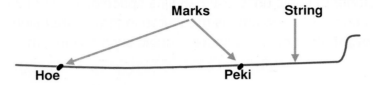

(**Note**: The distance from Hoe to Peki on the string is an approximate distance.)

Step 3: **Use a centimeter ruler to measure the distance between the two marks on the string as shown**.

The distance between the two marks on the string is about 5.2 cm.

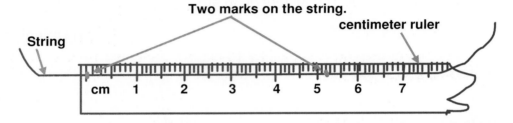

Step 4: **Use equivalent ratios to find the actual distance as shown**:

$$\frac{1}{10} = \frac{5.2}{k}$$

k is the actual distance in kilometers.

Hint: Review the chapter/section on equivalent ratios.

$1 \times k = 10 \times 5.2$ Cross multiply.

$k = 52$ km

Therefore, the distance from Peki to Hoe is 52 km.

Team Project 2

Goal of the project: To use the scale drawing and the map scale to find the actual distance between Peki and Tepa by using equivalent ratios. Use the map provided under Team Project 1. Use the same method as in Team Project 1 to find the distance between Peki and Tepa.

Example 1

Complete the map scale ratio table.

Map distance (cm)	1	?	5	?
Actual distance (km)	15	30	?	105

Solution

To find the map distance when the actual distance is 30 km

Step 1: From the table, the map scale is 1 cm = 15 km or $\dfrac{1\ cm}{15\ km}$.

Step 2: When the actual distance is 30 km, let the map distance be k.

Step 3: Use equivalent ratios to find the map distance as shown:

$$\frac{1\ cm}{15\ km} = \frac{k}{30\ km} \hspace{4cm} [A]$$

Step 4: Cross multiply equation $[A]$ because **cross products of equivalent ratios are equal** as shown:

$$\frac{1\ cm}{15\ km} \bowtie \frac{k}{30\ km}$$

$$15\ km \times k = 1\ cm \times 30\ km \hspace{3cm} [B]$$

Divide both sides of the equation $[B]$ by 15 km in order to isolate k and also to obtain the value of k as shown:

$$\frac{15\ km \times k}{15\ km} = \frac{1\ cm \times 30\ km}{15\ km}$$

$$\frac{\overset{1}{\cancel{15\ km}} \times k}{\underset{1}{\cancel{15\ km}}} = \frac{1\ cm \times \overset{2}{\cancel{30\ km}}}{\underset{1}{\cancel{15\ km}}}$$

$$k = 1\ cm \times 2$$
$$k = 2\ cm$$

Therefore, when the actual distance = 30 km, the map distance = 2 cm.

To find the actual distance when the map distance is 5 cm.

Step 1: From the table, the map scale is 1 cm = 15 km or $\dfrac{1\ cm}{15\ km}$.

Step 2: When the map distance is 5 cm, let the actual distance be n.

Step 3: Use equivalent ratios to find the actual distance as shown:

$$\frac{1\ cm}{15\ km} = \frac{5\ cm}{n} \hspace{4cm} [C]$$

Step 4: Cross multiply equation [C] because cross products of equivalent ratios are equal as shown:

$$\frac{1 \text{ cm}}{15 \text{ km}} \diagdown \diagup \frac{5 \text{ cm}}{n}$$

1 cm × n = 15 km × 5 cm. _____[D]

Divide both sides of equation [D] by 1 cm in order to obtain the value for n as shown:

$$\frac{1 \text{ cm} \times n}{1 \text{ cm}} = \frac{15 \text{ km} \times 5 \text{ cm}}{1 \text{ cm}}$$

$$\frac{\overset{1}{\cancel{1 \text{ cm}}} \times n}{\underset{1}{\cancel{1 \text{ cm}}}} = \frac{15 \text{ km} \times \overset{5}{\cancel{5 \text{ cm}}}}{\underset{1}{\cancel{1 \text{ cm}}}}$$

n = 15 km × 5
n = 75 km

Therefore, when the map distance is 5 cm, the actual distance is 75 km.

To Find the Map Distance When the Actual Distance is 105 km

Step 1: From the table, the map scale is 1 cm =15 km or $\frac{1 \text{ cm}}{15 \text{ km}}$.

Step 2: When the map distance is 105 km, let the map distance be w.

Step 3: Use equivalent ratios to find the actual distance as shown:

$$\frac{1 \text{ cm}}{15 \text{ km}} = \frac{w}{105 \text{ km}} \qquad \text{_____[E]}$$

Step 4: Cross multiply equation [E] because cross products of equivalent ratios are equal as shown:

$$\frac{1 \text{ cm}}{15 \text{ km}} \diagdown \diagup \frac{w}{105 \text{ km}}$$

1 cm × 105 km = 15 km × w _____[F]

Divide both sides of equation [F] by 15 km in order to isolate w and also to obtain the value of w as shown:

$$\frac{1 \text{ cm} \times 105 \text{ km}}{15 \text{ km}} = \frac{15 \text{ km} \times w}{15 \text{ km}}$$

$$\frac{\overset{7}{1 \text{ cm}} \times \overset{1}{105 \text{ km}}}{\underset{1}{15 \text{ km}}} = \frac{15 \text{ km} \times w}{\underset{1}{15 \text{ km}}}$$

$$1 \text{ cm} \times 7 = w$$
$$7 \text{ cm} = w$$

Therefore, when the actual distance is 105 km, the map distance is 7 cm.
Therefore, the completed table is:

Map Distance (cm)	1	2	5	7
Actual distance (km)	15	30	75	105

Example 2

Using the map, an inch ruler and the map scale, find the distance from Peki to Jawa to the nearest mile. Hint: Assume that the distance between any two cities is a straight line, and therefore, the distance can be measured directly with a ruler to the nearest inch.

Map of some cities.

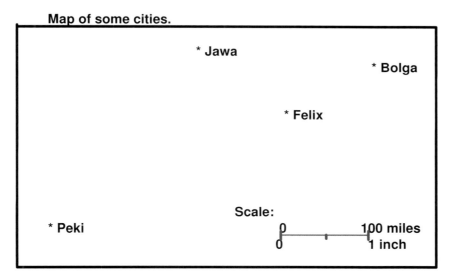

Solution

Step 1: Read the map scale.

The map shows a scale of 1 inch =100 miles or $\dfrac{1 \text{ inch}}{100 \text{ miles}}$.

Step 2: Use an inch ruler to measure the distance from Peki to Jawa on the map. The distance from Peki to Jawa on the map is approximately 2 inches to the nearest inch.

Step 3: When the map distance from Peki to Jawa is 2 inches, let the actual distance from Peki to Jawa be n.

Step 4: Use equivalent ratios to find the actual distance as shown:

$$\frac{1 \text{ inch}}{100 \text{ miles}} = \frac{2 \text{ inches}}{n} \hspace{4cm} [\text{A}]$$

Step 5: Cross multiply equation [A] because cross products of equivalent ratios are equal as shown:

$$\frac{1 \text{ in.}}{100 \text{ mi}} \diagup\!\!\!\!\!\diagdown \frac{2 \text{ in.}}{n}$$

$$1 \text{ in.} \times n = 100 \text{ miles} \times 2 \text{ in.} \hspace{3cm} [\text{B}]$$

Step 6: Divide both sides of the equation [B] by 1 in. in order to isolate n and also to obtain the value of n as shown:

$$\frac{1 \text{ in.} \times n}{1 \text{ in.}} = \frac{100 \text{ miles} \times 2 \text{ in.}}{1 \text{ in.}}$$

$$\frac{1 \cancel{\text{in.}} \times n}{1 \cancel{\text{in.}}} = \frac{100 \text{ miles} \times 2 \cancel{\text{in.}}}{1 \cancel{\text{in.}}}$$

$$n = 100 \text{ miles} \times 2$$
$$= 200 \text{ miles}$$

Therefore, the distance from Peki to Jawa is 200 miles.

Exercises

1. Explain what is meant by a scale drawing.
2. Explain what is meant by a map scale.
3. Copy and complete each ratio table. Hint: See Example **1**.

a.

Scale length (cm)	1	2	?	4
Actual length (km)	4	?	12	?

b.

Scale length (cm)	1	3	4	?
Actual length (km)	20	?	80	100

c.

Scale length (in.)	1	2	?	4
Actual length (ft)	5	?	15	?

4. Using the map in Example 2, find the:
   a. distance from Peki to Bolga.
   b. distance from Jawa to Bolga.
   Hint: See Example 2. The map distance should be to the nearest whole number.
   Assume that the road between any two cities is straight and therefore a ruler
   could be used to measure the map distance.

5. Copy and complete the ratio tables.

a.

Scale length (cm)	1	3	?
Actual length (km)	10	?	50

b.

Scale length (in.)	1	3	?	?
Actual length (ft)	4	?	24	48

6. Explain how to find the actual distance between two cities on a map.

CHAPTER 28

LINES AND ANGLES

New Terms

1. Plane.
2. Parallel lines.
3. Intersecting lines.
4. Perpendicular lines.

Quick Review

1. The unit of measure for an angle is called d——— and the symbol is ^{0} .
2. An angle is formed by two r—— that ——— .
3. A ray is ——————— .
4. A point is ——————— .
5. A line is ——————— .
6. A segment is ——————— .

A **plane** is a continuous flat surface. Three points that are not on a line are used to name a plane such as "plane ABC." The diagram of plane ABC is shown below.

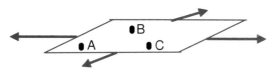

The diagram shows plane ABC.

The arrows in the diagram indicate that **the plane continues in all directions**.

Line Relationships
The three kinds of line relationships are:
(**a**) **parallel lines**
(**b**) **intersecting lines**
(**c**) **perpendicular lines**

Table of line relationships

Line type	Description	Diagram
Parallel lines	Parallel lines are lines in a plane that never intersect.	Line AB is parallel to line CD.
Intersecting lines	Intersecting lines are lines that cross each other at a point.	Line AB intersects line CD at point E.
Perpendicular lines	Perpendicular lines are lines that intersect at a point to form four right angles.	Line WX is perpendicular to line YZ at point P. ⌐ is the symbol for perpendicular lines, 90° or right angle.

Symbols and Concepts

The symbol ‖ means "is parallel to".

Example 1

Use symbols to write that the line AB is parallel to the line CD.

Solution

Line AB is written with a symbol as $\overleftrightarrow{AB}$.

Line CD is written with a symbol as $\overleftrightarrow{CD}$.

The symbol for "is parallel to" is ‖.

Therefore, use symbols to write that line AB is parallel to line CD as shown:

$$\overleftrightarrow{AB} \parallel \overleftrightarrow{CD}$$

Example 2

Use symbols to write that the segment AB is parallel to the segment CD.

Solution

Segment AB is written with a symbol as $\overline{AB}$.

Segment CD is written with a symbol as $\overline{CD}$.

The symbol for "is parallel to" is ‖.

694

Therefore, to use symbol to write that the segment AB is parallel to the segment CD is as shown:

$$\overline{AB} \parallel \overline{CD}$$

The symbol $\perp$ means "is perpendicular to". Note that perpendicular lines form 90^0 angles or right angles.

Example 3

(**a**). Use symbols to write that the segment WX is perpendicular to the segment YZ.

(**b**). Show in two ways how a segment WX can be perpendicular to the segment YZ in a diagram.

(**c**). Use symbols to write that segment PK is perpendicular to a line RC.
Use symbols to write that segment PK is parallel to a line RC.
Show in a diagram that segment PK is perpendicular to a line RC.
Show in a diagram that segment PK is parallel to a line RC.

Solution

(**a**). Segment WX is written with a symbol as $\overline{WX}$.

Segment YZ is written with a symbol as $\overline{YZ}$.
The symbol for "is perpendicular to" is $\perp$.
Therefore, to use a symbol to write that the segment WX is perpendicular to the segment YZ is as shown:

$$\overline{WX} \perp \overline{YZ}$$

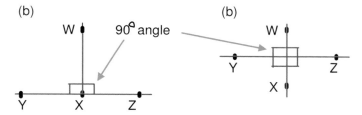

(**c**). Segment PK is written with a symbol as $\overline{PK}$.

Line RC is written with a symbol as $\overleftrightarrow{RC}$.
The symbol for "is perpendicular to" is $\perp$.
Therefore, segment PK is perpendicular to the line RC is written with a symbol as shown:

$$\overline{PK} \perp \overleftrightarrow{RC}$$

The symbol for "is parallel to" is $\parallel$.
Therefore, segment PK is parallel to the line RC is written with a symbol as shown:

$$\overline{PK} \parallel \overleftrightarrow{RC}$$

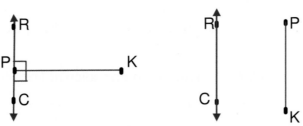

Segment PK is perpendicular to the line RC.

Segment PK is parallel to the line RC.

Key Facts
1. The angle formed by two perpendicular lines or two segments or a line and a segment is a right angle and the measure of a right angle is 90^0.
2. The understanding of two perpendicular segments is very important because it helps us later to understand that the angles of a rectangle or a square are formed by two perpendicular segments and that is why each angle of a rectangle or a square is 90^0.
3. The arrowheads at the ends of the symbol of a line shows that the line continues at both directions or that a line is endless.

Critical Geometric Points
The solution to Example **4** is long, but it is designed to provide the students with useful geometric points.

Group Exercise - Example 4
Using a diagram drawn on a square grid paper or a paper, explain the geometric condition for any two lines or any two segments or any line and any segment to be parallel.

Solution
The solution to this question is long, however, the solution is intentionally designed to provide the students with important geometric concepts. (**If Example 4 were to be a class test, the key answer would be just the last paragraph of this solution**).
The class should be divided into four teams, Team A, Team B, Team C, and Team D.
Each team should use a pencil, $8\frac{1}{2}$ inches × 11 inches square grid paper, and a ruler to draw figure 1 by using Step **1** to Step **4**.

Figure 1

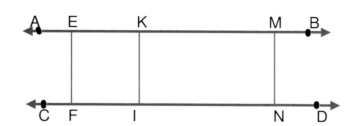

Step 1: Pick one of the horizontal grid lines on the grid paper and draw the line CD which should be 6 inches long by placing one of the edges of the ruler along the horizontal grid line that you have selected. Mark a point C, which should correspond to the 0 mark on the ruler and then mark a point D on the same horizontal grid paper which should correspond to the 6 inches marking on the ruler. With the edge of the ruler still on the same horizontal grid line, draw a line through the points C and D.

Step 2: Pick another horizontal grid line which should be about 2 inches from the line CD that you have drawn in Step 1. Place the edge of the ruler on this horizontal grid and mark point A approximately above point C, also mark point B approximately above point D, and then draw a line through points A and point B.

Step 3: Pick 3 vertical grid segments and label them EF, KL, and MN such that segment EF should be close to point A and point C, and the segment MN should be close to point B and point D as shown in figure 1. Place one edge of a ruler on point E and point F and draw the segment EF. Place one edge of the ruler on point K and point L and draw the segment KL. Place one of the edges of the ruler on point M and point N and draw the segment MN.

Step 4: Measure segments EF, KL, and MN as shown:

Place the edge of the ruler on segment EF such that point E should be on the 0 mark of the ruler, and then read the number of the mark on the ruler that corresponds to point F, and this number is the length of segment EF. Record the length of the segment EF.

Place the edge of the ruler on segment KL such that point K should be on the 0 mark of the ruler, and then read the number of the mark on the ruler that corresponds to point L, and this number is the length of segment KL. Record the length of the segment KL.

Place the edge of the ruler on segment MN such that point M should be on the 0 mark of the ruler and then read the number of the mark on the ruler that corresponds to point N, and this number is the length of segment MN. Record the length of the segment MN.

Step 5: **Analysis and conclusion**

(**a**). From the measurements of the segment EF, segment KL, and segment MN, it should be found that:

length of segment EF = length of segment KL = length of segment MN

(**b**). Line AB or segment AB is parallel to line CD or segment CD because horizontal grid lines are parallel. Note that line AB can become segment AB without the two arrowheads at the ends of the diagram of the line AB.

(**c**). The segments EF, KL, and MN form 90^0 angle with the lines AB and CD because the horizontal grid lines and the vertical grid lines form 90^0, and therefore, the segments EF, KL, and MN are called the **perpendicular distances** between lines AB and CD.

The geometric condition for any two lines or any two segments or any line and any segment to be parallel is that the **perpendicular distance** at any point between the two lines or the two segments or the line and the segment must be the same. Also, recall that in the "table of line relationships," parallel lines are described as "lines in a plane that never intersect."

Group Exercise

Bricklayers use the idea of parallel lines to lay bricks when they are building brick walls as shown in the picture.

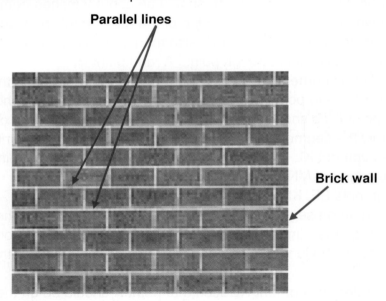

Parallel lines

Brick wall

The class should be divided into four groups. Each group should write about how the idea of parallel lines are used to:

       1. make roads
       2. make the floor of stairways
       3. make your math textbook.

Exercises

1. What symbol means "is parallel to?"

2. A right angle has the same angle measure as a 90^0 angle. True or false?

3. A plane is a cont_____ flat surf_____. Complete the statement.

4. Select the correct answer. How many points are used to name a plane?

Answer: (a) 1   (b) 4   (c) 3

5. What symbol means "is perpendicular to?"

6. The arrowheads at the ends of a line indicate that the line is endl_____

7. What are parallel lines?

8. What are intersecting lines?

9. What are perpendicular lines?

10. Use symbols to write that line WX is parallel to line YZ. Hint: See Example **1**.

11. Use symbols to write that segment AD is parallel to segment EF. Hint: See Example **2**.

12. Use symbols to write that segment PK is perpendicular to segment LM. Hint: See Example **3**.

13. Use symbols to write that segment GK is parallel to line AB. Hint: See Example **3**.

14. What is meant by the perpendicular distance of a segment?

15. What is the geometric condition for two segments to be parallel?

Group Exercises

1. The class should be divided into four teams and each team should draw the following diagrams and write all the segments that appear to be parallel using the symbol ∥ and also write all the segments that appear to be perpendicular using the symbol ⊥. Explain why the segment KH and the segment JI appear not to be parallel.

(a)   (b)   (c)
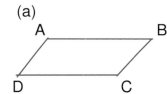   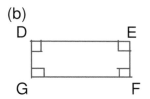   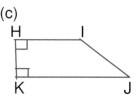

2. Each team should classify the following angles as acute, obtuse or right angle. Explain your answer.

   (**a**) ∠AFE   (**b**) ∠AFG   (**c**) ∠ HAL   (**d**) ∠HAB

   (**e**) ∠ABE   (**f**) ∠IBA   (**g**) ∠BED   (**h**) ∠FEJ

   (**i**) Explain why $\overline{FA}$ does not appear to be parallel to $\overline{EB}$.

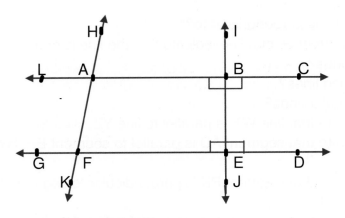

Solutions to the "Group Exercises."

The solution to the "Group exercises" is provided so as to provide the students with more understanding of the problem solving methods.

1. (a) $\overline{AB} \parallel \overline{DC}$, $\overline{AD} \parallel \overline{BC}$

There are no perpendicular segments because none of the angles are 90^0.

(b) $\overline{DE} \parallel \overline{GF}$, $\overline{DG} \parallel \overline{EF}$

$\overline{DE} \perp \overline{EF}$ because $\overline{DE}$ forms 90^0 angle with $\overline{EF}$.

$\overline{EF} \perp \overline{FG}$ because $\overline{EF}$ forms 90^0 angle with $\overline{FG}$.

$\overline{FG} \perp \overline{GD}$ because $\overline{FG}$ forms 90^0 angle with $\overline{GD}$.

$\overline{GD} \perp \overline{DE}$ because $\overline{GD}$ forms 90^0 angle with $\overline{DE}$.

(c) $\overline{HI} \parallel \overline{KJ}$, $\overline{KH}$ does not appear to be parallel to $\overline{JI}$ because $\overline{KH}$ and $\overline{JI}$ do not appear to be going in the same direction. So, if we extend $\overline{KH}$ and $\overline{JI}$, they will intersect at a point, but parallel lines are not supposed to intersect as explain with a diagram as shown:

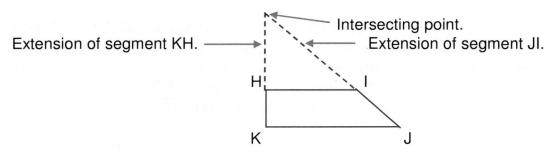

Extension of segment KH. ⟶

Intersecting point.

Extension of segment JI.

$\overline{IH} \perp \overline{HK}$ because $\overline{IH}$ forms 90^0 angle with $\overline{HK}$.

$\overline{HK} \perp \overline{KJ}$ because $\overline{HK}$ forms 90^0 angle with $\overline{KJ}$.

2. (a) $\angle AFE$ is an acute angle because it is less than 90^0.

(b) $\angle AFG$ is an obtuse angle because it is greater than 90^0.

(c) $\angle HAL$ is an obtuse angle because it is greater than 90^0.

(d) $\angle HAB$ is an acute angle because it is less than 90^0.

(e) $\angle ABE$ is a right angle because it is 90^0.

(f) ∠IBA is a right angle because it is 90⁰.

(g) ∠BED is a right angle because it is 90⁰.

(h) ∠FEJ is a right angle because it is 90⁰.

(i) $\overline{FA}$ does not appear to be parallel to $\overline{EB}$ because $\overline{FA}$ and $\overline{EB}$ do not appear to be going in the same direction, and therefore, if we extend $\overline{FA}$ and $\overline{EB}$, they will intersect at a point, but parallel lines are not supposed to intersect as shown:

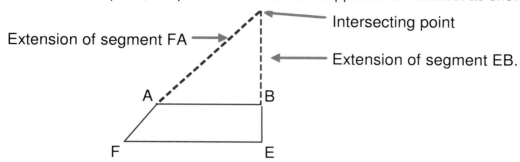

Example 1
What is the difference between parallel lines and perpendicular lines?

Solution

Parallel lines will never intersect or meet each other, but perpendicular lines intersect or meet each other at a point.

Example 2

Can the opposite edges (sides) of the standard $8\frac{1}{2} \times 11$ inches paper be considered parallel? Explain your answer.

Solution

Yes, the opposite edges (sides) of the standard $8\frac{1}{2} \times 11$ inches paper can be considered parallel because the perpendicular distance at any point of the opposite edges are the same. (Review perpendicular distances.)

Exercises

1. Draw (a) parallel lines AB and XY, (b) intersecting lines PQ and KL and (c) perpendicular lines JK and XY

2.

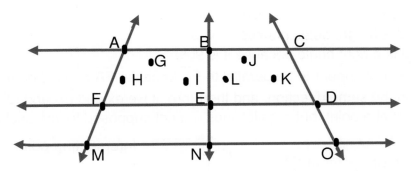

Using the diagram, name two examples of each term or statement.
Hint: Review this chapter.

(**a**) plane   (**b**) perpendicular lines   (**c**) Intersecting lines
(**d**) right angles   (**e**) parallel lines   (**f**) line segments
(**g**) rays   (**h**) acute angles   (**i**) obtuse angles
(**j**) points   (**k**) straight angles   (**l**) intersecting point.

Sum of the Measure of the Angles on a Straight Line

A straight angle measures 180^0 and this means that the sum of the measure of the angles on a straight line is 180^0 as shown below.

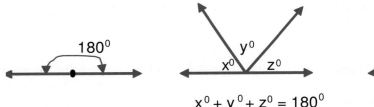

$$x^0 + y^0 + z^0 = 180^0 \qquad n^0 + m^0 = 180^0$$

Example 1
Find the value of the angle measure of x^0 in the diagram.

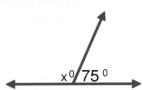

Solution
The sum of the measure of the angles on a straight line $= 180^0$.
Therefore, $x^0 + 75 = 180^0$

$\quad\quad\quad x^0 + 75^0 - 75^0 = 180^0 - 75^0$ (Subtract 75^0 from each side of the equation
$\quad\quad\quad x^0 + 0 = 105^0$ in order to eliminate 75^0 from the left side
$\quad\quad\quad x^0 \; = 105^0$ of the equation.)

Example 2
Find the value of x^0 in the diagrams.

(a)

(b)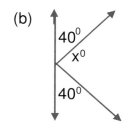

40^0

x^0

40^0

70^0

60^0 x^0

Solution
(**a**) The sum of the measure of the angles formed on a straight line $= 180^0$.

Therefore, $60^0 + 70^0 + x^0 = 180^0$

$$130^0 + x^0 = 180^0 \qquad (70^0 + 60^0 = 130^0)$$
$$x^0 + 130^0 - 130^0 = 180^0 - 130^0 \quad \text{(Subtract } 130^0 \text{ from each side of the equation in order to eliminate the } 130^0 \text{ from the left side of the equation.)}$$

$$x^0 + 130^0 - 130^0 = 180^0 - 130^0$$
$$x^0 + 0 = 50^0 \qquad (130^0 - 130^0 = 0, \text{ and } 180^0 - 130^0 = 50^0)$$
$$x^0 = 50^0$$

(**b**) The sum of the measure of the angles formed on a straight line $= 180^0$.

Therefore, $40^0 + x^0 + 40^0 = 180^0$

$$x^0 + 80^0 = 180^0 \qquad (40^0 + 40^0 = 80^0)$$
$$x^0 + 80^0 - 80^0 = 180^0 - 80^0 \quad \text{(Subtract } 80^0 \text{ from each side of the equation in order to eliminate the } 80^0 \text{ at the left side of the equation.)}$$

$$x^0 + 80^0 - 80^0 = 180^0 - 80^0$$
$$x^0 + 0 = 100^0 \qquad (80^0 - 80^0 = 0, \text{ and } 180^0 - 80^0 = 100^0)$$
$$x^0 = 100^0$$

Example 3
Find the value of x^0 in the diagram.

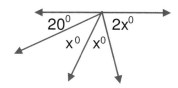

20^0 $2x^0$

x^0 x^0

Solution
Consider the diagram as angles formed on a straight line but the diagram is inverted
The sum of the measure of the angles on a straight line $= 180^0$.

Therefore, $20^0 + x^0 + x^0 + 2x^0 = 180^0$

$$20^0 + 4x^0 = 180^0 \qquad (x^0 + x^0\ 2x^0 = 4x^0)$$

$$20^0 - 20^0 + 4x^0 = 180^0 - 20^0$$ (Subtract 20^0 from each side of the equation in order to eliminate 20^0 from the left side of the equation.)

$$20^0 - 20^0 + 4x^0 = 160^0$$ $(180^0 - 20^0 = 160^0)$

$$0 + 4x^0 = 160^0$$ $(20^0 - 20^0 = 0)$

$$4x^0 = 160^0 \quad\text{————————————} [A]$$

Divide each side of equation $[A]$ by 4 in order to obtain the value of x^0 as shown:

$$\frac{4x^0}{4} = \frac{160^0}{4}$$

$$\frac{\overset{x^0}{\cancel{4x^0}}}{\underset{1}{\cancel{4}}} = \frac{\overset{40^0}{\cancel{160^0}}}{\underset{1}{\cancel{4}}}$$

$$x^0 = 40^0$$

Example 4

Find the value of x^0

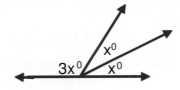

Solution

The sum of the measure of the angles on a straight line is $= 180^0$.

Therefore, $3x^0 + x^0 + x^0 = 180^0$

$$5x^0 = 180^0 \qquad (3x^0 + x^0 + x^0 = 5x^0).$$

$$5x^0 = 180^0 \quad\text{————————} [B]$$

Divide each side of equation $[B]$ by 5 in order to obtain the value of x^0 as shown:

$$\frac{5x^0}{5} = \frac{180^0}{5}$$

$$\frac{\overset{x^0}{\cancel{5x^0}}}{\underset{1}{\cancel{5}}} = \frac{\overset{36^0}{\cancel{180^0}}}{\underset{1}{\cancel{5}}}$$

$$x^0 = 36^0$$

Exercises

1. Find the value of x^0 in the following diagrams Hint: See Example **1**.

(a)

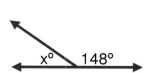

x^o 148°

(b)

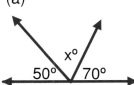

120' x^o

(c)

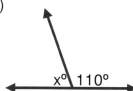

x^o 110°

2. Find the value of x^0 in the following diagrams. Hint: See Example **2**.

(a)

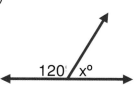

x^o
50° 70°

(b)

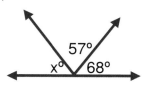

57°
x^o 68°

(c)

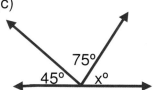

75°
45° x^o

3. Find the value of x^0 in the diagrams. Hint: See Example **3**.

(a)

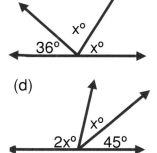

x^o
36° x^o

(b)

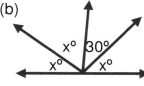

x^o 30°
x^o x^o

(c)

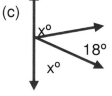

x^o
18°
x^o

(d)

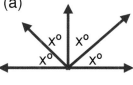

x^o
2x^o 45°

(e)

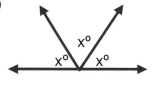

33°
3x^o 61°

(f)

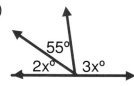

55°
2x^o 3x^o

4. Find the value of x^0 in the diagrams. Hint: See Example 4.

(a)

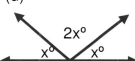

x^o x^o
x^o x^o

(b)

x^o
x^o x^o

(c)

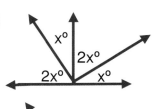

x^o
2x^o
2x^o x^o

(d)

2x^o
x^o x^o

(e)

x^o 3x^o
x^o

Challenge Questions

5. Find the value of x and the measure of the angle ABC in the diagrams. Hint: Note that the measure of the angle ABC is a multiple of x.

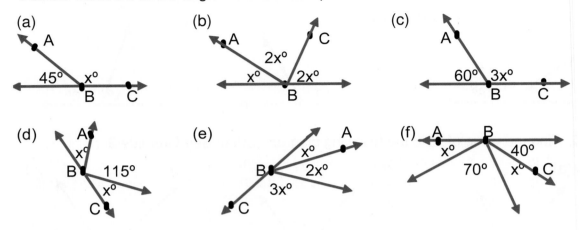

Answers to Selected Questions

1(a) 32^0 **2(a)** 60^0 **3(a)** 72^0 **4(a)** 45^0

Sum of the Measure of the Angles at a Point

Recall that a straight angle measures 180^0 and this means that the sum of the angles on a straight line is 180^0. When we say that a straight angle measures 180^0, we only consider one side of the straight line. If we consider both sides of the straight line, we can say that the sum of the angle measures on both sides of a straight line.

$$= 2 \times 180^0$$
$$= 360^0$$

One side of the straight line.

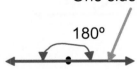

180°

180° above the line

180° below the line.

Sum of the measure of the angles on one side of a straight line = 180^0.

Sum of the measure of the angles on both sides of a straight line = $180^0 + 180^0 = 360^0$ or $2 \times 180^0 = 360^0$.

Since the sum of the measure of the angles on both sides of a straight line is really the same as the sum of the angles at a point, we can conclude that the sum of the angles at a point = 360^0 as shown:

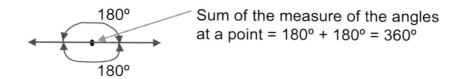

Sum of the measure of the angles
at a point = 180° + 180° = 360°

180°

180°

Group Exercises

The class should be divided into four teams, Team A, Team B, Team C, and Team D.
Each team should:

1. Use a ruler to draw a line which is 6 inches long.
2. Use a protractor to measure the angles on both sides of the straight line.
3. Add up the angles on both sides of the straight line.
4. Repeat this project five times and record the sum of the measure of the angles on both sides of the straight line.

Analysis of the Group Exercises

1. Are the sum of the measures of the angles on both sides of a straight line $= 360^0$?
2. Can we conclude that the sum of the measures of the angles at a point $= 360^0$?
Let us examine the following examples to see what types of questions could be asked regarding the sum of angles at a point and how they can be solved.

Example 1

Find the value of x^0 in the diagram.

(a)

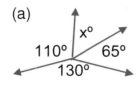

x^0

110°   65°

130°

(b)

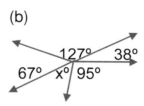

127°   38°

67° x^0 95°

Solution

(**a**) The sum of the measure of the angles at a point $= 360^0$.

Therefore,

$$x^0 + 65^0 + 130^0 + 110^0 = 360^0$$
$$x^0 + 305^0 = 360^0 \quad (65^0 + 130^0 + 110^0 = 305^0)$$
$$x^0 + 305^0 - 305^0 = 360^0 - 305^0 \quad \text{Subtract } 305^0 \text{ from each side of}$$

the equation in order to eliminate
the 305^0 at the left side of the
equation.)

$$x^0 + 0 = 55^0 \quad (305^0 - 305^0 = 0, \text{ and } 360^0 - 305^0 = 55^0)$$
$$x^0 = 55^0$$

(**b**) The sum of the measure of the angles at a point $= 360^0$.

Therefore,

$$x^0 + 67^0 + 127^0 + 38^0 + 95^0 = 360^0$$

$$x^0 + 327^0 = 360^0 \qquad (67^0 + 127^0 + 38^0 + 95^0 = 327^0)$$
$$x^0 + 327^0 - 327^0 = 360^0 - 327^0 \quad \text{Subtract } 327^0 \text{ from each side of}$$

the equation in order to eliminate the 327^0 at the left side of the equation.)

$$x^0 + 0 = 33^0 \qquad (327^0 - 327^0 = 0 \text{ , and } 360^0 - 325^0 = 33^0)$$
$$x^0 = 33^0$$

Example 2

Find the angle measure for x^0 in the diagrams. Find the measure of $\angle ABC$. The angles are formed at point B which is not shown in the diagram.

(a) 3x° 30° 110° x° 80° C A

(b) x° x° 2x° 2x° A C

Solution

(**a**) The sum of the measure of the angles at a point $= 360^0$

Therefore,

$$x^0 + 110^0 + 3x^0 + 30^0 + 80^0 = 360^0$$
$$x^0 + 3x^0 + 110^0 + 30^0 + 80^0 = 360^0 \qquad \text{(Group all the } x^0 \text{ together.)}$$
$$4x^0 + 220^0 = 360^0 \qquad (x^0 + 3x^0 = 4x^0, 110^0 + 30^0 + 80^0 = 220^0)$$
$$4x^0 + 220^0 - 220^0 = 360^0 - 220^0 \qquad \text{Subtract } 220^0 \text{ from each side of the}$$

equation in order to eliminate the 220^0 at the left side of the equation.)

$$4x^0 + 0 = 140^0 \qquad (220^0 - 220^0 = 0 \text{ , } 360^0 - 220^0 = 140^0)$$

$$4x^0 = 140^0 \text{ ──────────────── } [A]$$

Divide each side of the equation $[A]$ by 4 in order to obtain the value of x^0 as shown:

$$\frac{4x^0}{4} = \frac{140}{4}$$

$$\frac{\overset{x^0}{\cancel{4x^0}}}{\underset{1}{\cancel{4}}} = \frac{\overset{35^0}{\cancel{140}}}{\underset{1}{\cancel{4}}}$$

$$x^0 = 35^0$$

$\angle ABC = 3x^0$, so, the measure of
$\angle ABC = 3 \times 35^0 = 105^0$

(**b**) The sum of the measure of the angles at a point $= 360^0$.
   Therefore,

$$x^0 + x^0 + 2x^0 + 2x^0 = 360^0$$
$$6x^0 = 360^0 \qquad\qquad (x^0 + x^0 + 2x^0 + 2x^0 = 6x^0)$$

$$6x^0 = 360^0 \text{——————————————————--} [B]$$

Divide each side of equation $[B]$ by 6 in order to obtain the value of x^0 as shown:

$$\frac{6x^0}{6} = \frac{360^0}{6}$$

$$\frac{\overset{x^0}{\cancel{6x^0}}}{\underset{1}{\cancel{6}}} = \frac{\overset{60^0}{\cancel{360}}}{\underset{1}{\cancel{6}}}$$

$$x = 60^0$$

$\angle$ ABC $= 2x^0$, therefore, the measure of
$\angle$ABC $= 2 \times 60^0 = 120^0$.

Exercises

1. What is the sum of the measures of the angles formed at a point?

2. Find the value of x^0 in the diagram. Hint: See Example **1**.

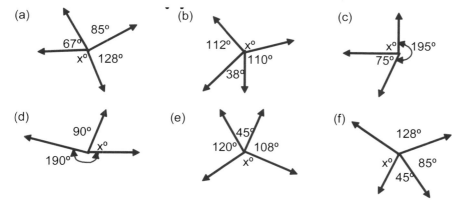

(a)   (b)   (c)   (d)   (e)   (f)

3. Find the angle measure for x^0 in the diagrams. Find the measure of $\angle$ABC given that B is the point where the angles are formed. Hint: See Example **2**.

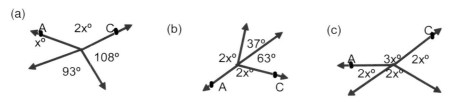

(a)   (b)   (c)

Challenge Questions

4. Find the angle measure for x^0 in the diagrams.

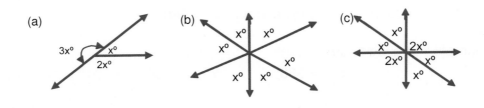

(a)   (b)   (c)

Answers to Selected Questions

2(a) 80^0 **2(d)** 80^0 **2(f)** 102^0 **3(c)** $x^0 = 45^0$, $\angle ABC = 135^0$

VERTICAL ANGLES

New Terms: vertical angle
Vertical angles are formed when two lines intersect as shown:

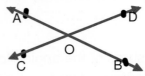

In the figure, $\angle AOD$ is vertically opposite to $\angle COB$
$\angle AOC$ is vertically opposite to $\angle DOB$
The measure of the vertically opposite angles are congruent. This means that the measure of the vertically opposite angles are equal.

Group Exercise
The class should be divided into four teams, Team A , Team B , Team C, and Team D.
1. Each team should draw two intersecting lines AB and CD so that the two lines intersect at point O as shown:

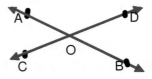

2. Each team should put the center of a protractor at the intersection point, which is O, and measure $\angle AOD$ and $\angle COB$. Is the measure of $\angle AOD$ the same as the measure of $\angle COB$? Can we say that the measures of the opposite angles are equal?
3. With the center of the protractor at the intersecting point , which is O again, measure $\angle AOC$ and $\angle DOB$. Is the measure of $\angle AOC$ and $\angle DOB$ the same? Can we say that the opposite angles are equal?

Example 1
Find the value of x^0 in each figure.

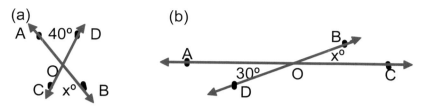

(a)

(b)

Solution

(**a**) $\angle$AOD is vertically opposite to $\angle$COB, and therefore, the measures of their angles are congruent. Therefore,

$$m\angle AOD = m\angle COB$$
Therefore, $40^0 = x^0$ $(m\angle AOD = 40^0,$ and $m\angle COB = x^0)$

(**b**) $\angle$AOD is vertically opposite to $\angle$BOC and therefore, the measure of their angles are congruent. Therefore,
$$m\angle AOD = m\angle BOC$$
Therefore, $30^0 = x^0$ $(m\angle AOD = 30^0,$ and $m\angle BOC = x^0)$

Example 2
Find the value of x^0 in each of the figures.

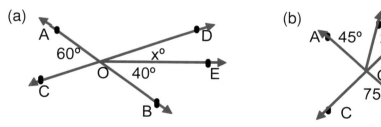

(a)

(b)

Solution

(**a**) $\angle$AOC is vertically opposite to $\angle$DOB
     Since vertically opposite angles are congruent,
$$m\angle AOC = m\angle DOB$$
$$60^0 = x^0 + 40^0 \qquad (m\angle AOC = 60^0, \text{ and } m\angle DOB = x^0 + 40^0)$$
$$60^0 - 40^0 = x^0 + 40^0 - 40^0 \qquad \text{(Subtract } 40^0 \text{ from each side of the equation}$$
in order to obtain the value of x^0.)
$$20^0 = x^0 + 0 \qquad (60^0 - 40^0 = 20^0, \text{ and } 40^0 - 40^0 = 0)$$
$$20^0 = x^0$$

(**b**) $\angle$AOD is vertically opposite to $\angle$COB.
     Since vertically opposite angles are congruent,

$$m\angle AOD = m\angle COB$$
$$45^0 + x^0 = 75^0$$
$$45^0 - 45^0 + x^0 = 75^0 - 45^0$$

$$0 + x^0 = 30^0$$
$$x^0 = 30^0$$

(m$\angle$AOD = $45^0+ x^0$, and m$\angle$COB = 75^0)
(Subtract 45^0 from each side of the equation in order to obtain the value of x^0.)
($45^0 - 45^0 = 0^0$, and $75^0 - 45^0 = 30^0$)

Example 3
Find the value of x^0 in each figure.

(a)

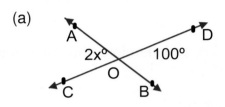

(b)

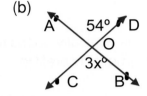

Solution
(**a**) $\angle$AOC is vertically opposite to $\angle$DOB.

Since vertically opposite angles are congruent,
$$m\angle AOC = m\angle DOB$$
Therefore, $2x^0 = 100^0$ (m$\angle$AOC = $2x^0$, m$\angle$DOB = 100^0)

$$\frac{2x^0}{2} = \frac{100^0}{2}$$

(Divide each side of the equation by 2 in order to obtain the value of x^0.)

$$\frac{\overset{x^0}{\cancel{2x^0}}}{\underset{1}{\cancel{2}}} = \frac{\overset{50^0}{\cancel{100^0}}}{\underset{1}{\cancel{2}}}$$

$$x^0 = 50^0$$

(**b**) $\angle$AOD is vertically opposite to $\angle$COB.

Since vertically opposite angles are congruent,
$$m\angle AOD = m\angle COB$$
Therefore, $54^0 = 3x^0$ (m$\angle$AOD = 54^0, m$\angle$COB = $3x^0$).

$$\frac{54^0}{3} = \frac{3x^0}{3}$$

(Divide each side of the equation by 3 in order to obtain the value of x^0.)

$$\frac{\overset{18^0}{\cancel{54^0}}}{\underset{1}{\cancel{3}}} = \frac{\overset{x^0}{\cancel{3x^0}}}{\underset{1}{\cancel{3}}} \ .$$

$$18^0 = x^0$$

Exercises

1. Vertically opposite angles are ——————.

2. The measure of the vertically opposite angles are ——————.

3. Find the value of x^0 in each figure. Hint: See Example **1**.

(a)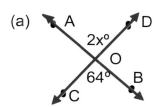

(b)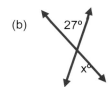

(c)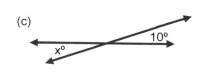

4. Find the value of x^0 in each figure. Hint: See Example **2**.

(a)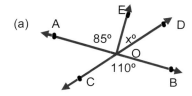

(b)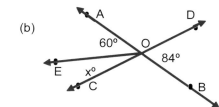

5. Find the value of x^0 in each figure. Hint: See Example **3**.

(a)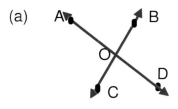

(b)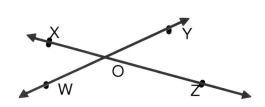

Challenge Questions

6. List all the vertically opposite angles in each figure.

(a)

(b)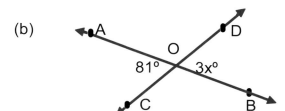

7. Find the value of x^0 in each figure, given that the lines join at point O.

(a)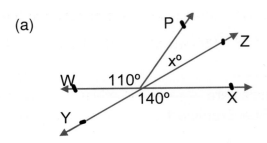

(b)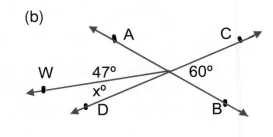

Cumulative Review
Draw each of the following diagrams.
1. Two parallel lines   **2.** A right angle   **3.** A segment
4. An isosceles triangle   **5.** Two perpendicular lines   **6.** A point
7. An acute angle   **8.** An obtuse angle   **9.** A ray
10. 180^0 angle   **11.** An equilateral triangle   **12.** A line

ASSOCIATE AN ANGLE WITH A CERTAIN AMOUNT OF TURNING

How to find $\frac{1}{4}$, $\frac{1}{2}$, $\frac{3}{4}$, and full turns

Recall that an angle is formed by the intersection of two rays and that a ray is a line that has a beginning point but no end point. **Angular measure** is obtained by dividing a circle into 360 equal parts and each part is called **one degree**.

If a circle is divided into two halves, then each half contains $\frac{360^0}{2} = 180^0$ as

shown in figure 1. Figure 1 shows that the angular measure of a straight angle or a straight line is 180^0. Figure 2 shows that if the circle is divided into four equal parts, then each part will contain 90°. Assume that the line AC intersects the line BD at the point X in figure 2 (X is not shown in the diagram), then:

1. a movement from the ray XC along the circle to the ray XB is a $\frac{1}{4}$ of a circle turn

which is 90°. Therefore, a $\frac{1}{4}$ turn is the same as 90°.

2. a movement from the ray XC along the circle to the ray XA is $\frac{1}{2}$ of a circle turn

which is 180°. Therefore, $\frac{1}{2}$ turn is the same as $90^0 + 90^0$ which is 180°.

3. a movement from the ray XC along the circle in anti-clockwise direction to the ray XD is $\frac{3}{4}$ of a circle turn, which is $90^0 + 90^0 + 90^0$ which is 270^0. Therefore, $\frac{3}{4}$ turn is the same as 270^0.

4. a movement from the ray XC along the circle in the anti-clockwise direction to the ray XC again is a full circle turn which is $90^0 + 90^0 + 90^0 + 90^0$ which is 360^0. Therefore, a full turn is the same as 360^0

Figure 1   **Figure 2.**

Exercises
1. A full turn is 360^0. How many degrees is a half turn?
2. A quarter turn is 90°. How many turns is 270^0?
3. Which is greater, $\frac{3}{4}$ turn or full turn? Explain your answer.

CHAPTER 29

POLYGONS AND ANGLES

Quick Review
1. What is the difference between a ray and a line?
2. What is the difference between a segment and a ray?

3. Solve: (**a**) $\frac{2}{3} \div \frac{1}{2}$ (**b**) $\frac{3}{4} \times \frac{2}{3}$ (**c**) $\frac{4}{7} + \frac{5}{14}$ (**d**) 25% of 120

4. Find the reciprocal of: (**a**) $\frac{3}{4}$ (**b**) 2   (**c**) 1

5. Find n in the equations;

(**a**) $\frac{n}{3} = \frac{6}{9}$ (**b**) $\frac{3}{5} = \frac{6}{n}$ (**c**) $4n = 24$

6. What is the difference between a right angle and a 90^0 angle?
7. What is the difference between an obtuse angle and an acute angle?

8. Choose the correct answer. In order to divide a number by a fraction,

   (**a**) multiply the number by the reciprocal of the fraction.

   (**b**) divide the number by the reciprocal of the fraction.

Polygons

A **polygon** is a closed figure formed by three or more line segments made on a flat surface and the line segments do not cross. Polygons are named by the number of their sides. Any polygon that has all sides equal and all angles equal is called a **regular polygon**. This means that a **regular polygon** has all sides congruent and all angles **congruent**. Congruent means having the same size or length and shape.

How Could You Tell That a Figure is a Polygon or is Not a Polygon?

The sides or the line segments of a polygon intersect at their endpoints and these intersection points are called **vertices**. Vertices is the plural of **vertex**.

(**a**). For example, the triangle in (a) shows a closed figure or the sides of the figure intersect at their endpoints and the sides of the figure is made up of line segments and therefore the triangle in (a) is a polygon.

(**b**). The figure in (b) shows a figure that is not closed and that means that all the sides of the figure do not intersect at their endpoints and therefore the figure in (b) is not a polygon.

(**c**). The figure in (c) is not a polygon because although the figure is a closed figure, a part of the figure is formed by a curve or an arc instead of line segments.

(**d**). The figure in (d) is not a polygon because the line segments of a polygon intersect only at the endpoints. Also, the description of the polygon states that the segments of the polygon do not cross but the figure (d) shows that two segments cross.

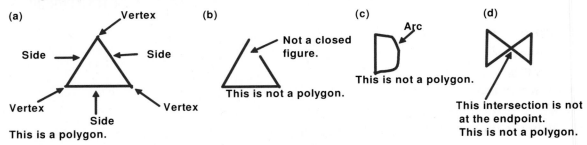

The Sum of the Interior Angles of a Polygon
The formula for finding the sum of the interior angles of a polygon is:

$(n - 2) \times 180^0$ where n is the number of sides of the polygon.

Some examples of polygons are listed in Figure 1.

Figure 1

Regular polygons	Polygons that are not regular	Name	Number of sides	Sum of the interior angles =(n - 2) × 180º
		Triangle	3	(3 - 2) × 180º = 180º
		Quadrilateral	4	(4 - 2) × 180º = 360º
		Pentagon	5	(5 - 2) × 180º = 540º
		Hexagon	6	(6 - 2) × 180º = 720º
?		Heptagon	7	(7 - 2) × 180º = 900º
	?	Octagon	8	(8 - 2) × 180º = 1080º
?	?	Nonagon	9	(9 - 2) × 180º = 1260º
?	?	Decagon	10	(10 - 2) × 180º = 1440º

Group Exercises

1. The class should be divided into four teams, Team A, Team B, Team C, and team D.

2. Each team should use the model of the other regular polygons in figure 1 to sketch regular heptagon, nonagon, and decagon. Hint: Do not use a ruler to measure the lengths of the sides of the polygons, but you should draw each length of the sides of the polygon to be approximately equal visually. If you could draw the sides of the polygons to be approximately equal visually, then each angle of the polygon will appear to be approximately equal visually.

3. Each team should use the model of the other polygons that are not regular in Figure 1 to sketch irregular octagon, nonagon, and decagon.

4. List the problems you have in sketching the polygons.

5. Could your sketches replace the missing polygons in Figure 1?

Sum of the Measures of the Angles in a Triangle
Group Exercise

It is possible to show that the sum of the angles in a triangle appear to be the same as the sum of the angles on a straight line or a straight angle which is 180^0 by using the following steps:

Step 1: Draw a straight line AB and with a protractor measure the straight angle which should be 180^0 as shown.

180°

A   B

Step 2: Draw an equilateral triangle XYZ with sides 3 inches and angles 60^0 as shown:

(**a**) With a pencil and a ruler, draw a line segment XY which is 3 inches long.

X   Y

(**b**) Place the center of the protractor on the endpoint X, measure and draw the 60^0 angle as shown. Hint: See the chapter/section on how to use a protractor to draw angles.

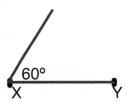

60°
X   Y

(**c**) Place the center of the protractor at the endpoint Y and measure and draw 120^0. Label the endpoint where the line from endpoint Y intersects the line segment from the endpoint X as Z.

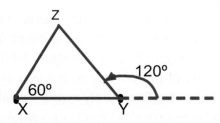

Z

60°   120°
X   Y

Since the sum of angles formed on a straight line is 180^0, the $\angle$XYZ

$$= 180^0 - 120^0 = 60^0$$

(**d**) With the center of the protractor on the vertex Z and aligning the base line (0^0) of the protractor with the line segment ZX, read the angle measure that corresponds to the angle XZY. This angle, XZY should be approximately 60^0.

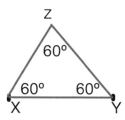

Step 3: Using a ruler, mark a point $1\frac{1}{2}$ inches from point X which is the middle of the line segment XY. Using a ruler, mark a point Q $1\frac{1}{2}$ inches from the point Y which is the middle of the line segment YZ. Using a ruler, mark a point R, $1\frac{1}{2}$ inches from point X which is the middle of the segment XZ. Join the points PQR with dotted line segments as shown:

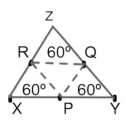

Step 4: Cut out the triangle XYZ. Cut off the angles X, Y, and Z along the dotted line segments RP, PQ, and QR respectively.

Step 5: Put the cut off angles together at a point to form a straight angle as shown.

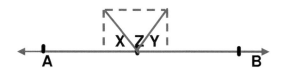

What conclusions can we make from the group exercise?

(**a**) The sum of the measure of the angles of a triangle is the same as the sum of the measures of the angles on a straight line which is 180^0. For example, from Step 2(d) $m\angle X = 60^0$, $m\angle Y = 60^0$, $m\angle Z = 60^0$, then,

$$m\angle X + m\angle Y + m\angle Z = 60^0 + 60^0 + 60^0$$
$$= 180^0$$

(**b**) Step 2(c), and Step 2(d) show that **the measure of the exterior angle of a triangle is equal to the sum of the measures of the two interior angles as shown**:

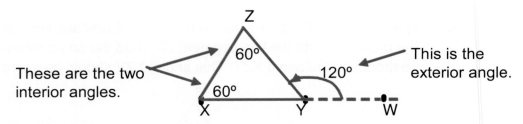

These are the two interior angles.

This is the exterior angle.

Measure of exterior angle of a triangle = Sum of the measures of the two interior angles. Therefore,

$m\angle WYZ = m\angle YXZ + m\angle XZY$

$120^0 = 60^0 + 60^0$ ($m\angle WYZ = 120^0$, $m\angle YXZ = 60^0$, and $m\angle XZY = 60^0$)

$120^0 = 120^0$

Example 1

Find the value of the angle measure for x^0.

(a)   (b)   (c)

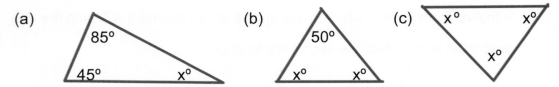

Solution

(**a**) The sum of the measures of the angles in a triangle = 180^0, therefore,

$45^0 + 85^0 + x^0 = 180^0$

$130^0 + x^0 = 180^0$ ($45^0 + 85^0 = 130^0$)

$130^0 - 130^0 + x^0 = 180^0 - 130^0$ (Subtract 130^0 from each side of the equation in order to obtain the value of x^0.)

$0 + x^0 = 50^0$ ($130^0 - 130^0 = 0$, $180^0 - 130^0 = 50^0$)

$x^0 = 50^0$

(**b**) The sum of the measures of the angles in a triangle = 180^0, therefore,

$50^0 + x^0 + x^0 = 180^0$

$50^0 + 2x^0 = 180^0$ ($x^0 + x^0 = 2x^0$)

$50^0 - 50^0 + 2x^0 = 180^0 - 50^0$ (Subtract 50^0 from each side of the equation in order to obtain the value of $2x^0$.)

$0 + 2x^0 = 130$ ($50^0 - 50^0 = 0$, and $180^0 - 50^0 = 130^0$)

$\dfrac{2x^0}{2} = \dfrac{130^0}{2}$ (Divide each side of the equation by 2 in order to obtain the value of x^0.)

720

$$x^0 \qquad 65^0$$
$$\frac{2x^0}{2} = \frac{130^0}{2}$$
$$\quad 1 \qquad\quad 1$$

$$x^0 = 65^0$$

(**c**) The sum of the measures of the angles in a triangle $= 180^0$, therefore,

$$x^0 + x^0 + x^0 = 180^0$$
$$3x^0 = 180^0 \qquad\qquad (x^0 + x^0 + x^0 = 3x^0)$$

$$\frac{3x^0}{3} = \frac{180^0}{3} \qquad\qquad$$ (Divide each side of the equation

by 3 in order to obtain the value of x^0.)

$$x^0 \qquad 60^0$$
$$\frac{3x^0}{3} = \frac{180^0}{3}$$
$$\quad 1 \qquad\quad 1$$

$$x^0 = 60^0$$

Example 2

Find the measure of $\angle C$.

(a)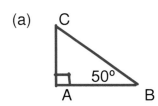

(b)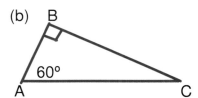

Hint: ⌐ **means 90º**

Solution

(**a**) The measure of $\angle A = 90^0$ (See the "hint" in the question.)

The measures of the sum of the angles in a triangle $= 180^0$, therefore,

$$m\angle C + 90^0 + 50^0 = 180^0 \qquad$$ ($m\angle C$ means the measure of angle C.)
$$m\angle C + 140^0 \qquad = 180^0 \qquad (90^0 + 50^0 = 140^0).$$
$$m\angle C + 140^0 - 140^0 = 180^0 - 140^0 \qquad$$ (Subtract 140^0 from each side of the
equation in order to obtain the value
of $m\angle C$.)

$$m\angle C + 0 = 40^0 \qquad\qquad (140^0 - 140^0 = 0, \text{ and } 180^0 - 140^0 = 40^0)$$
$$m\angle C = 40^0$$

(**b**) The measure of $\angle B = 90^0$ (See the "hint" in the question.)

The measures of the sum of the angles in a triangle $= 180^0$, therefore,

$$m\angle C + 90^0 + 60^0 = 180^0$$ (m∠C means the measure of angle C.)
$$m\angle C + 150^0 \qquad = 180^0$$ ($90^0 + 60^0 = 150^0$)
$$m\angle C + 150^0 - 150^0 = 180^0 - 150^0$$ (Subtract 150^0 from each side of the equation in order to obtain the value of $m\angle C$.)
$$m\angle C + 0 = 30^0$$ ($150^0 - 150^0 = 0$, and $180^0 - 150^0 = 30^0$)
$$m\angle C = 30^0$$

Example 3

Find the value of x^0. Hint: Use the measure of the exterior angle of a triangle property.

(a)

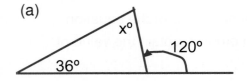

(b)

Solution

(a) The measure of the exterior angle $= 120^0$

The two interior angles are 36^0 and x^0

The measure of the exterior angle of a triangle is equal to the sum of the measures of the two interior angles, so that,

$$120^0 = 36^0 + x^0$$
$$120^0 - 36^0 = 36^0 - 36^0 + x^0$$ (Subtract 36^0 from each side of the equation in order to obtain the value of x^0.)

$$84^0 = 0^0 + x^0$$ ($120^0 - 36^0 = 84^0$, and $36^0 - 36^0 = 0^0$)
$$84^0 = x^0$$
$$x^0 = 84^0$$

(b) The measure of the exterior angle $= x^0$

The two interior angles are 42^0 and 78^0.

The measure of the exterior angle of a triangle is equal to the sum of the measures of the interior angles, so that,

$$x^0 = 42^0 + 78^0$$
$$x^0 = 120^0$$

Exercises

1. Give reasons why each figure is not a polygon. Hint: See the preceding notes, also match each figure with the description of a polygon to determine if the figure is a polygon or not.

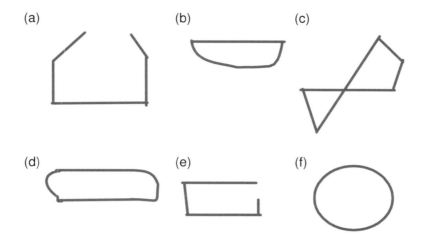

| (a) | (b) | (c) |
| (d) | (e) | (f) |

2. Give reasons why each figure is a polygon and state the name of each figure. Hint: See the preceding notes and also match the description of a polygon with each figure to determine if the figure is a polygon or not.

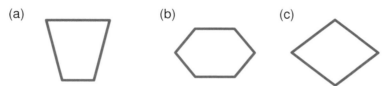

| (a) | (b) | (c) |

3. Find the value of the angle measure for x^0. Hint: See Example **1**. Match a similar question to a similar example in Example **1**.

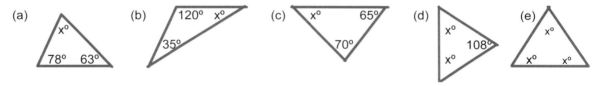

4. Find the measure of $\angle$B. Hint: See Example **2**.

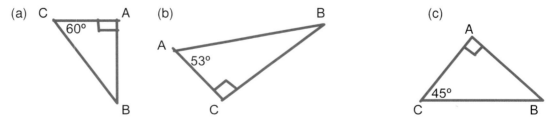

5. Find the value of x^0. Hint: Use the measure of the exterior angle of a triangle property. See Example **3**. Match a similar example in Example **3** with a similar exercise.

(a)

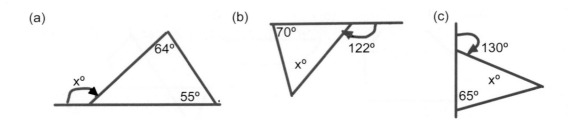

(b)

70°

122°

x°

(c)

130°

65°

x°

Challenge Questions

6. Find the measure of x^0

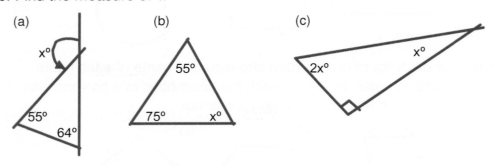

(a)

x°

55°

64°

(b)

55°

75°   x°

(c)

2x°   x°

To find the Sum of the Angles in a Quadrilateral

Group Exercise

Step 1: Draw a quadrilateral WXYZ.

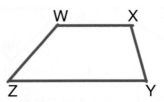

Step 2: Draw a line from Z to X to make two triangles.

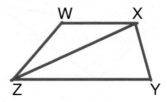

Step 3: We have two triangles in step 2 which are triangles WXZ and XYZ. We have already shown that the "sum of the measures of the angles in a triangle " is 180^0 and therefore the sum of the measures of the angles in the two triangles $= 2 \times 180^0 = 360^0$. The two triangles form a quadrilateral because **a quadrilateral is a closed figure which has 4 sides**. Therefore, a quadrilateral has the sum of the measures of angles (or interior angles) $= 360^0$

Sum of the Measures of the Angles of a Quadrilateral

We can use the sum of the measures of the angles of a quadrilateral $= 360^0$ to solve many problems.

Example 1

Find the angle measure of x^0.

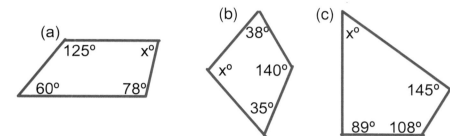

(a)

(b)

(c)

Solution

(a) The sum of the measures of the angles of a quadrilateral $= 360^0$, therefore,

$x^0 + 78^0 + 60^0 + 125^0 = 360^0$

$\quad\quad x^0 + 263^0 = 360^0$ $(78^0 + 60^0 + 125^0 = 263^0)$

$x^0 + 263^0 - 263^0 = 360^0 - 263$ (Subtract 263^0 from each side of the equation in order to obtain the value of x^0.)

$\quad\quad x^0 + 0 = 97^0$ $(263^0 - 263^0 = 0^0$, and $360^0 - 263^0 = 97^0)$

$\quad\quad x^0 = 97^0$

(b) The sum of the measures of the angles of a quadrilateral $= 360^0$, therefore,

$x^0 + 38^0 + 140^0 + 35^0 = 360^0$

$\quad\quad x^0 + 213 = 360^0$ $(38^0 + 140^0 + 35^0 = 213^0)$

$x^0 + 213^0 - 213^0 = 360^0 - 213^0$ (Subtract 213^0 from each side of the equation in order to obtain the value of x^0.)

$\quad\quad x^0 + 0 = 147^0$ $(213^0 - 213^0 = 0$, and $360^0 - 213^0 = 147^0)$

$\quad\quad x^0 = 147^0$

(c) The sum of the measures of the angles of a quadrilateral $= 360^0$, therefore,

$x^0 + 145^0 + 108^0 + 89^0 = 360^0$

$\quad\quad x^0 + 342^0 = 360^0$ $(145^0 + 108^0 + 89^0 = 342^0)$

$x^0 + 342^0 - 342^0 = 360^0 - 342^0$ (Subtract 342^0 from each side of the equation in order to obtain the value of x^0.)

$\quad\quad x^0 + 0 = 18^0$ $(342^0 - 342^0 = 0^0$, and $360^0 - 342^0 = 18)$

$\quad\quad x^0 = 18^0$

Example 2

Find the value of x^0.

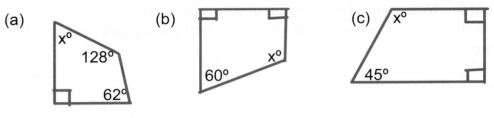

(a)

(b)

(c)

Hint: ⌐ **means 90º**

Solution

(**a**) The sum of the measures of the angles of a quadrilateral $= 360^0$, therefore,

$$x^0 + 128^0 + 62^0 + 90^0 = 360^0$$ (See the "hint" in the question regarding 90^0.)

$$x^0 + 280^0 = 360^0$$ ($128^0 + 62^0 + 90^0 = 280^0$)

$$x^0 + 280^0 - 280^0 = 360^0 - 280^0$$ (Subtract 280^0 from each side of the equation in order to obtain the value of x^0.)

$$x^0 + 0 = 80^0$$ ($280^0 - 280^0 = 0$, and $360^0 - 280^0 = 80^0$)

$$x^0 = 80^0$$

(**b**) The sum of the measures of the angles of a quadrilateral $= 360^0$, therefore,

$$x^0 + 60^0 + 90^0 + 90^0 = 360^0$$ (See the "hint" in the question regarding 90^0.)

$$x^0 + 240^0 = 360^0$$ ($60^0 + 90^0 + 90^0 = 240^0$)

$$x^0 + 240^0 - 240^0 = 360^0 - 240^0$$ (Subtract 240^0 from each side of the equation in order to obtain the value of x^0.)

$$x^0 + 0 = 120^0$$ ($240^0 - 240^0 = 0$, and $360^0 - 240^0 = 120^0$)

$$x^0 = 120^0$$

(**c**) The sum of the measures of the angles of a quadrilateral $= 360^0$, so that,

$$x^0 + 90^0 + 90^0 + 45^0 = 360^0$$ (See the "hint" in the question regarding 90^0.)

$$x^0 + 225^0 = 360^0$$ ($90^0 + 90^0 + 45^0 = 225^0$)

$$x^0 + 225^0 - 225^0 = 360^0 - 225^0$$ (Subtract 225^0 from each side of the equation in order to obtain the value of x^0.)

$$x^0 + 0 = 135^0$$ ($225^0 - 225^0 = 0^0$, and $360^0 - 225^0 = 135^0$)

$$x^0 = 135^0$$

Exercises

1. Find the value of x^0. Hint: See Example 1.

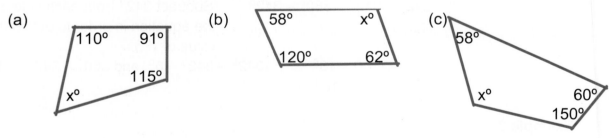

(a)

(b)

(c)

2. Find the value of x^0. Hint: See Example **2**.

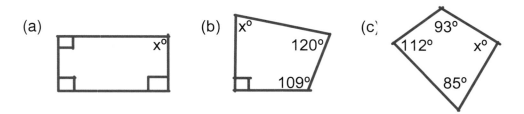

(a) [figure with angles showing right angles, x^0, and 48^0]

(b) [figure showing x^0, 128^0, and right angles]

(c) [figure showing 88^0, 130^0, right angle, and x^0]

Challenge Questions

3. Find the value of x^0.

(a) [rectangle figure with right angles and x^0]

(b) [figure showing x^0, 120^0, 109^0, and right angle]

(c) [kite figure showing 93^0, 112^0, x^0, and 85^0]

Review

1. Draw: (**a**) a hexagon, (**b**) an octagon, and (c) a pentagon.

2. State whether the measure of the angle is an acute, an obtuse, or a right angle.

  (**a**) 90^0 (**b**) 25^0 (**c**) 101^0

Sum of the Measures of the Angles of a Polygon

The sum of the measures of the angles of a triangle $= 180^0$

The sum of the measures of the angles of a quadrilateral $= 360^0$. Let us find a general formula for finding the sum of the measure of the angles of a polygon as shown:

1. Sum of measures of the angles of a triangle $= 180^0$

$$= (n - 2) \times 180^0, \text{ where n} = \text{number}$$
$$\text{of sides of a triangle.}$$
$$= (3 - 2) \times 180^0, \quad (n = 3)$$
$$= 1 \times 180^0$$
$$= 180^0$$

  Put n = 3 because a triangle has 3 sides.

2. Sum of the measures of the angles of a quadrilateral $= 360^0$

$$= (n - 2) \times 180^0, \text{ where n}$$
$$\text{is the number of sides}$$
$$\text{of a quadrilateral.}$$
$$= (4 - 2) \times 180^0, \quad (n = 4)$$
$$= 2 \times 180^0$$
$$= 360^0$$

Put n = 4 because a quadrilateral has 4 sides.

3. Therefore, **the general formula for finding the sum of the measures of the angles of any polygon is $(n-2) \times 180^0$.**

   where n is the number of sides of the polygon.

4. The general formula $(n-2) \times 180^0$ is used to find the sum of the measures of the angles of any polygon, but this formula is used specifically for the sum of the interior angles of the polygon. The interior angles of a polygon is the same as the angles inside the polygon as shown:

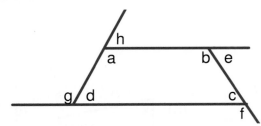

The angle measures of a, b, c and d are inside the polygon and they are called **interior angles**. The angle measures of e, f, g, and h are outside the polygon and they are called **exterior angles**.

Some important formulas and facts about a polygon are as shown:

1. The sum of the measures of the interior angles of a polygon = $(n-2) \times 180^0$, where n is the number of sides of the polygon.

2. The interior angle of a regular polygon = $\dfrac{(n-2) \times 180^0}{n}$,

   where n is the number of sides of the polygon.

3. The sum of the measures of the exterior angles of a polygon is 360^0.

4. All the exterior angles of a regular polygon are equal.

5. An exterior angle of a regular polygon = $\dfrac{360^0}{n}$,

   where n is the number of the sides.

Example 1

Find the sum of the measures of the interior angles of:

(**a**) a pentagon.

(**b**) a heptagon.

Solution

(**a**) The number of sides of a pentagon = 5.

   The sum of the measures of the interior angles of a polygon = $(n-2) \times 180^0$ where n is the number of the sides.

   Therefore, the sum of the measures of the interior angles of the pentagon

   $= (n-2) \times 180^0$

   $= (5-2) \times 180^0$ (Substitute n = 5, because a pentagon has 5 sides.)

$$= 3 \times 180^0$$
$$= 540^0$$

(**b**) The number of sides of a heptagon = 7.

The sum of the measures of the interior angles of a polygon = $(n - 2) \times 180^0$, where n is the number of the sides.

Therefore, the sum of the measures of the interior angles of the heptagon

$$= (n - 2) \times 180^0$$
$$= (7 - 2) \times 180^0 \quad \text{(Substitute n = 7, because a heptagon has 7 sides.)}$$
$$= 5 \times 180^0$$
$$= 900^0$$

Example 2

A polygon has 12 sides. Find the sum of the of the measures of the interior angles.

Solution

The sum of the measures of the interior angles of a polygon = $(n - 2) \times 180^0$ where n is the number of sides of the polygon.

Therefore, the sum of the measures of the angles of the 12 sided polygon

$$= (n - 2) \times 180^0$$
$$= (12 - 2) \times 180^0 \quad \text{(Substitute n = 12, because the polygon has 12 sides.)}$$
$$= 10 \times 180^0$$
$$= 1800^0$$

Example 3

The sum of the measures of the interior angles of a polygon is 540^0.

(**a**) Find the number of sides of the polygon.

(**b**) What is the name of the polygon in (a)?

Solution

(**a**) The sum of the measures of the interior angles of a polygon = $(n - 2) \times 180^0$, where n is the number of the sides of the polygon.

From the question, the sum of the measures of the interior angles of the polygon
$$= 540^0.$$

Therefore, $(n - 2) \times 180^0 = 540^0$

$180^0 \times n - 2 \times 180^0 = 540^0$	Multiply (n – 2) by 180^0.
$180n^0 - 360^0 = 540^0$	($180^0 \times n = 180n^0$, and $2 \times 180^0 = 360^0$)
$180n^0 - 360 + 360^0 = 540^0 + 360^0$	(Add 360^0 to each side of the equation in order to eliminate -360^0 from the left side of the equation.)
$180n^0 = 900^0$	($-360^0 + 360^0 = 0$, and $540^0 + 360^0 = 900^0$)
$\dfrac{180n^0}{180^0} = \dfrac{900^0}{180^0}$	(Divide each side of the equation by 180^0

in order to obtain the value of n.)

$$\begin{array}{cc} n^0 & 5 \\ \dfrac{180n^0}{180^0} = & \dfrac{900^0}{180^0} \\ 1 & 1 \end{array}$$

$$n = 5 \text{ sides.}$$

(**b**) From solution (a), n = 5 sides, therefore, the polygon is a pentagon.

Exercises

1. Identify the figure as a triangle, a quadrilateral, a pentagon, a hexagon, or a heptagon, and give reasons for your answer.

 (a) 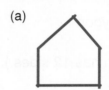 (b) 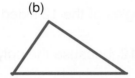 (c) 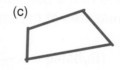 (d) 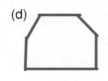 (e)

2. Find the sum of the measure of the interior angles of (a) a hexagon, (b) an octagon. Hint: See Example **1**.

3. A polygon has 7 sides, find the sum of the measure of the interior angles. Hint: See Example **2**.

4. The sum of the measure of the interior angles of a polygon is 720^0.
 (**a**) Find the number of sides of the polygon.
 (**b**) What is the name of the polygon?
 Hint: See Example **3**.

5. Given the measure of the 3 exterior angles of each polygon (convex polygon), find the measure of the fourth exterior angle of each polygon (convex polygon).
 Hint: See Example **4** and also note that the sum of the exterior angles of a polygon (convex polygon) is 360^0.
 a. 126^0, 75^0, and 54^0 **b.** 106^0, 75^0, and 94^0 **b.** 56^0, 88^0, and 132^0
 d. 66^0, 59^0, and 129^0 **e.** 101^0, 85^0, and 94^0 **f.** 50^0, 83^0, and 123^0

6. Find the missing measure of angle in each polygon (convex polygon). Hint: See Example **4**.
 a. $m\angle a = 112^0$ **b.** $m\angle e = 135^0$
  $m\angle b = ?$ $m\angle f = 73^0$
  $m\angle c = 110^0$ $m\angle g = ?$
  $m\angle d = 68^0$ $m\angle h = 58^0$

 c. $m\angle i = ?$ **d.** $m\angle m = 90^0$

$m\angle j = 118^0$ $m\angle n = 90^0$
$m\angle k = 67^0$ $m\angle o = ?$
$m\angle l = 68^0$ $m\angle p = 90^0$

a.

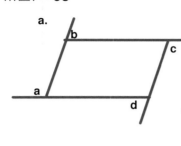

b.

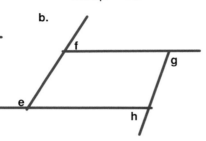

c.

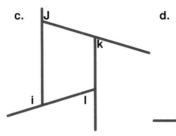

d.

7. Find the missing measure of angle in each polygon (convex polygon). Hint: See Example 5.

   (**a**). $m\angle a = 140^0$ (**b**). $m\angle d = 79^0$
   $m\angle b = ?$ $m\angle e = 142^0$
   $m\angle c = 85^0$ $m\angle f = ?$

   (**c**). $m\angle g = 130^0$ (**d**). $m\angle j = ?$
   $m\angle h = ?$ $m\angle k = 128^0$
   $m\angle i = 90^0$ $m\angle l = 95^0$

(a).

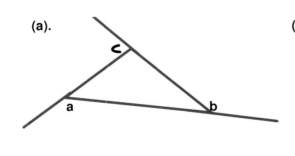

(b).

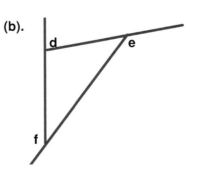

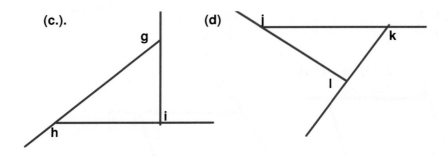

Challenge Questions

8. What is the name given to a polygon with the following number of sides:

    (a) 8 sides   (b) 6 sides   (c) 9 sides.

9. Find the sum of the measure of the interior angles of an octagon.

10. A polygon has 10 sides, find the sum of the measure of the interior angles.

11. Find the missing measure of angle in each polygon (convex polygon).

    (a). $m\angle a = 144^0$ **(b).** $m\angle d = 84^0$

         $m\angle b = ?$ $m\angle e = 140^0$

         $m\angle c = 83^0$ $m\angle f = ?$

    (c). $m\angle g = 133^0$ **(d).** $m\angle j = ?$

         $m\angle h = ?$ $m\angle k = 129^0$

         $m\angle i = 89^0$ $m\angle l = 92^0$

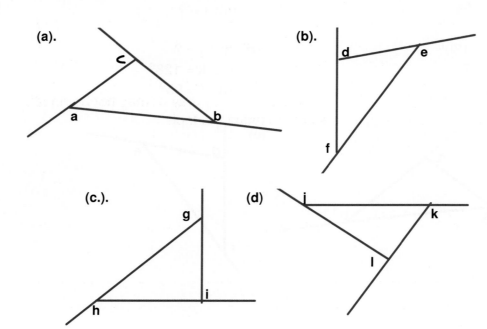

Answers to Selected Questions
5a. 105^0 **6a.** 70^0 **7a.** 135^0

Critical Geometrical Facts
1. The sum of the measures of the interior angles of a triangle $= 180^0$
2. The sum of the measures of the exterior angles of a triangle $= 360^0$
3. The sum of the measures of the exterior angles of a polygon including triangles and quadrilaterals $= 360^0$
4. The sum of the interior angles of any quadrilateral $= 360^0$

Classification of Triangles Using the Sides and the Angles of the Triangle
You may read more information on the classification of triangles under the chapter "Geometric Figures."
The sides and the angles of a triangle can be used to classify triangles as:
　　Equilateral triangle.
　　Isosceles triangle.
　　Scalene triangle.
　　Right-angle triangle.
An equilateral triangle has all sides and all angles equal.
An isosceles triangle has two or more sides equal and two or more angles equal.
A scalene triangle has no sides equal and no angles equal .
A right angle triangle has one 90^0 angle and the sides may or may not be equal.
The classification of the triangles is summarized in the table.

The table for the classification of triangles is on the next page.

Triangle type	Sample diagram	Description
Equilateral triangle	 60° 60° 60° ✕ indicates the sides that are equal.	All sides are equal and all angles are equal.
Isosceles triangle	 20° 80° 80° ✕ indicates the sides that are equal	Two or more sides are equal and two or more angles are equal.
Scalene triangle	 96° 54° 30°	No sides are equal and no angles are equal.
Right-angle triangle	 ⌐ indicates 90°	There is one angle which is 90°

Exercises

Classify the following triangles as an equilateral, an isosceles, a scalene or a right-angle triangle. Give reasons for your classifications. Hint: See the preceding section or the table and also match each figure with the description of each classification of the triangles to determine the classification of each figure.

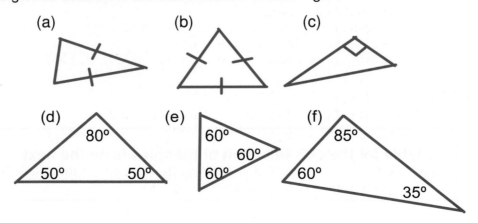

(a)　　　　　　(b)　　　　　　(c)

(d)　　　　　　(e)　　　　　　(f)
80°　　　　60°　　　　85°
50°　　50°　　60°　60°　60°　35°

Classification of Quadrilaterals

Quadrilaterals can be classified by the number of parallel sides, length of sides and the measure of the angles as shown in Figure 2.

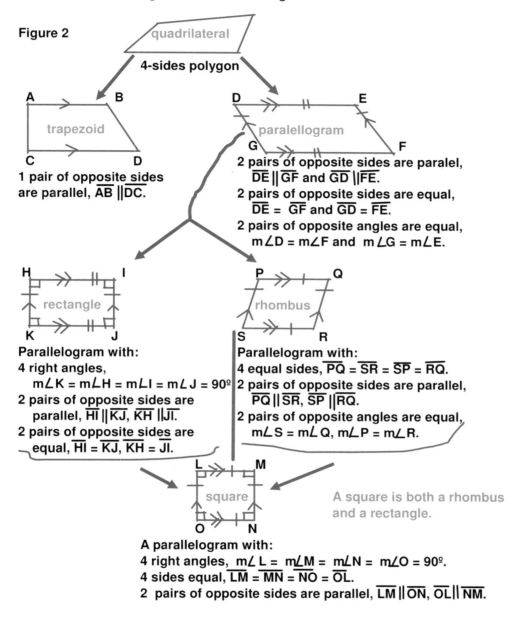

Figure 2

quadrilateral

4-sides polygon

trapezoid

1 pair of opposite sides are parallel, $\overline{AB} \parallel \overline{DC}$.

paralellogram

2 pairs of opposite sides are paralel, $\overline{DE} \parallel \overline{GF}$ and $\overline{GD} \parallel \overline{FE}$.
2 pairs of opposite sides are equal, $\overline{DE} = \overline{GF}$ and $\overline{GD} = \overline{FE}$.
2 pairs of opposite angles are equal, $m\angle D = m\angle F$ and $m\angle G = m\angle E$.

rectangle

Parallelogram with:
4 right angles, $m\angle K = m\angle H = m\angle I = m\angle J = 90^\circ$
2 pairs of opposite sides are parallel, $\overline{HI} \parallel \overline{KJ}$, $\overline{KH} \parallel \overline{JI}$.
2 pairs of opposite sides are equal, $\overline{HI} = \overline{KJ}$, $\overline{KH} = \overline{JI}$.

rhombus

Parallelogram with:
4 equal sides, $\overline{PQ} = \overline{SR} = \overline{SP} = \overline{RQ}$.
2 pairs of opposite sides are parallel, $\overline{PQ} \parallel \overline{SR}$, $\overline{SP} \parallel \overline{RQ}$.
2 pairs of opposite angles are equal, $m\angle S = m\angle Q$, $m\angle P = m\angle R$.

square

A square is both a rhombus and a rectangle.

A parallelogram with:
4 right angles, $m\angle L = m\angle M = m\angle N = m\angle O = 90^\circ$.
4 sides equal, $\overline{LM} = \overline{MN} = \overline{NO} = \overline{OL}$.
2 pairs of opposite sides are parallel, $\overline{LM} \parallel \overline{ON}$, $\overline{OL} \parallel \overline{NM}$.

The explanation of the symbols in figure 2 are:

means a group of segments that are parallel.
means a second group of segments that are parallel.
means a group of segments that are equal in length.
means a second group of segments that are equal in length.
means a right angle or a 90º angle.

735

Exercises

1. Select the correct word to complete each statement. Hint: See the preceding notes and Figure 2.

(**a**) A quadrilateral is a 4-sided **polygon** or a 4-sided (opened, closed) figure.

(**b**) A quadrilateral that has two pairs of opposite sides parallel is called a (trapezoid, parallelogram).

(**c**) A quadrilateral that has exactly one pair of opposite sides parallel is called a (parallelogram, trapezoid.)

(**d**) A quadrilateral or a parallelogram that has all sides the same length with the angles not right angles is called a (rhombus. square.)

(**e**) A quadrilateral or a parallelogram that has all sides of the same length with the angles being right angles is called a (rhombus, square.)

(**f**) A quadrilateral or a parallelogram that has 2 pairs of opposite sides equal and all the measures of the angles are right angles is called a (trapezoid, rectangle, square.)

(**g**) A square is both a rhombus and a rectangle. (true or false)

(**h**) What is the difference between a square and a rhombus? (All sides are equal, the angles of the rhombus are not 90^0 but the angles of the square are 90^0.)

2. Classify each figure as a rectangle, a square, a trapezoid, a parallelogram or a rhombus. Give detailed reasons for your classification. Hint: See Figure 2.

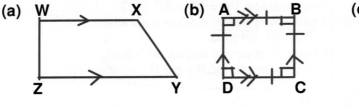

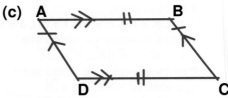

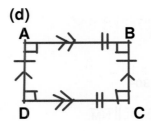

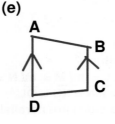

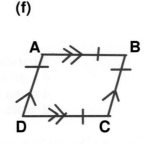

3. A regular polygon has equal sides and equal measure of angles. Does each figure appear to be a regular polygon? Explain your answer. Hint: See Figure 1 at the beginning of this chapter.

(a)   (b)   (c) 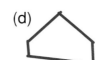 (d)   (e) ⬜

4. Sketch an example of each polygon. Hint: See Figure 1 at the beginning of this chapter and Figure 2.

(**a**) equilateral triangle   (**b**) rectangle   (**c**) regular pentagon   (**d**) quadrilateral

CHARPTER 30

GEOMETRIC FIGURES

Cumulative Review

1. $17 + 43 =$ **2.** $50 \div 10 =$ **3.** $32 - 18 =$ **4.** $9 \times 4 =$

5. $44 \div 4 =$ **6.** $28 - 12 =$ **7.** $60 \div 6 =$ **8.** $33 - 8 =$

9. $\begin{array}{r} 240 \\ \times\ 4 \\ \hline \end{array}$ **10.** $\begin{array}{r} 144 \\ +\ 195 \\ \hline \end{array}$ **11.** $\begin{array}{r} 29 \\ -\ 14 \\ \hline \end{array}$ **12.** $\begin{array}{r} 33 \\ \times\ 4 \\ \hline \end{array}$

13. $36 \div 3 =$ **14.** $28 \div 7 =$ **15.** $13 + 35 =$ **16.** $4^2 - 8 =$

17. $5.9 + 3.8 =$ **18.** $5.7 \times 3 =$ **19.** $2.9 \times 3.6 =$ **20.** $27.7 - 1.8 =$

21. $\dfrac{2}{3} \times \dfrac{2}{5} =$ **22.** $\dfrac{2}{3} \div \dfrac{7}{3} =$ **23.** $\dfrac{3}{4} - \dfrac{2}{3} =$ **24.** $2\dfrac{2}{3} + 2\dfrac{3}{4} =$

Geometric Figures

The are four basic geometric figures which are:

1. **A point**
2. **A ray**
3. **A line**
4. **A segment**

The four basic geometric figures can be represented in a table as shown:

737

Geometric Figures - Table

Diagram (figure)	Name	Symbol	Description
· X	Point X	X	A point is the smallest specific location in space.
X Y (ray)	Ray XY	$\overrightarrow{XY}$	A ray is a part of a line that starts at a point and continues in one direction.
X Y (line)	Line XY or line YX	$\overleftrightarrow{XY}$ or $\overleftrightarrow{YX}$	A line is a straight continuous arrangement of points in opposite directions.
X Y (segment)	Segment XY or segment YX	$\overline{XY}$ or $\overline{YX}$	A segment is a part of a line that starts at a point and ends at another point.

Group Exercises

1. Every student should take a 11 × 8 inches of paper and divide it into four sections.

2. Each student should draw one of the four basic geometric figures on one of each section of the paper. Cut out the four sections of the paper and put the individual sections into a container.

3. The class should be divided into four groups, such as group A, B, C, and D. "Group A" should compete against "group D" and "group B" should compete against "group C." A student in "group A" should pick one of the sections of the paper in the container and change the statement on the paper into a question for "group B" to answer. For example, if the section of the paper shows the diagram of line XY, then the "group A" student should ask "group B" students, "what is meant by a line XY and draw the line XY on the blackboard.

4. Record each correct answer on the tally table as shown. Each group should ask at least 20 questions.

Group	A	B	C	D
Tally	///	////	//	////

1. Which group understands the concept of the four basic geometric figures best?
2. Which figure do many students have problems with?
3. Which figure do many students have no problems with?

Example 1

Match the letters A, B, and C with the correct basic geometric figure.

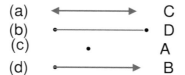

(a)	A. Point
(b)	B. Ray
(c)	C. Line
(d)	D. Segment

Solution

The letters are matched with the correct basic geometric figures as shown:

(a)	C
(b)	D
(c)	A
(d)	B

Example 2

By referring to the diagrams/figures of a ray, a segment and a line:
(**a**) What is the difference among a ray, a segment, and a line?
(**b**) Are a ray, a segment and a line alike?
(**c**) What is the difference between a line and a ray?
(**d**) What is the difference between a line and a segment?
(**e**) What is the difference between a segment and a ray?

Solution

(**a**) A ray, a segment and a line are different because by referring to the diagram/figure of a ray, a segment and a line, the one arrow head in the diagram of a ray shows that the **ray is continuous in one direction**. The diagram of a segment does not show any arrow head, therefore **a segment is not continuous**. The diagram of a line shows two arrows in opposite directions. Therefore, **a line continues in opposite directions**.

(**b**) A ray, a segment, and a line are alike in the sense that all of them are made up of points in a close and straight arrangements as shown:

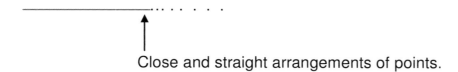

Close and straight arrangements of points.

(**c**) The two arrow heads of the diagram of a line show that **a line is continuous in opposite directions** but a ray which has one arrow head shows that **a ray is continuous just in one direction**.

(**d**) The two arrow heads of the diagram of a line shows that **a line is continuous in opposite directions** but a diagram of a segment has no arrow heads, and therefore, **a segment is continuous in neither directions**.

(**e**) There are no arrow heads in the diagram of a segment and therefore **a segment continues in neither directions** but the diagram of a ray has one arrow head, and therefore, **a ray continues in one direction**.

Group Exercises

The class should be divided into four groups, A, B, C, and D. Each group should use the table for the four basic geometric figures to complete the following statements:

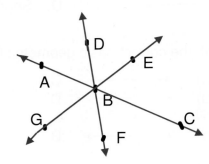

1. $\overline{GB}$ is s_____ GB. The answer to question 1 as example is: $\overline{GB}$ is segment GB.

2. $\overline{GE}$ is s_____ GE.

3. $\overleftrightarrow{GE}$ is l_____ GE.

4. $\overrightarrow{GE}$ is r_____ GE.

5. B is p_____ B.

6. C is p_____ C.

7. $\overleftrightarrow{AC}$ is l_____ AC.

8. $\overrightarrow{AC}$ is r_____ AC.

9. $\overline{AC}$ is s_____ AC.

10. $\overrightarrow{FD}$ is r_____ FD.

11. $\overrightarrow{DF}$ is r_____ DF.

12. D is p_____ D.

13. $\overleftrightarrow{DF}$ is l_____ DF.

16. $\overleftrightarrow{FD}$ is l_____ FD.

15. $\overrightarrow{BF}$ is r_____ BF.

17. The symbol for ray FB is ————-

18. The symbol for ray DF is ———

19. The symbol for point E is ————-

20. The symbol for point A is ————-

21. The symbol for segment CA is ———

22. The symbol for segment EG is ———

23. The symbol for line GE is ———

24. The symbol for line FD is ———

25. The symbol for ray GE is ———

26. The symbol for ray EG is ———

Group A should check group B's answers, group B should check group A's answers, group C should check group D's answers and group D should check group C's answers.

Analysis of the Group Exercises

1. Which group did best?
2. Which answers did all the groups get wrong?

3. How many answers did each group get correct?

4. How many answers did each group get wrong? Review the table of Geometric Figures to correct the wrong answers.

Example 3

(**a**) $\overline{AB}$ is the same figure as $\overline{AB}$? True or False.

(**b**) $\overleftrightarrow{BD}$ is the same figure as $\overleftrightarrow{BD}$? True or False.

(**c**) $\overrightarrow{AC}$ is the same figure as $\overrightarrow{CA}$? True or False. Explain your answer.

(**d**) Name all the rays in the diagram.

Solution

(**a**) True   (**b**) True

(**c**) False, because the direction of the ray AC is opposite to the direction of the ray CA.

(**d**) The rays in the diagram are $\overrightarrow{XZ}$, $\overrightarrow{XY}$, and $\overrightarrow{YZ}$.

Exercises

1. Sketch: (**a**) A ray   (**b**) A line   (**c**) A segment. Hint: See Example **1**.

2. Use symbols to write the following: See the table under the section Geometric Figures. (**a**) A line PK   (**b**) A ray PK   (**c**) A segment PK   (**d**) A point P.

3. List all the possible rays in the diagram. Hint: See Example **3**(**d**).

Challenge Questions

4. John's house is 200 feet from his school. Can the distance from John's house to the school be considered as a ray, a segment or a line? Assume that the direction from John's house to the school is straight. Explain. Hint: The distance starts from John's house, and then ends at the school. How many endpoints are involved with the distance from John's house to his school? **Note also that from the geometric diagram, a ray has one end point, a segment has two end points and a line has no end points**.

5. Is the light from a flashlight a segment, a ray or a line? Hint: The ray from a flashlight has a start point and then it continues.

6. Explain what is meant by a line.

7. Name all the lines, rays, points and segments in the diagram.

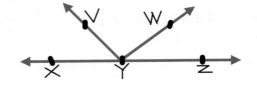

ANGLES

CLASSIFICATION OF TRIANGLES BY USING THE LENGTH OF THE SIDES

A triangle is a three sided figure.
The three types of a triangle according to the length of its sides are:
1. **equilateral triangle**
2. **isosceles triangle**
3. **scalene triangle**

Equilateral triangles are triangles that have all the three sides of equal length.
Isosceles triangles are triangles that have two or more sides of equal length.
Scalene triangles are triangles that have no sides of equal length.

Summary of Types of Triangles

Triangle Types	Description	Diagrams	Examples
Equilateral triangle	An equilateral triangle is a triangle that has all the three sides of equal lengh.		6cm, 6cm, 6cm
Isosceles triangle	An isosceles triangle is a triangle that has two or more sides of equal length.		6cm, 6cm, 6cm / 8cm, 8cm, 5cm
Scalene triangle	A scalene triangle has no sides of equal length.		3cm, 12cm, 10cm

Group Exercises — Construction

The class should be divided into four teams. The teams should be named Team A,

742

Team B, Team C, and Team D. Every team should use scissors to cut strips of colored paper measuring $\frac{1}{4}$ inch wide and 4 inches long, $\frac{1}{4}$ inch wide and 5 inches long and $\frac{1}{4}$ inch wide and 6 inch long. Each team should cut 24 pieces of each measurement.

Using the 24 pieces of each of the three types of the measurements of the paper strips, each team should:

(**a**) Join the strips at the ends to form 3 types of equilateral triangles. Sketch each type of the equilateral triangle that you have formed with the strips showing the measurements.

(**b**) Join the strips at the ends to form 3 types of isosceles triangles. Sketch each type of the isosceles triangle that you have formed with the strips showing the measurements.

(**c**) Join the strips at the ends to form 3 types of scalene triangles. Sketch each type of the scalene triangle that you have formed with the strip showing the measurements.

(**d**) All the teams should compare their sketches with the measurements.

(**e**) How many teams got all the exercises correct? Which exercises are wrong? Review the table on geometric figures to form the strips according to how an equilateral triangle, an isosceles triangle and a scalene triangle are described.

(**f**) Can you identify an equilateral triangle, an isosceles triangle, and a scalene triangle and can you describe what they are after these exercises?

TRIANGLE INEQUALITY
Test of the Requirements of the Lengths of the Sides of a Triangle to Form a Triangle

Group Exercises
The class should be divided into Team A and Team B. Each team should:

(**a**) Cut a strip of colored paper which should be $\frac{1}{4}$ in. wide with the following lengths:

   (**i**) 4 in., 6 in., 5 in.   (**ii**) 7 in., 4 in., 5 in.

(**b**) Each team should form a triangle with each set of dimension in (**a**)(**i**) and (**a**)(**ii**), by joining the ends of the paper strips.

(**c**) Is it possible to form the triangle in (**a**)(**i**) and (**a**)(**ii**) ? Explain your answer. Hint: See the rule as shown:

   Rule: The sum of the lengths of the shortest two sides of a triangle must be greater than the longest side in order to form the triangle.

Example 3
Using the rule above write an inequality regarding the lengths of the following triangles:

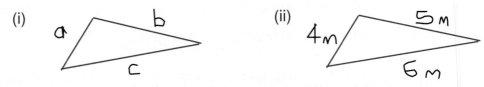

(i)   a   b   c

(ii)   4m   5 M   6 M

Note that this inequality is the condition that the side lengths of a triangle can form a triangle.

Solution

The rule contains the words "greater than" and therefore we can use the greater than sign ($>$) to write the inequality as follows:

(i) $a + b > c$ (The sum of the shortest lengths "a " and " b" is greater than the longest length c.)

(ii) 5 m. + 4 m. > 6 m.   (The sum of the shortest lengths, 5 m. and 4 m. is greater than the longest length of 6 m.)

   11 m. > 6 m.

Exercises

1. State the Rule for the Triangle Inequality.

2. Explain if each combination of side lengths can or cannot form a triangle. Hint: See Example **3**.

   (**a**) 3 ft, 6 ft, 5 ft   (**b**) 2 ft, 3 ft, 8ft   (**c**) 12 in., 5 in., 9 in.   (**d**) 6 yd, 10 yd, 8 yd

Challenge Question

3. Considering the description of an isosceles triangle and an equilateral triangle, can we say that the equilateral triangle is also an isosceles triangle? Explain.

Cumulative Review

1. Divide.

   a. 2⟌94   b. 3⟌64   c. 4⟌125

2. Add or subtract.

   a. 74   b. 226   c. 8.06
      + 38   + 491   - 2.17

3. What are parallel lines?

4. Are vertical angles equal? Explain your answer with a diagram.

5. Mary said that the median of three numbers is the middle number when the numbers are arranged in order from the lowest number to the largest number. Is her statement correct?

TYPES OF ANGLES

New Terms: **Acute angle**, **right angle**, **obtuse angle and straight angle**

The types of angles are as shown:

Acute angle

Right angle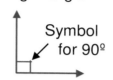

Symbol for 90º

Obtuse angle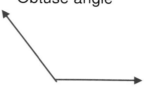

Straight angle

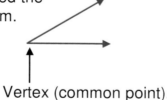

The measure of an acute angle is greater than 0º but less than 90º.

The measure of a right angle is 90º.

The measure of an obtuse angle is greater than 90º but less than 180º.

The measure of a straight angle is 180º

By observing the diagrams of the types of angles:

(1) We can write that "m∠acute < m∠right < m∠obtuse < m∠straight, where "m" stands for "measure of".

  ∠ is the symbol for angle.

  < is the symbol for "is less than"

  "m∠acute" stands for "measure of an acute angle".

  "m∠right" stands for "measure of a right angle".

  "m∠obtuse" stands for "measure of an obtuse angle".

  "m∠straight" stands for " measure of a straight angle".

(2) It can be concluded that **an angle is formed by two rays that have a common endpoint**.

This common endpoint is called the vertex as shown in the diagram.

Vertex (common point).

(**3**) A right angle is the same as an angle which has a measure of 90⁰.

Also, if two lines or two rays intersect or meet at a point such that the two lines or the two rays form a 90⁰angle, then the two lines or the two rays are said to be perpendicular to each other.

(**4**) A straight angle is the same as an angle which has a measure of 180⁰.

Review:

1. Is it true that an angle is formed by two rays that have a common endpoint? True or False? Explain.
2. Can we say that angles are classified by comparing them to 90⁰? True or False? Explain.

Exercises

1. Sketch an acute angle, an obtuse angle, a right angle and a straight angle. Hint: See section under "types of angles".
2. Classify the angles as an acute, an obtuse, a right or a straight angle. Hint: See the section on "types of angles".

(a)   (b)   (c)   (d)

3. Write a connection involving the symbol <, straight angle, acute angle, obtuse angle and right angle. Hint: See the section on "types of angles."

Measuring Angles

Angles are measured in units called degrees and the degrees are presented by the symbol ⁰. For example 90 degrees can be written using the symbol for degrees (⁰) as 90⁰. **Angles can be measured with a protractor**. Figure 1 shows the protractor with the features.

Figure 1

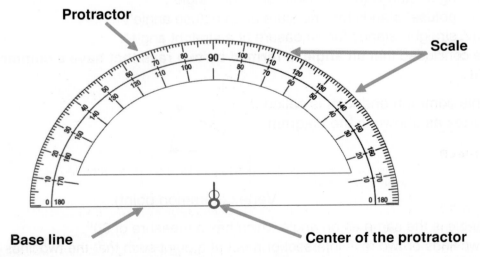

Protractor

Scale

Base line   **Center of the protractor**

There are several shapes of the protractor. However, the base line of a protractor is always the segment joining the 0⁰ and the 180⁰. The point at the middle of the segment joining the 0⁰ and the 180⁰ is the center of the protractor.

Example 1

Measure angle ABC as shown in step 1 with a protractor.

Solution

Step 1: Place the protractor on the angle to be measured so that the straight line of 0^0 and 180^0 (base line) on the protractor should be on one of the rays (the rays are BC and BA) that form the angle. The point at the middle of the 0^0 and 180^0 segment on the protractor should be on the vertex of the angle to be measured as shown in the diagram.

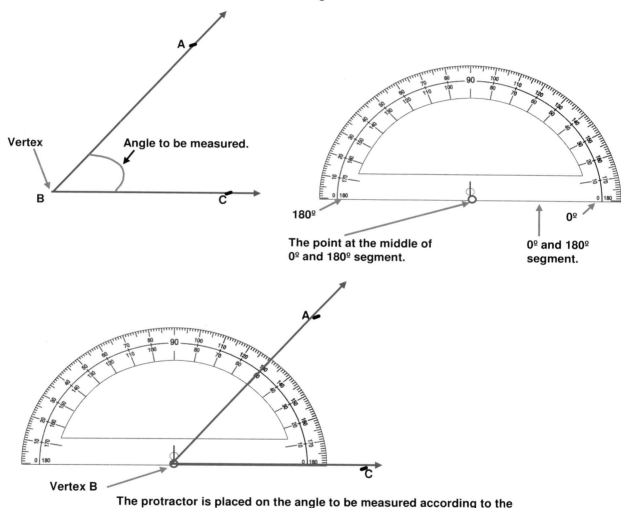

The protractor is placed on the angle to be measured according to the instructions in Step 1.

The protractor is placed on the angle to be measured according to the instructions in Step 1.

Step 2: Read the measure of the marking on the protractor that coincides with the ray BA as the measure of the angle ABC (m∠ABC). Since the ray BA coincides with the measure of 50^0 on the protractor, the measure of angle ABC is 50^0 as shown:

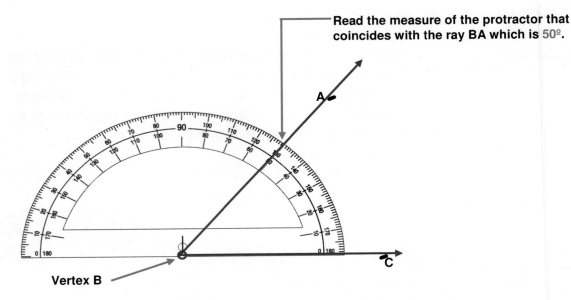

Read the measure of the protractor that coincides with the ray BA which is 50°.

Vertex B

Group Exercises

The class should be divided into four teams, Team A, Team B, Team C, and Team D.

1. Each team should use the method of "measuring angles" to measure the following angles and the measurements should be recorded. From the recorded data, indicate the angles that are acute, obtuse, right, or straight.

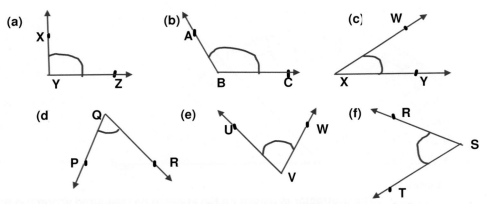

Note that the arcs specify the required angles to be measured as shown below.

Arc (required angle to be measured)

Hint: One of the rays of each of the triangles (a), (b), and (c) are horizontal as in Example 1 which makes it convenient to align and place the protractor on the angle ABC. However, triangles (d), (e), and (f) do not have one of their rays at the horizontal position, but still the angles can be measured by placing the middle of the segment joining the 0° and the 180° on the protractor on the vertex of angle ABC so that the segment (base line of the protractor) should be placed on one of the rays that forms the angle, and then follow step 2 of Example **1**.

How to Draw Angles Using a Protractor

Example 2
Use a protractor to draw an angle ABC which measures 45^0.
Solution
Step 1: Draw the ray BC of the triangle ABC horizontally.

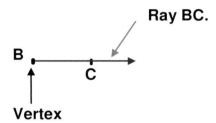

Step 2: Take a protractor and place it on the ray BC such that the point at the middle of the protractor from 0^0 to 180^0 marking coincides with the vertex (point B) and that the segment from the 0^0 to 180^0 marking on the protractor should be on the ray BC.

Take a pencil and make a dot at the location where the 45^0 marking on the protractor coincides with the paper, and label this dot as point A.

Place the protractor on the ray BC.

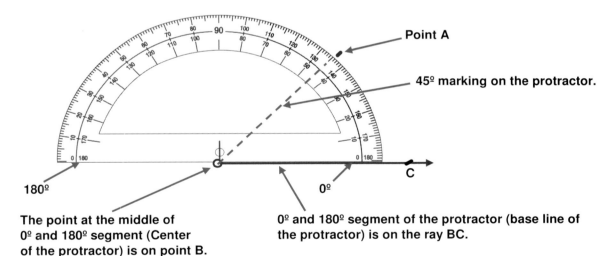

Step 3: Remove the protractor from the ray BC and set it aside. Take a pencil and a ruler. Place the edge of the ruler on point A and on the vertex B. Draw a line through point A to the vertex B. Angle ABC is the required angle which should be 45^0.

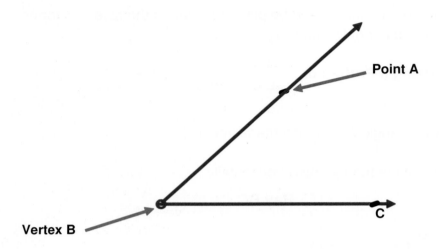

Point A

Vertex B

C

Group Exercises
The class should be divided into four teams. Each team should use a protractor to draw the following angle measures:

   (**a**) 30^0 (**b**) 42^0 (**c**) 68^0 (**d**) 90^0 (**e**) 151^0
   Hint: See Example **2**.

Exercises
1. Use the protractor to measure the following angles Hint: See Example **1**.

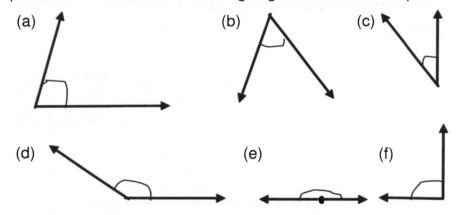

(a)   (b)   (c)

(d)   (e)   (f)

2. Use a protractor to draw $15^0, 25^0$, 28^0, 51^0, and 145^0. Hint: See Example **2**.

How to Name Angles and Measure of Angles
The symbol that represents an angle is $\angle$. The symbol that represents the measure of an angle is "$m\angle$."
The tables show how the angle and the measure of the angle Y, angle XYZ, and angle ZYX can be named in words and using symbols as shown:

Table A

Name in words	Name in symbols
Angle Y	$\angle Y$
Angle XYZ	$\angle XYZ$
Angle ZYX	$\angle ZYX$

Table B

Name in words	Name in symbols
Measure of angle Y	$m\angle Y$
Measure of angle XYZ	$m\angle XYZ$
Measure of angle ZYX	$m\angle ZYX$

Exercises

Using the fact that angle XYZ and angle ZYX represent the same angle:

1. How many possible ways can an angle be named? (one way, two ways, three ways).

2. The position of the vertex in naming an angle is at the middle, or we can say that the vertex is the middle alphabet when the angle is named using symbols; true or false? Hint: See the diagrams in Example **1** or Example **2**.

3. Use the symbols to write the following:

(**a**) Angle A   (**b**) Angle C   (**c**) Angle ABC   (**d**) Angle BCD

Hint: See Table A.

4. Use the symbols to write the following:

(**a**) measure of angle A   (**b**) measure of angle ABC   (**c**) measure of angle BCD

Hint: See Table B.

Classification of Triangles by Using the Angles

The three classifications of triangles by angles are:

1. **Acute triangle**   2. **Right triangle**

3. **Obtuse triangle**

Triangle Type	Description	Diagrams	Examples
Acute triangle	An acute triangle has three acute angles. (This means that each angle of the acute triangle is less than 90°).		
Right triangle	A right triangle has one right angle. (This means that a right triangle has one angle which is 90°).		
Obtuse triangle	An obtuse triangle has one obtuse angle. {This means that one of the angles of an obtuse triangle is more than 90°).		

Exercises

By using the table under the section Classification of "Triangles by Using the Angles," name each triangle as acute, right, obtuse triangle, or it is difficult to tell. Explain the reason for your answer.

(a) 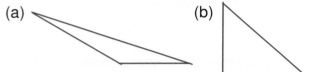   (b)   (c) 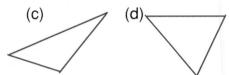   (d)

Classification of Triangles by Using Both the Length of the Sides and the Angles

The length of the sides of triangles can be used to classify triangles as equilateral, isosceles and scalene triangles, similarly, the angles of triangles can be used to classify triangles as acute, right or obtuse triangles. It is therefore, possible to give two names to a triangle as shown:

(a) **right and isosceles triangle**   (b) **acute and scalene triangle**

(c) **obtuse and scalene triangle**   (d) **right and scalene triangle**

(e) **acute and isosceles triangle**

Example 1

Use a diagram to explain each of the following statements:

(a) right and isosceles triangle   (b) acute and scalene triangle

(c) obtuse and scalene triangle   (d) right and scalene triangle

(e) acute and isosceles triangle

Solution

(a)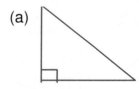

This is a right triangle because it has one right angle. This is also an isosceles triangle because it has two sides equal.

(b)

This is an acute triangle because it has three acute angles. This is also a scalene triangle because it has no sides of equal lengths.

(c)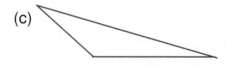

This is an obtuse triangle because it

(d)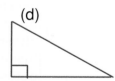

This is a right triangle because it has

has one obtuse angle. This is also a scalene triangle because it has no sides of equal lengths.

one right angle. This is also a scalene triangle because it has no sides of equal lengths.

(e)

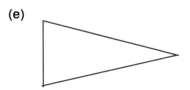

This is an acute triangle because it has three acute angles. This triangle is also an isosceles triangle because it has two sides that are equal.

Exercises

1. Complete these statements. Hint: See the section on the "Classification of Triangles by Angles."
  (**a**) An obtuse triangle has ————————————
  (**b**) A right triangle has ————————————
  (**c**) An acute triangle has ————————————
2. Sketch the following triangles. Hint: See the section on the "Classification of Triangles by Using Angles" and Example **1**.
  (**a**) Right angle triangle.   (**b**) Acute triangle.   (**c**) Obtuse triangle.
  (**d**) A triangle which is both a right and an isosceles.
  (**e**) A triangle which is both an obtuse and a scalene.
  (**f**) A triangle which is both an acute and a scalene.
  (**g**) A triangle which is both a right and a scalene.

Challenge Questions

3. How many obtuse angles does an obtuse triangle have?
4. How many right angles does a right triangle have?
5. Is it correct to say that a scalene triangle has three equal angles? Explain.

HOW TO SOLVE FOR UNKNOWN ANGLES IN GEOMETRIC SHAPES

Triangles

To solve for the unknown angle in a triangle, the following properties of the triangle are used:

1. The sum of the measures of the angles in any triangle is 180^0.
2. One of the measures of the angles of a right triangle is 90^0.
3. An isosceles triangle has at least two congruent sides, and therefore, an isosceles triangle has at least two angles of equal measures.
4. An equilateral triangle has three congruent sides, and therefore, an equilateral triangle has three equal measures of angles.

To Solve for the Unknown Angle of a Triangle by Using the Property of the Sum of the Measures of the Angles in Any Triangle is 180^0.

Example 1
Write and solve an equation to find x.

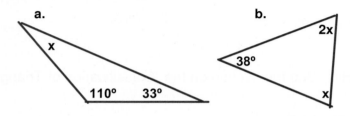
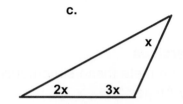

Solution
a. An equation can be written in order to find x as shown:

$x + 110^0 + 33^0 = 180^0$ Because the sum of the measures of angles in any triangle is 180^0.

$x + 110^0 - 110^0 + 33^0 - 33^0 = 180^0 - 110^0 - 33^0$ Move similar or like terms to one side of the equation by subtracting 110^0 and 33^0 from both sides of the equation.

$x = 180^0 - 143^0$ $- 110^0 - 33^0 = -143^0$
     $110^0 - 110^0 = 0$ and $33^0 - 33^0 = 0$.

$x = 37^0$ $180^0 - 143^0 = 37^0$

b. An equation can be written in order to find x as shown:

$x + 2x + 38^0 = 180^0$ Because the sum of the measures of angles in any triangle is 180^0.

$x + 2x + 38^0 - 38^0 = 180^0 - 38^0$ Move similar or like terms to one side of the equation by subtracting 38^0 from both sides of the equation.

$x + 2x = 180^0 - 38^0$ Now we have the like terms in x on the left side of the equation and the like terms in degrees are on the right side of the equation.

$3x = 142^0$ Simplify both sides of the equation, $x + 2x = 3x$ and $180^0 - 38^0 = 142^0$.

754

$$\frac{3x}{3} = \frac{142^0}{3}$$

Divide both sides of the equation by 3 in order to obtain the value of x.

$$\frac{3\overset{x}{\cancel{3x}}}{\underset{1}{\cancel{3}}} = \frac{142^0}{3}$$

$$x = \frac{142^0}{3} = 47\frac{1}{3}^0$$

c. $x + 2x + 3x = 180^0$

Because the sum of the measures of the angles of any triangle is 180^0.

$6x = 180^0$

Simplify or add the like terms.

$$\frac{6x}{6} = \frac{180^0}{6}$$

Divide both sides of the equation by 6 in order to obtain the value of x.

$$\frac{\overset{x}{\cancel{6x}}}{\underset{1}{\cancel{6}}} = \frac{\overset{30^0}{\cancel{180^0}}}{\underset{1}{\cancel{6}}}$$

Do the division by 6

$$x = 30^0$$

To Solve for the Unknown Angle of a Triangle by Using the Property of One of the Measures of a Right Angle of a Triangle is 90^0

Example 2

Write and solve an equation to find x.

a.

30°

2x

b.

x

2x

c.

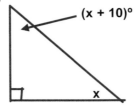

(x + 10)°

x

Solution

Special Note: A right angle may be written as 90°.

 This is the symbol for a right angle which is 90°.

a. The triangle is a right triangle and therefore one of the angles is 90^0.
Therefore, an equation can be written to solve for x as shown:

$2x + 30^0 + 90^0 = 180^0$
        Because the sum of the measures of the angles of any triangle is 180^0.

$2x + 30^0 - 30^0 + 90^0 - 90^0 = 180^0 - 30^0 - 90^0$

        Move similar or like terms to one side of the equation by subtracting 30^0 and 90^0 from both sides of the equation.

$2x = 180^0 - 120^0$ $-30^0 - 90^0 = -120^0$

$2x = 60^0$ $180^0 - 120^0 = 60^0$

$$\frac{2x}{2} = \frac{60^0}{2}$$ Divide both sides of the equation by 2 in order to obtain the value of x.

$$\frac{\overset{x}{\cancel{2x}}}{\underset{1}{2}} = \frac{\overset{30^0}{\cancel{60^0}}}{\underset{1}{2}}$$ Do the division.

$$x = 30^0$$

b. The triangle is a right triangle and therefore one of the angles is 90^0.
Therefore, an equation can be written to solve for x as shown:

$2x + x + 90^0 = 180^0$ Because the sum of the measures of the angles of any triangle is 180^0.

$2x + x + 90^0 - 90^0 = 180^0 - 90^0$ Move similar or like terms to one side of the equation by subtracting 90^0 from both sides of the equation.

$2x + x = 180^0 - 90^0$ Now we have like terms on both sides of the equation. $90^0 - 90^0 = 0$

$3x = 90^0$ $2x + x = 3x$ and $180^0 - 90^0 = 90^0$

$$\frac{3x}{3} = \frac{90^0}{3}$$ Divide both sides of the equation by 3 in order to obtain the value of x.

$$\frac{3\overset{x}{\cancel{3x}}}{\underset{1}{\cancel{3}}} = \frac{90^0 \overset{30^0}{}}{\underset{1}{\cancel{3}}}$$ Do the division by 3

$$x = 30^0$$

c. The triangle is a right triangle and therefore one of the angles is 90^0.
Therefore, an equation can be written to solve for x as shown:

$x + (x + 10)^0 + 90^0 = 180^0$ Because the sum of the measures of the
                                                    angles of any triangle is 180^0.

$x + x^0 + 10^0 + 90^0 = 180^0$ $(x + 10)^0 = x^0 + 10^0$

$x + x + 10^0 + 90^0 = 180^0$ Let x^0 be x.

$x + x + 10^0 - 10^0 + 90^0 - 90^0 = 180^0 - 10^0 - 90^0$

Move similar or like terms to one side of the
equation by subtracting 10^0 and 90^0 from
both sides of the equation.

$x + x = 180^0 - 10^0 - 90^0$ Now we have similar or like terms on each side
                                            of the equation. $10^0 - 10^0 = 0$ and $90^0 - 90^0 = 0$.

$2x = 180^0 - 100^0$ Simplify, $x + x = 2x$ and $- 10^0 - 90^0 = -100^0$.

$2x = 80^0$ Simplify, $180^0 - 100^0 = 80^0$.

$$\frac{2x}{2} = \frac{80^0}{2}$$ Divide both sides of the equation by 2 in order to
                                        obtain the value of x.

$$\frac{2\overset{x}{\cancel{2x}}}{\underset{1}{\cancel{2}}} = \frac{80^0 \overset{40^0}{}}{\underset{1}{\cancel{2}}}$$ Do the division.

$$x = 40^0$$

**To solve for the unknown angle of a triangle by using the property of an
isosceles triangle which states that an isosceles triangle has at least two
congruent sides and therefore, an isosceles triangle has at least two angles of
equal measures, and also by using the property of the sum of the measures
of the angles in any triangle is 180^0 as similarly done in Examples 1 and 2.**

**To solve for the unknown angle of a triangle by using the property of an
equilateral triangle which states that an equilateral triangle has three congruent
sides, and therefore an equilateral triangle has three equal measures of angles,**

and also by using the property of the sum of the measures of the angles in any triangle is 180^0 as similarly done in Examples 1 and 2.

Exercises

1. Write and solve an equation to find x. Hint: See Example **1a**.

a.
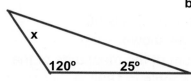

b.
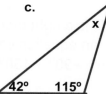

c.
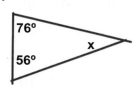

d.
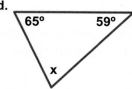

e.
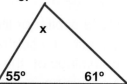

f.
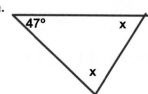

2. Write and solve an equation to find x. Hint: See Example **1b**.

a.
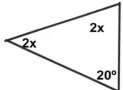

b.
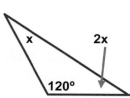

c.
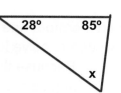

3. Find the value of x in each triangle.

a.
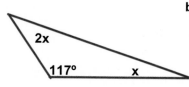

b.
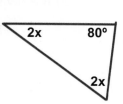

c.
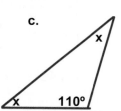

4. Write and solve an equation to find x. Hint: See Example **1c**.

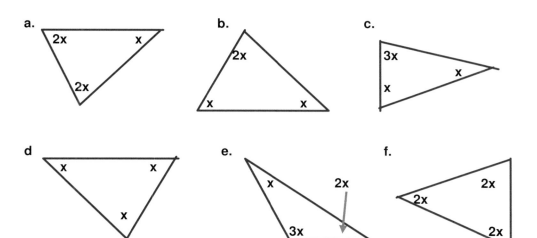

5. Write and solve an equation to find n. Hint: See Example **2a**.

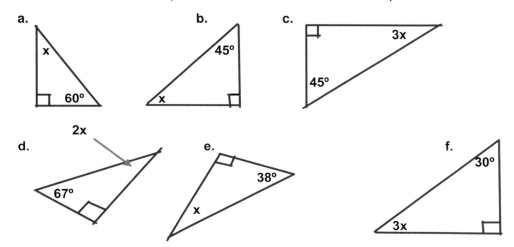

6. Write and solve an equation to find x. Hint: See Example 2b.

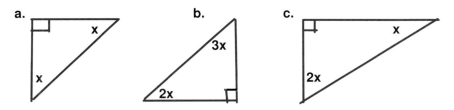

7. Write and solve an equation to find n. Hint: See Example 2c.

a.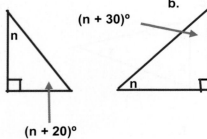

$(n + 30)°$

b.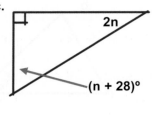

c.

$2n$

$(n + 28)°$

$(n + 20)°$

Answers to Selected Questions

1a. 35^0 **2a.** $66\frac{1}{2}^0$ **3a.** 21^0

4a. 36^0 **5a.** 30^0 **6a.** 45^0 **7a.** 35^0

Challenge Questions

7. Find the value of x in each triangle.

a.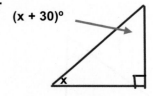

$(x + 30)°$

x

b.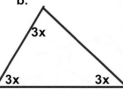

3x

3x   3x

c.

60°

x

x

d.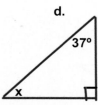

37°

x

e.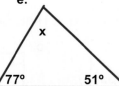

x

77°   51°

f.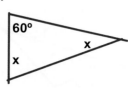

69°

42°   x

g.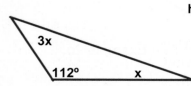

3x

112°   x

h.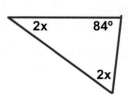

2x   84°

2x

i.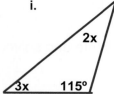

2x

3x   115°

PARALLELOGRAMS

To solve for the unknown angle in a parallelogram, the following properties of the parallelogram are used:

1. The sum of the measures of the angles in any quadrilateral, including the parallelogram is 360^0. A rectangle is also a parallelogram. Recall that a quadrilateral is a four sided figure.

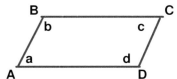

Parallellogram ABCD is a quadrilateral and the sum of the measure of the angles of any quadrilalteral is 360º.

> **Therefore, $m\angle A + m\angle B + m\angle C + m\angle D = 360^0$,**
> or **$a + b + c + d = 360^0$.**

2. The measure of the opposite angles of any parallelogram are equal.

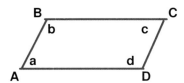

> In the parallelogram ABCD, $\angle$**A is opposite to** $\angle$C **and** $\angle$B **is opposite to** $\angle$**D.**
> **Therefore, $m\angle A = m\angle C$ and $m\angle B = m\angle D$,**
> or **$a = c$ and $b = d$.**

3. The consecutive angles of a parallelogram are supplementary.
   Two angles are supplementary if the sum of their measures is 180^0.

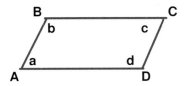

> In the parallelogram ABCD, the consecutive angles are:
> $\angle$**A and** $\angle$**B,** $\angle$**B and** $\angle$**C,** $\angle$**C and** $\angle$**D,** $\angle$**D and** $\angle$**A.**
> Therefore, **$m\angle A + m\angle B = 180^0$, or $a + b = 180^0$.**
> **$m\angle B + m\angle C = 180^0$, or $b + c = 180^0$.**
> **$m\angle C + m\angle D = 180^0$, or $c + d = 180^0$.**
> **$m\angle D + m\angle A = 180^0$, or $d + a = 180^0$.**

To solve for the unknown angle of a parallelogram by using the property of the sum of the measures of the angles in any quadrilateral, including the

parallelogram is 360^0. A rectangle is also a parallelogram.

Example 1

Find the measure of angle C and also find the value of n in each parallelogram.

a.

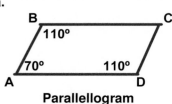

Parallellogram

b.

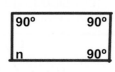

Rectangle

Solution

a. $70^0 + 110^0 + m\angle C + 110^0 = 360^0$ Because the sum of the measures of the angles in any parallelogram is 360^0.

$70^0 - 70^0 + 110^0 - 110^0 + m\angle C + 110^0 - 110^0 = 360^0 - 70^0 - 110^0 - 110^0$.

Move similar or like terms to one side of the equation by subtracting 70^0, 110^0, and 110^0 from both sides of the equation.

$m\angle C = 360^0 - 70^0 - 110^0 - 110^0$.   Now we have similar or like terms on each side of the equation. $70^0 - 70^0 = 0$ and $110^0 - 110^0 = 0$.

$m\angle C = 360^0 - 270^0$ Simplify, $- 70^0 - 110^0 - 110^0 = -270^0$.
$m\angle C = 90^0$ Simplify, $360^0 - 270^0 = 90^0$.

b. $n + 90^0 + 90^0 + 90^0 = 360^0$ Because the sum of the measures of the angles in any parallelogram is 360^0.

$n + 90^0 - 90^0 + 90^0 - 90^0 + 90^0 - 90^0 = 360^0 - 90^0 - 90^0 - 90^0$

Move similar or like terms to one side of the equation by subtracting 90^0, 90^0 and 90^0 from both sides of the equation.

$n = 360^0 - 90^0 - 90^0 - 90^0$ Now we have similar or like terms on each side of the equation. $90^0 - 90^0 = 0$.

$n = 360^0 - 270^0$ Simplify, $- 90^0 - 90^0 - 90^0 = -270^0$
$n = 90^0$ Simplify, $360^0 - 270^0 = 90^0$

How to Solve for the Unknown Angle of a Parallelogram by Using the Property of the Measure of the Opposite Angles of any Parallelogram are Equal

Example 2
Find the measure of the angles represented by b and x.

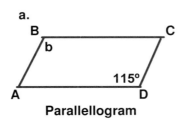

a.

Parallellogram

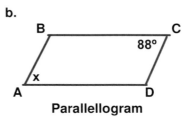

b.

Parallellogram

a. $\angle$B is opposite to $\angle$D and since the measure of the opposite angles of a parallelogram are equal, the m$\angle$B is equal to the m$\angle$D.
Therefore m$\angle$D $= $ m$\angle$B $= $ b $= 115^0$

b. Using similar reasoning as in Example 2a, x $= 88^0$.

How to Solve for the Unknown Angle of a Parallelogram by Using the Property of the Consecutive Angles of a Parallelogram are Supplementary

Two angles are **supplementary** if the sum of their measures is 180^0.

Example 3
Find the angle measure represented by n and x in the parallelograms.

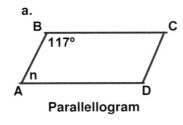

a.

Parallellogram

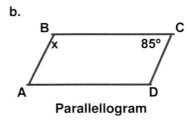

b.

Parallellogram

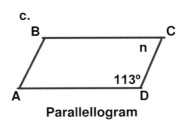

c.

Parallellogram

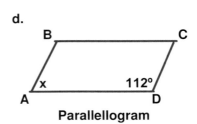

d.

Parallellogram

Solution
a. $\angle$A and $\angle$B are consecutive angles because there are no other angles between them. In any parallelogram, the consecutive angles are supplementary, and

763

therefore:

$n + 117^0 = 180^0$ Two angles are **supplementary** if the sum of their measures is 180^0.

$n + 117^0 - 117^0 = 180^0 - 117^0$ Move similar or like terms to one side of the equation by subtracting 117^0, from both sides of the equation.

$n = 180^0 - 117^0$ Now we have similar or like terms on each side of the equation. $117^0 - 117^0 = 0$.

$n = 63^0$.

b. $\angle B$ and $\angle C$ are consecutive angles because there are no other angles between them. In any parallelogram, the consecutive angles are **supplementary**, and therefore:

$x + 85^0 = 180^0$ Two angles are **supplementary** if the sum of their measures is $180^?$

$x + 85^0 - 85^0 = 180^0 - 85^0$ Move similar or like terms to one side of the equation by subtracting 85^0, from both sides of the equation.

$x = 180^0 - 85^0$ Now we have similar or like terms on each side of the equation. $85^0 - 85^0 = 0$.

$x = 95^0$.

c. $\angle B$ and $\angle C$ are consecutive angles because there are no other angles between them. In any parallelogram, the consecutive angles are **supplementary**, and therefore:

$x + 85^0 = 180^0$ Two angles are **supplementary** if the sum of their measures is 180^0.

$x + 85^0 - 85^0 = 180^0 - 85^0$ Move similar or like terms to one side of the equation by subtracting 85^0, from both sides of the equation.

$x = 180^0 - 85^0$ Now we have similar or like terms on each side of the equation. $85^0 - 85^0 = 0$.

$x = 95^0$.

c. $\angle C$ and $\angle D$ are consecutive angles because there are no other angles between them. In any parallelogram, the consecutive angles are supplementary, and therefore:

$n + 113^0 = 180^0$ Two angles are **supplementary** if the sum of their measures is 180^0.

$n + 113^0 - 113^0 = 180^0 - 113^0$ Move similar or like terms to one side of the equation by subtracting 113^0, from both sides of the equation.

$n = 180^0 - 113^0$

Now we have similar or like terms on each side of the equation. $113^0 - 113^0 = 0$.

$n = 67^0$.

d. $\angle A$ and $\angle D$ are consecutive angles because there are no other angles between them. In any parallelogram, the consecutive angles are supplementary, and therefore:

$x + 112^0 = 180^0$

Two angles are **supplementary** if the sum of their measures is 180^0.

$x + 112^0 - 112^0 = 180^0 - 112^0$

Move similar or like terms to one side of the equation by subtracting 112^0, from both sides of the equation.

$x = 180^0 - 112^0$

Now we have similar or like terms on each side of the equation. $112^0 - 112^0 = 0$.

$x = 68^0$

Exercises

1. Write all the three properties of the parallelogram that are used to find the unknown angles of a parallelogram.
2. Explain what is meant by the consecutive angles of a parallelogram.
   Hint: See Example **3a**.
3. The measure of the opposite angles of a parallelogram are equal. True or false?
   Hint: See Example **2**.
4. The sum of the measure of supplementary angles is 180^0. True or false?
   Hint: See Example **3**.
5. The measure of any consecutive angles of a parallelogram is supplementary.
   True or false? Hint: See Example **3**.
6. Find the measure of the unknown angle in each parallelogram. Hint: See Example **1**.

   a.
   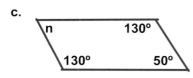

   b.
   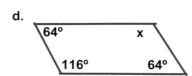

   c.
   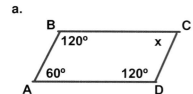

   d.
   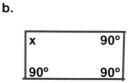

7. Find the measure of the angles represented by b and x. Hint: See Example **2**.

a.

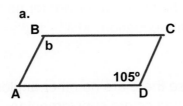

b.

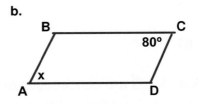

c.

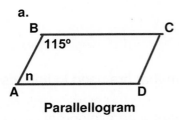

d.

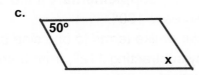

8. Find the angle measure represented by n and x in the parallelogram.
Hint: See Example **3**.

a.

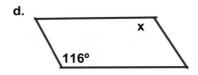

Parallellogram

b.

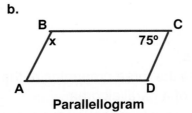

Parallellogram

c.

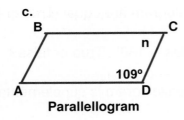

Parallellogram

d.

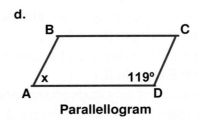

Parallellogram

e.

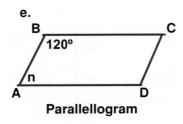

Parallellogram

f.

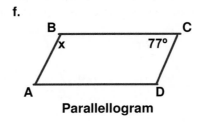

Parallellogram

g.

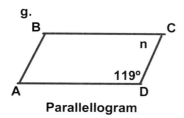

Parallellogram

h.

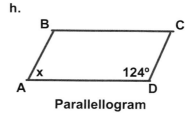

Parallellogram

Answers to selected questions

6a. 60^0 **7a.** 105^0 **8a.** 65^0

RHOMBUSES

To solve for the unknown angle in rhombuses, the following properties of the rhombuses are used:

A rhombus is an equilateral quadrilateral and all rhombuses are parallelograms. Since all rhombuses are parallelograms, the three preceding properties of the parallelograms that are listed under the section "Parallelograms" is also true for the rhombuses as shown:

1. The sum of the measures of the angles in any parallelogram is 360^0. A rhombus is also a parallelogram.

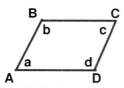

A rhombus is also a parallelogram.

Rhombus ABCD is a quadrilateral and the sum of the measures of the angles of any quadrilalteral is 360°.

Therefore, $m\angle A + m\angle B + m\angle C + m\angle D = 360^0$,
or $a + b + c + d = 360^0$.

2. The measure of the opposite angles of any parallelogram, including the rhombus are equal.

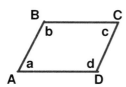

A rhombus is also a parallelogram.

In the rhombus ABCD or In the parallelogram ABCD, $\angle A$ is opposite to $\angle C$,

767

Therefore, m∠A = m∠C and m∠B = m∠D,
or **a = c and b = d.**

3. The consecutive angles of a parallelogram, including a rhombus are supplementary.

Two angles are **supplementary if the sum of their measures is 180^0.**

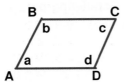

A rhombus is also a parallelogram.

In the rhombus ABCD or in the parallelogram ABCD, the consecutive angles are:
∠**A and** ∠**B,** ∠**B and** ∠**C,** ∠**C and** ∠**D,** ∠**D and** ∠**A.**
Therefore, **m∠A + m∠B = 180^0, or a + b = 180^0.**
m∠B + m∠C = 180^0, or b + c = 180^0.
m∠C + m∠D = 180^0, or c + d = 180^0.
m∠D + m∠A = 180^0, or d + a = 180^0.

Note that two angles form **consecutive angles** if there is no other angle between them.

To solve for the unknown angle of a rhombus by using the properties of the rhombus, see the worked examples under the section "Parallelograms" because rhombuses are also parallelograms. Also, the exercises under the section "Parallelograms" apply to the rhombuses.

TRAPEZOIDS

To solve for the unknown angle in a trapezoid, the following properties of the trapezoid are used:

1. The trapezoid, including the isosceles trapezoid is a quadrilateral that has one pair of parallel sides and the sum of the measures of the angles in any quadrilateral is 360^0.

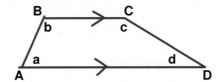

Segment BC and segment AD are the parallel sides of the trapezoid ABCD.

Trapezoid ABCD is a quadrilateral and the sum of the measures of the angles of any quadrilalteral is 360º.

Therefore, **m∠A + m∠B + m∠C + m∠D = 360⁰**,
or **a + b + c + d = 360⁰**.

2. The **isosceles trapezoid** is a trapezoid that has **a pair of equal legs and the measure of each pair of base angles are equal.**

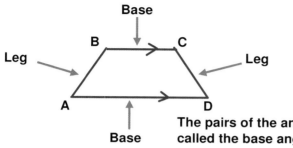

Segment BC and segment AD are the parallel sides of the trapezoid ABCD. The parallel sides of a trapezoid are called the bases and the nonparallelel sides are called the legs. The pairs of the angles that include each base are called the base angles. In trapeziod ABCD, the two pairs of the base angles are:

∠B and ∠C
∠A and ∠D

The measure of the base angles of a trapezoid do not have any special relationship unless the legs of the trapezoid are equal. In the trapezoid ABCD, the length of the leg AB is equal to the length of the leg CD. Therefore, the correct name of the trapezoid ABCD is isosceles trapezoid. Therefore, an isosceles trapezoid is a trapezoid that has equal legs.

In an **isosceles trapezoid**, each **pair of the base angles are equal**.
Therefore, in the isosceles trapezoid ABCD:

m∠B = m∠C and,
m∠A = m∠D

To solve for the unknown angle of a trapezoid by using the property of the trapezoid, that states that the measures of the angles in any quadrilateral is 360⁰, see the worked examples under the section "Parallelograms" because trapezoids and parallelograms are quadrilaterals. Also, the exercises under the section "Parallelograms" apply to the trapezoids.

To solve for the unknown angle of a trapezoid by using the property of the trapezoid, that states that the isosceles trapezoid is a trapezoid that has a pair of equal legs and the measure of each pair of base angles are equal.

Example 1
Find the value of n in each isosceles trapezoid.

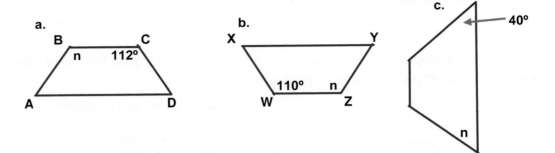

Solution

a. n = 112⁰ because the measures of the two pairs of the base angles of an isosceles trapezoid are equal. The two pairs of the equal measures of the base angles are as shown:

$$m\angle B = m\angle C \text{ and}$$
$$m\angle A = m\angle D$$

b. n = 110⁰ because the measures of the two pairs of the base angles of an isosceles trapezoid are equal. The two pairs of the equal measures of the base angles are as shown:

$$m\angle X = m\angle Y \text{ and}$$
$$m\angle W = m\angle Z$$

c. n = 40⁰ because the measures of the two pairs of the base angles of an isosceles trapezoid are equal.

Example 2

Find the value of x in each isosceles trapezoid. Hint: Use the combination of two properties of the isosceles trapezoid to find x. The two isosceles trapezoid properties are the measures of the two pairs of the base angles of an isosceles trapezoid are equal and the sum of the measures of the angles in a quadrilateral, including the trapezoid is 360⁰.

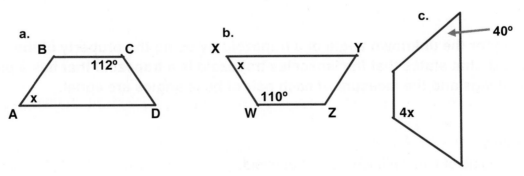

Solution

a. The measures of the two pairs of the base angles of an isosceles trapezoid are equal. Therefore, $m\angle B = m\angle C$ and $m\angle A = m\angle D$ and this can be shown in diagram form as shown:

The sum of the measures of the angles in a quadrilateral, including the trapezoid is 360^0, and therefore:

$$112^0 + 112^0 + x + x = 360^0$$

$$224^0 + 2x = 360^0 \qquad \text{Simplify, } 112^0 + 112^0 = 224^0 \text{ and } x + x = 2x.$$

$$224^0 - 224^0 + 2x = 360^0 - 224^0 \qquad \text{Subtract } 224^0 \text{ from both sides of the equation in order to isolate } 2x.$$

$$2x = 360^0 - 224^0 \qquad \text{Now, we have isolated } 2x, 224^0 - 224^0 = 0.$$

$$2x = 136^0 \qquad 360^0 - 224^0 = 136^0$$

$$\frac{2x}{2} = \frac{136^0}{2} \qquad \text{Divide both sides of the equation } 2x = 136^0$$
by 2 to obtain the value of x.

$$\frac{\overset{x}{\cancel{2x}}}{\underset{1}{\cancel{2}}} = \frac{\overset{68^0}{\cancel{136^0}}}{\underset{1}{\cancel{2}}} \qquad \text{Do the division. Review the section on division.}$$

$$x = 68^0$$

b. The measures of the two pairs of the base angles of an isosceles trapezoid are equal. Therefore, $m\angle X = m\angle Y$ and $m\angle W = m\angle Z$ and this can be shown in diagram form as shown:

The sum of the measures of the angles in a quadrilateral, including the trapezoid is 360^0, and therefore:

$$x + x + 110^0 + 110^0 = 360^0$$

$$2x + 220^0 = 360^0 \qquad \text{Simplify, } x + x = 2x \text{ and } 110^0 + 110^0 = 220^0.$$

$$2x + 220^0 - 220^0 = 360^0 - 220^0 \qquad \text{Subtract } 220^0 \text{ from both sides of the equation}$$
$$2x + 220^0 = 360^0 \text{ in order to isolate } 2x.$$

771

$$2x = 360^0 - 220^0$$
$$2x = 140^0$$

Now, we have isolated 2x, $220^0 - 220^0 = 0$. $360^0 - 220^0$.

$$\frac{2x}{2} = \frac{140^0}{2}$$

Divide both sides of the equation $2x = 140^0$ by 2 in order to obtain the value of x.

$$\frac{\overset{x}{\cancel{2x}}}{\underset{1}{\cancel{2}}} = \frac{\overset{70^0}{\cancel{140^0}}}{\underset{1}{\cancel{2}}}$$

Do the division by 2.

$$x = 70^0$$

c. The measures of the two pairs of the base angles of an isosceles trapezoid are equal. Therefore, this can be shown in diagram form as shown:

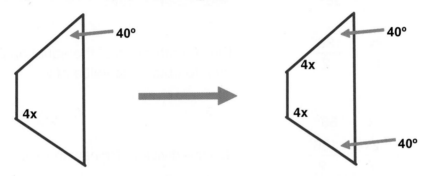

The sum of the measures of the angles in a quadrilateral, including the trapezoid is 360^0, and therefore:

$$4x + 4x + 40^0 + 40^0 = 360^0$$
$$8x + 80^0 = 360^0$$
$$8x + 80^0 - 80^0 = 360^0 - 80^0$$

Simplify, $4x + 4x = 8x$ and $40^0 + 40^0 = 80^0$.
Subtract 80^0 from both sides of the equation $8x + 80^0 = 360^0$ in order to isolate 8x.

$$8x = 360^0 - 80^0$$
$$8x = 280^0$$

Now, we have isolated 8x, $80^0 - 80^0 = 0$. $360^0 - 80^0 = 280^0$

$$\frac{8x}{8} = \frac{280^0}{8}$$

Divide both sides of the equation $8x = 280^0$ by 8 in order to obtain the value of x.

$$\frac{\overset{x}{\cancel{8x}}}{\underset{1}{\cancel{8}}} = \frac{\overset{35^0}{\cancel{280^0}}}{\underset{1}{\cancel{8}}}$$

Do the division. Review the chapter on division.

$$x = 35^0$$

Exercises

1. A trapezoid is a quadrilateral. True or false?
2. What is an isosceles trapezoid?
3. The sum of the measures of the angles of a trapezoid is 360^0. True or false.
4. Explain what is meant by the bases of a trapezoid?
5. Explain what is meant by the base angles of a trapezoid.
6. The pairs of base angles of an isosceles trapezoid are equal. True or false.
7. Find the value of x in each isosceles trapezoid. Hint: See Example **1**.

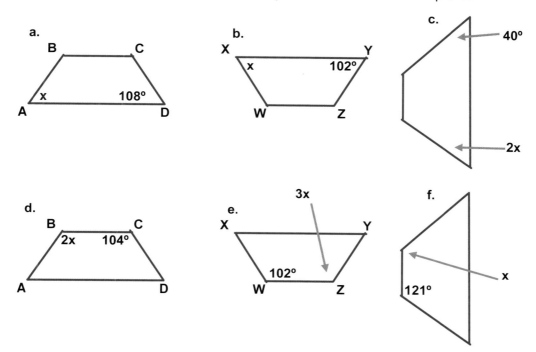

8. Find the value of x in each isosceles trapezoid. Hint: Use the combination of two properties of the isosceles trapezoid to find x. The two isosceles trapezoid properties are the measures of the two pairs of the base angles of an isosceles trapezoid are equal and the sum of the measures of the angles in a quadrilateral, including the trapezoid is 360^0. Hint: See Example 2.

a.

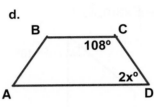

B   C
108°
x
A   D

b.

X   Y
x
102°
W   Z

c.

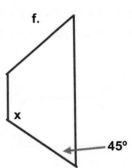

40°
2x

d.

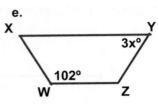

B   C
108°
2x°
A   D

e.

X   Y
3x°
102°
W   Z

f.

x
45°

Answers to Selected Questions
7a. 108^0 **8a.** 72^0

Challenge Questions
9. Find the value of x in each isosceles trapezoid.

a.

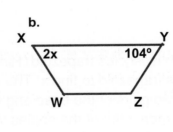

B   C
116°
x
A   D

b.

X   Y
2x   104°
W   Z

c.

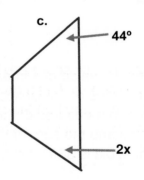

44°

2x

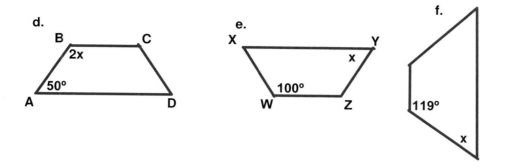

d.

e.

f.

CIRCLES

RADIUS, DIAMETER, AND CHORD

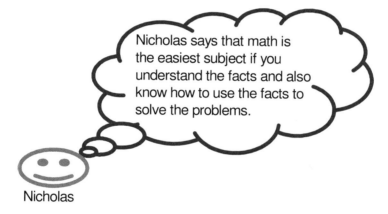

Nicholas says that math is the easiest subject if you understand the facts and also know how to use the facts to solve the problems.

Nicholas

A **circle** is a closed plane figure such that all the points on it are the same distance from the center. A **radius** (plural of radius is radii) is the distance from the center of a circle to any point on the circle. Therefore, we can also say that the radius of a circle is the line segment with one endpoint on the circle and the other endpoint at the center of the circle.

Could you give two examples of objects that are in the form of a circle?

An example of an object in the form of a circle is the bicycle wheel. The spokes of the wheel represent the radii of the circle and the spokes join at a fixed point called the center of the wheel or hub, as shown in the drawing on the next page.

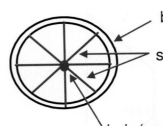 bicycle wheel (the wheel is like a circle).

spokes (the spokes are similar to the radius of a circle).

hub (center of the wheel, which is similar to the center of the circle).

The **chord** of a circle is the line segment that connects two points on a circle.

The **diameter** of a circle is the chord that passes through the center of the circle.

In the diagram,

(1) The fixed point O is the center of the circle.

(2) $\overline{AB}$ is the diameter.

(3) $\overline{AO}$ is a radius.

(4) $\overline{OB}$ is a radius.

(5) $\overline{EO}$ is the radius.

(6) $\overline{CD}$ is the chord.

(7) $\overline{AB}$ and $\overline{CD}$ are chords.

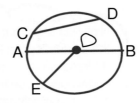

In any specific circle,

1. all radii have the same length
2. any radius = the diameter ÷ 2
3. the radius is one half of the diameter
4. all the diameters have the same length
5. the longest chord is the diameter
6. diameter = 2 × radius
7. all the radii meet at a fixed point, all the diameters intercept at a fixed point and all the radii and the diameters meet at a fixed point called the center.

Example 1

In the diagram, O is the center of the circle.

(a) $\overline{AB}$ is a diameter?

(b) $\overline{AO}$, $\overline{OG}$, and $\overline{OB}$ are radii?

(c) $\overline{CD}$, $\overline{CE}$, $\overline{DE}$, $\overline{EF}$, and $\overline{DF}$ are chords?

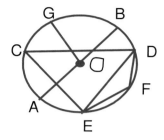

Solution

(**a**) $\overline{AB}$ is a diameter because $\overline{AB}$ passes through the center of the circle at point O, and $\overline{AB}$ is a chord. (**Note** that a chord is a line segment that connects two points on a circle and the chord that passes through the center of the circle is the diameter.)

(**b**) $\overline{AO}$, $\overline{OG}$, and $\overline{OB}$ are radii because they are line segments with one endpoint at the center of the circle, which is point O, and the other endpoints on the circle at points A, G and B.

(**c**) $\overline{CD}$, $\overline{CE}$, $\overline{DE}$, $\overline{EF}$, and $\overline{DF}$ are chords because they are line segments that connect two points on the circle and they do not pass through the center of the circle.

Example 2

(**a**) The diameter of a circle is 4 inches. How long is the radius?

(**b**) The radius of a circle is 9 inches. How long is the diameter?

Solution

(**a**) Diameter = 4 inches

Diameter = 2 × radius   (Review the preceding notes.)

$$\frac{\text{Diameter}}{2} = \frac{2 \times \text{radius}}{2}$$ (Divide each side of the equation in order to obtain the value of the radius.)

$$\frac{\text{Diameter}}{2} = \frac{\overset{1}{2} \times \text{radius}}{\underset{1}{2}}$$

$$\frac{\text{Diameter}}{2} = \text{radius} \quad\rule{3cm}{0.4pt}[\,A\,]$$

$$\frac{4 \text{ inches}}{2} = \text{radius}$$ (Substitute diameter = 4 inches Into equation $[\,A\,]$.)

$$\frac{\overset{2}{\cancel{4 \text{ inches}}}}{\underset{1}{\cancel{2}}} = \text{radius}$$

2 inches = radius

(**b**) Radius   = 9 inches

Diameter = 2 × radius   ─────────────────[B]

Diameter = 2 × 9 inches   (Substitute radius = 9 inches into equation [B].)

Diameter = 18 inches.

Exercises

1. In the diagram, the center of the circle is point O.

(**a**) List two line segments that passe through the center of the circle.

(**b**) List all the diameters, radii and chords. Hint : See Example **1**.

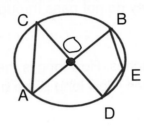

2. In the diagram, classify the line segments as radius, diameter or chord. Give reasons for your answer. The center of the circle is point O. Hint: See Example **1**.

(a) $\overline{DE}$ (e) $\overline{CO}$

(b) $\overline{AO}$ (f) $\overline{BD}$

(c) $\overline{AE}$ (g) $\overline{OB}$

(d) $\overline{AB}$

3. (**a**) The diameter of a circle is 10 inches. How long is the radius? Hint: See Example 2.

(**b**) The radius of a circle is 7 cm. How long is the diameter? Hint: See Example 2.

How to Draw a Circle
Group Exercise

Objective: To draw a circle which has a radius of 3 centimeters.

Materials that are needed in order to construct a circle are a ruler, a pencil, and a compass. A compass is a device for drawing circles. There are many types of compasses.

778

A Compass

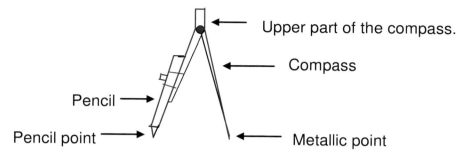

Step 1: Take a pencil and mark a point P which will be the center of the circle.

Step 2: Take a compass and a ruler. Put the ruler on the table with the centimeter scale showing upwards. Put the metallic point of the compass on the zero mark of the centimeter scale of the ruler, and then open the compass such that the pencil point should be on the 3 centimeter mark on the ruler. (**Note** that how much the compass is opened determines the length of the radius.)

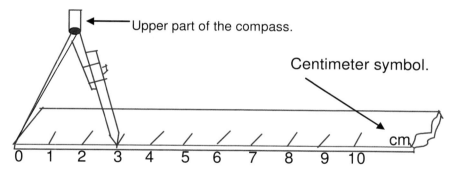

(The smaller markings on the centimeter scale have been omitted.)

Step 3: (**Caution**: we must keep the compass opening from Step 2 the same in order to maintain the 3 centimeter radius of the circle by holding only the upper part of the compass.)

By holding the upper part of the compass, put the metallic point of the compass on point P and with the pencil point touching the paper, swing the pencil point of the compass around (through 360°) to draw a circle.

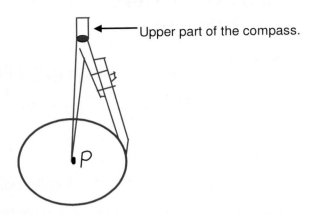

Upper part of the compass.

We can draw a diameter to the circle by drawing a line segment through the center of the circle at point P such that the line segment should touch the two opposite sides of the circle at points A and B.

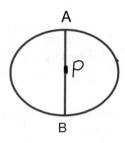

Analysis of the Group Exercise

1. Use a ruler to measure the diameter AB. Is the diameter 3 cm.? Note that the diameter AB of the circle in this book is not 3 cm. because the circle is not drawn to scale and also note that the book just shows you how to draw a circle with any specific radius.
2. Could you show that the relationship between the radii AP and PB and the diameter AB of a circle by measuring the radii AP and PB and the diameter AB. The relationship is:

$$\text{Diameter} = 2 \times \text{radius}$$

Exercises

1. A circle has a radius of 20 cm. How long is the diameter? Hint: See Example 2.
2. Draw a circle with each of the radius using a compass. Measure each diameter.
   (a) **2 cm**..   (b) 2 ins.   (c) 1 in.
   Hint: See the steps under the section "how to draw a circle."

Challenge Questions

4. Given the following diameter of each circle, find the radius of each circle.
   (a) 100 cm.   (b) 50 ins.   (c) 15 cm.   (d) 21 cm.
5. Given the following radius of of each circle, find the diameter of each circle.

(a) 5 cm.   **(b)** 9 ins.   **(c)** 2 cm.   **(d)** 11 cm.

Sum of the Measure of the Angles in a Circle

The sum of the measure of the angles in a circle is 360^0. The sum of the measures of the angles in a circle is similar to the sum of the measures of the angles at a point. The sum of the angles of the circle is: $w^0 + x^0 + y^0 + z^0 = 360^0$.

Rule 1: To find the unknown measure of an angle in a circle, find the sum of the measure of the angles that are given in the circle and then subtract that sum from 360^0.

Example 3

Find the value of x^0 in each diagram.

(a)
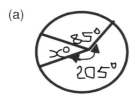

(b)
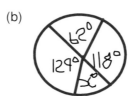

Solution

(a) The sum of the measure of the angles in a circle $= 360^0$, and therefore,

$x^0 + 85^0 + 205^0 = 360^0$

$x^0 + 290^0 = 360^0$ $(85^0 + 205^0 = 290^0)$

$x^0 + 290^0 - 290^0 = 360^0 - 290^0$ (Subtract 290^0 from each side of the equation in order to eliminate the 290^0 at the left side of the equation and also to obtain the value of x^0.) This is also the application of Rule 1.

$x^0 + 0 = 70^0$ $(290^0 - 290^0 = 0, 360^0 - 290^0 = 70^0)$

$x^0 = 70^0$

(b) The sum of the measure of the angles in a circle $= 360^0$, and therefore,

$x^0 + 118^0 + 62^0 + 129^0 = 360^0$

$x^0 + 309^0 = 360^0$ $(118^0 + 62^0 + 129^0 = 309^0)$

$x^0 + 309^0 - 309^0 = 360^0 - 309^0$ (Subtract 309^0 from each side of the equation in order to eliminate the 309^0 at the left side of the equation and also to obtain the value of x^0. This is

$$x^0 + 0 = 51^0$$
$$x^0 = 51^0$$

also the application of rule 1.)
$$(309^0 - 309^0 = 0, 360^0 - 309^0 = 51^0)$$

Exercises

1. Find the unknown angle measure of each circle.
Let the unknown angle measure be x^0. Hint: See Example **3**.

(a)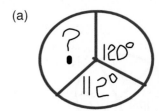

(b)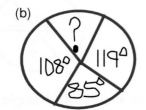

(c)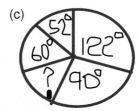

Challenge Questions

2. Find the unknown angle measure of each circle.

(a)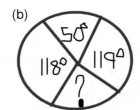

(b)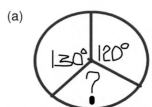

(c)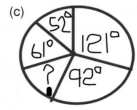

Answers to Selected Questions

1(a) 110^0 **2(b)** 73^0

Mixed Review

1. Two lines that intersect to form right angles are called perpendicular lines. True or False.

2. Reduce each fraction to the lowest term.

(a) $\dfrac{3}{9}$ (b) $\dfrac{5}{25}$ (c) $\dfrac{6}{36}$

3. What is the difference between an acute angle and an obtuse angle?

4. Solve:

(a) $-2 - 6 =$ (b) $-9 \div 3 =$ (c) $-12 \times 2 =$

5. Solve:

(a) $27 - 2 \times 4 + 3 =$ (b) $2 + 18 - 4 \times 2 =$ (c) $3^2 \times 2^3 =$

6. Explain what is meant by a regular hexagon.

7. What is the sum of the measure of the angles in a triangle?

8. What is the sum of the measure of the angles in a quadrilateral?

9. What is the sum of the measure of the angles formed in a circle?

10. To divide a number by a fraction, we have to multiply the number by the reciprocal of the fraction. True or false?

11. Solve:

(**a**) $6 \div \dfrac{1}{3} =$ (**b**) $\dfrac{3}{4} \div \dfrac{1}{8} =$ (**c**) $3 - 1\dfrac{1}{5}$ (**d**) $\dfrac{2}{3} \times \dfrac{3}{2} =$

CHAPTER 33

CIRCUMFERENCE

Nicholas asks if you could use some facts under "Place Values" section to solve some problems in this chapter?
What about giving an answer to the nearest tenth?

Nicholas

The **circumference** is the distance around a circle or a circular object. The ratio of the circumference to the diameter of a circle is called pi which has a symbol π. The value of $\pi = \dfrac{22}{7}$ **which is approximately 3.14.**

Find the Distance Around an Evaporated Milk Can and the Value of π.
Group Exercise.
Step 1. The materials needed for the exercise are a can, a string, a ruler, and a pen.
  Each group should take a can and wrap a string around the can.
  Make a mark on the string at a point where the string first overlaps.

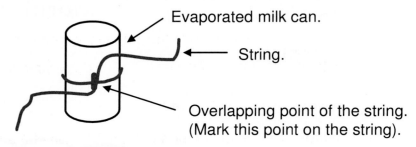

Evaporated milk can.

String.

Overlapping point of the string.
(Mark this point on the string).

Step 2. Put the ruler on the table and stretch the string on the ruler so that one of
  the marks on the string should be on zero marking and then read the
  marking on the ruler that corresponds to the second marking on the string.
  This reading is the length of the string around the evaporated milk can and
  this is, therefore the circumference.

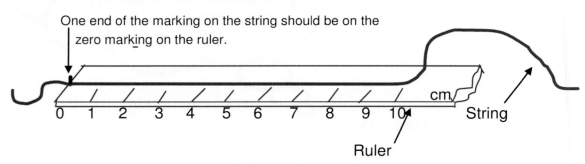

One end of the marking on the string should be on the
zero marking on the ruler.

0 1 2 3 4 5 6 7 8 9 10   cm

String

Ruler

  Record the circumference and let us represent the circumference by C.
Step 3. Use a pencil to trace the base of the can on a piece of paper. This trace
  is the distance around the can. With the zero mark of the ruler on one
  part of the trace (circle) at point A, move the other end of the ruler on
  the other side of the trace until you can find the longest distance on the
  ruler that coincides with the other side of the trace at point B. This
  distance is the diameter because we can recall that the **longest chord
  of a circle is the diameter**.
  $\overline{AB}$ is the longest chord, which is the diameter. Record the length of the
  diameter, and let us represent the diameter by the letter d.

Place the zero mark on the ruler on one part of the trace (circle).

Trace the base of the can.

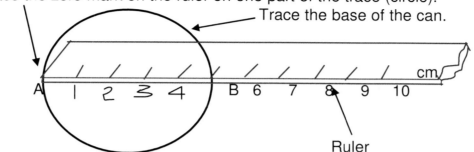

Ruler

Step 4. Find the ratio of the circumference to the diameter of the circle by dividing the circumference by the diameter which is $= \dfrac{c}{d}$. Record your value for the ratio $\dfrac{c}{d}$. Is your answer approximately 3.14?

Step 5: Find the circumference, the diameter and then the ratio of the circumference to the diameter of four more different size cans using steps 1 to 4 and record all the data for the group project in the table that shown:

Can type	Circumference(c)	Diameter(d)	Ratio $= \dfrac{c}{d}$
1			
2			
3			
4			
5			

Conclusion: The standard ratio $\dfrac{c}{d}$ is approximately $= 3.14 = \pi$.

Therefore, $\mathbf{c = \pi d}$ \qquad\qquad (**Important formula**)

(circumference $= \pi \times$ diameter where π is called pi)

Example 1

Find the circumference of a circle that has a diameter of 5 cm.

Solution

The circumference of a circle is given by the formula:

$C = \pi d$, where C is the circumference, $\pi = 3.14$ and d = diameter.

$C = \pi d$ ———————————— $[A]$

$C = 3.14 \times 5$ cm \qquad (Substitute $\pi = 3.14$, and d = 5 cm into equation $[A]$.)

$C = 15.7$ cm

Example 2

The circumference of a circle is 18.84 in. (**a**) Find the diameter. (**b**) Find the radius.

Solution

(**a**) The circumference of a circle is given by the formula:

$$C = \pi d \quad\text{————————————————}\quad [A]$$

$$18.84 = 3.14 \times d \qquad \text{(Substitute } C = 18.84 \text{ in. and } \pi = 3.14 \text{ into equation } [A].)$$

$$\frac{18.84}{3.14} = \frac{3.14}{3.14} \times d \qquad \text{(Divide each side of the equation by 3.14 in order to}$$

obtain the value of d.)

$$\frac{\overset{6}{18.84}}{\underset{1}{3.14}} = \frac{\overset{1}{3.14}}{\underset{1}{3.14}} \times d \qquad \text{(You may use the calculator to divide.)}$$

$$(18.84 \div 3.14 = 6, 3.14 \div 3.14 = 1)$$

$$6 = d$$

Diameter = 6 in.

(**b**) Diameter ÷ 2 = radius. Therefore, the radius = 6 in. ÷ 2 = 3 in.

Exercises

1. Find the circumference of each circle that has the following diameter to the nearest tenth. Hint: See Example 1 and review the chapter/section on "Place Values."
   (**a**) 3 cm   (**b**) 4 ft   (**c**) 6 in.   (**d**) 2.4 cm
2. The circumference of a circle is 9.42. Find the diameter of the circle.
   Hint: See example 2.
3. Find the diameter of a circle that has a circumference of 6.28 cm.
   Hint: See example 2.

Challenge Questions

4. Find the diameter of a circle that has a circumference of 31.4 cm.
5. Find the circumference of a circle that has a radius of 2.3 cm.
   Hint: Change the radius to the diameter first.
6. Find the circumference of each circle.

(a)

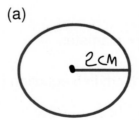

(b)

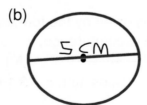

(c)

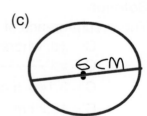

CHAPTER 34

SIMILAR AND CONGRUENT FIGURES

New Terms: **similar**, **congruent**, **corresponding sides**, **corresponding angles**

Similar figures are figures that have the same shape but they do not necessarily have to be the same size. In the diagrams, Figure A is similar to Figure B because they have the **same shape** but they do not have the **same size**. The symbol ~ means "is similar to."
 In the diagram, Figure A is similar to Figure B because they have the same shape but not the same size. Similarly, Figure C is similar to Figure D because they have the same shape but not the same size.

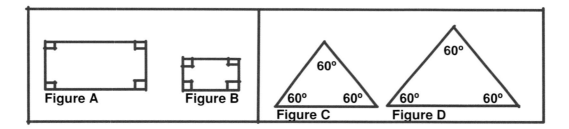

Congruent figures are figures that have the same shape and size. In the diagrams, Figure E is congruent to Figure F because they have the same shape and size. The symbol ≅ means "is congruent to."

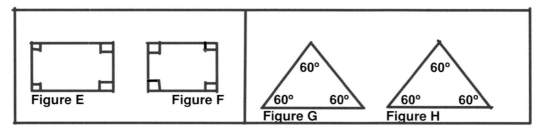

In the diagram, Figure I and Figure J are neither similar nor congruent because they have different shapes and different sizes. Similarly, Figure K and Figure L are neither similar nor congruent because they have different shapes and different sizes.

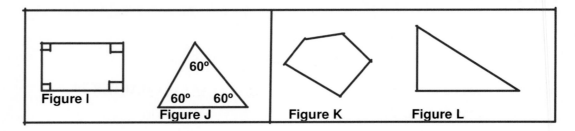

Figure I
Figure J
Figure K
Figure L

Critical Conclusions
1. Figures E and F or Figures G and H show that congruent figures are also similar figures.
2. Figures A and B or Figures C and D show that similar figures are not necessarily congruent figures.

Writing Similar Figures and Congruent Figures Using Symbols
The symbol for a triangle is △.
1. We can write that triangle ABC is similar to triangle DEF by using the symbols as shown: △ABC ~ △DEF

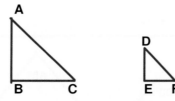

2. We can write that triangle PQW is congruent to triangle XYZ by using symbols as shown: △PQW ≅ △XYZ

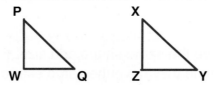

Group Discussion
Triangles ABC and triangles DEF are similar.
Similar polygons have corresponding angles and corresponding sides.
Note that when two figures are similar, for each part of one figure, there is a corresponding part on the other figure. To determine the corresponding angles and the corresponding sides of similar polygons, compare the shape of the polygons and then determine how each pair of angles and each pair of sides form corresponding parts as shown:

Corresponding Angles	Corresponding sides
∠A corresponds to ∠D	$\overline{AB}$ corresponds to $\overline{DE}$
∠B corresponds to ∠E	$\overline{BC}$ corresponds to $\overline{EF}$
∠C corresponds to ∠F	$\overline{AC}$ corresponds to $\overline{DF}$
∠ is the symbol for angle.	

Note that the angles in △ABC are congruent to the corresponding angles in △DEF and the length of the sides of △DEF are about twice the length of the corresponding sides in △ABC.

Conclusion: Note that in similar figures the **corresponding angles are congruent** (the same measure of angles), and the ratio of the lengths of the corresponding sides are **equal**.

Group Exercise
Given that △ABC is similar to △DEF, copy and complete the statements:

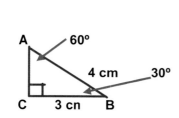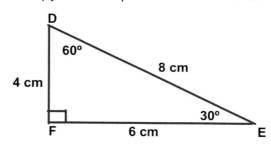

Corresponding Angles

∠A corresponds to ∠D

∠B corresponds to ∠?

∠C corresponds to ?

Corresponding sides

$\overline{AC}$ corresponds to $\overline{DF}$

$\overline{AB}$ corresponds to ?

$\overline{BC}$ corresponds to ?

Example 1
Given that the trapezoid ABCD is similar to the trapezoid EFGH, list all the pairs of the corresponding sides.

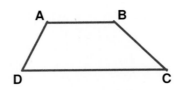
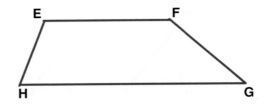

Solution
By comparing the shapes of the trapezoids ABCD and EFGH,

$\overline{AB}$ corresponds to $\overline{EF}$

$\overline{BC}$ corresponds to $\overline{FG}$

$\overline{CD}$ corresponds to $\overline{GH}$

$\overline{DA}$ corresponds to $\overline{HE}$

Example 2
Given that △ABC is congruent to △DEF,

a. What side of △DEF corresponds to side $\overline{AC}$?

b. What is the perimeter of △DEF ?

c. What is the length of $\overline{DF}$?

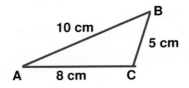
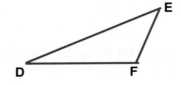

Solution
a. By comparing the shapes of △ABC and △DEF, $\overline{DF}$ corresponds to $\overline{AC}$.

b. The perimeter of △ABC is the distance around △ABC.

Therefore, the perimeter of △ABC $= \overline{AB} + \overline{BC} + \overline{AC}$

$= 10 \text{ cm} + 5 \text{ cm} + 8 \text{ cm}$

$= 23 \text{ cm}$

Since △ABC and △DEF are congruent, they have the same size and shape, and therefore, the perimeter of △DEF is also 23 cm.

Example 3
Write whether each pair of figures appear to be similar, congruent, both, or neither.

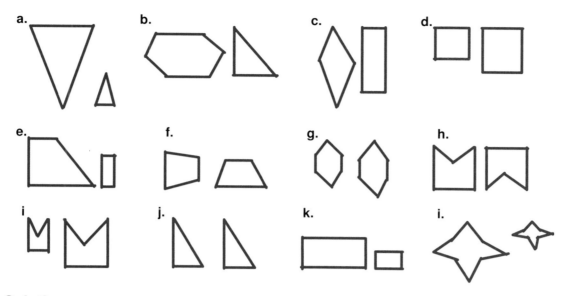

Solution

a. The two triangles appear to be similar because they have the same shape but not the same size.

b. The hexagon and the triangle are neither similar nor congruent because they have neither the same shape nor the same size.

c. The rhombus and the rectangle are neither similar nor congruent because they have neither the same shape nor the same size.

d. The two rectangles appear to be similar because they have the same shape but not the same size.

e. The trapezoid and the rectangle are neither similar nor congruent because they have neither the same shape nor the same size.

f. The two quadrilaterals appear to be similar and congruent because they have the same shape and the same size.

g. The two hexagons appear to be similar because they have the same shape but not the same size.

h. The two figures appear to be similar and congruent because they have the same shape and the same size.

i. The two figures appear to be similar because they have the same shape but not the same size.

j. The two triangles are similar and congruent because they have the same shape and the same size.

k. The two rectangles appear to be similar because they have the same shape but not the same size.

l. The two figures appear to be similar because they have the same shape but not the same size.

Exercises

1. We can say that in similar figures the corresponding angles are c _____ and the ratio of the lengths of the corresponding sides are e _____. Hint: See the section on "Group Discussion."

2a. Explain what is meant by similar figures.

2b. Sketch two similar right triangles. Hint: A right triangle has one right angle.

3a. Explain what is meant by congruent figures.

3b. Sketch two congruent rectangles and explain why they are congruent.

4. Congruent figures are also similar figures. True or False? Hint: See the preceding notes.

5. Similar figures are not necessarily congruent figures. True or False? Hint: See the preceding pages.

6. Two figures are neither similar nor congruent because they have different sh___ and different si____.

7a. What is the symbol for a triangle?

7b. What is the symbol for "is similar to?"

7c. What is the symbol for "is congruent to?"
    Hint: See the preceding pages.

8. Using symbols, write that:
    a. Triangle XYZ is similar to triangle ABC.
    b. Triangle ABC is congruent to triangle XYZ.
    Hint: See the preceding pages.

9. Similar polygons have corresponding angles and corresponding sides. True or False? Hint: See the preceding pages.

10. When two figures are similar, for each part of one figure, there is a corresponding p____ on the other figure.
    Hint: See the preceding pages.

11. In similar figures, the corresponding ang___ are congruent (the same measure of angles), and the ratio of the r____ of the corresponding s____ are equal. Hint: See the preceding pages.

12. Trapezoid WXYZ is similar to trapezoid ABCD. List all the pairs of corresponding sides. Hint: See Example **1**.

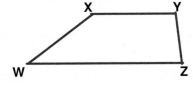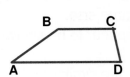

13. Given that △ABC ≅ △XYZ.
    (**a**) What side of △XYZ corresponds to side $\overline{YZ}$?
    (**b**) What is the perimeter of △XYZ?
    (**c**) What is the length of $\overline{XY}$?
    Hint: See Example **2**.

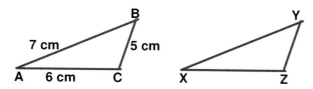

14. Write whether each pair of figures appear to be similar, congruent, both, or neither and give the reason for your choice.
Hint: See Example **3**.

a.

b.

c.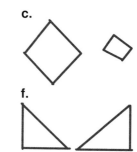

d.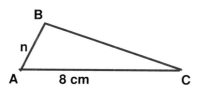

e.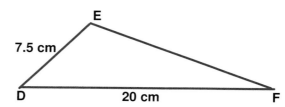

f.

How to Use Proportion to Solve Similar Figure Problems

What is a proportion? A **proportion** is an equation that states that **two ratios are equal**. Therefore, the **cross products** of a proportion are **equal**. Examples 1, 2 and 3 show and explain how a proportion and the cross products of a proportion can be used to solve similar figure problems.

Example 1

Given that the two figures are similar, write and solve the proportion to find the length of n.

Solution

By observing the shape of the figures,

$\overline{AB}$ corresponds to $\overline{DE}$

$\overline{AC}$ corresponds to $\overline{DF}$

We can find the value of n by using the fact that in similar figures, the ratios of the corresponding sides are equal.

Step 1: We can therefore, write two ratios or a proportion as shown:

smaller figure

$$\frac{\overline{AB}}{\overline{DE}} = \frac{\overline{AC}}{\overline{DF}} \qquad \text{———————} \quad [A]$$

↙ smaller figure

↗ bigger figure ↖ bigger figure

(**Note**: It is very important to remember the order of the two ratios so that for this specific example, the smaller figure value divides the bigger value on both sides of the equation as shown in equation $[A]$.)

From the figures, $\overline{AB} = n$, $\overline{DE} = 7.5$ cm, $\overline{AC} = 8$ cm, and $\overline{DF} = 20$ cm.

Substitute $\overline{AB} = n$, $\overline{DE} = 7.5$ cm, $\overline{AC} = 8$ cm, and $\overline{DF} = 20$ cm into equation $[A]$ as shown:

$$\frac{n}{7.5 \text{ cm}} = \frac{8 \text{ cm}}{20 \text{ cm}} \qquad \text{———————} \quad [B]$$

Step 2: Solve the equation $[B]$ or the proportion $[B]$ to obtain the value of n as shown:

$$\frac{n}{7.5 \text{ cm}} \diagdown \frac{8 \text{ cm}}{20 \text{ cm}}$$

Cross products of proportions are equal.
Hint: Review the chapter/section on proportion.

$$n \times 20 \text{ cm} = 7.5 \text{ cm} \times 8 \text{ cm} \quad \text{———————} \quad [C]$$

Divide each side of the equation $[C]$ by 20 cm in order to obtain the value of n as shown:

$$\frac{n \times 20 \text{ cm}}{20 \text{ cm}} = \frac{7.5 \text{ cm} \times 8 \text{ cm}}{20 \text{ cm}}$$

$$\frac{n \times \overset{1}{\cancel{20 \text{ cm}}}}{\underset{1}{\cancel{20 \text{ cm}}}} = \frac{7.5 \text{ cm} \times \overset{2}{\cancel{8 \text{ cm}}}}{\underset{5}{\cancel{20 \text{ cm}}}}$$

$20 \div 20 = 1$, $8 \div 4 = 2$, and $20 \div 4 = 5$

$$n = \frac{7.5 \text{ cm} \times 2}{5}$$

$$n = \frac{\overset{1.5}{\cancel{7.5 \text{ cm}}} \times 2}{\underset{1}{\cancel{5}}}$$

Divide by 5, $7.5 \div 5 = 1.5$, $5 \div 5 = 1$.

$$n = 1.5 \text{ cm} \times 2$$

794

$$n = 3.0 \text{ cm}$$

Example 2

The two figures are similar. Find the length of n.

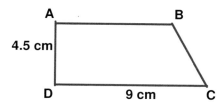
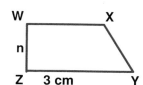

Solution

By observing the shape of the two figures, $\overline{AD}$ corresponds to $\overline{WZ}$ and $\overline{DC}$ corresponds to $\overline{ZY}$. We can find the value of n by using the fact that in similar figures, the ratios of the corresponding sides are equal.

Step 1: We can therefore, write two ratios or a proportion as shown:

Bigger figure

Bigger figure

$$\frac{\overline{AD}}{\overline{WZ}} = \frac{\overline{DC}}{\overline{ZY}} \qquad\qquad [A]$$

Smaller figure

Smaller figure

(**Note**: It is very important to remember the order of the two ratios so that for this specific example, the bigger figure value divides the smaller figure value on both sides of the equation [A] as shown.)

From the figures, $\overline{AD} = 4.5$ cm, $\overline{WZ} = n$, $\overline{DC} = 9$ cm, and $\overline{ZY} = 3$ cm.

Substitute $\overline{AD} = 4.5$ cm, $\overline{WZ} = n$, $\overline{DC} = 9$ cm, and $\overline{ZY} = 3$ cm into equation [A] as shown:

$$\frac{4.5 \text{ cm}}{n} = \frac{9 \text{ cm}}{3 \text{ cm}} \qquad\qquad [B]$$

Step 2: Solve the equation [B] or the proportion [B] to obtain the value of n as shown:

$$\frac{4.5 \text{ cm}}{n} \diagup\!\!\!\!\diagdown \frac{9 \text{ cm}}{3 \text{ cm}}$$

Cross products of a proportion are equal.
Hint: Review the chapter/section on proportion.

$$n \times 9 \text{ cm} = 4.5 \text{ cm} \times 3 \text{ cm} \qquad\qquad [C]$$

Divide both sides of equation [C] by 9 cm in order to obtain the value of n as shown:

$$\frac{n \times 9 \text{ cm}}{9 \text{ cm}} = \frac{4.5 \text{ cm} \times 3 \text{ cm}}{9 \text{ cm}}$$

$$\dfrac{n \times \overset{1}{\cancel{9 \text{ cm}}}}{\underset{1}{\cancel{9 \text{ cm}}}} = \dfrac{4.5 \text{ cm} \times \overset{1}{\cancel{3 \text{ cm}}}}{\underset{3}{\cancel{9 \text{ cm}}}}$$

9 can divide the left hand side of the equation and 3 can divide the right hand side of the equation.

$$n = \dfrac{4.5 \text{ cm}}{3}$$

$$n = 4.5 \div 3 = 1.5 \text{ cm} \qquad \text{(You may use a calculator.)}$$

$$n = 1.5 \text{ cm}.$$

Example 3

The two figures are similar. Find the length on n.

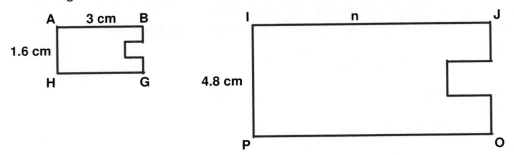

Solution

By observing the shape of the figure,

$\overline{AB}$ corresponds to $\overline{IJ}$

$\overline{AH}$ corresponds to $\overline{IP}$

We can find the value of n by using the the fact that in similar figures, the ratios of the corresponding sides are equal.

Step 1: We can therefore write two ratios or a proportion as follows:

Smaller figure　　　　　Smaller

$$\dfrac{\overline{AB}}{\overline{IJ}} = \dfrac{\overline{AH}}{\overline{IP}} \qquad\qquad\qquad [A]$$

Bigger figure　　　Bigger figure

(**Note**: It is very important to remember the order of the ratios so that for this specific example, the smaller figure value divides the bigger figure value on both sides of the equation [A] as shown.)

From the figures, $\overline{AB} = 3$ cm, $\overline{IJ} = n$, $\overline{AH} = 1.6$ cm, and $\overline{IP} = 4.8$ cm.

Substitute $\overline{AB} = 3$ cm, $\overline{IJ} = n$, $\overline{AH} = 1.6$ cm, and $\overline{IP} = 4.8$ cm into equation [A] as shown:

$$\frac{3 \text{ cm}}{n} = \frac{1.6 \text{ cm}}{4.8 \text{ cm}} \text{———————————————} [B]$$

Step 2: Solve equation $[B]$ or the proportion $[B]$ to obtain the value of n as shown:

$\frac{3 \text{ cm}}{n} \times \frac{1.6 \text{ cm}}{4.8 \text{ cm}}$ **Cross products of a proportion are equal.**
Hint: Review the chapter/section on Proportion.

$$n \times 1.6 \text{ cm} = 3 \text{ cm} \times 4.8 \text{ cm} \text{———————————} [C]$$

Divide both sides of equation $[C]$ by 1.6 cm in order to obtain the value of n as shown:

$$\frac{n \times 1.6 \text{ cm}}{1.6 \text{ cm}} = \frac{3 \text{ cm} \times 4.8 \text{ cm}}{1.6 \text{ cm}}$$

$$\frac{n \times 1.6 \overset{1}{\cancel{\text{ cm}}}}{\underset{1}{1.6 \cancel{\text{ cm}}}} = \frac{3 \text{ cm} \times 4.8 \cancel{\text{ cm}}}{1.6 \cancel{\text{ cm}}}$$

$1.6 \div 1.6 = 1$

$$n = \frac{14.4 \text{ cm}}{1.6}$$

$3 \times 4.8 \text{ cm} = 14.4 \text{ cm}$

$$n = 14.4 \div 1.6 = 9 \text{ cm}$$ (You may use a calculator.)
$$n = 9 \text{ cm}.$$

Exercise

1. Each pair of figures are similar. Write and solve the proportion to find the length n.
  Hint: See Example **1**.

(a).

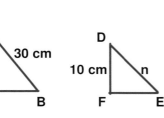

(b).

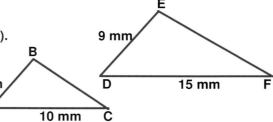

(c).

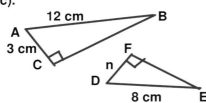

(d).

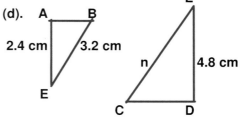

2. Each pair of figures are similar. Write and solve the proportion to find the length n.
Hint: See Example **2.**

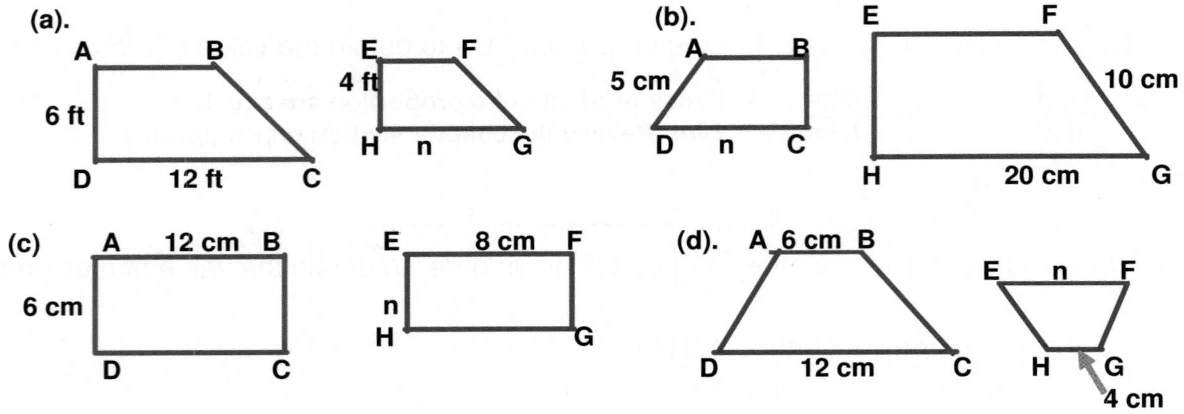

(a).

(b).

(c)

(d).

3. Each pair of figures are similar. Write and solve the proportion to find the length n.
Hint: See Example **3.**

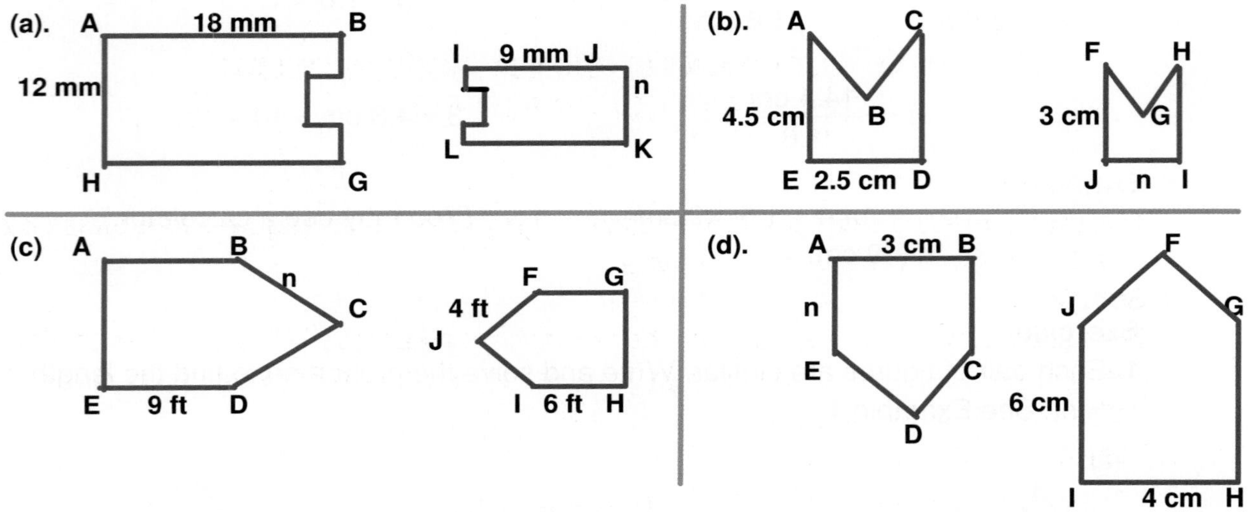

(a).

(b).

(c)

(d).

Answers to Selected Questions

1c. 2 cm   **2d.** 8 cm   **3d.** 4.5 cm

Challenge Questions

4. Each pair of figures are similar. Write and solve the proportion to find the length of n.

798

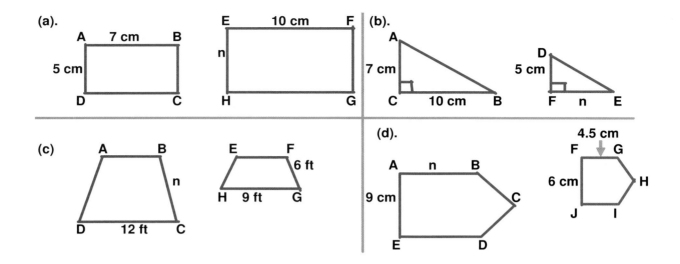

REAL WORLD APPLICATIONS - WORD PROBLEMS
SIMILAR AND CONGRUENT FIGURES

Example 1

1. A man 6 feet tall casts a 4-foot shadow. A lady who is standing next to the man casts a 3-foot shadow. How tall is the lady?

Solution

We assume that both the man and the lady form right angles with the horizontal floor. We can then use pairs of similar right triangles to find how tall the lady is as shown:

Let the height of the lady be n

Step 1: Sketch the diagram.

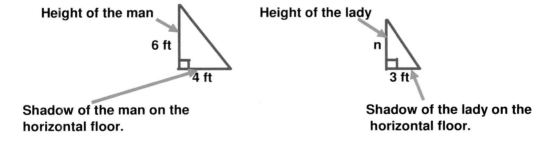

Step 2: The right triangles are similar, and therefore, write a ratio relating the shadow of the man and the shadow of the lady and also write a ratio relating the height of the man and the height of the lady because the ratios of the corresponding sides of similar figures are equal as shown:

Height of the
lady ↘   ↗ Shadow of the lady

$$\frac{n}{6 \text{ ft}} = \frac{3 \text{ ft}}{4 \text{ ft}} \qquad \underline{\hspace{4cm}} \; [A]$$

↗   ↖ Shadow of the man
Height of the man

(**Note**: It is very important to remember the order of the ratios so that for this specific example, the lady's height is divided by the man's height and the lady's shadow is divided by the man's shadow as shown in the equation $[A]$.)

Step 3: Solve the proportion as shown:

$$\frac{n}{6 \text{ ft}} \underset{\nearrow}{\overset{\searrow}{\times}} \frac{3 \text{ ft}}{4 \text{ ft}}$$

Cross products of a proportion are equal.
Hint: Review the chapter/section on Proportion.

$$n \times 4 \text{ ft} = 6 \text{ ft} \times 3 \text{ ft} \qquad \underline{\hspace{4cm}} \; [B]$$

Divide both sides of equation $[B]$ by 4 ft in order to obtain the value of n as shown:

$$\frac{n \times 4 \text{ ft}}{4 \text{ ft}} = \frac{6 \text{ ft} \times 3 \text{ ft}}{4 \text{ ft}}$$

$$\frac{n \times \overset{1}{\cancel{4 \text{ ft}}}}{\underset{1}{\cancel{4 \text{ ft}}}} = \frac{\overset{3}{\cancel{6 \text{ ft}}} \times 3 \text{ ft}}{\underset{2}{\cancel{4 \text{ ft}}}} \qquad (4 \div 4 = 1, \; 4 \div 2 = 2, \; 6 \div 2 = 3)$$

$$n = \frac{3 \times 3 \text{ ft}}{2} = \frac{9 \text{ ft}}{2} = 4.5 \text{ ft.}$$

$$n = 4.5 \text{ ft.}$$

Exercises

Hint: Use the solution method for Example 1 (pair of similar right triangles) to solve the following problems. Give your answer to the nearest tenth.

1. A girl 5 ft tall casts a 3 ft shadow, a boy who is standing next to her casts a shadow of 2 ft. How tall is the boy?

2. A tower is 20 meters high and casts a shadow which is 5 meters. How tall is a nearby building that casts a 3-meter shadow?

3. When a tree casts a 6-meter shadow, a man 2 meters tall casts a 1.4-meter shadow. How tall is the tree?

4. When a 2.5-meter sign post casts a 4.2-meter shadow, a man nearby casts a 3.2-meter shadow. How tall is the man?

5. John is 6.2 ft tall and casts a 10 ft shadow. A stop sign post nearby casts a 12 ft shadow. How tall is the stop sign post?

Answer to a Selected Question
1. 3.3 ft

CHAPTER 35

SYMMETRIC FIGURES

A geometric figure that can be divided into two identical parts is **symmetric** The line that divides the geometric figure into two identical parts is called the **line of symmetry**. If the geometric figure is folded along the line of symmetry, the two halves will match exactly. **A line of symmetry divides a geometric figure into exactly two matching halves**.

A figure has symmetry if it can be folded into two matching halves exactly. A geometric figure can have any number of lines of symmetry as shown in the following diagrams.

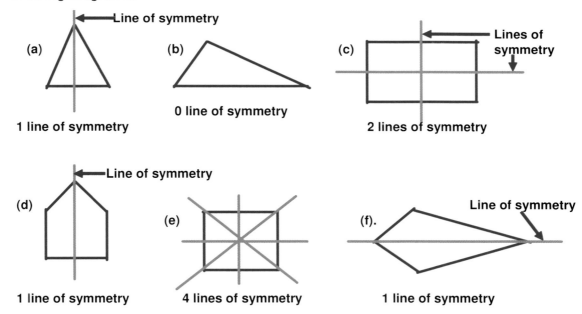

Group Project
Obtain a kite, fold it into two matching halves similar to diagram (f).
  • Are you able to fold the kite into exactly two matching halves?
  • Can you conclude that a kite has symmetry?

• Compare an airplane to the kite. Does the airplane have symmetry? Sketch an airplane and draw the line of symmetry.

Symmetry of Letters

The diagrams (a) and (b) show some lines of symmetry of some letters as shown:

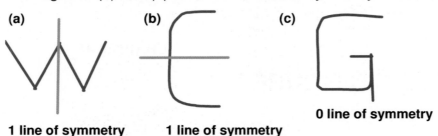

(a)
1 line of symmetry

(b)
1 line of symmetry

(c)
0 line of symmetry

Exercises

1. Explain what is meant by:
- **a**. Symmetry.
- **b**. Line of symmetry.
- **c**. Number of lines of symmetry.

2. In each diagram, is the dashed line along the line of symmetry? Explain your answer. Hint: See the notes provided.

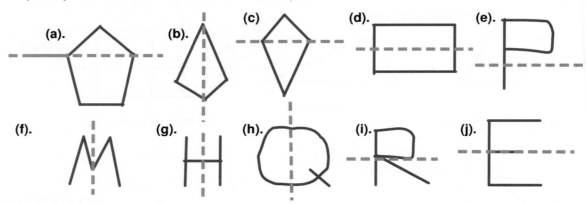

(a). (b). (c) (d). (e).

(f). (g). (h). (i). (j).

3. Sketch the following diagrams and draw all the possible lines of symmetry. Hint: See the notes provided.

(a). (b). (c)

Answer to a Selected Question

2a. The dashed line is not along the line of symmetry because the dashed line does not

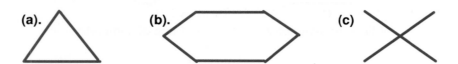

divide the figure exactly into two matching halves.

Cumulative Review

1. 95% of 20 =   **2**. 4% of 50 =   **3**. 6% of 16.2 =

4. .09% of 100 =   **5**. 900 − 398 =   **6**. What is an acute angle?

7. The sum of the measures of the angles in a triangle =

8. The sum of the measures of the angles on a line =

9. $4^2 − 2^2$ =   **10**. 24 − 2 × 4 + 1 =

11. The sum of the measures of the angles in a rectangle =

12. Find the missing angle.

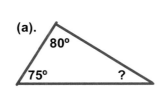
(a).

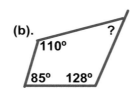
(b).

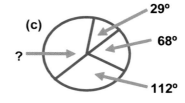
(c)

13. Sketch and label a figure for each symbol.

    a. ∠ABC   **b**. $\overrightarrow{DC}$ **c**. $\overleftrightarrow{XY}$ **d**. $\overline{AR}$

CHAPTER 36

COMPLEMENTARY AND SUPPLEMENTARY ANGLES

Cumulative Review

a. 4 - 2.138 =   **b**. 5.58 + 17.97 + 2.2 =   **c**. 7.68 × 3 =

d. John said that $\dfrac{2}{5} + \dfrac{1}{3} = \dfrac{7}{20}$. Is his statement correct? Explain your answer.

e. Mary said that the average of 4, 6, 8, 2, and 1 is 10. Is her statement correct? Explain your answer.

f. Explain how you would find the average of three numbers.

g. Explain what is meant by the mean and the mode of a data.

COMPLEMENTARY ANGLES

New Term: complementary angles

803

Two angles are **complementary** if their measures add to 90^0. For example, if the measures of angle A and angle B add to 90^0, then angle A and B are complementary angles, and such angles are called complements of each other. **We can find the measure of the complement of an angle by subtracting the measure of the angle from 90^0.**

Example 1
Find the complement of each angle.

a. 50^0 **b**. 2^0

Solution

a. Let the complement of $50^0 = x$.

Two angles are complementary if their measures add to 90^0.

Therefore,

$50^0 + x = 90^0$	Sum of the measures of complementary angles $= 90^0$
$50^0 - 50^0 + x = 90^0 - 50^0$	Subtract 50^0 from both sides of the equation
	$50^0 + x = 90^0$ to obtain x.
$0 + x = 40^0$	$50^0 - 50^0 = 0$, $90^0 - 50^0 = 40^0$.
$x = 40^0$	

Therefore, the complement of 50^0 is 40^0

Note: We can also find the measure of the complement of an angle by simply subtracting the measure of the angle from 90^0 as shown:

The complement of $50^0 = 90^0 - 50^0$

$$= 40^0$$

b. Let the complement of $2^0 = y$

Two angles are complementary if the sum of their measure is 90^0.

Therefore,

$2^0 + y = 90^0$	Sum of the measures of the complementary angles $= 90^0$
$2^0 - 2^0 + y = 90^0 - 2^0$	Subtracting 2^0 from both sides of the equation
	$2^0 + y = 90^0$ to obtain y.
$0 + y = 88^0$	$2^0 - 2^0 = 0$, $90^0 - 2^0 = 88^0$
$y = 88^0$	

Therefore, the complement of 2^0 is 88^0

Note: We can find the measure of the complement of an angle by simply subtracting the measure of the angle from 90^0 as shown:

The complement of $2^0 = 90^0 - 2^0$

$$= 88^0$$

Example 2
In the diagram, what is the value of x for x and 36^0 to be complementary angles?

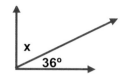

Solution

Two angles are complementary if the sum of their measures is 90^0.
Therefore,

$$x + 36^0 = 90^0$$
$$x + 36^0 - 36^0 = 90^0 - 36^0$$

Subtract 36^0 from both sides of the equation $x + 36^0 = 90^0$ to obtain x.

$$x + 0 = 54^0$$
$$x = 54^0$$

$36^0 - 36^0 = 0$, $90^0 - 36^0 = 54^0$.

Therefore, $x = 54^0$ for x and 36^0 to be complementary angles.

Exercises

1. Explain what is meant by complementary angles.

2. Find the complement of each angle. Hint: See Example 1.

   a. 28^0 **b**. 1^0 **c**. 89^0 **d**. 16^0

   e. 31^0 **f**. 7^0 **g**. 77^0 **h**. 92^0

3. If angle A and angle B are complementary angles, and the measure of angle B is 65^0, what is the complement of angle B? Hint: See Example 1.

4. In each diagram, find the value of x for x and the measure of the given angle to be complementary angles. Hint: See Example 2.

   a.

   b.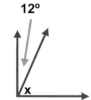

   c.

   d.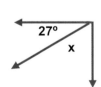

   e.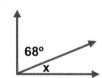

   f.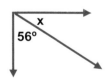

Answers to Selected Questions

   2a. 62^0 **4a**. 60^0

Challenge Questions

5. In each diagram, find the value of y for y and the measure of the given angle to be complementary angles.

a.

y

67°

b.

19°

y

c.

y

28°

d.

40°

y

e.

71°

y

f.

y

52°

6. Find the complement of each angle.

a. 59^0	b. 2^0	c. 31^0	d. 43^0	e. 69^0
f. 21^0	g. 11^0	h. 75^0	i. 66^0	f. 5^0

SUPPLEMENTARY ANGLES

New Term: **supplementary angles**

Two angles are **supplementary** if their measures add to 180^0. For example, if the measures of angle A and angle B add to 180^0, then angle A and angle B are supplementary angles and such angles are called supplements of each other. **We can find the measure of the supplementary angle by subtracting the measure of the angle from 180^0.**

Example 1

$\angle$A and $\angle$B are supplementary. If the $m\angle A = 120^0$, what is the $m\angle B$?
($\angle$A means angle A, $\angle$B means angle B, $m\angle A$ means measure of angle A, and $m\angle B$ means measure of angle B).

Solution

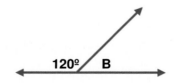

120° B

806

The sum of the supplementary angles is 180^0, therefore:

$$120^0 + m\angle B = 180^0$$

$120^0 - 120^0 + m\angle B = 180^0 - 120^0$ Subtract 120^0 from both sides of the

equation $120^0 + m\angle B = 180^0$ to obtain 120^0.

$$0 + m\angle B = 60^0$$ $120^0 - 120^0 = 0$ and $180^0 - 120^0 = 60^0$

$$m\angle B = 60^0$$

Example 2

Find the supplement of:

a. 5^0 **b**. 110^0

Solution

a. Let the supplement of 5^0 be x.

Two angles are supplementary if the sum of their measures is 180^0.

Therefore:

$$5^0 + x = 180^0$$

$5^0 - 5^0 + x = 180^0 - 5^0$ Subtract 5^0 from both sides of the equation

$5^0 + x = 180^0$ to obtain the value of x.

$$0 + x = 175^0$$ $5^0 - 5^0 = 0$ and $180^0 - 5^0 = 175^0$.

$$x = 175^0$$

Therefore, the supplement of 5^0 is 175^0.

b. Let the supplement of 110^0 be y.

Two angles are supplementary if the sum of their measures is 180^0.

Therefore: $110^0 + y = 180^0$

$110^0 - 110^0 + y = 180^0 - 110^0$ Subtract 110^0 from both sides of the equation

$110^0 + y = 180^0$ to obtain y.

$$0 + y = 70^0$$ $110^0 - 110^0 = 0$ and $180^0 - 110^0 = 70^0$

$$y = 70^0$$

Therefore, the supplement of 110^0 is 70^0

Example 3

a. In the diagram, name two pairs of supplementary angles.

b. In the diagram, name a pair of complementary angles.

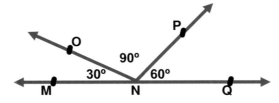

Solution

a. The sum of the measure of any two angles in the diagram are supplementary if their measure is 180^0.

Let us find the first supplementary angles:

$m\angle MNO = 30^0$ and $m\angle ONQ = m\angle ONP + m\angle PNQ$ See the diagram
$$= 90^0 + 60^0$$ See the diagram
$$= 150^0$$ $90^0 + 60^0 = 150^0$

Therefore,
$$m\angle MNO + m\angle ONQ = 30^0 + 150^0$$
$$= 180^0$$
Since the sum of $m\angle MNO$ and $m\angle ONQ$ is 180^0, then $\angle MNO$ and $\angle ONQ$ are supplementary angles.

Let us find the second supplementary angles:

$m\angle QNP = 60^0$ and $m\angle MNP = m\angle MNO + m\angle ONP$ See the diagram
$$= 30^0 + 90^0$$ See the diagram
$$= 120^0$$ $30^0 + 90^0 = 120^0$

Therefore,
$$m\angle QNP + m\angle MNP = 60^0 + 120^0$$
$$= 180^0$$ $60^0 + 120^0 = 180^0$
Since the sum of $m\angle QNP$ and $m\angle MNP$ is 180^0, then $\angle QNP$ and $\angle MNP$ are supplementary angles.

b. Two angles are complementary if the sum of their measures is 90^0.
A pair of complementary angles are $\angle MNO$ and $\angle PNQ$ because $m\angle MNO = 30^0$ and
$m\angle PNQ = 60^0$ and $m\angle MNO + m\angle PNQ = 30^0 + 60^0$ From the diagram
$$= 90^0$$ $30^0 + 60^0 = 90^0$
Since the sum of $m\angle MNO$ and $m\angle PNQ$ is 90^0, then $\angle MNO$ and $\angle PNQ$ are complementary angles.

Example 4
In the diagram, given that $m\angle 1 = 60^0$ find the
a. $m\angle 4$ **b**. $m\angle 3$

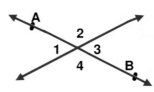

Solution
a. $m\angle 1 = 60^0$ Given in the question.
   $m\angle 1 + m\angle 4 = 180^0$ Sum of the measure of the angles on a straight line (AB) is 180^0 or supplementary.

   $60^0 + m\angle 4 = 180^0$ The question states that $m\angle 1 = 60^0$
$60^0 - 60^0 + m\angle 4 = 180^0 - 60^0$ Subtract 60^0 from both sides of the equation
                         $60^0 + m\angle 4 = 180^0$ to obtain the value of $m\angle 4$.

$$0 + m\angle 4 = 120^0 \qquad 60^0 - 60^0 = 0, \ 180^0 - 60^0 = 120^0$$
$$m\angle 4 = 120^0$$

b. $m\angle 1 = m\angle 3 \qquad \angle 1$ and $\angle 3$ are vertical angles and the measure
of the vertical angles are equal.

Since it is given in the question that $m\angle 1 = 60^0$, then $m\angle 3$ is also 60^0.

Exercises

1. Explain what is meant by supplementary angles.

2. If $\angle A$ and $\angle B$ are supplementary angles, for each case, find the missing angle.
Hint: See Example 1
  a. $m\angle A = 38^0$, $m\angle B = ?$ **b.** $m\angle A = ?$, $m\angle B = 100^0$
  c. $m\angle A = ?$, $m\angle B = 50^0$ **d.** $m\angle A = 110^0$, $m\angle B = ?$
  e. $m\angle A = 99^0$, $m\angle B = ?$ **f.** $m\angle A = ?$, $m\angle B = 104^0$

3. Find the supplement of each of the following angles. Hint: See Example 2.
  a. 101^0 **b.** 110^0 **c.** 1^0 **d.** 3^0 **e.** 55^0 **f.** 121^0

4. a. In each diagram name two pairs of supplementary angles.
  b. In each diagram name a pair of complementary angles.
  Hint: See Example 3.

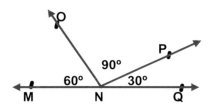 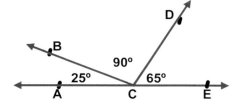

5. In the diagram, given that $m\angle 4 = 15^0$
  a. find $m\angle 3$
  b. find $m\angle 2$
  Hint: See Example 4.

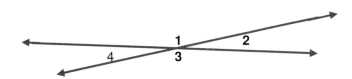

Answers to Selected Questions
2a. 142^0 **3a.** 79^0

Challenge Questions
6. What is the difference between complementary angles and supplementary angles?
7. Find the complement of each of the following angle measures.

a. 1^0 **b.** 32^0 **c.** 75^0 **d.** 89^0 **e.** 50^0

8. What is the supplement of each of the following angle measures.

     a. 1^0 **b.** 100^0 **c.** 179^0 **d.** 50^0 **e.** 121^0

ANGLES FORMED BY A TRANSVERSAL

A transversal is a line that intersects two or more other lines. A transversal that intersects two parallel lines is shown:

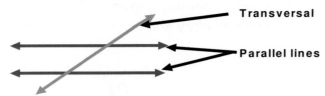

Group Exercise

The angles formed by the transversal that intersects parallel lines have special properties with respect to:

     a. Alternate interior angles.

     b. Alternate exterior angles.

     c. Corresponding angles.

First let us measure the angles formed by the transversal $\overleftrightarrow{XY}$ that intersects the two parallel lines $\overleftrightarrow{AB}$ and $\overleftrightarrow{BC}$, and then record the measurement of each angle in table 1. (**Note**: Draw your own diagram.) Use a protractor to measure the angles, and note that measuring with a protractor may not give the exact measurements.

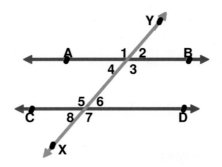

Table 1

Angles	Angle measurements	Acute or supplementary angle
∠1	m∠1	
∠2	m∠2	
∠3	m∠3	
∠4	m∠4	
∠5	m∠5	
∠6	m∠6	
∠7	m∠7	
∠8	m∠8	

Note: ∠ is the symbol for an angle and m∠ is the symbol for "measure of an angle".

1. List the angles that appear to have the same measurements as shown:

∠1, ∠?, ∠? and ∠? have about the same angle measure.

∠2, ∠?, ∠? and ∠? have about the same angle measure.

2. When you add the measure of any acute angle to the measure of any obtuse angle, is the sum approximately 180⁰?

Critical Conclusion

From your measurements, it can be concluded that:

Rule 1: The even number angles are the acute angles and the measure of their angles are equal, so their angles are congruent to each other.

Rule 2: The odd number angles are the obtuse angles and the measure of their angles are equal and, so their angles are congruent to each other.

Rule 3: Any acute angle is **supplementary** to any **obtuse** angle: (**Note**: The sum of the measures of two angles that add up to 180⁰ are said to be **supplementary**. The sum of the measures of two angles that add to 90⁰ are **complementary** angles.)

From the group exercise, we can conclude that:

  a. The acute angles are congruent to each other, and therefore,

∠2 ≅ m∠4 ≅ m∠6 ≅ m∠8.

  b. The obtuse angles are congruent to each other, and therefore,

m∠1 ≅ m∠3 ≅ m∠5 ≅ m∠7.

Note: ≅ is the symbol for "is congruent to". **Congruent** means figures that have the same size and shape.

How to Find the Measure of Angles Formed by a Transversal that Intersects Two or More Parallel Lines.

To find the measure of angles formed by a transversal that intersects two or more parallel lines, use the following two facts:

1. All the acute angles formed by the transversal are congruent to each other, so we can write in general that the **measure of any acute angle** = the **measure of any other acute angle**, and then solve the equation as needed.

2. All the obtuse angles formed by the transversal are congruent to each other, so we can write in general that the **measure of any obtuse angle** = the **measure of any other obtuse angle**, and then solve the equation as needed.

3. Any acute angle is **supplementary** to any obtuse angle, and therefore, we can then write that the **sum of the measures of any obtuse angle and any acute angle is 180^0** , and then solve the equation as needed.

Example 1

In the figure, given that $\overleftrightarrow{PQ}$ is a transversal and $\overleftrightarrow{XY}$ is parallel to $\overleftrightarrow{WZ}$, find the measure of
    a. each obtuse angle.   **b.** $\angle 5$.
    c. each acute angle.

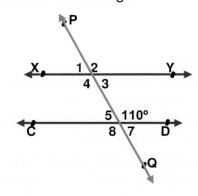

Solution

a. All the obtuse angles are congruent to each other, so
    $m\angle 2 = m\angle 4 = m\angle 8 = 110^0$ Hint: **See Rule 1.**

b. Any acute angle is supplementary to any obtuse angle, so
    $m\angle 5 + 110^0 = 180^0$ $\angle 5$ is supplementary to 110^0.
                                Hint: **See Rule 3.**

    $m\angle 5 + 110^0 - 110^0 = 180^0 - 110^0$ Subtract 110^0 from both sides of the equation in order to isolate $m\angle 5$.

               $m\angle 5 = 70^0$ $110^0 - 110^0 = 0$ and $180^0 - 110^0 = 70^0$.

c. $\angle 5$ is an acute angle and all the acute angles are congruent to each other and therefore, $m\angle 1 = m\angle 3 = m\angle 5 = m\angle 7 = 70^0$. Hint: **See Rule 2** and also, we have already shown in the solution of Example 1b that $m\angle 5 = 70^0$.

Example 2

Find x in the diagram. $\overleftrightarrow{XY}$ is parallel to $\overleftrightarrow{CD}$.

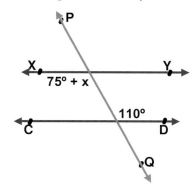

Solution

$75^0 + x = 110^0$ — Recall from the group exercise that, all the obtuse angles are congruent to each other.

$75^0 - 75^0 + x = 110^0 - 75^0$ — Subtract 75^0 from both sides of the equation in order to isolate x.

$x = 35^0$ — $75^0 - 75^0 = 0$ and $100^0 - 75^0 = 35^0$.

Example 3

Find x in the diagram. $\overleftrightarrow{XY}$ is parallel to $\overleftrightarrow{CD}$.

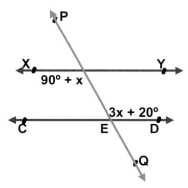

Solution

$90^0 + x = 3x + 20^0$ — Recall from the group exercise that, all the obtuse angles are congruent.

$90^0 + x - x = 3x - x + 20^0$ — Subtract x from both sides of the equation in order to eliminate the x on the left side of the equation, and also to gather the unknown terms only at the right side of the equation.

$90^0 = 2x + 20^0$ — $x - x = 0$ and $3x - x = 2x$.

$90^0 - 20^0 = 2x + 20^0 - 20^0$ — Subtract 20^0 from both sides of the equation in order to eliminate the 20^0 on the right side of the equation.

$70^0 = 2x$ — $90^0 - 20^0 = 70^0$ and $20^0 - 20^0 = 0$.

$$\frac{70^0}{2} = \frac{2x}{2}$$

Divide both sides of the equation by 2 in order to obtain the value of x.

$$\frac{\overset{35^0}{\cancel{70^0}}}{\underset{1}{\cancel{2}}} = \frac{\overset{x}{\cancel{2x}}}{\underset{1}{\cancel{2}}}$$

$$35^0 = x$$

The value of x is 35^0.

Example 4

a. Find x in the diagram. $\overleftrightarrow{AB}$ is parallel to $\overleftrightarrow{CD}$.
b. Find $m\angle AEY$.
c. Find $m\angle CFX$.

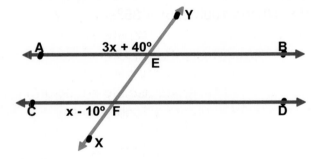

Solution

a. $m\angle AEY + m\angle CFX = 180^0$

Recall from the group exercise that any acute angle is **supplementary** to any obtuse angle.

$$3x + 40^0 + x - 10^0 = 180^0$$
$$4x + 30^0 = 180^0$$

$m\angle AEY = 3x + 40^0$ and $m\angle CFX = x - 10^0$
Combine like terms, $3x + x = 4x$ and $40^0 - 10^0 = 30^0$

$$4x + 30^0 - 30^0 = 180^0 - 30^0$$

Subtract 4x from each side of the equation in order to isolate 4x.

$$4x = 150^0$$

$30^0 - 30^0 = 0$ and $180^0 - 30^0 = 150^0$.

$$\frac{4x}{4} = \frac{150^0}{4}$$

Divide both sides of the equation by 4 to isolate x.

$$\frac{\overset{x}{\cancel{4x}}}{\underset{1}{\cancel{4}}} = \frac{150^0}{4}$$

$$x = 37.5^0 \qquad\qquad 150 \div 4 = 37\frac{1}{2} = 37.5$$

b. $m\angle AEY = 3x + 40^0$ Given in the diagram.
    $m\angle AEY = 3(37.5^0) + 40^0$ From the solution of Example **4a**, $x = 37.5^0$.
    $m\angle AEY = 112.5^0 + 40^0$
    $m\angle AEY = 152.5^0$

c. $m\angle CFX = x - 10^0$ Given in the diagram.
    $m\angle CFX = 37.5^0 - 10^0$ From the solution of Example **4a**, $x = 37.5^0$.
    $m\angle CFX = 27.5^0$

Corresponding, Alternate Interior, and Alternate Exterior Angles
When a transversal intersects two or more parallel lines, the angles formed are classified as **corresponding**, **alternate interior** or **alternate exterior** angles.
    1. Corresponding angles are congruent, and this can be used to set up an equation, and then solve for the measures of corresponding angles.
    2. Alternate interior angles are congruent, and this can be used to set up an equation, and then solve for the measures of alternate interior angles.
    3. Alternate exterior angles are congruent, and this can be used to set up an equation, and then solve for the measures of alternate exterior angles.

Corresponding angles.
$\angle 1$ corresponding to $\angle 5$
$\angle 4$ corresponding to $\angle 8$
$\angle 2$ corresponding to $\angle 6$
$\angle 3$ corresponding to $\angle 7$

Alternate Interior angles
$\angle 4$ is alternate interior to $\angle 6$
$\angle 3$ is alternate interior to $\angle 5$

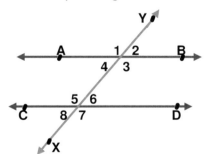 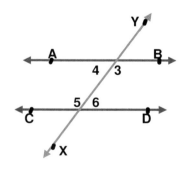

$\overleftrightarrow{AB}$ is parallel to $\overleftrightarrow{CD}$, and this is written as $\overleftrightarrow{AB} \parallel \overleftrightarrow{CD}$. The symbol for "is parallel to" is $\parallel$.

Alternate exterior angles
$\angle 1$ is alternate exterior to $\angle 7$
$\angle 2$ is alternate exterior to $\angle 8$.

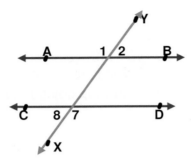

$\overleftrightarrow{AB}$ is parallel to $\overleftrightarrow{CD}$, and this is written as $\overleftrightarrow{AB} \parallel \overleftrightarrow{CD}$. The symbol for "is parallel to" is $\parallel$.

The Conditions for Two Lines to be Parallel

The five conditions for two lines to be parallel are:

1. If any of the corresponding angles are congruent.

2. If any of the alternate interior angles are congruent.

3. If any of the alternate exterior angles are congruent.

4. If the perpendicular distance at any point on the parallel lines are the same.

5. If the two lines will never meet if they are produced indefinitely.

Group Exercise

Try this!!, draw perpendicular lines or 90^0 lines to two parallel lines at different points on the line, and measure the perpendicular distances, and you will find that the perpendicular distances are the same only if the two lines are parallel.

Exercises

1. What is a transversal? What are the conditions for two lines to be parallel?

2. In the figure, $\overleftrightarrow{AB}$ is parallel to $\overleftrightarrow{CD}$.

   a. Which line is the transversal?

   b. List three pairs of supplementary angles. Hint: See Example 1**b**.

   c. List all the angles that are congruent to $\angle 3$. Hint: See Example 1c.

   d. List all the angles that are congruent to $\angle 6$. Hint: See Example 1a.

   e. If $m\angle 7$ is 125^0, find $m\angle 8$. Hint: See Example 1**b**.

   f. If $m\angle 3$ is 63^0, what is $m\angle 1$? Hint: See Rule 1.

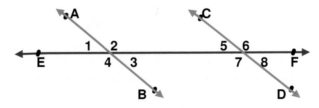

3. Given that in the figure $\overleftrightarrow{AB} \parallel \overleftrightarrow{CD}$, find the measure of each angle. Remember that $\parallel$ is the symbol for "is parallel to."

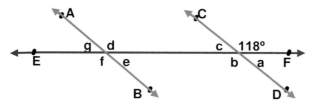

a. m∠d   **b.** m∠b   **c.** m∠f   **d.** m∠g   **e.** m∠c.

Hint: See Example 1. Note that m∠ is the symbol for the "measure of an angle".

4. Given that in the figure, $\overleftrightarrow{AB}$ ∥ $\overleftrightarrow{CD}$,

  a. List all the alternate exterior angles.

  b. List all the alternate interior angles.

  c. List all the corresponding angles.

  Hint: See the notes under "Corresponding, Alternate Interior and Alternate Exterior Angles". Hint: See Example 1.

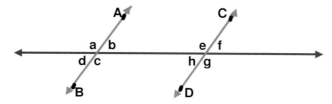

5. $\overleftrightarrow{AB}$ ∥ $\overleftrightarrow{CD}$, find the measure of each obtuse and each acute angle.

  Hint: See Example 1.

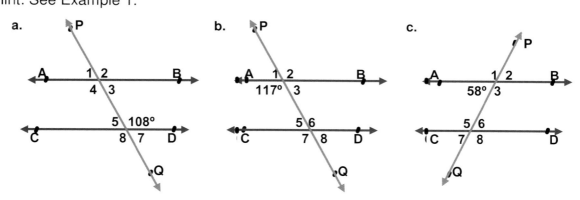

6. $\overleftrightarrow{AB}$ ∥ $\overleftrightarrow{CD}$, find x in each diagram. Hint: See Example 2.

a.

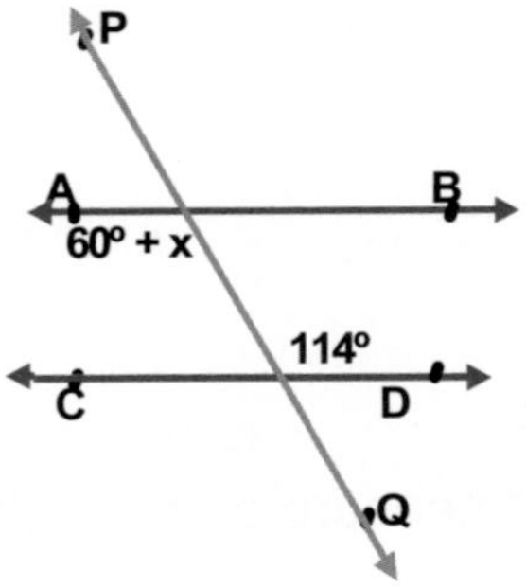

P

A   B
60° + x

114°
C   D

Q

b.

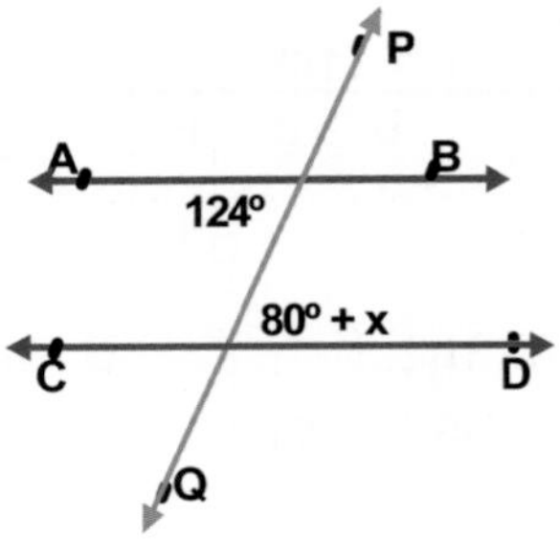

P

A   B
124°

80° + x
C   D

Q

c.

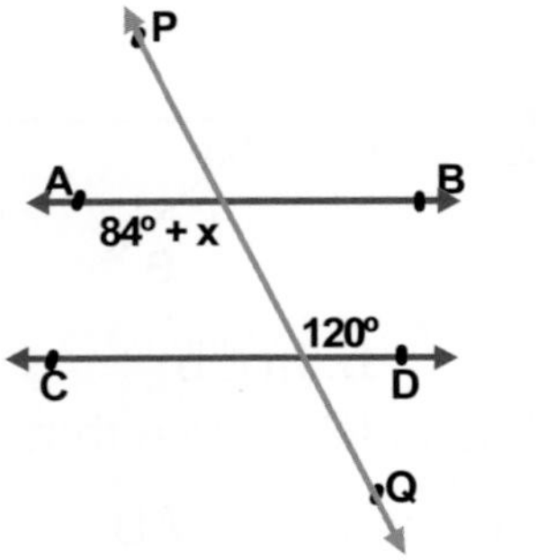

P

A   B
84° + x

120°
C   D

Q

7. Find x. $\overleftrightarrow{AB} \parallel \overleftrightarrow{CD}$. Hint: Round your answer to the nearest tenth. See Example 3.

a.

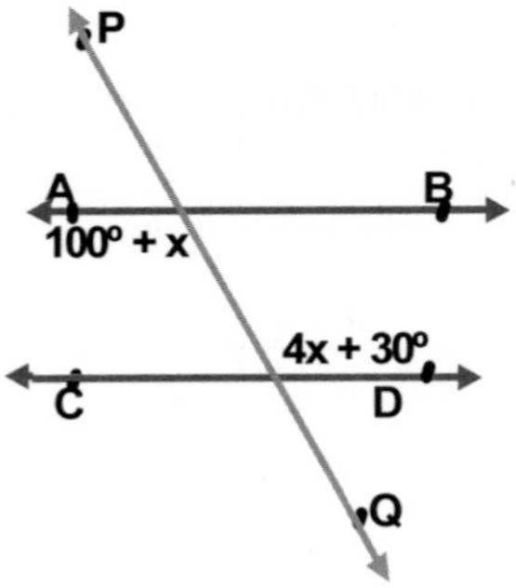

P

A   B
100° + x

4x + 30°
C   D

Q

b.

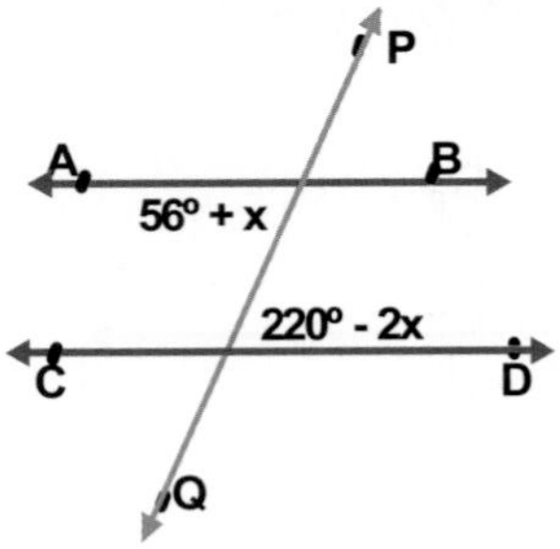

P

A   B
56° + x

220° - 2x
C   D

Q

c.

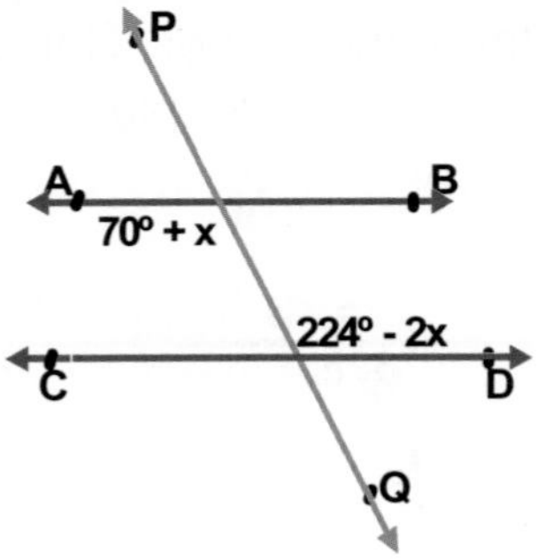

P

A   B
70° + x

224° - 2x
C   D

Q

8. $\overleftrightarrow{AB} \parallel \overleftrightarrow{CD}$. In the diagram **a**, find x and also find the m∠PEB and the m∠QFD.
        In the diagram **b**, find x and also find the m∠AEP and the m∠PFD.
        In the diagram **c**, find x and also find the m∠CFQ.

   Hint: See Example 4. Round your answers to the nearest tenth.

a.

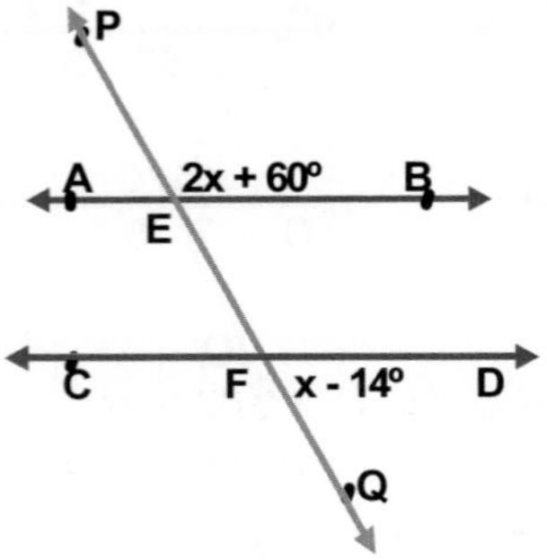

P

A   2x + 60°   B
   E

C   F   x - 14°   D

Q

b.

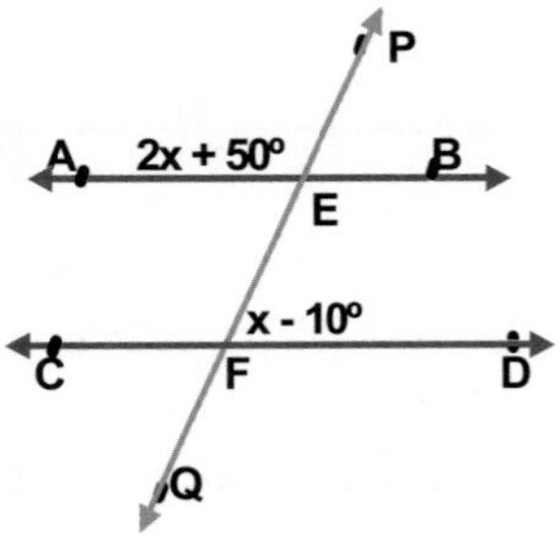

P

A   2x + 50°   B
     E

x - 10°
C   F   D

Q

c.

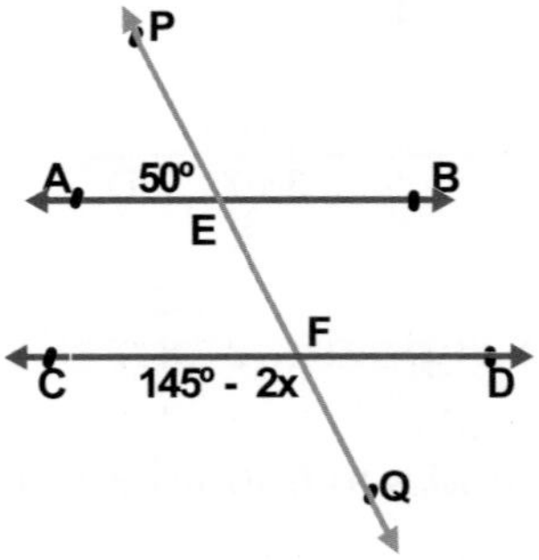

P

A   50°   B
   E

     F
C   145° - 2x   D

Q

Challenge Questions

9. $\overleftrightarrow{AB} \parallel \overleftrightarrow{CD}$, find the value of x. Round your answer to the nearest tenth.

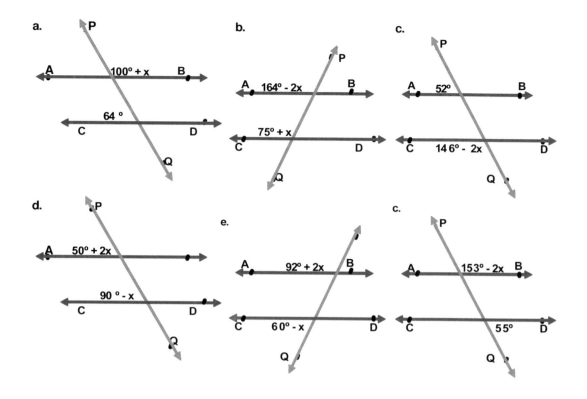

Answers to Selected Questions
2e. 55^0 **5a.** $m\angle 1 = m\angle 3 = m\angle 5 = m\angle 7 = 72^0$, $m\angle 2 = m\angle 4 = m\angle 8 = 108^0$.
6a. $80°$ **7a.** 23.3^0 **8a.** $x \approx 44.7^0$ $m\angle PEB \approx 149.3^0$ $m\angle QFD \approx 30.7^0$

TRANSFORMATION

New Terms: **rigid transformation**, **translation**, **slide**, **reflection**, **rotation**
A movement of objects without changing the size or the shape of the object is called **rigid transformation**. Since during transformation, the size and the shape of the object does not change, **the image is congruent to the preimage or the preimage is congruent to the image**. We can slide (translation), flip (reflection) and turn (rotation) an object as shown:

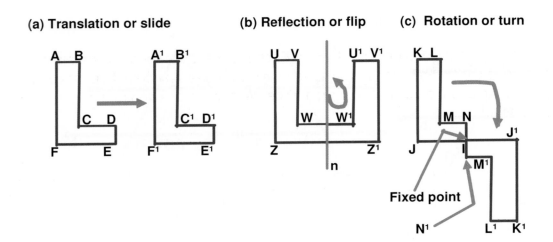

(a) Translation or slide **(b) Reflection or flip** **(c) Rotation or turn**

In diagram (c), I is a fixed point and it is also the point of rotation.

Slide (translation) - diagram (a)
A slide or a translation is the movement of an object along a straight line. Figure ABCDEF can slide to a new location at A^1 B^1 C^1 D^1 E^1 F^1. We say that figure A^1 B^1 C^1 D^1 E^1 F^1 is the translation of figure ABCDEF.
The figure ABCDEF is called the preimage and A^1 B^1 C^1 D^1 E^1 F^1 is called the image of ABCDEF. During translation, **every point of the preimage is moved in the same direction and by the same distance**.

Flip (reflection) - diagram (b)
A flip or a reflection is the movement of an object by flipping it over a line. We can also think of placing a mirror along line n. The mirror image of the object UVWXYZ is the object $U^1V^1W^1X^1Y^1Z^1$. We say that $U^1V^1W^1X^1Y^1Z^1$ is a reflection of UVWXYZ. The figure UVWXYZ is called the preimage and the figure $U^1V^1W^1X^1Y^1Z^1$ is called the image of the figure UVWXYZ. During reflection, **every point of the preimage is moved across the mirror line so that the perpendicular distance from the preimage to the mirror line is equal to the perpendicular distance from every corresponding points of the image to the mirror line**. The mirror line is also known as line of reflection.

Turn (rotation) - diagram (c)
A turn or a rotation is the movement of an object by turning or rotating it around a fixed point. In diagram (c) the object IJKLMN is turned or rotated at the fixed point I, until the object stops at a new position $I^1J^1K^1L^1M^1N^1$. We say that $I^1J^1K^1L^1M^1N^1$ is the rotation of the object IJKLMN. The object IJKLMN is called the preimage and the object $I^1J^1K^1L^1M^1N^1$ is called the image. During rotation, **every point of the preimage is moved by the same angle through a circular direction at a given fixed point known as the center of rotation**.

Group Project 1

The class should be divided into four teams. Each team should put a set-square on a paper and trace the first position of the set-square. Each team should then move the set-square to the second position and then trace the second position of the set-square as shown:

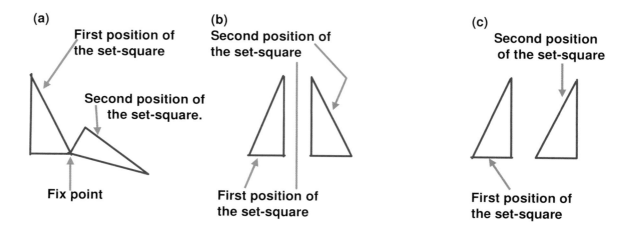

(a)
First position of the set-square

Second position of the set-square.

Fix point

(b)
Second position of the set-square

First position of the set-square

(c)
Second position of the set-square

First position of the set-square

- In each case, write down how the first set-square was moved to the second position of the set-square. Use the terms flip (reflection), slide (translation) and turn (rotation) to explain each movement as applicable.
- Each team should report the result of their project to the whole class.

Group Project 2 - a. How to draw the reflection of points.

      b. How to find the relationship between the angle formed by the preimage and the mirror line and the angle formed by the image and the mirror line.

      c. How to find the relationship between the perpendicular distance from the preimage to the mirror line and the perpendicular distance between the image and the mirror line.

Solutions

a. Draw the reflection of the points W, X, Y, and Z across the mirror line n.

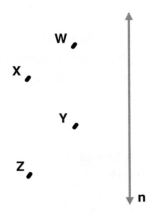

Method: Fold the paper along the mirror line n. Use a sharp object to punch holes through the paper at points W, X, Y, and Z. Unfold the paper and label the new points W^1, X^1, Y^1, and Z^1 as demonstrated:

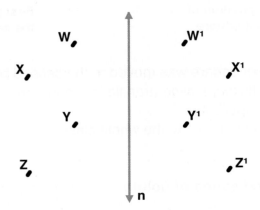

W^1 is the reflection or the image of W, X^1 is the reflection or the image of X, Y^1 is the reflection or the image of Y, and Z^1 is the reflection or the image of Z.

b.To find the relationship between the angle formed by the preimage and the mirror line and the angle formed by the image and the mirror line, draw $\overline{WW^1}$, $\overline{XX^1}$, $\overline{YY^1}$ and $\overline{ZZ^1}$. Label the intersection of $\overline{WW^1}$ and the mirror line as A. Label the intersection of $\overline{XX^1}$ and the mirror line as B. Label the intersection of $\overline{YY^1}$ and the mirror line as C. Label the intersection of $\overline{ZZ^1}$ and the mirror line as D as shown:

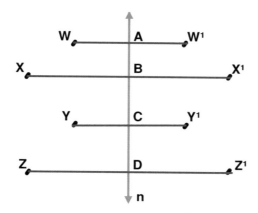

Let us measure the angle formed by $\overline{ZD}$ and the mirror line n by placing the center of the protractor at intersection D. The base line of the protractor should be over $\overline{ZZ^1}$, and then read the number of degrees on the protractor at where the mirror line crosses the protractor degree scale. The reading on the protractor should be 90^0, and this 90^0 shows that $m\angle ZDA = 90^0$ and $m\angle ADZ^1 = 90^0$ also. Similarly, read the $m\angle YCA$, $m\angle ACY^1$, $m\angle XBA$, and $m\angle ABX^1$, and complete the table shown:

Reading of the angles formed by the preimage and image line with the mirror line.	
Preimage side	Image side
$m\angle ZDA = 90^0$	$m\angle ADZ^1 = 90^0$
$m\angle YCA = ?$	$m\angle ACY^1 = ?$
$m\angle XBA = ?$	$m\angle ABX^1 = ?$

We can conclude from the reading of the angles formed by the preimage and the image line with the mirror line that **the preimage and the image line form 90^0 with the mirror line**. Since any two lines that forms 90^0 are called perpendicular lines, we can similarly say that the reflection of a point or the preimage and the image of a point are at a perpendicular distance from the mirror line. Further we can state that the **distance from every point of the preimage to the corresponding points of the image form 90^0 with the mirror line**.

c. To find the relationship between the perpendicular distance from the preimage to the mirror line and the perpendicular distance between the image and the mirror line. Take a ruler and measure the following segments from solution b: $\overline{WA}$ and $\overline{AW^1}$, $\overline{XB}$ and $\overline{BX^1}$, $\overline{YC}$ and $\overline{CY^1}$, $\overline{ZD}$, and $\overline{DZ^1}$, and record each pair of the measurements as shown:

Measurements of the perpendicular distances from the preimage to the mirror line and from the corresponding image to the mirror line.

$$\overline{WA} = ?$$ $$\overline{AW}^1 = ?$$

$$\overline{XB} = ?$$ $$\overline{BX}^1 = ?$$

$$\overline{YC} = ?$$ $$\overline{CY}^1 = ?$$

$$\overline{ZD} = ?$$ $$\overline{DZ}^1 = ?$$

We can conclude that since the perpendicular distance from each preimage to the mirror line and the perpendicular distance from each corresponding image to the mirror line is the same, **the perpendicular distance from any preimage to the mirror line is the same as the perpendicular distance from the corresponding images to the mirror line**.

Reflection Followed by Another Reflection Across Parallel Mirror Lines.
The transformation type when an object is reflected across two parallel mirror lines is **translation**. This is shown by Example 1.

Example 1
a. Reflect the triangle PQR through two parallel mirror lines.
b. Explain why the transformation across the first mirror line that produces triangle STU is not a translation.
c. Show that the type of transformation that results from the reflection of the triangle PQR through two parallel mirror lines that produces triangle VWX is a translation by visual inspection.

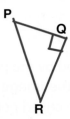

Solution
a. The reflection of the triangle PQR through two parallel mirror lines is shown in the diagram.

The reflection of the triangle PQR throw two mirror lines is shown in the diagram on the next page.

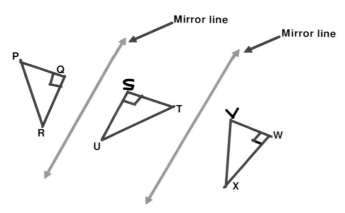

b. The transformation across the first mirror line that produces triangle STU is not a translation because although triangle STU is the image of PQR with the same shape and size, every point of the preimage PQR is not moved the same distance and in the same direction to form the image STU. For example, $\overline{QS}$ is shorter than the $\overline{PT}$ and triangle STU faces the opposite direction to triangle PQR. Translation requires that every point of the preimage which is PQR must be moved **the same distance** and in the **same direction**.

c. Show that the type of transformation that results from the reflection of the triangle PQR through two parallel mirror lines that produces triangle VWX is a translation by visual inspection because every point of the preimage which is triangle PQR is moved the same distance and in the same direction to form the new image which is triangle VWX. Translation requires that every point of the preimage which is PQR must be moved the **same distance** in the **same direction**.

Example 2
a. Reflect the alphabet F through two parallel mirror lines.
b. Explain why the transformation across the first mirror line is not a translation.
c. Show that the type of transformation that results from the reflection of the alphabet F through two parallel mirror lines is a translation by visual inspection.
Solution
a. The reflection of the alphabet F through two parallel mirror lines is shown as shown:

(The reflection of the alphabet F is shown on the next page.)

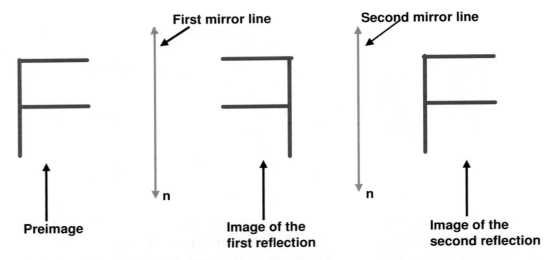

First mirror line

Second mirror line

n

n

Preimage

Image of the first reflection

Image of the second reflection

b. The transformation across the first mirror line is not a translation because although the image of the first reflection is of the same shape and size of the preimage, every point of the preimage is not moved the same distance to form every point of the image of the first reflection and this is evident because the image of the first reflection is facing the opposite direction to the preimage of the alphabet F. Translation requires that every point of the preimage must be moved the same distance in the same direction.

c. The type of the transformation that results from the reflection of the alphabet F through two parallel mirror lines is a translation by visual inspection because every point of the preimage is moved the same distance and in the same direction to form the new image after the reflection through two parallel mirror lines. Translation requires that every point of the preimage must be moved the same distance in the same direction.

Reflection Followed by Another Reflection Across Two Intersecting Mirror Lines.
The transformation type when an object is reflected across two intersecting mirror lines is **rotation**. This is shown in Example 3.

Example 3
a. Sketch the reflection of a right-angle triangle across two intersecting mirror lines.
b. Explain why the transformation that occurs when the reflection of a right-angle triangle across two intersecting mirror lines is a **rotation**.
Solution
a. The reflection of a right-angle triangle across two intersecting mirror lines is shown as shown:

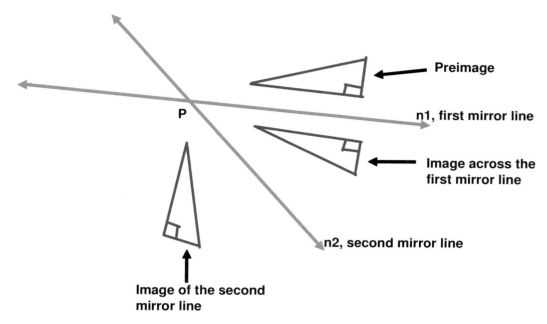

b. The transformation that occurs during the reflection of a right-angle triangle across two intersecting mirror lines is a rotation because every point of the preimage is moved by the same angle through a circular direction at a fixed point P.

Translation Followed by Reflection

Example 4
a. Sketch the translation of figure ABCD to form the image EFGH, followed by a reflection across the line n to form the image IJKL.
b. Give reasons why the figure EFGH is the translation of figure ABCD by visual inspection.
c. Give reasons why the figure IJKL is the reflection of the figure EFGH by visual inspection.

Solution
a. The translation of figure ABCD to form the image EFGH, followed by a reflection across the line n to form the image IJKL is sketched as shown:

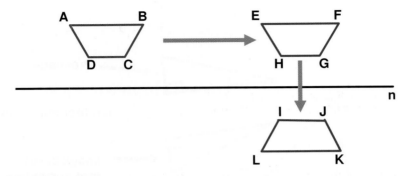

b. The figure EFGH is the translation of figure ABCD because every point of the figure ABCD is moved the same distance in the same direction.

c. The figure IJKL is the reflection of the figure EFGH because every point of the figure EFGH is moved across the mirror line n so that the perpendicular distance from every point of the figure EFGH to the mirror line n is equal to the perpendicular distance from the corresponding points of the image IJKL to the mirror line n.

Example 5
Sketch the image of each figure after the given rotation about the point P.

a. 90º rotation

b. 180º rotation

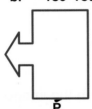

c. 90º rotation

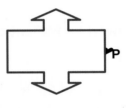

Solution
a. The sketch of the 90⁰ rotation is as shown:

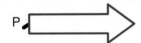

Note that if we join the point of rotation of the preimage and the point of rotation of the image, the angle between the preimage and the image should be be 90⁰ as shown:

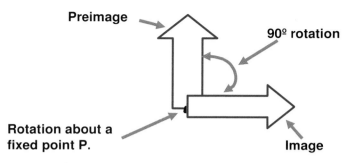

Preimage

90º rotation

Rotation about a
fixed point P.

Image

b. The sketch of the 180^0 rotation is as shown:

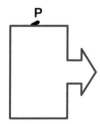

P

Note that if we join the point of rotation of the preimage and the point of rotation of the image, the angle between the preimage and the image should be 180^0, or the image will be under the preimage as shown:

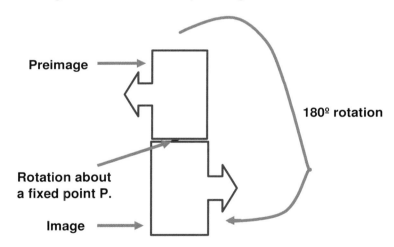

Preimage

180º rotation

Rotation about
a fixed point P.

Image

c. The sketch of the 90^0 rotation is as follows:

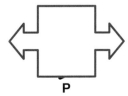

P

Note that if we join the point of rotation of the preimage and the point of rotation of the image, the angle between the preimage and the image should be 90^0 as shown:

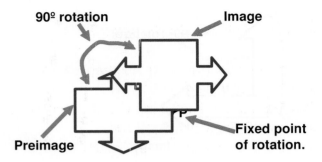

90º rotation　　**Image**

Preimage　　**Fixed point of rotation.**

Exercise

1. Explain the following terms using a diagram of your own:
   (a) Translation
   (b) Reflection
   (c) Rotation
   Hint: See the preceding notes.
2. Explain how the first figure was moved to the position of the second figure by using the terms rotation, reflection, or translation as applicable.

(a.)　　**(b.)**　　**(c.)**

Fix point

   Hint: See the preceding notes.
3. A polygon is translated, explain if the image of the polygon is congruent to the preimage. Hint: See the information about rigid transformation.
4. How would you classify the following actions using the terms rotation, reflection, or translation as applicable.
   (a) Opening a car door. Hint: Opening a car door is a rotation about a fixed point.
   (b) Opening the door to your house. Opening a car door is a rotation about a fixed point
   (c) When you see yourself in the mirror
   (d) When a book is moved horizontally in a straight line on a table to a position 6 inches away.
5. The lines from every point of the preimage to the image during reflection is perpendicular to the mirror line. True or false? Hint: See Group Project 2.
6. The perpendicular distance from the preimage to the mirror line is the same as or equal to the perpendicular distance from the image to the mirror line. True or false? Hint: See Group Project 2.
7. The mirror line is also known as the line of reflection. True or false? Hint: See notes on rigid transformations.

8. What is rigid transformation?

9. During rigid transformation, the size and the shape of the objects are not changed? True of false?

10. During rigid transformation, the preimage is congruent to the image or the image is congruent to the preimage. True or false?

11. Judith said that when a polygon is rotated about a fixed point, the image is congruent to the preimage. Is she correct? Explain your answer.

12. Translate each figure along the given line. Hint: See Group Project 1c.

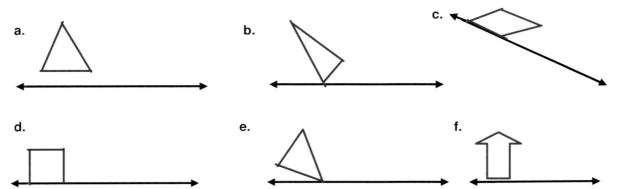

13. Reflect each figure across the given line. Hint: See Group Project 1b.

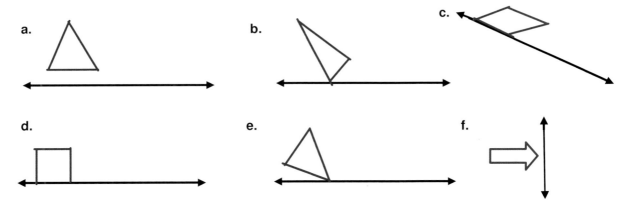

14. Rotate each figure about the given fixed point P. Hint: See Group Project 1c.

15. **a**. Reflect each figure through two parallel mirror lines.
    b. Explain why the transformation across the first mirror line is not a translation.
    c. Show that the type of transformation that results from the reflection of each figure through two parallel mirror lines a translation by visual inspection.
    Hint: See Example 1.

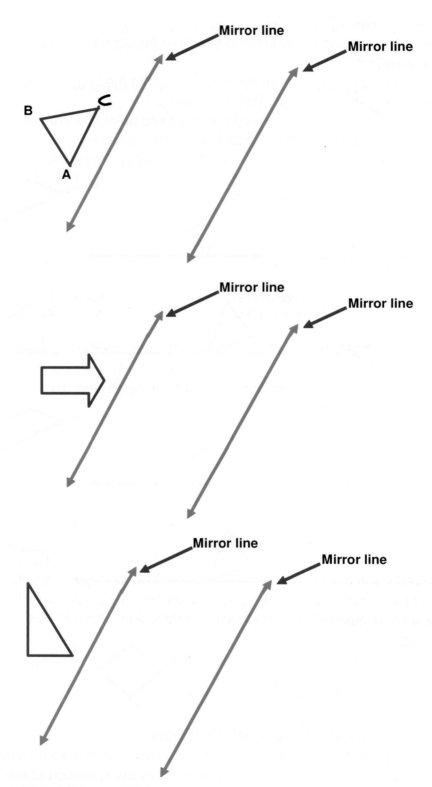

16. **a**. Reflect each alphabet through two parallel mirror lines.
    b. Explain why the transformation across the first mirror line is not a translation.
    c. Show that the type of transformation that results from the reflection of each

alphabet through two parallel mirror lines is a translation by visual inspection.
Hint: See Example 2.

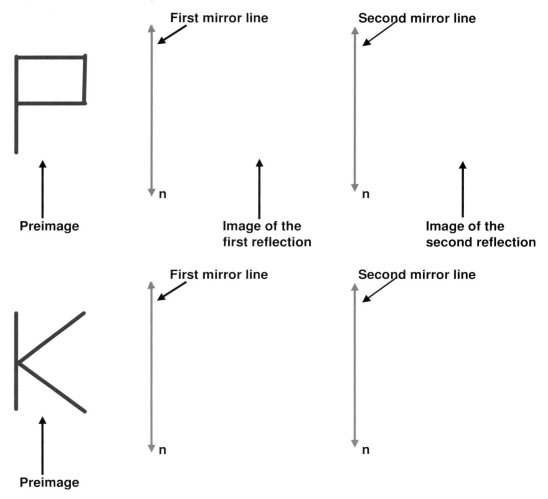

17. a. Sketch the reflection of each figure across two intersecting mirror lines.
    b. Explain why the transformation that occurs when the reflection of each figure across two intersecting mirror lines is a **rotation**.
    Hint: See Example 3.

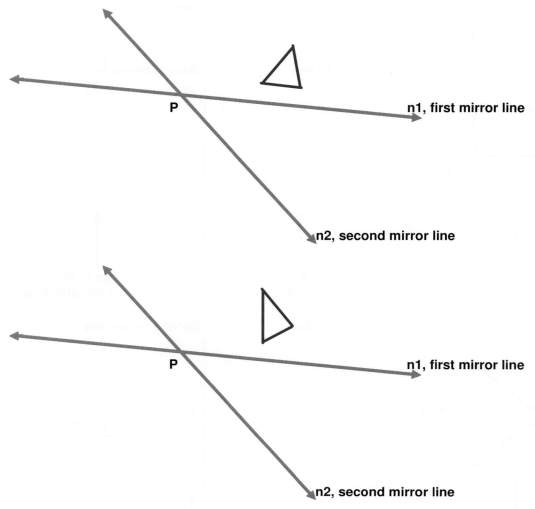

n1, first mirror line

n2, second mirror line

n1, first mirror line

n2, second mirror line

18 a. Sketch the translation of each figure to form an image, followed by a reflection across the line n to form a second image.

   b. Give reasons why the first image is a the translation of the preimage by visual inspection.

   c. Give reasons why the second image is the reflection of the first image by visual inspection.

   Hint: See Example 4.

i   ii   iii

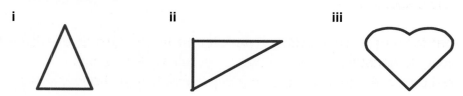

19. Sketch the image of each figure after the given rotation about the point P.
   Hint: See Example 5.

a. 90° rotation

P

b. 180° rotation

P

c. 90° rotation

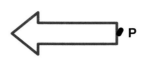

P

20. Draw the reflection of the points A, B, and C across the mirror line n by copying the diagram and folding the paper. Hint: See Group Project 2. Explain your method.

a.

A

n

b.

B

n

c.

C

n

Cumulative Review

1. $\dfrac{3}{4} \div \dfrac{7}{4} =$

2. $\dfrac{6}{7} \times \dfrac{1}{2} =$

3. $\dfrac{5}{6} - \dfrac{1}{4} =$

4. $\dfrac{1}{4} + \dfrac{1}{2} + \dfrac{3}{4} =$

CONSTRUCTION

New Terms: Angle bisector, bisect

How to use paper folding to construct perpendicular lines - Group Exercise 1.
To use paper folding to construct perpendicular lines, follow these steps:

1. Get a squared paper. A squared paper is a paper that has all the four sides equal and all the four corners are 90^0.

2. If you cannot get a squared paper, you can make one by getting an $8\dfrac{1}{2}$ inches by 11 inches standard paper and label the corners WXYZ and then

measure $8\frac{1}{2}$ inches along both sides of the of the length of the paper from W to A, and then from Z to B.

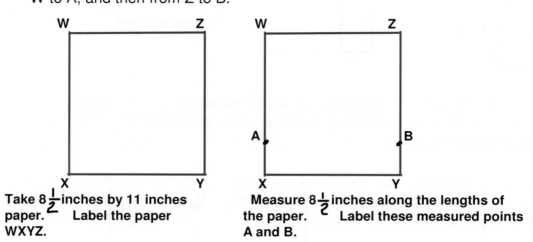

Take $8\frac{1}{2}$ inches by 11 inches paper.   Label the paper WXYZ.

Measure $8\frac{1}{2}$ inches along the lengths of the paper.   Label these measured points A and B.

3. With a pencil and a ruler, draw a line from A to B. Take a pair of scissors and cut along the line AB.

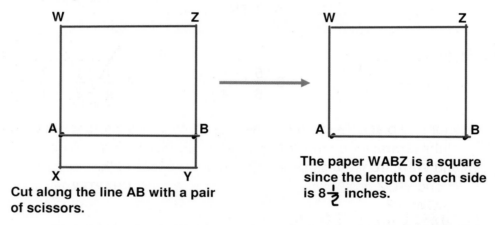

Cut along the line AB with a pair of scissors.

The paper WABZ is a square since the length of each side is $8\frac{1}{2}$ inches.

4. Fold the square paper WABZ along the diagonal AZ over such that the corners W and B should coincide as shown:

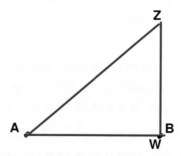

Firmly press on the side AZ to form a crease. A crease is a line made by folding.

5. Fold the paper folding in Step 4 over such that the vertex Z should coincide with the

vertex A and label the new vertex created as O as shown:

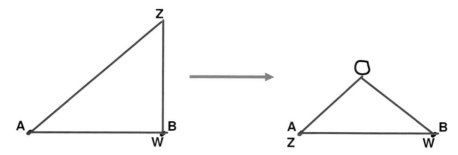

Firmly press on the sides AO and OB to form creases. A crease is a line made by folding.

6. Completely unfold the final folding in Step 5 to form the square paper WABZ again with O as the intersection point between the diagonals WB and AZ that are formed by the crease created by pressing on the sides AO and OB in Step 5.

Completely unfolding

Creases

7. Take a protractor and place the center of the protractor on the intersection O with the base line of the protractor on the line or crease AZ. Read the measures of the angles AOW and WOZ from the scale on the protractor. Record the measurements of angles AOW and WOZ as shown:

$$m\angle AOW = ?$$
$$m\angle WOZ = ?$$

Conclusion: Your measurements for angle AOW and angle WOZ should be 90^0. Two lines are perpendicular if they intersect to form 90^0, so lines AZ and WB are perpendicular lines. We have therefore just completed constructing perpendicular lines by using paper folding.

How to Use Paper Folding to Construct the Midpoint of a Segment - Group Exercise 2

To use paper folding to construct the midpoint of a segment, follow these steps:
1. Draw a segment AB of any convenient length (about 4 inches) on a piece of paper.
2. Take a pointed object and punch a hole at point A and then punch another hole at point B.

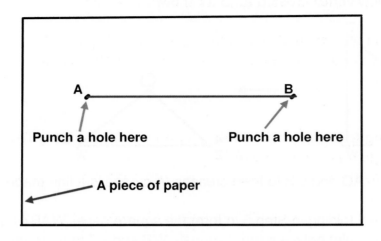

3. Fold the piece of paper over such that the hole A coincides with the hole B, and then firmly press the folded piece of paper to form a crease. A crease is a line made by folding. Label the intersection of the broken line and the crease o.

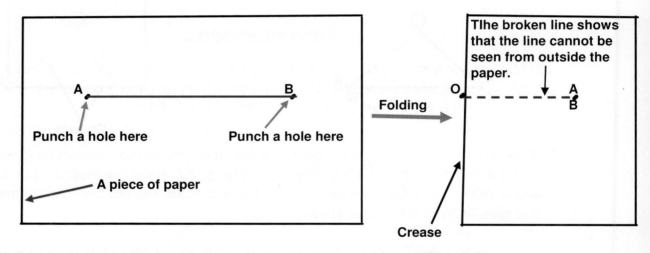

4. Unfold the paper and take a ruler and measure the segments AO and OB. Is segment AO the same length as segment OB? _____ (yes or no?).

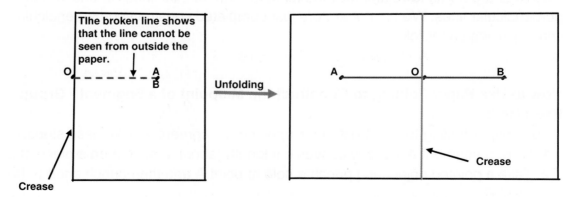

5. Can we say that the point O divides the segment AB into two equal parts? (yes or no).

6. Can we say that the point O is the midpoint of the segment AB? (yes or no).

Conclusion: Steps 1 to 4 use paper folding to construct the midpoint O of the segment AB.

How to Use Paper Folding to Produce an Angle Bisector or How to Use Paper Folding to Bisect an Angle - Group Exercise 3.

To use paper folding to produce an angle bisector or to use paper folding to bisect an angle follow these steps:

1. Draw any measure of an angle (about 60^0) on a piece of paper and label the angle ABC.

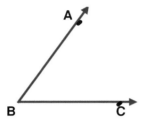

2. Take a ruler and measure the same distance from the point B along the segment AB and label this distance as BX, and then measure the same distance from the point B along the segment BC and label this distance as Y.

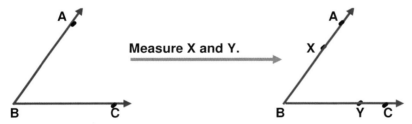

3. Take a pencil and punch a hole at the points B, X, and Y. Then fold the paper over such that the crease passes through the point B and also such that the hole at point X coincides with the hole at point Y.

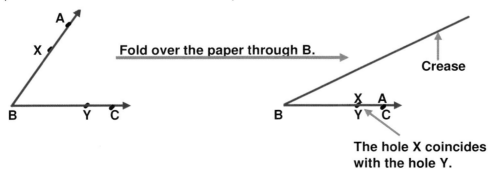

4. Unfold the paper and label a point P on the cease. Take a protractor, place the

839

center of the protractor at point B and with the base line of the protractor on the segment BC, read the protractor scale at where the crease crosses the protractor scale and this is the measure of angle PBC. Now measure angle ABP by placing the center of the protractor on point B such that the base line of the protractor is on the crease. Read the protractor scale at where the segment BA crosses the protractor scale.

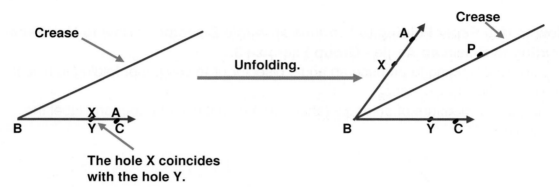

The hole X coincides with the hole Y.

Record your angle measurements as shown:

$$m\angle ABP = ?$$
$$m\angle PBC = ?$$

Is the measure of $\angle ABP$ equals to the measure of angle $\angle PBC$?

Conclusion: You should find that $m\angle ABP = m\angle PBC$ and therefore, the segment BP divides the measure of the angle ABC into two equal parts. The segment BP is called the angle bisector because any line or segment that divides an angle into two equal parts is called an **angle bisector**. The word **bisect** means to divide into two equal parts. We can therefore, bisect an angle or a segment. We can divide the angle or the segment into two equal parts.

Exercises

1. Use paper folding to draw a line that is perpendicular to each given segment. Give detailed explanations. Hint: See Group Exercise 1.

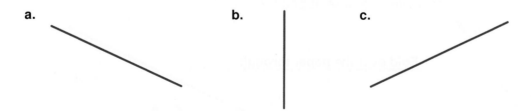

2. Two segments or lines are perpendicular if they intersect to form (180^0, 90^0, 75^0). Select the correct answer.

3. Use paper folding to construct the midpoint of each segment. Give detailed explanation. Hint: See Group Exercise 2.

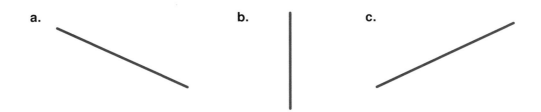

4. Explain what is meant by the midpoint of a segment.
5. Explain what is meant by angle bisector. Hint: See Group Exercise 3
6. Explain what is meant by the word bisect. Hint: See Group Exercise 3
7. Copy each angle and use paper folding to bisect each angle. Explain your method. Hint: See Group Exercise 3.

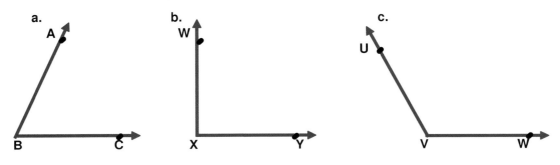

INDEX

A

D

E

F

G

H

hundredths 374, 376, 377, 399 - 407, 409, 417 - 423, 426, 427

I

impossible event 571
improper fraction 216, 238, 268, 272, 290, 293, 296, 315, 317 - 329, 331 - 336, 338, 344 - 353, 356 - 358, 360 - 363, 365, 469, 470, 476, 477, 497
inch 531 - 534
inequality 105, 106, 109, 110, 112
integer 163, 167, 168
integers 172 - 176, 189
interior angles 728 - 730, 733
intersecting lines 693, 694, 810
intersection 838
isosceles trapezoid 769, 770, 772 - 774
isosceles triangle 752 - 754
isosceles triangles 733, 734, 742, 743

K

kilogram 539 - 541
kilometer 520, 521, 523 - 528, 545, 548

L

leap year 555
least common denominator (LCD) 89, 226 - 228, 231 - 236, 239 - 242, 246 - 257, 259, 260 - 262, 264, 266, 284 - 287, 367 - 369
least common denominator 573
least common multiples 223 - 225, 228, 245
length 104, 638 - 657, 662, 665 - 668, 672, 674 - 684, 686, 687, 790, 792
line 738 - 741
line graph 596 - 598, 603, 604, 607, 611 - 618
line plot 57, 61
linear 686
liter 545 - 551
lowest terms 206 - 208, 276, 277, 285, 286, 290, 291, 293, 294, 316, 317, 319 - 324, 326 - 332, 334, 347, 350, 353 - 357, 360, 362, 363, 365, 392 - 396, 468 - 477, 488, 513, 514, 564, 570, 574 - 576, 580, 583 - 586, 656

M

map scale 687, 691
mean 55, 56, 58 - 61, 465
median 57, 59 - 61, 465
meter 519, 521, 523 - 531
metric cups 545 - 551
metric length 518
metric ton 539 - 541

N

O

P

Q

R

S

T

U

V

W

whole number 43, 258, 262 - 266, 270 - 274, 289, 293 - 309, 311, 312, 314, 317 - 334, 336, 351, 352, 356 - 366, 371 - 373, 375, 386, 387, 408, 409, 412 - 423, 437, 438, 440 - 442, 444 - 460, 463, 464, 467, 468, 486, 487, 490, 503, 511, 512, 516, 517, 529
whole Numbers 410, 443
width 104, 638 - 656, 662, 665 - 668, 675 - 684, 687
word phrases 63, 64 395, 396

X

x-axis 619, 621 - 632
x-coordinate 620 - 632

Y

yard 531 - 534
y-axis 619, 621 - 632
y-coordinate 620 - 632
year 555

Z

zero pair 172, 173, 175, 187
zero pairs 183,
zero slope 633 - 636

APPLICATION OF TECHNOLOGY BY USING TI-15 - REFERENCE

After the logic of mathematics is understood, students may use calculators and other computer softwares as applications of technology. Some of the applications of the TI-15 are shown. Refer to the manual of your calculator or computer program for detail applications.

Basic Operations

Keys

1. ⊞ adds.

2. ⊟ subtracts.

3. ⊠ multiplies.

4. ⊡ divides. The result may be displayed as a decimal or fraction depending on the mode setting you have selected.

5. Int÷ divides a whole number by a whole number and displays the result as a quotient and remainder.

6. Enter completes the operation.

7. (−) lets you enter a negative number.

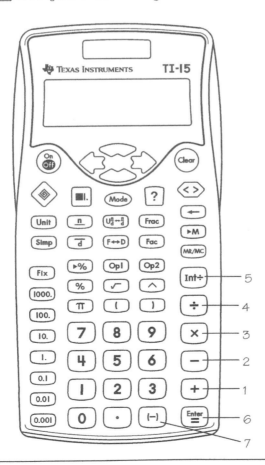

Notes

- The examples on the transparency masters assume all default settings.

- The result of Integer Divide Int÷ always appears as quotient and remainder (__ r __).

- The maximum number of digits for quotient or remainder (**r**) is 5. Quotient, remainder, and the **r** character cannot total more than 10 characters.

- If you use the result of integer division in another calculation, only the quotient is used. The remainder is dropped.

- All numbers used with Int÷ must be positive whole numbers.

- If you attempt to divide by 0, an error message is displayed.

- ⊞, ⊟, ⊠, ⊡, Enter, and Int÷ work with the built-in constants.

Display, Scrolling, Order of Operations, and Parentheses

Keys

1. ⟮ ⟯ opens a parenthetical expression. You can have as many as 8 parentheses at one time.

2. ⟮ ⟯ closes a parenthetical expression.

3. ← and → move the cursor left and right.

   ↑ and ↓ move the cursor up and down through previous entries and results.

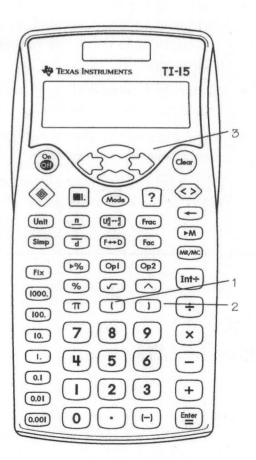

Notes

- The examples on the transparency masters assume all default settings.

- The EOS™ transparency master demonstrates the order in which the TI-15 completes calculations.

- When using parentheses, if you press ⟮Enter⟯ before pressing ⟮ ⟯, **Syn Error** is displayed.

- Operations inside parentheses are performed first. Use ⟮ ⟯ or ⟮ ⟯ to change the order of operations and, therefore, change the result.

  Example: $1 + 2 \times 3 = 7$
  $(1 + 2) \times 3 = 9$

- The first and second lines display entries up to 11 characters plus a decimal point, a negative sign, and a 2-digit positive or negative exponent. Entries begin on the left and scroll to the right. An entry will always wrap at the operator.

- Results are displayed right-justified. If a whole problem will not fit on the first line, the result will display on the second line.

TI-15: A Guide for Teachers

Equation Operating System

Priority	Functions
1 (first)	( )
2	Frac
3	^ √
4	(−)
5	× ÷
6	+ −
7	$U\frac{n}{d} \leftrightarrow \frac{n}{d}$ F↔D
8 (last)	Enter

Because operations inside parentheses are performed first, you can use ( ) to change the order of operations and, therefore, change the result.

Basic operations

$2 + 54 - 6 =$

Press	Display
2 ⊞ 54 ⊟ 6 [Enter]	`2+54-6=     50`

$3 \times 4 \div 2 =$

Press	Display
3 ⊠ 4 ⊟ 2 [Enter]	`3×4÷2=      6`

Add, Subtract

Multiply, Divide

Equals

Order of Operations

$1 + 2 \times 3 =$

Press	Display
1 [+] 2 [×] 3 [Enter]	`1+2×3=` `7`

$(1 + 2) \times 3 =$

Press	Display
[(] 1 [+] 2 [)] [×] 3 [Enter]	`(1+2)×3=` `9`

Division with remainders

Chris has 27 pieces of gum.
He wants to share the pieces evenly among himself and 5 friends. How many pieces will each person get? How many pieces will be left over?

Press	Display
27 [Int÷] 6 [Enter]	`27÷6=` `4 r 3`

Add

Multiply

Parentheses

Integer Divide

TI-15: A Guide for Teachers

Division with decimal result

Set the division display option to decimal and divide 27 by 6.

Press	Display

 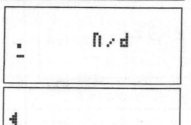

(Mode) [Enter]

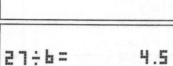

(Mode)

27 [÷] 6 [Enter]

27÷6=   4.5

Division with fractional result

Set the division display option to fraction and divide 27 by 6.

Press	Display

(Mode) ➡ [Enter]

(Mode)

27 [÷] 6 [Enter]

27÷6=   4 _5_
                  10

[Simp] [Enter]

4 _5_   4 _1_
   10   2

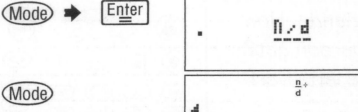

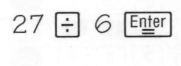

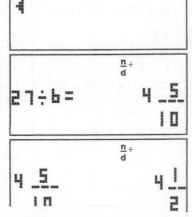

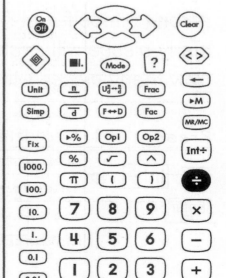

Quick Reference to Keys A

Key	Function
ⓞⁿ	Turns on the calculator. If already on, turns the calculator off.
(Clear)	Clears display and error condition.
ⓞⁿ (Clear)	To reset the calculator, hold down ⓞⁿ and (Clear) simultaneously for a few seconds and release. **MEM CLEARED** shows on the display. This will completely clear the calculator, including all mode menu settings, all previous entries in history, all values in memory, and the display. All default settings will be restored.
➡ ⬅	Moves the cursor right and left, respectively, so you can scroll the entry line or select a menu item.
	Moves the cursor up and down, respectively, so you can see previous entries or access menu lists.
⬅	Deletes the character to the left of the cursor before Enter is pressed.
(Mode)	Displays menu to select format of results of division:　　　　.　n/d
(Mode)	Displays menu to show or hide (?) in Op1 or Op 2:　　+1　Op　?
(Mode)	Displays menu to clear Op1 or Op2:　　Op1　Clear　Op2
(Mode)	Displays menu to reject or accept Reset:　　N　Y
0 1 2 3 4 5 6 7 8 9	Enters the numerals 0 through 9.
+	Adds.
−	Subtracts.
×	Multiplies.
÷	Divides.
Enter	Completes operations. Enters the equal sign or tests a solution in Problem Solving.
·	Inserts a decimal point.
(−)	Enters a negative sign. Does not act as an operator.
(	Opens a parenthetical expression.
)	Closes a parenthetical expression.

Quick Reference to Keys (Continued) | A

Key	Function
Int÷	When you divide a positive whole number by a positive whole number using Int÷, the result is displayed in the form **Q r R**, where **Q** is the quotient and **R** is the remainder. If you use the result of integer division in a subsequent calculation, only the quotient is used; the remainder is dropped.
n	When pressed after entering a number, designates the numerator of a fraction. The numerator must be an integer. To negate a fraction, press (-) before entering numerator.
d	When pressed after entering a number, designates the denominator of a fraction. The denominator of a fraction must be a positive integer in the range 1 through 1000. If you perform a calculation with a fraction having a denominator greater than 1000, or if the results of a calculation yield a denominator greater than 1000, the TI-15 will convert and display the results in decimal format.
Unit	Separates a whole number from the fraction in a mixed number.
Frac	Displays a menu of settings that determine how fraction results are displayed. • **U n/d** (default) displays mixed number results. • **n/d** displays results as a simple (improper) fraction. If **N/d→n/d** is displayed after you convert a fraction to a mixed number, you can further simplify the fractional portion of the mixed number.
Frac ◄	Displays a menu to select the method of simplifying fractions: • **Man** (default) allows you to simplify manually (step-by-step). • **Auto** automatically reduces fraction results to lowest terms.
Simp	Enables you to simplify a fraction.
Fac	Displays the factor that was used to simplify a fraction.
U n/d ↔ n/d	Converts a mixed number to an improper fraction or an improper fraction to a mixed number.
F↔D	Converts a fraction to a decimal, or converts a decimal to a fraction, if possible. Converts π to a decimal value.
%	Enters a percentage.

Quick Reference to Keys (Continued) | A

Key	Function
▸%	Converts a decimal or a fraction to a percent.
√⁻	Calculates the square root of a number.
^	Raises a number to the power you specify.
π	Enters the value of **π**. It is stored internally to 13 decimal places (3.141592653590). In some cases, results display with symbolic **π**, and in other cases as a numeric value.
▸M	Stores the displayed value for later use. If there is already a value in memory, the new one will replace it. When memory contains a value other than 0, **M** displays on the screen. (Will not work while a calculation is in process.)
MR/MC	Recalls the memory value for use in a calculation when pressed once. When pressed twice, clears memory.
Op1 Op2	Each can store one or more operations with constant value(s), which can be repeated by pressing only one key, as many times as desired. To store an operation to **Op1** or **Op2** and recall it: • Press Op1 (or Op2), enter the operator and the value, and press Op1 (or Op2) to save the operation. • Press Op1 (or Op2) to recall the stored operation. To clear the contents of **Op1** or **Op2**, press Mode ◂ ◂ , select **Op1** or **Op2**, and press Enter. New operations can now be stored for repeated use.
Fix 1000.	Rounds off results to the nearest thousand.
Fix 100.	Rounds off results to the nearest hundred.
Fix 10.	Rounds off results to the nearest ten.
Fix 1.	Rounds off results to the nearest one.
Fix 0.1	Rounds off results to the nearest tenth.
Fix 0.01	Rounds off results to the nearest hundredth.
Fix 0.001	Rounds off results to the nearest thousandth.
Fix ·	Removes fixed-decimal setting and returns to floating decimal.

Display Indicators

B

Indicator	Meaning
◈	Calculator is in Problem Solving mode.
▣	Calculator is in place-value mode.
Fix	The calculator is rounding to a specified number of places.
M	Indicates that a value other than zero is in memory.
▸M	Value is being stored to memory. You must press [+], [−], [×], [÷], or [Enter] to complete the process.
Op1, Op2	An operator and operand is stored.
Auto	In calculator mode, **Auto** simplification of fractions to lowest terms is selected. In ◈, Problem Solving function is in **Auto** mode.
I	Integer division function has been selected (appears only when cursor is over division sign).
n/d ÷	Division results will be displayed as fractions.
N//d→n/d	The fraction result can be further simplified.
↑ ↓	Previous entries are stored in history, or more menus are available. Press – to access history. Press – and – to access additional menu lists.
← →	You can press ⬅ and ➡ to scroll and select from a menu. You must press [Enter] to complete the selection process.